AF412790

ARTISTS' MAGAZINES

ARTISTS' MAGAZINES

AN ALTERNATIVE SPACE FOR ART

GWEN ALLEN

THE MIT PRESS
CAMBRIDGE, MASSACHUSETTS
LONDON, ENGLAND

MIT Press books may be purchased at special
quantity discounts for business or sales promotional
use. For information, please email special_sales@
mitpress.mit.edu or write to Special Sales
Department, The MIT Press, 55 Hayward Street,
Cambridge, MA 02142.

This book was set in Helvetica Neue and Minion Pro
by The MIT Press. Printed and bound in Spain.

Library of Congress Cataloging-in-Publication Data
Allen, Gwen, 1971–
Artists' magazines : an alternative space for art /
Gwen Allen.
p. cm.
Includes bibliographical references and index.
ISBN 978-0-262-01519-6 (hardcover : alk. paper)
1. Art, Modern—20th century—Periodicals.
2. Art, Modern—20th century—Historiography.
I. Title.
N6490.A58 2011
709.04´5—dc22

2010022787
10 9 8 7 6 5 4 3 2

CONTENTS

ACKNOWLEDGMENTS

I wish to thank the following artists and editors who generously offered their recollections and insights, especially those who agreed to be interviewed for this project: Vito Acconci, Liza Béar, AA Bronson, Benjamin Buchloh, Edit deAk, Dan Graham, Friedrich Heubach, Thomas Lawson, Bernadette Mayer, Susan Morgan, Brian O'Doherty, Walter Robinson, and Willoughby Sharp. Others who willingly gave of their time and helped with my research include Leonard Abrams, Michael Andre, Rasheed Araeen, Anna Banana, Elliott Barowitz, Sally Beers, Julian Blaine, Mel Bochner, Yve-Alain Bois, Daniel Buren, Victor Coleman, Tricia Collins, David Dalton, Debbie DeStaffan, Herbert George, Jeremy Gilbert-Rolfe, Andy Graham, Suzanne Hammer, Naoyoshi Hikosaka, David Hlynsky, James Hugunin, Ron Kolm, William Leavitt, Steven Leiber, Philip Leider, Les Levine, Lucy Lippard, Gerhard Johann Lischka, Harley Lond, Tom Marioni, Raul Marroquin, Dick Miller, Alan Moore, Cynthia Navaretta, Suzanne Ostro, Otto Piene, Howardena Pindell, David Platzker, Lucio Pozzi, Judy Rifka, David Robbins, Dorothea Rockburne, Nancy Schoocraft, Pamela Seymour Smith Sharp, Ingrid Sischy, Terise Slotkin, Terry Smith, Carol Squiers, Philip Steadman, Betsy Sussler, Gerhard Theewen, Reiko Tomii, Herman de Vries, Brian Wallis, Helene Winer, Bob Witz, and Judith Wong.

The research, writing, and publishing of this book were made possible by fellowships from the Henry Luce/American Council of Learned Societies and the Stanford University Art and Art History Department. I was also fortunate to receive a Getty Library Research grant. I am especially thankful for release time from teaching made possible by a San Francisco State University Vice Presidential Award and a Presidential Award. A San Francisco State University Mini-Grant subsidized permission and licensing fees for this book's illustrations.

Portions of chapter 4 were published in *Artforum* and *Art Journal,* and I thank the editors of these publications, and especially Tim Griffin, Don McMahon, and Patricia Phillips, for their feedback. I also thank the archivists and librarians at the Getty Research Library, the Museum of Modern Art Library, the San Francisco Museum of Modern Art Library, and the National Gallery of Canada for their patience and help with my research.

This book began as a dissertation under the direction of Pamela M. Lee, and it is profoundly indebted to her intellectual guidance and inspired by her own scholarship and writing. I also thank the other members of my dissertation committee, Maria Gough, Michael Marrinan, and Nicholas Jenkins, for their feedback and support.

I feel fortunate to have worked alongside dear friends and colleagues at the Maine College of Art, especially Joe Begnaud, Aimée Bessire, Adriane Herman, Beata Niedzialkowska, Chris Thompson, and Ling-Wen Tsai. At San Francisco State University I am thankful for the support of my colleagues in the Art Department, particularly fellow art historians Judith Bettelheim, Whitney Chadwick, Mark Johnson, Santhi Kavuri-Bauer, and Richard Mann. I am also grateful for my students, both MECA and SFSU, whose enthusiasm for the book's topic helped sustain my own engagement with it.

I wish to acknowledge several others who have been crucial to the completion of this book and to the well-being of the author. First, I must single out Karen Rapp, who read the entire manuscript at various stages and provided invaluable feedback and insights (not to mention moral support); this book would be impossible without her. Jill Dawsey and Julian Myers also read portions of the manuscript and offered incisive comments. Tirza Latimer offered wise and generous suggestions at a key moment. Geoff Kaplan was an important interlocutor in the field of graphic design, and also helped with the images for the book. Eda Čufer's friendship has been important, even over a distance. Kerry Hanlon has been there for me in many ways over many years. Others whom I wish to thank for various kinds of encouragement and assistance include Fabienne Adler, Zachary Barowitz, Kelly Baum, Hsiao-Yun Chu, Carlton Evans, David Henkin, Corey Keller, Carrie Lambert-Beatty, Rael Lewis, Sheila Lyons, Sarah Malakoff, Gabriela Muller, Kaz Okada, Dana Ospina, Jessica Riley, Andre de Abreu Serrao, and Cherise Smith.

It seems somehow fitting that a book that is so much about the processes of publishing and editing has benefited so greatly from the support of my own editor at the MIT Press, Roger Conover. His knowledge and acute understanding of the topic informed the conceptualization and realization of this project, and enriched the experience of writing it. For this I am most appreciative. Also at the MIT Press, I sincerely thank Matthew Abbate, who saw this book to press, and Margarita Encomienda, who designed it, as well as Paula Woolley and Anar Badalov for their efforts in the preparation of this book.

For their love and support, I thank my family: my parents, Anne and William Allen; my sisters Elizabeth Allen and Rebecca Allen; Peter Pocagar; John Esteves; and my nieces and nephews, Jacob, Liam, Benjamin, Lauren, and Jillian.

This book is dedicated to Phyllis Johnson, whom I unfortunately never knew, but who would have been pleased and surprised, I think, to know that her little magazine was not forgotten.

     ACKNOWLEDGMENTS

INTRODUCTION

The expectation of failure is connected with the very name of a Magazine.
NOAH WEBSTER

In 1788 the American publisher and dictionary writer Noah Webster, founder of several short-lived periodicals, lamented the precarious enterprise of publishing a magazine.[1] The average life span of a magazine in the United States between 1741 and 1850 was only eighteen months, and it was not until well into the nineteenth century that the advertising industry made magazine publishing a reliably profitable business.[2] Yet the ephemerality that defined the magazine at the dawn of its invention has remained fundamental to the social possibilities inherent in this particular form of printed matter. To publish a magazine is to enter into a heightened relationship with the present moment. Unlike books, which are intended to last for future generations, magazines are decidedly impermanent. Their transience is embodied by their unprecious formats, flimsy covers, and inexpensive paper stock, and it is suggested by their seriality, which presumes that each issue will soon be rendered obsolete by the next.

During the 1960s and 1970s magazines became an important new site of artistic practice, functioning as an alternative exhibition space for the dematerialized practices of conceptual art. Abandoning canvases, pedestals, and all they stood for in the established institutions of modernism, this art sought out lightweight and everyday media, and relied heavily on texts, photographs, and other kinds of documents. Conceptual art depended upon the magazine as a new site of display, which allowed it to be experienced by a broader public than the handful of people actually present to witness a temporary object, idea, or act—or in the case of earth art, ambitious enough to make the trek to the remote locations where this work tended to reside. As the art historian David Rosand observed of the pivotal new role of the art magazine during this period, "you read it. But you read it because it told you what was going on partly because so much of what was going on was *not* to be seen in the galleries."[3]

While artists used the magazine to document their work, they also began to explore it as a medium in its own right, creating works expressly for the mass-produced page. These original artists' contributions (sometimes called artists' projects, artists' pages, or magazine art)[4] investigated the distinct materiality of the magazine as well as its unique properties as a form of communication. The everyday, throwaway form of the magazine mirrored art's heightened sense of its own contingency in the 1960s and 1970s: its insistence on the actual time and place in which was it encountered. Inexpensive and accessible, the magazine was an ideal expressive vehicle for art that was more concerned with concept, process, and performance than with final marketable form. Indeed, the ephemerality of the magazine was central to its radical possibilities as an alternative form of distribution that might replace the privileged space of the museum with a more direct and democratic experience. As Joseph Kosuth described his *Second Investigation* (1968), which took the form of advertisements in various newspapers and magazines, "people can wrap dishes in my work."[5]

This book explores the significance of artists' magazines in art of the 1960s through the 1980s by examining magazines that were published by artists and their supporters as alternatives to the mainstream art press and commercial gallery system. These publications, scores of which began—and more often than not ended—during this period, were driven not by profit motives but by an earnest and impassioned belief in the magazine's capacity to radicalize the reception of art. As Benjamin Buchloh recalled of *Interfunktionen* (a magazine that he took over in 1974 and edited for just two issues before a controversial work within its pages led to its financial undoing): "I think you have to be very young and very naive and very lunatic to do a magazine in the first place."[6] If this observation captures something of the utopian hopes artists and critics pinned to the magazine during this time, it also suggests how these aspirations paradoxically acknowledged—and even in some sense depended upon—the very fleeting and precarious nature of the magazine itself.

Like the relationships and communities they embody, artists' magazines are volatile and mutable. They seek out the leading and precarious edges; they live at the margins rather than in the stable and established center. They thrive on change and impermanence, favor process over product, and risk being thrown away. They court failure. Yet this book argues that such failure should be understood not as an indication of defeat, but as an expression of the vanguard nature of these publications and their refusal of commercial interests. Moving beyond the literal failure of magazines, it will examine how this quality took on metaphorical and ideological significance as a rejection of standard measures of art world success, and as a different way of imagining art's power and potential.

DESIGNED FOR REPRODUCIBILITY

Walter Benjamin was among the first to observe that when art is reproduced and distributed through the mass media, it becomes a qualitatively different form of communication, one with profound aesthetic and political repercussions. In his 1936 essay "The Work of Art in the Age of Mechanical Reproduction," he argued that when a work of art is mechanically duplicated, it loses its aura, or its unique existence in time and space. However, at the same time, he insisted, it gains a new—and highly ambivalent—political function, one that is predicated upon its greatly expanded public. Speaking of the new technical capabilities of photography and film, Benjamin declared that "the work of art reproduced is now becoming the work of art designed for reproducibility"[7]—a phrase that presciently describes many of the artistic practices that are discussed in this book. Benjamin's understanding of the social possibilities of art and media was rooted in his nuanced attention to the material conditions of production and distribution, and the way these structure the social relationships between the author or artist and the audience—ideas he also discussed in "The Author as Producer" (1934). (In fact, Benjamin even planned, along with Bertolt Brecht, to publish a magazine, *Krise und Kritik* [Crisis and criticism], that would have allowed him to explore these ideas not only in theory but in practice—a project that unfortunately never materialized.)[8]

Benjamin's observations are pertinent to the arguments of this book, and they shed light on the important role of magazines in the history of art—a role that has arguably been as vital as that of the works of art themselves. One of the first artists' periodicals was the *Propyläen* (1798–1800), founded by Johann Wolfgang von Goethe and Johann Heinrich Meyer. As Goethe explained, its title referred to "the step, the door, the entrance, the antechamber, the space between the inner and the outer, the sacred and the profane[;] this is the place we choose as the meeting-ground for exchanges with our friends"—a description that indicates the magazine's important role as both a portal and gathering place for people and ideas.[9] The title of *The Germ*, another important early artists' magazine, started in England by the Pre-Raphaelites and published for a mere four issues in 1850, likewise suggests the formative role of magazines: it was here that artistic ideas were not only recorded and exchanged, but germinated; here that avant-garde movements originated and gained momentum. With the development of new printing technologies, the twentieth century saw a flourishing of periodicals for which artists served as publishers, editors, writers, typographers, and designers. Some of the most important of these included prewar avant-garde magazines such as *Lacerba* (1913–1915), *Blast* (1914–1915), *291* (1915–1916), *Cabaret Voltaire* (1916), *The Blind Man* (1917), *Dada* (1917–1921), *De Stijl* (1917–1932), *L'Esprit Nouveau* (1920–1925), *Zenit* (1921–1926), *Mécano* (1922–1923), *Merz* (1923–1932), *Lef* (1923–1925), *La Révolution Surréaliste* (1924–1929), *Tank* (1925), *Novyi Lef* (1927–1929), *Internationale Revue i10* (1927–1929), *Minotaure* (1933–1939), *View* (1940–1947), and *VVV* (1942–1944), as well as the postwar abstract expressionist periodicals, including *Iconograph* (1946), *The Tiger's Eye* (1947–1949), *Possibilities* (1947–1948), *Instead* (1948), and *It Is* (1960–1965).[10] Important avant-garde artists' magazines, such as *Gutai* (1955–1965) in Japan and *Boa* (1958–1960) in Argentina, were also being published outside of Europe and the United States during these years.

Even as these publications implicitly questioned the division between fine art and design, insisting upon the magazine as an important site of artistic production, they remained, for the most part, a means to an end—vehicles for defining artistic agendas and circulating ideas, rather than works of art in themselves. Clive Phillpot stressed this difference in a 1980 article, noting of these earlier periodicals that artists "simply used their skills to produce magazines, however handsome or unconventional they might be. Unlike artists in the '60s they were not consciously using the production of a magazine to question the nature of artworks, nor were they making art specifically for dissemination through a mass-communication medium."[11] By contrast, he argued, artists' magazines in the 1960s manifested "a wholly different attitude of artists towards the magazine and towards the nature of what constituted art."[12]

Indeed, while the magazines featured in this book are in many ways heir to these earlier artists' periodicals, they also signal something different, demonstrating an unprecedented experimentation with the formal and conceptual possibilities of the magazine, and a new kind of self-reflexivity about its status as a medium. This novel understanding of the artists' magazine can be traced back to several periodicals from the late 1950s and early 1960s, including *Spirale, Zero, Gorgona, Revue Nul = 0, Revue Integration, Diagonal Cero, KWY, Revue Ou, material, dé-coll/age, V TRE,* and *Fluxus,* as well as Wallace Berman's *Semina.* These publications, many of which had exceedingly small print runs of just a few hundred copies per issue, exemplify a radical new kind of experimentation with the formal and conceptual possibilities of the magazine,

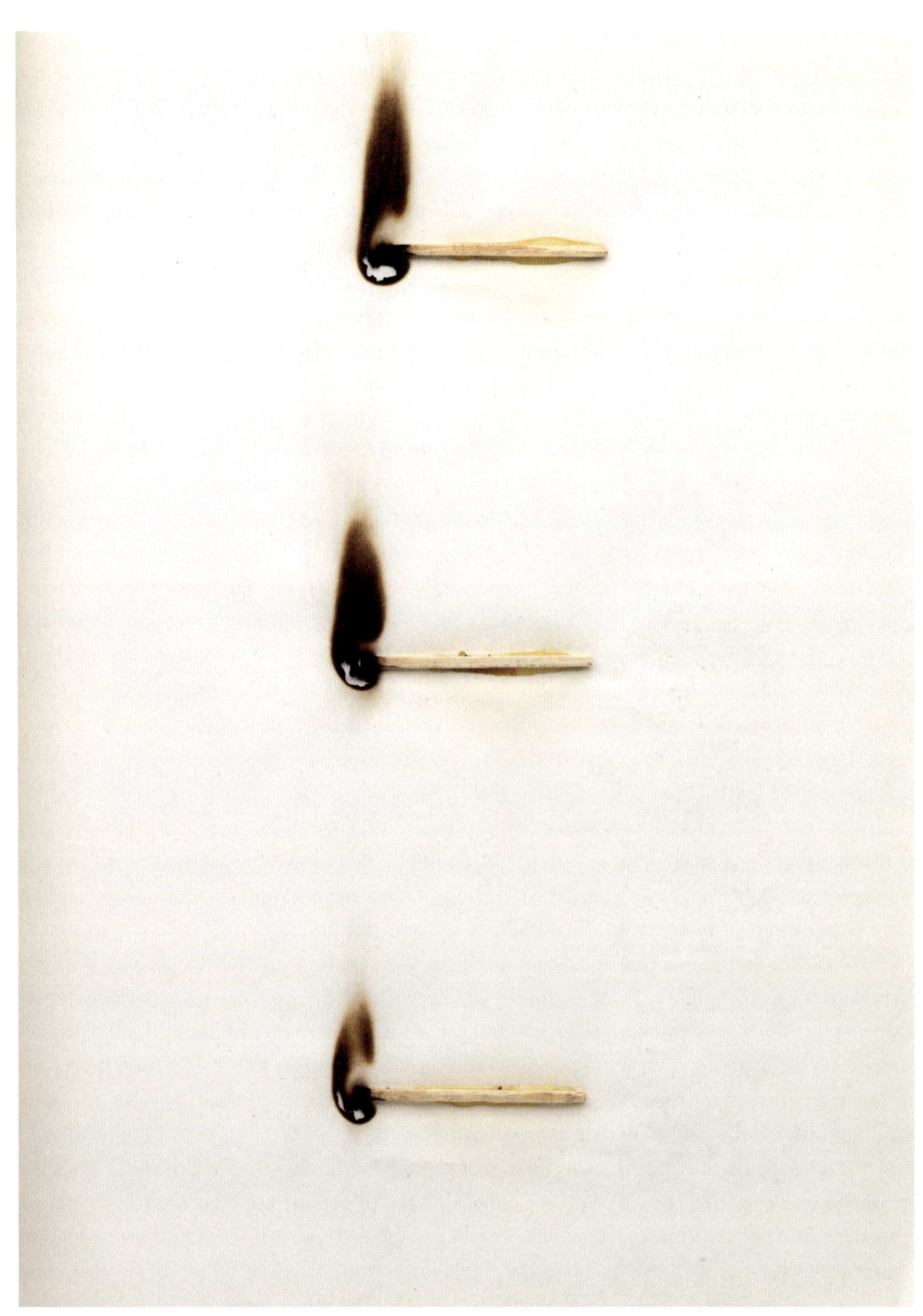

I.1
Bernard Aubertin, page in *Revue Integration,*
no. 4, 1965. Courtesy of the artist. Research Library,
The Getty Research Institute, Los Angeles
(86-S1545 v.4).

as artists utilized unbound, die-cut, and embossed pages, glued objects onto pages, tore them, and even burned them. Bernard Aubertin, for example, glued three matches to a page of *Revue Integration* and lit them, leaving three scorch marks on the page. Such investigations of the materiality and temporality of the printed page (which very much overlapped with the practices of concrete poetry) coincided with new understandings of artistic medium itself in the postwar period. As the meaning of art was increasingly seen to reside in a performative, temporal, and conceptual experience rather than a strictly formal, visual one, artists found new ways to express these experiences in the magazine, breaking away from the traditional limits of the static, two-dimensional page.

In the late 1960s and 1970s, artists approached the magazine with the same inventiveness with which they embraced other media in the "expanded field." They experimented with format, design, and typography, reveled in the materiality of language and print, emphasized the tactility and interactivity of the magazine, and foregrounded the acts of reading and turning the page. Robert Smithson, for example, understood the magazine as a quasi-sculptural medium, likening its dense layers of texts and images to geological strata; Sol LeWitt invited viewers to draw on the page; Vito Acconci conceived of the magazine as a performative realm within which language was an event as much as an object; Dan Graham explored what he called "the physicality of print" as well as its social and economic conditions.[13] Other artists explored unbound, multimedia formats that challenged the very definition of the magazine itself. Whereas Benjamin argued that reproduction ruins the aura of the original work of art, replacing its unique existence in time and space with a mediated experience that at once diminishes its authenticity and renews its significance and potential in the present, these experiments open onto a new set of possibilities. In some cases, artists imbued the reproduced page with a new kind of auratic presence; in others, they destabilized the hierarchy between original and reproduction altogether.

For these artists, as for Benjamin, the social and political implications of art's reproducibility were paramount: their understanding of the magazine as a new kind of artistic medium was accompanied by a profound recognition of its possibilities as a distribution form that might circumvent the expertise of the critic and the exclusivity of the gallery space, and thus radically transform the reception of art. Yet the possibilities of the media for artists during this time were also vastly different from those that Benjamin identified—not only because of their remove from the political conditions of Europe in the 1930s that gave his writing its particular urgency, but also because of important changes in media culture itself. The reproduction of art was no longer the relatively new and uncharted phenomenon it had been in Benjamin's time, and artists' understanding of the magazine in the 1960s and 1970s was modulated by an entirely different set of historical circumstances. The reproduction of art had become ubiquitous within an advanced spectacular media culture in which not only works of art but social relationships more generally were increasingly mediated—a situation about which Guy Debord famously observed, "Everything that was directly lived has moved away into a representation."[14] At the same time, advances in printing technology made processes such as offset, mimeo, and Xerox inexpensive and widely available to nonspecialized producers, leading to a burgeoning alternative and underground press.

Artists' investigations of the magazine took place within this context, internalizing the new possibilities of mass communication technology, whether utopian or dystopian. The very notion of the work of art and of artistic medium and how they might express meaning to an audience were understood differently against and within this new media culture. Magazines were certainly not the sole site for such investigations—similar and overlapping concerns attended artists' explorations of film, video, and television, as well as cybernetics and systems theory (not to mention more traditional mediums such as painting and sculpture) during this time. However, the magazine played an especially pervasive and pivotal role in the dramatic transformations in artistic production, reception, and distribution in an age of information. By taking stock of this role, this book contributes to a growing body of scholarship that has begun to critically examine the relationship between art and media during the 1960s and 1970s.[15] It also reconsiders the political significance of conceptual art's use of language, documentation, and publicity by examining the specific ways in which the magazine as a medium and distribution form engendered a critique of art's institutions and audiences.[16] By approaching these strategies through the lens of the magazine's distinct material conditions and social relationships, this book strives to more fully grasp the successes as well as failures of these practices, while complicating the way in which these very terms are mobilized to assess art's significance and value.

ARTISTS' MAGAZINES AS ALTERNATIVE SPACES

This book attests to the historicity of the artists' magazine as a particular kind of oppositional site during the 1960s, 1970s, and 1980s. The magazines that comprise its case studies—*Aspen* (1965–1971), *o to 9* (1967–1969), *Avalanche* (1970–1976), *Art-Rite* (1973–1978), *FILE* (1972–1989), *Real Life* (1979–1994), and *Interfunktionen* (1968–1975)—suggest that the significance of the artists' magazine during this time was deeply tied to the evolving notion of the alternative space.[17] This term neatly captures how the two-dimensional printed page functioned as a substitute exhibition space for conceptual art—a corollary to the architectural interior of the gallery or museum. However, it also expresses the ways in which magazines paralleled and furthered the ideological and practical objectives of alternative spaces. Like other artist-run, independent, and nonprofit exhibition spaces and collectives, magazines challenged the institutions and economies of the mainstream art world by supporting new experimental forms of art outside the commercial gallery system, promoting artists' moral and legal rights, and redressing the inequities of gender, race, and class.[18] Indeed, as will become clear in the pages that follow, magazines were not merely secondary or supplementary to other kinds of alternative spaces and institutions but were deeply enmeshed within the new cultural economies these institutions helped to bring about. To publish art—to literally make it public—was a political act, one that challenged the art world and the world at large.

Central to the oppositional character of artists' magazines was the way in which they both drew on and defined themselves against mainstream media and, in particular, the commercial art magazine. While art magazines such as *Artforum* witnessed the reign of formalist criticism as well as the integration of this criticism within the spectacular economy of advanced media culture, artists' magazines insisted on a different set of conditions and criteria for evaluating art. Like the underground press in the 1960s and 1970s—which undoubtedly served as an important model— they expressed their differences from mainstream publications in both form and content.

Artists' magazines were produced and distributed not according to the motives of profit but according to the artistic, social, and political ideals they sought to convey. Edited and designed in loft spaces and distributed at independent and artist-run bookstores such as Printed Matter in New York and Art Metropole in Toronto—or sometimes given away for free—these publications were influential well beyond their limited circulations and brief life spans. Against the slickness of mainstream art magazines with their glossy finish and high-quality color reproductions, artists' magazines expressed anticommercial, egalitarian sentiments through their unpretentious, do-it-yourself formats, such as mimeograph and newsprint. Often penniless, they relied on grants, meager advertising, and subscription revenue and the (usually uncompensated) intellectual labor of their editors and contributors.

Their advertising sections were more likely to broadcast political statements or promote nonprofit spaces than to sponsor commercial galleries. Criticism and exhibition reviews were replaced by artists' projects, writings, and interviews, through which artists "talked back" to critics and took charge of the public discourse around their work. Letters to the editor became sites of protest, expressions of solidarity, and occasions for inside jokes. Mastheads reveal how the divisions of labor between editors, critics, designers, and writers blurred and overlapped, giving way to new kinds of collaboration rooted in intellectual exchange and camaraderie. Magazines track the formation of such relationships, and record conflicts and differences of opinion—disagreements over which editors resigned, friendships dissolved, and sometimes publications themselves even came to an end.

This book's center of gravity lies in magazines that were strongly associated with conceptual art's aesthetic and ideological concerns as they developed in North America in the 1960s and 1970s, as well as the legacy of these practices in the 1980s. While previous accounts of conceptual art have emphasized the important role of printed matter more generally, subsuming magazines within a broader category of artists' publications—including artists' books and exhibition catalogs—this book contends that the magazine is a very specific form of printed communication that merits its own study.[19] I argue that the distinct physical and communicative properties of the magazine—its reproduced, serial format, its collective nature, its inherent publicness, and its close connection with the economies of art and art criticism—made it an especially compelling medium for artists during this period.

Even as I stress the ways in which artists' magazines so often deliberately rejected standard measures of artistic quality, individual genius, greatness, and monetary worth, I insist on their value as sites of artistic meaning, and argue for the importance of the often overlooked creative work of editing, publishing, and designing magazines. Magazines demand the same kind of close attention to their form, content, and conditions of production and reception as more traditional works of art. I take into account their materiality as printed objects with an identifiable set of attributes and elements, such as covers, mastheads, bindings, editorial pages, and advertising sections. I pay close attention to factors such as typography and design, format, printing technologies, paper stock, and examine how magazines structure meaning through sequence and juxtaposition. I analyze these formal aspects of magazines alongside their titles, editorial statements, and contents, to shed light on editorial goals and policies and intended readership. However, I also consider the complex "social lives" of publications, to borrow Arjun Appadurai's term, indicating how objects are animated in their circulation through time and space.[20] I explore how magazines were produced and distributed, and the human relationships that they not only recorded but occasioned. A case study approach makes it possible to examine individual issues of magazines but also to understand how they function in a series, over the entire run of a publication; to look at how magazines begin and how they end, and how they evolve over time.

Five of the chapters focus on New York-based publications, enabling an examination of the relationships between several magazines which referenced and reacted to one another over the course of two decades, and the charting of their changing role within the artistic community in lower Manhattan. However, the book also counteracts this narrow geographical scope by looking outside of the United States to consider the Canadian magazine *FILE* in chapter 6, and the German magazine *Interfunktionen* in the epilogue. Both of these chapters address the question of geography in ways that expand upon and complicate the stories being told in the other chapters. The appendix further supplements the book's main case studies with examples of artists' magazines from around the world.

Chapter 1 situates the artists' magazine historically and theoretically in relationship to the commercial art magazine and 1960s media politics. I draw on Jürgen Habermas's account of the public sphere as well as Oskar Negt and Alexander Kluge's subsequent critique of Habermas in order to consider the function of the magazine as a site of both publicity and counterpublicity during this time. Using *Artforum* as its primary case study, the introduction examines the art magazine's contradictory function in the reception of art: on the one hand, its role in the promotion and spectacular consumption of art, and on the other, its publication of artists' writings and "interventions" that challenged this role.

Chapter 2 examines *Aspen* (1965–1971), a multimedia magazine housed in a cardboard box, containing Super-8 films, flexi-disc records, critical writings, and artists' projects. *Aspen* suggests, in ways that resonate powerfully throughout the rest of the book, the transformation of the magazine from a two-dimensional bound object into a three-dimensional exhibition space. Artists did not merely use *Aspen* to document and distribute their work; they also explored the magazine as a temporal, interactive medium. This chapter focuses on the issues of *Aspen* that were guest-edited by the artist and critic Brian O'Doherty (issue 5+6) and the artist Dan Graham (issue 8), to consider the politics of reception that were at the heart of conceptual art's understanding of the magazine as medium and exhibition space.

Chapter 3 discusses *o to 9* (1967–1969), a mimeographed poetry magazine founded by the poet and performance artist Vito Acconci and the poet Bernadette Mayer. *o to 9* featured poetry and experimental writing alongside conceptual art. This chapter considers the magazine's role in the investigations of the materiality of language, so important to both art and poetry at this moment. As the concrete vehicle of such investigations, *o to 9* embodied the evolving understanding of the printed page from a static surface to a performative realm of actions and events.

Avalanche (1970–1976) is the subject of chapter 4, which considers the formative role of this publication in the alternative art practices that emerged in SoHo in the 1970s, including conceptual art, earth art, performance, video, dance, and music. This chapter analyzes the artists' projects, interviews, and advertisements published in *Avalanche*, demonstrating how they functioned as alternatives to the discourse published in the mainstream commercial press. Circumventing the authority of the critic, *Avalanche* fostered a more direct channel for the artist's voice and helped to forge a new understanding of the artists' magazine as a site of artistic identity and community that would be influential throughout the 1970s.

Chapter 5 looks at *Art-Rite* (1973–1978), an eclectic zine-like publication that was founded to counter the market-driven concerns and egotistical posturing its editors perceived in the commercial art press of the time. *Art-Rite* forged an irreverent, experimental style of criticism, publishing loft reviews that covered younger, then-less-known artists in SoHo. This chapter examines the editorial and artistic policies that defined *Art-Rite* and looks at how the magazine functioned as an alternative space alongside other alternative artist-run spaces and collectives within the art world at this time, including Printed Matter and Artists' Space.

Chapter 6 examines *FILE* (1972–1989), founded by the Canadian collective General Idea as a vehicle for mail art and the Canadian art scene. Later the magazine became a means to document and publicize the group's own projects, such as the Miss General Idea Pageant. Employing strategies such as masquerade, *détournement*, and viral media tactics, *FILE* parodied and critiqued mainstream media and sought to exploit the magazine's spectacular visual economy to construct and express countercultural and queer identities.

Chapter 7 examines *Real Life* (1979–1994), which featured artists associated with the Pictures generation as well as the activist-oriented collectives of the 1980s in the South Bronx and East Village. In its attempt to provide a noncommercial critical discursive space for art, *Real Life* self-consciously looked back to artists' magazines of the 1960s and 1970s. It not only chronicled the new postmodernist media and appropriation practices of artists in the 1980s, but was an important primary site for such investigations.

The epilogue expands the book's vista outside of North America to examine the Cologne-based magazine *Interfunktionen* (1968–1975). Founded to protest the conservative curatorial strategies of Documenta, *Interfunktionen* was a crucial vehicle for international and especially transatlantic exchange in the 1960s and 1970s. However, the magazine also provided opportunities for German artists to reflect upon the very problematic question of their own national identity and history. This chapter examines the tensions between international exchange and national, local, and regional artistic identity that *Interfunktionen* manifested—a dynamic that resonates strongly in today's global art world.

The book includes an appendix consisting of an illustrated list of artists' magazines founded around the world between 1945 and 1989, which provides basic publication information and describes editorial objectives, notable contributors, format, and design. (The exact parameters for inclusion are discussed in more detail in the headnote to the appendix.) The appendix both augments and complements the book's main case studies and themes, contextualizing them within a broader geographical and historical field. It reinforces the significance of the magazine as a site of artistic practice by indicating the much wider milieu, both inside and outside the United States, within which artists' magazines proliferated.

Many of the qualities that made magazines such a compelling medium for artists—such as their temporality and their process-oriented nature—also make them fascinating art historical documents. Besides precisely situating the reception of art within specific places and times—not only the year but often the exact month—they also open onto the contingency of history itself, stressing its conditional, fragmented, and subjective nature. Magazines provide a different kind of information about the past than more objective or totalizing accounts: they emphasize the role of the accidental, the happenstance, the unintended in what often gets passed down as inevitable. They show us things that might otherwise get lost, that might not be considered important enough at the time to get recorded in more authoritative documents, such as books or exhibition catalogs. This book attempts to make this vast archive of magazines more known and accessible, and to situate these publications within the historical conditions in which they were first produced and encountered.

1

1

THIS IS NOT TO BE LOOKED AT

ARTFORUM IN THE 1960S
AND 1970S

In 1969 Lee Lozano wrote the following instructions for a performance called *Throwing Up Piece*: "Throw the last twelve issues of *Artforum* up in the air." This simple directive and the irreverent image that it evokes—magazines being violently tossed skyward, the sound of flapping, tearing pages, and the sudden, sickening thud of them landing on the floor, spines warped, covers bent back—conveyed the artist's exasperation with *Artforum*'s reign in the New York art world at the time. In this sense, Lozano spoke for a generation of artists who were frustrated by the promotional role of the magazine and, perhaps, spoke especially for women artists, whose exclusion from the upper echelons of the art world *Artforum* and other commercial art magazines had done little to redress and had, if anything, perpetuated.

The unprecedented authority of the magazine in the art world at this moment was widely noted. A 1972 article in *Newsweek* singled out *Artforum*'s "predominant" influence, and attested to "the growing, seminal importance of the art magazine. No longer the passive judge and recorder of art, it is now a part of the action."[1] In 1976 the critic John Walker went so far as to claim that "the power of the art magazine to define and legitimize new developments in art has become greater than that of the art gallery and museum."[2] Artists took account of this new role of the media in the reception of their work in various and contradictory ways. On the one hand, as Lozano's *Throwing Up Piece* suggests, they resented the magazine's power, and its role in an economic system that benefited galleries and dealers instead of artists and viewers. However, they also sought to harness—or, alternatively, to subvert—the magazine's power by appropriating it as a new kind of medium and exhibition space.

In this chapter, I examine the art magazine's contested status during the 1960s and 1970s, focusing on the history of *Artforum*. I consider several factors that played into the new power of the art magazine, including conceptual art's reliance on photographic and textual documentation, the politics of art criticism, and the intensification of spectacular media culture. While *Artforum* has frequently been cast as a straw man in cautionary tales about the art magazine's promotional function, I hope to complicate this familiar story by showing that the magazine was a highly ambivalent site in which multiple kinds of publicity—both promotional and progressive—coexisted.

NO MORE REPRODUCTIONS: CONCEPTUAL ART AND THE MAGAZINE

A standard card file. A photostat of a dictionary definition. A set of instructions to be carried out by the viewer. Sculptures made out of steam, frost, and growing grass. A reel of transparent film. A canceled performance. An empty gallery. This is the kind of art that Lucy Lippard and John Chandler had in mind when they coined the term "dematerialization" in 1968, writing:

1.1

Lee Lozano, *Throwing Up Piece*, 1969 (detail of
notebook page). Ink from ball-point and felt-tip
pen on note paper. Collection of Richard Tuttle,
New York. © The Estate of Lee Lozano. Courtesy
of Hauser & Wirth.

During the 1960s, the anti-intellectual, emotional/intuitive processes of art-making characteristic
of the last two decades have begun to give way to an ultra-conceptual art that emphasizes the
thinking process almost exclusively. … Such a trend appears to be provoking a profound domaterioli-
zation of art, especially the art object, and if it continues to prevail, it may result in the art object's
becoming wholly obsolete.[3]

The prospect of the disappearance of the art object carried with it the utopian promise that art might escape its status as commodity and circumvent the gallery to become a truly accessible and democratic form of expression. While Lippard and Chandler did not fully explore these political implications of dematerialization in their 1968 article, by December 1969 Lippard would state in an interview with Ursula Meyer, "The artists who are trying to do non-object art are introducing a drastic solution to the problem of artists being bought and sold so easily, along with their art."[4]

And yet the dematerialization of art did not, as the critics predicted, result in the evaporation of art into thin air, but produced, in lieu of traditional art objects, a strange subset of documents—texts, photographs, maps, lists, and diagrams—which served as evidence, as stand-in, as archival trace of the artistic act. With its reliance on textual and photographic documentation, conceptual art ushered in a dramatically new set of exhibition practices—practices that no longer revolved around the display of unique objects but were instead based on the reproduced page. Lippard later recalled, "one of the things we often speculated about in the late sixties was the role of the art magazine. In an era of proposed projects, photo-text works, and artists' books, a periodical could be the ideal vehicle for art itself, rather than merely for reproduction, commentary and promotion."[5] The dealer Seth Siegelaub was among those to pioneer the use of printed publications—including books, posters, catalogues, Xeroxed booklets, and magazines—in the display and distribution of conceptual art, explaining in a 1970 interview:

For many years it has been well known that more people are aware of an artist's work through
(1) the printed media or (2) conversation than by direct confrontation with the work itself. …
When art concerns itself with things not germane to physical presence, its intrinsic (communicative)
value is not altered by its presentation in printed media. The use of catalogues and books to
communicate (and disseminate) art is the most neutral means to present the new art. The catalogue
can now act as primary information for the exhibition, as opposed to secondary information about
art in magazines, catalogues, etc., and in some cases the "exhibition" can be the "catalogue."[6]

Siegelaub explored these ideas in his "July/August 1970," an exhibition that took place solely in the British art magazine *Studio International* and featured works made expressly for the page. (I discuss this exhibition in the epilogue.) Siegelaub's pragmatic embrace of the art magazine as a new site of display highlights the contradictions inherent in conceptual art's utopian attempt to escape the market, since the magazine's promotional publicity was central to Siegelaub's ability to market this art.[7] However, while conceptual art relied upon and even exploited the magazine's promotional function, it also disrupted the magazine's conventions as a form of communication.

The critic Gregory Battcock drew attention to the subversive potential of such practices in his 1970 *Arts Magazine* article "Documentation in Conceptual Art," observing:

The following documentations introduce serious questions concerning the function of an art magazine in a Conceptual Art environment. They seem to threaten the continuing vitality of traditional art criticism and the role of art illustration. … After all, in this instance, the works of art are not reproductions; the pages that follow are works of art. There are no more reproductions. There is no more criticism. No more aesthetics. Only art. … These artists have provided yet another positive contribution to the ultimate and long overdue reidentification of the medium of the art magazine.[8]

The pages that the critic so emphatically declared "only art" looked more or less like ordinary magazine pages, comprising an impartially delivered list of statements by Sol LeWitt, a hand-drawn diagram by Mel Bochner, a set of instructions by Lawrence Weiner, and a theoretical essay by Daniel Buren. And yet it was precisely this ordinariness—this indistinguishability from the surrounding pages—that made these works so radical. By dissolving the distinctions between art and art criticism, reproduction and original, these works implicitly challenged the magazine's hierarchy of authority and, not least, the authority of the art critic. While Battcock affirmed with a wink his own role as co-conspirator in this project, he simultaneously alluded to the larger politics of the art magazine and the tensions between artists and critics that made the questions raised by these works so pointed.

A BRIEF HISTORY OF THE ART MAGAZINE: TO PUBLISH = "TO MAKE PUBLIC"

The art magazine had its origin in the self-published pamphlets that were distributed on the occasion of the Salon, the first free public exhibition of art, which opened at the Louvre in 1737. Indeed, art criticism was central to the progressive nature of the public sphere as it emerged in eighteenth-century Europe, as described by Jürgen Habermas in his classic account of the formation of a new kind of critical publicity that allowed the bourgeois class to oppose the ruling power's authority. One of the primary roles of criticism, according to Habermas, was to provide a kind of practice round, which would sharpen the capacity of individuals to think critically and prepare them to engage in "real" juridical and ethical debates in the public sphere: "In the institution of art criticism … the lay judgment of a public that had come of age … became organized. … The art critics could see themselves as spokesmen for the public."[9]

Early art criticism was deeply tied to the social experience of the exhibition space of the Salon—a notoriously crowded and noisy place, where the people-watching rivaled the art on view.[10] As Habermas describes, "the innumerable pamphlets criticizing or defending the leading theory of art built on the discussions of the salons and reacted back on them—art criticism as conversation."[11] This interplay between printed criticism and spoken language was key to how art criticism distinguished itself from its elitist predecessor, connoisseurship, since, unlike the latter, art criticism was not intended to impose the critic's opinion on the viewer, but to encourage the viewer's own critical judgment.

The first periodicals stressed this interconnectedness between the spoken and printed word. In particular, Habermas describes how the periodical fostered a participatory sort of communication among a public too large to converse face to face, by allowing individual readers to see themselves as part of a larger, ongoing conversation. Periodicals were "so intimately interwoven with the life of the coffee houses," he claims, that "periodical articles were not only made the object of discussion by the public of the coffee houses but were viewed as integral parts of this discussion."[12] Habermas cites the dialog form used by many of the articles and the practice of publishing letters to the editor as evidence of the distinct reciprocity of public discourse fostered by these early periodicals: "One and the same discussion transposed into a different medium was continued in order to reenter, via reading, the original conversational medium."[13] The periodical's progressive function in the public sphere was thus tied to its unique distribution form—its circulation and seriality—which extended the thread of a conversation through space and time to be picked up by different groups of readers.

While some of these early periodicals contained art criticism alongside more general cultural and political topics, periodicals devoted solely to art did not arise until the middle of the eighteenth century. Indeed, as Thomas Crow notes, the very idea of a regularly published art journal was initially deemed outlandish by Academy officials, who feared it would "degenerate in no time to criticisms, mockery, and baseless judgments" and become "no more than a periodical series of insults which would aggrieve our artists, close the studios and ruin public exhibitions."[14] Due to its libelous potential, art criticism was officially censored between the 1750s and the beginning of the 1770s, during which time it was available to only an exclusive few. Denis Diderot's criticism, for example, was circulated clandestinely in the *Correspondance littéraire*, a handwritten newsletter with a secret subscription list of fifteen names.[15] Clearly, within the rigidly controlled world of academic painting in the eighteenth century, the art magazine—and the new public it was seen as capable of rousing—threatened to upset the established relationship between artists and their patrons.

It is telling, then, that when the first magazines devoted solely to art did arise, first in Germany and then throughout Europe and the United States, they were largely sponsored by art academies themselves, and were concerned with news, information, and promotion rather than critical commentary. Art periodicals during the nineteenth century largely followed this model of the academy-sanctioned press. They ranged from scholarly art historical and antiquarian journals to those addressed to a more general public, containing articles on art history, connoisseurship, aesthetics, and the biographies of artists, as well as exhibition reviews, news, and obituaries.[16] While a handful of early art magazines stood out as important critical vehicles— among them Johann Wolfgang von Goethe's *Propyläen* (1798–1800); the Parisian magazine *L'Artiste* (1831–1904), which published writers such as Charles Baudelaire and Honoré de Balzac; the American Pre-Raphaelite magazine *The Crayon* (1855–1861), which published John Ruskin and Henry James; and art nouveau magazines such as the London-based *The Studio* (1893–) and the Berlin-based *Pan* (1895–1900)—these were the exception rather than the rule. A far cry from the scandalous self-published pamphlets of Salon criticism, art magazines in the nineteenth century were increasingly geared toward an upper-middle-class audience interested in art as pastime or decoration; according to one account, they were "brought into being to grace the cultivated drawing rooms" of the time.[17] Meanwhile, the rise of advertising in the 1830s had radically restructured the entire business of the press. As Carl Bücher argued, "the paper assumes the character of an enterprise which produces advertising space as a commodity that is made marketable by means of an editorial section."[18] The rise of advertising precipitated the disintegration of the public sphere from a site of true critical publicity into the ersatz "pseudopublicity" that Habermas observed in the twentieth-century culture industry.

This admittedly abbreviated gloss on the history of the art magazine sheds some light on its initial promise as a site of critical publicity. Part of what made *Artforum* so exceptional in the 1960s was the way in which it harked back to the Enlightenment model of the public sphere described by Habermas—and, one could argue, in some measure succeeded in realizing it, at least for a time. Begun in San Francisco as a renegade alternative to the mainstream art press (then consisting of *Art in America, Arts Magazine,* and *Art News*), *Artforum* self-consciously invoked the democratic principles that guided the founding of art criticism in the eighteenth century. Its very title implied that the magazine sought to function, like the ancient Roman marketplace which was its namesake, as a space for public debate and discussion. Such a space was originally literally embodied within the publication in its special "forum" section, demarcated by colored paper, which an editorial note promised would "contain a lot of divergent and contradictory opinion." These aspirations were echoed by formalist criticism's own ambitions to reclaim its public purpose in the 1960s. Meanwhile, artists began to participate in the discourse surrounding their work in unprecedented ways, challenging not only the claims of criticism but the very model of the bourgeois public sphere on which it depended. By the end of the decade, some increasingly questioned whether the criticism in *Artforum* had been overshadowed by the promotional aspect of the magazine and its role in the spectacular consumption of art. It was largely due to such concerns that several *Artforum* critics broke away from the magazine and founded the dissident journal *October* in 1976.

ARTFORUM: PROBLEMS OF CRITICISM

In June 1962 *Artforum* hit the newsstands. The square-shaped glossy periodical, with its name boldly printed in the top right-hand corner in capitalized black sans serif lettering, was considerably slighter and sparer than it is today, with a stapled spine and just a few small black-and-white gallery advertisements. On its cover, against an ochre background, was a barely discernible detail of a kinetic sculpture by Jean Tinguely: a dark, mysterious, tenebrous form that in its very indistinctness suggested the inchoate identity of the fledgling publication itself. With a circulation of around 3,000, the first issue of this unknown magazine published in California gave few indications of the decisive role it would play in the 1960s art world.[19]

Charles Cowles, *Artforum*'s publisher from 1965 to 1970, was only mildly exaggerating when he claimed that the magazine was founded by "several people in San Francisco who knew nothing about art or the art world."[20] These included Philip Leider, a law school dropout working in a local gallery, who was the magazine's first editor; a printing salesman named John Irwin, who convinced his boss at Pisani Printers to back the project financially; and the artist John Coplans, who would succeed Leider as editor in 1971. *Artforum* was founded as a mouthpiece for West Coast artists who felt overlooked by the mainstream New York-based art press, and especially as "a counterpoint to *Art News*," which under the editorship of Thomas Hess in the 1950s had become the leading art magazine in the United States at that time.[21] A statement printed in the first issue indicated the editorial mission of the new publication: "*Artforum* is an art magazine published in the West—but not only a magazine of Western art. We are concerned first with Western activity but claim the world of art as our domain. *Artforum* presents a medium for free exchange of critical opinion."[22]

THIS IS NOT TO BE LOOKED AT

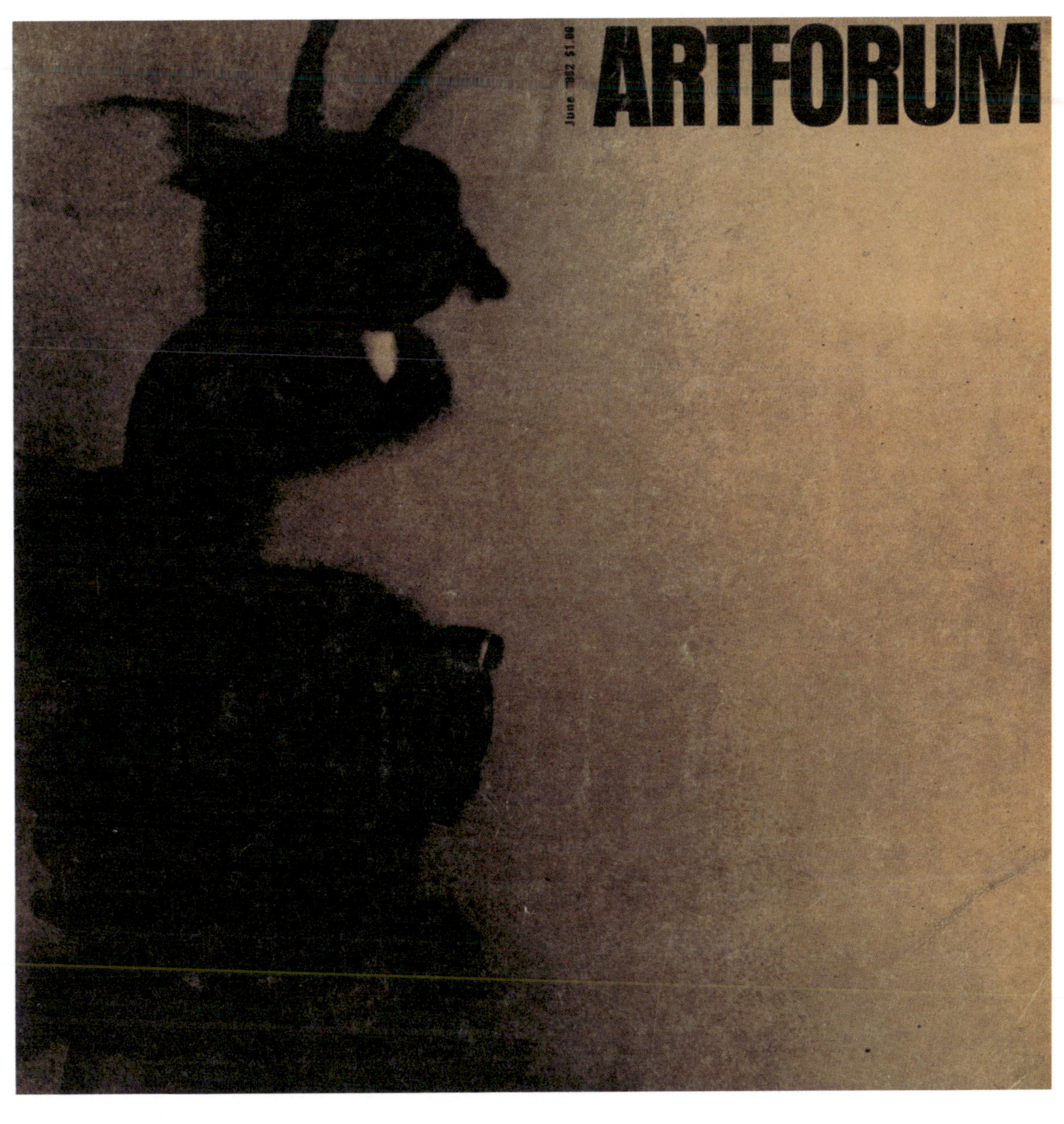

1.2

Artforum 1, no. 1, June 1962, cover. © *Artforum*.
Courtesy of *Artforum*.

Early issues of the magazine, with their typos and the occasional upside-down picture, attest to a period of trial and error as Leider and the other staff members confronted the steep learning curve of the task at hand. As Leider recalled, "I can't tell you how green I was. I didn't know what typesetting was, I didn't know what photo-engraving was. I didn't know anything. … I had to learn *everything*."[23] The magazine's remove from both the publishing business and the New York art world played a role in the editorial risks that made *Artforum* so remarkable during the 1960s. It was the publication's initial aloofness from East Coast art world politics—its "purity"—that appealed to the group of New York critics who began writing for the magazine in the mid-1960s, a group that included Max Kozloff, Barbara Rose, Lucy Lippard, Sidney Tillim, Michael Fried, Robert Pincus-Witten, Annette Michelson, and Rosalind Krauss. According to Kozloff, who was among the first New York critics to be hired, *Artforum* was "a thin, local—and therefore, it seemed, a marginalized thing."[24]

As it gained a reputation and increased its advertising and subscriptions, the magazine soon followed the art world's gravitational pull; it moved to Los Angeles in 1965 and then to New York in 1967, earning accusations of having abandoned the West Coast art scene for East Coast prestige and advertising revenue. Yet it is difficult to imagine that Leider was enticed by fame or fortune. He initially wanted *Artforum* to be advertisement-free, and he once described his near-phobic avoidance of the art world's social scene: "I … prefer correspondence to other forms of communication, hate using the telephone, am terrified of meeting people, … [and] get physically sick at all social functions, especially art world parties and openings."[25] Nevertheless, once in New York *Artforum* was not merely swept into the centripetal force of the art world; in many ways, the publication became the center of its orbit. Donald Judd, writing in 1969, complained, "*Artforum* since moving to New York has seemed like *Art News* in the 1950s. There's serious high art and then there's everybody else, all equally low. … Bell and Irwin hardly exist; Greenbergers such as Krauss review all the shows. … *Artforum* is probably the best art magazine but it's depressing that it's gotten so bad and close to the others."[26]

While Greenberg rarely wrote for *Artforum*, his influence dominated the magazine during the 1960s. Greenberg's method of formalist criticism distinguished itself from the belletristic "purple prose" favored by *Art News* in the 1950s. "Art writing and art criticism as such are becoming discredited," Greenberg had warned in his influential 1962 article "How Art Writing Earns Its Bad Name," singling out the "rhetoric and logical solecisms" published in *Art News* as the worst offenders.[27] By contrast, Greenberg's formalist criticism sought to reinvigorate the public purpose of art criticism through a renewed commitment to objectivity achieved through a nearly scientific elaboration of art's form that would validate its aesthetic superiority in empirical terms.

Greenberg's influence was especially evident in the writings of Michael Fried, toward whom Leider felt an intense allegiance. *Artforum*'s editorial sponsorship of Fried was evident in both the frequency of his articles and the prominence they were given within the magazine. As Leider remembered of choosing the cover image, "I wanted to direct the reader's attention to the most important thing in the magazine. As often as I could I would tie it to an article by Michael."[28] *Artforum* covers from the mid- to late 1960s were in fact disproportionately devoted to the late modernist artists Fried championed, including Olitski, Noland, Caro, Louis, and perhaps most conspicuously Stella, to whom three covers were devoted between 1966 and 1970.

One of the striking things about the formalist criticism published in *Artforum* in the 1960s is its heightened sense of moral and ethical urgency—a criticality that reestablished criticism's connection, implicit in its etymology, to a state of crisis. For example, Fried famously ended "Art and Objecthood" with the phrase, "Presentness is grace," describing the experience of modernist art through the theological concept of salvation. As he later recalled, "I was sure that what I was doing mattered—in fact I thought that nothing less than the future of Western civilization was at stake in 'Art and Objecthood' and the other essays of 1966–67."[29] Thomas Crow has characterized the moral fervor of this criticism as "compensatory," suggesting how it served as a marker for the political dimension of modernist art and criticism that had been central to their origins in the Enlightenment but that had since been lost or repressed: "Modernist criticism brought into the 1960s a surplus of moral commitment that was the relic of an earlier dream of art as the focus of an ideal public sphere."[30]

However, as the 1960s wore on, the moral claims of formalist criticism began to ring hollow in the face of its total exclusion of social and political issues. Moreover, this criticism was revealed to be inadequate as an interpretive framework for art that was no longer formal but conceptual in nature. Such quandaries were documented in a ten-part series of articles published in *Artforum* between 1967 and 1971 entitled "Problems of Criticism." In its very title, this series signaled the new kind of seriousness and self-scrutiny that characterized the practice of art criticism in this period, as well as the growing lack of consensus over precisely what was at stake. The articles gave voice to stark differences of opinion, as Greenberg defended his increasingly apoliticized brand of formalism, claiming, "You cannot legitimately want or hope for anything from art except quality."[31] Meanwhile, Barbara Rose attacked formalist criticism as elitist and inadequate in the face of new conceptual and performance-based art—art that, she pointed out, "challenges not only the market mechanism, but also the authority of the critic by rendering superfluous his role of connoisseur of value or gourmet of quality."[32] And Rosalind Krauss revealed her break with the doctrine of Fried and Greenberg as she became intrigued by the temporality of minimalist and postminimalist art.

Leider expressed his own misgivings about formalist criticism and his increasing fascination with antiformalist, conceptual practices in an article he published in the September 1970 issue, entitled "How I Spent My Summer Vacation, or, Art and Politics in Nevada, Berkeley, San Francisco and Utah (Read about It in *Artforum*!)." The article chronicled his cross-country trip through the deserts of Nevada and Utah, where he visited recently executed earthworks including Michael Heizer's *Double Negative* (1969) and Robert Smithson's *Spiral Jetty* (1970). Written in the present tense, it recreates for the reader the rush of disconnected events and sights Leider experienced and contemplated on his journey. Peppered with quotations from Abbie Hoffman, the article returns repeatedly to the relationship between art and politics, trying, if unsuccessfully, to reconcile these terms. The most salient political reference is to the Vietnam War—the war saturates the essay, forming the backdrop against which Leider's reflections take place—but he also mentions Kent State, Altamont, the Weather Underground, the Manson murders, the feminist movement, and the ecology movement.

Leider wonders "whether the times were not forcing us to a completely new set of ideas about what an artist was and what an artist did," and in an assessment that breaks completely with formalist criteria, he notes that "the question of what is revolutionary art isn't too different,

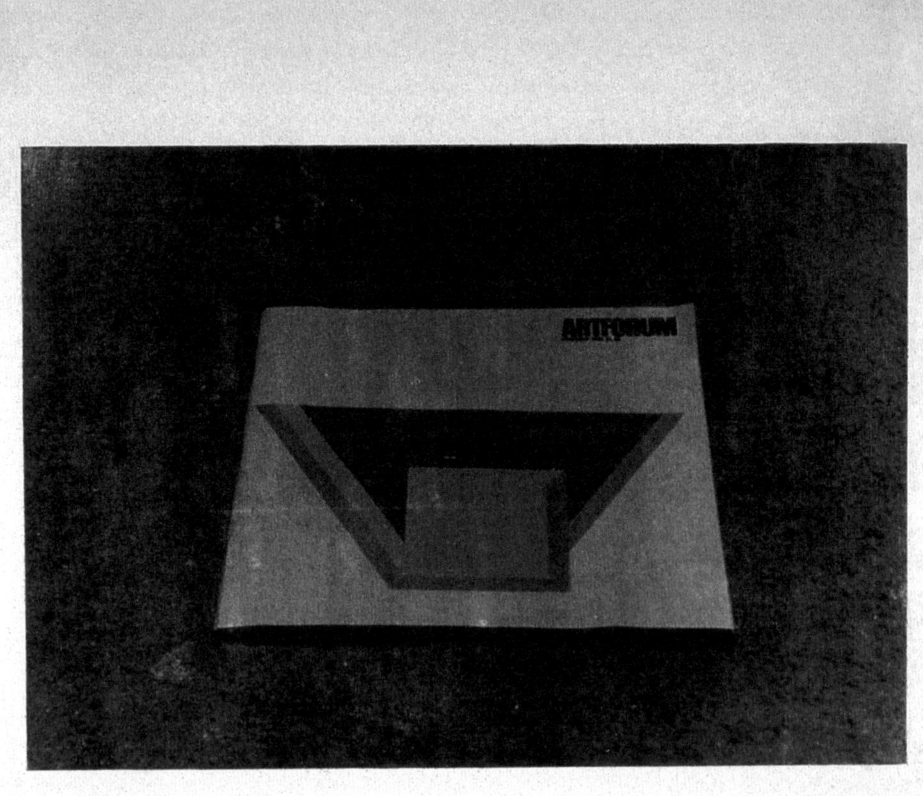

1.3

John Baldessari, *THIS IS NOT TO BE LOOKED AT*,
1966–1968. Acrylic, photo-emulsion on canvas,
59 × 45 inches. Courtesy of Marian Goodman Gallery.

in the end, from the question of what is good art."[33] If Leider's article conveys his disillusionment
with formalist criticism, it also hints at his growing disenchantment with the magazine itself, for
the self-deprecating subtitle "Read about It in *Artforum!*" sarcastically compares the magazine to
a sensationalist tabloid. Leider's article implies that the sense of crisis that pervaded art criticism
at this moment was not merely related to changes in art's medium; it was also deeply tied to a
transformation in the *media* of criticism: the art magazine.

In his 1968 work *THIS IS NOT TO BE LOOKED AT,* the artist John Baldessari paired an image
of the cover of the November 1966 issue of *Artforum* with the text, appropriated from Francisco
Goya's *Disasters of War* series, "THIS IS NOT TO BE LOOKED AT." This work is emblematic
of conceptual art's rejection of the exclusively visual concerns of modernist art and art criticism,
exemplified by Greenberg's influential notion of opticality. Indeed, the particular issue of the
magazine Baldessari chose to depict featured Frank Stella's painting *Union III* (1966) on its cover,
and contained Michael Fried's important essay "Shape as Form: Frank Stella's Irregular Polygons,"
in which the critic hailed Stella's work as the pinnacle of modernist painting because of the way
that it announces its medium by making shape a function of visual rather than tactile apprehen-
sion—in other words, because of the way that it privileges vision above the other senses. However,
if conceptual art's iconoclasm was directed against the "opticality" of art and art criticism in the
1960s, Baldessari implies that it was also aimed at the visuality of the magazine itself.

Driven by advances in printing technology and the demands of a growing readership, art
magazines boasted larger formats, coated pages, and an abundance of high-quality, and increasingly color, reproductions during the 1950s and 1960s, establishing a new visual culture within
which art and art criticism were experienced. A 1962 study entitled "Periodicals in the Visual
Arts" included among the current trends for art magazines "an emphasis upon visual communication," observing that "art periodicals are being designed to be 'seen' rather than 'read.'"[34] *Artforum* in
particular underscored this new salience of the image in its format and layout (which happened
to be designed by Ed Ruscha during the 1960s, under the pseudonym Eddie Russia). *Artforum's*
signature square shape and Helvetica-derived logo were indebted to modernist principles of
Swiss design.[35] Driven by the mandate of legibility, Swiss design replaced the traditional vertical
orientation of print with a gridded expanse in which text and image were integrated as equal,
interchangeable elements. Through its graphic design, *Artforum* not only declared itself a modern
publication with an up-to-date look and sensibility; it also insisted that the basis of this novelty
resided in its function as a new kind of visual field.

The new visual character of the art magazine in the 1960s proved auspicious for modernist
criticism's formalist methodology. As Rosalind Krauss later remarked, "new criticism in art depended on the magazine—on the availability of good reproductions as evidence."[36] However, this
new visuality also altered the magazine's role in the evaluation of art, greatly amplifying its promotional tendencies. To take an often-cited example, in 1958 Jasper Johns's painting *Target with
Four Faces* (1955) appeared in full color on the cover of *Art News* on the occasion of the artist's
first solo exhibition at the then-unknown Leo Castelli Gallery. The show promptly sold out, and
Alfred Barr purchased three paintings, including the one reproduced on the magazine cover, for

the Museum of Modern Art.[37] Most tellings of this story don't mention what was actually written about Johns's work (a measly paragraph-long review); rather, it was the appearance of the work on the magazine cover that allegedly accounted for its sudden rise in stature, proving the adage that "A reproduction in a magazine is worth two one-person shows."[38]

As this example demonstrates, the integration of criticism within the spectacular economy of the commercial art magazine greatly accelerated the process of evaluating art. Whereas early criticism depended on the duration of the dialog form as well as the uncertainty of a conclusion that is central to the unfolding of spoken conversation, the newly visual character of the art magazine replaced the unhurried pace of thought and conversation with the immediacy of an overnight sensation. This new speed undoubtedly contributed to the acculturation of the avant-garde that Clement Greenberg in 1967 dubbed "novelty art," to suggest the way in which artistic movements increasingly mimicked consumer products in cycles of planned obsolescence. "I find myself back in the realm of Good Design, where Pop Art, Assemblage, and the rest of novelty art live," he complained, suggesting that the radical nature or "far-out"-ness of art had itself become formulaic and predictable, merely another fashion.[39] Greenberg singled out minimalism as the prime example of novelty art. As James Meyer has shown, this sculpture, despite its unconventional form, proved surprisingly easy to consume as a look or style, influencing even designer dresses and living room furniture.[40] The minimalist discourse that circulated in magazines, while crucial to the aesthetic significance of this art, was also inevitably a factor in the spectacular consumption of minimalist art, suggesting the dialectical nature of the art magazine as a site of publicity in the 1960s and 1970s. However unfamiliar or "far-out" its medium (a steel cube, a row of bricks, a pile of dirt), when this sculpture was encountered in a magazine's well-designed pages and expertly cropped photographs, it was instantly and automatically recognized as art. Dan Graham aptly expressed this power of the art magazine:

> Through the actual experience of running a gallery [the John Daniels gallery, where minimalist artists such as Dan Flavin, Robert Smithson, and Sol LeWitt exhibited in the mid-1960s], I learned that if a work of art wasn't written about and reproduced in a magazine it would have difficulty attaining the status of "art." It seemed that in order to be defined as having value—that is, as "art"—a work had only to be exhibited in a gallery and then to be written about and reproduced as a photograph in an art magazine. Then this record of the no longer extant installation, along with more accretions of information after the fact, became the basis for its fame, and to a large extent, its economic value.[41]

Art criticism had always been enmeshed in the market, a fact that is not necessarily at odds with its progressive function but, one could argue, has actually been central to it, since criticism mediated between aesthetic and economic value, preventing art from being reduced to pure investment potential.[42] However, the promotional capacity of criticism intensified during the 1960s as the art market escalated, as reflected by *Artforum*'s swelling advertisement section.[43] As Krauss recalled, "the whole issue of the promotional ends to which art writing was put … was in the air at the time. And I remember feeling very anguished about this. You know, to what degree was writing about someone a factor in raising his or her price."[44] Such concerns were compounded by the revelation, in the October 1970 issue of *Artforum*, of Greenberg's own work as a paid consultant to the New York gallery French and Company. In the article, Ad Reinhardt referred to Greenberg as a dealer—an exaggeration, perhaps, but one that contained enough truth to be embarrassing to Greenberg. Infuriated, Greenberg stopped speaking to both Leider and Fried, who also somehow stopped speaking to one another over the incident when Fried refused to choose sides—a rift in personal friendships that served as a microcosm of the larger fault lines within the practice of criticism, and within the magazine itself, at this time.[45] Leider resigned from *Artforum* a year later, in fall 1971.

LYNDA BENGLIS'S *ARTFORUM* AD AND THE FOUNDING OF *OCTOBER*

If the spectacular visuality of the art magazine diminished its function as a site of critical publicity, it also produced a novel set of conditions through which art might engage its public. This was made clear in an advertisement taken out by the artist Lynda Benglis in the November 1974 issue of *Artforum*. In this well-known image, Benglis appears nude, suggestively brandishing a large, double-headed dildo. The work was a response to the hypermasculine publicity images being circulated by Robert Morris and other male artists at the time, such as Morris's poster for his April 1974 Castelli-Sonnabend exhibition, which showed the artist bare-chested, in chains, and wearing a German war helmet (this image had been reproduced in an article about Morris's work in the September 1974 issue of *Artforum*). Well aware of the vexed role of publicity in the art world at the time, Benglis intended the ad to function, at least in part, as a parody, "mocking the commercial aspect of the ad, the art-star system, and the way artists use themselves, their persona to sell the work. … The placement of the ad, in an art magazine, was important."[46] Benglis originally requested that the photograph be included in an article about her work by Robert Pincus-Witten. However, when then-editor John Coplans refused to run the image in the editorial space according to her specifications, he suggested that she take out an ad instead.

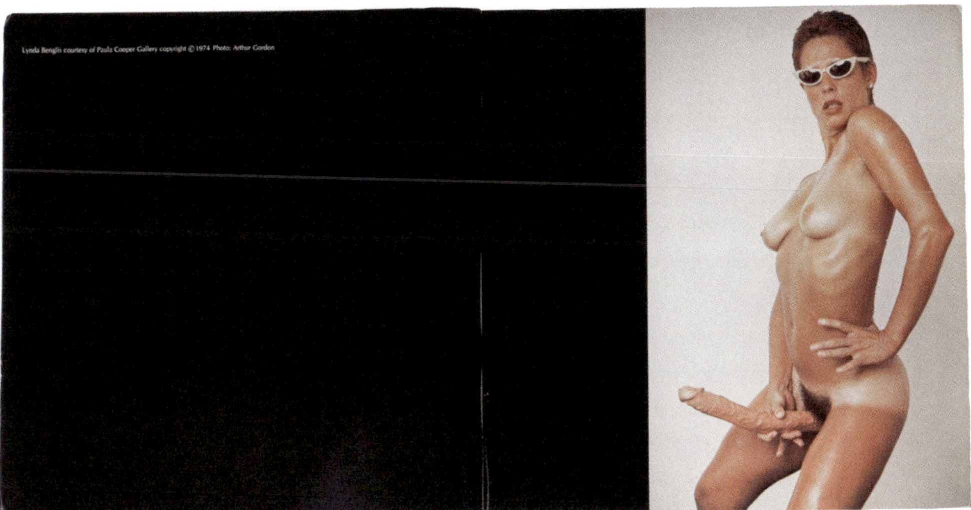

1.4

Lynda Benglis, *Artforum* advertisement, 1974.
Courtesy of Cheim & Read, New York. © *Artforum*,
November 1974.

Though Coplans evidently intended to preserve the integrity of the magazine's editorial section, Benglis's advertisement had precisely the opposite effect. It caused a commotion among *Artforum*'s editorial staff, becoming a point of cathexis for a host of anxieties and frustrations, chief among them the promotional role of criticism and the gender politics of the art world. Several critics wrote an angry letter to the editor in which they expressed their indignation, stating that they "felt compelled to publicly dissociate themselves" from the magazine. While the critics objected to the vulgarity of the ad, what they found most disturbing, they wrote, was the "crudeness with which the advertisement has pictured the journal's role as devoted to the promotion of artists in the most debased sense of that term."[47] By equating the advertising space of the magazine with a form of sexual solicitation, the ad implied, as the critic Annette Michelson explained, "that the magazine itself is the brothel within which things are for sale. And I did not see myself as the inhabitant of an intellectual brothel."[48]

And yet, if Benglis's ad functioned as a canny metaphor for the promiscuous trafficking of aesthetic and economic value taking place between the covers of the magazine (the gendered implications of which were especially charged, given the high percentage of *Artforum* critics who were women),[49] its ability to shock depended on more than mere metaphor. Part of what made the ad so unsettling was the way in which it simultaneously exploited and critiqued the spectacular visuality of the magazine itself, using it to stage a different kind of public address. As Benglis insisted, "Context was a very important issue: it was an *artwork*, not a picture of the artist."[50] Indeed, the impact of Benglis's image depends quite specifically on the distinct format of the magazine: its full-page color reproductions and the vividness with which its glossy pages convey colors and textures; the way in which the image takes the viewer by surprise when the page is turned, as well as its inescapable associations with a pornographic centerfold. As Richard Meyer has incisively observed of Benglis's photograph, it "does not document a performance so much as it enacts one."[51] Importantly, this performance takes place not only within the photograph, but very much within the communicative medium of the magazine itself.

Benglis's advertisement was a catalyst in the subsequent resignation of several *Artforum* editors—including Krauss, Michelson, and Jeremy Gilbert-Rolfe—who went on to found the journal *October*. The ad was "the last straw," according to Krauss, in the growing dissatisfaction and discord among the *Artforum* editorial staff under Coplans.[52] In particular, there was resentment over his perceived lack of commitment to newer media such as film, video, and performance (which were pervasive in the pages of magazines such as *Avalanche* by that point) and his aversion to the kind of intensive, lengthy academic articles that had appeared in the magazine under Leider. Both of these qualities were indirectly related to the fact that Coplans was attempting to create a more sellable, easily consumable product (he had, after all, taken over a nearly bankrupt magazine).[53] In the first issue of *October*, published in Spring 1976, the editors revealed their newfound wariness about the role of images in the practice of art criticism, confessing, "Long working experience with major art journals has convinced us of the need to restore to the criticism of painting and sculpture, as to that of the other arts, an intellectual autonomy seriously undermined by emphasis on extensive reviewing and lavish illustration."[54] Against the visual excess of the mainstream art press, *October* carried no gallery advertisements and vowed to be "plain of aspect, its illustrations determined by considerations of textual clarity."[55]

OCTOBER

1

Michel Foucault — *"Ceci n'est pas une pipe"*

Richard Foreman — *The Carrot and the Stick*

Noël Burch — *To the Distant Observer:*
Towards a Theory of Japanese Film

Richard Howard — *The Giant on Giant-Killing*

Rosalind Krauss — *Video: The Aesthetics of Narcissism*

Jeremy Gilbert-Rolfe
and John Johnston — *Gravity's Rainbow and the Spiral Jetty*

Jean-Claude Lebensztejn — *Star*

Hollis Frampton — *Notes on Composing in Film*

Spring 1976 $3.00

1.5

October, no. 1, Spring 1976, cover.

October's very title suggested its aspirations to revolutionize artistic discourse: "We have named this journal in celebration of that moment in our century when revolutionary practice, theoretical inquiry and artistic innovation were joined in a manner exemplary and unique."[56] Notably, the journal referenced not only the October revolution itself but specifically its memorialization in Sergei Eisenstein's 1927–1928 film, thus suggesting *October*'s commitment to new media and interdisciplinary inquiry. Indeed, in direct opposition to formalist criticism's insistence on medium-specificity, *October* sought to counter the segregation of different media within "various overspecialized reviews," and to "reopen an inquiry into the relationship between the several arts which flourish in our culture. … Thus, innovations in the performing arts have been inflected by the achievements of painters and sculptors, those of film-makers have been shaped by poetic theory and practice."[57]

The artist Lucio Pozzi, who was involved in the very early planning stages of *October*, though he would drop out of the project before the first issue was published, designed the magazine's layout and logo.[58] The subdued design, consisting of elegant black Baskerville lettering on a cream background with the issue number in red, was a dead ringer for the Parisian avant-garde literary journal *Tel Quel*—an homage that signaled the kind of intensive critical discourse that October sought to foster. In addition to texts by art historians, critics, and theorists, including Jacques Derrida, Michel Foucault, Julia Kristeva, Douglas Crimp, and Craig Owens, *October* published texts by artists, filmmakers, and writers including Eisenstein, Daniel Buren, Tricia Brown, Laurie Anderson, Hollis Frampton, Michael Snow, Samuel Beckett, Yvonne Rainer, Robert Morris, and Carl Andre, demonstrating the intersection between theory and practice that the publication sought to chart and advance.

Founded as the result of an editorial mutiny that produced a seismic shift in the way art criticism was practiced, *October* suggests how magazines both stem out of such ruptures in discourse and perpetuate them, by allowing ideas that were once nascent or marginal to surface and become influential, sometimes even dominant, prompting a subsequent generation of revolts—and new magazines. Magazines not only embody collective ideals and goals, but also register conflict and schisms (Gilbert-Rolfe disappeared from the masthead of *October* after the third issue, explaining, "I wanted it to be a journal of divergent approaches, and by the time we got to number three it was clear that it wasn't going to be that").[59] The beginnings of magazines are frequently dialectically linked to their endings, which often indicate not so much the dissolution of their original editorial goals as their realization—a realization that in some sense renders the magazine itself less necessary—which may be one reason why so many little magazines are so fleeting. This dynamic will play out again and again in many of the case studies in the chapters that follow.

The SoHo bookseller Jaap Rietman, known for stocking rare and alternative artists' books and periodicals, helped to finance the first issue of *October*, and was its sole distributor.[60] Rietman's bookstore, at West Broadway and Spring Street, was a "cramped but snug" space, where artists frequently worked as cashiers.[61] As one writer described the shop, "books were piled high on shelves and counters. They burst into the aisle and caught at your clothes. A perfectly innocent gesture could sweep a whole bundle of magazines underfoot."[62] If one had wandered into Rietman's bookstore in the 1970s, one would have seen, in addition to *October*, an array of other independently published magazines, including several of the artists' magazines that will be discussed in subsequent chapters. These publications attest to the fact that the revolutionary changes in artistic discourse in the 1960s and 1970s were generated not only by critics and art historians, but by artists themselves.

A MUSEUM OF LANGUAGE: ARTISTS' WRITINGS AND INTERVENTIONS

As critics were debating the meaning of art and criticism in the pages of *Artforum* in the 1960s, artists had begun to take part in the discussion, too. It is a testament to Philip Leider's insightfulness, but also perhaps to his plucky indifference toward the art world's chain of command, that he opened the magazine up as a laboratory for the experimental writings of artists, including Dan Flavin, Robert Morris, Robert Smithson, and Sol LeWitt. LeWitt prefaced his "Paragraphs on Conceptual Art" by explaining, "the editor has written to me that he is in favor of avoiding 'the notion that the artist is a kind of ape that has to be explained by the civilized critic.' This should be good news to both artists and apes."[63] Indeed, with Leider's encouragement, artists began to "talk back" to critics, writing about their own work and that of their peers, participating to an unprecedented degree in the critical debates around their work, challenging, as LeWitt called it, "the secret language that art critics use when communicating with one another through the medium of art magazines."[64]

According to Leider, the artists who wrote for *Artforum* during his tenure did so "as a reaction to the state of affairs in criticism: the artists who wrote for me were artists directly opposed to the criticism I was publishing (and the artists the critics liked didn't feel the need to write). Artists who wrote for *Artforum* wrote defensively, against what they took to be misguided critics. So you could say with some truth that the state of affairs in criticism is the most immediate cause of the rash of artist's writings I published."[65] Alternately campy, parodic, manifesto-like, and grammatically adventurous, these writings were stylistically at odds with the dispassionate, exacting prose of formalist criticism. The first installation of Morris's "Notes on Sculpture," published in *Artforum* in February 1966, for example, began as a spoof on formalist criticism, burlesquing its authoritative tone and linear historiography.[66] Even the layout of these articles on the page—which at times playfully mimicked the forms of the artists' work itself—communicated their unusual status. As Smithson would describe artists' writings from this period, they formed a "museum of language" in which "language covers rather than discovers its sites and situations, here language closes rather than discloses doors to utilitarian interpretations and explanations."[67] In Carl Andre's writings, Smithson notes, "thoughts are crushed into a rubble of syncopated syllables. Reason becomes a powder of vowels and consonants."[68] Robert Morris "enjoys putting sham mistakes into his language systems."[69] Donald Judd uses a "language full of holes—a language that ebbs from the mind into an ocean of words." Dan Flavin's "language falls toward its final dissolution like the sullen electricities in Flavin's lights."[70] "LeWitt is very much aware of the traps and pitfalls of language."[71] Even as minimalist artists participated in the critical debates around their work, Smithson suggests that they questioned the very grounds of this debate by challenging the principles of rational and objective communication upon which formalist criticism—and the bourgeois public sphere itself—rested. In this sense these writings attempt to stake out a different kind of communication within the discursive space of the art magazine.

One of the ways they do this is by challenging the very distinction between art and criticism. Smithson's own writings, such as "A Tour of the Monuments of Passaic, New Jersey" (*Artforum*,

1.6

Sol LeWitt, "Paragraphs on Conceptual Art."
© *Artforum*, Summer 1967, page 79. © 2010
The LeWitt Estate / Artists Rights Society (ARS),
New York.

    THIS IS NOT TO BE LOOKED AT

December 1967) and "Incidents of Mirror-Travel in the Yucatan" (*Artforum*, November 1969), emphasized their ambiguous status, in between criticism and works of art. The latter chronicles a recent trip to Mexico, where Smithson made a series of nine temporary sculptural installations by arranging a set of square mirrors in various locations. It included several photographs that Smithson took of these installations (one of which appeared on the magazine's cover). The square photographs are organized in a gridded layout that echoes the arrangement of the mirrors themselves, a visual rhyming that suggests the blurring between the physical site of the installations and the discursive site of the magazine. Leider, who became a close friend and supporter of Smithson during the late 1960s, described the article as "a form of that work of art. ... This wasn't simply a record of it, this was another version of it."[72] Indeed, the article does not merely document these sculptures in the typical sense of that term; rather, it is their sole intended format. As Smithson writes, "the mirror displacements were dismantled right after they were photographed. The mirrors are somewhere in New York. The reflected light has been erased. ... It is the dimension of absence that remains to be found."[73]

Not surprisingly, "Incidents of Mirror-Travel in the Yucatan" lampooned formalist criticism, undermining its faith in the objectivity of optical truth by insisting on the inadequacies, distortions, and blind spots of vision. The landscape Smithson describes is a place of "anti-vision" in which "Sight turned away from its own looking. ... The eyes became two wastebaskets" and "Vision sagged, caved in, and broke apart."[74] And, in a direct jab at Greenberg, Smithson observes of the Mexican landscape that "Flatness was nowhere to be found."[75] Moreover, language, prized by formalist critics for the precision with which it might explicate the visual, is here rendered useless as a means to reveal truth: "To reconstruct what the eye sees in words, in an 'ideal language' is a vain exploit," he insists. "Why not reconstruct one's inability to see?"[76] But the article also, in its very premise, thwarts the promotional role of the visuality of the magazine itself, since the reproductions that illustrate the article and appear on the magazine cover cannot contribute (at least not straightforwardly) to the market value of the work.

In investigating the magazine page as a new kind of artistic medium, Smithson was not alone. Several articles published in commercial art magazines (and also occasionally in fashion magazines) around the same time occupied similarly ambiguous ground in between magazine articles and works of art. Drawing on strategies such as parody, pastiche, appropriation, and mimicry, these articles intervened in the dominant discourse of the magazine, challenging both the authority of criticism and the promotional role of the magazine. For example, Mel Bochner and Robert Smithson's joint article "The Domain of the Great Bear" (*Art Voices*, Fall 1966) is a campy essay on the Hayden Planetarium embedded with found publicity materials. Bochner's "Beach Boys—100%" (*Arts Magazine*, June 1967) is a text collage pilfered from publicity materials from the pop band. Dan Graham's *Figurative* (1965) is a found receipt flanked by two advertisements published in the June 1968 issue of *Harper's Bazaar*. Smithson's "Quasi-Infinities and the Waning of Space" (*Arts Magazine*, November 1966) is an esoteric meditation on physics, architecture, art history, and science fiction.[77] These articles functioned in various ways, and were, no doubt, motivated by different objectives—from Brechtian efforts at estrangement, to opportunistic attempts to capitalize on the magazine's publicity, to some combination of the two. What these diverse writings share is that they represent the new way in which artists took charge of the publicity surrounding their work at this time.

INCIDENTS OF MIRROR-TRAVEL IN THE YUCATAN

ROBERT SMITHSON

Of the Mayan ideas on the forms of the earth we know little. The Aztec thought the crest of the earth was the top of a huge saurian monster, a kind of crocodile, which was the object of a certain cult. It is probable that Mayan had a similar belief, but it is not impossible that at the same time they considered the world to consist of seven compartments, perhaps stepped as four layers.
—J. Eric S. Thompson, *Maya Hieroglyphic Writing*

The characteristic feature of the savage mind is its timelessness: its object is to grasp the world as both a synchronic and a diachronic totality and the knowledge which it draws therefrom is like that afforded of a room by mirrors fixed on opposite walls, which reflect each other (as well as objects in the intervening space) although without being strictly parallel.
—Claude Levi-Strauss, *The Savage Mind*

Driving away from Merida down Highway 261 one becomes aware of the indifferent horizon. Quite apathetically it rests on the ground devouring everything that looks like something. One is always crossing the horizon, yet it always remains distant. In this line where sky meets earth, objects cease to exist. Since the car was at all times on some leftover horizon, one might say that the car was imprisoned in a line, a line that is in no way linear. The distance seemed to put restrictions on all forward movement, thus bringing the car to a countless series of standstills. How could one advance on the horizon, if it was already present under the wheels? A horizon is something else other than a horizon; it is closedness in openness, it is an enchanted region where down is up. Space can be approached, but time is far away. Time is devoid of objects when one displaces all destinations. The car kept going on the same horizon.

Looking down on the map (it was all there), a tangled network of horizon lines on paper called "roads," some red, some black. Yucatan, Quintana Roo, Campeche, Tabasco, Chiapas and Guatemala congealed into a mass of gaps, points, and little blue threads (called rivers). The map legend contained signs in a neat row: archeological monuments (black), colonial monuments (black), historical site (black), bathing resort (blue), spa (red), hunting (green), fishing (blue), arts and crafts (green), aquatic sports (blue), national park (green), service station (yellow). On the map of Mexico they were scattered like the droppings of some small animal.

The *Tourist Guide and Directory of Yucatan-Campeche* rested on the car seat. On its cover was a crude drawing depicting the Spaniards meeting the Mayans, in the background was the temple of Chichén Itzá. On the top left-hand corner was printed " 'UY U TAN A KIN PECH' (listen how they talk)—EXCLAIMED THE MAYANS ON HEARING THE SPANISH LANGUAGE," and in the bottom left-hand corner " 'YUCATAN CAMPECHE'—REPEATED THE SPANIARDS WHEN THEY HEARD THESE WORDS." A caption under all this said "Mayan and Spanish First Meeting 1517." In the "Official Guide" to Uxmal, Fig. 28 shows 27 little drawings of "Pottery Found at Uxmal." The shading on each pot consists of countless dots. Interest in such pots began to wane. The steady hiss of the air-conditioner in the rented Dodge Dart might

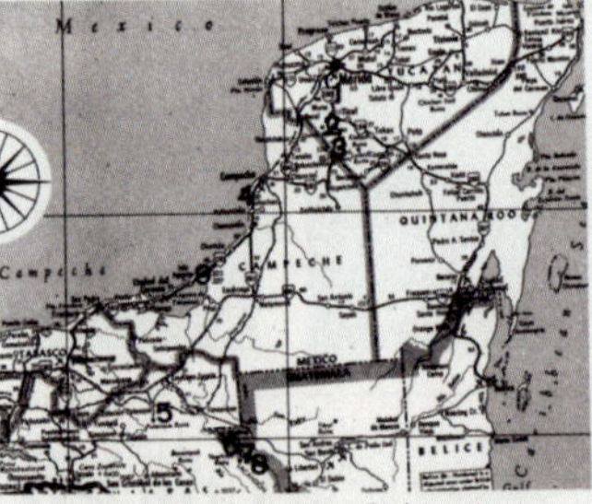

Vicinities of the Nine Mirror Displacements.

have been the voice of Eecath — the god of thought and wind. Wayward throughts blew around the car, wind blew over the scrub bushes outside. On the cover of Victor W. Von Hagen's paperback *World of the Maya* it said, "A history of the Mayas and their resplendent civilization that grew out of the jungles and wastelands of Central America." In the rear-view mirror appeared Tezcatlipoca — demiurge of the "smoking-mirror." "All those guide books are of no use," said Tezcatlipoca, "You must travel at random, like the first Mayans, you risk getting lost in the thickets, but that is the only way to make art."

Through the windshield the road stabbed the horizon, causing it to bleed a sunny incandescence. One couldn't help feeling that this was a ride on a knife covered with solar blood. As it cut into the horizon a disruption took place. The tranquil drive became a sacrifice of matter that led to a discontinuous state of being, a world of quiet delirium. Just sitting there brought one into the wound of a terrestrial victim. This peaceful war between the elements is ever present in Mexico — an echo, perhaps, of the Aztec and Mayan human sacrifices.

The First Mirror Displacement:

Somewhere between Uman and Muna is a charred site. The people in this region clear land by burning it out. On this field of ashes (called by the natives a "milpa") twelve mirrors were cantilevered into low mounds of red soil. Each mirror was twelve inches square, and supported from above and below by the scorched earth alone. The distribution of the squares followed the irregular contours on the ground, and they were placed in a random parallel direction. Bits of earth spilled onto the surfaces, thus sabotaging the perfect reflections of the sky. Dirt hung in the sultry sky. Bits of blazing cloud mixed with the ashy mass. The displacement was *in* the ground, not *on* it. Burnt tree stumps spread around the mirrors and vanished into the arid jungles.

The Second Mirror Displacement:

In a suburb of Uxmal, which is to say nowhere, the second displacement was deployed. What appeared to be a shallow quarry was dug into the ground to a depth of about four to five feet, exposing a bright red clay mixed with white limestone fragments. Near a small cliff the twelve mirrors were stuck into clods of earth. It was photographed from the top of the cliff. Again Tezcatlipoca spoke, "That camera is a portable tomb, you must remember that." On this same site, the Great Ice Cap of Gondwanaland was constructed according to a map outline on page 459 of Marshall Kay's and Edwin H. Colbert's *Stratigraphy and Life History*. It was an "earth-map" made of white limestone. A bit of the Carboniferous period is now installed near Uxmal. That great age of calcium carbonate seemed a fitting offering for a land so rich in limestone. Reconstructing a land mass that existed 350 to 305 million years ago on a terrain once controlled by sundry Mayan gods caused a collision in time that left one with a sense of the timeless.

Timelessness is found in the lapsed moments of perception, in the common pause that breaks apart into a sandstorm of pauses. The malady of wanting to "make" is *unmade*, and the malady of wanting to be "able" is disabled. Gondwanaland is a kind of memory, yet it is not a memory, it is but an incognito land mass that has been *unthought* about and turned into a Map of Impasse. You cannot visit Gondwanaland, but you can visit a "map" of it.

The Third Mirror Displacement:

The road went through butterfly swarms. Near Bolonchen de Rejon thousands of yellow, white and black swallowtail butterflies flew past the car

1.7

Robert Smithson, "Incidents of Mirror-Travel in the Yucatan," *Artforum*, November 1969.
Text © Estate of Robert Smithson / Licensed by VAGA, New York, NY.

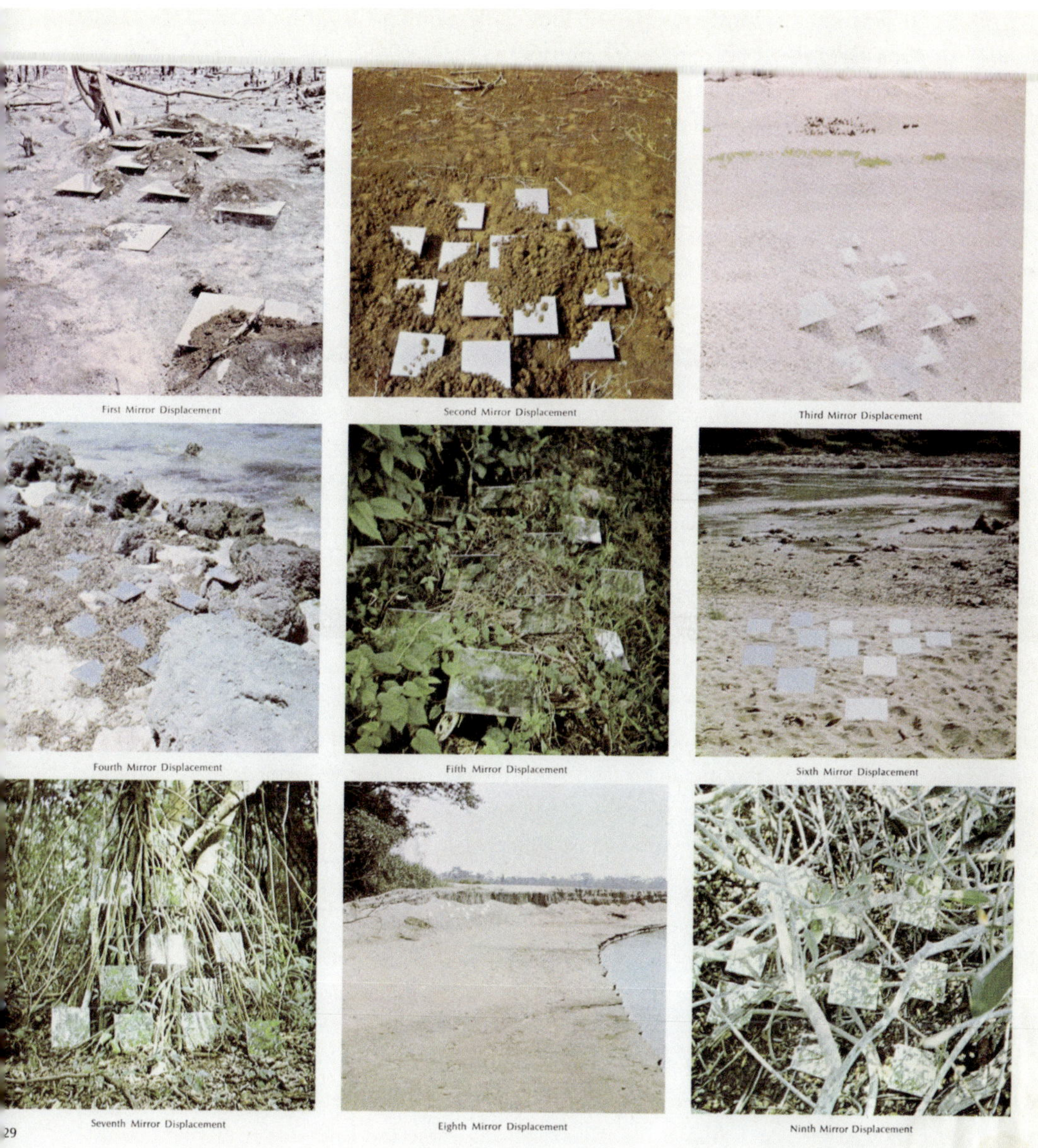

First Mirror Displacement

Second Mirror Displacement

Third Mirror Displacement

Fourth Mirror Displacement

Fifth Mirror Displacement

Sixth Mirror Displacement

Seventh Mirror Displacement

Eighth Mirror Displacement

Ninth Mirror Displacement

One of the earliest and most important of these "interventions" was Dan Graham's *Homes for America*, published in the December 1966–January 1967 issue of *Arts Magazine*. At first glance, the article appeared to be an ordinary magazine article. However, it did not quite square with the usual run of criticism and reviews in the art magazine. For one thing, nowhere in the article does Graham mention art. Instead, he discusses the suburban tract-housing developments that had become ubiquitous in the United States during the postwar era. Furthermore, there is something odd about the article's tone, about the deadpan way in which it describes, with the detached precision of a *nouveau roman*, the serial logic of these devalued homes, which, the artist writes, "exist apart from prior standards of 'good' architecture … and were not built to satisfy individual needs or tastes."[78] At the same time, there is something vaguely—even uncannily—familiar about Graham's account of the industrially produced buildings of suburbia, which evokes the rhetoric and formal sensibility of minimalist art with its serial logic of "one thing after another," as Judd famously described this art.[79] Even the layout of the article—its lists of LeWitt-like permutations and photographs of repetitive, industrial architectural structures—graphically expresses and almost caricatures this serial logic, an effect that was most obvious in Graham's own paste-up for the article, showing how he intended it to appear (in the version published in *Arts Magazine*, Graham's own photographs were omitted and a Walker Evans photograph was substituted instead).

In reflecting recently upon his choice to use the magazine as a medium, Graham stressed the way in which its mass-produced, serialized, and inherently temporal form echoed the materials and formal procedures of minimalism, explaining, "Flavin said we should go back to the hardware store. LeWitt said we should use his work for firewood. And I thought, why don't I just use a magazine page."[80] If minimalism challenged the conventions of the museum or gallery space, however, Graham instead intervened into the communicative conditions of the magazine itself. *Homes for America* also illustrates the important role of discourse in defining minimalism, enacting Graham's observation, cited earlier, that a work of art only had to appear in a magazine in order to be considered art. At the same time, by literalizing this fact, the piece short-circuits the role of magazines in defining the value of art: as Graham insisted, "the fact that *Homes for America* was, in the end, only a magazine article, and made no claims for itself as 'Art,' is its most important aspect."[81]

Tucked away among the typical run of criticism and reviews, the articles by Graham, Bochner, and Smithson, among others, invited the possibility of being overlooked—a camouflage strategy that allowed them to infiltrate the magazine's discourse and catch the reader off guard, "like intellectual time bombs to be discovered later," as Bochner put it.[82] The status of these articles is uncertain, their genre indeterminate. They exist somewhere in between criticism and works of art, a confusion exacerbated by the fact that many of these artists also published more conventional art criticism. Bochner, for example, was regularly writing reviews for *Arts Magazine* during this time, following in the footsteps of Judd, who began writing for *Arts* in 1959 in a terse, aphoristic style that prompted comparisons with the reductive forms of his sculpture. However, while for Judd writing criticism was merely a job—"I wrote criticism as a mercenary, and would never have written it otherwise," he claimed[83]—these stealth interventions had a much different purpose. Even as they exploited the publicity medium of the magazine, they used it against the grain, subtly tweaking readers' expectations.

Homes for America

Early 20th-Century Possessable House to the Quasi-Discrete Cell of '66

D. GRAHAM

Belleplain	Garden City
Brooklawn	Garden City Park
Colonia	Greenlawn
Colonia Manor	Island Park
Fair Haven	Levitown
Fair Lawn	Middleville
Greenfields Village	New City Park
Green Village	Pine Lawn
Plainsboro	Plainview
Pleasant Grove	Plandome Manor
Pleasant Plains	Pleasantside
Sunset Hill Garden	Pleasantville

Large-scale 'tract' housing 'developments' constitute the new city. They are located everywhere. They are not particularly bound to existing communities; they fail to develop either regional characteristics or separate identity. These 'projects' date from the end of World War II when in southern California speculators or 'operative' builders adapted mass production techniques to quickly build many houses for the defense workers over-concentrated there. This 'Cali-

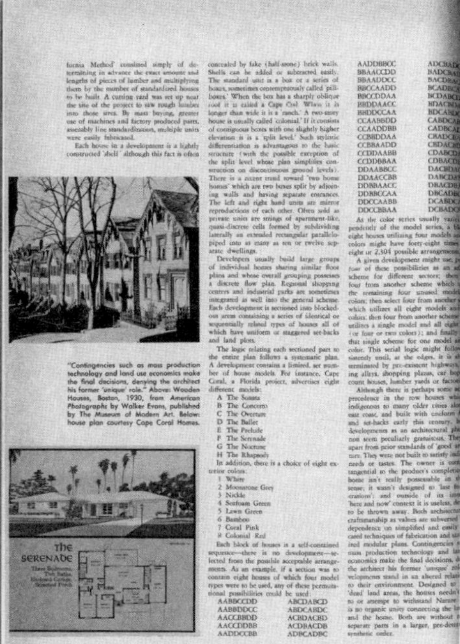

"Contingencies such as mass production technology and land use economics make the final decisions, denying the architect his former 'unique' role." Above: Wooden Houses, Boston, 1930, from *American Photographs* by Walker Evans, published by The Museum of Modern Art. Below: house plan courtesy Cape Coral Homes.

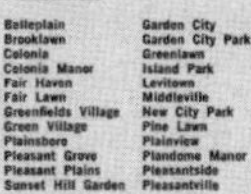

A The Sonata
B The Concerto
C The Overture
D The Ballet
E The Prelude
F The Serenade
G The Nocturne
H The Rhapsody

In addition, there is a choice of eight exterior colors:

1 White
2 Moonstone Grey
3 Nickle
4 Seafoam Green
5 Lawn Green
6 Bamboo
7 Coral Pink
8 Colonial Red

1.8

Dan Graham, *Homes for America,* in *Arts Magazine,*
December 1966–January 1967.

Homes for America

D. GRAHAM

Belleplain
Brooklawn
Colonia
Colonia Manor
Fair Haven
Fair Lawn
Greenfields Village
Green Village
Plainsboro
Pleasant Grove
Pleasant Plains
Sunset Hill Garden

Garden City
Garden City Park
Greenlawn
Island Park
Levitown
Middleville
New City Park
Pine Lawn
Plainview
Plandome Manor
Pleasantside
Pleasantville

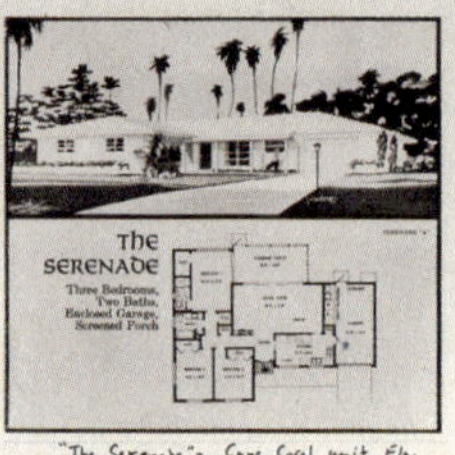

"The Serenade"– Cape Coral unit, Fla.

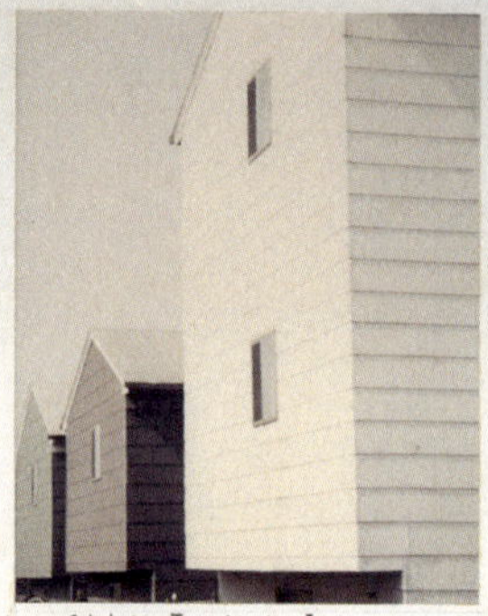

Set-back, Jersey City, New Jersey

Each house in a development is a lightly constructed 'shell' although this fact is often concealed by fake (half-stone) brick walls. Shells can be added or subtracted easily. The standard unit is a box or a series of boxes, sometimes contemptuously called 'pillboxes.' When the box has a sharply oblique roof it is called a Cape Cod. When it is longer than wide it is a 'ranch.' A

Large-scale 'tract' housing 'developments' constitute the new city. They are located everywhere. They are not particularly bound to existing communities; they fail to develop either regional characteristics or separate identity. These 'projects' date from the end of World War II when in southern California speculators or 'operative' builders adapted mass production techniques to quickly build many houses for the defense workers over-concentrated there. This 'California Method' consisted simply of determining in advance the exact amount and lengths of pieces of lumber and multiplying them by the number of standardized houses to be built. A cutting yard was set up near the site of the project to saw rough lumber into those sizes. By mass buying, greater use of machines and factory produced parts, assembly line standardization, multiple units were easily fabricated.

The logic relating each sectioned part to the entire plan follows a systematic plan. A development contains a limited, set number of house models. For instance, Cape Coral, a Florida project, advertises eight different models:

A The Sonata
B The Concerto
C The Overture
D The Ballet
E The Prelude
F The Serenade
G The Noctune
H The Rhapsody

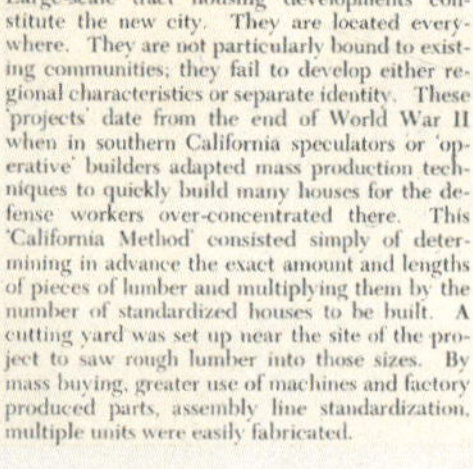

Two Entrance Doorways, 'Two Home Homes', Jersey City, N.J.

two-story house is usually called 'colonial.' If it consists of contiguous boxes with one slightly higher elevation it is a 'split level.' Such stylistic differentiation is advantageous to the basic structure (with the possible exception of the split level whose plan simplifies construction on discontinuous ground levels).

There is a recent trend toward 'two home homes' which are two boxes split by adjoining walls and having separate entrances. The left and right hand units are mirror reproductions of each other. Often sold as private units are strings of apartment-like, quasi-discrete cells formed by subdividing laterally an extended rectangular parallelopiped into as many as ten or twelve separate dwellings.

Developers usually build large groups of individual homes sharing similar floor plans and whose overall grouping possesses a discrete flow plan. Regional shopping centers and industrial parks are sometimes integrated as well into the general scheme. Each development is sectioned into blocked-out areas containing a series of identical or sequentially related types of houses all of which have uniform or staggered set-backs and land plots.

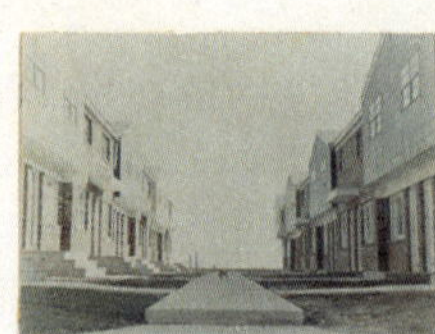

Center Court, Entrance, Development, Jersey City, N.J.

In addition, there is a choice of eight exterior colors:
1 White
2 Moonstone Grey
3 Nickle

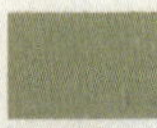

4 Seafoam Green
5 Lawn Green
6 Bamboo
7 Coral Pink
8 Colonial Red

As the color series usually varies independently of the model series, a block of eight houses utilizing four models and four colors might have forty-eight times forty-eight or 2,304 possible arrangements.

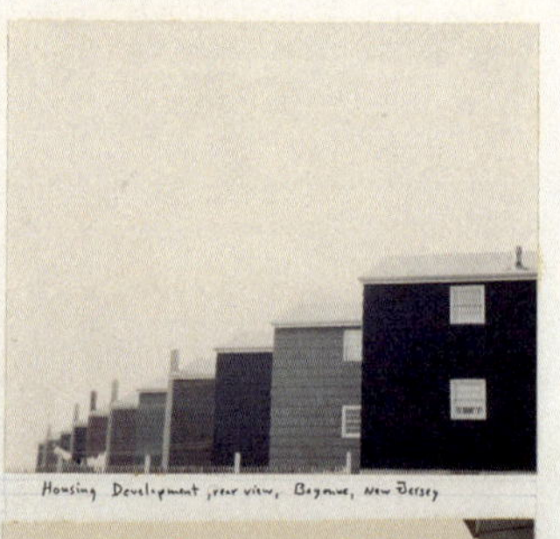

Housing Development, rear view, Bayonne, New Jersey

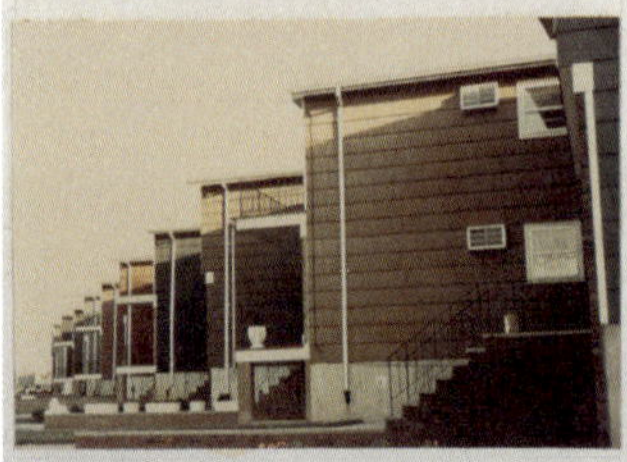

Housing Development, front view, Bayonne, New Jersey

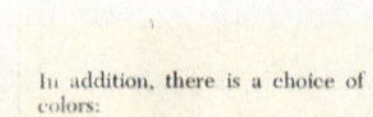

Dan Graham

1.9

Dan Graham, *Homes for America*, 1966–1967. Printed matter. Variable according to publication. Courtesy of the artist and Marian Goodman Gallery.

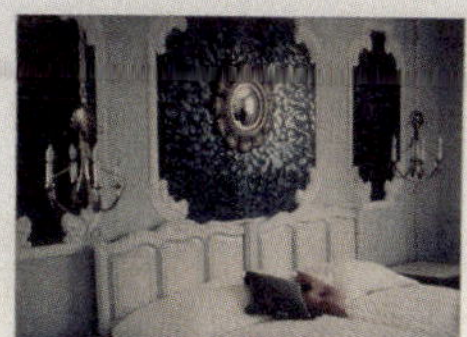

Interior of Model Home, Staten Island, N.Y.

Each block of houses is a self-contained sequence — there is no development — selected from the possible acceptable arrangements. As an example, if a section was to contain eight houses of which four model types were to be used, any of these permutational possibilities could be used:

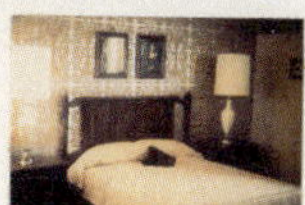

Bedroom of Model Home, S.I., N.Y.

AABBCCDD	ABCDABCD
AABBDDCC	ABDCABDC
AACCBBDD	ACBDACBD
AACCDDBB	ACDBACDB
AADDCCBB	ADBCADBC
AADDBBCC	ADCBADCB
BBAADDCC	BACDBACD
BBCCAADD	BCADBCAD
BBCCDDAA	BCDABCDA
BBDDAACC	BDACBDAC
BBDDCCAA	BDCABDCA
CCAABBDD	CABDCABD
CCAADDBB	CADBCADB
CCBBDDAA	CBADCBAD
CCBBAADD	CBDACBDA
CCDDAABB	CDABCDAB
CCDDBBAA	CDBACDBA
DDAABBCC	DACBDACB
DDAACCBB	DABCDABC
DDBBAACC	DBACDBAC
DDBBCCAA	DBCADBCA
DDCCAABB	DCABDCAB
DDCCBBAA	DCBADCBA

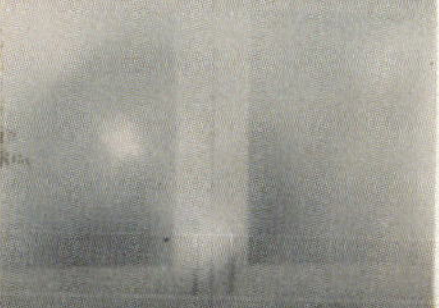

Basement Area, Home, New Jersey

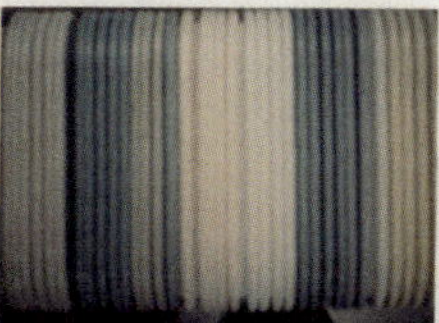

'Discount Store', Sweaters on Racks, New Jersey

The 8 color variables were equally distributed among the house exteriors. The first buyers were more likely to have obtained their first choice in color. Family units had to make a choice based on the available colors which also took account of both husband and wife's likes and dislikes. Adult male and female color likes and dislikes were compared in a survey of the homeowners:

'Like'

Male	Female
Skyway	Skyway Blue
Colonial Red	Lawn Green
Patio White	Nickle
Yellow Chiffon	Colonial Red
Lawn Green	Yellow Chiffon
Nickle	Patio White
Fawn	Moonstone Grey
Moonstone Grey	Fawn

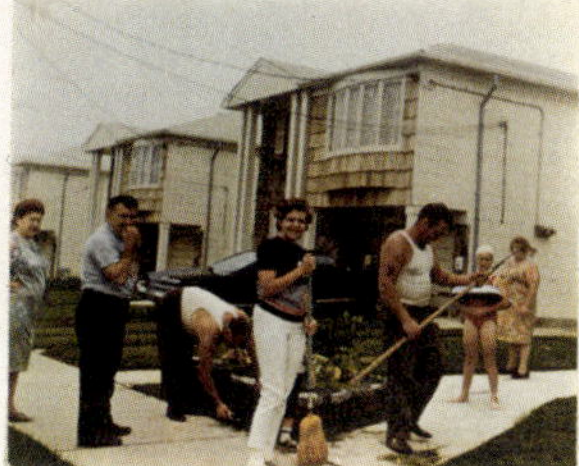

Two Family Units, Staten Island, N.Y.

'Dislike'

Male	Female
Lawn Green	Patio White
Colonial Red	Fawn
Patio White	Colonial Red
Moonstone Grey	Moonstone Grey
Fawn	Yellow Chiffon
Yellow Chiffon	Lawn Green
Nickle	Skyway blue
Skyway Blue	Nickle

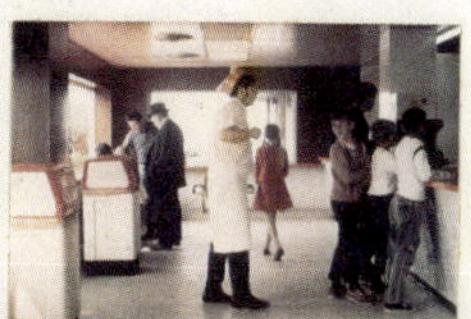

Car Hop, Jersey City, N.J.

A given development might use, perhaps, *four* of these possibilities as an arbitrary scheme for different sectors; then select four from another scheme which utilizes the remaining four unused models and colors; then select four from another scheme which utilizes all eight models and eight colors; then four from another scheme which utilizes a single model and all eight colors (or four or two colors); and finally utilize that single scheme for one model and one color. This serial logic might follow consistently until, at the edges, it is abruptly terminated by pre-existent highways, bowling alleys, shopping plazas, car hops, discount houses, lumber yards or factories.

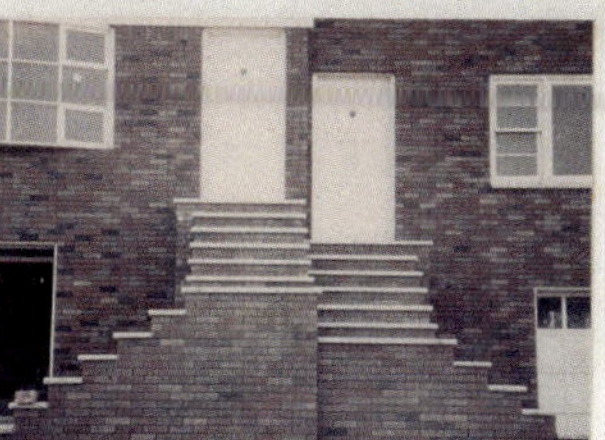

'Split-Level', 'Two Home Homes', Jersey City, N.J.

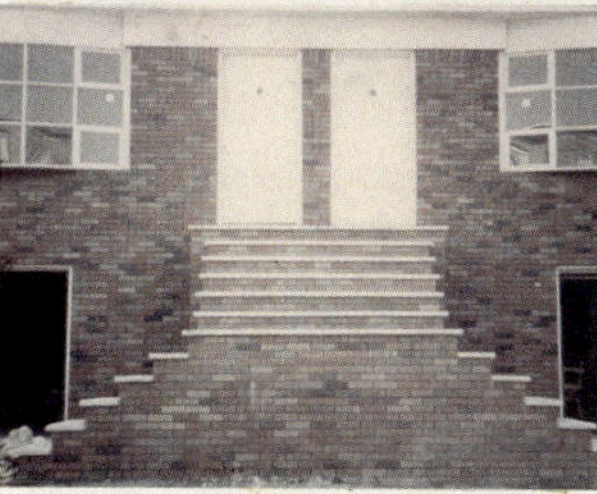

'Ground-Level', 'Two Home Homes', Jersey City, N.J.

Although there is perhaps some aesthetic precedence in the row houses which are indigenous to many older cities along the east coast, and built with uniform façades and set-backs early this century, housing developments as an architectural phenomenon seem peculiarly gratuitous. They exist apart from prior standards of 'good' architecture. They were not built to satisfy individual needs or tastes. The owner is completely tangential to the product's completion. His home isn't really possessable in the old sense; it wasn't designed to 'last for generations'; and outside of its immediate 'here and now' context it is useless, designed to be thrown away. Both architecture and craftsmanship as values are subverted by the dependence on simplified and easily duplicated techniques of fabrication and standardized modular plans. Contingencies such as mass production technology and land use economics make the final decisions, denying the architect his former 'unique' role. Developments stand in an altered relationship to their environment. Designed to fill in 'dead' land areas, the houses needn't adapt to or attempt to withstand Nature. There is no organic unity connecting the land site and the home. Both are without roots — separate parts in a larger, predetermined, synthetic order.

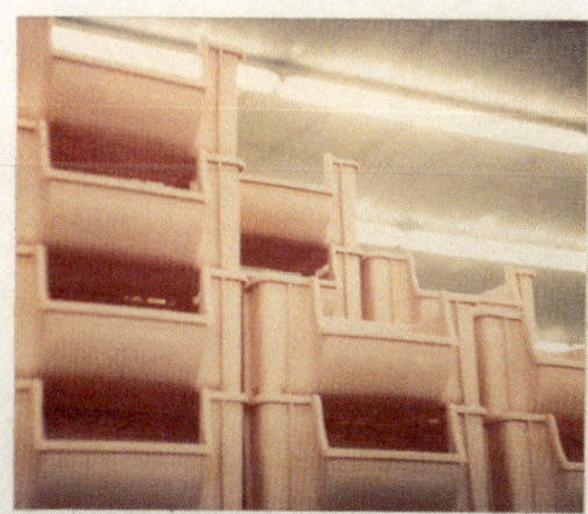

Kitchen Trays, 'Discount House', New Jersey

ARTS MAGAZINE/December 1966-January 1967

Dan Graham

wagon train into the wilderness through bogs of bumpkin comedy and tinsel wooing. Later, after a brief moment at a campsite, all these people are mysteriously back in the fort as though they'd never left it.

It's incredible, the amount of leeway that is allowed. If a prop man locates a bench from an antique store next to a tree in a just-set-up campsite, the scene stays in though the film for the preceding five minutes has been insisting on formidable wilderness. This is studio moviemaking at its slackest.

All these gauche, careless skills — the uglification of actors (padding a buxom barmaid, Annelle Hayes, so that her bust line starts angling out from the collarbone and doesn't turn in till it reaches her waist), the jerky progress from melodrama to bathos to camp, the TV Western feeling of no flow, outdoors, or sense of period (Stewart is wearing a jacket from Abercrombie, all Indians and their tents are from a psychotics' Halloween Ball)—are the responsibility of John Ford, a director generally noted for making movies with a poetic and limitless knowledge of Indians, ranging farthest across the landscape of the American past, and being the moviemaker's Mr. Movie.

There's no question that there's a new crowd-pleasing movie around that has to do with a disenchanted cop, a city in which no corner is untainted, and an artichoke plot. Wrapped around a heart that is just a procedural cop story, police routines in Washington (*Pendulum*), San Francisco (*Bullitt*), Phoenix (*Coogan's Bluff*), and Manhattan (*Madigan* and *The Detective*), is a shrubwork of *Daily News* stories, the whole newspaper from beginning to end: the sensationalism, sentimentality, human interest, plus some liberal editorials. Each film has its mini-version of the drug scene, investigating committees, philandering wives, some of it as wrong as the psychedelic dance orgy in *Coogan's Bluff*, the weirdness there being the thousand equally frenzied participants, or the two senators (Robert Vaughn in *Bullitt*, Paul McPrissy in *Pendulum*) who are played odiously and with heavy messages.

Superficially, it's a straight Bogart story with Sinatra (interestingly mediocre), McQueen (you could buy back

Manhattan for the Indians with his blue eyes), or Peppard (unfulfilled, slightly sedentary) playing the ace detective role, but playing it less mythically and with much more defeat. The real juice of the films is their ranginess, that they give you a lot, the zest for what a city contains, and the flatness.

These movies work partly because they are exploiting the fairly unplumbed field of pessimistic observing rather than action, or, for that matter, acting of the traditional or method variety. The work often goes overdone, as when Bullitt is shown waking up and McQueen, trying for a bent-over feeling, does a St. Vitus dance while suggesting a wave of nausea spreading across his face. But in a long, near-silent and very good stretch in U.C. Hospital, which is almost excessive in the way it sticks like plaster to the mundaneness of the place, the movie hits into about seventeen verities: faces looking out as though across the great divide of 20th-century lousiness.

These movies use Hollywood bodies in a new way which could be called city physical: unglamorous, a lot of self-contempt (although I don't see Jean Seberg as anything shy of complacency), naturalness emphasized or pushed to the front of the screen without losing its ordinariness (both Peppard and McQueen have great rooted-to-the-earth stances). The boy rapist in *Pendulum*, the young cop who gets shot in the beginning of *Bullit*, Lee Remick (too nice and too frail for a nympho), Don Stroud's very ungraceful, unused to running in *Coogan's Bluff*—all these actors seem to work towards an ideal of anonymity through a kind of unweighted gesture and great stretches of silent resistance to the material around them. There's nothing better in these films than Peppard rifling the yellow pages for the telephone number of his wife's beauty parlor, or McQueen eating a sandwich and drinking a glass of milk, very tense and guilty about having lost his prize hood to a pair of hired killers.

The scripts are written with the lore of a taxi driver, his head filled with routes, the difficulty of getting through crowds, and the cold, confusing congestion to be expected at any monument, terminal, or bedroom. These are not stingy films. If

1.10

Stephen Kaltenbach, "Build a Reputation," from the *Artforum* ads series. Courtesy of *Artforum* and the artist. © *Artforum,* May 1969, page 73.

The articles by such artists published in *Arts Magazine* during the 1960s were supported by a maverick editor named Sam Edwards, who also published several important underground newspapers during this period.[84] As Bochner recalled of Edwards's support, "*Arts* gave you permission to change the rules. It was my sense that by publishing these interventions, that this was a political gesture, anti–art world, antiestablishment."[85] Like the radical media practices of the underground press of the late 1960s, these articles were guerrilla tactics that attempted to commandeer the commercial publicity of the magazine by manipulating its form, content, mode of address, and audience.

In a similar vein, artists began to tap into the advertising space of commercial magazines during this period, a practice that Graham discussed in his 1967 proposal for *Aspen* magazine. Lee Lozano, who was working closely with Graham at the time, succinctly described this practice: "Buy space in the publication of your choice … for the time duration of your choice. Use the space in each issue as a box for the idea or ideas of your choice. Part of the page of the art mag is as good a material for an artist to use as any other … and your ideas, piggyback as they go, would have guaranteed, fast, wide distribution."[86] If the idea of using the magazine advertisement as a way to distribute work had a pragmatic appeal, it also had an antagonistic dimension. Taking out paid advertisements was a way for artists to siphon off the commercial publicity of the art magazine and repurpose it for their own interests. Graham, who created several ads and also proposed ads between 1966 and 1969—including *Detumescence* (1966), *Likes (A Computer-Astrological Dating-Placement Service)* (1967–1969), and *Income (Outflow) Piece* (1969)—claimed that these works were meant to function like "holes in the topography of the magazine," suggesting that they were intended to puncture or disrupt its discourse, allowing other kinds of messages to surface.[87] The advertisements taken out by conceptual artists must have come across as cryptic to many of their readers. For example, Joseph Kosuth published excerpts from *Roget's Thesaurus* in the advertising space of various newspapers and periodicals, including the *New York Times, Artforum, Museum News,* and *The Nation,* as part of his *Second Investigation* (1968). Stephen Kaltenbach placed a series of advertisements in twelve consecutive issues of *Artforum* from November 1968 to December 1969 in order to circulate his "micro-manifestos," consisting of pithy and ironic phrases such as "Art Works," "Build a Reputation," and "Become a Legend," that foregrounded the role of the art magazine in careerism and promotion.[88]

Artists' advertisements attest to the complexity of the magazine as a site of publicity. On the one hand artists used advertisements, as Lozano described, to reach a broader public. Kaltenbach explained to Patricia Norvell in a 1969 interview, "there are fourteen thousand copies of *Artforum,* so instead of simply sitting down and talking to you, if I have an idea that could be used, why I'm sitting down and talking to fourteen thousand people."[89] And yet in reality, such "accessibility" was less straightforward than this statement implies. As the artist admitted of his puzzling *Artforum* ads later in the same interview, "a lot of the things I put in *Artforum* are not understandable to an awful lot of people who read the magazine."[90] This qualification highlights the contradictions of conceptual art's more general aspirations toward universal legibility. It suggests that, rather than attempting a universal form of address, Kaltenbach was using the magazine as a coded form of communication that might be legible to some readers and not others. In fact, he said, "the ads were aimed at artists."[91] This statement suggests that the art magazine might be conceived not as a single universal discursive space but as a site of multiple, competing modes of communication.

Such a model was evoked by Robert Smithson's 1968 description of an art magazine (and the fact that he designates it as square suggests he has *Artforum* in mind):

> If you read this square magazine long enough, you will soon find a circularity that spreads into a map devoid of destinations, but with land masses of print (called criticism) and little oceans with right angles (called photographs). Its binding is an axis, and its covers paper hemispheres and you, like Gulliver and Ulysses, will be transported into a world of traps and marvels. The axis splits into a chasm in your hands, thus you begin your travels by being immediately lost. In this magazine is a series of pages that open into double terrains, because "we always see two pages at once" (Michel Butor). Writing drifts into stratas [*sic*], and becomes a buried language.[92]

Smithson's geological metaphors suggest the materiality of print he explored extensively in works such as *A Heap of Language* (1966), insisting that we see the art magazine as a concrete physical object, and even a quasi-sculptural medium. Against the rational, objective principles of formalist criticism, the artist imagined the magazine as a deeply disorderly and entropic discursive landscape, littered by "continental critical drift," "swamps of 'isms,'" "dunes of words," and "intellectual lava flows."[93] The reader must navigate these conflicting viewpoints, and split attention between words and images—a vertiginous and disorienting, but also potentially revelatory experience. Smithson conjures an entropic model of reading and seeing that depends on the materiality of the magazine itself, which is meant to be flipped through, read backward as well as forward—and perhaps, in the ultimate entropic act, even thrown away. He also, however, speaks to the magazine's complex character as a representational and communicative medium. Indeed, Smithson's description suggests a model of the art magazine not as a single, unified field of discourse, but as a fractured, heterogeneous space in which multiple, overlapping, and contradictory types of communication compete and collide.

Such heterogeneity and multiplicity have been central to theories of alternative or counterpublic spheres. In their 1972 book *Öffentlichkeit und Erfahrung* (*The Public Sphere and Experience*), Oskar Negt and Alexander Kluge point to the many alternative sites of publicity that arose alongside and in opposition to the dominant universal, homogenous public sphere described by Habermas. Such counterpublics, to cite Nancy Fraser's useful definition, constitute "parallel discursive arenas where members of subordinated social groups invent and circulate counter discourses to formulate oppositional interpretations of their identities, interests, and needs."[94] Whereas for Habermas, the corporate structure of contemporary mass media precluded the possibility that such media might be used progressively, Negt and Kluge take the opposite tack. For them, the counterpublic sphere depends on precisely those forms of industrially advanced communication media that Habermas dismissed as pseudopublicity. Their concern is with how the media might be appropriated for "counterproductions" that compete with the dominant media "at the most advanced technological level."[95] The artists' interventions and advertisements discussed in this chapter functioned as such counterproductions. They were attempts—albeit tactical and short-lived ones—to wrest from the spectacular publicity function of the art magazine a different kind of communication.

Artists' growing disillusionment with art magazines in the late 1960s was part of their wider dissatisfaction with the exclusionary policies of elitist art institutions, evident in the numerous activist groups founded during this time to assert artists' moral and legal rights over their work and to fight racism and classism within the art world.[96] While much of this protest dealt with the museum and gallery space, the art magazine was central to the struggles over artistic identity and self-determination at this time. Indeed, at the Art Workers' Coalition Open Hearing in April 1969, several artists expressed indignation at the magazine's role in the art world status quo. Lee Lozano called for an "art revolution," declaring: "I cannot consider a program of museum reforms without equal attention to gallery reforms and art magazine reforms which would aim to eliminate *stables* of artists and writers."[97] At the same event, Dan Graham observed: "art magazines … depend exclusively for their economic existence on selling ads to galleries for the most part. For what it's worth to the readers who will buy it, the critic who must sell it, quality in art is all that counts."[98] And Carl Andre advocated boycotting magazines entirely, demanding: "No more reproductions. Reproductions lead to a false and destructive kind of 'fame' which separates artists from the community of artists by making them 'famous' and rich. Reproductions give rise to a body of people who 'know your work' without ever seeing it. This is an abomination. Artists should forbid people to snap pictures of their work."[99]

In response, artists not only intervened in commercial art magazines but published their own magazines, through which they sought to contest the institutions and economies of the mainstream art world and to create an alternative set of conditions for art and art criticism. As Ron White and Andrew Menard explained in the artist-run magazine *The Fox*, "trade journalism doesn't encourage creative participation, it encourages a voyeuristic consumption" and produces "art as exchange value. … If we really don't want to capitulate to the consciousness industry we have to use the media differently."[100] At stake in the chapters that follow is what it meant to "use the media differently." Unlike earlier avant-garde artists' periodicals, which were founded to support specific artistic movements, the magazines discussed in this book were motivated less by the need to promote a narrow aesthetic agenda than by a desire to transform the art magazine itself.

If the magazine was a new kind of medium for artists in the 1960s and 1970s, it was equally a radical media practice—and the two, while not reducible to one another, were deeply intertwined. Even as artists sought to make their work legible and accessible through the magazine, they questioned the latter's status as a neutral, universal public space, insisting on the specificity and contingency of both the magazine and its audience. In doing so, they challenged the ideal public sphere in which formalist art criticism imagined its ethical function as working, replacing its universal and abstract subject with the reality of new artistic identities, communities, and counterpublics. In this sense, artists' magazines resonated with alternative media practices outside of the art world, and especially with the countless underground publications founded to support countercultural social and political movements during this era, such as the *Whole Earth Catalog, Off Our Backs, The Body Politic, The Black Panther* newspaper, and the *San Francisco Oracle*. Within the art world as outside of it, magazines documented and helped to construct these new identities and experiences. In this sense, these temporary publications had an enduring effect on the social relationships among artists, critics, curators, dealers, and—not least—viewers and readers.

2

THE MAGAZINE AS A MEDIUM
ASPEN, 1965–1971

In 1964 a New York journalist and editor named Phyllis Glick was spending the year in Aspen, Colorado, where, in between skiing and working as a photographer, she attended the Aspen International Design Conference. Perhaps it was here, while encountering some of the most innovative trends in contemporary graphic design, that she had an idea for a new magazine. It was a whimsical idea. She imagined a three-dimensional publication housed in a cardboard box with all kinds of unbound contents, including flexi-disc records, films, souvenirs, and other objects, such as "blueprints, a bit of rock, wildflower seeds, tea samples, an opera libretti [*sic*], old newspapers, jigsaw puzzles."[1] When she returned to New York, she founded *Aspen: The Magazine in a Box*, using her maiden name, Phyllis Johnson, as a *nom de plume*. "In calling it a 'magazine,'" she explained to her readers in the first issue, "we are harking back to the original meaning of the word as a 'storehouse, a cache, a ship laden with stores.'"[2]

This fundamental capacity of the magazine to bring together different types of things also appealed to a number of artists around the same time. Wallace Berman's *Semina* (1955–1964), Henri Chopin's experimental sound-poetry magazine, *Revue Ou* (1958–1974), George Maciunas's Fluxus publications, Wolf Vostell's *dé-coll/age* (1962–1969), and William Copley's *S.M.S.* (1968) are just a few examples of artists' magazines that experimented with multimedia or unbound formats in the 1960s. Whether or not Johnson was aware of these publications, she would soon discover for herself that the expanded category of the periodical she envisioned had a special resonance within the 1960s art world. Commissioning contemporary artists to design and guest-edit the magazine, she transformed *Aspen* into a miniature traveling gallery, enthusiastically announcing, "*Aspen* gives you actual works of art! Exactly as the artist created them. In exactly the media he created them for."[3] If *Aspen* attests to the potential of the magazine as a new kind of artistic medium and exhibition space in the 1960s, this chapter argues that its significance must be understood in relationship to the expanded categories of artistic medium during this time, witnessed in minimalism, conceptual art, and related practices—practices that were most evident in *Aspen* 5+6, edited by Brian O'Doherty, and *Aspen* 8, edited by Dan Graham.

....

While today the town of Aspen, Colorado, is perhaps best known as an upscale ski resort, in the 1960s it emerged as a vibrant, offbeat center of cultural and technological innovation.[4] It was this spirit with which Johnson sought to associate her magazine. To her, Aspen represented more than just a place; it was "a point of view, a state of mind, a symbol of the free-wheeling eclectic life (much as the *New Yorker* uses New York)."[5] A former mining settlement, the town was reinvented in the 1950s by the Chicago industrialist Walter Paepcke, who founded both the Aspen Ski Company and the Aspen Institute, a progressive humanistic think tank that sponsored programs and

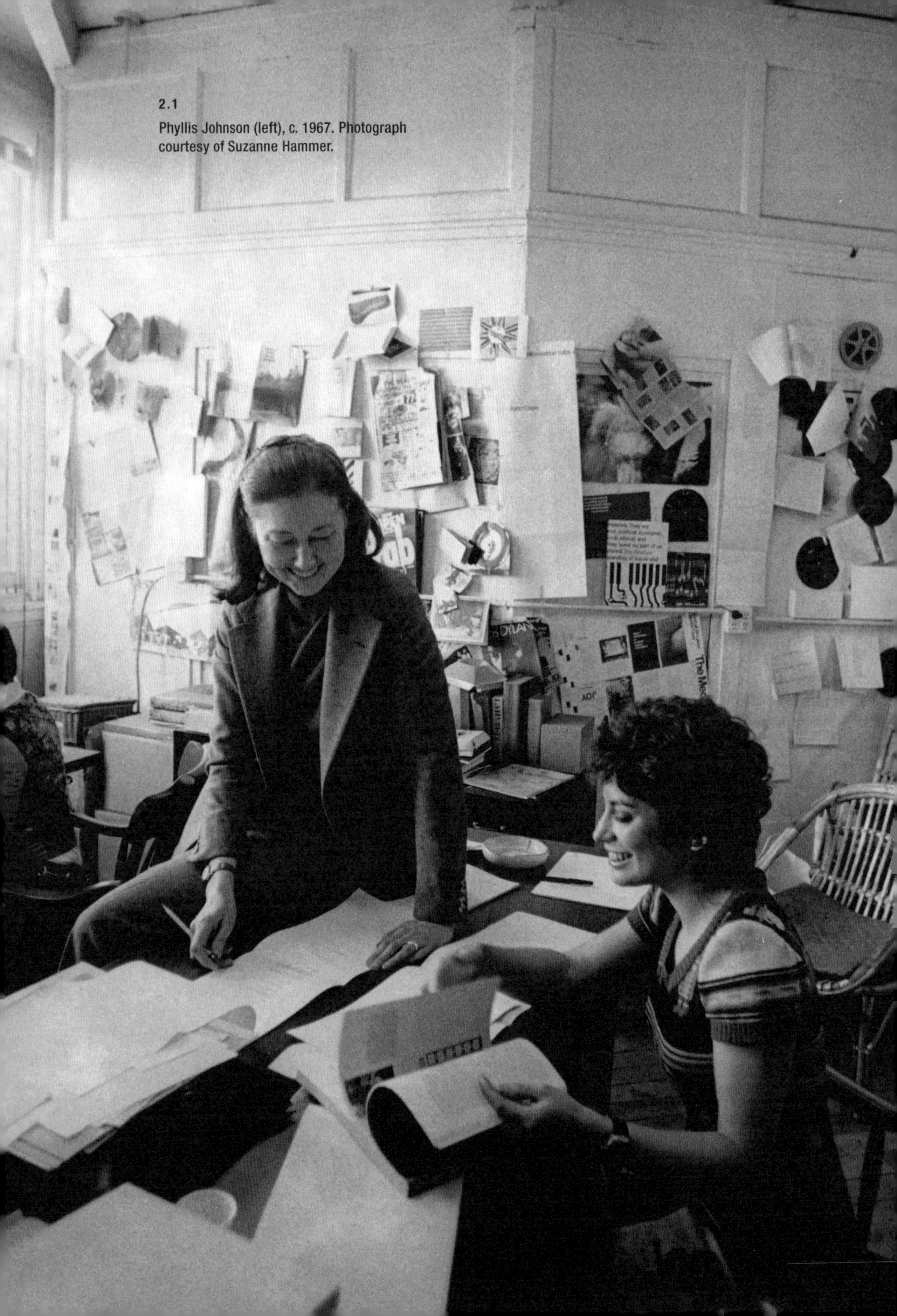

2.1
Phyllis Johnson (left), c. 1967. Photograph
courtesy of Suzanne Hammer.

seminars on a broad variety of topics including the arts, communications, justice, education, and the environment. Hosting the annual International Design Conference, music and film festivals, and an artist-in-residence program, the Aspen Institute greatly contributed to the city's reputation as a meeting ground for artists, scientists, and writers, including Herbert Bayer, Hunter S. Thompson, and Buckminster Fuller.

Aspen's rich cultural and recreational offerings provided ample editorial material for the new magazine, which initially reported on proceedings at the Aspen Institute and on other local attractions. The first issue, published in 1965, was a flat, laminated, black cardboard box that hinged on the left side, opening to reveal an assortment of pamphlets and booklets in different formats and sizes, on topics such as cross-country skiing, Colorado wildlife, regional architecture, and recipes, alongside lengthy excerpts from the 15th Annual Aspen International Design Conference, plus a jazz record. George Lois, who designed the first issue, remembers Johnson's enthusiasm as she animatedly described its novel boxed format to him (though to him, he admitted, it sounded a bit like "trying to reinvent the wheel").[6] This issue, and the second—a white box containing excerpts of papers delivered at the Aspen Film Conference, an article on downhill skiing, and a record of works by the classical composer Alexander Scriabin—seemed to cater to the wealthy, educated residents and tourists of Aspen, for whom Johnson claimed she wanted to provide "culture along with play."[7] And yet the editor seems to have had other things in store for the magazine from the beginning—even if she herself was not yet sure exactly what they would be; as she explained to her readers, "for this first issue, we've started out with a rather dignified format, but who knows what the next issue will be!"[8]

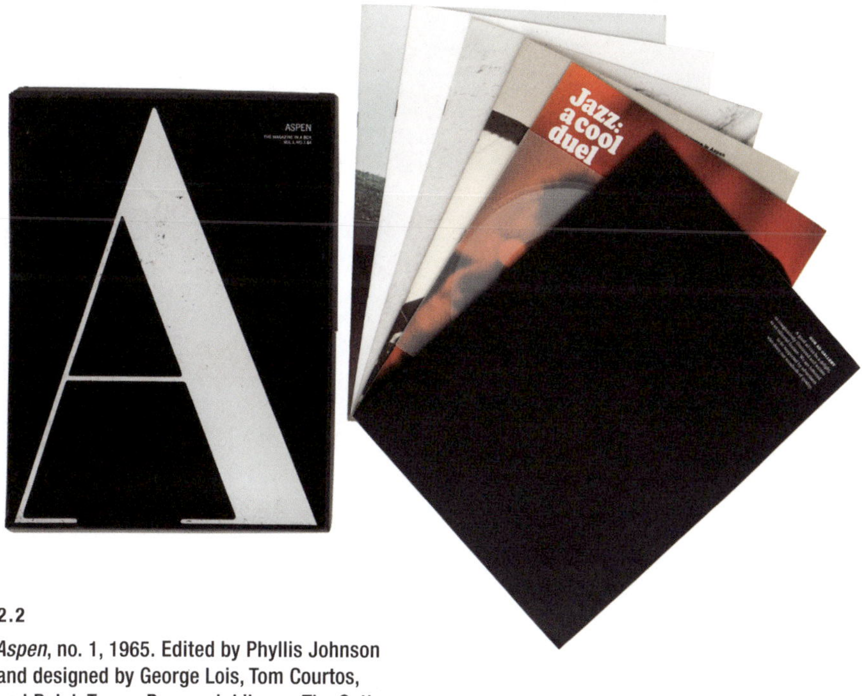

2.2

Aspen, no. 1, 1965. Edited by Phyllis Johnson and designed by George Lois, Tom Courtos, and Ralph Tuzzo. Research Library, The Getty Research Institute, Los Angeles (86-S1350 no. 1).

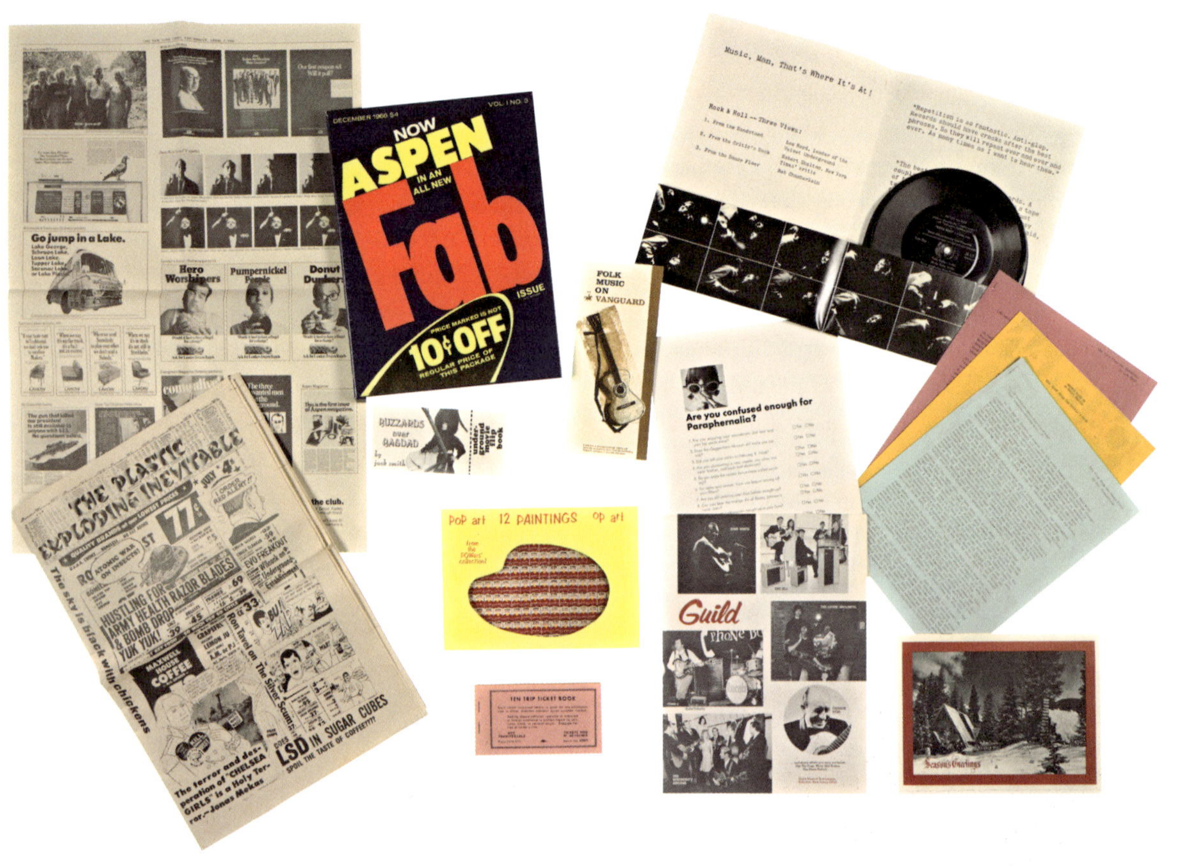

2.3

Aspen, no. 3, December 1966. Designed by Andy
Warhol and David Dalton. © 2009 The Andy Warhol
Foundation for the Visual Arts / Artists Rights
Society (ARS), New York. Research Library, The Getty
Research Institute, Los Angeles (86-S1350 v.1 no.3).

Johnson asked Andy Warhol, who was prominently featured in the collection of eminent Aspen art collector John Powers, to design issue 3, a task the pop artist largely delegated to the rock critic David Dalton, who was his studio assistant at the time (and who would soon go on to become a founding editor of *Rolling Stone* magazine).[9] A drastic departure from the previous two issues, *Aspen* 3 was designed in the form of a box of Fab laundry detergent, and was steeped in the underground, countercultural milieu of the Factory. It contained a reversible movie flipbook with excerpts from Warhol's film *Kiss* on one side and Jack Smith's *Buzzards over Baghdad* on the other; a set of postcard reproductions of paintings from the Powers collection; a "Ten Trip Ticket Book" with excerpts from the Berkeley conference on LSD; the first (and only) issue of the *E.P.I. Newspaper*; and a flexi-disc of the first Velvet Underground release, *Loop*, a never-ending (because it ends in a locked groove), feedback-infused, instrumental drone. Providing a mélange for both ears and eyes, *Aspen* 3 emulated the multisensory experience of Warhol's intermedia performance group, the Exploding Plastic Inevitable, which toured the country in 1966 and 1967.[10]

Within the 1960s art world, *Aspen*'s multimedia format was clearly a boon, promising to not only document but also simulate the proliferating forms of new media art. Another multimedia magazine published in New York at around the same time and featuring some of the same artists as *Aspen* was William Copley's bimonthly *S.M.S.* (1968), which contained intricate, limited-edition artists' objects and multiples in a cardboard portfolio. "Art has left the canvas. It's expanded its activity and every kind of activity has become art," Copley observed, suggesting that the new malleability of the category of the periodical mirrored developments within the art world itself, as artists questioned and blurred previously distinct categories of medium.[11] A review of *Aspen* and *S.M.S.* by the intermedia artist Jud Yalkut captures artists' excitement about the new periodical formats at this moment:

> **What possibilities for the further evolution of the magazine format lay ahead in the challenges of new technologies now opening to the artist? More films, slides, film-strips, tape recordings as well as records and tape-loops, inflatable models and sculpture-structures may comprise a complete multimedia package with magazine "box" covers. … In our foreseeable future, the perfection of three-dimensional color videotape may well, in the words of Nam June Paik, make *Life* magazine as obsolete as *Life* made *Collier's*.[12]**

Yalkut enthusiastically embraces the new artistic possibilities of the magazine, and suggests the way in which these possibilities were deeply connected to new communication and information technologies being developed within the broader context of 1960s media culture. And yet, while Yalkut imagines how these technologies might transform and improve upon the traditional printed magazine, he also raises the specter that they might, in effect, render it extinct. Indeed, *Aspen*'s strange, hybrid format in between old and new media speaks rather poignantly to the anxiety of print at this time—an anxiety that was all too real to magazine publishers, who watched their profits plummet as television cut into advertising revenue.[13]

As many pointed out at the time, *Aspen* epitomized the ideas of the Canadian media theorist Marshall McLuhan, who heralded the end of print in an electronic age. *Aspen* 4 was in fact dedicated to the ideas of McLuhan. Designed by Quentin Fiore, the issue referenced the perceptual effects of hallucinogens as much as the visual signifiers of computer circuitry, showcasing the decade's countercultural lifestyles and music, where McLuhan believed the seeds of the new social forms of the global village were being sown. It contained a double-sided poster version of McLuhan's 1967 bestseller *The Medium Is the Massage*, with the book's pages spread out mosaic-like so that they can be viewed all at once, and featured articles on the Haight-Ashbury psychedelic scene, outlaw motorcycle culture, and the geodesic-domed, pro-LSD alternative community of Drop City, Colorado. Also included in the issue were John Cage's lecture from the 1966 Aspen International Design Conference entitled "Diary: How to Improve the World (You Will Only Make Matters Worse)" and a flexi-disc recording of electronic music by Mario Davidovsky and Gordon Mumma.

McLuhan argued that new "cool" media, such as television, offered participatory, nonlinear, and multisensory experiences that would supersede the linear, static format of the phonetic alphabet, which "must be strung together bead-like, and in a prescribed order."[14] However, as Nam June Paik pointed out, McLuhan's "biggest inconsistency is that he still writes books."[15] *Aspen* 4 appeared to resolve this contradiction, exemplifying McLuhan's notion that technology would "extend" the nervous system by activating the aural and tactile capacities of the human sensorium, which, he argued, had suffered attrition during print's reign of visuality. And yet, while *Aspen* clearly alluded to the multimedia technologies of the electronic age—and was, no doubt, conceived, at least in part, in order to compete with them—it also utterly failed to rival the simultaneity and speed of broadcast or digital information. Against the virtual, integrated audiovisual experience of the television screen, *Aspen* insisted on a concrete materiality and an actual engagement with the human senses. As Phyllis Johnson proclaimed about the magazine, "you don't just read it: you hear it, hang it, feel it, fly it, sniff it, taste it, fold it, wear it, shake it, even project it on your living room wall."[16]

With its cardboard-box cover, *Aspen* appeared markedly—and captivatingly—primitive as an example of multimedia. It explored the communicative possibilities of the future by looking backward, serving as a reliquary for those very media—records, films, and print—that threatened to become obsolete in an emerging digital age. However, while McLuhan is often remembered for predicting the end of print, he also raised the possibility that, as it was rendered anachronistic by newer technologies, the medium of print might release its true artistic potential. Echoing Walter Benjamin's notion of the outmoded, he observed: "the movie and TV, as much as radio and gramophone, have by-passed the printed word. That is to say they have turned the printed word into an art form just as Gutenberg turned the manuscript into an art form."[17]

Aspen certainly seemed to instantiate this possibility. Each subsequent issue of the magazine was sui generis: issue 5+6, edited by O'Doherty, focused on minimalism and conceptual art; issue 6A was a reprint of the single-issue Judson Church magazine *Manipulations*, documenting the performance series "12 Evenings of Manipulations"; issue 7 was a game-filled "British Box" issue edited by Mario Amaya, which included an Eduardo Paolozzi coloring book, recordings by John Lennon and Yoko Ono, and kitsch souvenirs by Peter Blake; Dan Graham edited issue 8, devoted to "Art/Information/Science"; issue 9 was a psychedelic "Dreamweapon" issue edited by musicians Angus and Hetty MacLise, which contained a photo-poetry poster by Gerard Malanga and a sheet of gummed stamps illustrated with rainbow-colored nudes by Don Snyder; and issue 10 (which did not have editorial credits) was an incense-scented "Far East" issue, complete with miniature Sung Dynasty landscape scrolls. A Buckminster Fuller issue in which each article would unfold into a geodesic dome was planned but—fittingly, perhaps—never realized.

Like many of Fuller's improbable inventions, *Aspen* seemed out of step with the demands of the practical world. Plagued by production issues, which were no doubt exacerbated by the complications of coordinating its various guest editors, the magazine was notoriously behind schedule. While billed as a quarterly, *Aspen* came out intermittently, once or maybe twice a year, prompting one reviewer to remark, "the publication date is as much a surprise as the contents."[18] In all likelihood, such unpredictability contributed to the demise of its advertising section, which started off strong as an unbound "ad gallery" in its own separate folder, but then dwindled, apparently ceasing completely after issue 5+6.[19]

In 1971, the U.S. Postal Service revoked the magazine's second-class mail license, forcing it to fold shortly after its tenth issue. Citing criteria established by Congress in 1879, which required that periodicals be dated, numbered, formed of printed sheets, and have consistency between issues and periodicity, the Postal Service objected in particular to *Aspen*'s erratic publication schedule and inconsistent format. While admitting that the publication was "a clever and imaginative idea," the Postal Service concluded that it was not a periodical.[20] More than just a matter of postage, this historical footnote suggests how radically *Aspen* differed from a standard periodical in both its physical properties and its circulation. Though these differences spelled the publication's commercial failure, they would prove central to its artistic significance.

ASPEN 5+6: A MINIATURE MUSEUM

"With conceptual art, you needed a magazine more than a gallery," the Irish expatriate artist and critic Brian O'Doherty recalled of his decision to edit *Aspen* 5+6.[21] The dematerialized forms of conceptual art, which largely consisted of texts, photographs, and other ephemeral documents, were perfectly suited for distribution in the reproducible printed format of the periodical. O'Doherty's expansive editorial vision soon spilled into a special double issue, published in Fall 1967, which contained four films, five records, critical texts, and several printed artists' projects, showcasing experimental art, dance, performance, film, music, and literature. Contained in a freestanding white cardboard box, *Aspen* 5+6 presented a cross section of the 1960s New York avant-garde, highlighting minimalism and conceptual art, while stressing its continental affinities and historical precedents. It included films by Hans Richter, László Moholy-Nagy, Robert Rauschenberg, and Robert Morris; flexi-discs of music by John Cage and Morton Feldman; texts and spoken word recordings by Samuel Beckett, Naum Gabo, William S. Burroughs, Alain Robbe-Grillet, Richard Huelsenbeck, and Marcel Duchamp; an interview with Merce Cunningham; printed artists' projects by O'Doherty, Dan Graham, Sol LeWitt, Mel Bochner, and Tony Smith; and critical articles by Susan Sontag, George Kubler, and Roland Barthes, whose landmark essay "The Death of the Author" was published here for the first time.

In his working notes for *Aspen* 5+6, O'Doherty referred to the magazine as a "miniature museum" and specified that it would contain diminutive works of art, such as dollhouse-sized sculptures by Oldenburg and Judd (neither of whom ended up participating in the final version).[22] One model he likely had in mind was Duchamp's *Boîte-en-valise* (1935–1941), a "portable museum" which consisted of sixty-nine facsimiles of the artist's works, including miniature versions of

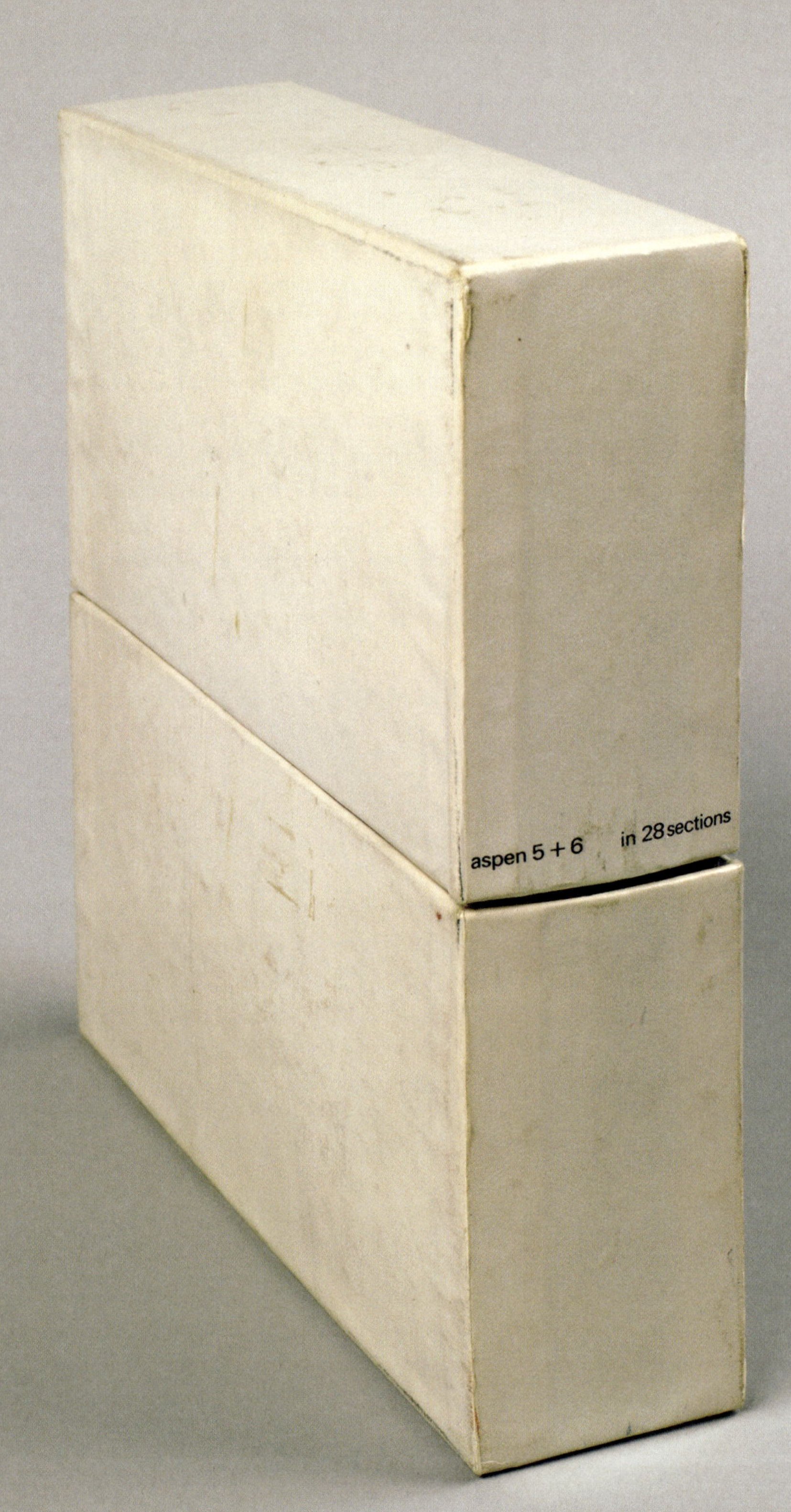
aspen 5 + 6   in 28 sections

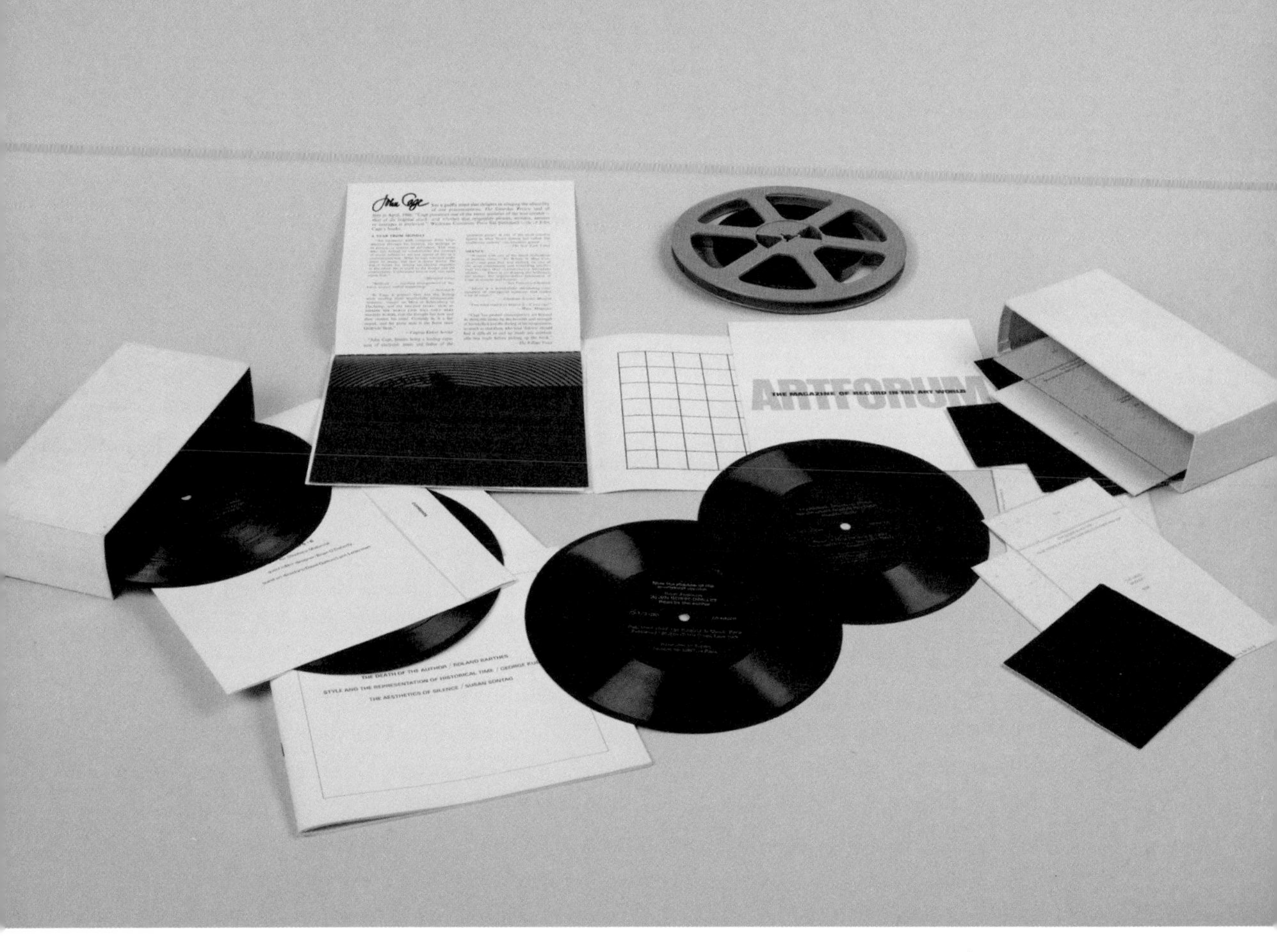

2.4 and 2.5

Aspen, no. 5+6, Fall 1967. Edited and designed by
Brian O'Doherty. Courtesy of Brian O'Doherty.
Research Library, The Getty Research Institute,
Los Angeles (86-S1350 no. 5–6).

his readymades, meticulously arranged in a small suitcase.[23] O'Doherty was a great admirer of Duchamp, whom he knew personally, and included in *Aspen* 5+6 recordings of the artist reading from "The Creative Act" (1956) and *À l'infinitif* (1912–1920). And yet, while the *Boîte-en-valise* was produced in special deluxe editions, creating an aura around mechanically reproduced works of art through collotype printing and hand-coloring techniques such as *pochoir*, *Aspen* was a very different kind of endeavor. At four dollars an issue, and with a stated circulation of 20,000 (albeit a figure that was probably greatly exaggerated),[24] it was not a limited-edition multiple, but a mass-produced museum, designed less to preserve and protect works of art than to set them free.

The square white cardboard cover of *Aspen* 5+6 evoked the proverbial white cube of the gallery space—which O'Doherty would later critique in his important series of essays "Inside the White Cube: The Ideology of the Gallery Space," published in *Artforum* in 1976. Here he denounced the sterile elitism of the commercial gallery, describing its "unshadowed, white, clean, artificial" environment in which "there is no time" and "the outside world must not come in."[25] In retrospect, *Aspen* 5+6 seems to prefigure O'Doherty's later interest in how art might escape the architectural and institutional strictures of the traditional gallery. Rather than cloistering art from everyday life, the magazine released it back into the world, countering the timeless, contemplative visuality of the modern museum with a distinctly temporal, interactive experience.

The issue, which was opened by lifting the top half of the box cover off of the bottom half, presented a peculiar challenge to its reader, requiring various types of concentration and hands-on interaction. Subscribers to the magazine could watch, in grainy, silent, black-and-white footage, Hans Richter's *Rhythm 21* (1921), an abstract film composed of staccato squares and rectangles; László Moholy-Nagy's *Lightplay* (1932), which documented the dazzling patterns of light and shadow of the artist's kinetic sculpture; Robert Rauschenberg's *Linoleum* (1967), a kind of performance collage involving dancers and live chickens; and Stan VanDerBeek's film of Robert Morris's performance *Site* (1964), in which the artist hauls away plywood panels to reveal a tableau of Edouard Manet's *Olympia* featuring Carolee Schneemann as its reclining female nude. They could listen to the high-pitched shrieks of electronic frequencies derived from chance operations in John Cage's *Fontana Mix* (1958), and to the dreamy, arrhythmic percussive sounds of Morton Feldman's *King of Denmark* (1965), which specified that no mallets or sticks, but only the performer's hands, fingers, and arms, be used to play instruments. The reader was required not only to play records and to project films, but to perform a play in Brian O'Doherty's *Structural Play #3*; to compose music in Cage's *Fontana Mix*; to complete a poem in Dan Graham's "Poem, March 1966"; to turn the pages of Mel Bochner's *Seven Translucent Tiers* (1967), a stack of translucent tracing paper printed with a grid that contained patterns of pluses and minuses to be "added up"; and even to construct a cardboard model of Tony Smith's sculpture *The Maze* (1957).

Set loose from the traditional codex form, *Aspen*'s unbound format encouraged multiple rhizomatic connections among its components. The table of contents inventoried a dizzying cornucopia of themes and movements, including constructivism, structuralism, conceptualism, traditions of paradoxical thinking, objects between categories, time (in art and "history"), silence and reduction, and language. Against the strict evolutionary chronology of the modern museum, expressed by Alfred Barr's famous flow chart, art history in *Aspen* unfolds in an uneven temporality. Artistic influences do not proceed in a neat, linear fashion, but ricochet back and forth, echoing among the various historical and neo-avant-garde practices juxtaposed in the publication, from minimalism and conceptual art to constructivism, Dada, and the French *nouveau roman*. The magazine as a whole manifests Kubler's claim in his essay "Style and the Representation of Historical Time," included in the issue, that "historically, every work of art is a fragment of some larger unit, and every work of art is a bundle of components of different ages, intricately related to many other works of art, both old and new, by a network of incoming and outgoing influences."[26]

O'Doherty's working notes for *Aspen* 5+6 bear witness to the complexities of his editorial process in the face of these myriad connections and cross-references. Scribbled with elaborate lists, diagrams, arrows, and doodles, as well as phone numbers and dollar amounts, these notes reveal the labyrinthine relationships between the components, as he decided who to include and how to organize the sections, and worked out the logistics and production costs of the issue. O'Doherty listed himself as guest editor and designer as well as a contributing artist; he also contributed as a critic under the pseudonym Sigmund Bode (this was one of many alter egos that he would take on throughout his career, later producing art under the alias Patrick Ireland). He was also clearly operating as a new kind of curator, envisioning how the works of art and writings would be arranged physically and conceptually within this novel discursive space.

Aspen 5+6 was dedicated to the modernist poet Stéphane Mallarmé, whose explorations with the materiality and sonority of language served as a model for the issue's experiments with the spoken and printed word. In particular, the magazine paid tribute to Mallarmé's *Le Livre*, the poet's idea for a three-dimensional book, which was to consist of a set of mobile sections contained in a box and meant to be read aloud and collectively by an audience. Never realized during his lifetime, *Le Livre* was described by Mallarmé in his posthumously published notes, which were translated into English in the German music journal *Die Reihe* in 1964, where American artists such as Dan Graham and Sol LeWitt first encountered them.[27] *Le Livre* served as a kind of blueprint for how *Aspen*'s unbound format transformed the semantic and social possibilities of print, bringing about a collective, indeterminate form of reading.

In his 1967 article "The Book as Object," Graham described *Le Livre* as

> a radical divergence from the traditional book, which attempts to translate its author's private viewpoint as re-presentation in the individual mind of its readers. The linear book's time is enclosed whereas Mallarmé's book exists in a moment-to-moment specificity, its duration and structure being formally identified with the constituent group of readers whose presence literally in-forms it. Unlike the old book, the "reader" does not work his way through in one direction.[28]

Likely written with *Aspen* in mind, Graham's discussion of Mallarmé sheds light on the particular appeal of the magazine's unbound format for artists at this time. Graham's description of reading resonates strongly with the phenomenological models of spectatorship being explored by minimalism—where, in the words of Robert Morris, "it is the viewer who constantly changes the shape by his change in position relative to the work."[29] However, Graham also clearly evokes a poststructuralist model of signification—suggesting that the meaning of a text is determined by the reader's experience rather than solely by the author's intention—as Barthes described in "The Death of the Author," published, as mentioned, in *Aspen* 5+6. The unparalleled significance of this particular issue of *Aspen* has to do not only with the way in which it crystallized the intersection between minimalism's phenomenological models of perception and poststructuralist investigations of language—an intersection that was pivotal for the emerging practice of conceptual art—but also with the implications of this convergence for the social and political possibilities of both art and media.

Published at the peak of minimalism's influence in the New York art world, *Aspen* 5+6 featured work by well-known minimalist artists including Sol LeWitt, Mel Bochner, Tony Smith, and Robert Morris. With its square white box cover and its reductive sans serif font, the magazine stylistically embodied the industrial, geometric forms of this work. O'Doherty conceived of the magazine's cover as itself a kind of miniature minimalist sculpture—a modular form that could be arranged in different ways by the reader.[30] In its metamorphosis from a flat, two-dimensional object into an unbound three-dimensional experience, *Aspen* in some sense paralleled the minimalist shift from an illusionistic pictorial realm to a physical or spatial reality, expressed by Judd's assertion that "three-dimensions are real space."[31] And like Judd's specific objects, which he asserted were "neither painting nor sculpture," *Aspen* 5+6 threw into question its own category or medium, insisting on its hybrid status with its multimedia components ("objects in between categories" was one of the themes listed on its table of contents).[32]

One of the most significant ways that *Aspen* 5+6 engaged with minimalist aesthetics was through its emphasis on temporality. In his working notes, O'Doherty repeatedly referred to the magazine as the "Art & Time issue of *Aspen*," and "time (in art and 'history')" was another theme listed in the table of contents. Indeed, *Aspen* vividly manifests the heightened engagement with temporality that, as Pamela Lee has argued, was central to 1960s art more generally, and that was perhaps most famously described in Michael Fried's scathing critique of minimalism, "Art and Objecthood," which appeared in the Summer 1967 issue of *Artforum*, just months before *Aspen* 5+6 was published.[33] Here Fried singled out minimalism's "endless, or indefinite, duration" as responsible for its "theatricality"—a new, and for the critic, deeply regrettable, relationship with the viewer.[34] Invaded by the mundane time and space of everyday life, minimalist works threatened to go on and on, refusing categorization or final meaning—and worse, failing to elicit conviction in the critic.

While all magazines might be considered temporal in that reading itself takes place in time, *Aspen* 5+6 dramatizes its temporality through its unbound, multimedia format. Consider the following review by Dore Ashton:

> The book O'Doherty creates must, in physical fact, be seen in irregular time masses. I, for instance, had to arrange a film showing in my school in order to see the films. ... I had to borrow a phonograph with extra-slow time speed in order to hear Gabo reading his manifesto and Duchamp reading his prescription for an anti-Bouvard and Pécuchet dictionary. And I had to wrap up the essays and "data" (as the work by the visual "artists" in the box is called) and take them on a train to read. ... Assimilating O'Doherty's creation in these disparate temporal circumstances, I nonetheless, perhaps through unshakeable habit, was reading—reading a pattern of modern art in its multiple perspectives.[35]

Ashton characterizes the experience of reading the magazine as explicitly temporal: it was impossible to view the magazine's contents all at once, or even in one sitting. Furthermore, the publication coincides with the reader's own duration, and is mediated by the "disparate temporal circumstances" of her own life, her teaching schedule, her daily commute.

Besides documenting works of art that might be considered quintessentially theatrical, such as LeWitt's *Serial Project #1 (ABCD)* (1966) and Morris's *Site* (1964), *Aspen* included documents—in the form of records, films, and printed materials—that were themselves distinctly time-based, requiring activation from the reader. Like the plywood slabs and beams, fabricated cubes, and found industrial objects of minimalist sculpture, which Fried abhorred because of the way they were driven by the spectator's interaction—in his words, this sculpture "*depends* on the beholder, is *incomplete* without him, it *has* been waiting for him"[36]—the magazine in a box relied on the reader to activate it, to open it up and bring its mute, static contents to life.

This interactivity was staged in an especially acute—and earnest—way by Smith's cardboard model of *The Maze*. The original sculpture, created for the exhibition "Schemata 7" at the Finch College Museum of Art in 1957, consisted of four large modules arranged in a square, to create a labyrinth-like experience for the viewer who could walk through the pathways in between the modules. While the miniature version included in *Aspen* 5+6 obviously does not recreate the sense of scale of the original sculpture, it does underscore how deeply the magazine's literal interactivity resonated with minimalism's radical new understanding of the work of art as something intrinsically driven by the experience of the spectator. A set of eight black cardboard pieces meant to be cut out and pasted together by the viewer, the piece literally enacts the dissolution of the gestalt form of the work into a kind of endlessness of its different sides, which never quite cohere in the viewer's phenomenological experience. Furthermore, judging by the complexity of the instructions, it is likely that the construction of this piece would actually have been, for all practical purposes, an endless process—or at least one that the reader might have given up on before finishing. Indeed, to imagine the reader, all thumbs, fumbling with these cardboard pieces (the artist recommends using a matte knife and Elmer's glue) is to envision a model of viewership rooted in the duration and tactility of the human body.

And yet while such contingency meant one thing in the context of a sculptural work encountered in the architectural space of the museum or gallery, it undoubtedly meant something very different in the discursive space of a magazine, where critics and readers interpret art through texts. Indeed, if *Aspen*'s unbound format evoked minimalism's new understandings of the viewer, it also powerfully conjured the new poststructuralist models of reception announced by Roland Barthes as "the birth of the reader," which insisted upon language itself as a contingent, interactive, and temporal medium.

THE BIRTH OF THE READER

The extraordinary importance of "The Death of the Author" for visual artists in the 1960s has long been acknowledged; to revisit it within its original site of publication in *Aspen* 5+6 allows us to more fully appreciate Barthes's influence on visual artists—and, perhaps, theirs on him. Brian O'Doherty had become familiar with Barthes's writings through the progressive literary magazine *Evergreen Review* (in which *Aspen* itself frequently advertised). He contacted the French

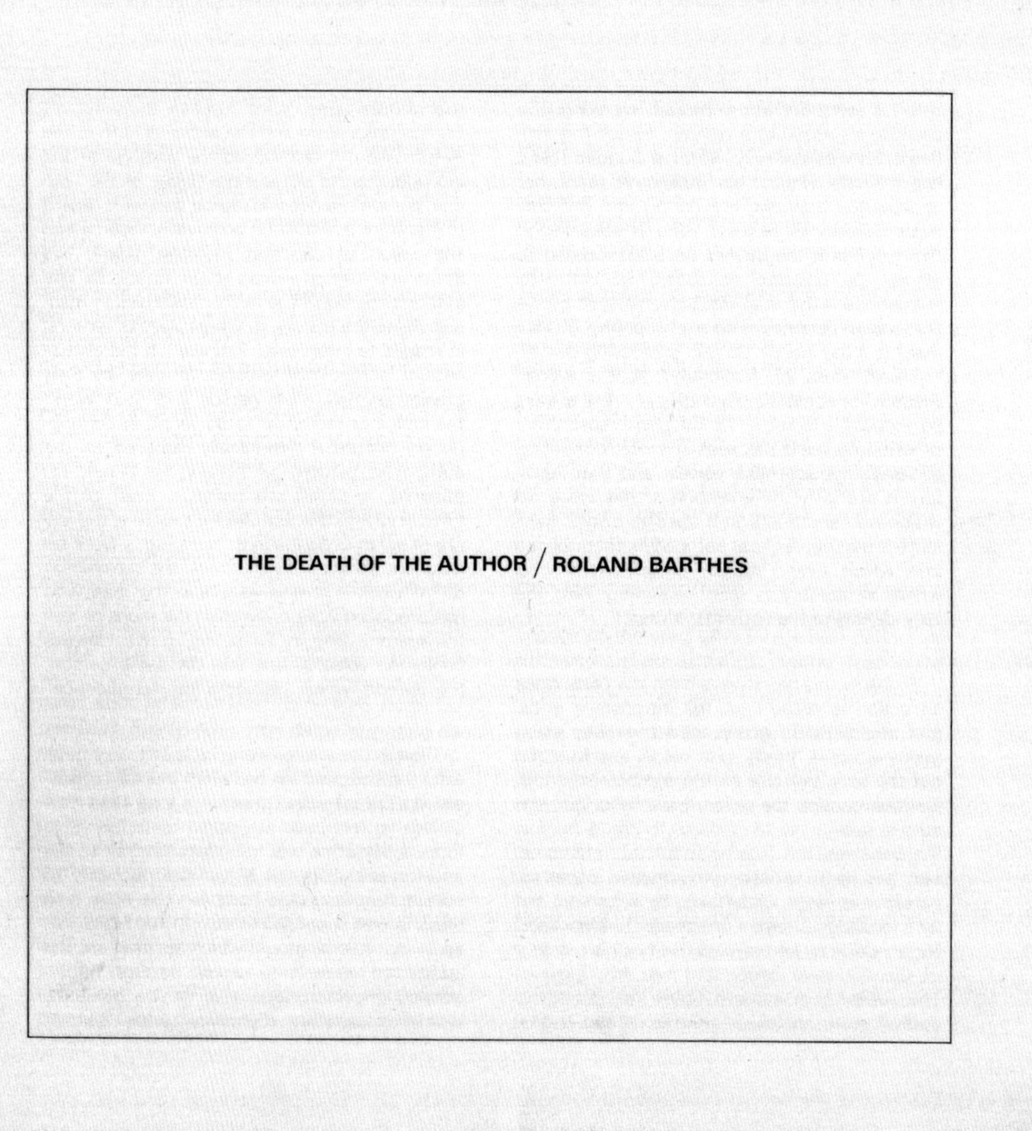

2.6

Roland Barthes, "The Death of the Author,"
title page, *Aspen*, no. 5+6, Fall 1967. Courtesy of
Brian O'Doherty.

theorist in the summer of 1967, inviting him to contribute to *Aspen* 5+6. Apparently O'Doherty encouraged Barthes to take advantage of the magazine's unique multimedia format, for Barthes replied, "your project is of much interest to me, but I for one hold a *radical* belief in writing, and cannot imagine doing anything but writing."[37] He sent "The Death of the Author" a few months later, with a note apologizing for its brevity and expressing his hopes that it would be acceptable and "in sufficient harmony with the issue."[38]

Commissioned specifically for *Aspen* 5+6, Barthes's famous essay must be understood as a deeply site-specific piece of writing, informed by and meant to be read alongside visual art, music, performances, and texts. To read "The Death of the Author" in the site of its original publication is to more fully comprehend Barthes's characterization of the modern text as "a multidimensional space in which a variety of writings, none of them original, blend and clash."[39] By leaving the sequence of the magazine up to the individual reader, who manipulates its various components, determining their arrangement and relationship to one another, *Aspen* echoes Barthes insistence on the primacy of reception—"the birth of the reader"—over and above the author's intention. As O'Doherty observed, "this discreteness will in effect measure the extent of the reader-listener-viewer's involvement."[40] The magazine's multimedia format attests to the important role of new communication technologies in the new models of authorship and reception announced by poststructuralist theory: to read (and listen to and watch) *Aspen* is to witness the death of the author as a casualty of the sixties' information society with its birth of new readers, who were also television watchers, radio listeners, and moviegoers. Even the layout and typography of the essay, printed in Univers font on square pages, embodies the stark, impersonal surface of the page as the locus of "that neutral composite, oblique space where our subject slips away, the negative where all identity is lost, starting with the very identity of the author, writing," as Barthes described the experience of the text.[41]

Aspen highlights the ways in which artists participated in the questioning of authorship, by using strategies such as chance operations, collage, deskilling, and serial procedures to displace artistic intention and engage the viewer as an active coproducer of meaning. (As Sol LeWitt explains in "Serial Project #1," published in *Aspen* 5+6, "the role of the artist is not to instruct the viewer, but to give them information. Whether the viewer understands this information is incidental to the artist; he cannot foresee the understanding of all his viewers.")[42] The magazine also illuminates the tensions surrounding art criticism in the 1960s, for the death of the author also marked the demise of the critic. Barthes argued that "Once the Author is gone, the claim to decipher a text becomes quite useless. … Criticism (be it new) is today undermined along with the Author."[43] This assertion would have had special resonance given the heated debates that were going on between artists and critics in the pages of magazines such as *Artforum* at this moment. Formalist criticism, as exemplified by the writings of Fried, established aesthetic value according to the critic's conviction of a visual truth: his or her ability to instantly and automatically recognize—or dismiss—the virtues of a work of art. As Fried wrote, "it is this continuous and entire presentness … that one experiences as a kind of instantaneousness" that allowed the critic to feel conviction.[44] Against this a priori recognition of aesthetic quality, *Aspen* 5+6 insisted on a less secure kind of knowledge, replacing a model of aesthetic judgment based on the consensus of a single, supposedly universal point of view with the unpredictability and indeterminacy of multiple viewpoints and subject positions.

Beyond demonstrating the intersection between 1960s art and poststructuralist theory, *Aspen* embodied the egalitarian politics underpinning both. Indeed, Barthes's call for the radical redistribution of cultural production was realized in a very tangible way by this magazine which sent art through the mail in a cardboard box, allowing artists to circumvent the museum or gallery and bring about a more direct, democratic relationship with the viewer or reader. Barthes himself was apparently satisfied with the way *Aspen* 5+6 turned out, writing in a postcard to O'Doherty the following summer, "it is *fascinating,* and for me, very good."[45] (He also mentioned that he was still awaiting payment; as O'Doherty recalled with regret, none of the contributors ever got paid.)[46]

CONCEPTUAL ART AND THE MAGAZINE: DAN GRAHAM'S *SCHEMA (MARCH 1966)*

Aspen 5+6 attests to the pivotal new role of language in 1960s art, as exemplified by Dan Graham's contribution to the issue, "Poem, March 1966"—a work better known as *Schema (March 1966)* (1966–1967). This work seems to graft the phenomenological investigations of minimalism onto the medium of language itself, demonstrating the "mapping of the linguistic model onto the perceptual model" which Benjamin Buchloh has identified as central to the development of conceptual art.[47] However, *Schema* also sheds light on the significance of the magazine itself as the vehicle of this exploration.

Schema consists of an algorithmic template: a generic list of variables—such as "(number of) adjectives," "(type of) paper stock," "(name of) typeface"—that self-referentially index its own appearance on the page, setting off a circular chain reaction in which the poem's form alters its content, which alters its form, and so on. The work, Graham stipulated, could be published in any magazine and was to be completed by the editor according to the design and layout of the particular publication in which it appeared. Originally typeset for *Arts Magazine*, it was pulled by the editor at the last minute. After its initial publication in *Aspen*, it appeared in numerous subsequent periodicals, including *Art-Language, Extensions, Interfunktionen, Studio International,* and *Flash Art.* In *Aspen* the template was printed, along with the completed poem, on a single sheet of 8-by-16-inch cardstock, folded in half.

Referred to as a "do-it-yourself poem" by one reviewer, *Schema* exemplifies Barthes's observation that "it is language that speaks, not the author."[48] As Graham himself observed about the piece, "there is no composition. No artistic or authorial 'insight' is expressed."[49] *Schema* enacts a profound emptying out of subjectivity from language: instead of communicating an author's ideas, it foregrounds the materiality of language itself, as it appears on the mass-produced page (in much the same way that minimalism's industrial forms and procedures removed the hand of the artist). To come across *Schema* in *Aspen* 5+6 is to be momentarily distracted from the meaning of words by the shapes of letters and numbers, and even by the density of the material on which they are printed. It is to observe the unadorned mechanical form of the font, to notice the texture and pliability of the page. Our automatic reading habits disrupted, we are reminded that reading is an activity that is not only conceptual but profoundly visual and tactile.

By foregrounding the medium of the magazine in this self-referential manner, *Schema* paralleled—and parodied—the reductive logic of the modernist work of art, which, critics such as Clement Greenberg claimed, revealed the purity of its medium by emphasizing its unique material properties—the flatness of painting, for example. Ultimately, however, *Schema* suggests a very different notion of medium, one that (again like minimalism) challenges the autonomy of the work of art implicit in this formalist definition, by insisting on its context-bound nature. As Graham wrote about the piece, "it is not art for art's sake" but "immediate, particular, and altered as it fits the terms (and time) of its system or (the) context (it may be read in)."[50]

By enacting in a very literal—almost didactic—way a poststructuralist model of language, *Schema* functioned as a site-specific investigation of the magazine, demonstrating that the meaning of language was contingent upon the material conditions of the printed page, as well as on the editor's interpretation of these conditions. Each time it was published, the piece was modified, registering the graphic design and typography of the specific magazine in which it appeared—adopting the stark modern style of sans serif, for example, or the bureaucratic, old-fashioned look of Courier. The work also draws attention to the distinct temporality and transience of the magazine—the fact that periodicals are linked to a specific window of time, after which they are relegated to the status of back issues. This limited duration was key to *Schema*'s critical function. As Graham wrote about the work, it "subverts value. Beyond its appearance in print or present currency, *Schema* is disposable, with no dependence on material (commodity), it subverts the gallery (economic system)."[51]

Just as minimalism and site-specific sculpture in the 1960s foregrounded the physical location of the work of art, insisting that the museum or gallery was not a neutral backdrop but a determinant factor in the work's reception, so *Schema* insisted that the magazine page was not merely a generic container for discourse. And, just as the practice of site-specific art led from a consideration of the physical circumstances of the gallery space to the exploration of its social and political conditions—a practice that would become known as institutional critique—so Graham's investigation of the material facts of the magazine page opened onto the ideological and institutional conditions of the art magazine and art criticism within the art world. His critique of these conditions would become more even more explicit in *Aspen* 8, which he went on to guest-edit.

ASPEN 8: ART AS IN-FORMATION

Organized around the theme "Art/Information/Science," *Aspen* 8 reflected the preoccupation with cybernetics and systems theory in the art world at this time, as signaled by numerous exhibitions including Kynaston McShine's "Information" and Jack Burnham's "Software," both in 1970. Dense with printed matter of various shapes, sizes, and formats, the magazine exemplified the propensity of art at this time to literally take the form of information and documentation. Among its contents were Robert Smithson's *Strata: A Geo-photographic Fiction*, a collage of horizontal layers of found text and photographs of fossils; Yvonne Rainer's choreographic diagrams, writings, and photographs; a poster version of Ed Ruscha's 1967 book *Thirty-four Parking Lots*; documents and proposals by Dennis Oppenheim, Robert Morris, and Richard Serra; a lecture/song by David and Eleanor Antin; a booklet by Terry Atkinson and Michael Baldwin; an "audio study" by Steve Reich; a score by Philip Glass; and flexi-disc recordings by Jackson Mac Low and La Monte Young. The magazine's cover, designed by Fluxus artist George Maciunas, was not a box but a large square folder, which appeared less a container of its contents than a vehicle for their dispersal.[52]

SCHEMA

(number of) adjectives
(number of) adverbs
(percentage of) area not occupied by type
(percentage of) area occupied by type
(number of) columns
(number of) conjunctions
(number of) depression of type into surface of page
(number of) gerunds
(number of) infinitives
(number of) letters of alphabet
(number of) lines
(number of) mathematical symbols
(number of) nouns
(number of) numbers
(number of) participles
(perimeter of) page
(weight of) paper sheet
(type) paper stock
(thinness of) paper stock
(number of) prepositions
(number of) pronouns
(number of point) size type
(name of) typeface
(number of) words
(number of) words capitialized
(number of) words italicized
(number of) words not capitalized
(number of) words not italicized

2.7

Dan Graham, *Schema (March 1966)*, 1966–1967, as
published in *Aspen*, no. 5+6, Fall 1967. Printed matter.
Variable according to publication. Courtesy of Marian
Goodman Gallery.

POEM

35 adjectives
7 adverbs
35.52% area not occupied by type
64.48% area occupied by type
1 column
1 conjunction
0 mms. depression of type into surface of page
0 gerunds
0 infinitives
247 letters of alphabet
28 lines
6 mathematical symbols
51 nouns
29 numbers
6 participles
8" x 8" page
80 lb. paper sheet
dull coated paper stock
.007" thin paper stock
3 prepositions
0 pronouns
10 point size type
Univers 55 typeface
61 words
3 words capitalized
0 words italicized
58 words not capitalized
61 words not italicized

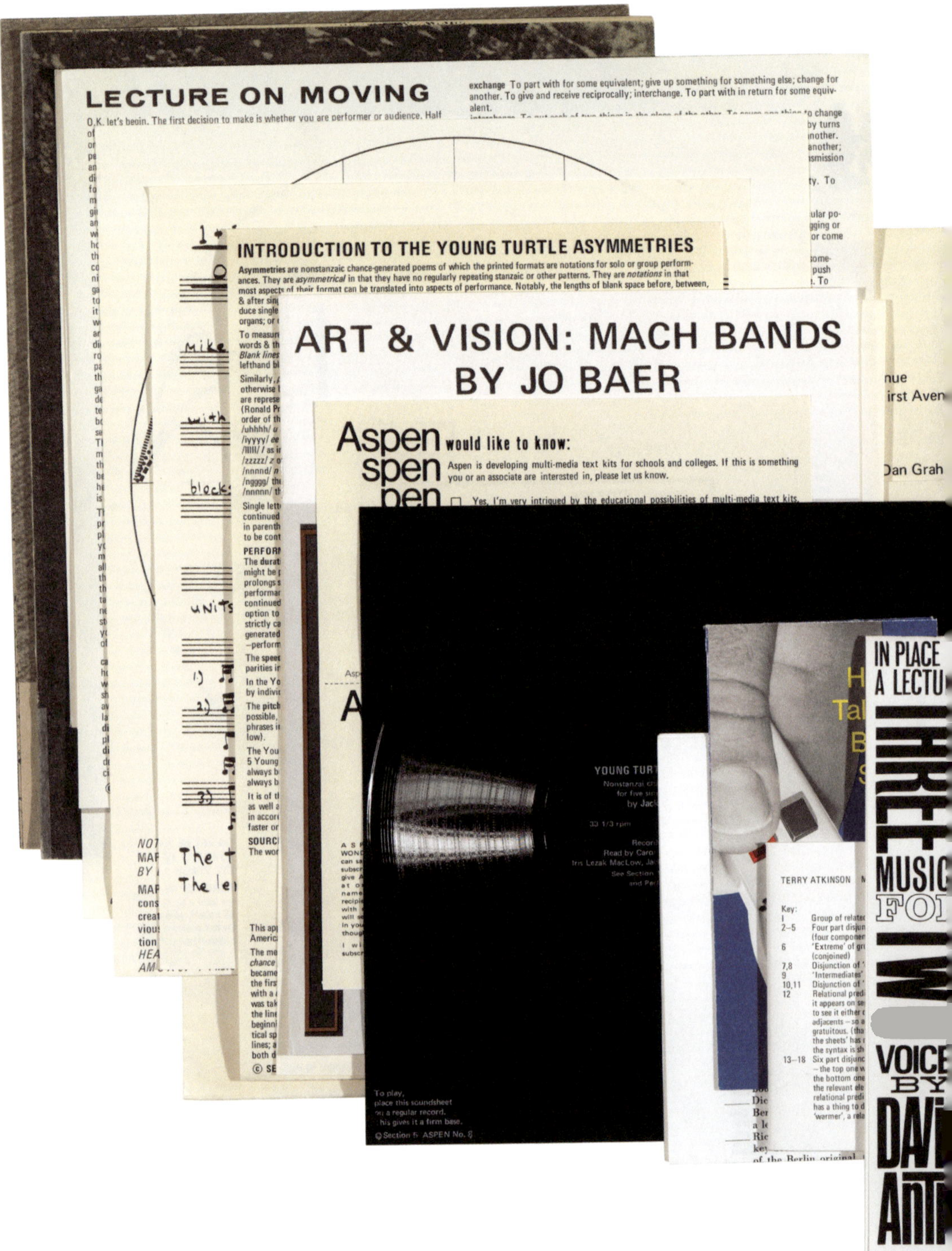
LECTURE ON MOVING
INTRODUCTION TO THE YOUNG TURTLE ASYMMETRIES
ART & VISION: MACH BANDS
BY JO BAER
Aspen would like to know:
Aspen is developing multi-media text kits for schools and colleges. If this is something you or an associate are interested in, please let us know.
Yes, I'm very intrigued by the educational possibilities of multi-media text kits.
THREE
MUSIC
FOR
VOICE
BY
DAVID
AntIn
IN PLACE
A LECTU
TERRY ATKINSON
YOUNG TURT

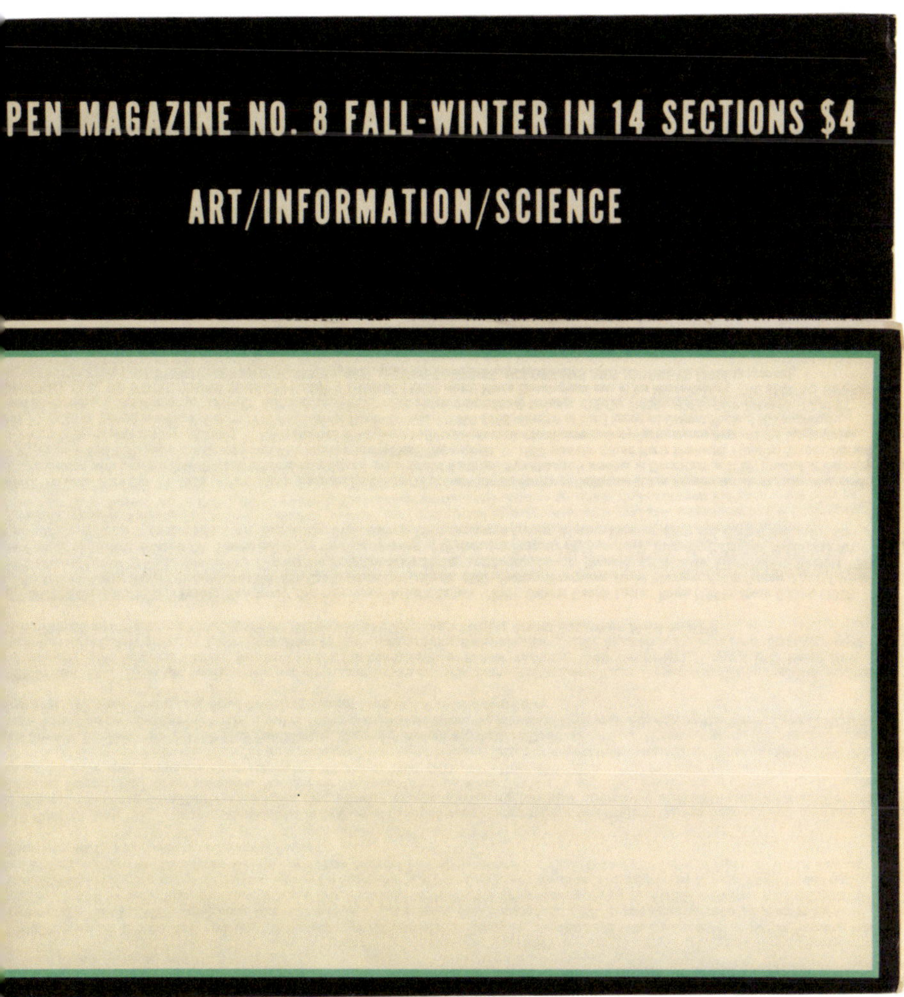

2.8

Aspen, no. 8, Fall-Winter 1970–1971. Edited by
Dan Graham and designed by George Maciunas.
Inside cover image by Jo Baer. Research Library,
The Getty Research Institute, Los Angeles
(86-S1350 no. 8).

However, while *Aspen* 8 explored art's new status as information, it also challenged the dominant conditions under which this information circulated in an art world that, as Jack Burnham pointed out in 1969, was itself an "information system" in which "critics, magazines, galleries, museums, collectors and historians exist to create information out of unprocessed art data. … The survival strategy of the art system is transforming preferred information into values."[53] Graham himself had condemned the role of the art magazine in perpetuating an economic system that benefited galleries and dealers instead of artists and viewers in his 1969 statement for the Art Workers' Coalition Open Hearing, discussed in chapter 1. With *Aspen* 8 he sought to challenge this system by reimagining the magazine's role both inside the art world and beyond it. As he explained in his editorial statement: "this issue where artists have conceived and (in part) designed their contributions … may aid in redefining the magazine's place in (and as) art in (and as participant in) the larger world."[54]

Specifically, Graham hoped that the publication's unbound format might emancipate the reader from the editorial and authorial monopoly on meaning, as it had in *Aspen* 5+6. Echoing his earlier writings on Mallarmé's *Le Livre*, he equates the literal mobility of the magazine's free-floating contents with a greater degree of interpretive leeway, explaining that "in reading … a reader's mind's eye is changing: his position continually shifting."[55] However, in *Aspen* 8, Graham also began to explore more specifically how the magazine's unconventional physical format might correspond to a radical restructuring of its socioeconomic organization. He points out that the meaning of a text in a magazine is controlled not only by the author, but also by the advertisers who underwrite it:

> While in the past the book and later the magazine form has served to represent (re-present) (contain) the author's privileged *insight* (or several authors' points of view) to the masses of individual readers who've bought and identified the *experience*, magazines serving as part and parcel of a socio-economic structure which necessitates and perpetuates this system of single dimension, single fixed point of view … its form assuming that enough private points of view—static—of its readers and its authors can be brought in line with the line of its advertisers whose ads support the magazine's existence.[56]

Graham's analogy between the way in which an author dictates the meaning of a text and the way in which the economic structure of a magazine circumscribes its editorial content recognizes how the relationship between individual authors and readers is tied to the larger socioeconomic conditions of the production and distribution of media. Barthes himself had implied as much, insisting that the figure of the author is "the epitome and culmination of capitalist ideology," a statement that hints at how the corporate ownership of media perpetuates the treatment of cultural meaning as private property rather than public knowledge.[57]

Graham further speculates that the traditional codex form of magazines might reinforce on a concrete level the integration of editorial content and advertising, ensuring that they are bound together and viewed in a set sequence. He condemns the "single dimension, single fixed point of view" as the traditional codex form, clearly referencing McLuhan's well-known comparison between print and *perspectiva artificialis* in *The Gutenberg Galaxy*. Here, McLuhan argues that the development of print resulted in an isolation of vision from the other senses that was analogous to the shift instantiated within visual representation by the fifteenth-century invention of perspective—a shift that resulted in "a reduction of experience to a single sense, the visual," leading to the viewer's detachment from the world and to contemporary attitudes of indifference and passivity.[58] And yet, against McLuhan's technological determinism—buried in his glib adage, "The medium is the message"—Graham insists that the technology of print does not determine its communicative possibilities, but rather is itself deeply contingent upon the social conditions of its production and distribution.

These were the conditions that Graham sought to challenge with *Aspen 8*. He proposed turning the economic structure of the commercial art magazine on its head, suggesting that artists might team up with corporations to produce works of art as advertisements, with the profits from the ads going directly to the artists (Graham and several other artists had already experimented with this idea by creating individual magazine advertisement pieces, as discussed in chapter 1). "This arrangement," he wrote, "would serve a twofold function: the artist might help the corporation in establishing its corporate image while the corporation might help the artist in freeing some of the limitations in relation to the reader and socio-economic frameworks."[59] He later admitted that this plan was idealistic, and it did not materialize in the published issue of *Aspen* 8, which seems to have had no advertisements.

Graham sought to create a publication that would not be dominated by a single overarching theme or motive—whether the editor's, the authors', or the advertisers'—but that would combine multiple interests and opinions, and would be further destabilized by the diverse perspectives of its readers. As he described *Aspen* 8, it "does not have a point of view (mine or a priori determined by the form); instead its point of view is continually shifting, feedback contingent in its place (time and context) and its relationship to the readership who individually and collectively compose or in-form its meaning."[60] Graham's concept of "in-formation," with its suggestion of an unfixed, indeterminate process rather than a concluded end state, clearly invokes the cybernetic concept of feedback. Defined as the necessary noise or interference in any communication system, feedback is a model of information as contaminated—but also enriched—by its own means of transmission, as well as by the conditions of its reception.[61] In the late 1960s, feedback was used widely as a paradigm for radical media practices that sought to redress the asymmetry between the producers and receivers of media, as evidenced, for example, by the video art magazine *Radical Software*, founded in 1970 to explore the progressive social potential of video and new media.[62]

While during the 1960s and 1970s cybernetics was most frequently associated with investigations of new electronic and digital technologies, *Aspen* 8 suggest that its implications were equally applicable to print media. Indeed, feedback was a metaphor that suggested to artists how the magazine might function as an interface that encouraged its readers to participate in its meaning, to interfere with its message: to talk back. Processes of feedback—messages rendered impure, disrupted, and distorted by their own means of transmission—are everywhere in evidence in *Aspen* 8, from the degraded reproductions of Smithson's *Strata* that threaten to dissolve into abstract patterns of mechanically reproduced dots, to Steve Reich's *Pendulum Music*, a score that uses receivers and microphones to amplify electronic feedback. However, feedback was also inherent in the very format of the magazine itself—its participatory nature as a container of objects to be touched and grasped. If *Aspen*'s interactive multimedia format challenged the conventions for viewing art within the museum space, it also challenged the spectacular regime of the media itself.

Ultimately, Graham wanted readers to participate not just in the magazine but in the world itself. He suggested that *Aspen* 8 might "point directly to the outside world—to products to be played (maybe records) and services to be rendered."[63] He conceived of the magazine not so much as an object or final product but as an intermediary—a broker between the reader and the world, connecting the two, however temporarily: "The signs on the page function simply as vectors: switching terminuses in the transaction between the activating authorial mover, the world out there and the activated moved reader who, finishing, left to shift for himself in another place—continues the transaction (in another time and space); reading isn't another order of time or experience apart."[64] To say that the reader finishes "in another place" is another way of saying that the reader does not finish, is never finished with reading this magazine, which is not an ends, but a means—a medium—for another experience, and another and another, marked not by discrete beginnings and ends but by relationships and conversations and actions and passage through time.

....

If *Aspen* suggests how the magazine functioned as a new kind of medium and distribution form that promised to radically transform the social and political possibilities of art, it also suggests the limitations and contradictions of this project. The magazine seems to have left some readers puzzled—and even exasperated. A review in *Time* magazine summed up issue 5+6 as follows:

> *Aspen* is a magazine for people who don't like to read much. ... *Aspen* assaults all the senses not just the visual. ... Any reader (participant, player, victim?) who takes the trouble to wade through the latest issue, designed by Brian O'Doherty, should find his senses fully exhausted. ... For those who seek refuge in conventional words, a few are supplied. They are, however, often as inscrutable as the rest of the contents.[65]

Clearly, for this reviewer at least, the "birth of the reader" was not a liberating experience as much as it was an aggressive affront to the reader. That the experimental and unfamiliar nature of *Aspen*'s contents puzzled uninitiated readers, or fatigued those accustomed to being lulled by mainstream media (such as *Time* magazine itself, perhaps), should come as no surprise; some might argue that this perplexity was precisely the point. However, this review is interesting because it lays bare the contradictions at the heart of conceptual art practices of the 1960s: while this art claimed to be more accessible to a wider audience by reducing art to language and seeking out alternative models of distribution, it too often appeared opaque to all but the most specialized of audiences. In fact, *Aspen* belies the conceit of legibility that so often accompanied the egalitarian claims of conceptual art.

And yet rather than foreclosing on the artistic possibilities of the magazine, *Aspen* very much leaves them open and unanswered—an open-endedness that was in some sense affirmed by the publication's own unfortunate ending when the U.S. Postal Service revoked its second-class mail license in 1971. According to the transcript from the legal hearing, the Postal Service claimed that *Aspen* was not a magazine but a "non-descript publication," that it was "not easily described; unclassifiable; belonging, or apparently belonging, to no particular class or kind."[66] *Aspen*'s breach of the bureaucratic category of the periodical illustrates the indeterminacy of the publication: the deep uncertainty about its format, contents, and publication schedule. This indeterminacy suggested how the conventions of the magazine—the rules that made it legible as such—might be conceived anew, so that the magazine was no longer merely a prescription for a given format, but a set of conditions rife with unforeseen possibilities. *Aspen* raises the question: What is a magazine? It suggests, in ways that parallel new understandings of artistic medium itself at this time, that a magazine might be something compelled by its own internal logic and rules, without determining ahead of time what kind of experience or object these rules will create.[67] This shift had implications for how artists understood the magazine as an artistic medium and also for how they used it as a communication medium, in ways that will be taken up in subsequent chapters.

Aspen's publisher, Phyllis Glick, née Johnson, moved on to other endeavors, losing touch with the artists with whom she was once close, and disappearing from the art world, virtually without a trace.[68] She eventually moved back to Colorado to help care for her aging mother and aunt, and helped to found a retirement home in Glenwood Springs, Colorado; she wrote and illustrated *The Mushroom Trail Guide*, a highly regarded book on mushrooms (an interest that was perhaps inspired by her acquaintance with John Cage, who was an avid mycologist as well as a composer); she traveled around the world, climbed mountains, and learned to tango in Argentina. She continued to support the arts, working as a docent at the Contemporary Museum Honolulu at the end of her life. Though her time in the art world was largely a passing interlude, her magazine had an impact well beyond its brief existence.

3
ART ON AND OFF THE PAGE
0 TO 9, 1967–1969

In the 1960s, art and poetry crossed paths. This convergence occurred, among other places, in the coffeehouses and galleries of New York's Lower East Side and SoHo districts, where poets and artists met and encountered one another's work at readings and exhibitions. However, the meeting of art and poetry also occurred in the pages of small-circulation and self-published magazines, where terms such as "visual poetry," "concrete poetry," "conceptual art," and "mail art" were used, sometimes interchangeably, to classify the sudden surge of new practices that flouted the distinction between visual art and language during this time.[1] The mimeographed magazine *o to 9*, published a total of six times by Vito Acconci and Bernadette Mayer between 1967 and 1969, was an especially important site for such investigations. Born out of the juncture between conceptual art and experimental poetry in lower Manhattan, it presented innovative writing alongside an eclectic mix of art, musical scores, choreographic notations, and performance documents. Along with other little magazines such as *The Black Mountain Review, Extensions, Caterpillar, Some/Thing*, and *Unmuzzled Ox, o to 9* attests to the crucial role of the periodical in both witnessing and encouraging the vital cross-fertilization of these practices.

o to 9 was named after Jasper Johns's stencil paintings, a series of canvases the artist began in the mid-1950s that depicted, in rich color and texture, the generic forms of letters and numbers, traced from store-bought stencils. When Leo Steinberg asked Johns, "Do you use these letter types because you like them or because that's how the stencils came?" he famously replied: "But that's what I like about them, that they came that way."[2] For Johns, the readymade nature of the stencils emphasized the concreteness of language, apart from the meaning it ordinarily expressed in the context of words and sentences. Freed from the responsibility of conveying human thought and emotion, these arbitrary letters and integers could be appreciated as the distinctly visual objects that they were. Johns "turned words into matter," observed Acconci, who began his own career as a writer, earning his M.A. from the prestigious Iowa Writer's Workshop.[3] He credited Johns with his turn from fiction to poetry in 1964, recalling of seeing the stencil paintings for the first time: "I could never write fiction again. I wanted words to be material, the way Johns let numbers and letters be material, and you had a chance to do that on one page, you couldn't sustain it for three-hundred pages."[4]

In *o to 9*, Acconci and Mayer, and those they invited to contribute to the magazine, pushed the materiality of language to its limit, vastly expanding the notion of what a poem could be. They emphasized the concrete aspects of language—its visual, phonetic, and kinetic qualities. They abandoned the regular meters and narrative form of traditional poetry, and used procedural verse techniques and found texts to undermine conventional notions of authorship. "We didn't want to be surrounded by 'regular' poetry," Mayer explained, adding, "there was little reason to write poetry at the time and not do something else, like be what they called a conceptual artist."[5]

0 TO 9

Indeed, their unorthodox approach to language dovetailed with the investigations of artists, such as Robert Smithson, Dan Graham, Adrian Piper, Lawrence Weiner, Douglas Huebler, and Robert Barry, whose work they discovered in exhibitions, including the series of four "Language" shows at the Dwan Gallery between 1967 and 1970. "Language to be Looked at and/or Things to be Read" was how Smithson described his own work and that of his peers in his 1967 press release for the first of the Dwan shows, a phrase that aptly describes his own approach to language as a sculptural material—something "built not written."[6]

Besides revealing the overlapping aesthetic concerns of poets and artists, *o to 9* also reflected the shared social spaces in which they became acquainted with one another and exchanged ideas. Such spaces included the coffeehouses on the Lower East Side, such as Les Deux Mégots and Le Metro; the Poetry Project at St. Mark's Church, where Mayer taught an influential series of workshops in the 1970s; and the lofts, alternative spaces, and galleries opening up in nearby SoHo. For example, in May 1968, a poetry event was held at Robert Rauschenberg's loft at which poets— including Acconci, John Perreault, and Clark Coolidge—participated in a Happening-like event utilizing media such as words, sounds, rubber, tape, film, slides, paper, flashlights, typewriter, shoes, ladders, decals, girls, helium, and signals.[7] And in June 1969, Acconci did a reading at the Paula Cooper Gallery, alongside films and performances by Bruce Nauman, Dan Graham, Dennis Oppenheim, Yvonne Rainer, Steve Reich, and Richard Serra.[8] *o to 9* documented and furthered such interdisciplinary commingling, transferring it from the din of casual meetings, conversations, and readings into a more formal arena of exchange. Acconci's own transition from a poet into a performance artist—a change that happened around 1969—took place in the permeable boundaries between art and poetry that *o to 9* helped to open up.

Acconci would later describe this transformation as follows: "I couldn't be on the page any more. Language took me out onto the street. I was moving on the page, now I wanted to move on the sidewalk, on the street. I was more thinking of the street as a field of activity rather than the page."[9] The six issues of *o to 9* chronicle how this interest in language evolved from something concrete and material to something increasingly dynamic and performative—a development that can be tracked in the progressively tactile and temporal covers of the magazine. The concrete materiality of the first four covers (an uncut mimeo stencil, a waterfall map of the United States, a typed list of the first line of every poem in the issue, and an actual book jacket selected from the editors' collections) suddenly gives way to the dynamism of issue 5's cover: a sheet of paper that has been crumpled into a ball and flattened out again so that it retains an abstract textual web of creases. The cover of issue 6—comprised of six blank pages—also emphasizes the ability of the page to register time and movement.

3.1

Cover of *0 to 9*, no. 5, January 1969. Edited by Vito Acconci and Bernadette Mayer. Research Library, The Getty Research Institute, Los Angeles (88-S1201 no. 5).

These final two covers emblematize Acconci's understanding of the magazine not as a static, two-dimensional thing but as a vehicle and locus for action—something to be moved through and beyond. If the aesthetic and poetic investigations in *o to 9* stressed its nature as a spatiotemporal vehicle that metaphorically propelled language over and ultimately off the page, they also depended upon the magazine's literal circulation of ideas within the artistic and poetic communities in lower Manhattan. The mimeographed, hand-assembled publication, which was produced in an edition of 250 to 300 copies, registered the tangibility of this community, suggesting that the materiality of language was key not only to the aesthetic significance of art and poetry in the 1960s but also to the larger social context in which these practices gained meaning.

THE POETICS AND POLITICS OF THE MIMEOGRAPH

In 1967 Acconci and Mayer were both relatively unknown poets working in the bohemian outpost of New York's Lower East Side. Related by marriage (Acconci was then married to Mayer's sister, the artist Rosemary Mayer), the two had known each other since high school in Brooklyn, and Bernadette had dated Acconci's good friend, the poet Robert Viscusi. They decided to publish a magazine for the same reasons that so many poets during this time founded little magazines: to define a community of writers and readers within which to seek out like-minded individuals and to discover an audience. "Vito and I created *o to 9* as an environment for our own work, which did not seem to exist anywhere else,"[10] Mayer recalled of the 8½-by-11-inch mimeographed, stapled publication—a low-fidelity format that was nearly identical to that of dozens, if not hundreds, of similar poetry magazines that sprung up in New York and elsewhere during this period.

The dizzying proliferation of small-circulation presses and mimeographed magazines—including *C: A Literary Review*, *Poems from the Floating World*, *Umbra*, and *Fuck You: A Magazine of the Arts*, to name just a few—were central to both the aesthetic innovations and the social world of second-generation New York School poetry. "I find it hard to keep up with their magazines coming out so irregularly & so much of who's published and where and when depending on mood & fraternity,"[11] one of the characters in Mayer's 1976 play *Cave of Metonymy* complains; and, in reality, such magazines were deeply embedded in unofficial networks of friends and acquaintances that constituted both their contributors and readers. About the decision to start *o to 9*, Acconci recalled, "Bernadette and I needed an outlet for what we did. At the same time we wanted a context for what we did (I'm not sure what came first). On the one hand, the magazines by and with the New York School poetry weren't publishing us. On the other hand, we didn't want to be in those magazines."[12]

A predecessor to the photocopy machine, the mimeograph was invented by Thomas Edison in 1876. Because it did not require specialized typesetting or printing equipment, the mimeograph allowed virtually anyone with a typewriter to become a printer. As Daniel Kane has shown in his important study of mimeograph magazines in the Lower East Side poetry scene, not only did these publications disseminate poetry, but they also shaped the social milieu in which this poetry was written and read, serving "as a kind of metaphorical extended meeting ground" for the poetic community.[13] Kane argues that the speed and spontaneity of the mimeograph was key to its significance as a medium for alternative poetry in the 1960s. Because they could be produced so rapidly and so inexpensively, mimeographed publications brought the experience of the printed page closer to the impromptu nature of the live poetry reading itself, capturing something of the informal, sociable atmosphere of these gatherings. For example, Kane writes that Rexograph sheets were passed out at readings, to be drawn or written on, or taken home and typed on, and then submitted, and the resulting magazine would be brought back and distributed the following week.[14] The production and circulation of poetry magazines was thus so deeply intertwined with the actual spaces in which poets interacted and socialized that in a very real sense the magazines both documented these spaces and helped to produce them.

While poets were exploring the reciprocity between the live poetry reading and the printed page during the 1960s, conceptual artists and performance artists were simultaneously investigating the entanglement between document and event in their own work. To use an example given earlier, in Smithson's "Incidents of Mirror-Travel in the Yucatan" (*Artforum*, November 1969), the magazine article not merely documented the artist's temporary, site-specific sculpture but was its sole intended format. *o to 9* elucidates how the relationship between what was on the page and what was off of it was central to both art and poetry at this time, and witnesses how the two practices powerfully resonated with and inflected one another.

Acconci and Mayer printed *o to 9* on a borrowed mimeograph machine late at night. They would drive to a friend's father's office in New Jersey, arriving after closing at 5 PM, and work until dawn, typing the stencils and running off and collating the magazine, sometimes with the help of friends or relatives. The crudeness of the mimeograph process lent the publication a distinct materiality, rife with smudges and blobs, incompletely formed letters, uneven ink distribution, and other flaws due to imprecision in the stencil-cutting and printing process. Besides stirring up associations with political broadsides and other radical publishing practices, this unrefined appearance gave language a kind of weight and corporeality that was in keeping with the poetic investigations published in the magazine. "Nothing was perfect about *o to 9* in its mimeograph form," Mayer observed. "We were trying to get far away from the idea, so promulgated, of the perfection of the poem with white space around it, set off from other things."[15] Indeed, in *o to 9* language is not pristine or idealized, but a messy, unruly substance that disregards conventional spacing and margins, to say nothing of proper grammar and syntax. Words do not remain well-behaved and silent couriers of meaning, but seem to make noise, to act things out.

The uncut mimeo stencil that served as the cover of the first issue of *o to 9* was an indigo-colored sheet of wax-coated mulberry paper that could be punched through by the type bar of a typewriter, or drawn on with a stylus. Not only did this cover stress the materiality of the magazine by referencing its printing process; it also made the subscribers of the magazine into potential contributors, since the stencil could, in theory, be removed, typed on, and sent back to the editors for publication in the next issue. While this possibility remained largely symbolic (according to Acconci, nobody actually used the cover in this way), it expressed a reciprocity between the production of the magazine and its reception that was central to the kind of participatory community *o to 9* strove to create among its readers.

As Acconci recalled of sending out the magazine, "we hoped that the people we distributed it to would contribute to it."[16] The editors did not keep an official subscription list, but sent the magazine to "people we wanted to be like, people we wanted to like us, people we wanted to be

TOP EDGE GUIDE FOR IMPRESSION PAPER

ELITE

0 TO 9

in the magazine."[17] They also dropped off copies at local bookstores, such as the Eighth Street Bookstore, the East Side Bookstore, Gotham Book Mart, and Sheridan Square—stores that also functioned as "gathering places for writers," according to Acconci[18]—thus placing the magazine within a social context of chance meetings, conversations, and other publications.

Of course, *o to 9* was also a kind of gathering place in and of itself. In it, Acconci and Mayer published their own work alongside poetry by those they knew or admired, including Robert Viscusi, Tom Clark, Ron Padgett, Clark Coolidge, John Giorno, Harry Mathews, Emmett Williams, Larry Freifeld, Barrett Shaw, Hannah Weiner, George Bowering, John Perreault, Jerome Rothenberg, Kenneth Koch, Larry Fagin, and Bern Porter. The magazine fostered writing that was even more theoretical and unconventional than most alternative poetry being produced at the time in the Lower East Side. Sometimes language appears to "cover the page" (as Acconci once observed of his own poetry) in densely typed passages that go right up to the edge of the paper. Other times, the page is nearly blank, as in Aram Saroyan's spare poems, which consisted of a single row of lowercase *i*'s typed across two facing pages, evoking a zipper; or the solitary word "dinner" printed in the middle of two facing pages; or simply two empty, white pages. Yet other contributions were more performative and conceptual, such as Jackson Mac Low's "biblical poems," which were created by chance operations, leaving both the composition and reading speed up to the reader, or Phil Corner's composition based on tape recordings of everyday sounds.

The editors also looked outside their immediate vicinity of colleagues and peers—and even outside of their own century—seeking contributions from "distant relations" and "imaginary friends," as Acconci described the idiosyncratic array of texts that appeared in the magazine, many of which were out of print and had no copyright.[19] They published writings by the Elizabethan poets Sir Walter Raleigh and Sir Arthur Gorges, the eighteenth-century German poet Novalis, Hans Christian Andersen, Lord Herbert of Cherbury, Lord Stirling, Gustave Flaubert, Gertrude Stein, and Guillaume Apollinaire. They printed excerpts from Raymond Queneau's *Exercises in Style*, which consisted of ninety-nine retellings of the same story, each in a different style, and Stefan Themerson's translation of Li Po's "Drinking Alone by Moonlight." Several issues included anonymous works from indigenous oral traditions, such as stories from the Native American Tillamook tribe of the Northwest Coast, "Eskimo Songs," and "Seneca Songs," reflecting the contemporary interest in ethnopoetics, which would later become the basis for Jerome Rothenberg and Dennis Tedlock's magazine *Alcheringa*.

3.2

Cover of *0 to 9*, no. 1, April 1967. Edited by Vito Acconci and Bernadette Mayer. Research Library, The Getty Research Institute, Los Angeles (88-S1201 no. 1).

3.3 (following page)

Vito Acconci, "Moving," *0 to 9*, no. 5, January 1969, page 5. © Vito Acconci. Research Library, The Getty Research Institute, Los Angeles (88-S1201 no. 5).

may be used as ideas for new works.

29.   The process is mechanical and should not be tampered with.   It
should run its course.

30.   There are many elements involved in a work of art.   The most
important are the most obvious.

31.   If an artist uses the same form in a group of works, and changes the material, one would assume the artist's concept involved the
material.

32.   Banal ideas cannot be rescued by beautiful execution.

33.   It is difficult to bungle a good idea.

34.   When an artist learns his craft too well he makes slick art.

35.   These sentences comment on art but are not art.

moving art
-V.H.A.

Acconci and Mayer also published visual artists, composers, and choreographers, whom they increasingly saw as fellow travelers. By the final two issues, the magazine's table of contents was dominated by artists—including Morton Feldman, Sol LeWitt, Robert Smithson, Dan Graham, Adrian Piper, Yvonne Rainer, Robert Barry, Alan Sondheim, Steve Paxton, Les Levine, Bernar Venet, Michael Heizer, Rosemary Mayer, Douglas Huebler, Lee Lozano, and Lawrence Weiner. Jasper Johns even agreed to submit some notes from his sketchbook.

While *0 to 9* was originally inspired by Jasper Johns's stencil paintings, which emphasized the materiality of typographical form, the magazine soon developed a novel understanding of what the materiality of language might entail, as poets and artists pushed language beyond its two-dimensional existence on the page. They explored, for example, the dynamic and three-dimensional objecthood of the magazine, the turning of its pages, and the conditions of its circulation and distribution. Acconci's own writings manifested this evolving understanding of language, from a purely visual form to a kinetic object—a shift that paralleled his own development from a poet into a performance artist.

Acconci's poem "Kay Price and Stella Pajunas," published in the first issue, suggests his interest in the capacity of language to express sound and motion through its typographical arrangement on the page. Named after two record-setting typists, the poem conveys the look and clamor of rapid, incessant typing through its irregular spacing, apparent typos, crossed-out characters, and onomatopoeic "clangs" and "ticks." While the kinetic and phonetic nature of this poem remains largely implied, taking place in the reader's imagination, Acconci soon found ways to make a sense of movement more palpable and literal, distancing himself slightly from the aims of concrete poetry, which focused on the purely visual character of language. He recalled, "Yes, I wanted stuff to be based on the page, but I still wanted words to be words, I didn't want words to be images; and the way I saw concrete poetry, it was making images out of words, whereas I was interested in motion through a page rather than an image on a page. I don't think I was ever particularly interested in something stilled. I didn't want to turn poetry into painting; I didn't want to turn it in into an image. I certainly didn't want to turn it into an object."[20]

Acconci increasingly saw language less as an object than as a site of action and motion: something to be animated. "Reading is uttering aloud printed or written matter … writing is forming or inscribing words, letters, symbols, etc. on a surface, as by cutting, carving, or, especially marking with a pen or pencil … writing is covering something with writing," he wrote in a set of untitled poems published in issue 4.[21] He began to conceive of the poem not as the end point of the writer's or reader's thought process but as an opportunity for transit, explaining that he "wanted to move, from number to number, from word to word, from line to line, from page to page."[22] He sought to literally embody such movement in his poetry. In his poem "ON," for example, published in issue 3, Acconci scattered the verses of the poem throughout the magazine so that the reader must leaf through the entire publication in order to read it. And, in "Moving," he appropriated words from other authors' texts, transplanting them to the bottom corner of the page, where they completed the phrase "moving _____."

Such works not only attest to Acconci's interest in the spatiotemporal possibilities of language on the page; they also speak to the crucial role of the magazine, in particular, in these investigations. Indeed, both "ON" and "Moving" depend upon their interaction with the other contributions in the publication—an interaction that could not have taken place within the pages of a single-author book. They thus highlight, in addition to its materiality, the magazine's collective, collaborative nature, which contributes so deeply to the social significance of this particular form of printed matter.

Acconci also explored how the magazine's conditions of circulation and distribution shape the spatiotemporal—and social—possibilities of language. In his poem "Act 3, Scene 4," for example, he typed each line of the 350-line poem onto a separate sheet of paper, and then bound each sheet into a different copy of the magazine. Instead of reproducing the poem in its entirety, the magazine contained a single verse in each copy, along with a note explaining the poem's unusual structure: "The line you have just read is the 208th of a 350 line piece; the rest appears in the other 349 copies of *o to 9* number 5." In order to read the poem from start to finish, one would have to track down every copy of issue 5, an idea that suggests in very concrete terms how magazines transport language through time and space in order to reach a collective readership—a public that is both held together and divided from one another by the particular circumstances of the magazine's circulation and distribution. "Act 3, Scene 4" conjures the various locations through which the magazine moves and the individuals it reaches—places and persons that, in the case of *o to 9*, were defined by a fairly small, local community of poets and artists in lower Manhattan. The poem calls to mind how the magazine embodied this readership, expressing its close-knit character and local scale through its own means of production and materiality—its nature as a small-circulation magazine that has been typed and assembled by hand.

ART ON THE PAGE

If Acconci's poetry during the late 1960s was, as he later put it, "moving through the magazine, off the page,"[23] art was unmistakably migrating in the opposite direction. Issue 5 of *o to 9* (January 1969) opened with Sol LeWitt's "Sentences on Conceptual Art" (which would also be published in the first issue of *Art-Language* later that year). Consisting of thirty-five typed statements, this cool-headed manifesto signaled the new prevalence of language in the ephemeral practices of conceptual art. As LeWitt declared, "the artist may use any form, from an expression of words (written or spoken) to physical reality, equally."[24] Like *Aspen*, discussed in the previous chapter, *o to 9* witnessed the important new role of the magazine as a site of distribution for such work.

For example: LeWitt contributed a working sketch scribbled with numbers and grids, and several finely cross-hatched drawings; Dan Graham arranged the numbers 0 through 9 in a pyramid in *Discrete Scheme without Memory*; Robert Smithson published his *Non-Site Map of Mono-Lake, California*, a photograph of his *Upside Down Tree*, and his *Urination Map*, which designated a series of points in the state of New Jersey where the artist planned to urinate; Adrian Piper presented an exhaustive set of permutational operations involving arranging the numbers 1 through 64; Michael Heizer listed the locations of his work *Nine Nevada Depressions*; Yvonne Rainer published "automatic writing from my movies"—strings of simple nouns and verbs prompting stream-of-consciousness-like associations; Alan Sondheim submitted studies for "various impossible machines"; Lawrence Weiner submitted a typed statement specifying an act that could be carried out by the reader: "Five gallons of red vegetable coloring poured into an eastward flowing stream on or near the Continental Divide U.S.A."; Steve Paxton contributed "Satisfyin' Lover," a choreographic notation that involved an indeterminate number of people walking and pausing across a space at intervals to be determined by the performers; and Rosemary Mayer created a visual record of the sound of firecrackers on the Fourth of July.

Many of these contributions served as evidence of an artistic thought, act, object, or event—the kinds of documents that had become synonymous with conceptual art, starting with Mel Bochner's *Working Drawings and Other Visible Things on Paper Not Necessarily Meant to Be Viewed as Art* (1966). Such documents were often necessary stand-ins for works which might exist in a remote location, such as earthworks, or which might not even manifest themselves physically at all. Perhaps the most extreme version of such dematerialization was exemplified by a group of artists associated with the dealer Seth Siegelaub.[25] For example, in his *Inert Gas Series* (1969), Robert Barry released volumes of invisible gas such as helium into the air—an act that was communicated to the public through a series of posters he sent out to individuals and institutions. Douglas Huebler, another artist represented by Siegelaub, likewise created highly ephemeral works which relied heavily on documentation like maps and photographs, such as his *Duration Piece #2*, a line of sand spread across a highway in New Hampshire which he photographed as it disappeared. As Huebler famously declared, "the world is full of objects ... I do not wish to add any more."[26]

While, as discussed in chapter 1, Siegelaub encouraged the new role of documentation in conceptual art, conceiving of such documentation as a new kind of primary site, he also maintained a distinction, however subtle, between the document and the work itself, explaining, "whether an artist chooses to present the work as a book or magazine or through an interview or with sticker labels or on billboards, it is not to be mistaken for the 'art.'"[27] This separation between work and document was also recognized by the artists themselves. As Huebler insisted, "I use the camera as a dumb copying device that only serves to document whatever phenomena appear before it. ... No 'aesthetic' choices are possible."[28] However, *o to 9* reveals a new approach to such documents, as artists began to consider the magazine page not only as a stand-in for a work of art located elsewhere, but as a site and medium in and of itself.

at 4:37 P.M., and will rise tomorrow at 7:20 A.M. The moon

(The line you have read is the 204th of
a 350 line piece; the rest appears in the
other 349 copies of 0 TO 9 number 5.)

THE POINT REPRESENTED ABOVE DRAWS TO ITSELF AND FIXES, FOR AN
INSTANT, EACH AND EVERY OTHER POINT LOCATED WITHIN THE PHYSICAL
SPACE OF THIS ROOM AND CONTINUES TO DO SO FOR THE ENTIRE TIME
THAT THIS PAGE IS OPEN BUT IT IMMEDIATELY CEASES TO EXIST WHEN
THE PAGE IS TURNED.

3.6

Douglas Huebler, untitled, *0 to 9*, no. 6, July 1969,
page 54. © 2010 Douglas Huebler, courtesy of Darcy
Huebler / Artists Rights Society (ARS), New York.

Barry's two contributions to issue 6, for instance, were listed in the table of contents as "The Space Between Pages 29 & 30" and "The Space Between Page 74 and 75." As the artist described the piece in his proposal to Acconci, "the first is the Space between any two facing pages, between two separate pieces. … No page is printed; no page is left blank. I do not have a page—I have the space between two pages. The other idea is similar but the space is between two pages on opposite sides of one sheet … (e.g. the space between this page, that I'm writing to you on and the opposite side of this page.)"[29] Though the two works appear at first glance to be conceptually identical, in practice they produce very different experiences. In the first instance, because pages 29 and 30 were two sides of a single page (which happened to contain the last page of a work by Bernar Venet and the first page of Dan Graham's essay "Eisenhower and the Hippies"), the "space between" them refers to the infinitesimal thickness of the sheet of paper. By contrast, pages 74 and 75 were facing pages that contained poems by Clark Coolidge and Bernadette Mayer. The space between them therefore depends upon the angle at which the magazine is opened—a space that fluctuates as the page is turned and disappears completely when it is closed. Like Barry's sculptural investigations, which focused not on sculptural objects but on the space around the object, or on virtually undetectable objects and acts, his contribution to *o to 9* emphasized the normally imperceptible, overlooked spaces of the magazine itself.

Huebler also emphasized the concrete existence of the magazine as a three-dimensional object in space in his contributions to issue 6, consisting of the following two sentences typed on otherwise blank pages:

LOCATED ON THE ABOVE SURFACE IS AN INDETERMINATE QUANTITY OF THREE DIMENSIONAL SPACE

and

THE POINT REPRESENTED ABOVE DRAWS TO ITSELF AND FIXES, FOR AN INSTANT, EACH AND EVERY OTHER POINT LOCATED WITHIN THE PHYSICAL SPACE OF THIS ROOM AND CONTINUES TO DO SO FOR THE ENTIRE TIME THAT THIS PAGE IS OPEN BUT IT IMMEDIATELY CEASES TO EXIST WHEN THE PAGE IS TURNED

By drawing attention to the relationship between the two-dimensional surface of the magazine page and the three-dimensional "real" space that surrounds it—a space that is completely variable depending upon where that particular issue of the magazine is located—Huebler highlights the magazine as an interactive and thus deeply contingent object.

Besides emphasizing the magazine's objecthood—its concrete materiality and its existence in three-dimensional space—the experimental poetry and conceptual art documents published in *o to 9* open, by extension, onto the larger historical context of the publication. *o to 9* was published in the late 1960s, when the New York art world was becoming politicized by organizations such as the Art Workers' Coalition, which protested the war in Vietnam, drew attention to artists' rights, and condemned the elitism, sexism, and racism of the art world. The self-published, mimeographed magazine was emblematic of this countercultural rejection of traditional artistic venues and values in ways that echoed the burgeoning underground press of the period. Indeed, Acconci recalls that he and Mayer were "obsessed with the Whole Earth Catalog," suggesting that their editorial aspirations resonated with the do-it-yourself, antiestablishment ethos of the underground press of the 1960s and 1970s.

One work that alluded explicitly to this larger sociopolitical context was Lee Lozano's *General Strike Piece*, published in issue 6. In this piece, the artist announced her intention to "gradually but determinedly avoid being present at official or public 'uptown' functions or gatherings related to the 'art world' in order to pursue investigation of total personal and public revolution."[30] In the same issue Lozano published *Dialogue Piece*, in which she stated her goal to initiate dialogs with people by inviting them to her loft—conversations which, she noted, would not be recorded, but would "exist solely for their own sake as joyous social occasions."[31] As different as they might seem, the *General Strike Piece* and *Dialogue Piece* were in fact linked by a common thread. At stake in both was the possibility—or more accurately, the difficulty—of communication within the professional realm of the art world, a world that Lozano described elsewhere as elitist and sexist. She protested against the art world by withdrawing completely from this public realm and into the privacy of her loft, where she sought out conversations that might escape the instrumentalized social relationships of the art world. And yet her choice to publish these works in *o to 9* complicates this strict opposition between public and private, drawing attention to the paradoxical nature of the limited-circulation magazine as a public site that allowed these performances to be witnessed by a larger audience while simultaneously limiting the scope and nature of this audience to the small group of artists and poets who constituted the magazine's readers.

Lozano's performances and her choice to publish them in *o to 9* must be understood in the context of her involvement with the Art Workers' Coalition and her disillusionment with the mainstream art world and especially the commercial art press, as expressed in her 1969 *Throwing Up Piece*, discussed in chapter 1. Her *General Strike Piece* and *Dialogue Piece* shed light on the importance of *o to 9* in empowering artists, supporting alternative art, and fostering artistic communities. Not only did *o to 9*'s do-it-yourself, mimeographed form contrast with the glossy pages of mainstream art magazines, but it embodied a notion of community that was very different from the anonymous and professional group of readers who subscribed to larger, more established publications. As Acconci recalled of the role of artists' magazines in the late 1960s and early 1970s, they "were important because you knew you were not working alone."[32]

STREET WORKS

Asked why *o to 9* ended after its sixth issue, Acconci offered the following reflections: "Why was it the last issue? It had to be—I wasn't on the page anymore."[33] Indeed, by the late 1960s, he had begun to venture further and further off the page and increasingly thought of himself as an artist rather than a poet, gaining notoriety within the art world for his conceptual and performance-based works, such as *Following Piece* (1969), *Trademarks* (1970), *Conversions* (1971), and *Seedbed* (1972). He described this transition in a letter to the poet Opal Nations in February 1968:

> my work changed
> get out of poetry
> written, context,
> into real space[34]

ART ON AND OFF THE PAGE

As many have observed, Acconci's metamorphosis from a poet into a performance artist was a gradual, even natural, progression.[35] Craig Dworkin has offered an important insight into the nature of this shift by reframing Acconci's performances as less of a break from his poetry than as its extension—"the continuation of poetry by other means."[36] Dworkin points not only to the increasingly performative quality of Acconci's poetry readings of the late 1960s (one of his last readings consisted of a series of telephone calls made from pay phones along the route from his apartment to the reading venue, which were transmitted on speakerphone to the audience) but also to the insistently printerly nature of his early performances. In *Trademarks,* for example, Acconci bit himself and then produced imprints of the bite marks by inking his skin and pressing it onto a piece of paper, literally making his body into a mark-making, or printing, device.

o to 9 provides a vivid document of Acconci's trajectory from a poet into a performance artist, tracking his increasingly performative experiments with language. The magazine did not merely record this evolution but participated profoundly in it, serving as a bridge that allowed language to cross over from the two-dimensional space of the page into the three-dimensional realm of human actions and events. A set of notes he published in *Avalanche* in 1972 offers further insight into the way in which Acconci began to conceive of the page as something to move both through and beyond: "Use this page as the start of an event that keeps going, off the page; use the page to fix the boundaries of an event, or a series of events, that takes place in outside space. ... Or the page can be used as a stopping-place—a place to regroup forces—for an outside event. I'm moving through the book, moving over another space."[37]

This transition was perhaps nowhere more clear than in "Street Works," a supplement to the final issue of *o to 9* that documented a series of public performances by artists and poets with the same title. In its very designation as a supplement, "Street Works" emphasized its liminal status with regard to the rest of the magazine, as something that marked a passage from one set of practices (poetry) into another (performance). It was an assembling, in which each contributor submitted a specific number of copies of his or her work to be collated by the editors— an insistently democratic form of publishing that gained much currency during the period, as witnessed by Richard Kostelanetz's magazine *Assembling,* founded the next year.[38] The "Street Works" supplement included typed and handwritten descriptions, notes, and lists, along with maps, photographs, diagrams, and other kinds of documents photocopied on various kinds and colors of paper. And yet, if the *Street Works* performances signaled the culmination of poetry's desire to move off the page, they also paradoxically insisted on the magazine's continued role in this new set of practices, as a form of documentation.

Organized by John Perreault, Marjorie Strider, and Hannah Weiner, the performances in *Street Works* took place in New York in four installments in March, April, May, and September of 1969.[39] The *Street Works* performances used urban space as the context for an action; many of them also involved language. While they drew on artistic precedents such as Happenings and earthworks, they were also inspired, Perreault wrote, by folk forms such as "parades, street fairs, and block dances."[40] As he defined it, the term "Street Work" referred to "anything that takes place in the street or is placed in the street, calls attention to the street, is temporary, and is designated or created by an artist as a Street Work."[41] Several poets used the events as an opportunity to circulate their poetry in a different context or for a different audience. Anne Waldman, for

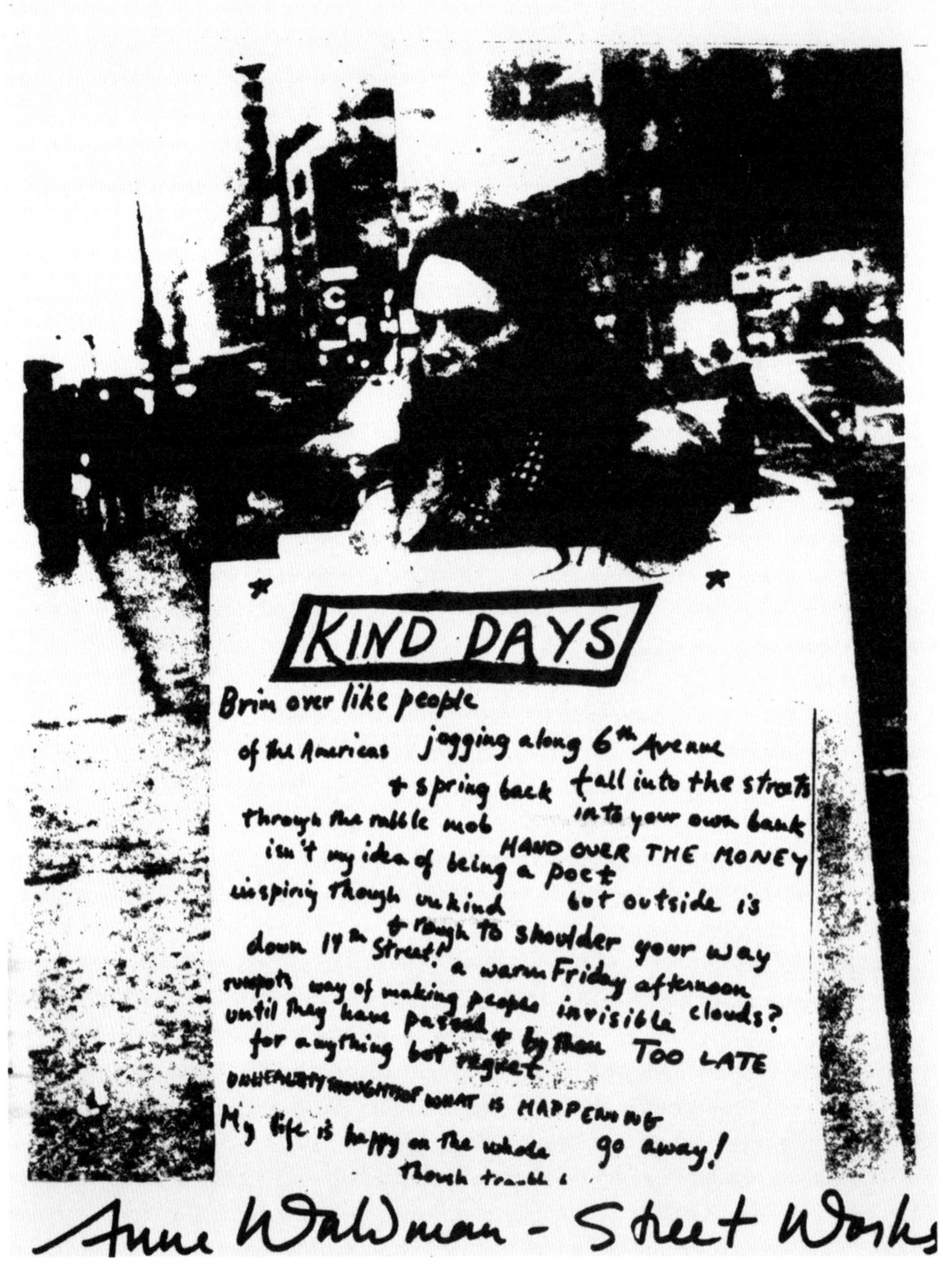

3.7

Anne Waldman, photocopied photograph of Anne
Waldman's performance as published in
"Street Works," supplement to *0 to 9*, no. 6, July 1969.
Courtesy of Anne Waldman.

example, printed her poem "Kind Days" on a sandwich board which she wore as she walked around handing out pinks slips of paper that said, "Happy Weekend Folks!" Madeline Gins distributed questionnaires, the responses to which she planned to incorporate into a "group novel." For his performance *T-shirt Alphabet*, Perreault convinced twenty-six people to wear t-shirts stenciled with letters of the alphabet, so that they spelled out words—deliberately or not—when they stood next to one another. An anonymous participant produced a "Trash Poem" by passing out 300 sheets of paper, each of which contained one word, and composing the poem from all of the words that appeared side up on the sidewalk. Artists such as Adrian Piper, Stephen Kaltenbach, and Les Levine also participated, as did the critic Lucy Lippard.

Street Works resonated, albeit indirectly, with the social and political upheavals of the late 1960s as protestors across the globe took to the streets. Acconci qualified this parallel, however: "Compared to a student revolution in Paris, I don't know if this was much, but that was the air of the time. It was the time of the Vietnam War. Not that the stuff in *Street Works* was directly political. … It wasn't directly political in terms of making political pronouncements, but I think a lot of us thought that that's not how you get people to change. If people are telling you something directly, why would you listen? You want a different kind of atmosphere."[42] While the *Street Works* performances were not explicitly political, they suggest how the metaphorical significance of the street as an emblem of the larger social and political transformations of the 1960s inflected the expanded fields of both art and poetry during this decade—and shaped the meaning of the magazine as a site of such practices. For example, in the first issue of the poetry magazine *Extensions*, in 1968 (to which both Acconci and Dan Graham contributed), photographs of graffiti on the walls of the Sorbonne from May 1968 appeared alongside art and poetry, stressing the analogy between the magazine page and the public spaces of social and political activism.

This association, exemplified by the "Street Works" supplement to *0 to 9*, reinforced the magazine's significance as a medium and distribution form that might precipitate the exodus of art from more traditional institutions into a wider social and political arena in the late 1960s. Artist-activist groups had begun to "take to the streets" to protest conditions both inside and outside the art world. And just as conceptual art itself depended on documentation to reach a wider audience, so too the Art Workers' Coalition (AWC) and other activist groups relied on the mass media as an important public space that functioned in tandem with "live sites" of protest. When the AWC famously protested the Vietnam War at the Museum of Modern Art—standing in front of Picasso's *Guernica* and holding the AWC poster *And Babies*, in which Ron L. Haeberle's graphic photograph of the My Lai massacre was superimposed with the text, "Q: And babies? A: And babies"—they also asked several art magazines to publish an image of the protest on their covers. *Studio International* (November 1970) was the only magazine that agreed to run the image—a fact that on the one hand suggests the importance of the print media as a site of artistic activism at this moment, and on the other highlights the inadequacy of the mainstream commercial art press in supporting such practices. To publicize and archive their activities, the Art Workers' Coalition published *Documents I* in April 1969—a publication that strikingly resembled *0 to 9* in its ad hoc, mimeographed form.

Acconci's own contributions to *Street Works* included several performances in which he placed language in the city or transported it through space by attaching gummed labels and notes

<u>A</u> <u>situation</u> <u>using</u> <u>streets</u>, <u>walking</u>, <u>running</u>

<u>General</u> circumstances: Street Works II; April 18, 1969; 5 to 6 PM; 13
St. to 14 St., Fifth Ave. to the Ave. of the Americas.
<u>Particular</u> circumstances: I stood on a corner, picked out (mentally)
a person walking from that corner to the next, noted the time, ran
from that corner to the next, noted when I reached the second corner,
waited, noted when the person walking reached the second corner (or
noted that he did not reach it if a certain time elapsed -- 5 minutes
for north-south blocks, 10 for east-west blocks -- without his arrival.
The action was performed six times.
Two <u>particular</u> instances: 1) 14 St.(N) & 6th Ave. -- A woman in a green
coat walking toward 5th Ave. -- Starting time, 5:24 -- My arrival at
5th Ave., 5:25 & 5 seconds -- The woman's arrival, 5:28 & 7 seconds;
2) 14 St.(S) & 6th Ave. -- A man in a blue & white T-shirt walking
toward 5th Ave. -- Starting time, 5:44 & 30 seconds -- My arrival at
5th Ave., 5:45 & 33 seconds -- At 5:54 & 30 seconds, the man had not
yet arrived.

1. When I choose the person walking, and know that I will reach the
   second corner before him, "I am beginning to shift the first corner," which he marks, to the second corner; until: when he moves
   ahead of me, as I stand timing him, "he is beginning to shift the
   first corner," which I mark; until: as I pass alongside him, and
   our lines of moving meet, "we are repeating the corner"; until: as
   I start to run ahead of him, "I am shifting the shift."
2. Corner: L <u>cornu</u> horn, end, point. Street: L, fem. of <u>stratus</u>, past
   part. of <u>sternere</u> to spread out, throw down.
   "Corner" as a revised version, a summary, of "street" : the street
   brought to a point.
   Street too large to be directly perceived: "street" as the result
   of a generalizing mental operation.
   Place: specific locality / an indefinite region or expanse.
   To place: to cause to rest or lie.
   "Lying low."
3. Place: a step in a sequence; an empty or vacated position.
4. "Watch" is activated as I look at my watch to time his starting
   point; the watch goes on to time each point he gets to while I am
   occupied lifting my notebook, writing the number down, etc.
   Time: a point when something occurs; an interval comprising a limited and continuous action, condition, or state of being; a reality that is an absolute flowing apart from the events filling it.
5. When I pull ahead of the person walking, "I lose touch," "he loses
   ground."
6. Touch: VL <u>toccare</u> to knock, strike, strike a bell, touch.
   Strike: to achieve by or as if by computaion or calculation; to
   succeed in reaching; to come upon in the course of drilling or
   prospecting.
   No clear signal; no "clear as a bell." (No "point"; nothing is
   "driven into a corner.")
   Mark; marksmanship; lose aim; marching; murk.
   "Street": (<u>slang</u>) release from confinement. (I am freed of him.)
7. When I get so far ahead of the person walking that he is no longer in sight, he is walking indeterminately; for all I know, "he
   may not be walking at all."
   My running is <u>after</u> <u>the</u> <u>fact</u> of his walking.
   Watch: a period of duty; shift; a portion of time during which a

to objects such as mailboxes, traffic lights, and the sides of the buses. He also used the circulation of the mail as a way to carry his words throughout the city, by sending postcards to all residents who lived on Thirteenth Street. In addition to these language-based performances, Acconci began to interact directly with people on the street. In his piece *A Situation Using Streets, Walking, Running*, Acconci would "pick out (mentally)" an unsuspecting person on the street and proceed to run ahead of that person until he reached the next corner, where he would wait for him or her, and repeat the process. The performances were described in densely typed, detailed sets of notes, published in the "Street Works" supplement. However, these notes are clearly more than just a straightforward set of instructions; in both their visual form and syntax they resemble Acconci's poetry from the period, as the following passage illustrates:

> When I choose the person walking, and know that I will reach the second corner before him, "I am beginning to shift the first corner," which he marks, to the second corner; until: when he moves ahead of me, as I stand timing him, "he is beginning the shift the first corner," which I mark; until: as I pass alongside him, and our lines of moving meet, "we are repeating the corner"; until: as I start to run ahead of him, "I am shifting the shift."

Indeed, as performative as Acconci's work had become in the spring of 1969, it still remained tied—however tenuously—to the practice of poetry, and to the experience of the page.

Shortly after this, the following October, Acconci first performed his *Following Piece* (1969) as part of *Street Works IV*. In this work, he again followed unsuspecting strangers on the street, sometimes for hours, until they entered a private residence, while documenting the experience photographically. This piece marked a new phase in his transition from poetry to performance art, which Acconci has described as follows: "In 1968 words like 'conceptual art' started being used and I thought, well if I'm writing it doesn't necessarily have to be on the page. And I asked myself a very obvious question. If I was so interested in movement why was I moving over an 8 ½ × 11 sheet of paper? There's a floor out there, there's a ground, there's a street, there's a whole city. And when I did *Following Piece* it was sort of a way to get myself off the writer's desk and into the city."[43]

Though Acconci's performances were a departure from the space of the page into the real space of the world, this passage was not in fact as absolute or irreversible as it might appear. For, if "Street Works" signaled the end of *o to 9*—the moment when poetry finally leapt right off of the pages of the magazine and into the street—it simultaneously heralded a crucial new role for the magazine in the documentation of such work. As Acconci observed of his first performances, most of which did not have a formal audience outside of passersby, or were performed within the confines of private spaces: "my early work depended on media. An action needed reportage; it didn't exist unless it was reported."[44] This idea would become key in *Avalanche*, which will be discussed in chapter 4.

4

AN ARTISTS' MAGAZINE

AVALANCHE, 1970–1976

Published only thirteen times over the course of seven years—from fall 1970 through summer 1976—*Avalanche* made every issue count. The magazine, founded by Liza Béar and Willoughby Sharp, functioned as a gallery without walls for art that eschewed architectural and institutional borders. From its vantage point in an industrial section of lower Manhattan then still known unassumingly as South of Houston, where the magazine made its home in a minimally renovated former thread warehouse at 93 Grand Street, *Avalanche* surveyed the new media art of the late 1960s and early 1970s, including conceptual art, performance, video, dance, and music.[1] Both chronicle and agent for these newly minted forms, *Avalanche* sought to put the media into the hands of artists—who, in turn, not only used the magazine to promote themselves and publicize their work but tapped its potential as a medium in and of itself.

By eliminating art criticism and exhibition reviews in favor of process documents and interviews, the publication fostered a direct channel for the artist's voice. According to Sharp, the magazine's raison d'être was "to amplify the artist[s], not merely by putting their faces on the cover but to go into some kind of dialogue with them and find out how the magazine could serve them. … *Avalanche* was an artists' magazine."[2] The artists' portraits that appeared on the cover of each issue—moody, filmic, black-and-white close-ups—peer out with startling directness: Lawrence Weiner frowns sardonically; Vito Acconci gloomily drags on his cigarette; Yvonne Rainer gazes at the camera with a matter-of-fact, penetrating intelligence. William Wegman, meanwhile, is humorously represented by a motion-blurred shot of his dog and frequent artistic collaborator, Man Ray, cocking his head in the canine equivalent of pensiveness.

While the stated goal of *Avalanche* was to empower the artist, its format echoed the cult of celebrity then sweeping American popular culture. Interviews and cover shots were, after all, defining features of *Playboy*, *Rolling Stone*, and of course, Andy Warhol's *Interview*. Looking back, we can also see in the magazine, albeit in nascent form, the contemporary art world's infatuation with the image of the artist as star. Yet *Avalanche* manifests a different kind of glamour: the unmade-up, unshaven faces, and defiant, brooding expressions and demeanor suggest a collective portrait of the artist as counterculture. Though the figure of the artist was increasingly being cast as a middle-class professional (as witnessed by mainstream representations, such as the fashionable photographs of minimalist artists published in *Harper's Bazaar* in the mid-1960s), *Avalanche* insisted on an alternative definition of artistic identity—an identity that would prove central to the politicization of the art world during this period.[3] The magazine emphasized the crossover between the antiestablishment lifestyles and politics of the 1960s and 1970s and the radical artistic practices of the period. With its ad hoc feel and relatively modest circulation of around five thousand, *Avalanche* revealed how the quintessential publicity form of the art magazine might foster a radical counterpublic within the alternative art community centered in SoHo in the early 1970s.[4]

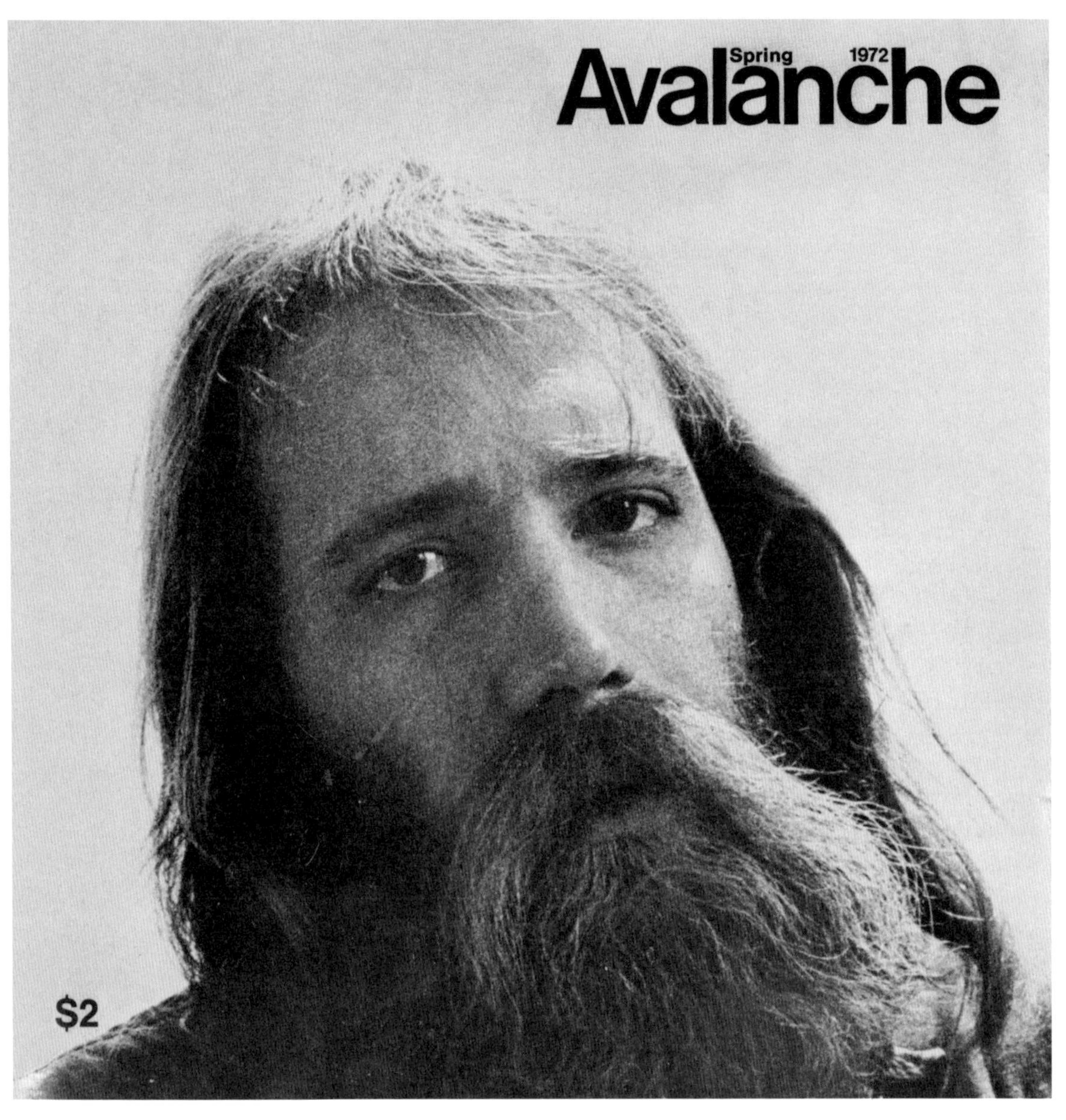

4.1

Photograph of Lawrence Weiner, cover of *Avalanche*,
no. 4, Spring 1972. Photograph by Doug Conner.
Courtesy of Liza Béar.

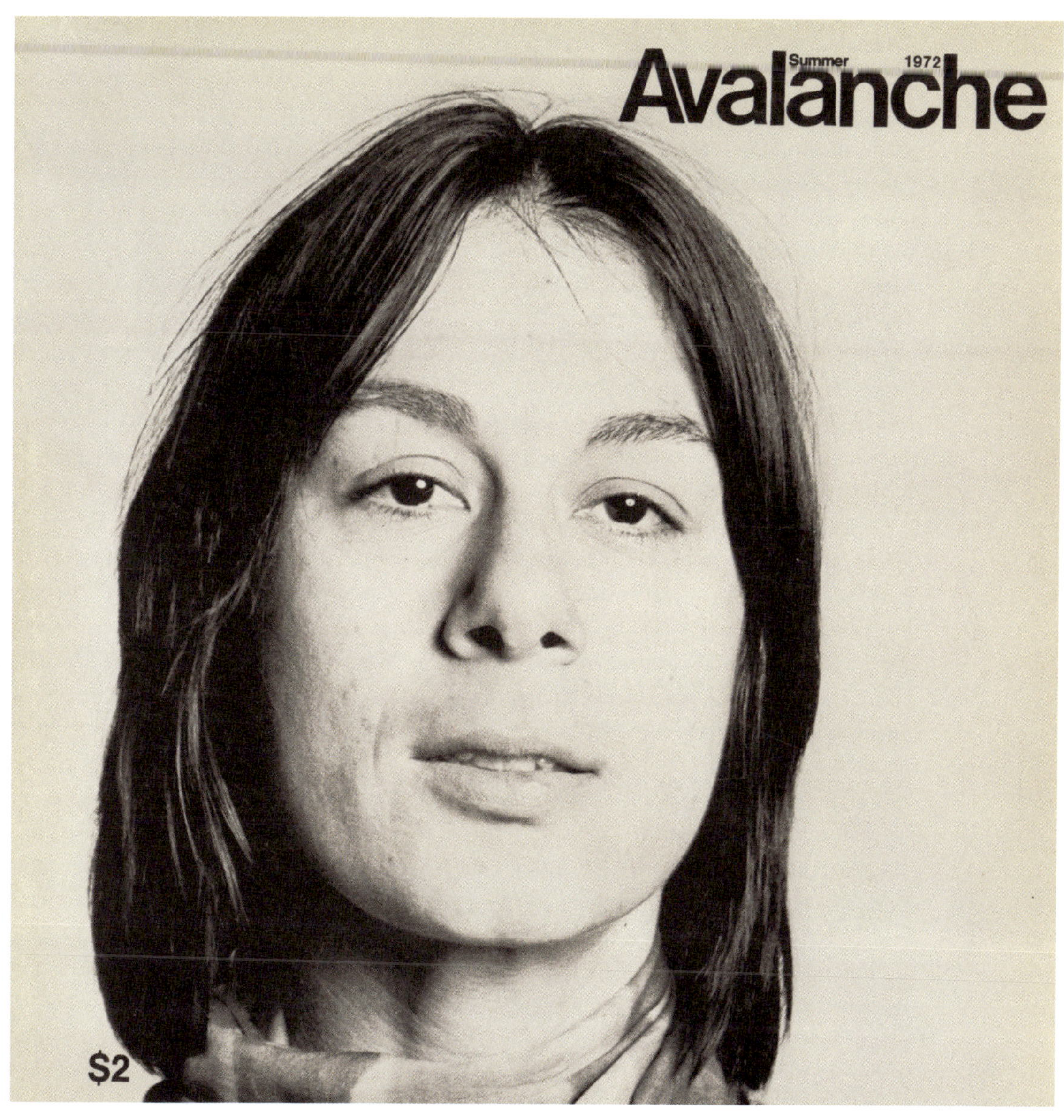

4.2

Photograph of Yvonne Rainer, cover of *Avalanche*,
no. 5, Summer 1972. Photograph by Gianfranco
Gorgoni. Courtesy of Liza Béar. Research Library,
The Getty Research Institute, Los Angeles (84-S1249).

Explaining the magazine's title—which he and Béar decided upon one night while brainstorming—Sharp observed in an interview, "The word 'avalanche' and what it signified was very appealing to me because I saw myself as a renegade. I had hair that I could sit on, I started smoking marijuana in '64 and was still smoking at that time, and I wanted this thing, this magazine, to represent a cultural breakthrough ... something that an avalanche does. It reconfigures, breaks down the old structure."[5] Indeed, the magazine was conceived as a groundbreaking rupture with the mainstream art world—one that might start off small but that would gain momentum as time went on, clearing a new path for art in its wake. The geological metaphor also referenced earth art, which was the theme of the first issue. Sharp originally wanted to call the magazine "Earthworm," but he and Béar eventually rejected that idea (according to Sharp, among other reasons, Robert Smithson expressed chagrin at the idea) and settled on *Avalanche* instead—a word that Béar preferred because it was "more evocative and typographically pleasing ... with its French derivation and feminine final *e*."[6] (Whether serendipitously or deliberately, *Avalanche* also echoed the title of another artists' magazine, *Landslide*, founded by Bas Jan Ader and William Leavitt in 1969.)

As guest curator of the seminal earth art exhibition at Cornell University's Andrew Dickson White Museum of Art in 1969 (the second in a series of exhibitions he conceived about the four astrological elements: air, earth, fire, and water), Sharp gained firsthand experience with the challenges art of the period posed for mainstream art institutions. As Thomas Leavitt explained at a symposium held on the occasion of the Cornell show, "What is implied with this type of art, and also many other types, incidentally, is a new kind of support for the artists—not based on possessiveness and also not based upon the idea of an art object. It becomes then perhaps the support of research or the support of interesting activity—whatever may be given—rather than the acquisition of something for the home or museums. It implies a whole different orientation of support."[7]

Avalanche was linked to this multi-inflected notion of a "different orientation of support." The magazine's role was twofold: first, it served as a crucial new physical support, or medium, providing a means to document and disseminate the new ephemeral, remotely located, and time-based works of the 1960s and 1970s. And second, it was central to the related search for new institutional supports, providing a way to advocate this work, to create patrons, audiences, and markets—a way to create public support. The very nature of earth art suggested to *Avalanche*'s editors how the magazine might constitute a new medium for this art, assuming a primary role in the works' communicability instead of the secondary, supplementary role it had performed traditionally as criticism or archive. Robert Smithson, for example, saw magazine pages as prime opportunities for "non-sites," the artist's term for the documentation—rock samples, maps, photographs, and texts—through which he frequently represented his remote, large-scale works to viewers. Asked to elaborate on the concept of the non-site during an interview published in the first issue of *Avalanche*, Smithson explains: "There's a central focus point which is the non-site; the site is the unfocused fringe where your mind loses its boundaries and a sense of the oceanic pervades, as it were. ... The interesting thing about the site is that, unlike the non-site, it throws you out to the fringes. ... One might even say that the place has absconded or been lost. ... This is a map that will take you somewhere, but when you get there you won't really know where you are. In a sense the non-site is the center of the system, and the site itself is the fringe or the edge."[8]

Smithson's site/non-site dialectic suggests a compelling model for the relationship between *Avalanche* and the art it documented in lower Manhattan. The SoHo art community, while not that far physically from the uptown gallery scene in Manhattan, was "in the fringes," as Smithson might say—situated outside the dominant art world centers, and largely excluded by its main vehicles of publicity. Although artists, lured by low rents and the uncharted feel of SoHo, had been illegally living in its abandoned factories and manufacturing loft spaces since the early 1950s—a story by now well known and oft-romanticized—the neighborhood still had relatively few inhabitants in the early 1970s. "At the time, there wasn't a car in SoHo at night," Jackie Winsor reminisced. "Usually if you saw someone on the street you'd know who they were. The buildings would be black except for red lights on the staircase."[9] As Béar characterized it, SoHo in those years was a "no-man's land not yet conquered by the forces of capitalism. ... Everything took place within a radius of a 10–12 minute walk. ... Prior to answering machines, computers, voice-mail, faxes, beepers, word of the first performances of Philip Glass's *Music in 12 Parts* at 10 Bleecker Street would be passed along by running into someone at the hardware store or the Canal Street post office."[10]

Avalanche served as a guide to SoHo, keeping the artists who lived and worked in SoHo informed about local goings-on, and promoting its emerging alternative spaces and performance venues. The magazine even hosted screenings and performances in its own headquarters, in a loft space on Grand Street, right around the corner from a constellation of brand-new alternative art venues. Sharp claimed, "*Avalanche* was more than a magazine, it was Willoughby Sharp and Liza Béar at 93 Grand Street on the ground floor. ... If *Avalanche* hadn't had offices in SoHo long before it was SoHo, it wouldn't have been what it was. You could knock on the window."[11] *Avalanche* was in the thick of it—on street level as a fledgling artistic community began to take hold. The *Avalanche* headquarters functioned as an occasional performance space and gallery, but also as a place, like other alternative spaces, such as 112 Greene Street or Food restaurant, where artists went for company, conversation, and various types of practical and moral support. As Béar described the *Avalanche* headquarters, "with sixteen-foot tin ceilings, a skylight in the back, a plate glass window onto the street and a usable basement, the space had charisma and a vaguely theatrical feel well-suited to performance as well as magazine production. ... The space stayed uncluttered with only a huge white plywood table, very few shelves and light tables in the front. The artist Van Schley had given *Avalanche* a 24" Setchell-Carlson black and white monitor, which had excellent definition and functioned as a light source in the cavernous space. It was usually left on with the sound off."[12]

However, if *Avalanche* functioned as a kind of map for the unmarked space of early SoHo, it was not merely an empirical record of this space. Instead, like Smithson's non-sites, it existed in a reciprocal and constitutive relationship to its site. Smithson was fond of describing printed matter through geological imagery and once characterized art magazines as "strata" with "land masses of print (called criticism) and little oceans with right angles (called photographs)."[13] Qua Smithson, *Avalanche* mined the materiality of printed matter. Designed as a series of double-page spreads, with advertising wrapped front and back around editorial content, the magazine unfolds in a dense, layered manner, with texts and photographs cascading across the page, full-bleed images alternating with spare, white pages. There is a cinematic quality to the magazine: in

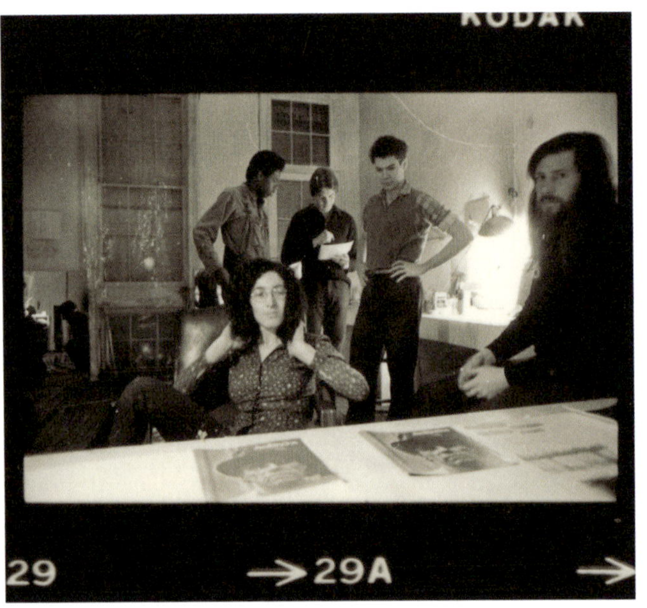

4.3

Liza Béar and Willoughby Sharp at 93 Grand Street,
c. 1973. In background, from left to right: Alfonia Tims,
musician; Barry Ledoux, sculptor; and Chris
Lethbridge. Photo: Cosmos; courtesy of Liza Béar.

fact, Béar explained that "it was designed as a film might be: sequentially from beginning to end. If you were to turn the pages one at a time, you would get a continuous and ever-changing, never repeated experience."[14] The sheer quantity of photographs published in *Avalanche* is remarkable. in the first issue, a conversation between Smithson, Michael Heizer, and Dennis Oppenheim is illustrated with no fewer than thirty-two photos, several of which bleed across two pages. To come across this layout in *Avalanche* is to comprehend more fully how the representational concerns of 1970s art were inflected by the communication forms of an emerging media culture.

Artists frequently designed their own contributions—one of the ways that "the artist took control," in Sharp's words.[15] They explored new ways to present their process-oriented and time-based work to the public, experimenting with layout and developing a visual rhetoric to signify the passage of time through the static medium of typography and photograph. Among these contributions were Richard Long's "Retrospective," eight pages of photographs recording his subtle interventions into the landscape (Fall 1970 issue); Robert Morris's "Document: Pace and Process," instructions for and photodocumentation of a performance that involved riding several ponies back and forth along a single line (Fall 1970); Richard Serra's "Verb List Compilation," a succession of verbs in the infinitive form describing sculptural processes (Winter 1971); Hanne Darboven's "Words," one of the artist's writing projects in which she marks the passage of time through lists of consecutive numbers typed out in Courier font over ten pages of the magazine (Spring 1972); Alice Aycock's "Four 36-38 Exposures," a series of contact sheets showing cloud formations moving and dissipating over a given time interval (Spring 1972); Gordon Matta-Clark's "Jacks," a set of photographs documenting the artist's junkyard performance (Fall 1971); Sol LeWitt's "Page Drawings," consisting of instructions for the reader to draw directly on the magazine page (Spring 1972); and Vito Acconci's "Trademarks," documenting a performance in which the artist produced prints from self-inflicted bite marks on his own skin (Winter 1971). The Fall 1972 issue was essentially given to Acconci in order to document his work—a minicatalog complete with bibliography and index.

One of the things that is fascinating about the artists' pages in *Avalanche* is the diverse— and sometimes contradictory—attitude toward the role of such documentation. While some artists, such as Smithson, acknowledged and embraced the primary role of media representation in the reception of art, others balked at the idea. For example, Carl Andre grumbled to Sharp and Béar in an interview in the first issue of the magazine, "I'm afraid we get a great deal of our exposure to art through magazines and through slides and I think this is dreadful, this is anti-art because art is a direct experience with something in the world and photography is just a rumor, a kind of pornography of art."[16] *Avalanche* participated in and even exacerbated such inconsistencies, destabilizing the opposition between original and reproduction and attesting to the complexity and uncertainty of the magazine as a new kind of artistic medium. Was it an art magazine? Was it an exhibition space? Was it some combination of the two? That *Avalanche* raises these questions about its own status without fully resolving them is part of what makes it such a fascinating and compelling document—one that allows us to witness the working out of these questions rather than their clear-cut resolution.

SOL LEWITT   PAGE DRAWINGS

ON THIS PAGE USING A PENCIL
OR A PEN, DRAW LINES FROM
EACH VOWEL IN THIS PARAGRAPH
TO EACH CORNER OF THIS PAGE.

18

4.4

Sol LeWitt, "Page Drawings," *Avalanche*, no. 4, Spring
1972. © The LeWitt Estate / Artists Rights Society
(ARS), New York.

DRAW A VERTICAL LINE FROM THE TOP
OF THIS PAGE TO THE BOTTOM, AND A
HORIZONTAL LINE FROM THE LEFT
SIDE OF THIS PAGE TO THE RIGHT.
DRAW A DIAGONAL LINE FROM THE
UPPER LEFT CORNER TO THE LOWER
RIGHT CORNER, AND ANOTHER
DIAGONAL LINE FROM THE UPPER
RIGHT CORNER TO THE LOWER RIGHT.

19

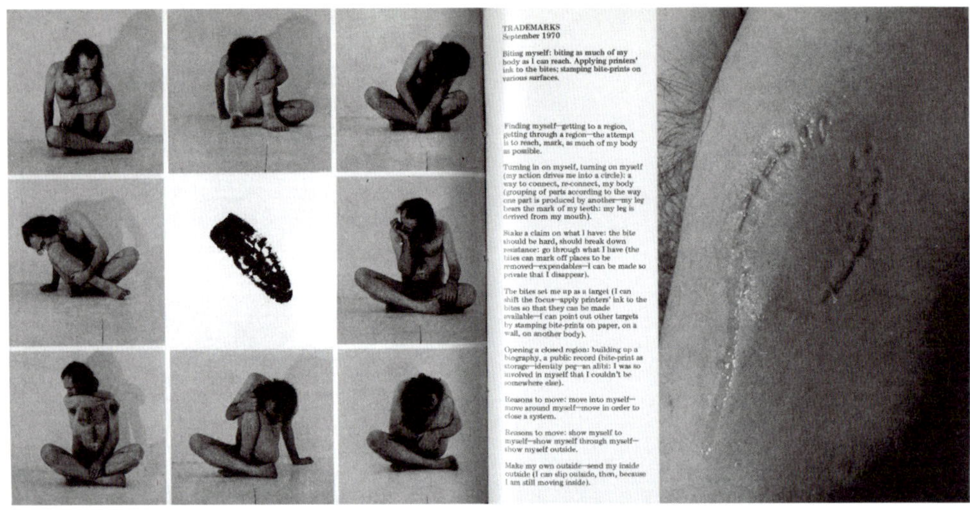

4.5

Vito Acconci, "Trademarks," *Avalanche*, no. 6, Fall 1972. Courtesy of the artist.

AN ARTISTS' MAGAZINE

Avalanche, like so many worthwhile endeavors, had its origins in a chance encounter. In 1968 Béar was a London-based magazine editor on her first trip to New York, where she contacted Sharp, an art historian working as an independent curator, to retrieve a film for an artist friend back home. This casual errand turned into a fortuitous meeting, as the two felt an instant rapport, discovering their common interests in art and media, and they almost immediately agreed to produce an art magazine together. Béar sold her return ticket to England and the two set up shop in Sharp's Gramercy Park apartment, where they pooled their respective expertise and went to work conceptualizing and designing the magazine, selling ads, and sorting through the huge quantity of mail that had started to flow in as word of the new magazine spread in the art world. Béar remembers, "We jumped right in and literally got down to work on the magazine's format, laying out early issues of *Life* and Dadaist publications on the floor. It never occurred to us to try to raise some money first."[17] They did virtually everything themselves: design, layout, typesetting, selling advertisements (as well as frequently designing the ads), conducting interviews, and selecting artists' projects. *Avalanche* was published under the imprint of Kineticism Press, which Sharp had co-founded with the German art dealer Paul Maenz in 1966 to "foster the total distribution of artistic information in all media."[18] On the masthead, Sharp is listed as publisher, Béar as editor, and one "Boris Wall Gruphy" (an anagram of Willoughby Sharp) as the designer of the publication; after issue 9, Sharp was listed as artist-in-residence. They worked as a team, collaborating closely on all aspects of the magazine; as Béar recalled, "it was a totally organic process of give and take."[19]

The first issue was on the newsstands in late October 1970. "When *Avalanche* came along, I said this is the first time there's a magazine that's more interesting than *Artforum*,"[20] remembered the critic Robert Pincus-Witten. *Avalanche* borrowed *Artforum*'s square format—a choice that reads in retrospect as both homage and challenge to the latter's authority. In many ways *Avalanche* can indeed be read as a tactical appropriation of the publicity form of the commercial art magazine. Printed on glossy, high-quality paper, the upstart had a solidity to it and even a degree of polish that stood in contrast to—almost contradicted—the process-oriented, unfinished quality of so much of the art it documented (even as it was the very vehicle of that art, or in some cases, actually was the art). It gave the offhand snapshots of performances and installations or video stills a sudden feeling of legitimacy, made their haphazard cropping and accidental blurring seem intentional, even stylized, once they were neatly framed by a bright white border and surrounded by immaculate lines of Univers font. The magazine came out somewhat sporadically: the first year there was one issue, the next year two, the third year three. In 1974, when printing costs skyrocketed, *Avalanche* switched to a newspaper format. Even, then, however, it was printed on substantial 50 lb. uncoated paper; according to Béar, *Avalanche* "was intended to last."[21]

The choice to put Joseph Beuys's portrait on the first cover signaled the editors' ambition for their magazine to be international in scope, which they fulfilled by lining up distribution and advertisers in Europe.[22] Sharp frequently traveled to Europe, and *Avalanche*'s international aspirations dovetailed with magazines such as the Cologne-based *Interfunktionen* and the Paris-based *Robho*, to which he contributed. In addition to Beuys, who was featured in issues 1 and 5, the magazine published interviews and projects by European conceptualists including Jannis Kounellis, Yves Klein, Hans Haacke, Daniel Buren, Gilbert and George, Stanley Brouwn, Jan Dibbets, David Tremlett, Braco Dimitrijević, Ulrich Rückriem, Ulrike Rosenbach, Klaus Rinke, and Franz Erhard Walther—a transatlantic roster that is especially impressive given the exceedingly limited coverage of Europe in other United States art magazines at the time. *Avalanche* also countered the New York bias of the mainstream press by covering artists elsewhere in the United States, especially in California, as well as in Canada, publishing interviews with General Idea and Image Bank. And yet, while *Avalanche*'s role in helping to open up the New York art world to developments elsewhere in North America and abroad should not be underestimated, the magazine's significance also remains deeply tied to its function in representing the local community of artists in SoHo.

Sharp's insistence that *Avalanche* was an "artists' magazine" reflects the growing demand by artists for more control in the display and distribution of their work—demands that catalyzed the formation of numerous activist groups in the late 1960s, including the Art Workers' Coalition, which Sharp and Béar were indirectly involved in founding. The Art Workers' Coalition crystallized in the winter of 1969 when the Greek kinetic sculptor Vassilakis Takis, disapproving of the Museum of Modern Art's unauthorized exhibition of his work *Tele-Sculpture* (1960) in the exhibition "The Machine as Seen at the End of the Mechanical Age," removed the piece from the museum in an act of civil disobedience. Béar and Sharp, an avid supporter of kinetic art, were instrumental in organizing the demonstration. Béar called the press, and Sharp gathered a group of friends and supporters, who watched in the MoMA sculpture garden as Takis unplugged his

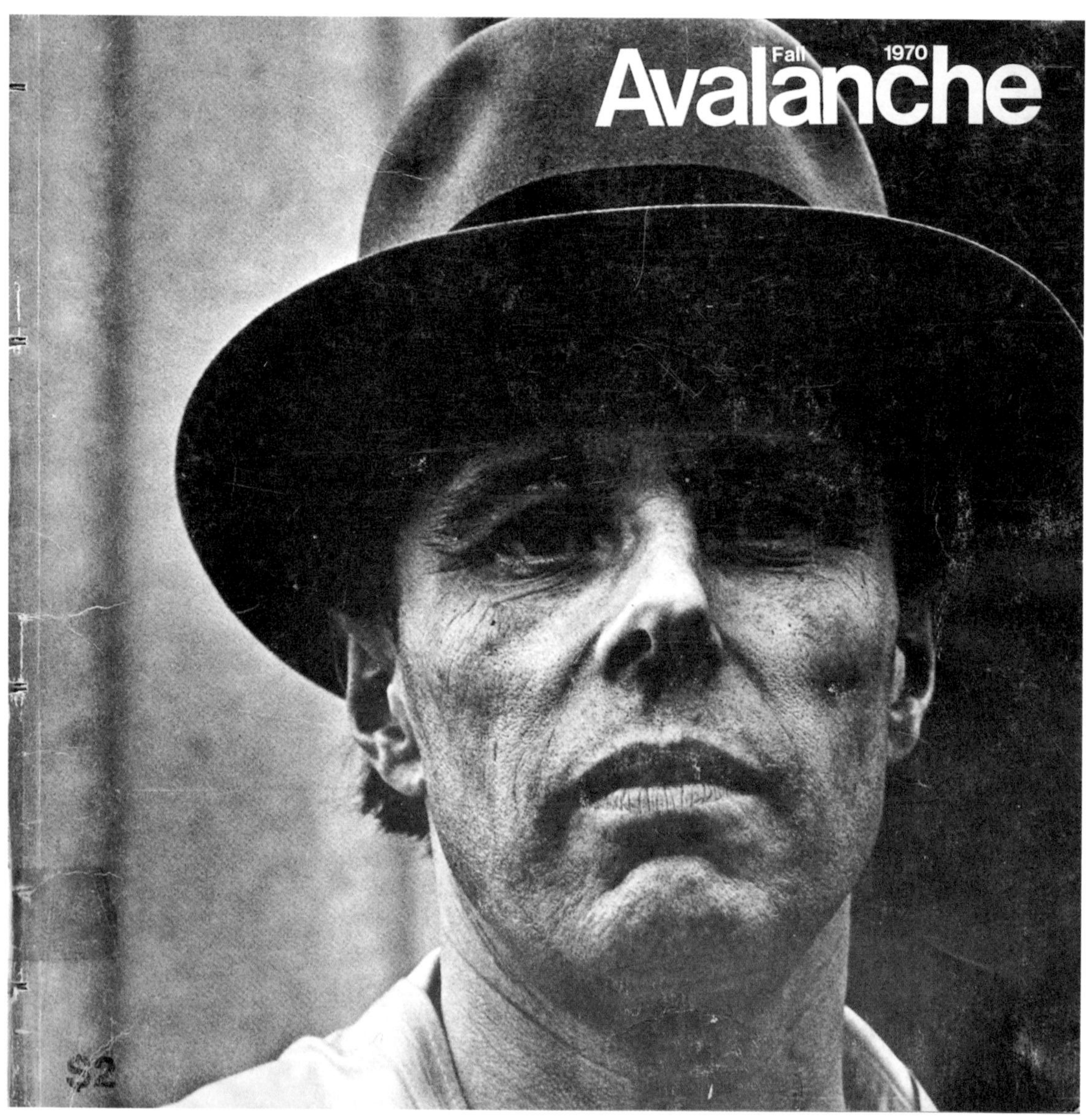

4.6

Photograph of Joseph Beuys, cover of *Avalanche*,
no. 1, Fall 1970. Photograph by Shunk-Kender.
© Roy Lichtenstein Foundation. Collection of Steven
Leiber, San Francisco.

sculpture and carried it out of the museum. And it was at their apartment, a few days later, that a group of artists and critics got together to draft the initial set of "13 Demands," which prompted the formation of the Art Workers' Coalition.[23] Among these demands were: "a section of the Museum, under the direction of black artists, should be devoted to showing the accomplishments of black artists"; "the Museum should be open on two evenings until midnight and admission should be free at all times"; and "a section of the Museum should be permanently devoted to showing the work of artists without galleries."[24]

As AWC member Carl Andre insisted, "The solution to the artist's problems is not getting rid of the turnstiles at the Museum of Modern Art, but in getting rid of the art world. This the artists can easily do by trusting one another and forming a true community of artists."[25] Andre's statement, issued in the context of an Art Workers' Coalition meeting, was tantamount to a call for secession from the art world. *Avalanche* suggests the importance of artists' magazines to the empowerment of artists during this moment—an empowerment that would also be realized in the alternative artist-run spaces that emerged in SoHo and across the country in the 1970s, offering new ways of making and exhibiting work outside of the venues of the mainstream art world. One of the earliest and most important alternative spaces was 112 Greene Street, founded in an old rag-salvaging building by Jeffrey Lew and Alan Saret in 1970. In an interview published in the second issue of *Avalanche*, Lew and Saret discussed the spontaneous, artist-focused, noncommercial character of 112 Greene Street, qualities that would be central to the numerous alternative spaces that proliferated throughout the 1970s. They explained their deliberate decision to cultivate the roughness of the space in opposition to the uptown "white cube" gallery spaces: "112 Greene Street is really funky and should be left funky. We're not going to touch it, except put in basic things like doors and lights, but we're not going to paint it and fix it up. Just take the dangerous elements out."[26] As this suggests, 112 Greene Street was conceived as a versatile, constantly changing space that would accommodate and echo the process-oriented art it exhibited. Asked whether anything had been sold, they replied, "No. If people want to buy something they have to say so. Because there's no one there asking, Would you like to buy it? There are no little red dots."[27] And queried about the issue of artists' control, they asserted, "The artist really wants that kind of freedom, of flexibility, and not to worry about backers influencing you or telling you what to make."[28]

The ideological goals of 112 Greene Street shed light on *Avalanche*'s own editorial mission to support artists—a mission that would subsequently prove central to numerous artists' magazine in North America throughout the 1970s. Artists didn't have to be at the mercy of their critics, *Avalanche*'s editors maintained; they could be proactive about their own portrayal in the media. This insight was timely, since artists had already begun to "talk back" to critics, penning articles and criticism such as the spate of minimalist writings famously appearing in *Artforum* in the mid- to late 1960s. *Avalanche* went even further by circumventing the critic altogether and pioneering a novel set of terms for critical discourse about art, based on nonhierarchical and cooperative forms of communication.

The alternative character of *Avalanche*'s artistic discourse was perhaps most evident in the interviews it published, through which artists were encouraged to talk frankly about their work without the mediation of critics. Over six years, *Avalanche* published sixty-one interviews with artists, including conversations with Carl Andre, Robert Smithson, Michael Heizer, Dennis Oppenheim, Bruce Nauman, Terry Fox, Barry Le Va, Jackie Winsor, Lawrence Weiner, Philip Glass, Janis Kounellis, Yvonne Rainer, General Idea, Vito Acconci, William Wegman, Ed Ruscha, Tina Girouard, Chris Burden, Meredith Monk, Daniel Buren, and Gordon Matta-Clark. Many of the interviews were abundantly illustrated with photographs of the artist's work. Béar and Sharp conducted all but one or two of the interviews themselves, preparing assiduously by doing weeks' worth of reading and research. Sharp recalled that they approached the work "almost from an historical sense before it was history. ... The attention that was paid to the artistic process, it was ludicrous!" For example, to prepare for their interview with Barry Le Va, published in issue 3 (Fall 1971), they asked the artist to lend them the ten most important books in his library, and then proceeded to read every single one. According to Béar, whose extremely candid interviewing style produced some of the most fascinating art historical documents of the period, the *Avalanche* conversations were "no kissing cousin of the celebrity interview, but a kind of investigative reporting that aimed to understand rather than to expose, in which the questioning voice was closely attuned to the artist's sensibility."[29] Questions are posed unpretentiously, sometimes bluntly. To Buren: "So what were you trying to do, exactly?" (December 1974); to Smithson: "What exactly is your concept of a non-site?" (Fall 1970); to Matta-Clark: "What's a metaphoric void?" (December 1974); to Girouard: "So in what ways does the choice of medium become significant?" (Summer/Fall 1973); to Weiner: "At what point did you see yourself as an artist?" (Spring 1972); to Andre: "Do you feel that your work is subversive in any way?" (Fall 1970); to Rainer: "Has being a woman made a difference to your work?" (Summer 1972).

Richly idiosyncratic, the *Avalanche* interviews convey something of the affective nuance and informal quality of the original exchanges they record, allowing us to imagine that we are eavesdropping on history, a fly on the wall of a loft in SoHo when the acronym was still novel. The interviews capture the rhythms and cadences of natural speech, brimming with pauses, non sequiturs, phatic expressions—those qualities that characterize actual conversations.[30] The closeness between interviewer and subject manifests itself as a kind of fluency and spontaneity largely absent from the curt, contrived-sounding interviews appearing in other art magazines at the time, which read as a drill of preconceived questions. The *Avalanche* interviews, by contrast, circle and ramble, the way real conversations do. Artist and interviewer think out loud, finish one another's sentences—a synergy that was typographically reinforced by the absence of initials identifying interviewer and interviewee, whose voices were instead indicated by different weights and styles of font in early issues. Often the interviews take place over a meal or over the course of a long afternoon; sometimes they begin with the lighting of a joint or hash. They seem to go beyond the mere communication of information to the communion of intellect—as well as the enjoyment of company.

GORDON MATTA-CLARK . . . .

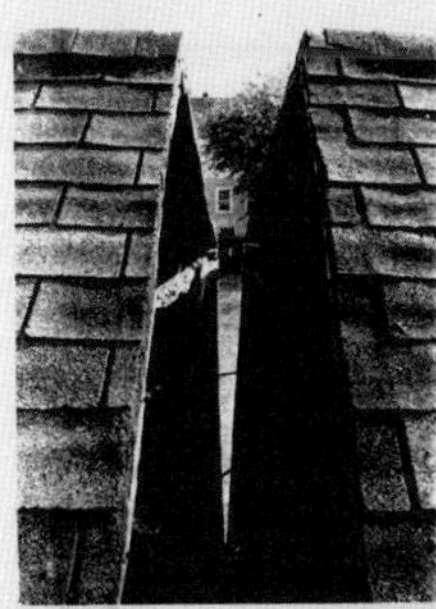

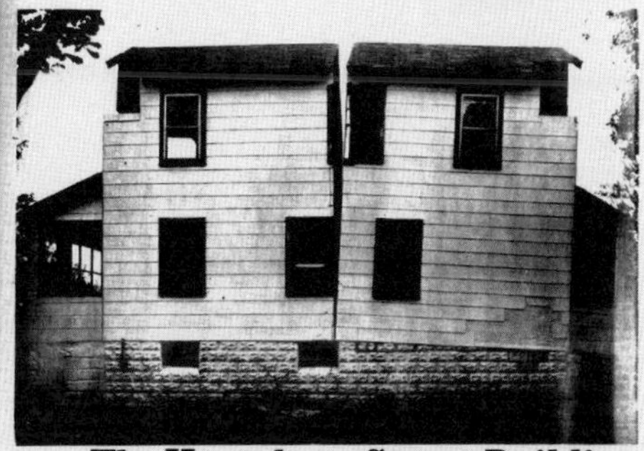

SPLITTING

The Humphrey Street Building

Tuesday, May 21st, 1974. Gordon Matta-Clark talked to Liza Bear at *The Fountain Service*, Englewood, New Jersey, and later at the Humphrey Street building.

GM: Holly and Horace Solomon gave me the Humphrey Street building in March. It's substandard housing in bedroom suburbia near the Lackawanna railroad. The community here is starting to thin out, people are selling their property and the city's buying up the land for redevelopment. Now it's getting back to a nice transitional grandiose... the area almost has a Southern quality because everything is so run down. The Solomon family had originally bought the house as an investment, and it's now been scheduled for demolition... One of the things that's clearest in my mind is how this interest in working with buildings originated. It evolved out of that period in 1970 when I was living in the basement at 112 Greene Street and doing things in different corners. Initially they weren't at all related to the structure, I was just working within a place, but eventually I started treating the place as a whole, as an object. One of the first times I did this was at the Boston Museum Art School in 1971, where I started to play with the plumbing as a system within the building. I intended one of the gas lines by bringing it around from behind a wall, so that there was a loop of contained gas in the gallery, and then I followed the gas lines back into the street with photographs, so the piece also had a photographic extension. When I was living at 4th Street a few years ago I was already thinking in terms of dealing with a whole building. At first what the nature of the activity would be seemed unclear, but gradually there was a logical progression through various kinds of local references to the whole building system.

LB: I've always thought of you as working within an architectural context.

GM: Not architectural in the strict sense. Most of the things I've done that have "architectural" implications are really about non-architecture, about something that's an alternative to what's normally considered architecture. The Anarchitecture show at 112 Greene Street last year — which never got very strongly expressed — was about something other than the established architectural vocabulary, without getting fixed into anything too formal.

LB: Do you see the Humphrey Street building as a piece of anarchitecture?

GM: No. Our thinking about anarchitecture was more elusive than doing pieces that would demonstrate an alternate attitude to buildings, or, rather to the attitudes that determine containerization of usable space. Those attitudes are very deep-set... Architecture is environment too. When you're living in a city the whole fabric is architectural in some sense. We were thinking more about metaphoric voids, gaps, left-over spaces, places that were not developed.

LB: What's a metaphoric void?

GM: Metaphoric in the sense that their interest or value wasn't in their possible use...

LB: You mean you were interested in these spaces on some non-functional level.

GM: Or on a functional level that was so absurd as to ridicule the idea of function... For example, the places where you stop to tie your shoe-laces, places that are just interruptions in your own daily movements. These places are also perceptually significant because they make a reference to movement space.

When I bought those properties at the New York City Auction the description of them that always excited me the most was "inaccessible." They were a group of fifteen micro-parcels of land in Queens, left-over properties from an architect's drawing. One or two of the prize ones were a foot strip down somebody's driveway and a square foot of sidewalk. And the others were kerbstone and gutterspace. What I basically wanted to do was to designate spaces that wouldn't be seen and certainly not occupied. Buying them was my own take on the strangeness of existing property demarcation lines. Property is an all-pervasive. Everyone's notion of

The simplest way to create complexity . . .

ownership is determined by the use factor.

But I was talking about how my work with buildings started. Some of the first pieces that actually dealt with impingements on buildings as a structural fabric were very small extractions. At that point I was thinking about surface as something which is too easily accepted as a limit. And I was also becoming very interested in how breaking through the surface creates repercussions in terms of what else it imposed upon by a cut. That's a very simple idea, and it comes out of some line drawings that I'd been doing.

LB: A cut is a simple thing if you see it in graphic terms only. What struck me about the Humphrey Street piece was how much information the cut seemed to reveal.

GM: Yes, a cut is very analytical. It's the probe! The essential probe. The scaffold of sharp-eyed inspectors. Initially I also wanted to go beyond visual things. Of course, there are visual consequences in cutting, certainly to removal, but it was kind of the thin edge of what was being seen that interested me as much, if not more than, the views that were being created.

LB: What do you mean exactly?

GM: Well, for example the layering, the strata, the different things that are being severed. Revealing how a uniform surface is established. The simplest way to create complexity was one of the formal concerns here, without having to make or build anything.

LB: Have you ever made things as such, or have you always worked

Physical wit and a trace of absurdity . . .

by removing or tampering with existing structures?

GM: I build in renovating lofts, but I've certainly not built any objects recently! That's one of the things I like about the Humphrey Street building, it has a curious object scale ambiguity to it. The cut makes the building into a manipulated thing, like an object, though it's as much the idea of a cut as the functional construct that interests me.

LB: Well, it's certainly not going to be functional very long.

GM: Not when it gets demolished it won't. But I think of it now as still being potentially functional. There's no reason why one shouldn't be able to live in that place. In fact, I would be very interested in translating cuts like this into still usable or inhabited space. It would change your perceptions for awhile, and it

would certainly modify privacy a great deal. You'd have to live on or as far away from the line as possible.

LB: It might be an answer to sharing living space problems. Beyond the gap.

GM: Yes — move out!

LB: What was the piece you did last fall in Genoa, was it related in any way to this?

GM: When I went to Italy I was searching for places to work, and Vinetto Rebora of Galleriaforma gave me the office and draughting room of his old factory, a little concrete building, very Mediterranean terra cotta shingle roof, a beautiful structure, in one of the heavy industrial areas in Genoa. But the concrete was a foot and a half thick — so it was a monstrous job trying to get it cut.

LB: How did you cut it?

GM: All by hand, with a chisel... Just before Genoa I did a piece in Milan while Carol Goodden was dancing with Trisha Brown. I was roaming around and I found these old masonry warehouses. I'd never dealt with masonry before. What seemed to happen quite naturally with masonry was that rather than dealing with a whole, the cuts became more and more palpable as things in themselves. The Milan piece was called *Infraform*. The building was made of terra cotta bricks with cement on either side. There was a certain intersection of walls that I cut out of. But although I removed the area that I'd cut away, there was a moment when it was still standing there described only by the line of the cut. That impressed me as much as anything I'd done up 'til then. First of all, it made it very

clear that the walls had been separated without anything being removed. But I took out the portion that I'd cut, because at the time I was still interested in that extraction process, making a reference to what wasn't there as much as to what was there. Positive and void balances. So when I went to Genoa, I dealt with the same basic problem more extensively. I cut horizontal lines that ran parallel with the floor throughout the interior of the space, so that all the walls were separated from the ceiling. The first line was these feet

off the floor and the other lines were eighteen inches above each other, so that the walls were cut into three parts. One was attached to the foundations, another suspended... There were a few points that remained holding it in place. Then what I tried to do was to somehow make a couple of pictures that would unify the whole building. I took the center out of the roof, and then another cut from the top of the roof down. So I was still dealing with an abstractive process, rather than making a physical shift in the structure as I

4.7

"Gordon Matta-Clark: Splitting," interview by Liza Béar,
Avalanche, no. 10, December 1974, pages 34–35.
Courtesy of Liza Béar.

Consider a 1972 interview with Ed Ruscha titled "… a Kind of a Huh?" in which Ruscha and Sharp discuss the meaning and even the spelling of the expression "huh?"—a word Ruscha used to describe his first book of photographs, *26 Gasoline Stations*:

ER: I realized that for the first time this book [*26 Gasoline Stations*] had an inexplicable thing I was looking for, and that was a kind of a "Huh?" That's what I've always worked around. All it is [is] a device to disarm somebody with my particular message. A lot of artists use that.

WS: Give me some examples of "Uh." […]

ER: I think that would be spelled H-U-H with a question mark …

WS: or H-U-H-U-H-U-H.

WR: Well, then that would be like a "yes," that would be like uh-huh.

WS: Uh-ha, right.

WS: Mmmmm. Right.

ER: I just use that word to describe a feeling that a lot of artists are attempting to bring out, and some are doing it very well.[31]

The "huh?" seems to capture for Ruscha the difficulties in inhabiting language: "huh" is a kind of phonetic lapse, signaling the experience of inaudibility—or even aporia. And yet the "huh?" in this instance signifies not so much a deficiency in communication but its inevitability: the fact that even when we can't quite find the right word, we manage to convey meaning through sounds and gestures and expressions. And yet such communication is radically different from the conventions of written language. Indeed, linguistic theorists say that deviation from conventional usage characterizes the social practice of conversation. As the linguist H. P. Grice argued in his 1967 lecture "Logic and Conversation," when speaking to one another, we often flout the rules of conventional language, using irony, understatement, hyperbole, ambiguity, obscurity, and prolixity to imply things that are outside its scope. Such tendencies, he concluded, make the meaning of conversations both context-bound and indeterminate. The meaning of conversations, Grice claimed, "is not carried by what is said but only by the saying of what is said, or by 'putting it that way.'"[32]

The model of communication represented in these interviews is a distinctly temporal and collaborative one: it depends on the fact that a conversation between two people always exceeds the sum of its parts, that it takes place according to the logic of interactivity and reciprocity rather than objectivity or rationality. In these interviews, Sharp and Béar come across less as critics than as interlocutors: curious, insightful, but not particularly anxious to forward a thesis. Sometimes they are awkward, or sometimes they meander, circling around a point without ever seeming to get to it. Other times they lead straight into dead ends, as in the following exchange between Sharp and the conceptual artist Lawrence Weiner:

[WS:] What does the photographic image of this work [*A Square Removal from a Rug in Use*] mean to you?

[LW:] Nothing, absolutely nothing …

[WS:] What experiences led you to want to deal with language as an art problem?

[LW:] None of your business ...

[WS:] The general concerns of your work have often been referred to as conceptual. How do you relate to that category?

[LW:] To be terribly frank, I don't understand it at all.[33]

Despite their informal and sometimes humorous character, the interviews were rooted in acute, detailed analysis of works of art—an inquiry in which both artist and interviewer participated equally. This is evident in a discussion between Béar and Vito Acconci about the artist's performance *Seedbed* (1972) in which he masturbated while hidden under a ramp installed at the Sonnabend Gallery:

LB: Why do you consider *Seedbed* your most important work?

VA: The physical situation of *Seedbed* allowed me to be with an audience, with a potential viewer, more than any situation I had come up with before. ... If their presence, their footsteps, had to cause my fantasies, I would have to be drawn to them in order to fantasize.

LB: So although you didn't know who the individual viewers were, who the footsteps corresponded to, and they couldn't be sure which of them your comments referred to, you think your fantasizing created an intimate rapport between you.

VA: Well, yeah, hopefully they were completely compromised as they walked into the gallery, onto the ramp—they were implicated.

LB: That's a peculiar kind of intimacy. They're put in the position, by coming to the gallery, of hearing you perform what's normally a private activity for which they may provide the stimulus. They're not there as voyeurs. So they're being more compromised than you are.[34]

The interviews can also be personal and moving. When Rainer describes her discovery of performance, the immediacy of her revelation is such that we can imagine being in the room with her:

YR: My first intense feeling of being alive was in performance and that's really what committed me to ...

WS: Could you describe that?

YR: Mmmmmm. It was my first dance. ... I stood waiting for the curtain to go up—no, it didn't go up, it parted, and I had the sense of uh ... it was like an epiphany of beauty and power that I have rarely experienced since. I mean, I knew I *had* them—the audience.[35]

While Béar and Sharp collaborated on most interviews from the beginning (with Béar doing most of the transcription and editing of interviews as well), in later issues they are credited individually. Béar's more visible profile coincides with the increasing prominence of the voices of women artists in the magazine's pages. Béar was especially attuned to the possibilities of the interview as an artistic form in its own right. For example, in her interview with Joel Shapiro,

WS: Mmmmm. Right.

ER: I just use that word to describe a feeling that a lot of artists are attempting to bring out, and some are doing it very well.

WS: Yes.

ER: The entire collection of my books just doesn't have that feeling of "Huh?" When you go through the whole collection it begins to make some sense; it shows more about the attitude behind them than one of them does. One of them will kind of almost knock you on your ass.

WS: *Nine Swimming Pools* does that . . . I see you have a book on Vermeer here.

ER: Well, I was curious about Vermeer's life and some of those pictures. The paintings in that book are all the ones he ever did, aren't they?

WS: Yes, I think he only did thirty-six. . . . Would you say that you pioneered the book form as an art work?

ER: Oh, I don't know. It's just that traditionally the book has not been accepted as a work to be put in an art gallery.

WS: I can't think of anyone else who used the book medium as an art vehicle.

ER: Well a lot of poets have done it but it hasn't been called gallery art art.

WS: Have your books been getting more frequent?

ER: Well last year I did three but *The Colored People* is the only one I've done this year. Everything in the media is paced for people's pace. *Time* magazine comes around once a week and that's about the time you've forgotten the last one. Or *Popular Mechanics* or what have you. A newspaper. I've gotten into the style of reading a newspaper in the morning for a couple of hours after I wake up. All the media are filtered that way to the cycles we live in. You know, we live in daily cycles; we live in weekly cycles; we live in monthly cycles so once a year an artist has a show; he might make ten shows a year but they'll be in different cities. It's all paced out. It's very natural the way all those things happen.

WS: Does that apply to your own work?

ER: The way to produce art is the same way as the media, to sort of go with that rhythm. That's why I don't do twelve books a year, because other people aren't ready for it and neither am I. I'm not ready to make twelve statements a year. I *could*, and possibly I could push my craft much further because I'm dedicated to this whole publishing thing. I really owe a lot to it. It's a responsibility, it's my baby. I have to develop it. When I did the books I had a complete feeling of creation in the same sense that a woman would have a child. I even wrote that down: "These books are my children." But when I got *Colored People* back from the press, I yawned, I just yawned.

WS: Was there a point in your career when you started losing interest in making things with your hands?

ER: Yeah, definitely. About three years ago, I just didn't have the desire to work with my hands, make a painting. I didn't want to take the time. Then it occurred to me that a way out was to find somebody who could paint and have him do it.

WS: Have you ever rejected anything that was already printed?

ER: Mmmmm. I've had practically a cardiac arrest over the reprint of one of my books, *The Sunset Strip*. I had to go get a lawyer. The original printer finished the job and it was gonna go to the bindery but they cut and folded the whole job wrong. Then I showed them the dummy so they could see that it was not folded right and I said, "You'll have to do this over," and they started to argue with me and I just broke out in hives. I really had spots on my face; I was ready to have a heart attack on the spot and I got a lawyer and they finally did the job over again. They had to pay for the cost of the paper and printing and all that. I've run into all kinds of problems working with people like that and I've had to buy color separations and other things on the outside.

WS: Then isn't it desirable to find a medium that doesn't even . . .

ER: No, no, unless I just want to sit back . . . painting a picture is a very simple thing to do. You don't have to rely on other people; you're in total control. But you don't pick a particular medium so you can have total control over it. If you can't work with those people, you're not going to get a good product.

WS: How could you make a better book?

ER: Better? I don't know how it can be better. I'm satisfied with the results that I've gotten so far. There are technical problems that I need to . . .

WS: Like?

ER: It's a job making sure the thing gets delivered properly and that they keep on schedule. For example, *Colored People* had to be finished in time for the November opening at Castelli and it was pretty close to the wire. I got them about four days before I left for New York.

WS: That book was your one-man show, but do you really need a gallery context for it?

ER: Uh, well, I don't know whether I need a gallery for the books to survive or not.

4.8

From "… a Kind of a Huh? An Interview with Edward Ruscha." Photographs by Carol Merserau. Spread from *Avalanche*, no. 7, Winter/Spring 1973. Research Library, The Getty Research Institute, Los Angeles (84-S1249).

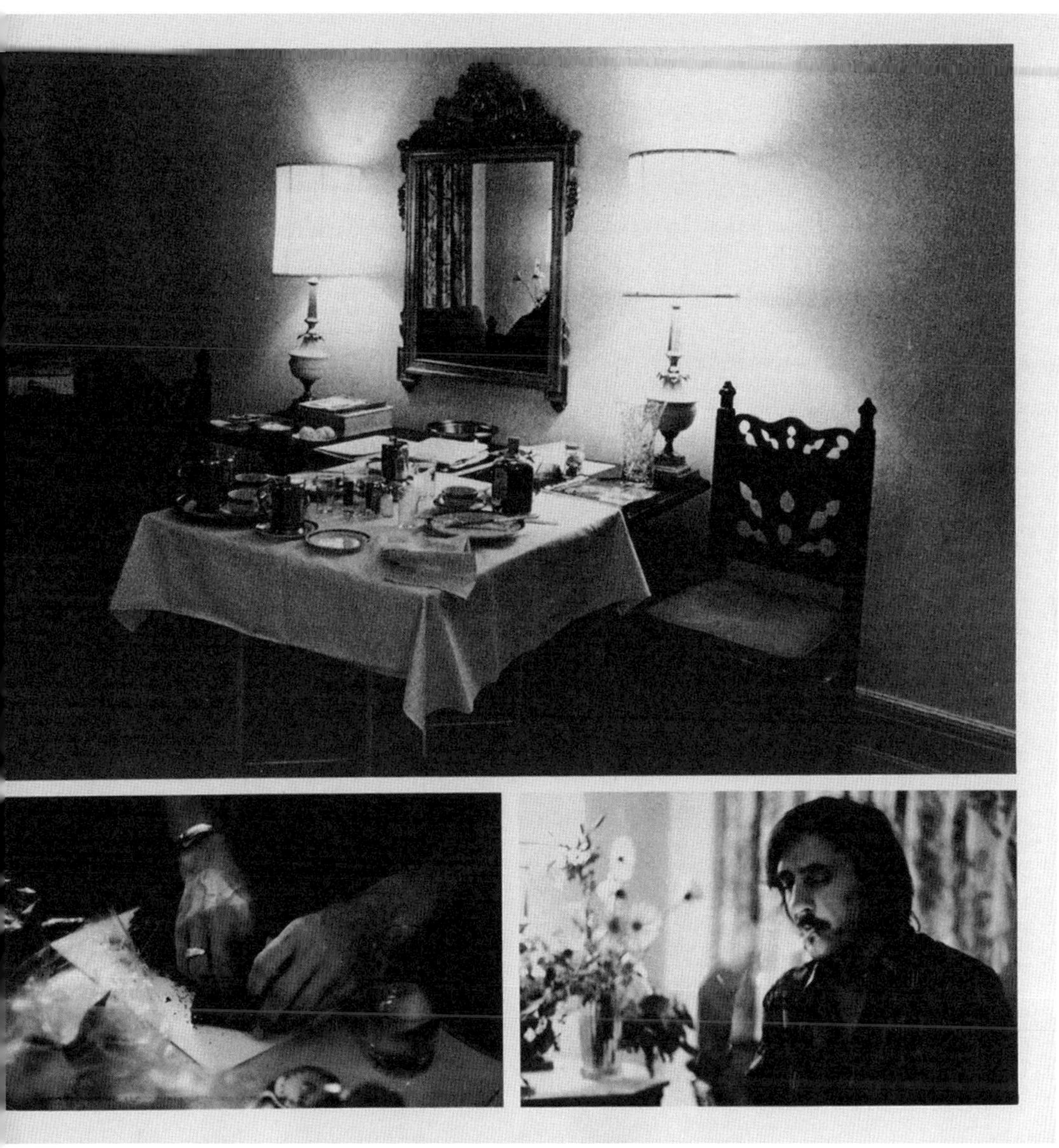

in *Avalanche* 12 (Summer 1975), she conceived of the conversation through the narrative and formal devices of film, recalling, "I treated it as 'takes' with cuts made for rhythm, cadence, content."[36] The interview has a kind of mise-en-scène, moving from setting to setting, and alternating between playful and serious "scenes" punctuated with the word "cut." The interview, entitled "Torquing"—a reference to a sculptural technique, but also a pun on the word "talking," alluding to a mishearing that takes place in the course of the interview itself—begins in the kitchen area of Shapiro's studio, where the following exchange takes place:

—Oh, you don't think anything from the outside can change it?

—What happens is that I work and then I get self conscious. … Sugar?

—No thanks.

—Do you want a cushion?

—No I want to sit on a hard chair that's the right height.

—I want something I can put my feet on.

—I sense we're both quite particular about our level of comfort.

—Usually I lie down right over there.

—To talk, you mean?

—It's hard for me to talk anywhere, standing up. … It's easier if I'm comfortable. (PAUSE)[37]

Several days later, the interview continues in a cab on the way to the foundry, where Shapiro is taking several models to be cast:

—Where are we going?

—Greenpoint. India Street.

—All I wanted to know was the general district. Is it Brooklyn?

—Yeah, Greenpoint. And the foundry guys are real brutes.

—Oh I can imagine.

—They never want to do what I want them to do.

—So which pieces are you having cast?

—All of them.

—You're going to have this cast solid …

—Yeah, if they'll do it. I don't know anything about it see, so I always bring in things and they say, we can't do that. It's impossible. … (Cut)[38]

Sure enough, as if on cue, the following exchange between the artist and the caster takes place later in the foundry:

—Can we do this in one piece?

—In one piece?

—Yeah, so it doesn't open. … Is that hard to do? The rest I want solid.

—Not hard to do, but impossible.

—It's impossible? Oh, well.[39]

Though the *Avalanche* interviews have an unedited, informal quality, paradoxically, they were carefully edited to preserve each artist's idiom and the nuances of spoken conversation. Such attentiveness reflects the magazine's commitment to providing an authentic channel for the artist's voice, even as it throws into question the very possibility of such authenticity, reinforcing—in a way that Smithson probably would have appreciated—the always already mediated nature of the magazine as a representational site. Beyond their value as primary art historical sources, the *Avalanche* interviews attest to the important role of conversation in the process of making and viewing art in SoHo in the 1970s. Laurie Anderson made this observation in her recollection of the period:

> The thing that I loved best about that time was how much people were involved in each other's work. All of us did a lot of talking and a lot of writing. … The talking was really a working method and a way of identifying with each other. … The talking is not only a way to figure out what you're doing, it's the work itself. In fact I felt really frustrated with Gordon [Matta-Clark]'s shows and the exhibitions of other friends. Because without the talk, the background, the thing was left really blank. The life was out of it.[40]

Anderson's insistence on the importance of conversation and her frustration with gallery exhibitions, which isolated the work, severing it from the vitality of this social context, points to a model of the work of art which exceeds a formal definition of medium as a tallying up of materials and procedures, and instead locates the significance of art in its social experience and effects. The talking, she states, is "the work itself."

RUMBLES, MESSAGES, AND ADS

Asked about the art market, Sharp countered, somewhat surprisingly, "If anything I was trying to encourage these artists to get into the market, helping them market their work. I'm not against the market."[41] Besides revealing a certain by-the-seat-of-his-pants pragmatism, without which the magazine couldn't have survived for as long as it did, this statement touches on one of the more arresting ironies of conceptual art: famous for its contempt for the market, this dematerialized art was ultimately more reliant on newer and perhaps even more insidious forms of publicity and spectacle. *Avalanche*'s biased sponsorship of particular artists in both its editorial and advertising sections (today one is struck by the strict correlation between the artists featured in prominent ad space and a not insignificant portion of the editorial content) provoked accusations that the magazine was "clannish, in the editors' protection of too few reputations" and "more a part of the continuum of promotion than it is a critical journal," in the words of critic Lawrence Alloway.[42]

4.9

Bykert Gallery's "Stop the War" ad and *Avalanche*
table of contents, spread from *Avalanche*, no. 1, Fall
1970. Research Library, The Getty Research Institute,
Los Angeles (84-S1249).

AN ARTISTS' MAGAZINE

Avalanche

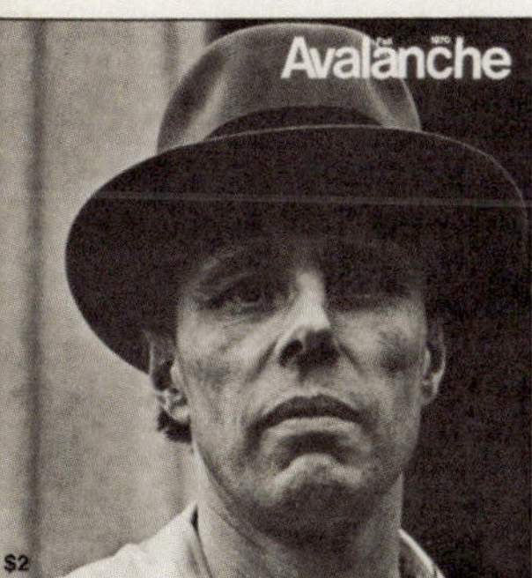

$2

Publisher: Willoughby Sharp
Editor: Elizabeth Béar
Designer: Boris Wall Gruphy
Photography: Shunk-Kender
Production: Richard Hogle
Circulation: Harold Klein

Photos: Adam Bartos **18-21**; Dirk Buwalde **14**; Richard Clark **50-52** bot., **60**; Pat Crowe **34, 40, 55, 59**; Robert Fiore **13, 15**bot. rt.; Terry Fox **11**; Andy Hardy **57**top & bot.; Mike Heizer **65, 68**bot., top & bot.; Barry Klinger **10, 16** top; Garry Krueger bot.; William C. Lipke **52-54** top; Peter Moore **17**; Dennis Oppenheim **51** top, **56** top & bot., **57**, **70-71**; Nathan Rabin **5** top; Shunk-Kender **4, 68**; Seth Siegelaub **22-23, 25**; John Weber **6, 48-49**

Courtesy: Andrew Dickson White Museum of Art, Cornell Univ., Ithaca, N.Y. **40, 51-55, 58-59, 62**; Oliver Andrews **2**; Keith Arnatt **3**; Luis Fernand Bene- **4** bot.; Bykert Gallery, N.Y. **5** top; Leo Castelli Gallery, N.Y. **15** bot.; It, **17** top; Jan Dibbets **34-39**; Dwan Gallery, N.Y. **6, 18-21, 44, 48, 60-61, 64-65**; Dwan Gallery, N.Y. **5** bot.; John Gibson **15** bot., **27, 43** bot., **51** top, **56-57, 70**; Mike Heizer **68-69**; Jewish Museum, N.Y. **8, 9** bot., **17**; Richard Long **42** & bot., **43** top, **45-47**; Bruce McLean **14**; Allan Kopersberg **7** bot.; Larry Smith **16**; Robert Smithson; William Wegman **9** top, **15** top.

Avalanche is published quarterly by Kineticism Press, 10 Park Avenue, Room 303 South, New York, N.Y. 10017. Editorial office: 204 East 20th St., N.Y.C. 10003. 674-5430. © 1970 Kineticism Press. All rights reserved. U.S. subscriptions $7 a year. Foreign subscriptions $9. Printed by Miller Printing & Litho Corp., 121 West 19th St., N.Y. 10011. U.S. national newsstand distribution by Eastern News Distributors, Inc., 155 West 15th St., New York, N.Y. 10011.

Fall 1970

Number One

Contents

1

However, while the benefits of the art world's information systems typically accrued to those at the top of pecking order, *Avalanche* worked to the artists' advantage. Indeed, the magazine inverted the typical relationship between advertising and editorial space. Instead of advertising dictating editorial content, the reverse was true: according to Béar, "our practice was to decide on the artist first then go after the ads, not the other way around." [43] Advertising space was also used for purposes other than promotion. For example, when the Guggenheim Museum censored Buren's work in 1971, *Avalanche* ran a full-page advertisement, courtesy of the German dealer Konrad Fischer, broadcasting the scandal (Winter 1971). In other instances, ad space was used for antiwar statements or was even left blank, paid for by galleries that wished to support the magazine without endorsing particular artists. In its unabashed and tactical use of publicity, *Avalanche* perspicaciously anticipated critical media practices of the 1980s and 1990s.

Instead of exhibition reviews, *Avalanche* published a section called "Rumbles," a communiqué from the frontlines of the art world to keep readers posted on performances, Happenings, exhibitions, openings, readings, and screenings. Compiled by the editors from correspondence they received from artists around the world, the "Rumbles" section provided invaluable eyewitness accounts of such goings-on through vignettes and newsflashes. "For his first New York show, San Francisco artist Terry Fox performed a 30 minute piece in a dilapidated part of Reese Palley's basement," read a dispatch in the inaugural issue. Other events reported in "Rumbles" included: "John Baldessari is burning all his paintings in a California crematorium" (Fall 1970); "William Wegman performed Three Speeds, Three Temperatures this May in the faculty men's room at the University of Wisconsin, Madison" (Fall 1970); and "the preliminary draft of an Artist's Reserved Rights Sale Agreement, drawn up by Seth Siegelaub … has been submitted to some five hundred people in the international art community for their approval" (Winter 1971).

Gossip and anecdotes of a more personal nature were printed in a section called "Messages," a kind of community newsletter where one could read such riveting facts as "Richard Long passed an afternoon watching hippopotami at the Central Park Zoo. … Gordon Matta served a bone dinner at Food on Sunday February 20. … Terry Fox has had his sternum removed" (Spring 1972). On a more sober note, issue 8 (Summer/Fall 1973) included news of Robert Smithson's accidental death in a plane crash as well as the birth of Food cofounder Rachel Lew's twins (complete with pictures of the newborn infants and information about their breastfeeding). The inclusion of such information gives a decidedly local and personal tenor to *Avalanche*'s mode of address. It presumes a level of familiarity, even intimacy, with and among its readers and the artists it covered.

The publicity generated by *Avalanche* benefited not only the artists it promoted but also the new galleries and alternative spaces that had begun cropping up in SoHo: 112 Greene Street and Paula Cooper were soon joined by Holly Solomon's 98 Greene Street Loft and the cluster of commercial galleries at 420 Broadway, including the new downtown branches of Dwan, the John Weber Gallery, Castelli, Sonnabend, and John Gibson. The *Avalanche* ads, many of which were designed by Sharp and Béar, did more than promote the art shown in these galleries; they also conveyed the distinct spatial and social character of the emerging downtown gallery scene. While ads in mainstream art magazines were timed to correspond to the rotation of gallery shows—which corresponded roughly to the magazines' own periodicity—*Avalanche*'s erratic publication schedule precluded such synchronization.[44] Though some *Avalanche* ads do announce specific shows or feature the work of particular artists, many instead emphasize the gallery itself, either by listing its entire stable of artists or by referencing its distinct architectural setting and location in SoHo through images of gallery interiors and storefront exteriors, street addresses, and floor plans.

Avalanche also advertised watering holes like Max's Kansas City; Fanelli's, an Italian working-class bar where artists would gather after openings; and Food, the cooperative eatery founded by artists Caroline Goodden, Tina Girouard, Suzanne Harris, Matta-Clark, and Lew. The latter establishment was especially significant for the downtown art community. Opening its doors in September 1971 (an event chronicled in the "Rumbles" section of the Fall 1971 issue of *Avalanche*), Food functioned as an important site of both social and artistic activity.[45] Artists served as guest chefs in a series of Sunday night dinners; one such dish—a concoction by Matta-Clark—featured a hard-boiled egg filled with live brine shrimp. Food regularly advertised in *Avalanche*, fortuitously leaving a record of its importance within the downtown art scene, while also suggesting the magazine's own role in this social context. The first ad for Food, published in Fall 1971, consists of a photograph taken before the place was fully renovated, with the sign still showing the name of its former occupant, a Creole eatery called Doris' Restaurant, with "FOOD" written in Magic Marker over it, suggesting the palimpsest quality of the urban neighborhood, as its original signs and placards were replaced with new ones. In a subsequent advertisement, "Food Fiscal Facts" are listed, including quantities of various goods—"tons of various flours used for bread: 4½," "oranges squeezed: 16,000"—but also "dogs asked to leave: 47," "rebellions: 2," "notices taped to windows: 1,175," "percentage of workers who are artists: 84%," and "free dinners given: 3,072." Later ads grow even more cryptic and amusing: a photograph of a dog sniffing at a plate filled with pills; or a bunch of cabbage leaves, with the phrase "Love Among the Cabbages," referring to a 1972 essay by Peter Tompkins and Christopher Bird which details the emotional and spiritual life of plants—an essay that fueled the ecology movement. The final ad, in the Spring 1973 issue, just before Food's ownership changed hands, shows the street corner at which Food was located, with the restaurant's simple banner and the signs for Wooster and Prince streets, as if the restaurant were somehow synonymous with this intersection itself, defined by this spot on the urban grid.

How we read *Avalanche*'s significance today comes back to historical context—specifically, the milieu of the alternative art community in SoHo. "This was the epoch of retail-free bliss," Béar recalls. "There was as yet no art scene as such for the public."[46] Part of what *Avalanche* did was to create this scene, to shape the character of the emerging art public as it metamorphosed from a loosely affiliated group of like-minded individuals into a thriving artistic community (which, as we know, would eventually evolve into a highly commercialized gallery scene). *Avalanche* not only witnessed the accumulation of value by both the art and the spaces in which it was shown in SoHo but was also a part of that escalation. Ultimately, this transformation eroded the very public sphere the magazine's editors had sought to cultivate, and artists soon began to imagine alternative scenarios for maintaining that sphere's viability.

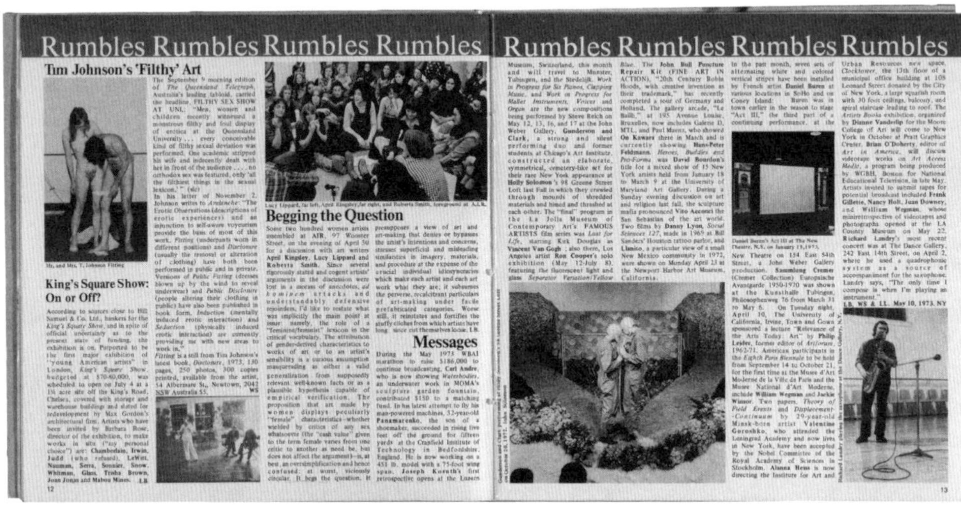

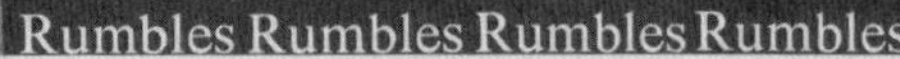

Tim Johnson's 'Filthy' Art

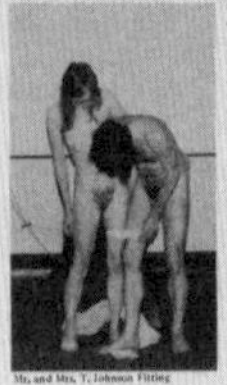

Mr. and Mrs. T. Johnson Fitting

The September 6 morning edition of *The Queensland Telegraph*, Australia's leading tabloid, carried the headline, FILTHY SEX SHOW AT UNI. "Men, women and children meanly witnessed a monstrous filthy and foul display of erotics at the Queensland University ... every conceivable kind of filthy sexual deviation was performed. One academic stripped his wife and indecently dealt with her in front of the audience ... no orthodox sex was featured, only 'all the filthiest things in the sexual lexicon.'" (sic)

In his letter of November 2, Johnson writes to *Avalanche*: "The Erotic Observations (descriptions of erotic experiences) and an injunction to self-aware voyeurism provide the focus of most of this work. Fitting (underpants worn in different positions) and *Dictionare* (usually the removal or alteration of clothing) have both been performed in public and in private. Versions of *Public Fitting* (dresses blown up by the wind to reveal underwear) and *Public Dictionare* (people altering their clothing in public) have also been published in book form. *Induction* (mentally induced erotic interaction) and *Seduction* (physically induced erotic interaction) are currently providing me with new areas to work in.

Fitting is a still from Tim Johnson's latest book, *Dictionare*, 1972, 130 pages, 250 photos, 300 copies printed, available from the artist, 54 Albermare St., Newtown, 2042 NSW Australia $5.

— WS

King's Square Show: On or Off?

According to sources close to Hill Samuel & Co. Ltd., bankers for the *King's Square Show*, and in spite of official uncertainty as to the present state of funding, the exhibition is on. Purported to be the first major exhibition of "young American artists" in London, *King's Square Show*, budgeted at $70–80,000, was scheduled to open on July 4 at a 1¾ acre site off the King's Road, Chelsea, crowded with storage and warehouse buildings and slated for redevelopment by Max Gordon's architectural firm. Artists who have been invited by Barbara Rose, director of the exhibition, to make works in situ ("my personal choice") are: Chamberlain, Irwin, Judd (who refused), LeWitt, Nauman, Serra, Sonnier, Snow, Whitman, Glass, Trisha Brown, Joan Jonas and Mabou Mines.

— J.B.

Begging the Question

Some two hundred women artists assembled at A.I.R., 97 Wooster Street, on the evening of April 30 for a discussion with art writers April Kingsley, Lucy Lippard and Roberta Smith. Since several rigorously stated and cogent artists' arguments in the discussion were lost in a morass of anecdotes, *ad hominem* attacks and understandably defensive rejoinders, I'd like to restate what was implicitly the main point at issue: namely, the role of a "feminine/feminist" lexicon in the critical vocabulary. The attribution of gender-defined characteristics to works of art or to an artist's sensibility is a curious assumption masquerading as either a valid generalization from supposedly relevant well-known facts or as a plausible hypothesis capable of empirical verification. The proposition that art made by women displays peculiarly "female" characteristics—whether wielded by critics of any sex, whatever [the] "cash value" given to the term female varies from one critic to another as need be, but does not affect the argument's—is, at best, an oversimplification and at worst, viciously circular. It begs the question. It presupposes a view of art and art-making that denies or bypasses the artist's intentions and concerns, stresses superficial and misleading similarities in imagery, materials, and procedure at the expense of the crucial individual idiosyncracies which make each artist and each art work what they are; it subsumes the perverse, recalcitrant particulars of art-making under facile prefabricated categories. Worse still, it reinstates and fortifies the stuffy clichés from which artists have long since cut themselves loose.

— L.B.

Messages

During the May 1973 WBAI marathon to raise $186,000 to continue broadcasting, Carl Andre, who is now showing *Waterholes*, an underwater work in MOMA's sculpture garden fountain, contributed $150 to a matching fund. In his latest attempt to fly his man-powered machines, 32-year-old Panamarenko, the son of a shoemaker, succeeded in rising five feet off the ground for fifteen yards at the Cranfield Institute of Technology in Bedfordshire, England. He is now working on a 451 lb. model with a 75-foot wing span. Joseph Kosuth's first retrospective opens at the Lucerne

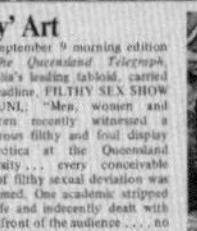

Lucy Lippard, far left, April Kingsley far right, and Roberta Smith, foreground at A.I.R.

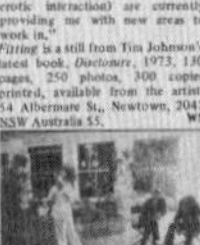

Gugelmeni and Clark, performance at Friday somewhere's via Valerani Street Loft on October 26, 1972. John Solomon

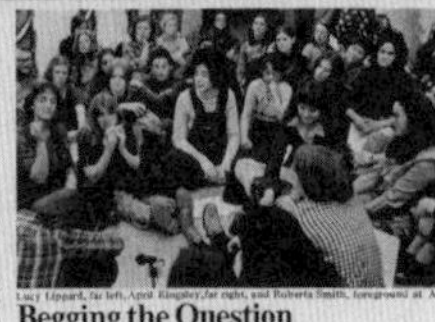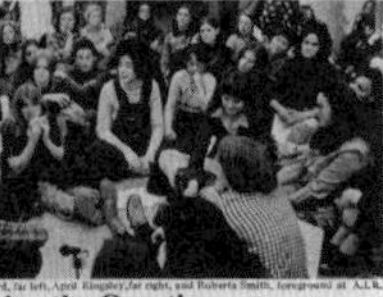

Museum, Switzerland, this month and will travel to Munster, Tubingen, and the Stedelijk. *Work in Progress for Six Pianos*, *Clapping Music*, and *Work in Progress for Mallet Instruments, Voices and Organ* are the new compositions being performed by Steve Reich on May 12, 13, 16, and 17 at the John Weber Gallery. Gunderson and Clark, a strong and former students of Chicago's Art Institute, constructed an elaborate symmetrical, ornamentry-like set for their rare New York appearance at Holly Solomon's 98 Greene Street Loft last Fall in which they crawled through mounds of shredded materials and hissed and thrashed at each other. The "final" program in the La Jolla Museum of Contemporary Art's FAMOUS ARTISTS film series was *Lust for Life*, starring Kirk Douglas as Vincent Van Gogh; also there, Los Angeles artist Ron Cooper's solo exhibition (May 12–July 8), featuring the fluorescent light and glass *Separator Variation/Yellow Blue*. The John Bull Puncture Repair Kit (FINE ART IN ACTION), "20th Century Robin Hoods, with creative invention as their trademark," has recently completed a tour of Germany and Holland. The gallery arcade, "Le Batik," at 195 Avenue Louise, Bruxelles, now includes Galerie D, MTL, and Paul Maenz, who showed On Kawara three in March and is currently showing Hans-Peter Feldmann. *Heroes, Buddies and Pro-Forma* was David Bourdon's title for a mixed show of 15 New York artists held from January 18 to March 9 at the University of Maryland Art Gallery. During a Sunday evening discussion on art and religion last fall, the sculpture mafia pronounced Vito Acconci the San Sebastian of the art world. Two films by Danny Lyon, *Social Sciences 127*, made in 1969 at Bill Sanders' Houston tattoo parlor, and *Llanito*, a particular view of a small New Mexico community in 1972, were shown on Monday April 23 at the Newport Harbor Art Museum, California.

In the past month, seven sets of alternating white and colored vertical stripes have been installed by French artist Daniel Buren at various locations in SoHo and on Coney Island; Buren was in town earlier in the season to stage "Act III," the third part of a continuing performance, at the

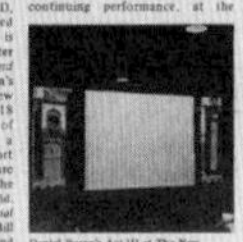

Daniel Buren's Act III at The New Theatre, N.Y. on January 13, 1973.

New Theatre on 154 East 54th Street, a John Weber Gallery production. Sammlung Cremer (Cremer Collection) Europäische Avantgarde 1950–1970 was shown at the Kunsthalle Tubingen, Philosophenweg 76 from March 31 to May 6. On Tuesday night, April 10, The University of California, Irvine, Town and Gown sponsored a lecture "Relevance of the Arts Today: Art" by Philip Leider, former editor of *Artforum*, 1962–71. American participants in the *Eighth Paris Biennale* to be held from September 14 to October 21, for the first time at the Musee d'Art Moderne de la Ville de Paris and the Musee National d'Art Moderne, include William Wegman and Jackie Winsor. Two papers, *Theory of Field Events* and *Displacement-Continuum* by 29-year-old Minsk-born artist Valentine Goroshko, who attended the Leningrad Academy and now lives in New York, have been accepted by the Nobel Committee of the Royal Academy of Sciences in Stockholm. Alessio Benn is now directing the Institute for Art and Urban Resources' new space, *Clocktower*, the 13th floor of a municipal office building at 108 Leonard Street donated by the City of New York, a large squarish room with 30 foot ceilings, balcony, and spiral staircase leading to roof. The *Artists Books* exhibition, organized by Dianne Vanderlip for the Moore College of Art will come to New York in October at Pratt Graphics Center. Brian O'Doherty, editor of *Art in America*, will discuss videotape works on *Art Across Media*, a program being produced by WGBH, Boston for National Educational Television, in late May. Artists invited to submit tapes for potential broadcast included Frank Gillette, Nancy Holt, Juan Downey, and William Wegman, whose miniretrospective of videotapes and photographs opened at the LA County Museum on May 22. Richard Landry's most recent concert was at The Dance Gallery, 242 East 14th Street, on April 2, where he used a quadrophonic system as a source of accompaniment for the saxophone. Landry says, "The only time I compose is when I'm playing the instrument."

— J.B., WS & LL. May 10, 1973. NY

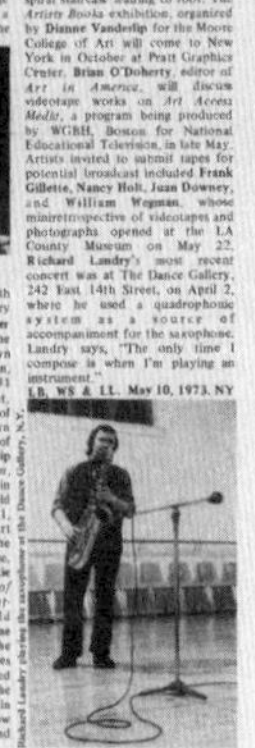

12   13

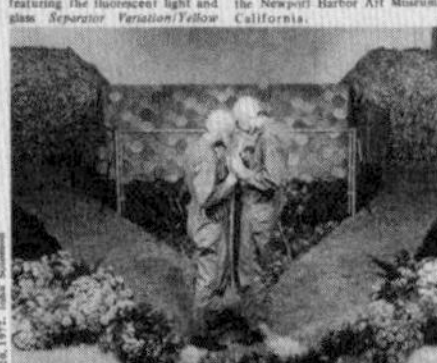

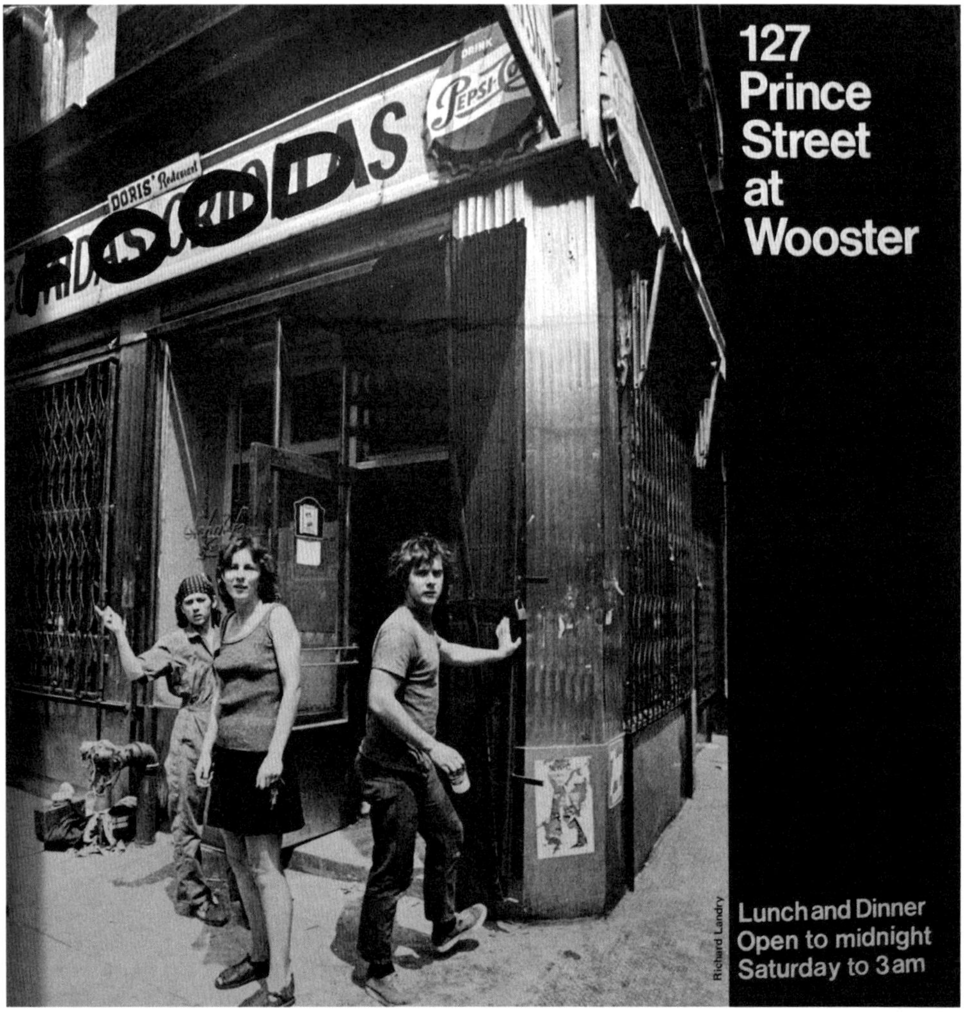

The effects of such processes—indeed, their intensification—are evident today: 93 Grand Street, the site of the original *Avalanche* workplace, is now a fashion boutique, its unfinished concrete floors both referencing the original use of the space and suggesting the fetishization of "process" as mere style. Yet the disappearance of *Avalanche* magazine—its own ephemerality— amounts to a kind of resistance to such conditions as well. With no major corporate sponsorship, *Avalanche* was supported solely by subscriptions, advertisements, public and private grants, and, not least, the intellectual labor of its editors and artists. The last issue, published in 1976, showed on its cover the financial ledger for the magazine, revealing its precarious fiscal straits—a situation cleverly reinforced by the visual pun of the magazine's title, printed in bright red. (Sharp also acknowledged that the winds of the art world were already starting to shift in a different direction— toward neo-expressionist painting—and, as he put it, he was no longer "with the art.")[47] The final cover image suggests that *Avalanche* quite literally refused to profit from its engagement with the artists it revered. Then, as if mimicking much of the art it had championed for the past six years, the magazine silently faded out of existence.[48]

4.10

"Rumbles" section. *Avalanche*, no. 7, Winter/Spring 1973. Research Library, The Getty Research Institute, Los Angeles (84-S1249).

4.11

Ad for Food restaurant, *Avalanche*, no. 3, Fall 1971. Courtesy of Liza Béar.

Avalanche

TRIAL BALANCE

Acct #	DESCRIPTION	1976 JAN	1976 FEB	1976 MAR	1976 APR	1976 MAY	1976 JUN
100	Revenue, total recorded & adjusted	1548 50	1031 15	667 =	1268 50	1170 30	1649 =
200	General factotum [suspense account]	11 64	136 89	-149 83	67 53	3 01	5 97
300	New subscriptions & renewals, individuals & institutions	158 =	288 =	210 =	135 50	62 =	128 =
301	Back issues, magazine & tabloid, nos 2 → 19	352 50	278 25	73 50	177 =	33 50	80 =
302	Newsstands & bookstores, in and out of town	133 =	115 30	208 50	17 =	12 =	48 =
303	Advertising, full, half & quarter page	350 =	—	75 =	589 =	450 =	1135 =
304	State funds: NYSCA						
305	Federal funds						
306	Contributions						
	Expenses, total	1635 34	820 =	731 38	1185 =	1199 25	1504 65
201	Chief consultant	103 91	220 =	267 =	—	25 =	143 =
400	Printing: negatives, stripping, plates, paper & press time	300 =	—	—	100 =	—	—
401	Typesetting: body copy, subheads & heads	12 =	—	—	—	55 02	304 08
402	Layout & paste-up				12 =		93 =
403	Photography					12 =	44 50
404	Audiotape & video		450	32 94	19 =	1 17	20 15
500	Fees for correspondence & transcribing	110 91	60 =	80 =	25 =	20 =	
501	Telephone contact	133 13		88 =		269 69	
502	Rent for ground floor & basement	300 =	350 =		400 =		100 =
503	Postage & shipping	64 45	13 06	12 54	58 71	65 75	13 18
504	Stationery & supplies	32 28	7 72		20 87	18 51	40 29
505	Xerox			4 =	8 03	3 85	4 =
506	Travel		1 =		25 42		8 50
507	Maintenance	35 =	9 01	16 18	100 =	24 50	3 78
508	Miscellaneous				25 =		

© WILSON JONES COMPANY   G7506 GREEN   PAT. APPL. FOR   G7506C COVERLESS   MADE IN U.S.A.

AN ARTISTS' MAGAZINE

4.12

Liza Béar, *Trial Balance*, cover of *Avalanche*, no. 13,
Summer 1976. Courtesy of Liza Béar.

5

THE MAGAZINE AS AN ALTERNATIVE SPACE

ART-RITE, 1973–1978

"Things are possible when you're young," Walter Robinson mused, thinking back on how he, Edit deAk, and Joshua Cohn—three recent college graduates with no previous publishing experience—founded *Art-Rite* magazine in 1973.[1] Reveling in its own disposability and its homespun, zine-like format, *Art-Rite* forged an iconoclastic, experimental style of criticism, focusing on younger, lesser-known artists in SoHo, whom the editors encouraged to write for the magazine and to use it as a medium. As implied by its title, *Art-Rite* sought to create a kind of criticism that would be, like the bargain products in a dime store, accessible and unpretentious. The magazine had a quaint, artless quality with its half-tabloid newsprint pages, hand-stenciled logo, and do-it-yourself layout. As the editors confided in the eighth issue: "I got the media coming out of my typewriter. It is a very special media, though. It is small and free and designed to look insignificant and void of the sixties ego tripping."[2]

Art-Rite's humble format and unassuming tone and temperament could not have been further from the coated, full-bleed pages and cinematic layout of *Avalanche*. The latter, though initially founded to champion the new alternative artistic practices emerging in the then-uncharted enclave of downtown Manhattan, had come within a few short years to represent its own brand of exclusivity within the up-and-coming SoHo art scene, as the neighborhood morphed from a marginal outpost of the art world into the new hot spot. Indeed, Stephanie Edens, writing in *Art-Rite*, described the groundbreaking cooperative gallery space 112 Greene Street, as "'sceney,' hard to get into, subsumed by an ingrouped clubiness," and observed that it "now attracts the kind of rad-chic audience it once repelled."[3] *Art-Rite*'s unostentatious, low-key bearing was more compatible with the egalitarian and inclusive attitude of a new crop of nonprofit, artist-run galleries that would become known as alternative spaces. One example of the new type of alternative space was Artists Space, described by Edens a few issues later as "[rising] above the promotional excitement which sells art in the commercial gallery while it also avoids the cliquishness which leaves us on the outside of some SoHo Cooperative spaces."[4]

By the time *Art-Rite* began, the salad days of conceptual art had begun to wane. In retrospect, the utopian claims surrounding art of the late 1960s seemed wide-eyed and idealistic—even to those who had initially espoused them. Whereas, in 1968, Lucy Lippard had hailed dematerialization as a strategy through which art might escape the gallery and market, five years later she was considerably more skeptical, writing, in her 1973 book *Six Years: The Dematerialization of the Art Object from 1966 to 1972*:

> Hopes that "conceptual art" would be able to avoid the general commercialization, the destructively "progressive" approach of modernism were for the most part unfounded. It seemed in 1969 …
> that no one, not even a public greedy for novelty would actually pay money, or much of it, for a Xerox sheet referring to an event past or never directly perceived, a group of photographs documenting

And yet, during the 1970s, the hopes of art of the 1960s were not abandoned altogether, so much as they were toned down and tethered to a new set of practical concerns, evident in the numerous alternative spaces and collectives that emerged during this decade.[6] As Brian O'Doherty, an important theorist and proponent of the alternative space (often credited with coining the term itself), stated, "A lot of the radical energies of the '60s fed into alternative spaces. They were started by people who asked a lot of questions in the '60s and are answering them in the '70s."[7] The rise of alternative spaces was encouraged by the new availability of public funding, which O'Doherty, as director of the National Endowment for the Arts' visual arts program from 1969 to 1976, was instrumental in allocating.[8] Relieved of the need to sell art, alternative spaces could afford to be experimental and open-ended in their programming, prioritizing the needs of artists over those of dealers and curators. They not only fostered experimental art, but supported the ideological and practical goals of political activism within the art world and promoted artists' moral and legal rights. As O'Doherty observed: "The artist-generated institution for making or showing work may be the single most important development of the seventies. Significantly, it is a social rather than an esthetic one."[9]

As artist-run cooperative galleries and collectives proliferated throughout North America during this period, artists' magazines complemented and reinforced their aesthetic and ideological goals, providing important discursive spaces within which art and art criticism opposed the values of the mainstream art world and commercial art press. As *Art-Rite*'s editors explained, "The editor of an establishment magazine confessed that 'vital aspects of present day art are not included in his pages simply because the commercial interests which persist in dominating the communication outlets, on every level, ensure that much relevant art activity fails to surface.' This indicates the raison d' être of the alternative periodicals vis-à-vis the '70s art superstructure."[10] Artists' magazines played a significant—yet often overlooked—role in supporting alternative spaces, by both providing crucial publicity for their cutting-edge exhibitions (which received scant attention in the mainstream art press) and bolstering their institutional objectives by promoting artists' rights. *Art-Rite*, along with countless other alternative artists' periodicals, functioned alongside bricks-and-mortar gallery spaces to challenge the social and economic exclusivity of the mainstream art world and to forge new artistic identities and criteria—a struggle that was especially crucial for artists confronting the racist and sexist institutions of the art world during this period.

In her 1977 article "Alternative Space: Artists' Periodicals," Howardena Pindell claimed that artists' magazine should be considered alternative spaces in their own right. While Pindell's article provided a historical overview and chronology of artists' periodicals since 1900, her use of the term "alternative space" clearly referenced the politicized, countercultural sense of this concept as it had evolved within the North American alternative space movement of the 1970s. Working as an assistant curator in the Museum of Modern Art library, Pindell was interested in the periodical as an alternative space not only as a scholar but as an artist and activist. A founding member of the AIR Gallery, the first nonprofit space dedicated to women artists, Pindell had witnessed firsthand the potential of alternative spaces to counter the social inequities of the mainstream art world, remembering, "At the time I was fighting against the art world as being both male and white-dominated."[11] Artists' periodicals, she observed, were crucial to this struggle, providing "a means for the artist to put him- or herself directly into art history without the aid of the critic or dealer or curator as mediator—an alternative space."[12]

BABY BLOOD

It was in O'Doherty's seminar on art criticism that deAk, Robinson, and Cohn first met, during the spring of their senior year at Columbia University. O'Doherty was an important mentor for *Art-Rite*, providing advice and various kinds of practical and editorial assistance for the fledgling publication. (His name even appears on the masthead of the first issue, though it is crossed out because he insisted that his young protégés take full credit for the new publication.) O'Doherty's role in *Art-Rite*'s beginnings is significant, suggesting that the publication inherited and furthered his efforts to create alternative structures within the art world—efforts that in many ways began with *Aspen* 5+6, discussed in chapter 2. O'Doherty had gone on to become editor in chief of *Art in America* in 1970, a post he held until 1974. Seeking to reinvigorate that magazine, he invited Cohn and Robinson to write reviews, prompting deAk to remark, "We realized that criticism must be in horrible shape if they're so hungry for baby blood, right?"[13] (The three even considered calling their magazine "Baby Blood.") One of the original ideas for *Art-Rite* was to produce the magazine as a newsprint insert in *Art in America*—a kind of Trojan horse that would smuggle alternative ideas into the bastions of the mainstream art press. This history testifies to the complicated relationship between mainstream and alternative institutions at this time—one of interdependence and mutual fascination as well as opposition. Ultimately, *Art-Rite*'s editors chose autonomy, recalling, "Of course, when we realized what we were doing, we had no need to be in *Art in America*. ... We wanted our own little rag, no matter how ugly or cheap-o or shitty it was gonna be."[14]

After graduating from college, the three editors enrolled in the Whitney Independent Study Program—an institutional affiliation that they exploited as they laid the foundations for the new magazine, approaching critics, artists, and gallery owners for support and advice, and asking fellow students to contribute articles. The first issue of *Art-Rite* was published in the spring of 1973. A mere eight pages long—so insubstantial as to be practically a flyer—this first issue consisted of one thousand copies printed for $100 and "distributed haphazardly through the galleries."[15] For the first cover, the editors tapped Les Levine, whose own magazine, *Culture Hero*, a gossipy, satirical tabloid that covered the downtown art scene, served as an inspiration for *Art-Rite*. Levine provided a droll, stream-of-consciousness text/image piece in which he recounts finding a little gold smile on the floor—a story that captured the whimsical, self-effacing character of the magazine itself.

ART–RITE

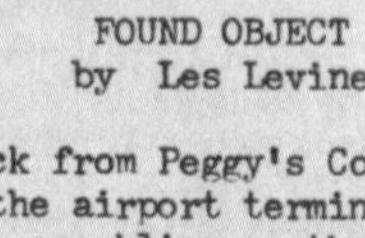

FOUND OBJECT
by Les Levine

On my way back from Peggy's Cove as I was
walking out the airport terminal door, I saw
a tiny object sparkling on the floor. I
have always believed that it is lucky to find
things so I bent down and picked it up. It
was a little gold smile. I inspected it. I
couldn't tell whether it was a tie pin or an
earring. On the back of it, it had stamped
the words: 14-K gold filled. So I put it in
my pocket and I began to think -- found
object, but you can't make a found object.
Marcel Duchamp has made that, but I do not
go around trying to find objects. I just
found this object and it was like finding a
smile. Duchamp went around finding objects
and he didn't find every object. He selected
objects so maybe they should have been called
"connoisseured objects." I didn't connoisseur this object. I just found it and I
wasn't trying to find it. And then I thought
what if my mother had called me Marcel. That
would make me Marcel Levine. But my mother
was a hairdresser so she probably would have
called me Marcel Wave. But her sense of humor
wasn't like that. One day my mother met my
Aunt Katie in downtown Dublin. And my Aunt
Katie said to my mother, "Nelly buried her
husband last week." And my mother answered,
"Well, of course, you have to once they're
dead. It's the law." And when I told someone about my mother's joke they said she must
have read James Joyce, but they were wrong.
James Joyce had listened to my mother. And
then I thought there's an artist named Jack
Levine and there's a film producer named
Joseph E. Levine and I have made a few films
myself. And then I finally thought being
born is not too original. It happens to the
best and worst of us.

THE MAGAZINE AS AN ALTERNATIVE SPACE

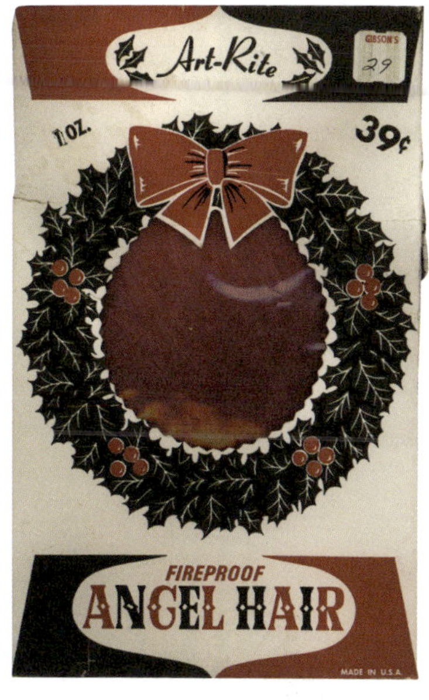

5.1

Les Levine, cover, *Art-Rite*, no. 1, April 1973.
Courtesy of the editors and the artist. Collection
of Steven Leiber, San Francisco.

5.2

Art-Rite corporation's angel hair package.

It has been suggested that the magazine may have taken its title from the Art-Rite corporation, which manufactured Christmas decorations, including an iridescent tinsel-like substance made of spun glass called angel hair that was popular in the 1950s. Another possible allusion is to an important little magazine and press: Anne Waldman and Lewis Marsh's *Angel Hair*.[16] In addition to its homophonic pun, *Art-Rite*'s potential association with the Christmas decoration manufacturer sheds light on the magazine's kitschy, nostalgic quality, and its fanciful, festive attitude. *Art-Rite* signaled a new self-consciousness about the magazine's status as a cheap, accessible medium, simultaneously hyperbolizing and ironizing conceptual art's utopian claims. In particular, the magazine's editors embraced the paradox of its commodified format, emphasizing its status as a mass-produced consumer product (like Warhol's Fab issue of *Aspen*), while simultaneously mobilizing this fact to redouble their efforts to deprivilege and democratize the experience of art.[17]

Early issues reveal how green the editors were. Their novice status led to some rather cringe-worthy faux pas. "I've really enjoyed both issues and think they're too cute for words. … I'd just like to point out that the critic I *think* we both have in mind is Clement Green*berg* not this mysterious anonimo Greenburg you keep talking about," Linda Nochlin wrote in a letter to the editor, published in the third issue.[18] While it was true that *Art-Rite*'s editors were literally young and inexperienced, their physical age was less important than the way in which they self-consciously staged these facts to signify their antiestablishment attitude toward the mainstream art world. As they explained, "Power trips were eliminated automatically by the nature of the givens: Our not knowing enough, being … unreliable, vocational (rather than professional) and having been motivated by belief—which is really quite different from power, mutually exclusive, really."[19] As Lippard vouched for the magazine in a grant application, "all the risks larger institutions don't and can't take, *Art-Rite* can and does."[20]

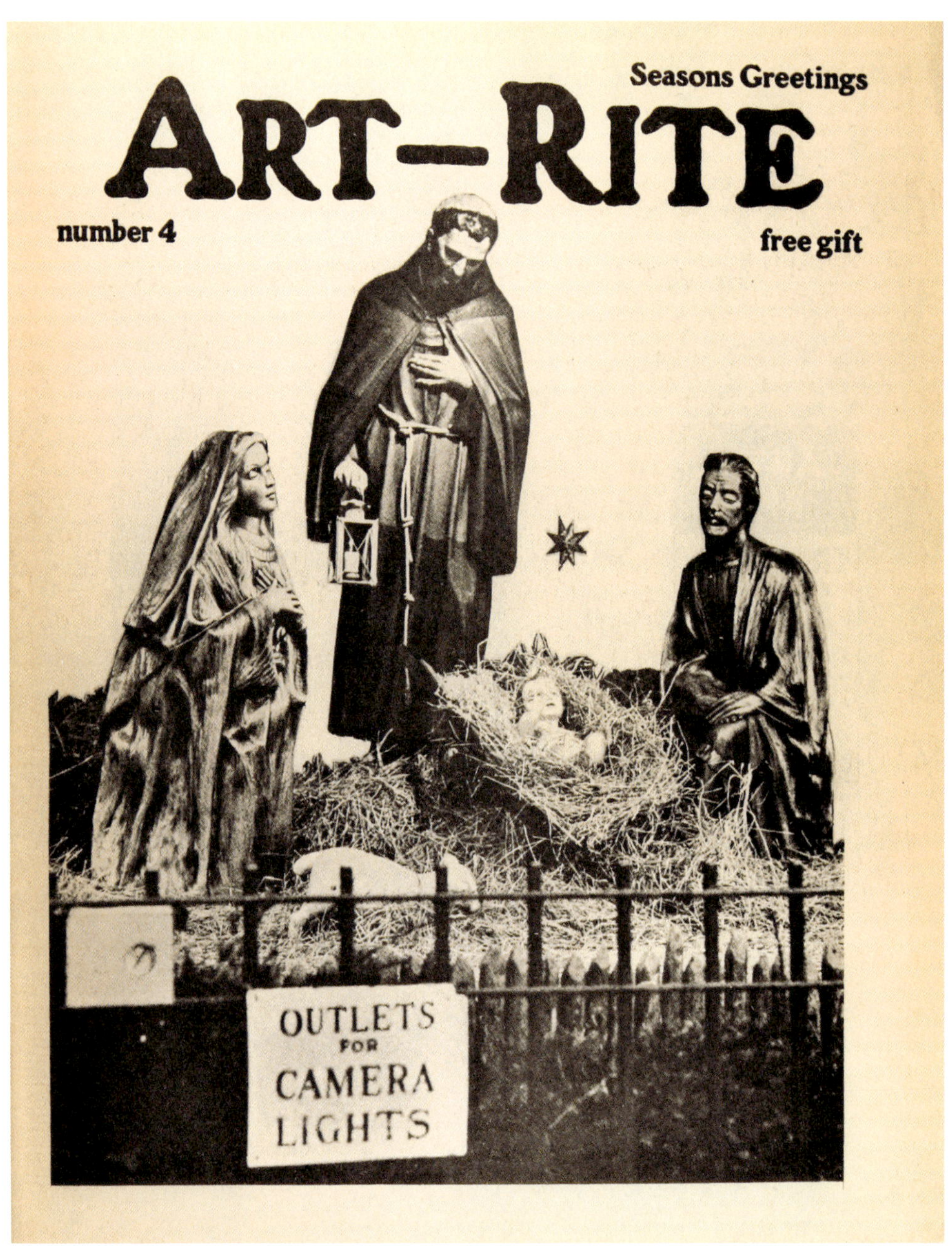

5.3
Yuri, cover, *Art-Rite*, no. 4, 1973. Courtesy of the
editors. Collection of Steven Leiber, San Francisco.

  THE MAGAZINE AS AN ALTERNATIVE SPACE

It was deAk, who had emigrated from Hungary when she was a teenager, crossing the border in the trunk of a car, who supplied much of the oomph for the new magazine. "She had all the ideas. She had all the drive," Robinson recalled of deAk, who would make phone calls to artists and critics, refusing to be intimidated by their stature relative to hers, and boldly walk into galleries to sell ads.[21] "It was about inventing possibilities for herself, I think," he reckoned.[22] The *Art-Rite* editors set up their headquarters in deAk's downtown loft at 149 Wooster Street, just down the block from Artists Space, and in the heart of SoHo's burgeoning new alternative gallery scene. A huge space with a darkroom in the back, the loft was the site of all-night writing sessions, wild dinner parties, and a rotating troupe of out-of-town guests. Because they could not afford to pay contributors very much, the editors tried to compensate with hospitality, offering to put them up, feed them dinner, and introduce them to other writers and artists. "A lot of our writers are first time writers who are trying to open doors for themselves. We do make sure that if we can do something for them we do," deAk explained.[23]

Discussing the collaborative nature of the publication, deAk observed, "We work closely together, put our minds all in one pot and stir it until it gets done."[24] Accordingly, many articles were unsigned or bylined "A-R." Robinson, who had a day job working at *Jewish Week*, an independent community newspaper, covertly used the facilities to do the layout and typesetting for *Art-Rite* (until he was fired for doing so). DeAk's husband at the time, the artist Peter Grass, did photography for the magazine, along with her cousin Yuri. As deAk observed of the magazine's do-it-yourself spirit, "You can dream for a while and write, and be psychologists for a while and edit other people's work … then you get down to manual labor. Then you become delivery boys and mailmen."[25] Producing the magazine became enmeshed also in the emotional complications of life and relationships; at various points both Cohn and Robinson were romantically involved with deAK, culminating in a fistfight between the two men that precipitated Cohn's departure from the publication in 1975.[26]

While *Art-Rite* underscored the magazine's commodified, mechanically reproduced status as an egalitarian form of distribution, it paradoxically affirmed the experience of the handcrafted. For example, issue 6 featured a hand-folded cover designed by Dorothea Rockburne; and issue 8, designed by Pat Steir, was decorated with potato-prints of cheerful flowers in primary colors, which the editors painstakingly hand-stamped on all six thousand copies. These vivid unexpected glimpses of the handmade gave the magazine an intimate quality that was in contrast to the standardized impersonal character of mainstream media. The editors cultivated a friendly, familiar tone, addressing their readers with affectionate salutations and expressions such as "you're the greatest"[27]—an attitude that also defined the circulation and distribution of the magazine, which was "given away in recognition of the community that nurtures it."[28] The fourth issue was even billed as a Christmas card—a "free gift" Season's Greetings issue (a possible allusion to the Art-Rite holiday decoration company) consisting entirely of pictures, with contributions by artists including Christo, Holt, and Matta-Clark.

Following the chaotic rhythms and distractions of its editors' hectic lives, *Art-Rite* was published irregularly, between four and nine issues per year, according to one subscription flyer. Some issues were published out of sequence, or not at all. The following apology was sent out with issue 17: "We know we are behind schedule—because of production snafus, money problems and other things. … If you have not received issue #16, our issue on art in Europe, it's because we haven't published it yet. It's taking longer than we planned to sink our claws into the entire continent!"[29] (The issue was never published.) *Art-Rite*'s idiosyncrasies distinguished it from the polished professionalism of trade journals, which, as deAk wrote, "come out on schedule with their well-directed art and their packaged glamour. They are rarely hot, rarely cold. They usually have no particular beauty other than the accepted norm; they rarely have charm, they rarely make mistakes."[30]

THE AESTHETICS AND POLITICS OF NEWSPRINT

When they got the first issue of *Art-Rite* back from the printer, the editors celebrated by lighting a cigar and gleefully tearing a copy in half—a sacrament to the magazine's disposability. "We wanted people to throw it away," deAk recalled. "We didn't want to contribute to raising the value of art. It wasn't made for collectors and galleries."[31] Unlike higher-quality papers, which are chemically processed to remove the lignon, a chemical compound naturally occurring in wood, newsprint still contains this organic substance, which causes the paper to deteriorate quickly when exposed to air and light, becoming discolored and brittle. Its high absorbency also means that reproductions are much coarser and cruder than those on coated papers. Speaking of the choice to print *Art-Rite* on newsprint, deAk stated, "For me it had a tremendously important aesthetic quality. I loved newsprint, I loved the look of it, the feel of it."[32]

Indeed, while *Art-Rite*'s half-tabloid format was certainly determined in part by economic necessity, the paper's impoverished appearance also carried important ideological connotations, signaling its affinity with the countercultural ethos of underground newspapers and flaunting its contrast with the spectacular visuality of the mainstream art press. The editors declared, "It is printed on newsprint in the belief that the low cost process will help deinstitutionalize and demystify the esoterica it contains"; they added that "coated stock is ecologically unsound for the mind as well as the earth."[33] As its name implies, newsprint has traditionally been used for only the most temporary of publications, such as newspapers, meant to last for a single day. This literal ephemerality dramatizes *Art-Rite*'s contingent nature as a document that sought to participate profoundly in the moment it recorded, by focusing on emerging art and artists. As the editors explained, "Where the commercial structure attempts to consolidate and codify, the alternatives try to accommodate; they deal with the live nerve endings of turmoil—with what is on the verge of formulation."[34]

Art-Rite characterized its editorial policy as "coverage of the uncovered"—a mandate it fulfilled with its "loft reviews," which promised to report on art before it had even left the studio.[35] Lippard compared the magazine to "off-off Broadway," observing that it "nurtures, encourages, and provokes the newest art and the youngest artists."[36] It revealed a predilection for eclectic, off-beat topics such as fashion, punk music, and knickknacks, and supported unknown and outsider artists, including the punk musician and artist Alan Suicide (a.k.a. Alan Vega), whose colorful kitschy arrangements of light bulbs at the gallery OK Harris were reviewed in the first issue, and Steve Hermedes, an eccentric autodidactic mailroom employee of Columbia University, who was proclaimed in issue 2 to be "an itinerant undeclared artist" who "lives his life to a personalized, original scheme which matches up integrally with conceptual art requirements."[37] Meanwhile,

THE MAGAZINE AS AN ALTERNATIVE SPACE

the magazine was not afraid to knock more established artists. A review in the first issue, entitled "Big Boys Downtown" (a pointedly gendered characterization that was not incidental), slammed new work by LeWitt, Bochner, and Judd, dubbing the artists "old masters of New Trends" and accusing them of pandering to the market by repeating the same "boring, frustrating, and useless" formulas that had gained them recognition the previous decade.[38] They reserved such venom for artists who had already achieved success: "because they were safe we couldn't hurt them and since we spent the rest of our life defending babies we had to attack someplace," deAk maintained, insisting, "the artists chosen for pole-axing … can't be hurt by it."[39]

Art-Rite promoted conceptual, antimarket artistic practices, hailing Douglas Huebler's tabloid-style book *Duration Piece #8* as "undoubtedly one of the masterpieces of the season, and not only because it costs $2.00."[40] Other artists who contributed to the magazine or were prominently featured in it were Yvonne Rainer, Gordon Matta-Clark, Vito Acconci, William Wegman, Alan Sondheim, Robert Morris, Chris Burden, Carl Andre, Adrian Piper, Philip Glass, Robin Winters, Richard Foreman, Laurie Anderson, Trisha Brown, Carolee Schneemann, Hannah Wilke, Lucinda Childs, Michelle Stuart, Charles Simmonds, Jack Smith, Joan Jonas, Nancy Holt, Eleanor Antin, and Rebecca Horn—a list that reveals, among other things, the prominence of women artists in *Art-Rite*'s pages, which is in striking contrast to their marginalization within the mainstream art world at the time. The magazine candidly drew attention to feminist art with a poll titled "Unskirting the Issue" (issue 5, Spring 1974), consisting of responses by several women artists to the question: "Do you think there is a shared female artistic sensibility in the work of female artists?" *Art-Rite* was also supportive of new media, publishing special issues on video (issue 7, guest-edited by Anna Canepa) and performance art (issue 10), and it registered the growing politicization of the art world with articles on artists' rights.

The magazine served as a rotating exhibition space for a series of artist-designed covers: clever, understated works for the page, many of which emphasized and exploited the publication's distinct, lightweight materiality. William Wegman's spare, simple line drawing for issue 2 created a visual rhyme out of V-shaped marks that signified seagulls and waves in a schematic seascape. Christo "wrapped" issue 5 with a trompe-l'oeil paper bag—an image that referenced the artist's monumental architectural and landscape wrappings, but also alluded wryly to the practice of concealing porn magazines in brown paper wrappers.[41] In 1976, *Art-Rite* inaugurated its Dollar Art Series, in which entire issues of the magazine were given over to an artist or artists—including Alan Suicide (issue 13), Rosemary Mayer (issue 15), Kim MacConnel (issue 17), Image Bank (issue 18), Demi (issue 20), and Judy Rifka (issue 21)—to create a mass-produced work of art available for less than a gallon of milk.

Among the most inspired of *Art-Rite*'s covers was Dorothea Rockburne's design for issue 6. Instead of printing something on the surface of the page, the artist explored its three-dimensional materiality, folding back the cover to diagonally bisect it into two triangles, limned by the slightest shadow. The editors diligently executed Rockburne's idea according to her instructions, creasing thousands of covers themselves, and readily donated two extra pages of precious editorial space to accommodate the design, which required that the first and second pages of the magazine be left blank. Deeply site-specific, Rockburne's cover emphasized the interactive, tactile dimension of the "handmade newspaper," as she called *Art-Rite*, as well as its quotidian,

ART–RITE

number 6

THE MAGAZINE AS AN ALTERNATIVE SPACE

throwaway character.[42] Heightening this effect, the exposed surface of the newsprint has yellowed over time, much like a photogram—a happy accident, according to the artist, but one that poignantly expresses the paper's fugitive quality.

Rockburne's cover cleverly referenced her *Drawing Which Makes Itself* series, begun in 1972, with which she reconceptualized the act of drawing as a fundamentally process-driven activity—less a means to render a preconceived object than a trace of the interaction between artist and materials. As Rosalind Krauss noted of these reductive, postminimalist works in which abstract marks were produced by creases and shadows on paper or carbon paper, they insist on the externality or "publicness" of meaning.[43] Rather than using paper as a surface on which to project her individual, a priori thoughts and feelings—a conduit for the private self—Rockburne allows that surface itself to generate meaning, locating artistic process in the external world as something equally available to all. If the democratization of aesthetic experience implied by Rockburne's drawings remained largely symbolic within the context of the gallery space, her *Art-Rite* cover demonstrates how this idea of publicness might gain significance within the medium—and media space—of the magazine itself, as a model of communication in which the meanings of art and art criticism were not dictated from above but accessible, nonhierarchical, and collaborative.

"A FLOATING ARTIST SPACE"

In its support of experimental, unsaleable art and unestablished artists, *Art-Rite* clearly paralleled the goals of alternative artist-run gallery spaces such as Artists Space, where deAk worked part time as assistant director from 1974 to 1975. As Irving Sandler recalled of Artists Space, one of the earliest and most influential publicly funded alternative spaces, which he and Trudy Grace founded in 1972, "The idea was that artists, who often felt victimized by juries, now would become the jury of the whole. They would choose."[44] Though there was no formal affiliation between the two, *Art-Rite* and Artists Space were deeply aligned ideologically. *Art-Rite* extensively covered exhibitions and performances at Artists Space, and the latter, in turn, frequently advertised in the magazine. Through deAk's position, *Art-Rite* even occasionally participated in Artists Space's programming. For example, in 1974 the magazine presented an evening performance series there called *PersonA*, a kind of after-hours guerrilla performance event with participants including Jennifer Bartlett, Eleanor Antin, Peter Hutchinson, Alan Sondheim, Kathy Acker, Laurie Anderson, Adrian Piper, Dennis Oppenheim, and Jack Smith.[45] Moreover, the magazine was distributed at Artists Space and other alternative venues, suggesting that its circulation coincided with the foot traffic in the alternative galleries.

5.4

Dorothea Rockburne, cover, *Art-Rite*, no. 6, Summer 1974. © 2010 Dorothea Rockburne / Artists Rights Society (ARS), New York. Collection of Steven Leiber, San Francisco.

However, while artists' magazines facilitated the institutional objectives of alternative spaces in the 1970s, and even constituted alternative spaces in their own right, they also differed from bricks-and-mortar institutions, opposing the monumentality that characterizes even the most rustic of architectural structures. Indeed, deAk insisted that, despite their many parallels, "Artists Space was not like *Art-Rite* … which came from the people, establishing our voice, our own style and category. Artists Space was something grown-ups and institutions like NYSCA dreamed up."[46] By contrast, with its relatively low overhead and quick turnaround, the magazine could afford to be more daring and spontaneous in its editorial decisions, featuring artists who were too unknown to make it into even the alternative spaces. DeAk was especially sympathetic to the plight of the countless artists who came in the door of Artists Space looking in vain for exhibition opportunities (as she later recalled of her position there, "I did everything from being the cleaning lady to making it possible for artists to breath the air there because they had so many rules and regulations").[47] She would sometimes invite such artists to publish in the magazine, explaining later: "Maybe nothing could happen for that artist at Artists Space, but we could do something in *Art-Rite* for them."[48]

The relationship between *Art-Rite* and Artists Space attests to the complex reciprocity between the two-dimensional, representational surface of the page and actual, three-dimensional alternative spaces and institutions in the 1970s. On the one hand, magazines functioned as a corollary or supplement to the physical gallery space. *Art-Rite*'s insistently do-it-yourself format and newsprint pages even suggested an analog to the raw, unfinished architectural interiors of so many alternative gallery spaces. Several alternative galleries published their own journals, and others used the printed page as a substitute exhibition space. For example, the Institute for Art and Urban Resources purchased seven pages of advertising space in the December 1976 issue of *Artforum* in which it presented "The Magazine Show"—the work of six artists (Richard Nonas, Alan Saret, Robert Ryman, Patrick Ireland, Susan Rothenberg, and Richard Tuttle) who created pieces that fit the format of the magazine page.

At the same time, however, magazines provide a model of space that is not limited to geometric or architectural definitions, but is rooted in their conditions of circulation and distribution, insisting on space as a temporal field of possibility—something that is itself contingent and mutable. Such a model informed the ideological goals of alternative spaces themselves, which not merely provided a physical place or architectural container for works of art but, as Martin Beck has argued, reconceptualized space as a means of social production.[49] As one critic pointed out at the time, "The 'alternative' these establishments provide is to be found in the word 'space'— a neutral, nonjudgmental, nonauthenticating, openly experimental and sympathetic place to house new ideas, a place unconcerned with traditional amenities like engraved invitations and plaques on the walls, or trustees with connections to IBM and XEROX."[50] In some ways, it might be argued, magazines did not merely serve an ancillary role to alternative gallery spaces, but were an original prototype for such spaces. (Brian O'Doherty's own exploration of *Aspen* magazine as an experimental, artist-driven exhibition space in the late 1960s suggests the primacy of the magazine in his own understanding of the alternative space.)

And yet, if the magazine functioned as a substitute for an exhibition space, offering a place that could transcend the architectural and institutional constraints of the gallery—a "floating

THE MAGAZINE AS AN ALTERNATIVE SPACE

artist space" as O'Doherty called one artists' publication[51]—its discursive space also remained deeply embedded in specific architectural and geographical places. As *Art Rite*'s editors asserted, "Our activities extend way off the pages of the magazine."[52] The magazine's local vantage point in SoHo was stressed in its editorial and advertising space, both of which were dominated by downtown alternative venues. Issue 11/12 featured, in lieu of traditional advertisements, fourteen pages of photographs of New York art spaces, taken from the street view—a kind of extended photo essay which provided a valuable visual record of the neighborhood during this period, while reinforcing *Art-Rite*'s own placement within this urban setting. The editors insisted: "Our communication is not long distance, we are in close proximity to the art."[53]

ART WRITING: *ART-RITE*'S CRITICISM

Art-Rite's editors were not nearly as guileless and unsophisticated as they sometimes liked to pretend. Having been steeped in critical theory and institutional critique in the Whitney Independent Study Program, they published a manifesto-like editorial statement entitled "Reorganizations" in the third issue, revealing an approach to art and art criticism that was broadly informed by systems theory and structuralism. "Art is a sign, a medium of communication. As such it is a node within the communicational matrix which includes primarily the viewer, the artist, the context, a history of art and art criticism, plus any other aspect of human experience either the artist or the viewer puts into the circuits," they wrote, offering the following set of propositions:

> Good art is proportional to the circuits it creates.
> Criticism tends to emphasize circuits art stands for (art–art history, art–its history, art–thought).
> Good criticism identifies the circuits art actually creates.
> Art–artness circuits alone are of a very low order.
> Art–self circuits are of a high order.
> Art–viewer–other people circuits are of a high order.
> High order art is hard for artists to make.[54]

"Reorganizations" attempted to account for the complex social world within which art and its interpretation takes place. In opposition to formalist criticism, *Art-Rite*'s editors insisted that art should not be judged in terms of some objective measure of aesthetic quality but according to its capacity to engender communication and connections between people—a capacity their magazine sought to enhance by making art and art criticism more accessible.

Denouncing the "tired, chewed up, self-referential intellectualism" they perceived in the mainstream press, and especially in the formalist criticism that had dominated *Artforum* during the late 1960s, *Art-Rite*'s editors fostered an unorthodox, decidedly unstuffy form of writing that eschewed the expert judgment of the critic in favor of the *sensus communis*.[55] As deAk explained, "It's cross-checking the art, taking it from the point of view of a layman walking into the gallery and not knowing any of the bullshit. What would he or she see?"[56] Drawing on market research techniques, they regularly used the poll as a format, locating the evaluation of art in the pooled, collective knowledge of the many rather than imposing the judgment of a single critic. They developed a style of criticism that was folksy, colloquial, and resolutely subjective, insisting, "We need not remain detached and analytical while looking at art."[57]

In its deliberate embrace of the amateur over the professional critic, *Art-Rite* harked back to the ethical function of art criticism as it had emerged in the eighteenth-century public sphere. As Jürgen Habermas has pointed out, the first art critics, who assumed the title of *Kunstrichter* (art judge), saw themselves as nonspecialists: "The *Kunstrichter* retained something of the amateur; his expertise only held good until countermanded; lay judgment was organized within it without becoming, by way of specialization, anything else than the judgment of one private person among all others who ultimately were not to be obligated by any judgment except their own. This is precisely where the art critic differed from the judge."[58] However, while the supposedly universal bourgeois public sphere of the eighteenth century that Habermas describes was largely limited to white middle-class men, *Art-Rite* appealed to the emancipatory claims of criticism in order to facilitate the advent of new counterpublics within the art world of the 1970s.

Art-Rite's experimental approach to criticism (combined with the editors' actual inexperience) inevitably resulted in some fairly jejune prose, especially early on. As an example, the following sentence about Alan Suicide's show appeared in the first issue: "This indecently capturing fancy paraphernalia becomes disenfranchised symbols, toys for a ritual of access."[59] Also somewhat sophomoric was a "fictional review" in issue 2, entitled "the Case of the Paint-Cast Shadows," about a woman who experiences flashbacks of an erotic rendezvous while visiting the loft space of a painter named Hilty. Over time, however, the editors developed a quirky and quite lyrical style, rooted in careful observation and vernacular language. For example, about Matta-Clark's *Splitting* they wrote: "It was very odd at Gordon Matta's house, a house as material, in the weeds and sunshine in a suburban slum, condemned, small cracked rooms, spacious yard, hair cream still in the bathroom, very concrete, very unreal."[60]

Against the animosity and suspicion that had so frequently characterized the relationship between artists and critics in the late 1960s, exemplified by the heated debates in *Artforum* or by *Avalanche*'s outright rejection of criticism, *Art-Rite* ushered in a new camaraderie between artists and critics. Its masthead did not segregate editorial staff, artists, and writers according to role or title, but listed them together under the cooperative, nonhierarchical heading "by, for, about, and thanks to."[61] Many of the articles the editors wrote were unsigned. Others were bylined "Edward Pursor," a pen name they sometimes used to represent the "rickety old critic" who was their alter ego.[62] As they explained, "There's no way, really, to sign those articles. … An idea would come and one person would write it. But it might not be that person's idea and the writing would go through changes. … Someone might bring in a finished article and say 'what do you think of it?' Or else someone would say, let's sit down at the typewriter and do an article, and then we'd all pump ideas out."[63] The practice of publishing articles anonymously, deAk noted, also prevented readers from elevating any one critic's opinion to an authoritative status: "We decided not to sign our articles so that people would not construct that kind of an image for us, or any kind of image for us, of who we were."[64] She added, "I really don't think that a critic is important," and vowed "to destroy the criticship of critics, so that people will learn to put things together for themselves. I want to take away criticism's importance and focus it back to the artwork."[65]

As part of their effort to demystify and deprivilege the practice of art criticism, *Art-Rite* published a column entitled "The Critics" that offered readers an up-close-and-personal glimpse of several of the period's best-known critics. As deAk described the column, "The idea was to

     THE MAGAZINE AS AN ALTERNATIVE SPACE

break the power. It was just to bring down the image of the critic as a person with proficiencies and with limitations like every person has. We wanted to show to the artists that if somebody writes a negative review about them, it's all right."[66] Accompanied by candid snapshots of each critic, the column discussed their critical approaches while revealing snippets about their personal history, art collections, and even sartorial preferences. They disclosed, for example, that Lawrence Alloway was the son of a London bookseller, was bedridden with tuberculosis at the age of eleven, and lived in two floors of a brownstone on West Twentieth Street, as well as the fact that Robert Pincus-Witten was "quite a snappy dresser."[67]

Among the critics *Art-Rite* profiled was Lucy Lippard, whose reputation as an "antiacademic rebel" was clearly a model for the publication's own renegade brand of criticism.[68] The profile recounted Lippard's beginnings as a page and research assistant at the Museum of Modern Art, where she spent her days carrying heavy piles of periodicals to curators and met Dan Flavin, Robert Ryman, and Sol LeWitt, who also worked there as museum guards; her political awakening on a trip to Argentina in 1968; her boycott of *Artforum* ("in protest against *Artforum*'s Greenbergian line and the fact that they didn't want articles on many artists who interested her, though some of these would soon become *Artforum*'s own cover boys");[69] her important work as an activist with political artists' organizations, such as the Art Workers' Coalition, which she helped to found in 1969; and her doubts about being part of the art world at all ("I can never figure out if I should keep on plugging for the work and the values I care about and provide at least a whisper of dissent from the artworld mainstream, or quit entirely in protest").[70] While Lippard was frank about her disillusionment with conceptual art, acknowledging that "conceptual art got co-opted too and I certainly don't blame any of the artists because artists should be able to make a living off what they do like everybody else," she also reaffirmed her ongoing commitment to the unrealized egalitarian promise of art in the late 1960s, insisting, "it is crucial that art acquire a broader audience or it will stifle in its own narrow confines."[71]

ISSUE 14: ARTISTS' BOOKS

Issue 14 (Winter 1976–1977) of *Art-Rite* was a special issue devoted to artists' books. Though the use of the book as an artistic medium was not entirely new, with historical precedents such as illuminated manuscripts and *livres d'artistes*, the artist's book was redefined in the 1960s and 1970s as an explicitly democratic medium. Lippard, who was an important advocate of artists' books, described the term "artists' book" as implying "mass produced, relatively cheap, accessible to a broad public. … Handmade, one-of-a-kind books were something else—often very beautiful, but the kind of 'precious objects' I hoped we'd escape."[72] In particular, Lippard was optimistic about the potential of artists' books to fulfill the unrealized goals of art of the late 1960s, observing, "One of the basic mistakes made by early proponents of Conceptual art's 'democratic' stance (myself included) was a confusion of the characteristics of the medium (cheap, portable, accessible) with those of the actual contents (all too often wildly self-indulgent or so highly specialized that they appeal only to an elite audience)."[73] By contrast, she argued, "the most important aspect of artists' books *is* their adaptability as instruments for extension to a far broader public than that currently enjoyed by contemporary art."[74]

too pointed. They carried more and less meaning than I wanted. They were always too personal. They were nobody's business but mine. So I stopped. And I made sculpture.

And that was better; more general, more diffuse, more ambiguous—but also more immediate. People could trip over them.

Yet something was lost. Something important to me: a narrative quality that moves and excites me. Something I can't get and don't want in my sculpture. It's a temporal quality; specific memories used as building blocks in sculpture that snakes through time.

So I make books too. But differently than I did before. My books are like sculpture now; built for the same reasons and in the same way. They aim at the same ambiguous feelings, work with the same not quite regular forms and the same preshaped materials—they are objects; objects to deal with. But, they do what my sculpture can't: they jump, they move, they snake with the richness of real incident—they are the space between the sculptures.

Adrian Piper

Cheap Art Utopia

Suppose art was as accessible to everyone as comic books? as cheap and as available? What social and economic conditions would this state of things presuppose?

(1) It would presuppose a conception of art that didn't equate spatiotemporal uniqueness with aesthetic quality. People would have to be able to discriminate quality in art without the trappings of preciousness, e.g. the gilt frame, the six-figure price tag, the plexiglass case, the roped-off area around the work, etc.

(2) It would presuppose a different economic status for artists. Since art would be cheap and accessible, artists could no longer support themselves by receiving high prices for their work. Their situation would be comparable to that of writers, for whom first editions, original manuscripts and the like play virtually no economic role during their own lifetime.

(3) Therefore art dealers would bear much the same sort of economic relationship to artists that agents bear to writers: perhaps just as symbiotic (we should no longer fool ourselves into thinking of the relationship as parasitic), but not nearly as lucrative an enterprise as art dealing is now. Economically, artists' and art dealers' profits would diminish proportionally.

(4) Since artists' revenue would depend more on volume of sales than on making a killing on the yearly masterpiece, artists would gradually feel increasingly disposed to make their work palatable or relevant to a larger segment of society than that which now constitutes the art world. Some would equate this increased popularity (literally) with a decline in aesthetic quality; these individuals would become bitter, dogmatically elitist, and comfort themselves with the thought that their work represented the last bastion of aesthetic integrity. Others would find that this state of things no longer fueled their images of themselves as rare and special persons, and so would

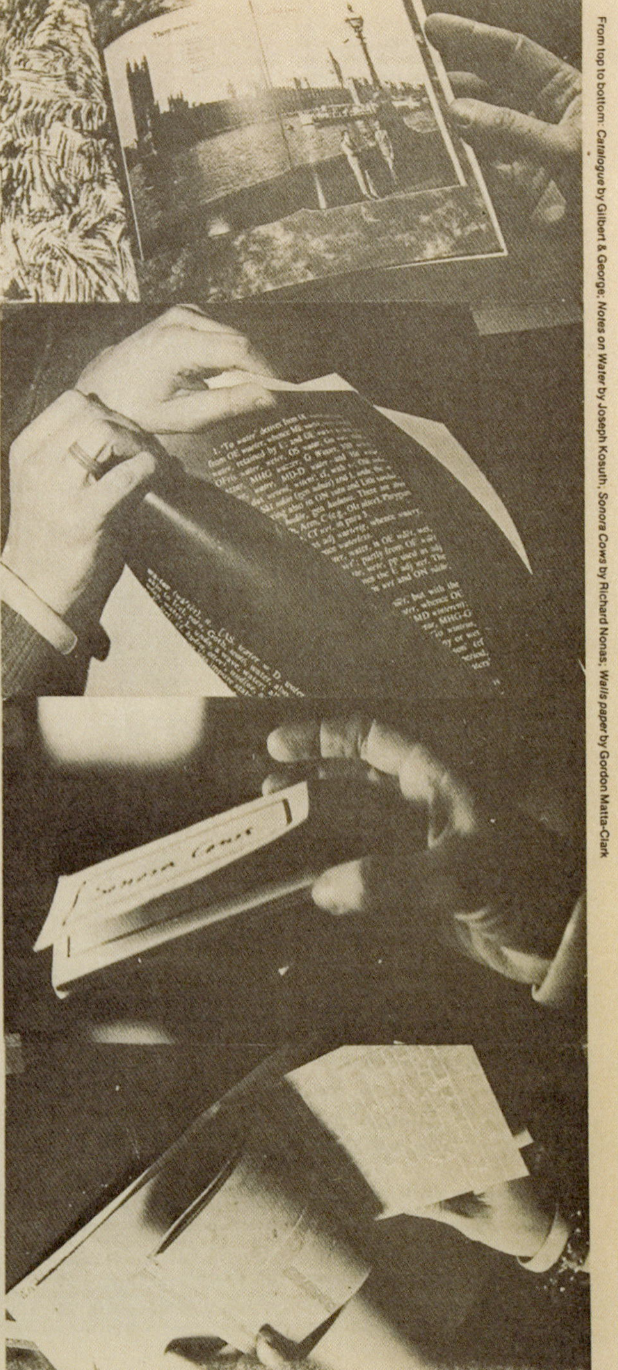

From top to bottom: *Catalogue* by Gilbert & George; *Notes on Water* by Joseph Kosuth; *Sonora Cows* by Richard Nonas; *Wallpaper* by Gordon Matta-Clark

5.5

Art-Rite, no. 14, Winter 1976–1977, page 11.
Courtesy of the editors. Collection of Steven Leiber, San Francisco.

 THE MAGAZINE AS AN ALTERNATIVE SPACE

In addition to serving as a crucial—if somewhat idiosyncratic—resource on artists' books, with an extensive catalog, statements by fifty artists and critics, and numerous articles and reviews, issue 14 of *Art-Rite* considered its own participation in the aesthetic and political possibilities it surveyed, offering a novel set of methodologies for representing and evaluating this important new medium. As deAk later recalled, "we were basically formulating how to write about a new medium that had not been dealt with before."[75] Instead of presenting a monolithic overview of the topic, they published a series of unedited artists' statements, ranging in length and tone from manifesto-like lists to more academic accounts, to informal, stream-of-consciousness responses, producing a heterogeneous, multivocal discourse that mirrored the collaborative, egalitarian ethos of artists' books themselves. As the editors noted in the issue: "The collective quality of these statements functions as the most basic and genuine definition of artists' books."[76] The editors also experimented with new ways of photographing books to convey their interactive, tactile dimension. Rather than splayed flat and cropped from their surroundings, books are shown being flipped through, going in and out of focus as their pages are turned.

Besides considering the aesthetic and formal properties of artists' books, issue 14 also emphasized the political potential of this accessible, low-cost medium. This was underscored by the poem by Carl Andre that appeared on the cover. Centered on the page, the poem consisted of a square grid of handwritten, capitalized block letters, quoting a passage from Karl Marx's *Capital*: "The life process of society which is based on the process of material production does not strip off its mystical veil until it is treated as production by freely associated men and women and is consciously regulated by them in accordance with a settled plan." The form of Andre's poem echoes its content, enacting the idea that the work of art might "strip off its mystical veil" and be freed from its status as commodity, emancipating artistic production and reception from their alienated condition within the capitalist system. Like the modular metal slabs of the artist's minimalist sculpture, the poem insists on the concrete facticity of its material—here, language, itself—detached from its capacity to express ideas and illusions. Devoid of punctuation and spacing, the poem encourages readers to connect its letters randomly, discovering new words hidden within it. As Liz Kotz has argued, Andre's poetry attempts to liberate language from the tyranny of authorial intention in order to bring about a radical democratization of meaning—an interpretation reinforced by the artist's own account: "The poetry I am trying to write is poetry which eliminates the poet. ... What I want to illuminate in my poetry are not those things which only I can see, but those things which any man can see."[77]

Though language might be considered the medium of Andre's poem, its meaning cannot be separated from its form of distribution—in this case, a free, self-published artists' magazine. By appearing on the newsprint cover of *Art-Rite*, the poem foregrounds the magazine's role in actually achieving the social transformation to which it refers, by giving artists more control over the production and distribution of their work and allowing them to reach different audiences. However, while artists embraced the printed page as an inherently accessible and public medium—a concept with roots in the Enlightenment model of the public sphere—they also began to question the universal character of this normative ideal, which masked its historical reality. (Andre's description above with its reference to "any man" reveals the gendered assumptions that underwrote his own concept of the public space of the printed page.) Other artists began to think instead

ART–RITE

artists' books

THELIFEPROCESSO
FSOCIETYWHICHIS
BASEDONTHEPROCE
SSOFMATERIALPRO
DUCTIONDOESNOTS
TRIPOFFITSMYSTI
CALVEILUNTILITI
STREATEDASPRODU
CTIONBYFREELYAS
SOCIATEDMENANDW
OMENANDISCONSCI
OUSLYREGULATEDB
YTHEMINACCORDAN
CEWITHASETTLEDP
LANKMARXCAPITAL

THE MAGAZINE AS AN ALTERNATIVE SPACE

about how printed matter might register not the mythical universal character of some abstract ideal of the public, but the actual subjectivities of artists and their viewers. Lippard, for example, was interested in the role artists' publications might play in the feminist art movement, observing:

> [Artists' books] open up a way for women artists to get their work out without depending on the undependable museum and gallery system (still especially undependable for women). They also serve as an inexpensive vehicle for feminist ideas. … The next step is to get the books out into supermarkets, where they'll be browsed by women who wouldn't darken the door of Printed Matter or read *Heresies* and usually have to depend on Hallmark for their gifts. I have this visual of feminist artists' books in school libraries (or being passed around under the desks), in hairdressers, in gynecologists' waiting rooms, in Girl Scout Cookies.[78]

Lippard's irreverent description captures how artists' publications, with their egalitarian, unpretentious formats, might oppose the patriarchal category of greatness and challenge the hierarchies of gender and class within the art world.[79] The model of the public sphere that she evokes is clearly not a universal Habermasian one, equally accessible to all, but a distinctly gendered realm which at times overlaps a more general public space (school libraries) and at other times asserts its separateness (gynecologists' offices). Indeed, as Peter Uwe Hohendahl has argued, for social groups that have been historically excluded from the official institutions of the public sphere, "a unified public sphere to which everybody has equal access is probably less a democratic achievement than a sign of repression, since the formal equality guaranteed by the Constitution had not prevented social and sometimes even legal discrimination."[80] Instead, Lippard suggests that artists' publications might produce a counterpublic sphere—an alternative space in which artistic communities, especially those marginalized by mainstream art institutions, might develop their own artistic criteria and forms of expression.

5.6

Carl Andre, *THELIFEPROCESSO*, 1976, cover, *Art-Rite*, no. 14, Winter 1976–1977. Courtesy of the editors. Art © Carl Andre/Licensed by VAGA, New York, NY. Collection of Steven Leiber, San Francisco.

Though artists' publications did not show up in the grocery store checkout line as Lippard had hoped, they did offer a crucial platform for women artists to publicize their work, define the politics of feminist art practice, and create a sense of solidarity and community. Lippard herself was a founding member of the Heresies collective which published *Heresies* magazine—one of several magazines founded to support feminist art practices during the 1970s.[81] The editorial statement in the first issue of *Heresies* asserted, "As a step toward the demystification of art, we reject the standard relationship of criticism to art within the present system, which has often become the relationship of advertiser to product. We will not advertise a new set of genius-products just because they are made by women."[82] As this statement demonstrates, artists' magazines sought not only to change the content of mainstream media, but to transform its socioeconomic relations of production. By insisting that the politics of art and art criticism were inseparable from their form of distribution, *Art-Rite* provided an influential model for such alternatives. (When several former *Artforum* editors founded *October* in 1976, even they paid close attention to the form of the magazine as well as its content, vowing to be visually austere and free of advertisements.)

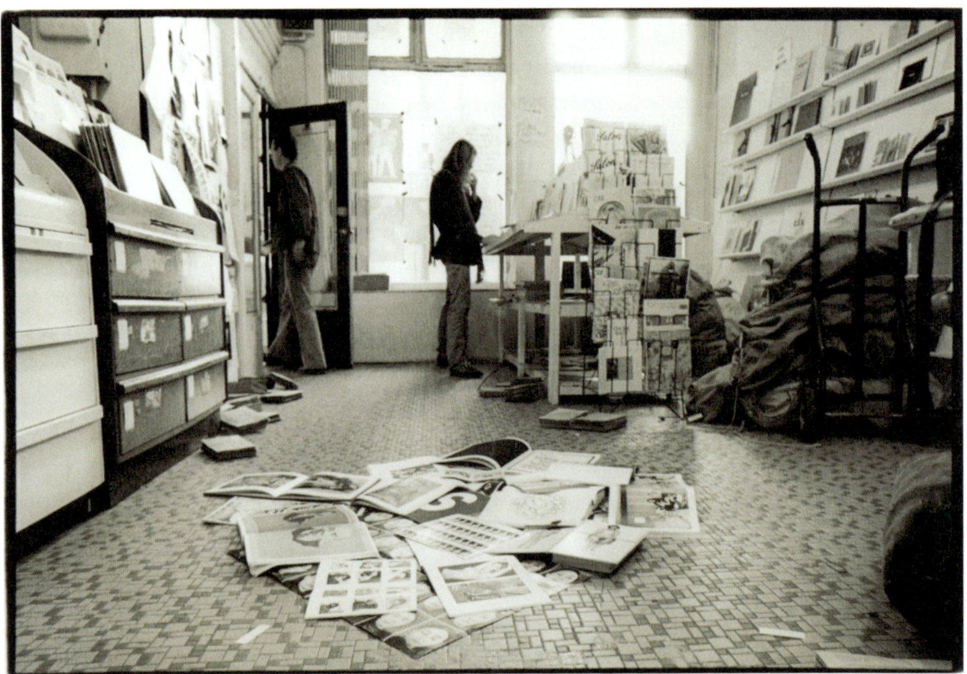

5.7

Printed Matter at 7 Lispenard Street. Photograph by Sarah Longacre, c. 1980. Courtesy of Printed Matter, Inc., and Sarah Longacre.

   THE MAGAZINE AS AN ALTERNATIVE SPACE

In 1976, deAk, Robinson, Lippard, and a few others founded Printed Matter, an alternative space devoted to publishing, promoting, and distributing artists' publications.[83] Like Martha Wilson's Franklin Furnace, which slightly preceded it, as well as like-minded institutions in other cities including Art Metropole in Toronto, Bookspace in Chicago, and Other Books & So in Amsterdam, Printed Matter was a hybrid space, combining the normally mutually exclusive categories of store and nonprofit and merging many different kinds of activities and functions, serving as a bookstore, a gallery for artists' books, a publisher, and an information center for self-publishing artists. These spaces provided important new models of publishing, distributing, and marketing artists' publications that allowed artists to maintain more control over these processes.[84] In addition, these spaces functioned as archives and distribution centers, organized exhibitions and events, and hosted performances, readings, and screenings—making it clear that the aesthetic potential of printed matter was deeply linked with other new time-based and ephemeral media such as performance, video, and film.

Institutions such as Printed Matter point to another way that the two-dimensional space of the page might intersect with and traverse real, three-dimensional space. By allowing artists and their readers to participate in a larger collective identity, Printed Matter contributed to the social function of artists' publications. According to Lippard, "Printed Matter was originally a community of radical/avant-garde/experimental (not always the same thing) artists. … Printed Matter was an incredible support system for artists."[85] Among the space's many other uses, the group Political Art Documentation and Distribution, discussed further in chapter 7, used Printed Matter as the site of its initial meetings. Printed Matter also sought to make artists' publications available to a wider audience outside the art world by giving them a more salient public presence within the urban community. It was with this in mind that the space, which was located during the late 1970s in Tribeca near a large Post Office facility, began to install a series of curated window exhibitions facing out onto the street, with the hope that intrigued passersby would be tempted to step inside.

Even though *Art-Rite* and other artists' publications clearly strove to reach a broader public outside of the art world, their true legacy is most evident within it. As editor Harley Lond wrote in the first issue of the L.A. artists' magazine *Intermedia*, "the vacuum in which artists have struggled for years is now being filled by a host of political and economic organizations striving to create a stronger representation and voice for artists everywhere. There is almost a grassroots movement among artists to take control over their destinies."[86] Much like the underground press of the period, artists' magazines helped to kindle new social formations in the art world in very practical ways, by circulating resource lists, publicizing political activities, and disseminating information about safety and hazardous materials, housing, and health insurance for artists. As Lippard observed, "Artists' publications were and still are important not only for their content and educational information but also for the networking they generate. At a time when little politics appeared in art magazines (and if it did, it was treated as a separate category) these portable objects could be mailed around the country, sparking actions in other contexts."[87] Both the collective nature of the periodical and its seriality made it an especially effective vehicle for the formation of artistic communities, since it could spread ideas through space and sustain dialog over time. As the artist-run magazine *The Fox* claimed of itself, it was "less a publication, a reified object, than the byproduct of a community of people. That is, there is some attempt to use it as an instrument of praxis, both as a cause and effect of self-determination."[88]

Throughout the 1970s, numerous alternative artists' magazines were founded, prompted by the same motives that propelled the founding of alternative spaces—to support the ideological and practical goals of political activism within the art world, and to foster new artistic communities and counterpublics. In addition to those already mentioned, magazines such as *Tracks, Art Workers News, Women Artists Newsletter, Appearances, Chrysalis, Black Art, New Observations, Big Deal*, and *Red-Herring* sprang up alongside the new alternative gallery spaces. Magazines outside of New York—including *Vision* and *La Mamelle* in San Francisco; *New Art Examiner* and *The Original Art Report* in Chicago; *Straight Turkey, The Dumb Ox, Intermedia, LAICA Journal, Performance Art Journal*, and *Choke* in Los Angeles; *Sunday Clothes* in South Dakota; *Criss Cross Communications* in Boulder; and *Art Papers* in Atlanta—were crucial for the development of local and regional art scenes. As Alan Moore noted in 1974, "art world centrism is undeniably breaking down … art periodicals in outlying communities have become increasingly conscious of their own potential to contribute to the enrichment of contemporary art."[89] As with alternative galleries, the increased number of independently published artists' magazines in North America was precipitated in part by the new availability of public funding during this time.[90] *Art-Rite*, for example, was funded by both the NEA and the New York State Council on the Arts. Unlike commercial publications, which competed for readers and advertisers, artists' magazines in the 1970s were guided by a cooperative spirit. They supported one another, publishing advertisements for one another and cultivating common editorial goals. They even occasionally collaborated, as *Art-Rite* and *LAICA Journal* did in 1978, taking advantage of their nearly identical formats to create a joint issue, distributed on both coasts.

In their 1978 article "Alternative Periodicals," deAk and Robinson sampled the profusion of new artists' magazines, offering a loose taxonomy with the following categories: Picture Magazines ("consist of artworks, usually graphics or photographs done in the magazine space"); Parochials and House Organs ("fledgling critical magazines and papers, often with strong artist participation, that fashion the scene in communities outside of mainstream centers"); the Voice of the New ("rebellious, enfranchising new art and artists that the commercial periodicals with their interests invested elsewhere, have resisted"); the Scholarly Ones ("misfortune: they continue to mystify analytical writing"); the Lobbyists ("periodical agent for the disenfranchised" which "conceive of their audience as a social unit, and one that needs protection"); and Newsletters ("alternative point: low overhead").[91] As this overview demonstrates, within the 1970s art world artists' magazines did not function as a single, unified public sphere, but as multiple, sometimes competing sites of counterpublicity. As deAk and Robinson themselves observed, "The time of a single forum for avant-garde art has ended."[92]

ALTERNATIVE AND MAINSTREAM

If *Art-Rite* helped to define the artists' magazine as an alternative space, it also suggested how publications wrestle with the same processes of institutionalization that other kinds of alternative spaces experience. Thus, in issue 8 (Winter 1975), an editorial statement recounted how the magazine had been founded to serve young and unknown artists, and then reflected:

    THE MAGAZINE AS AN ALTERNATIVE SPACE

Indeed, though the term "alternative" connotes an opposition to what is mainstream, in practice this opposition often proves highly unstable. As deAk recalled of the origins of the publication, "We came in without a big bang. We just put our magazine around. People up to date thought we had money. We were riding on the absurdity of the situation—that we were three nobodies, had no money, had no fame, and didn't know anybody in the art world. But it was perfect—we were totally free."[94] As Cohn and Robinson then observed, "It's easy to start a magazine. It becomes harder and harder to stay free once you become known."[95] These comments point to the precariousness of alternative enterprises more generally—the fact that, in the process of publicizing and supporting what is marginal, they often transform the margins into the center. If they are successful, they render themselves obsolete. In its support of "young, unknown artists," *Art-Rite* inadvertently participated in the marketing of these very qualities, feeding the art market's appetite for novelty.

This dilemma was highlighted during a conference on alternative publishing that took place on February 20, 1977, at San Francisco's alternative space, 80 Langton Street. Here a group of magazine publishers from California and New York gathered to exchange information about their involvement in the activity of alternative art publishing. *Art-Rite*'s editors were invited, as were the publishers of *Vision, La Mamelle, Choke, The Dumb Ox, Intermedia*, and *Assembling*. Tables were set up with current and back issues of each periodical, and at four o'clock that afternoon a panel discussion took place. An audience member asked: "Is there any unifying notion of an alternative magazine in these publications?"[96] This seemingly innocent question prompted a rather exasperated retort from Tom Mandel, the publisher of *Arts Biweekly*: "What does the word 'alternative' mean? It don't mean shit."[97] Another audience member cynically chimed in: "It's hype for grant applications." DeAk offered the following observation: "If you unify alternatives you get a mainstream and that's not what we're about. … Our position is somewhat ambiguous. We are not people with a very specific jargon. We don't make easy issues. We are navigating and trying to float and be open. That is our position."[98]

The next year, in 1978, *Art-Rite* would float right out of existence, with as little fanfare as it had begun five years before. According to Robinson, the magazine "petered out. We kind of ran out of energy. It's just one of those things. We never really made any money out of it, it ran its course."[99] Likewise, when asked why the magazine ended, deAk explained, "We were getting older. We had to work all the time. … The magazine wouldn't pay anything for us. I just got tired."[100] While these remarks attest to the burnout that is endemic to alternative enterprises more generally, they also suggest how impermanence might actually safeguard such enterprises, in essence preempting the processes of acculturation that would inevitably overtake them. The final issue of *Art-Rite*, designed by Judy Rifka, consisted of two thousand original mixed-media drawings, collages, and stencils, each on a single sheet of paper folded in half, sent out like a handmade card.[101]

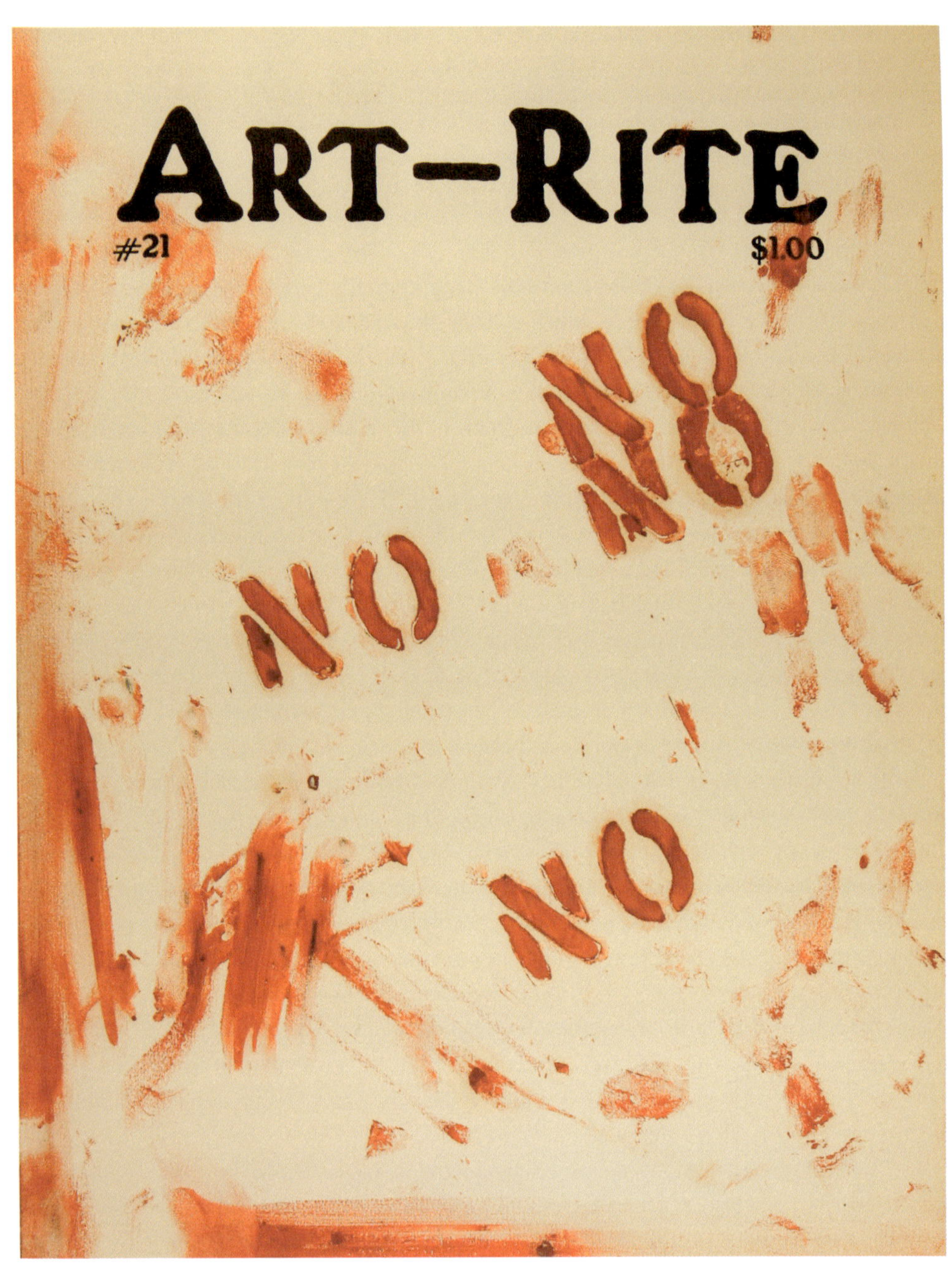

5.8

Judy Rifka, *Art-Rite*, no. 21, 1978, cover. Courtesy of
the artist and the editors. Collection of Steven Leiber,
San Francisco.

Meanwhile, the notion of the magazine as an alternative space was becoming an increasingly mainstream idea. A little over a year after *Art-Rite* ceased publication in late 1978, *Artforum*'s February 1980 issue, under the direction of its brand-new editor, Ingrid Sischy, was nearly entirely given over to artists' projects—a feature that would become a mainstay in *Artforum* throughout the 1980s. Several of the works originally created for *Art-Rite*'s Dollar Art Series, including Rifka's drawings, were reproduced as artists' projects for the issue, alongside artists' projects by Dan Graham, Art & Language, Ed Ruscha, Laurie Anderson, Jenny Holzer, Peter Nadin, and others. As Sischy, who had been the director of Printed Matter, wrote in her editorial statement, "Apart from the reviews, none of the pages in this issue is a reproduction of a work of art, all are primary art intended for this and only this format."[102] DeAk herself contributed an article in which she reflected back on her experience publishing *Art-Rite* in the 1970s, describing it as "a reaction against what I saw as the monolithic art infrastructure and about my means to circumvent it."[103] But she pointed out that "now we are in an opposite situation. The power of art's statements and contributions to culture has to be sent beyond the art world's boundaries," and went on to express her optimism about the art magazine as a medium, explaining, "The presence of art directly in a magazine could be like a bass drum, a thumping existence that could lock the whole enterprise into a meaningful track."[104]

On the one hand, the February 1980 issue of *Artforum* suggests the assimilation of alternative practices by mainstream institutions, and the art market's black-hole-like capacity to turn even the most valueless object into a cipher for monetary worth (an irony that is only amplified today by the fact that *Art-Rite* and other artists' magazines and ephemera from the 1960s and 1970s have become collectors' items, appraised at thousands of dollars).[105] And yet it also hints at a shift in the relationship between the nonprofit and commercial sectors that would define a new generation of alternative practices in the late 1970s and early 1980s, such as Colab (of which Robinson was a member). Among other things, these new practices would demonstrate not only that mainstream institutions co-opt alternative ones, but that alternatives also borrow from and exploit commercial spaces. Maybe in this sense the February 1980 issue of *Artforum* can be read not solely as the cooptation of *Art-Rite* but also as its final issue—an ending that was also the beginning of a new chapter in the history of the magazine as an alternative space.

6
THE MAGAZINE AS MIRROR
FILE, 1972–1989

In the Winter/Spring 1973 issue of *Avalanche*, the Toronto-based group of artists known as General Idea (AA Bronson, Felix Partz, and Jorge Zontal) were interviewed by Willoughby Sharp. Sharp prefaced the interview by noting that it took place while "sitting at the General Idea kitchen table, smoking their grass and my hash"[1]—a fact that may have contributed to the "Who's on First" quality of the conversation, which began:

> WS: I want to ask for the first question, what's the general idea?
> AA: None of your business. (Ha, ha, ha.)
> WS: When was the first Miss General Idea Pageant, then?
> AA: The first time was in 1968, and we don't talk about it.
> WS: Well, let's talk about it.
> AA: Miss Page was chosen Miss General Idea 1968 in a private ceremony,
> the details of which are not revealed.
> WS: Aha! So it's a phony first pageant. No first pageant, you guys.
> JS: The full details will be revealed in 1984.
> WS: Really, so you mean we'll have to wait?
> JS: Yes.
> RG: The next year, '69, was also a secret pageant.
> AA: Grenada Gazelle was chosen Miss General Idea 1969.
> WS: A second phony Miss Pageant? (Hahaha.)
> PJ: Phony secret, fake.
> AA: Fake mystery.
> WS: You're propagating fake mysteries, aren't you?
> JS: All over the place.
> WS: And Mannerist decadence?
> AA: Unquote.
> RG: We're writing history.
> WS: You're writing history.
> AA: History's what you make it.[2]

The interview reveals the wisecracks, wordplay, and cryptic layers of fact and fiction that characterized General Idea's varied artistic production, including their magazine, *FILE*, published from 1972 to 1989. The magazine—or "megazine," as it was frequently called—reported on the group's eclectic, evolving interests and activities, from the Canadian mail art scene and elaborate preparations for a campy, "fake" beauty contest known as the 1984 Miss General Idea Pageant, to the Canadian new wave and punk music scene. Anticipating the critical approaches of queer theory, General Idea explored masquerade and performance as subversive strategies to denaturalize dominant cultural categories of gender, class, beauty, and artistic production—and to investigate the role of the media in upholding such categories.

FILE was central to these explorations. According to Bronson, the magazine "was very much an artwork by General Idea. It wasn't a magazine in the normal sense of the word. It was one of our projects, and it was very much integral to our project as a whole."[3] Appropriating *Life* magazine's red and white logo—an act of cultural piracy for which Time Inc. later threatened to sue—*FILE* can itself be understood as a kind of performance, an impersonation of this quintessential example of American mass media. Flaunting its glossy, full-color cover, which disguised a cheap tabloid interior, the magazine suggested a "queering" of the media that at once exaggerated and undermined its spectacular visual regime.

As Bronson described *FILE*'s editorial impetus, "We wanted to create a Canadian art scene when there wasn't one. There were the beginnings of one, but there wasn't a real scene, but we thought if we could create the image of a scene then in fact it would exist."[4] Much as *Avalanche* had done for the SoHo art community, *FILE* sought to provide a publicity vehicle for alternative Canadian artists, who were, in many ways, doubly marginalized, not only within the Canadian art scene but by Canada's own subordination to the United States. Willoughby Sharp was a friend of General Idea, and *Avalanche* was mentioned frequently in *FILE*, suggesting the affinities between the two publications. However, if *FILE* was inspired by *Avalanche*'s example, it also resonated with Andy Warhol's *Interview* and Les Levine's *Culture Hero* in the way that it self-consciously lampooned the role of publicity in the art world, adopting the sensationalistic tone and flashy visual appearance of advertising and consumer culture. General Idea's cynicism toward the mass media was coupled with optimism about its untapped egalitarian possibilities. As they wrote in one of their many manifesto-like editorials, "To win a mass audience does not require art appreciation classes or longer gallery hours or lower prices. ... To have effect, art must reposition itself in competition with other mass audiences. Artists of the world—sell out—sell out before it's too late!"[5]

In their appreciation for the possibilities of the magazine as a new kind of medium and distribution form, General Idea was especially influenced by the work of Robert Smithson, whose article "Incidents of Mirror-Travel in the Yucatan" (discussed in chapter 1) they came across in the November 1969 issue of *Artforum*. As Bronson recalled, "we read and reread that essay, and it was reflected in everything we did after that."[6] In homage to Smithson, General Idea produced *Light On* (1971), a project they later documented in *FILE*. They designed and had custom-built two large mirrors mounted on double-rotating mechanisms which they lugged around southern Ontario in the back of a truck, aiming beams of light at various historical and tourist sites. While actual mirrors would continue to play a role in their subsequent pieces, the mirror arguably functioned most powerfully in their work as a metaphor. They conceived of *FILE* magazine itself "as a mirror held out to the Canadian network, which had been building up in the previous months. It had built up to such a point that it only needed an awareness of itself as a network of people across Canada to actually exist. In other words, *FILE* brought that network of Canadian artists into existence by showing them they were there."[7]

General Idea's understanding of the magazine as a mirror evoked the self-perpetuating, circular logic that numerous media theorists have seized upon as one of spectacular media's most insidious characteristics—what Guy Debord described in his 1967 book *The Society of the Spectacle* as the "basically tautological" character of the spectacle, observing that "it says nothing more than 'what appears is good; what is good appears.'"[8] (The journal *Internationale Situationniste* itself had metallic paper covers, which Debord once compared to a "deforming mirror," suggesting the intent to simultaneously literalize and warp this reflective, tautological capacity of the media.)[9] For General Idea, *Life* magazine epitomized the media's ability to mirror reality, and thus generate its own news. Founded by Henry Luce in 1936, *Life* relegated texts to captions for page upon page of photographs; indeed, the magazine's motto, "See *Life*, See the World," said it all. As General Idea explained in an editorial, "LIFE was the Coca-Cola of the picture magazines … the first and instant précis of lifestyle the emerging manner the reflective possibilities of mass media. … The news that made LIFE was made news by LIFE."[10] The artists were especially fascinated by a series of human-interest stories from the 1950s entitled "*Life* Goes to a Party" which reported on the minutiae of suburban life during that decade—a feature they would later mock with their *FILE* parties.[11] As they later explained, "We were interested in *Life* magazine because it was the first magazine to create news rather than just report it. They would take fairly mundane events and turn them through the photo-story process into news stories … so we were interested in the fact that *Life* was cognizant of their ability of creating news."[12]

FILE seized upon the media's capacity to generate its own news, harnessing it as a viral tactic that might sabotage the media's spectacular regime from within. Emblematic of this approach was the cover of the first issue, which showed the Planter's Peanut logo, Mr. Peanut (or rather, the artist Vincent Trasov wearing a large papier-mâché shell and tights), posing nonchalantly against the Toronto skyline. As Bronson described the photogenic advertising anthropomorph, "It is the very emptiness of the image, its very lack of content, that creates its desirability: although the image has no connection to any specific event, production, or opinion, its lack of substance combined with its familiarity leaves it an open receptacle, an empty mirror onto which the media can project anything they want. And they do."[13] In fact, Trasov's Mr. Peanut persona would become a darling of the media, appearing on the covers of mainstream magazines, including *Esquire* and the *Village Voice*. He would even run for mayor of Vancouver in 1974, with the official platform "No comment." In its parasitic dependence on media coverage, the Mr. Peanut performance harkens back to the "pseudo-events" staged by the Yippies, such as their famous nomination of a pig named Pigasus as a presidential candidate at the 1968 Democratic National Convention—events that, as David Joselit has discussed, resonated with artistic investigations of media at the time.[14] Unlike the Yippies' pseudo-events, however, Mr. Peanut was appropriated from the media to begin with, at once hyperbolizing the media's informational structure, and turning it back in on itself.

Likewise, FILE critiqued the media by inhabiting and amplifying its own representational systems: if *Life* mirrored life, FILE mirrored *Life*. And yet this reflection was not perfect, but slightly off, slightly distorted, just as the title was not an exact replica of *Life*, but an anagram that transposed two letters. Like Smithson, General Idea conceived of the mirror not simply as a blank, narcissistic reflection but as a metaphor for a critical form of self-reflexivity that might prompt a new kind of self-awareness.[15] Indeed, FILE's imitation of *Life* was a subversive form of mimicry that undermined the latter's representational formula, denaturalizing it and rendering it strange. By mirroring the self-perpetuating logic of the spectacular media and exaggerating it to the point of absurdity, FILE attempted to undermine its authority, encouraging readers to become more active participants in this image world.

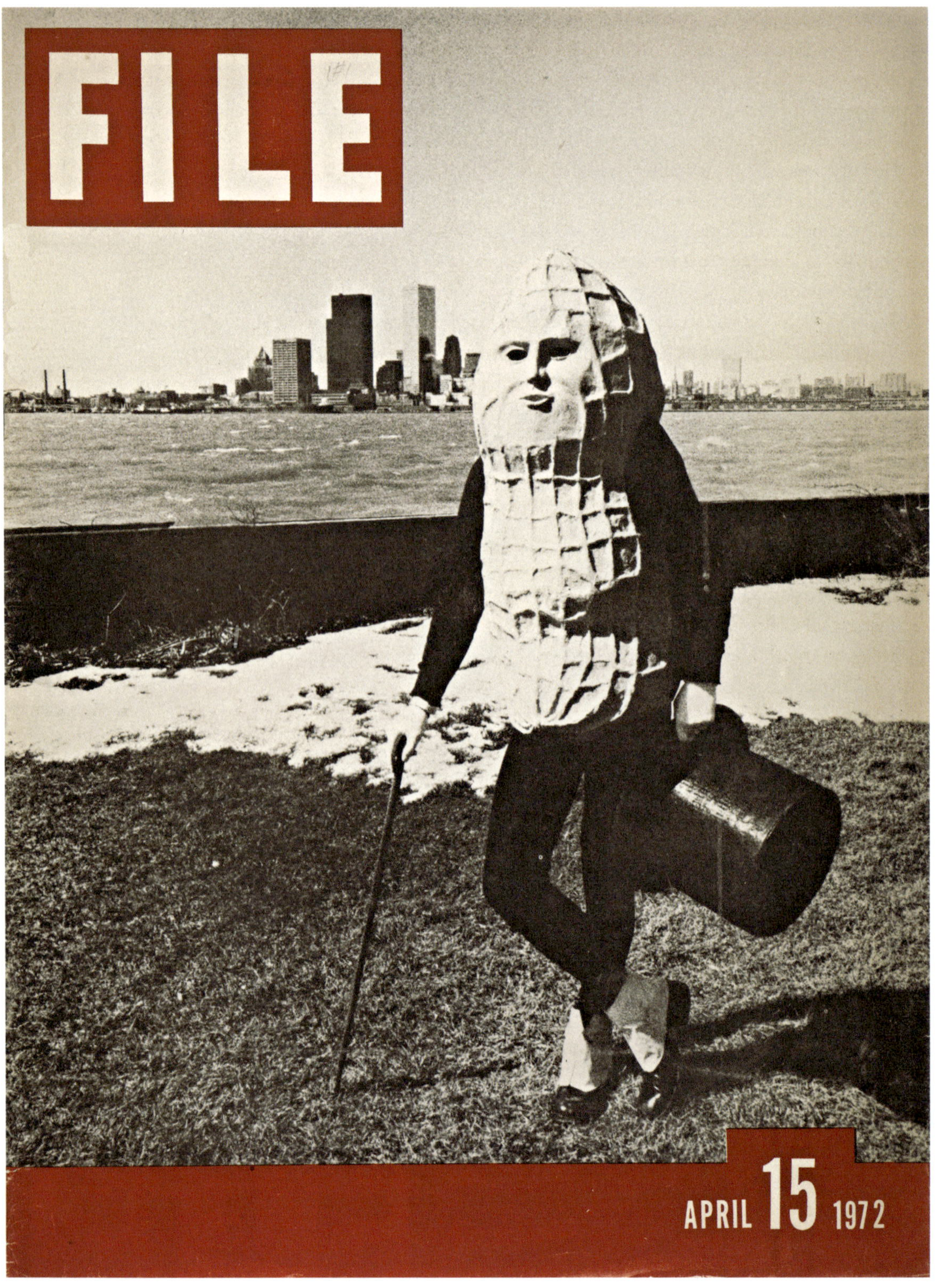

                                    THE MAGAZINE AS MIRROR

In the late 1960s, Bronson, Partz, and Zontal (all of whom had previously changed their names—from Michael Tims, Ronald Gabe, and George Saia, respectively) began to work together under the corporate-sounding moniker General Idea. With backgrounds in publishing, film, and architecture, they were involved in the intellectual and countercultural scene centered around Rochdale College, a radical "free university" which arose, initially under the auspices of the University of Toronto, as a cooperative, student-run alternative to traditional education.[16] Though short-lived, Rochdale College left a lasting mark on the Toronto cultural scene through institutions such as the experimental theater group Passe Muraille, with which General Idea performed, and the influential alternative publisher Coach House Press, which published several important artists' magazines including *Image Nation, Is, Snore Comix,* and *Open Letter,* to which the members of General Idea contributed.

Starting in 1969, the three artists rented a house at 78 Gerrard Street West in Toronto, where they began to collaborate with a loose circle of friends and artists including Mimi Page, Granada Gazelle, Miss Honey (a.k.a. Honey Novick), and Pascal (a.k.a. Stuart Murray, a transsexual female singer who was then undergoing hormone treatments), many of whom would be featured in the early issues of *FILE.* During this time they conceived of their artistic production as a kind of *Gesamtkunstwerk*—one extended performance in which they dressed up in unusual costumes, created a series of window displays in their apartment's storefront facade, sold clothing in an Oldenburg-like Happening called *Betty's,* and began to mine imagery from a found scrapbook from the 1930s that had belonged to a military captain, which would form the basis of the iconography for much of their subsequent work.[17]

General Idea also started to participate in the Canadian correspondence art scene, centered around the Vancouver-based collective Image Bank—founded in 1970 by the artists Michael Morris (a.k.a. Marcel Dot/Marcel Idea), Gary Lee Nova (a.k.a. Artimus Rat), and Vincent Trasov (a.k.a. Myra Peanut)—as well as Dana Atchley's Ace Space Company. Canadian mail art was influenced by and closely connected to mail artists in the United States, such as Ray Johnson, who was often considered the founder of mail art, Ken Friedman, and the Bay Area Dadaists.[18] Correspondence or mail artists—or networkers, as they were sometimes called—used the postal system as a medium and mode of distribution, exchanging personal correspondence such as postcards, letters, and collaged, rubberstamped, or photocopied images. Operating roughly on the principle of a chain letter, mail art depended upon the exchange of correspondence between artists—correspondence that would, in principle, increase over time as more individuals became part of the network. As Bronson recalled of the large volume of clippings and collages that began to pour in: "In the early days of General Idea, we used to get up rather late in the morning, get ourselves coffee and sit and open the mail, and opening the mail could easily take two or three hours."[19]

6.1

General Idea, *FILE* 1, no. 1, April 15, 1972, cover.
Photograph by David Hlynsky. Courtesy of AA Bronson
and David Hlynsky. Research Library, The Getty
Research Institute, Los Angeles (87-S274 no. 1).

FILE started off as a way to archive—or file—this deluge of mail art, as well as to chronicle General Idea's activities more generally.[20] It was one of several mail art magazines founded in the early 1970s, a number that would soar into the hundreds by the end of the decade. Among the best-known publications were *Info, N.Y.C.S. Weekly Breeder, West Bay Dadaist/Quoz, Rubber, Ephemera, Arte Postale!* and *Commonpress*. Usually produced in very limited editions of a couple hundred at most, these publications tended to have a handmade character, and included original collages, drawings, hand-stamped pages, and even objects pasted onto pages or contained in plastic bags. Others were crudely photocopied zines, or assemblings, with completely open submission processes in which contributors would submit a given number of copies of their work, which would then be compiled by the editor. Due to their limited circulation and unusual editorial procedures, most mail art magazines were distributed mainly among the mail artists who contributed to them. *FILE*'s insistently mass-produced format and much higher circulation are exceptional in this regard. While mail art was rooted largely in private correspondence between individuals, *FILE* sought to enlarge this network through the mass media, making mail art available to a much broader public.

In 1970 General Idea moved into the top two floors of an abandoned office building at 87 Yonge Street in Toronto's financial district—a rambling series of dilapidated rooms in which they managed to rig up a shower and kitchen and created a number of dramatic, themed rooms. The result was a kind of ornate sculptural environment that Bronson described in an unpublished text from the time: "Painted jungles and deco mirrors, feathers and bats, lizards and a profuse collection of esoterica have transformed this unlikely location into the Jungle Room, the Blue Ball Room, and other absurd delights."[21] It was here that they began to publish *FILE*. The first three issues of the magazine, funded by a $17,000 "local initiatives" grant from the Canadian Department of Manpower and Immigration, were printed in an edition of three thousand copies each, which were given away at local Toronto galleries and bookstores and mailed free to artists, galleries, and critics worldwide.

FILE in many ways echoed the ad hoc, do-it-yourself character of the underground press. (Bronson had previously edited the Winnipeg underground newspaper *The Loving Couch Press*, which he founded with several fellow architectural students who had dropped out of the University of Manitoba School of Architecture to found a commune.) Borrowing typesetting equipment from some friends of friends who were publishing a women's magazine, General Idea enlisted the entire ensemble of roommates, neighbors, and visitors who regularly congregated at 87 Yonge Street to contribute. As Bronson recalled, "whoever happened to be around at the time would be involved."[22] The collaborative nature of the magazine was an extension of the group's collective approach to artistic production, more generally; as they once declared, "being a trio frees us from the tyranny of individual genius."[23]

The editorial policy set out in the first issue of *FILE* suggested the magazine's artist-centered ethos: "All contributions will be considered, but emphasis is placed on evidence of research or other activity in progress, rather than on criticism, aesthetics, or historical considerations."[24] The first few issues provided free ad space to artists and artist-run organizations, reviewed alternative spaces and alternative publications, and offered logistical tips on public and private funding sources. Such serious, practical information was largely eclipsed, however, by commentary of a much different sort. Characterized by a profusion of pseudonyms, inside jokes, double entendres,

and spoofs and puns of every variety, the magazine tracked the humorous, outrageous, and sometimes ribald antics of General Idea and their friends.

As they explained in an editorial in the first issue: "In order to grasp the FILE phenomenon it is necessary to realize the extent of concerns involving the invisible network that bind
the world of Dr. Brute and Alex the Holy, Marcel Idea and Miss General Idea, Clara the Bag Lady
and Lady Brute, the Swedish Lady and Mr. Cones, Dadaland and Dada Long Legs, A. A. Bronson
and Dr. Fluxus, Ray Johnson and Sunny Bunny, Anna Banana and Honey Banana, Bum Bank and
Art Rat, Burtiful Buropia and Canadada."[25] Many of the articles in FILE came across as decidedly private and diaristic, as did the candid snapshots of General Idea and the rest of the mail art
scene. For example, a column entitled "Miss Honey's Diary" divulged the secret confessions of a
thirteen-year-old girl in the early 1960s, including her teenage crushes, love of Hollywood film,
and dread of nuclear war. Letters to the editor were often rambling personal notes filled with
confidential disclosures and quotidian details, and signed "Love" or "Love and Kisses." Given the
magazine's professed commitment to democratizing the art scene, FILE's cultivation of an exclusive
aura around a coterie of insiders seems paradoxical. As Bronson himself admitted, "FILE is, at
best, ambiguous and requires explication for the uninitiated."[26] And yet the magazine promoted a
much different in-crowd from that which dominated the pages of *Artforum* and other mainstream
art magazines at the time.

For the first several years, FILE remained closely tied to the mail art scene, which was a
means to generate both subscribers and content for the magazine. For example, it circulated an
international artists' directory (a kind of white pages for the art world) and a series of Image Bank
image request lists through which artists could join the network and request images to use in
mail art activities. It also published selected examples of mail art, and solicited reader participation and feedback in the form of "reader responses pages." The enigmatic, blurry photograph on
the cover of issue 2 was itself a response to General Idea's mail art project *Manipulating the Self*, in
which participants were asked to take photographs of themselves holding a rather awkward pose
which involved wrapping one's arm around one's head to grab one's own chin. Another mail art
project became the basis for FILE's food column, which published bizarre and sometime crude
recipes, such as a maraschino cherry and peanut butter sandwich, Ukrainian frog rolls, "faggot
pudding," and "Art Historian a La Mode De Caen" (which called for stoning an art historian to
death and was meant "to be eaten only by Fine Arts students").

With its reliance on such techniques as collage, rubberstamps, and photocopying, mail
art thumbed its nose at received definitions of aesthetic quality and competence, welcoming
amateur and dilettante efforts. While this approach earned it epithets such as "quick-kopy-krap"
and "junk mail" (sometimes well deserved), mail art must also be seen within the context of other
artistic practices of the 1960s as an example of deskilling: the deliberate attempt to eliminate
mastery and virtuosity from the work of art, witnessed, for example, in the tasklike dance of the
Judson dancers or the industrially produced, reductive forms of minimalist sculpture. FILE participated in mail art's radical rejection of the criteria and categories of the professional art world,
especially class-based notions of artistic expertise, by publishing contributions from "practicing
non-artists," such as Valerie of Winnipeg, whose "Collection of Groovy Guys" (ten snapshots of
grinning men with sideburns and shaggy hairstyles) appeared in the second issue.

IMAGE BANK IMAGE REQUEST LIST

"Words beget image and image is virus–"

The complete Image Bank Image Request Lists are being published in book format by the Talon Press, Vancouver, B.C., Canadada.

Image requests for issues of FILE should be directed to FILE Magazine, 87 Yonge Street, Toronto Canadada M5C 1S8.

A

A SPACE/MARIEN LEWIS
85 St. Nicholas St., Toronto, Canadada
Pictures of people biting their nails, yourself biting your nails, when in Toronto pay A Space a visit.

AARON
2271 Edgelow Rd., Victoria, B. C. Canadada
Pictures of mouths.

ACCUMULATION/KAREN KORELL
R. D. 1, Sugar Run, Pa. 18846, U. S. A.
Map drawings and pictures of the Canadian border.

ACE SPACE COMPANY/DANA ATCHLEY
Box 183, Crested Butte, Colorado 81224, U. S. A.
Slides of your space and/or slides of the following: rainbows, stars, palm trees, lightning bolts, wheels, corn, crabs, clouds, roses, cactus and on-the-road shots.

AIRPRESS
1075 Jassamine Way, Fort Lee, New Jersey 07024, U. S. A.
Pictures of zebras and post cards of classical works of art.

DIETRICH ALBRECHT/REFLECTIONS PRESS
Raichberg 7, 7 Stuttgart 61, Germany
Images of politicians in action and state funerals.

ALEATORY NOVELTIES/BARRY McCALLION
130 N. Brooks Ave., Claremont, Calif. 91711, U. S. A.
Alfred Jarry memorial air lift project, The Marcel Duchamp Fan Club West, images and information regarding images of "this is not the oars mistress".

MARIO AMAYA/N.Y.C.C.
2 Columbus Circle, N. Y., N. Y., U. S. A.
Images of bullet wounds, bondage and billiard tables.

AMOS, EVERYTHING ASS.
283 Brunswick Ave., Toronto, Canadada
Requests images of the Statue of Liberty, diamond head in the background of Waikiki, dense postcards, Maytag families, camels, gas pumps, sep. with hose attached, double esp. with hose in car flanks, and maybe FEMALE ATTENDUNTS???

ANT FARM c/o HUDSON
2255 Lyon St., San Francisco, Calif. 94115, U. S. A.
Requests race images and items, negro cartoons, famous bigots and pics of Larry Rivers.

ANT FARM, c/o DOUG & CHIP
224 North Arcola St., Angleton, Texas 77515, U. S. A.
Comparisons, photos of classic cars and pics of cars with their owners, pictures of yourself in front of your television set, stylized maps of the USA, motels.

ELEANOR ANTIN
201 Pacific Ave., Solana Beach, Calif. 92075, U. S. A.
Suggestions on ways of recycling her 100 boots.

ARAKAWA
124 West Houston St., N. Y., N. Y., U. S. A.
calendars.

ARCHIGRAM
59 Aberdare Gardens, London N.W. 6, England.
Images of "other world" fairs, examples of Mondo Artie design.

BOX ARNOLD
R. R. 1, Winlaw, B. C., Canadada.
Images of the earth from outer-space.

ART FOR ALL, c/o GILBERT & GEORGE
12 Fournier St., London E. 1, England
Images of nest eggs nesting.

ART RAT
1919 Granville St., Vancouver 9, B. C., Canadada.
Dead letters, forking paths, shark fins becoming telephones, drive-in theatres, baseball and sport photos.

MARY ASHLEY/OH SHIT!
2520 Webster St., Berkeley, Calif. 94705, U. S. A.
Image loss.

BARBARA ASTMAN
56 Beverley St., Toronto 26, Canadada
Requests images of cows.

AVENUE B SCHOOL OF ART
Box 277, North Bennington, Vermont, U. S. A.
Pictures of the Invisible Man and Woman to be forwarded to the North West Mounted Valise.

B

B & R
2263 York St., Vancouver 9, B. C. Canadada
Requests gull, merry-go-round and canoe images.

AL BALKAVIND
Fine Arts Gallery, University of British Columbia, Vancouver 8, B. C., Canadada
Images of vampires and shop windows.

ANNA BANANA
c/o 44 West 6th Ave., Vancouver, B. C., Canadada
Images of foolish things, images and information on bananas, everything you ever dreamt about bananas, Queen of Hearts images, rainbows.

HONEY BANANAS
Box 614, Sausalito, Calif. 94965, U. S. A.
Buster Brown and dog tags, wolves, dogs, ducks, foxes, Mr. and Mrs. Peanuts, home made toys from Oglalla, Nebraska.

G. BARRENHOLTZ
c/o O. C. A., 100 McCaul St., Toronto, Canadada
Requests information on "Who has heard of Royden Rabinowich?"

MARTIN BARTLETT
557 East 13th Ave., Vancouver, B. C., Canadada
Images of earth, air, fire, water, ether, music for flutes, drums, bells and horns.

SCOTT & FREUDE BARTLETT
57 Harriet Alley, San Francisco, Calif. 94103, U. S. A.
Stills and information from your movies.

BUFFALO BARTON
c/o Ms. Generality, 24 Bayview, Wards Island, Toronto, Canadada.
Anything pertaining to Ms. Generality, Vic d'Or and the Coleman saga.

MAX BATES
931 Lakeview Rd., Victoria, B. C. Canadada
Memories and photos of the Grande Hotels.

DON BATTERSHALL
Hotel Damiot, 6235 Primrose, Los Angeles, Calif. 90068, U. S. A.
Polaroids of the color of the sky, must have the time and place of the photo.

IAIN BAXTER/N.E. THING CO.
1419 Riverside Dr., North Vancouver, B. C. Canadada
Suggestions for what to do with everything that is left after everything has become art.

PHILIP BEARD
8 Ifield Rd., West Brompton, London S.W. 10, England.
Pics of rabbits and helicopters, not necessarily participating in the same space-time continuum, but should they coincide then so much the better.

DONALD M. BELL
5 Cortleigh Blvd., Toronto 310, Canadada
Images of Humphrey Bogart and anything from the film Casablanca.

GARY BELL
1330 Harwood, Apt. 1807, Vancouver 5, B. C., Canadada
Pictures of highrise apartments and lobbys.

ANTHONY BENJAMEN/THE NORTH POLE PROJECT
369 Berkeley St., Toronto 225, Canadada
Pictures taken at the North and South Poles, information pics on prisms.

JOHN BENSON
1937 Mt. Vernon St., Philadelphia, Pa. U. S. A.
Images of head bands and the Pacific Northwest.

JEFF BERNER/INNERSPACE PROJECT
55 Mountain View, Mill Valley, Calif. U. S. A.
Ideas for a book on ways to use the postal system and old pornographic pics from between 1880 - 1939.

JOSEPH BEUYS
4 Dusseldorf - Iberkassel, Drakeplatz 4, West Germany
Everything you ever received from Ken Friedman and Fluxus West that was xeroxed.

STAN BEVINGTON/COACH HOUSE PRESS
401 Huron St. (rear), Toronto, Canadada
Images of the closest thing to "the pipe", images of beavers (not the split species).

BILL BISSETT/BLEWOINTMENT PRESS
Box 8590, Station H, Vancouver 5, B. C., Canadada
Images of 8½ x 11 paintings, drawings, photos, anything.

CHICKEN & AURORA BOREALIS/CRESCENT MOON NOVELTIES
61 West 70th, #3A, N. Y., N. Y. 10023, U. S. A.
Images of the crescent moon.

DAVID BOURDON
33 Greenwich Ave., N. Y., N. Y. 10014, U. S. A.
Images of people at home in Locust Valley.

DAVID BRIERS/PAGES MAGAZINE
15 Park Mansions, Prince of Wales Drive, London S. W. 11, England
Nothing by mouth, moustache and thin nostril images.

EDWIN BRIGGS
136 Middle Road, Southborough, Mass. 01772, U. S. A.
Pics of lady and midget wrestlers, pics of people getting hit by pitched balls.

HOWARD BROOMFIELD/ACOUSTIC ECOLOGY
1750 East 2nd Ave., Vancouver 12, B. C., Canadada
Tapes recorded in urban situations.

WALT BROWN
29 Crescent Rd., Madison, N. J. 07940, U. S. A.
Images in black & white of machines of any kind, living environment fantasies.

DR. BRUTE/B.B.I.
44 West 6th Ave., Vancouver, B. C., Canadada
Pictures of Brutopia, leopard skin, fayhaye neighhaye pics, anything brutiful.

BRIAN BUCZAK
14040 Garfield, Detroit, Michigan 48239, U. S. A.
Requests any or all white rimmed or pointed or rhinestone trimmed glasses. Broken or otherwise. Photos or drawings of glasses would be nice also. Also any unwanted or damaged photos.

BETH OF BURNABY
Box 6811, Station S, Vancouver, B. C., Canadada
Images of sunflowers.

WILLIAM BURROUGHS
8 Duke St., St. James, London S.W. 1, England
Ideas for camouflage in 1984.

RUSSEL L. BUTLER
310 S. Smith St., Gurdon, Ark. 71743, U. S. A.
Images of Marilyn Monroe, Coca-Cola, newspaper clippings of movie ads, esp. the Bijou.

6.2

"Image Bank Image Request List," *FILE* 2, nos. 1 and 2, May 1973, page 15. Courtesy of AA Bronson.

Despite all of its joking around, *FILE* was rooted in a serious political objective: to create an alternative, decentralized informational structure that would oppose the hierarchies of the art world establishment, a goal that was central to the mail art network more generally. As Ken Friedman observed, "It seemed to us that certain individuals at the center of the art world media—critics, curators, dealers—could reach anyone, while the rest of us had a hard time finding jealously guarded mailing lists to reach others."[27] Exemplary of *FILE*'s challenge to the hierarchies of the mainstream art world was its "Top Ten Chart," which originated with a mass mailing that invited recipients to vote by sending back the bottom half of a serrated postcard, printed with the following call for participation:

> *FILE*, the tabloid for Artists by Artists extends an invitation to help choose today's TOP TEN ARTISTS. Would you like to see all of your top favorite Artists in every issue of *FILE*? Well you can if you just follow these simple instructions. First, choose your ten favorites and write their names on the attached coupon. Second, write your name and address, cut out the coupon and mail to *FILE*, 87 Yonge Street, Toronto 1, Ontario.[28]

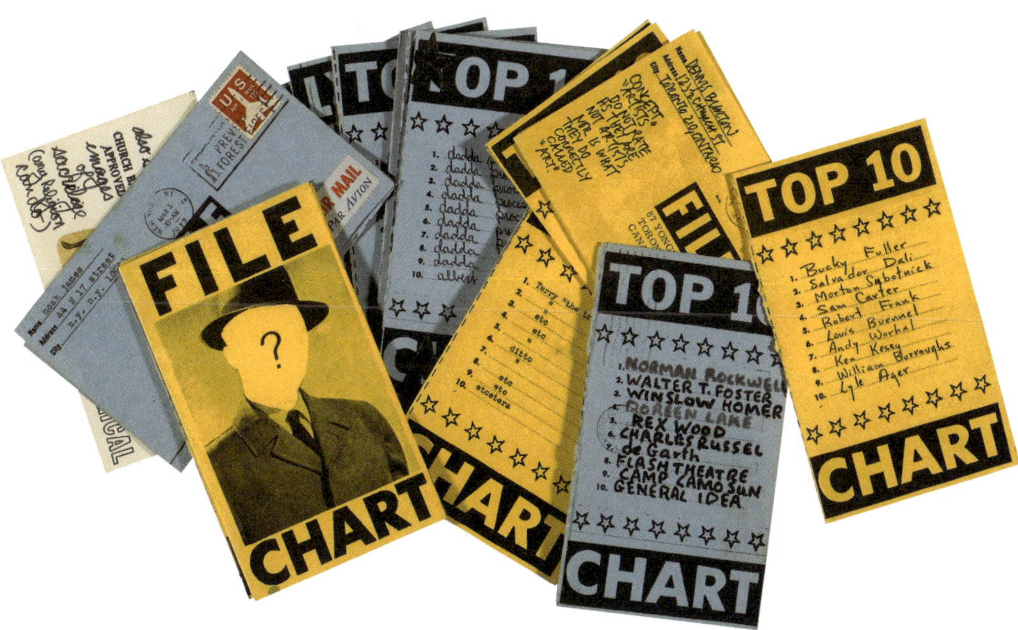

6.3

General Idea, *FILE* "Top Ten Chart" mailers, 1972,
National Gallery of Canada Library and Archives,
Photo © NGC, Ottawa.

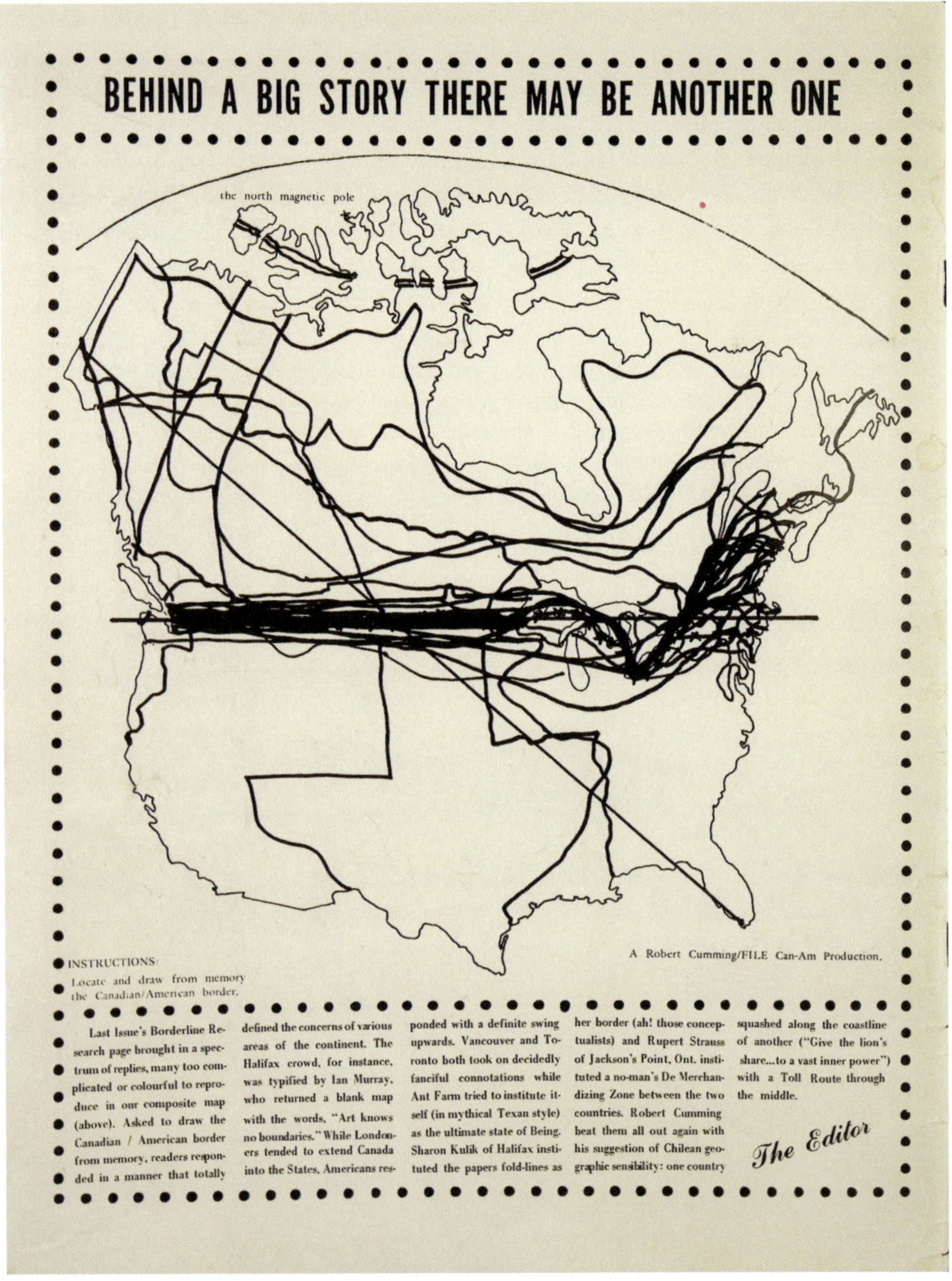

6.4

General Idea, composite map, "Borderline Research"
reader response project, *FILE* 1, nos. 2 and 3,
May-June 1972. Courtesy of AA Bronson.

A regular feature in the first several issues, the "Top Ten Chart" illustrates *FILE*'s populist approach to determining artistic merit, based not on the expert judgments of critics, dealers, and collectors, but on the opinions of its readers. Accordingly, the magazine revealed a social order vastly different from that of the mainstream art world. Not surprisingly, the "Top Ten Chart" was dominated by members of the mail art network, with Ray Johnson in first place. "The only concession to high art," the editors insisted, was Andy Warhol, who placed fifth.[29] Also notable was the prevalence of women artists. As the editors explained, "The female gender rises through the medium of the mailing chain with an elegant ease, establishing itself with mundane eloquence in the arena of our affliction"—a fact they celebrated in the second issue with a section of "women's pages," featuring notable "fe-mail" artists such as Anna Banana.[30]

The "Top Ten Chart" also gave prominence to Canadian artists, suggesting that mail art's rejection of the hierarchies of the art world had a special significance for Canadian artists, who tended to be overshadowed by their colleagues in the United States. The proximity of the majority of Canadians to the U.S. border (according to an often cited if seldom verified statistic, 90 percent of Canadians live within 100 miles of the border) gave them a unique vantage point onto American culture, which they were simultaneously immersed in and marginalized from. The first issue of *FILE* drew attention to the charged nature of the border in the Canadian collective psyche in a reader response project consisting of a blank map of North America with the instructions, "Draw from memory the Canadian/American border." The resulting composite map was a comical and telling portrayal of U.S. cultural imperialism, with borders designated as far north as the Arctic Circle. As General Idea observed, "readers responded in a manner that totally defined the concerns of various areas of the continent. ... While Londoners tended to extend Canada into the United States, Americans responded with a definite swing upwards."[31]

General Idea's fascination with the border as both a literal and a metaphorical construct was evident in a series of projects they called "borderline cases," ten of which were published in the September 1973 issue. These collages of found media images were studies of various types of representational procedures—including mirroring, mimicry, masquerade, and parody—which were capable of bringing about radical shifts in perspective by destabilizing received social categories, rendering them ambiguous and strange. As the artists described in their accompanying editorial, such ambiguity was "not a symptom of a schizophrenic who travels back and forth across the line but a quality of the border dweller who performs in the stolen moments."[32] With their "borderline cases," General Idea reclaimed the experience of marginalization as a positive thing and an opportunity for critical engagement—an idea that not only concerned geography but resonated with other experiences of marginalization as well. As Partz would later observe, "I think that being gay forces you into an outside position on society, culture, whatever ... it can be a negative thing, but on the other hand it can be a positive thing."[33] The border was thus more than just a physical boundary between countries; it was a trope for the gulf between signifier and signified, intrinsic to any representational medium. By offering the possibility of manipulating or distorting meaning, the border suggested a liminal zone of transformation—an opportunity for border crossings concerning not only nationality or geography, but all kinds of social codes and identities including gender, sexuality, class, beauty, taste. With its alternative, queer, Canadian perspective, *FILE* was perhaps the ultimate borderline case.

General Idea, "Pablum for the Pablum Eaters," *FILE* 2,
nos. 1 and 2, May 1973. Courtesy of AA Bronson.

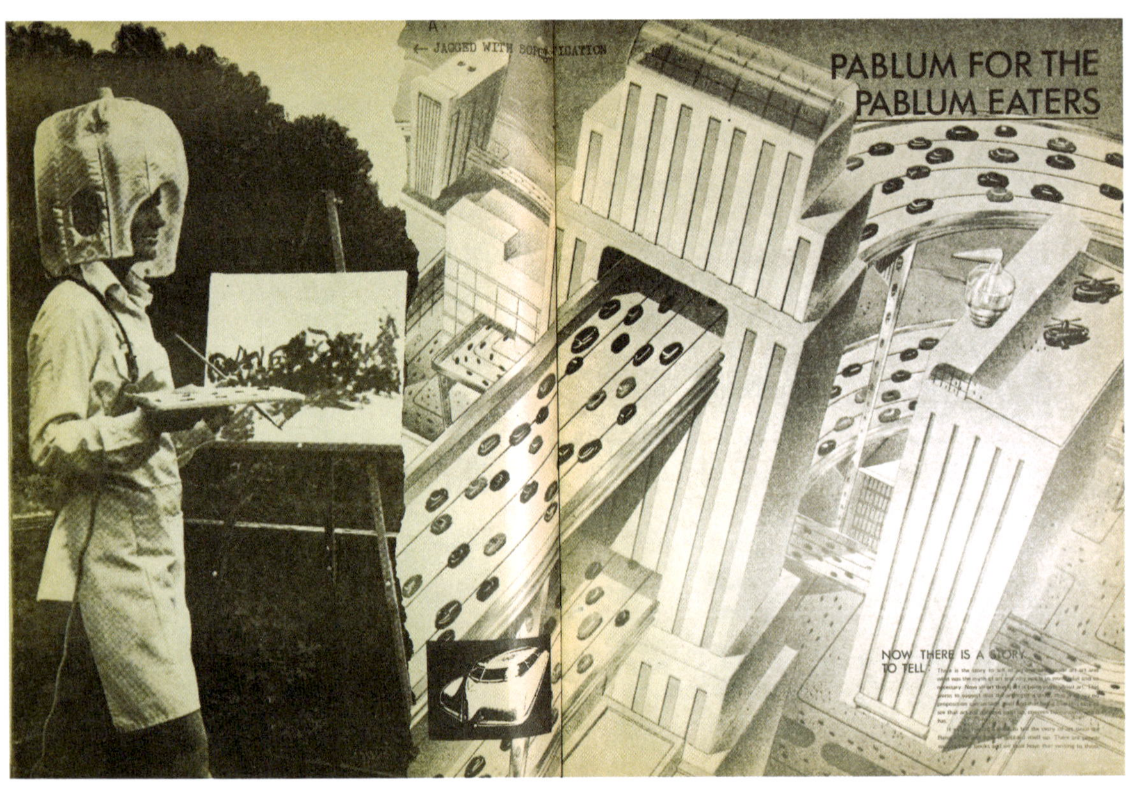

THE MAGAZINE AS MIRROR

Mail art depended heavily on the practices of appropriating and repurposing mass media imagery through collage and other methods of *détournement*, as suggested by two popular mail art slogans, "Collage or perish" and "Cut up or shut up." In the May 1973 issue of *FILE*, General Idea published a lengthy editorial entitled "Pablum for the Pablum Eaters" in which they laid out the intellectual and theoretical framework for such practices. Pablum, a popular Canadian brand of baby cereal, connoted the infantilizing quality of the mainstream media. And yet, as the editorial made clear, General Idea (along with their cohorts, Image Bank) saw mail art as the basis for a radical media that encouraged ordinary people—"Pablum eaters"—to become empowered producers of images instead of passive consumers. The sixteen-page editorial was an extended collage of found media imagery, much of it from old *Fortune* magazines, which combined futuristic superhighways, mad scientists, time capsules, a man-eating cactus, an elephant safari, and the *Manneken Pis*, to create a phantasmagoric yet vaguely recognizable mediascape within which the viewer was invited to free-associate.

The essay superimposed on top of this sequence was itself a kind of textual montage which lifted ideas and quotations from numerous other writers and theorists, among them Claude Lévi-Strauss, William S. Burroughs, and Marshall McLuhan.[34] Among other ideas, the editors pointed out parallels between the tactical media strategies of mail art and Lévi-Strauss's notion of bricolage, which he observed in the myth making of indigenous cultures in North and South America.[35] In *The Savage Mind*, Lévi-Strauss stressed that myths were not inferior versions of modern scientific knowledge but were equally valid forms of taxonomy through which to categorize and understand the world. Unlike the totalizing methods of science, however, myth relied on bricolage—a creative making-do with the "remains and debris" of preexisting languages and symbols. In *FILE*, General Idea encouraged readers to become bricoleurs—"culture criminals" and intellectual cannibals" who fabricated "alternative myths" out of official cultural representations. "History is the story of the 'great' and the wealthy and the powerful few. The poor and the renegade are left with myth, legend and folklore," they wrote.[36]

Another important point of reference was Brion Gysin's cut-up method, a technique of writing—most famously employed in William Burroughs's novel *The Nova Express*—that depended on folding in excerpts from preexisting texts. The cut-up method exemplified Burroughs's concept of language as a virus—the idea that language is not a neutral vehicle for communication but infects the speaker, parasitically invading the act of communication and distorting the message.[37] Within the context of *FILE*, viral language implied the possibility of interfering with the transmission of mass media, using its structure to spread rogue messages. As General Idea explained in "Pablum for the Pablum Eaters," they were concerned with "establishing a culture that relates to official culture as a virus does to an organism."[38] (Burroughs would himself subscribe to *FILE* and participate in the image request lists, and eventually he published several short stories in the magazine.)

Within this context, the Image Bank image request lists published in *FILE* can be seen as a central part of the radical media practices that the magazine encouraged. Described as a "decentralized clip art center," the image request lists cataloged specific types of images (such as "Palm Trees," "Pineapples," "19th century Hot Air Balloons," "Easter Eggs," "tattoo pics and porno") that

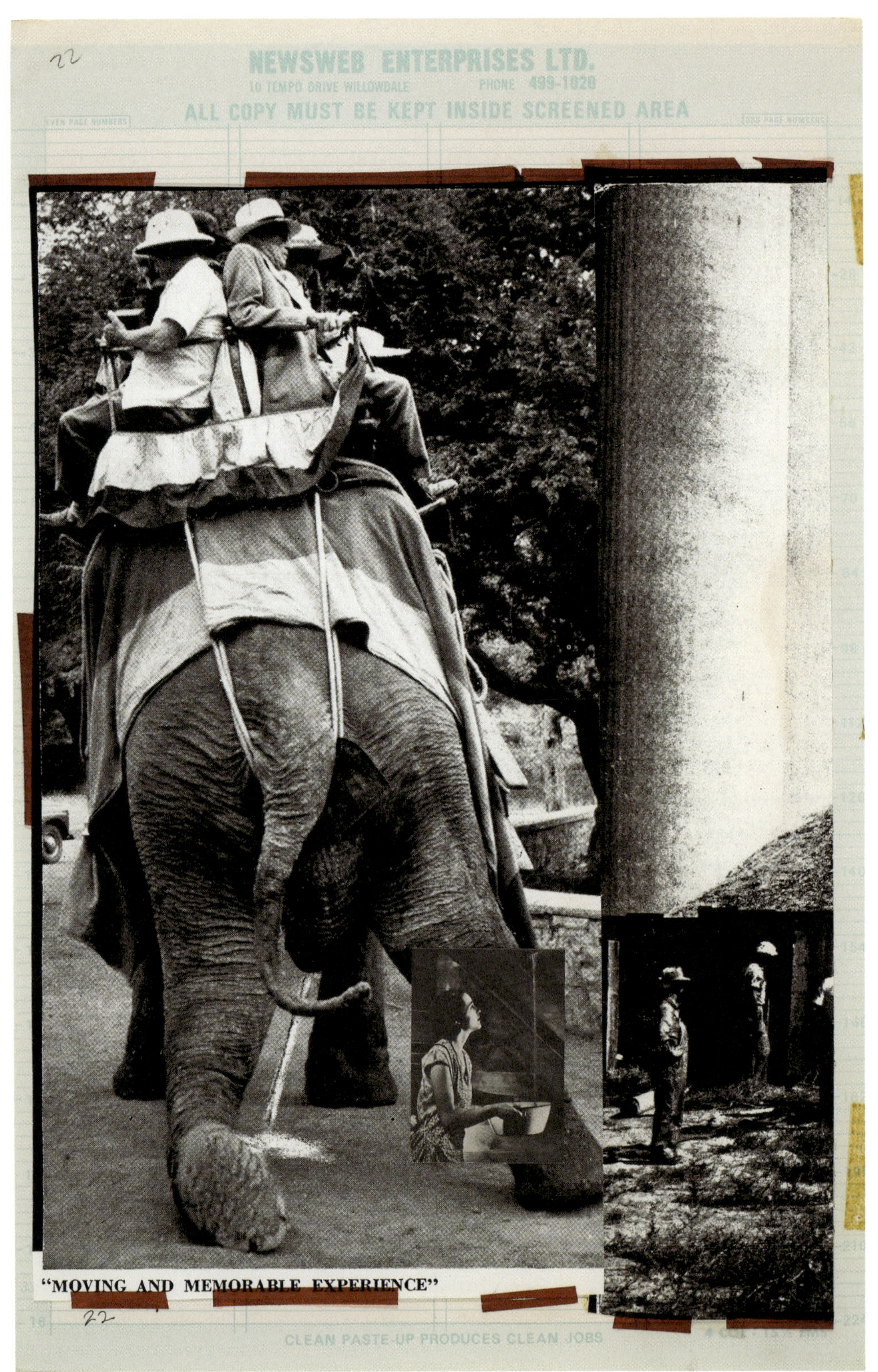
NEWSWEB ENTERPRISES LTD.
10 TEMPO DRIVE WILLOWDALE
PHONE 499-1020
ALL COPY MUST BE KEPT INSIDE SCREENED AREA
"MOVING AND MEMORABLE EXPERIENCE"
CLEAN PASTE-UP PRODUCES CLEAN JOBS

artists requested to use as source material in their work.[39] By literally cutting these images out of their original context, General Idea and Image Bank believed that artists might free the images from their bondage as commodity fetishes, prompting new kinds of meanings and desires. As Bronson insisted, "It's not just a matter of publishing, it's making people aware of new needs or people making you aware of some new need."[40] *FILE* featured particularly successful instances of appropriated and transformed images in its "Image of the Month" column. In issue 1, for example, Robert Cummings published a photomontage of a Ritz cracker with anuses dotting its indented surface—an image whose uncanny sexual punning rivaled surrealist objects such as Meret Oppenheim's famous fur-lined teacup, emblematizing the transgressive power of such practices.

FILE not only reproduced and circulated examples of détourned media imagery; it was itself a prime example of such practices, as its confiscated *Life* logo suggests. The magazine's own layout emphasizes that the magazine page is itself a form of bricolage within which different kinds of texts and images—headlines, columns, photographs, and illustrations—collide and intermingle. The original paste-up sheets for the magazine—light-blue gridded sheets, onto which images and columns of text have been pasted or waxed—appear as relics of the pre-digital era, when physical cutting and pasting were an intrinsic part of magazine layout. Indeed, the techniques of montage and collage were invented not by artists, but by anonymous producers of advertisements, magazines, and other forms of commercial culture.

While art historians and critics have distinguished between the ubiquitous commercial use of montage and collage in mass media and the aesthetically and politically progressive practices of montage pioneered by avant-garde artists such as John Heartfield and Hannah Höch, *FILE* complicates this strict opposition between commercial and avant-garde techniques by inhabiting them both at once.[41] This is evident in the "Pablum for the Pablum Eaters" spread, which relies on the visual vocabulary of mainstream consumer culture, using sophisticated super-overlay techniques, for example, to seamlessly combine imagery and text, while at the same time rupturing the illusion of the page as a single, continuous surface, revealing its constructed nature. The layout uses abrupt shifts in scale and size to create jarring juxtapositions, and accentuates the jagged, torn edges where images come together. By playing these two techniques off of one another, the magazine refuses to settle too comfortably into either one, highlighting the dialectical relationship between them.

6.6

General Idea, paste-up sheet for "Pablum for the Pablum Eaters," *FILE* 2, nos. 1 and 2, May 1973, page 22. National Gallery of Canada Library and Archives, Ottawa.

By late 1973, the correspondence art phenomenon had begun to run its course in the pages of *FILE*. In the September 1973 issue, Ray Johnson announced the "death" of his New York Correspondence School in a mock obituary notice.[42] Robert Cummings likewise bid farewell to the mail art scene, expressing his chagrin at the deteriorating aesthetic quality of the "junk mail" he received and at its potential ecological impact, confessing, "I get stuff every day that barely makes it out of the envelope and into the trash it is so terrible. It's not the terribleness of the art that worries me, but the enormous waste of paper."[43] *FILE* would continue to publish the Image Bank image request lists until its Fall 1975 issue, but it would gradually distance itself from the mail art scene, prompting a string of takeoffs, including *VILE*—started, according to editor Anna Banana, in response to "*FILE*'s growing disdain for mail art"—and later *BILE* and *SMILE*.[44]

However, General Idea continued to support mail art—and all kinds of artists' publications—through Art Metropole, the artists' distribution center they founded in 1974. Art Metropole distributed magazines, artists' books, videos, mail art, and other ephemera, and also served as General Idea's new artistic headquarters. As General Idea announced in the December 1973 issue of *FILE*, Art Metropole would function as "an extension of *FILE* Megazine, taking over and diversifying the functions of reflection and connection."[45] Housed in a building at 241 Yonge Street which had been constructed in 1911 for Toronto's first major art supplier (from which the center took its name), Art Metropole anticipated artists' spaces such as Franklin Furnace and Printed Matter, both founded in New York in 1976.

Meanwhile, *FILE* began to focus more exclusively on General Idea's own evolving artistic interests and activities, as well as on the alternative scene in Toronto. Among other things, *FILE* documented the overlap between artists and the punk and new wave music scene centered around bands like the Dishes, the Viletones, and Rough Trade, who played at the Beverley Tavern on Queen Street in Toronto, which the members of General Idea frequented in the mid-1970s.[46] Attesting to *FILE*'s significance within the experimental music scene, the group the Residents distributed a promotional flexi-disc of their first album, *Meet the Residents*, in the February 1974 issue. In 1977 General Idea produced the "Punk 'til you Puke" issue of *FILE*, featuring the Sex Pistols, the Clash, the Talking Heads, Throbbing Gristle, and Richard Hell and the Voidoids. The issue also included reviews of several punk zines, such as *Sniffin Glue*, *Punk*, and *Search and Destroy*, and mimicked in its own layout the layered, crude aesthetic of such do-it-yourself publications. In their editorial, General Idea compared their own strategies of alternative distribution to the punk ideology: "it's cheap ... it's easy ... go do it!"[47]

The magazine continued to hone its imitation of sensationalistic public relations jargon, inaugurating its "Bzzz Bzzz Bzzz" column in the Spring 1976 issue, which caricatured tabloid gossip columns with namedropping, art world celebrity sightings, photo ops, and mock scandals. For example: "The controversial critic Benjamin Buchloh explained to his date that 60's Minimalism is at the root of all performance art including his appearance in this gossip column. Filmmaker Ross McLaren overheard October critic Douglas Crimp tell Parachute critic Thierry de Duve that the party was simultaneously subversive and complicit hence postmodern."[48] It also staged a series of semifictionalized *FILE* parties by condensing separate social interactions into a single evening—a takeoff on the *Life* magazine column "Life Goes to a Party." As Bronson later recalled about the magazine, "We built up a whole mythical world, and only the tip of that iceberg existed in reality."[49]

Throughout much of the 1970s, this mythical world largely revolved around an event known as the 1984 Miss General Idea Pageant, which entailed an increasingly intricate and convoluted series of preparations, objects, and performances; many of these were generated solely for the purpose of being covered in the magazine, creating a kind of self-enclosed bubble. As Bronson described *FILE* at the time: "Now the focus has stepped up. It's gone from mirroring the community to mirroring the mirroring of the community. In other words, most of the material we are now covering is material generated by *FILE*. *FILE* now is primarily about *FILE*."[50] The 1984 Miss General Pageant was conceived as a sequel to a series of earlier performances, the most elaborate of which was the *1971 Miss General Idea Pageant*, held at the Art Gallery of Ontario. A meticulously orchestrated affair, the 1971 pageant involved a flurry of promotional documentation and publicity, with official-looking contestant "entry kits" and acceptance forms which were mailed out to sixteen preselected finalists—all of which culminated in a campy awards ceremony complete with limousines, searchlights, live musical performances, judges, trophies, and prizes. Bronson was the master of ceremonies, and Marcel Dot was crowned as the winning contestant. General Idea initially planned to do the pageant annually, but soon realized that this was unrealistic given the complicated and time-consuming nature of the event. Instead, they decided that the next one would occur in "the future"—a concept symbolized by the Orwellian year 1984. Much of their work over the next half-decade or so, including performances, sculpture, architecture, videos, as well as *FILE* magazine itself, was thus contrived as an extensive buildup to the 1984 Miss General Idea Pageant.

More than just a fake beauty contest, the Miss General Idea Pageant was an allegory for the art world itself—part of an elaborate mythical cosmology, a kind of parallel universe that General Idea devised in order to caricature the conventions of the mainstream art world. Through the medium of the beauty pageant and its various architectural and mass media permutations, General Idea both mobilized and made fun of the art world's systems of taste and aesthetic value, and especially the roles of fame, money, and publicity in this system. The unifying concept behind all of these was glamour. As they wrote in an editorial in the "Glamour Issue" of *FILE* (Autumn 1975):

> We wanted to be artists and we knew that if we were famous and glamorous we could say we were artists and we would be. We never felt we had to produce great art to be great artists. ... We knew Glamour was not an object, not an action, not an idea. We knew Glamour never emerged from the "nature" of things. There are no glamorous people, no glamorous events. We knew Glamour was artificial. We knew that in order to be glamorous we had to become plagiarists, intellectual parasites.[51]

General Idea's fixation on glamour had partly to do with the fact that it was such a taboo subject within the art world of the 1970s. As they later recalled, "It was in extremely bad taste to talk about glamour. It was the last subject in the world that anybody would mention. And the same with money and fame. ... It would have meant the end of their careers probably, if [artists] were demonstrably any of those things. Although secretly, of course, they wanted all three."[52] Like a return of the repressed, glamour appeared in the Miss General Idea project as an uncanny version of itself, familiar yet strange, marked by perversions and compulsive repetitions. Indeed, the

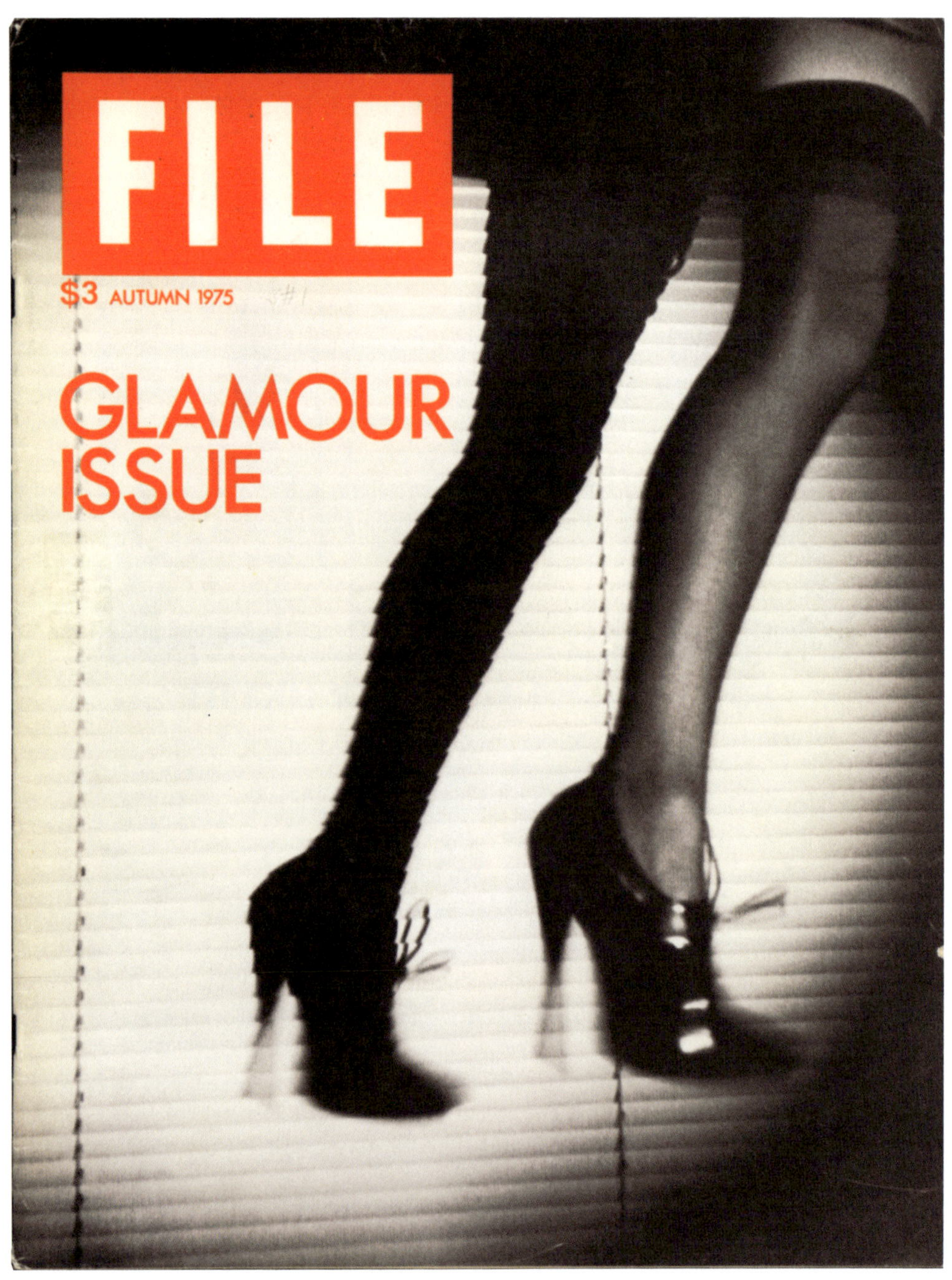
FILE
$3 AUTUMN 1975
GLAMOUR
ISSUE

6.7

General Idea, *FILE* 3, no. 1, Autumn 1975, the
"Glamour Issue." Research Library, The Getty Research
Institute, Los Angeles (87-S274).

winning contestant of the Miss General Idea Pageant most frequently represented in the pages of *FILE* was Miss General Idea 1971, Marcel Idea, wearing a liver-colored *Miss General Idea Gown* bunched up around his neck. And the spirit of Miss General Idea was played by Anna Depuis, the former Miss Montreal, decked out in full bondage gear including a cat mask, a black bathing suit, and high-heeled boots.

FILE participated in General Idea's *détournement* of conventional notions of glamour by reporting on the preparations for the 1984 Pageant and showcasing various costumes and props, such as the *Luxon V.B.* (1973), a large venetian blind with double-sided mirrored slats, and the *Miss General Idea Shoe* (found, c. 1973), a brown and black patent leather stiletto-heeled pump. However, the magazine also played a crucial role in the restructuring of the relationship between artist and audience that the project sought to bring about. Using the reader response pages initially developed within the context of mail art, General Idea solicited feedback from readers on various aspects of the pageant preparations. By far the most elaborate of these was the design and construction of the Pavillion—a structure that would house the 1984 pageant and its 1,984 audience members. Conceived as both a literal architectural structure and an allegorical construct, the Pavillion was a kind of decentralized museum or archive composed of the collective submissions or "image tenders" of reader's proposals and blueprints.

In the September 1973 issue, a sheet of blank graph paper was provided as a centerfold insert to be used by readers to submit designs for the Pavillion's grand stairway. The other side of the insert showed a mockup of the future January 1984 cover of *FILE* featuring Marcel Idea as Miss General Idea, stressing the strange proleptic temporality of the project and the magazine's role in documenting this event which had not yet occurred. The proposals received back (about twenty or so) ranged from the mythical to the extravagant to the simply preposterous. One reader described a futuristic structure consisting of nine spheres connected by tubes that would be solar-powered with fiber optic lamps. Another suggested glass stairs that sparkled with Mylar, a red carpet, and singing plants. The most expensive proposal was by Lagtek, who suggested a TV Totem tower made out of over two thousand large-screen televisions for an estimated cost of $84 million.[53] Like much of General Idea's work, the Pavillion existed at the crossroads between metaphor and reality, keeping the two realms in a productive tension.

Perhaps it was testimony to their success in confusing the distinction between representation and reality that General Idea's audience sometimes took things a little too literally. Bronson recalled, "As 1984 came closer, we realized that people were expecting us to build an actual pavilion."[54] Their solution, fittingly enough, was to construct another fiction as an escape route from the first, staging a fake fire in which the mythical Pavillion burned to the ground. They made a dummy mock-up of the ruins in Kingston, Ontario, set off smoke bombs, and even collaborated with the local fire department, who responded to the scene as if it were an actual fire. Covered extensively in the Summer 1978 issue (as if it were happening in 1984) with images of the structure's charred remains, the destruction of the Pavillion further exacerbated the project's temporal dissonances and inversions. Like Smithson's "ruins in reverse"—as the artist called the unfinished construction sites of Passaic, New Jersey, which "don't *fall* into ruin *after* they are built but rather *rise* into ruin before they are built"[55]—the Pavillion of the future had become an artifact of the past without ever having passed through the present.

As the primary archive of the 1984 Miss General Idea Pageant, *FILE* participated crucially in its disturbance of teleological time. As General Idea wrote, "All archives are a means of making present, of establishing the past as an existing presence."[56] Indeed, the magazine functioned as an intervention into the historical process that might disrupt modernity's rational ideology of progress, suggesting a model of the archive not merely as a receptacle or repository for history but as an active process of making history.

QUEERING THE MAGAZINE: *FILE*'S PERFORMATIVITY

The Summer 1978 issue of *FILE*, featuring the burning of the Pavillion building, marked the tenth anniversary of General Idea. As such milestones have a tendency to do, the occasion seemed to prompt a mood of self-reflection and reassessment for the group. While *FILE* would continue to publish occasional articles about excavations from the Pavillion, its drawn-out anticipation of the future 1984 Miss General Idea Pageant had lost much of its momentum. In other ways as well, the magazine's initial editorial impetus had shifted. Its goal of creating a Canadian art scene no longer felt as urgent, now that thriving artistic communities had taken hold in Toronto and other cities across Canada, as witnessed by the proliferation of new art spaces and galleries, as well as a handful of new alternative art periodicals such as *Centerfold, Parallelogramme, Art Communication Edition / Strike, Image Nation, Only Paper Today, Is, Open Letter, Parachute, Queen Street Magazine, Rampike,* and *Impulse.*

Even *FILE*'s physical appearance had changed, after repeated legal threats by Time Inc. had forced General Idea to redesign the magazine's logo. The publishing giant sent its first "cease and desist" letters in June 1974, arguing that the "unauthorized simulation of the cover of *LIFE* magazine constitutes trademark infringement and unfair trading upon and appropriation of the goodwill and reputation of *LIFE* magazine."[57] In its characteristic smart-alecky manner, General Idea published the official legal correspondence in *FILE* as letters to the editor. Eventually, however, faced with mounting legal fees, they conceded—choosing "life over *LIFE*," as they put it in their editorial—and unveiled a new cover design (selected through an international *FILE* logo contest) in the Spring 1977 issue.[58] The new logo, which changed color from issue to issue, seemed symbolic of a deeper transformation in the magazine's editorial approach. As General Idea explained, "the legal battle merely punctuated a change of vision that was already occurring for *FILE*."[59]

Among other things, this change of vision coincided with a shift in the magazine's representation of gay identity and sexuality. While it had always embraced gay themes and iconography, featuring, for example, references to bondage, leather, and drag, much of this had been at the level of innuendo and inference—subtext rather than text. By contrast, the Fall 1979 issue, a special issue on "Transgressions" coedited with Rodney Werden, suggested a more explicit editorial commitment to exploring the politics of gender and sexual identity. Among other things, the issue included an essay by the French theorist Guy Hocquenghem (whose 1972 book *Homosexual Desire* might be considered an early example of what would later be called queer theory) in which he discussed the 1975 murder of the Italian gay intellectual Pier Paolo Pasolini, allegedly by a seventeen-year-old hustler. In what surely would have been perceived as an affront to dominant gay and lesbian politics at the time, Hocquenghem made the provocative claim that homosexuality ought to preserve and embrace its marginality—and even its associations with

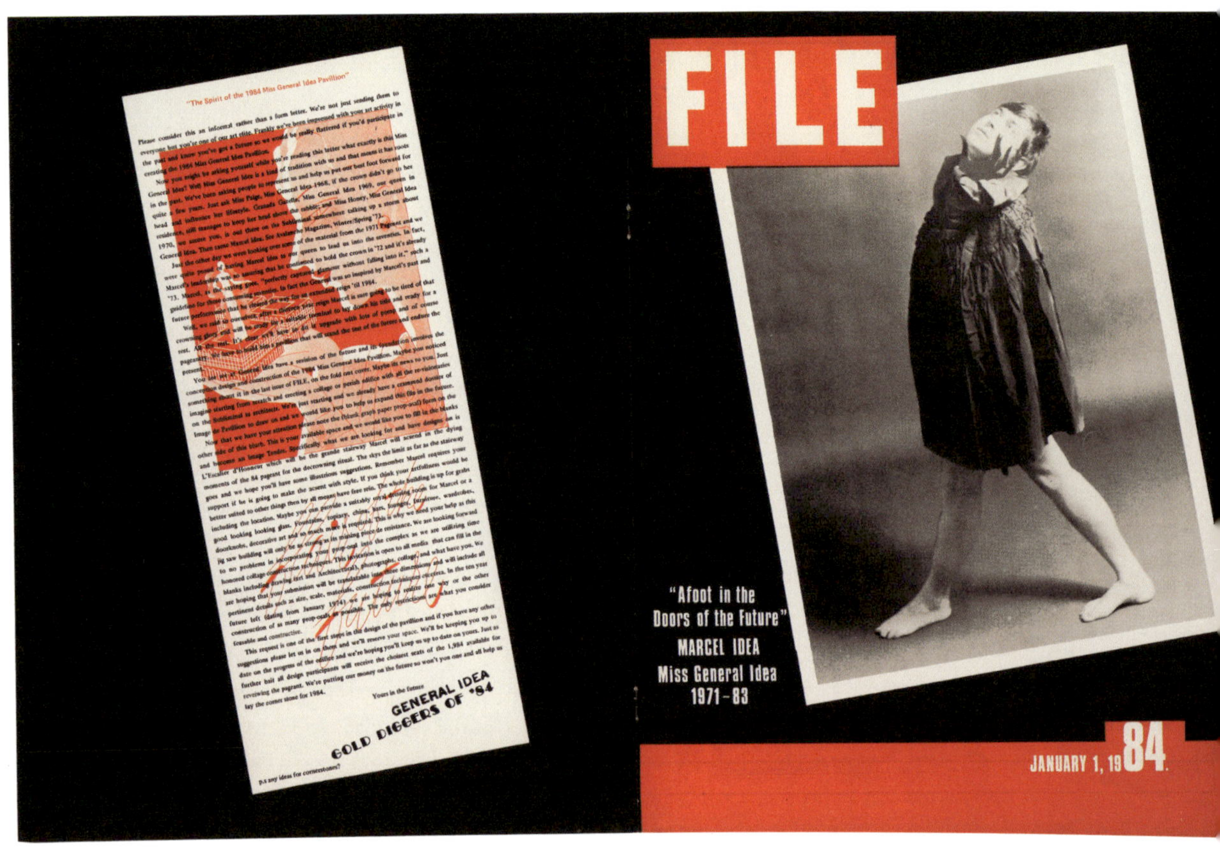

6.8

General Idea, "A Foot in the Doors of the Future"
(front and back cover of insert), *FILE* 2, no. 3,
September 1973. Courtesy of AA Bronson.

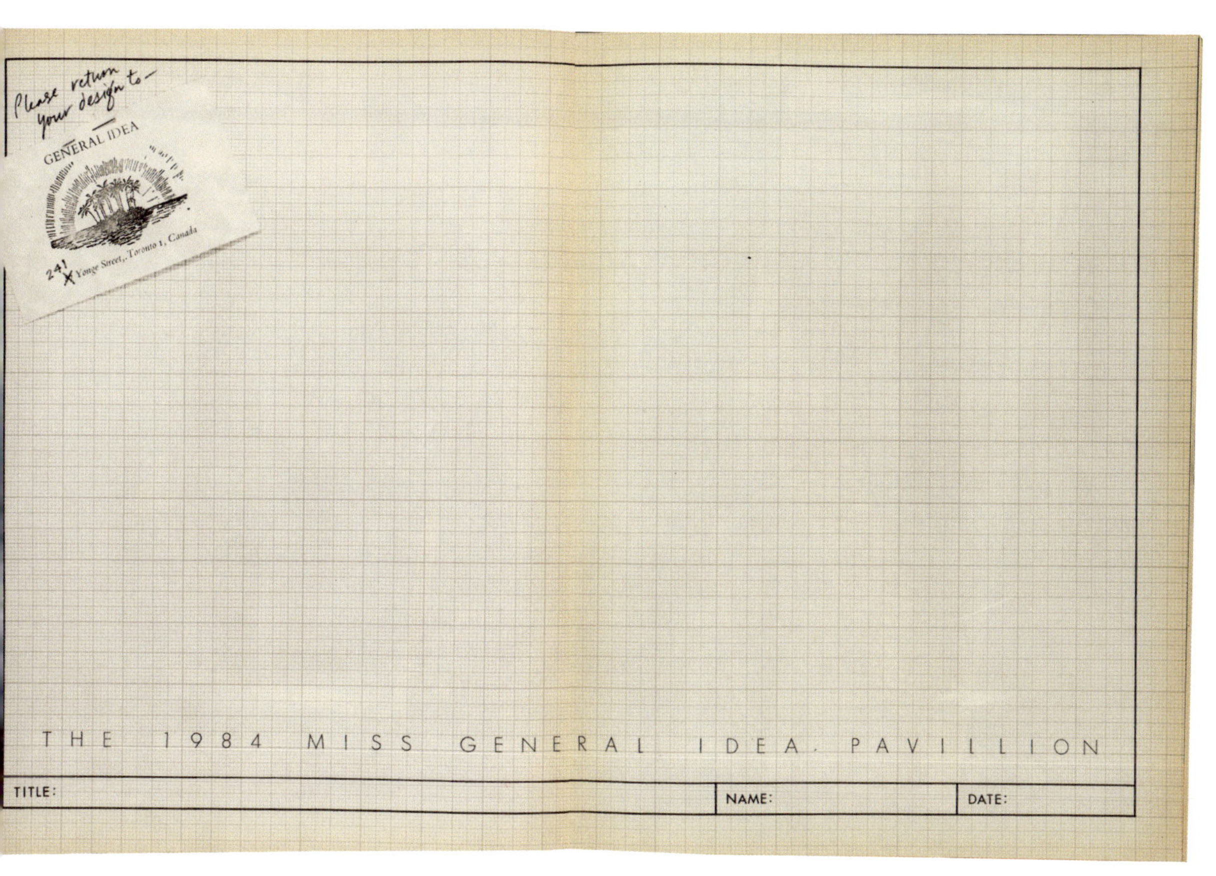

6.9

General Idea, "A Foot in the Doors of the Future"
(inside of insert), *FILE* 2, no. 3, September 1973.
Courtesy of AA Bronson.

criminality—rather than assimilating into the heterosexual norms of mainstream society.[60] The essay was followed by two photographs by Robert Mapplethorpe, both titled *Richard NYC*, which graphically depicted S&M activities, accompanied by the artist's statement: "I'm dealing in these photographs with sexual pleasure—the people in them do indeed enjoy the activity—They are not models hired for the occasion—they are on an adventure—exploring new realms of reality— they are proud people—art transcends morality."[61]

While it would be over a decade before Mapplethorpe's photographs were infamously censored in the United States, another notorious censorship case was raging in Toronto in the late 1970s against one of Canada's most renowned and important gay liberation magazines, *The Body Politic*. Obscenity charges filed against the magazine had prompted demonstrations and fundraisers in support of the beleaguered publication across Canada and in cities around the world. General Idea donated a full-page ad in the Summer 1978 issue of *FILE* to the "Body Politic Free the Press Fund," describing the police raid on the magazine's editorial offices during which manuscripts, mail, and subscription lists had been seized, and urging readers to oppose this appalling repression of free speech.

FILE's expression of solidarity with *The Body Politic* was not at all surprising, given General Idea's involvement in gay intellectual life in Toronto in the late 1960s and 1970s. *FILE* was, after all, founded at the height of the organized fight for equality known as the gay liberation movement that emerged in the wake of the Stonewall riots in 1969, the same year in which homosexuality was decriminalized in Canada.[62] There, as in the United States, the early 1970s saw protests and demonstrations in support of gay and lesbian rights, the founding of numerous gay and lesbian organizations, and a thriving gay and lesbian alternative press. This historical context throws into relief the radicalism of *FILE*'s engagement with themes of gay sexuality in the early 1970s.[63] And yet, despite this, the gay liberation movement itself went virtually unmentioned in its pages. As Bronson recalled, "We were not in support of gay liberation in its usual mainstream manifestation."[64]

While General Idea certainly supported the goals of gay liberation in a broad sense, a close look at *FILE*'s approach to gender and sexual identity does reveal its differences from the prevailing representational strategies of the identity-based gay liberation movement, which largely focused on affirming lesbian, gay, bisexual, and transgender identity, as well as on civil rights and antidiscrimination legislation. The identity-based approach was exemplified in a brief entitled "We Demand" printed in the first issue of *The Body Politic* (November-December 1971). Among the demands were calls for an end to prejudice and discrimination, as well as for equality in employment, immigration, child custody, and service in the armed forces. As this list makes clear, even as the gay liberation movement forged new understandings of gender and sexual identity that questioned heteronormative definitions and upset clear distinctions between gay and straight, it also necessarily relied, however strategically, on essentialist categories of identity in order to fight for legal recognition and rights.[65] By contrast, General Idea's gender-bending play with categories of sexual identity challenged such essentialist and legalistic definitions, and in fact thwarted fixed notions of identity altogether.

FILE's unorthodox approach to the politics of sexual identity—including its use of exaggerated or stereotypical representations of homosexuality, in order to subvert them—was at odds with the proud, celebratory images found in gay and lesbian liberation publications such as *Vector*, *Come Out!*, *Amazon Quarterly*, *The Furies*, and *Gay Sunshine*. As General Idea later explained, they liked to question "the correctness" of so much political art—"the smugness one can so easily fall into. … Even if our political consciousness is completely correct, we still like to play at being incorrect now and then."[66] The images in *FILE* were closer to the transgressive sexualities represented in such publications as Ed Sanders's *Fuck You: A Magazine of the Arts*, the Amsterdam-based sexual liberation paper *Suck*, and numerous queer zines of the 1970s, including Dennis Cooper's *Little Caesar* and Boyd MacDonald's *Straight to Hell*.[67] (MacDonald was interviewed in the Spring 1982 issue of *FILE*.) *FILE*'s unconventional representations of gay sexuality prompted outrage in some readers, as exemplified by an anonymous 1972 review (widely believed to have been written by Dennis Wheeler, a curator at the Vancouver Art Gallery), entitled "*FILE*: The Great Canadian Art Tragedy." Condemning what he saw as General Idea's frivolous attitude, the reviewer declared: "Shitting on their own homosexuality they have done an inestimable disservice by re-repressing what remains for many a serious and actual struggle within this society. They have paraded their homosexuality as though that in itself gave the mag. some bizarre status within the enigma of the alternative society. Instead the problem of homosexuality as an actual way of life recedes into the pageantry of camp parody."[68] With typical irreverence, General Idea responded by appropriating the review, and sending out an annotated copy as part of a mail art project entitled *The Great Canadian Art Tragedy Project, Performed for General Idea by Dennis Wheeler, May 1972* (1972).

While General Idea's insistence on the artificiality and ambiguity of gender may have challenged identity-based approaches to gay liberation politics in the 1970s, it simultaneously anticipated queer theory's destabilization of gender identity in the 1990s. In particular, General Idea's investigations of performance as central to social and sexual identity resonate with notions of gender performativity developed by theorists such as Judith Butler. Butler maintains that gender is not a natural category but one rooted in behaviors, gestures, clothing, and other signifiers, as exemplified by the practice of drag, which, she has argued, suggests the performative dimension of all gender. She writes, "To claim that all gender is like drag, or is drag, is to suggest that 'imitation' is at the heart of the *heterosexual* project and its gender binarisms, that drag is not a secondary imitation that presupposes a prior and original gender, but that hegemonic heterosexuality is itself a constant and repeated effort to imitate its own idealizations."[69]

Butler's understanding of gender performativity sheds light on the visual and representational strategies developed in *FILE*. In a way, the magazine might itself be conceived as a kind of performance: with its glossy color cover wrapped around its cheap newsprint interior, *FILE* was, in a sense, itself in drag, masquerading as *Life*. As Bronson recalled, "I wanted it, on a newsstand, to be a simulacrum of a real magazine; more than a real magazine. So we made this very cheap tabloid interior and wrapped a glossy cover around it."[70] This statement sheds light on *FILE*'s effectiveness as a radical media practice that functioned by "queering" mainstream media. Just as drag, through imitation, undermines heterosexuality's claims to be "real," *FILE*'s mimicry of mainstream media destabilized the media's representational structure, questioning its authority and exposing its artificiality. The resulting ambiguity led to a radical semiotic instability, as General Idea articulated in an editorial in their tenth-anniversary issue:

We wanted to point out the wildly fluctuating interpretations you, our public, impose on us. Under your gaze we become everything from frivolous nightlifers to hard-core post-Marxists theoreticians. We wanted to point out the function of ambiguity in our work, the way in which ambiguity "flips the meaning in and out of focus," thus preventing the successful deciphering of the text (both visual and written) except on multiple levels. … Since we give a wide range of choices (and we are conscious of the politics of choice) we are never sure which side you, our readers, will take.[71]

FILE's destabilization of the categories of gender thus took place alongside its challenges to the hierarchical structures of language and communication—suggesting that the participatory artistic and media practices developed in the late 1960s and 1970s must be seen within the context of other forms of social critique and liberation, such as the gay liberation, feminist, and civil rights movements that came about during these decades. Indeed, the radical new social identities and formations that arose during this time were inseparable from the radical new modes of communication through which they were expressed.

MOVING TO NEW YORK

During the late 1970s and 1980s, *FILE* gradually began to focus less on General Idea's own work and more on artists' projects and pages that they curated. Several special issues were published, including "Foreign Agents" (Fall 1980), a section of which was guest-edited by Sylvère Lotringer, the editor of *Semiotexte*; the "Mondo Cane Kama Sutra Issue" (1983), given over entirely to reproductions of General Idea's series paintings of three Day-Glo poodles in a mind-boggling number of X-rated permutations; the "*FILE* Retrospective" issue (1984); an issue devoted to a series of drawings by John Scott (1985); and a joint issue with the Australian journal *Art & Text* (1986). The group began to spend more time in New York, where they would relocate permanently in 1986, a fact that was reflected in the increasing number of American artists featured in the magazine during the 1980s—especially the so-called Pictures artists whose media-savvy strategies of appropriation General Idea had anticipated.

The final four issues, produced after they moved to New York, were smaller and more commercial-looking, with lavish special endpapers, foldouts, and high-quality color reproductions. *FILE* continued to satirize art world conventions and the role of publicity. The cover of issue 26 (dated "Xmas 1986"), for example, replicated the cover of the May 1986 issue of *Artnews*, which featured a photograph of Sherrie Levine. As the editors explained, "*Artnews* focused attention on appropriation with their Sherrie Levine cover this spring. We focus attention on the focusing of attention with this appropriation of the *Artnews* cover of Sherrie Levine."[72] The issue included work by Levine, Jeff Koons, Sarah Charlesworth, Richard Prince, Louise Lawler, Ken Lum, Jim Welling, and Elaine Sturtevant. The next year, in issue 28 (1987), they focused on the art market, featuring artists who addressed issues of commodification in their work—including Andy Warhol, Rosemarie Trockel, Silvia Kolbowski, Haim Steinbach, Barbara Kruger, Antoni Muntadas, Alan Belcher, and Group Material—while simultaneously foregrounding the magazine's own commodified status, stating, "This issue of *FILE* we present as a commodity and it is a commodity." Yet plaguing both of these issues was the nagging suspicion that the line between appropriator and appropriated had begun to erode. In fact, the critical distance from the art world that General Idea had cultivated in *FILE* was more difficult to maintain once they were in

THE MAGAZINE AS MIRROR

the center of this world. Reflecting on the last few years of the publication, Bronson observed: "As soon as we moved to New York, we were no longer observers of culture; we were participants. … *FILE* was more of a real magazine."[73]

General Idea's own work had also begun to move in a different direction. They devoted more and more of their energy to addressing the AIDS crisis, seeking out new public spaces and methods of dissemination better suited to their activist aims. Their best-known work from this period was their *AIDS Project* (1987–1994) in which they appropriated Robert Indiana's iconic LOVE image, replacing the word "Love" with the acronym "AIDS," printed in red letters and arranged, as in the original work, within a blue and green square. Imitating the populist distribution of Indiana's original image, they created postage stamps, monumental public sculpture, posters, and magazine covers. The juxtaposition of Indiana's ubiquitous symbol of 1960s free love with the charged and, at that point, still highly stigmatized subject of AIDS created a shocking image that both raised awareness of the epidemic and detonated the word's taboo status. Like General Idea's previous projects, it was a deeply polysemous work in which meanings and connotations proliferated, and not necessarily in predictable or politically correct ways.[74]

Issue 27 of *FILE* (Spring 1987) was designated "The Journal of the New Mortality." The issue began and ended with eight black endpapers, symbolizing the experience of death and loss surrounding AIDS. Works that dealt directly or indirectly with this topic by artists Ross Bleckner, Marina Abramović and Ulay, Peter Nagy, and Mike Kelley were included, alongside Freud's 1917 essay "Mourning and Melancholia" and excerpts from Yve-Alain Bois's "Painting: The Task of Mourning." Ultimately, General Idea's shifting artistic interests and priorities in the face of the AIDS epidemic (which would claim the lives of Partz and Zontal in 1994) played a role in the decision to end the magazine. As Bronson recalled, "We had friends who had died and the whole impetus of creating work that related to the AIDS situation was really driving all that we did and we didn't feel that *FILE* could really help with that project. So we purposefully let it die at that point."[75]

In the final issue, published in 1989, the editors observed that while *FILE* had begun as "an alternative to the alternative press," it ended up as "an agent provocateur caught by surprise in the spotlight, ensconced in the very gallery it sought to avoid, as the art audience emerged as a major cultural force in the 1980s. … In this era of corporate culture, the culture *is* corporate: *FILE* cannot continue without becoming enmeshed in the deadlines, managing editors, international correspondents, advertising representatives and other signifiers of the mundane world."[76] This last issue, devoted to "the City," looked at various artistic interventions into urban space, including Matt Mullican's urban designs, Dennis Adams's bus shelter, Alan Belcher's public art proposals, and Krzysztof Wodiczko's *Homeless Vehicle Project*—interventions that echoed the new direction General Idea's own work had begun to take in the form of AIDS-related cultural activism. Though the magazine ended, the radical media strategies that it had introduced as a way to transform the conditions of the art world did not cease altogether, but continued to operate outside its bounds.

7

ARTISTS' MAGAZINES IN THE 1980S
REAL LIFE, 1979–1994

On the cover of the Autumn 1981 issue of *Real Life* magazine is a mysterious photograph. Attributed to Louise Lawler, the image appears vaguely architectural, yet withholds any obvious contextual or perspectival cues, remaining abstract, flat, indecipherable. As it wraps around to the back cover of the magazine, where a bed and table are visible, the image becomes legible as the wall and tiled floor of a domestic space. The space is Lawler's loft, where, on Thursday, June 25, 1981, from 7 to 9 p.m., Sherrie Levine installed her *After Eliot Porter* series of photographs—photographs that are themselves almost completely cropped out of the magazine cover, appearing as a curious sliver above the *Real Life* logo.

The evening was part of a series of extremely fleeting events and exhibitions that Lawler and Levine organized during the early 1980s. In addition to exhibiting their work in private lofts, they organized outings and social gatherings. They invited some people to the ballet on a Sunday afternoon; they served glasses of Dubonnet at the tiny painting studio of a deceased Russian émigré named Dmitri Merinoff; once they mailed out a card printed with the sentence, "His gesture moved us to tears." These events left little residue outside of invitations and memory traces, and occasional documents published in small-circulation artists' magazine, such as *Real Life* or *Wedge*, where the artists published another series of photographs in 1982.

The artists named their sporadic collaboration *A Picture Is No Substitute for Anything*, a phrase that referenced Hollis Frampton's statement to Carl Andre in their book *12 Dialogues*, "A photograph is no substitute for anything."[1] As Levine recalled of the project, "it was a way of distancing ourselves from the art world. In those days I didn't think the art world was the real world."[2] Yet if Levine and Lawler, like so many of their avant-garde and neo-avant-garde predecessors, sought to reconcile the age-old opposition between art and life, by the 1980s this opposition had been irrevocably triangulated by a third term: the media. For the group of artists known as the Pictures generation—so named after Douglas Crimp's 1977 "Pictures" exhibition at Artists Space—the question of the relationship of art to the pervasive visual culture of the mass media had become a pressing one. As Crimp wrote in his catalog essay for the "Pictures" exhibition:

7.1 and 7.2 (following pages)

Real Life, no. 7, Autumn 1981, back and front cover.
Photograph by Louise Lawler. Courtesy of the artist.

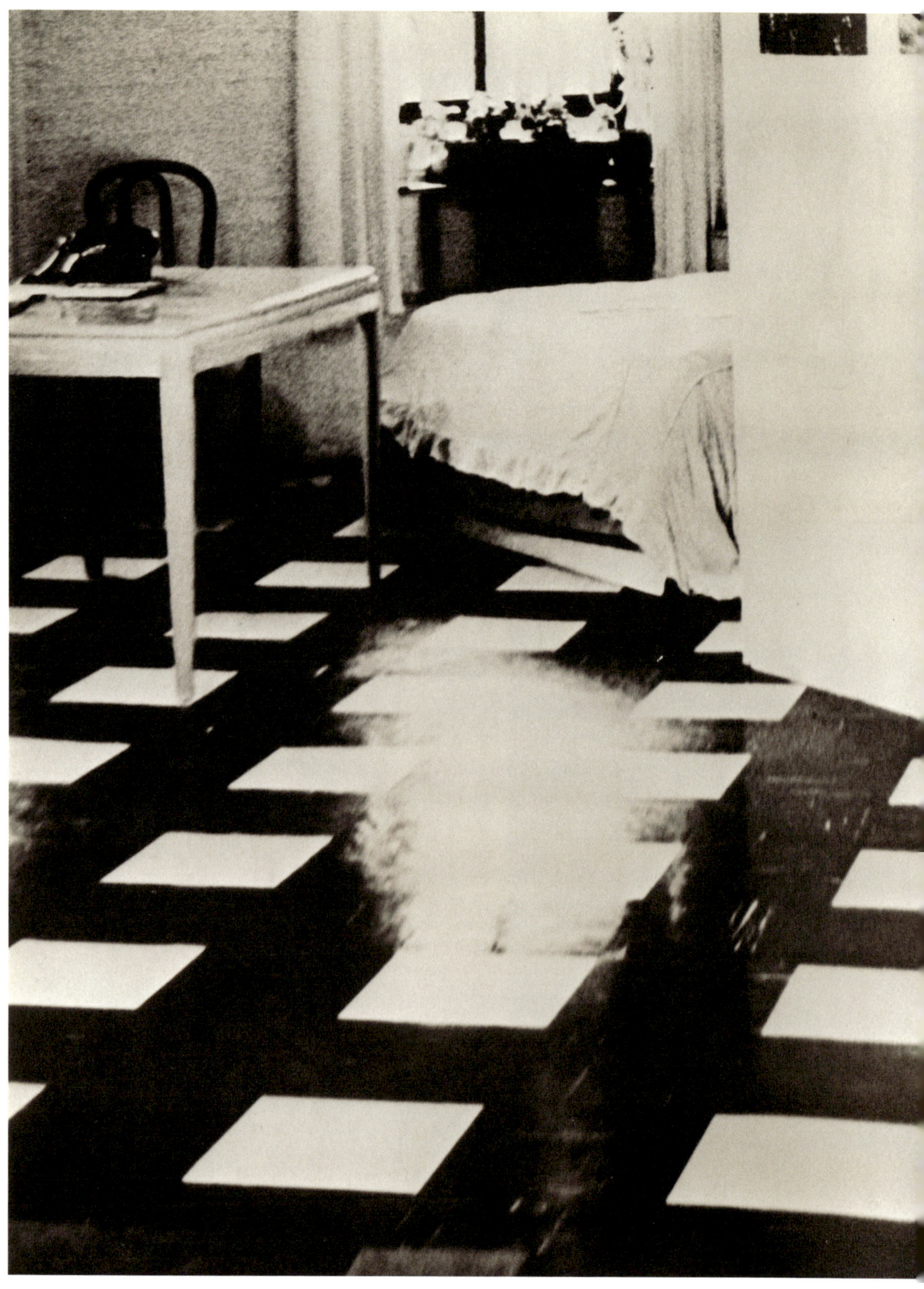

REAL LIFE Magazine
Autumn 1981 $2.00

"To an ever greater extent our experience is governed by pictures, pictures in newspapers and magazines, on television and in the cinema. Next to these pictures firsthand experience begins to retreat, to seem more and more trivial. While it once seemed that pictures had the function of interpreting reality, it now seems that they have usurped it."[3] However, if these artists were, as Crimp insisted, concerned with representations—with pictures—they were also, it seems, interested in testing the limits of these pictures, and in exploring what could not be represented or usurped in this manner. Indeed, *A Picture Is No Substitute for Anything* raises the possibility that reality might evade representation, that it might exist outside of the visual economies of both art and media—a possibility that the *Real Life* cover, in its very indecipherability, seems to uphold, refusing to be a surrogate for witnessing Levine's installation in person. And yet, if the magazine cover was not merely a substitute for reality, what was its role? Might it then constitute its own reality? And if so, what was the nature of this reality, and what was its relationship to both art and life?

Real Life magazine was published by Thomas Lawson and Susan Morgan from 1979 to 1994. As Lawson recalled of the plain-spoken black-and-white magazine, it "was generated out of numerous late-night discussions circling around our questions, attitudes, and desires. … Our idea was to provide a forum for our generation to speculate on the general culture, a place for artists to talk about and with artists, discuss each other's work and consider the work that had influenced us. But conversation is inherently ephemeral and even gallery exhibitions are fleeting: somehow it seemed that all of our talk was directing us toward the printed page."[4] While the magazine served as an archive, capturing ephemeral events and conversations in the more permanent medium of print, it was also a document that was itself highly transitory and unfixed, capturing the informal, unguarded quality of the dialog between artists that had inspired it. *Real Life* provided a perspective on the contemporary moment that did not pretend to be removed from or outside of it, but that drifted, unmoored, among the turbulent eddies and ripples of the present. As the editors observed of the magazine, which they published out of Lawson's loft space at 41 John Street in the financial district of lower Manhattan, it "always had an aleatory quality—contributions came from people we encountered in the city and as we traveled. The editorial process occurred somewhere between intention and happenstance."[5]

Perhaps more than any other publication, *Real Life* crystallized the sensibilities and interests of the artists of the Pictures generation. And yet the magazine provides a different view onto this moment than more canonical accounts, revealing a sincerity that gives pause to received ideas about the decade's market- and media-fueled hype. As Sherrie Levine recalled,

> There were no commercial venues for the things we were interested in, which I now think made for, in many ways, a very wholesome atmosphere. … The economy was "recessed," and most of us had crappy day jobs. We lent each other money and lived in dumps. We believed we were the only audience for one another's work. We were young, energetic, generous, and ambitious. I use the word "ambitious" in the best sense; we wanted to make a difference, to show some resistance to the status quo. With not much at stake yet, outside of group approbation, I experienced an exhilarating sense of community and purpose.[6]

Real Life both arose from and reinforced this sense of community and purpose. With a circulation of one to two thousand and just a handful of ads, mainly for emerging galleries and nonprofit spaces such as Artists Space, Metro Pictures, and the Kitchen (many issues have no ads at all), the magazine published a diverse range of material, including artists' writings and projects, criticism, working notes, reproductions, and interviews. The magazine's heavyweight, matte paper and understated design reinforced Lawson's goal "to collect written and visual material which reflects the actual concerns of the artists I associate with, a clearing house for ideas as free as possible from the strictures of self-promotion and commodity fetishism."[7] *Real Life* was initially designed by Debbie DeStaffan, a photographer and graphic designer who lived down the block from Lawson's studio, and who got to know him and other artists when she was hired to photograph exhibition openings at Artists Space.[8] The simple, clean layout that she created set the magazine apart from the slickness of commercial publications such as *Esquire* and *Rolling Stone*, where she freelanced the rest of the time. Her liberal use of the white page offered a respite from the loud, crowded surfaces of mainstream media, providing space within which to observe and read and think. As DeStaffan described it, "*Real Life* was a magazine that one wanted to hold and keep, and spend some time with."[9]

The title *Real Life* perfectly captured the charged ambivalence of the concept of the real for the Pictures generation—that "mixture of love and contempt for the ever present images of capitalist consumerism," as Lawson put it.[10] The magazine's title was Sherrie Levine's idea, one of several that were tossed around over the course of many evenings spent brainstorming in different bars (runners-up included *This Magazine*, *True Art Magazine*, and *Untitled*). Lawson recalled, "I think when we hit on [the title], it resonated because it could do that—it could be taken in that complex way, and that seemed to address the kind of art that we were interested in, this work that had that kind of complexity to the world."[11] Thick with irony, the phrase reads like a hackneyed quotation from some unacknowledged source—which, in fact, it was: Levine borrowed it from a book by her University of Wisconsin-Madison MFA classmate Michael Lesy, *Real Life: Louisville in the Twenties* (1976). The magazine's title was thus appropriated—an aesthetic strategy that would, of course, become a hallmark of the Pictures artists, and of Levine's work in particular, most famously exemplified by her photographs of photographs, such as the *After Walker Evans* series (1979), two of which were published in issue 5 (Winter 1980) of *Real Life*.

Though the critic Valentin Tatransky did not use the word "appropriation" in his article on Levine's work, which appeared in the inaugural issue of *Real Life*—the artist's first substantial review—he described precisely the procedure that this term would come to name. Describing Levine's series of painted and collaged silhouettes (one of which was reproduced on the cover of that issue) and her mechanical reproductions from a how-to-draw book, Tatransky observed that the work manifested "a desire to express an attitude to an image, combined with the desire to leave the image alone."[12] As Benjamin Buchloh has argued, appropriation is a deeply ambivalent form of communication, related to both allegory and montage, that can simultaneously negate and preserve meaning.[13] According to Buchloh, because it extracts an image or linguistic sign wholesale from its original context, depleting it of its initial signified and substituting a new one

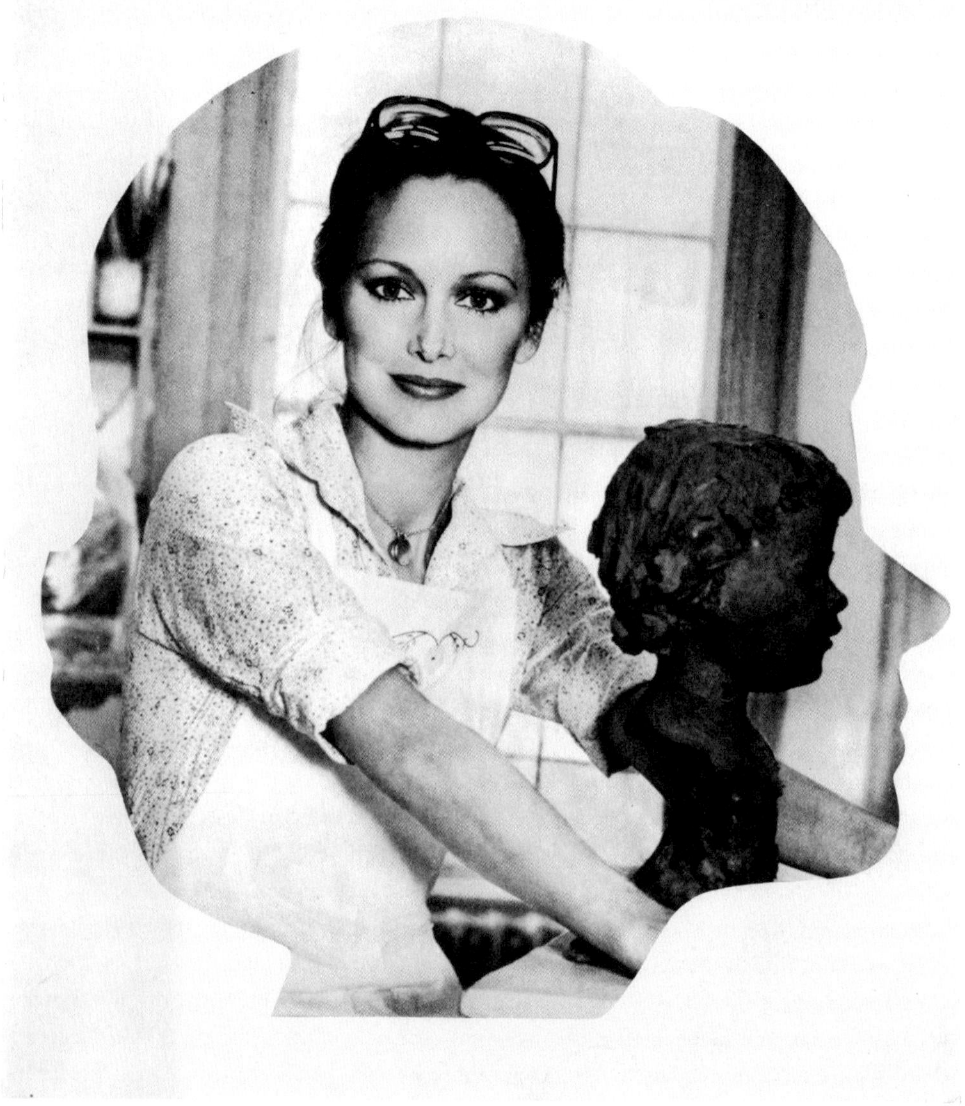

7.3

Sherrie Levine, *Untitled*, 1979, *Real Life*, no. 1,
Spring 1979, cover. Courtesy of Thomas Lawson.
©Sherrie Levine.

while keeping the signifier more or less intact, appropriation does not erase the first meaning but layers a new meaning on top of it. It is out of this juxtaposition that appropriation gains its dialectical ability to convey two things at once. As Levine herself wrote of her *After Walker Evans* series, "I appropriate these images to express my own simultaneous longing for the passion of engagement and the sublimity of aloofness. I hope that in my photograph of photographs an uneasy peace will be made between my attraction to the ideals these pictures exemplify and my desire to have no ideals or fetters whatsoever. It is my aspiration that my photographs, which contain their own contradiction, would represent the best of both worlds."[14]

Likewise, the phrase "real life" betrays a deeply contradictory impulse, one that both retains and cancels the original meaning of the expression. Pronounced disingenuously, the magazine's title suggests the detached skepticism with which the Pictures artists dismissed the very possibilities of originality, authenticity, and self-expression in a media-saturated world. And yet, if for theorists such as Guy Debord and Jean Baudrillard the loss of the real was a foregone conclusion, things were much less resolved in the pages of *Real Life*, as artists sought—in an unexpectedly genuine way—to understand and come to terms with the very real effects of this media culture on people's lives, on their experiences and emotions.[15] As Lawson recalled, "I think it was one of those periods when artists feel that art has become too rarefied and abstract and needs to reconnect to everyday activities and to real life. But how do you do that, and what is real life? Is it our experience, or is it the stories that are told to us? I think that's what people were trying to work through."[16]

On the cover of the first issue was a reproduction of Levine's *Untitled* (1978), a collage consisting of a cut-out magazine advertisement, framed by a silhouette of a child's head. One of a series of similar works that the artist produced at the time, this particular image featured a model wearing an apron and sculpting a bust of a young child, symbolically conflating the creativity of the female artist with the domestic tasks of housekeeping and childrearing. Juxtaposing several different types and levels of representation—from the model posing as an artist, to the sculpted portrait of the child, to the silhouetted profile—Levine's *Untitled* suggests the dizzying layers of mediation that filter the experience of so-called reality, as well as the gender politics that underlie these representations (a situation that was humorously compounded when some viewers mistakenly identified the model in the advertisement as a self-portrait of Levine herself).[17] The silhouette that frames the image creates a sense of peering through an opening, like a keyhole or camera viewfinder, interrupting the transparency of the photograph, and accentuating the tension between the illusionist depth of the photograph and the flatness of the two-dimensional surface on which it is reproduced—here, the magazine cover. The image insists that this surface is not merely a neutral window onto the world but itself a representation.

Indeed, the magazine cover implicitly raises the question of its own status in relationship to the work of art that it reproduces—a work that was, after all, created from a magazine reproduction to begin with. While there is no evidence that Levine herself considered the appearance of *Untitled* on the cover of *Real Life* anything other than a straightforward reproduction, a mere illustration of the work, the image itself complicates things, suggesting another possibility. In fact, Crimp singled out Levine's silhouetted collages in his revised "Pictures" essay, published in the Spring 1979 issue of *October* (which coincided exactly with the first issue of *Real Life*), as exemplary of how this new work undermined the distinction between original and reproduction. About the collages, one of which was reproduced in his essay, he asked, "What was the medium of … the work? … A cut-out picture from a magazine? Or is the medium of this work perhaps its reproduction here in this journal? And if it is impossible to locate the physical medium of the work, can we then locate the original artwork?"[18]

While Crimp's ultimate concern was with the medium of Levine's *Untitled*, the image, as it appears on the cover of *Real Life*, also raises the question of the medium of the magazine itself. For the *Real Life* cover repeats and extends the operations of Levine's original collage, superimposing upon the work a third element: the title *Real Life,* printed across the top of the page. Among the things being juxtaposed in this cover, then, are two magazines: the glossy fashion magazine from which the image was initially pilfered, and the limited-circulation artists' magazine in which it is now being seen. The cover plays these two very different contexts off of one another, underscoring the discrepancy between them. Against the staged fakeness of the magazine advertisement, there is something steadfast and down-to-earth about *Real Life*. And yet one cannot say that the latter was more authentic or real, because the magazine destabilizes the very terms of this opposition, revealing the interpenetration of media and reality rather than privileging one over the other.

Even as *Real Life* separated itself from mainstream publications on the newsstand, it simultaneously referenced and tweaked this wider visual culture, in ways that strikingly paralleled the media-based artistic practices it supported. As Lawson described his own paintings and the work of many of his peers, "It is an art which disrupts and displaces our routine ways of seeing and talking about the pictures which inform our lives, and which dominate us from the mass media. … An art which raises questions which reveal that the methods of production and reproduction of these all-powerful images … are profoundly ideological and riddled with promises which cannot be kept."[19] In an important sense, the magazine constituted a parallel site, or even another medium, in which these questions about the media were being raised. In their writings for *Real Life* (as in the contemporaneous British magazine *ZG*), artists considered the visual culture of Hollywood films and commercial television with the same kind of critical scrutiny once reserved for the domain of high art. Barbara Kruger wrote "Game Show," a biting appraisal of television game shows and their insidious effect on the well-being of housewives, and "Devils with Red Dresses On," an analysis of the gender politics of the film *Gentlemen Prefer Blondes*. Richard Prince contributed "Menthol Pictures," in which he described movies watched in various situations including while ingesting drugs and in a peep show booth, observing the psychological and physical effects of cinema on its viewers. And in his article "Going Places," Lawson analyzed the film *American Gigolo* as an allegory for contemporary consumer society.

Moreover, in its graphic form the magazine twinned the artistic investigations of media that it published. For example, the soft porn image of an amorous couple floating eerily on the cover of issue 3, and the image of a murdered gangster that fills the front and back covers of issue 5 were taken from the pulp magazines that Lawson was using as source imagery in a series of paintings at the time, in which he investigated how mass-media images of sex and violence, in different—or maybe not so different—ways, titillated the viewer. As they appear on the cover of *Real Life*, these images are so obviously extracted from elsewhere, so estranged from their original context (the scissor marks are clearly visible in the image on issue 3), that they prompt the viewer to notice and confront their meaning in a new way. Likewise, the small rectangular photograph of Brigitte Bardot that appears on the cover of issue 6 both enacts and interrupts the conventions of the cover girl. Instead of filling the page, Bardot's come-hither countenance appears tiny and far away against the otherwise blank cover, while establishing a "peek-a-boo" relationship with the full-page image, a few pages later, of the star stepping out of a bathtub, drawing attention to the way that magazines manipulate the readers' attention not only on individual pages but through the sequencing of multiple pages. Such examples suggest the acute self-reflexivity with which *Real Life* commented on and critiqued its own mass-cultural form.

A SPACE FOR ARTISTS TO TALK AND WRITE

Lawson had moved to New York from Scotland in 1975 to pursue his career as a painter. Later he recalled:

> I came with an idea of community, and in search of fellow artists. Fuelled by movies like *An American in Paris*, I imagined a free-floating sexy world where ideas and passions were exchanged, and the problems of daily life were somehow taken care of. What I imagined was a fantasy. The thing is, Lower Manhattan in the late 1970s came close to fulfilling that fantasy. The city was near-bankrupt, the collapsed Westside Highway only the most visible sign of widespread corruption and decay. After dark the vast warehouse districts below Houston Street were all but deserted, and a newcomer soon came to recognize that the few people on the streets were artists and musicians and dancers who lived and worked there. It was easy to find the bars and restaurants that stayed open late, and in these places, easy to strike up conversation and eventually friendships with others seeking the classic bohemian life.[20]

Through a social network of bars and clubs such as Magoo's, Barnabus Rex, and the Mudd Club and alternative exhibition and performance venues such as Artists Space, 3 Mercer Street, and the Kitchen, Lawson found himself part of a group of young artists, many of whom were also new to the city. A university-educated artist who had already earned master's degrees in English and art history in Scotland, Lawson pursued his interest in art history and theory as a Ph.D. student at the City University of New York. While studying under Rosalind Krauss and Robert Pincus-Witten, he met fellow students Craig Owens and Douglas Crimp. Part of his thesis research on Joseph Cornell was published in the journal *October*, which Krauss had cofounded, and where Crimp and Owens became regular contributors. Ultimately, however, he sought to create a different kind of forum with *Real Life*: "a space for artists to talk and write, rather than art historians or art critics."[21]

Lawson met Morgan in 1976 in the downtown neighborhood bar and artists' hangout Barnabus Rex. At the time, she was cooking in restaurants and writing stories for little magazines. She had moved to New York from Nantucket, where she read vintage issues of *Harper's Bazaar*, *Vanity Fair*, and *Flair* in the houses she would caretake during the off-season, and discovered books by the Nova Scotia College of Art and Design Press, which were stocked by a small progressive bookstore on the island. She recalled that she had always viewed magazines as "an expanded conversation, providing access to a much wider world. … I liked the cross fertilization of ideas and disciplines and the democratic accessibility of the page."[22]

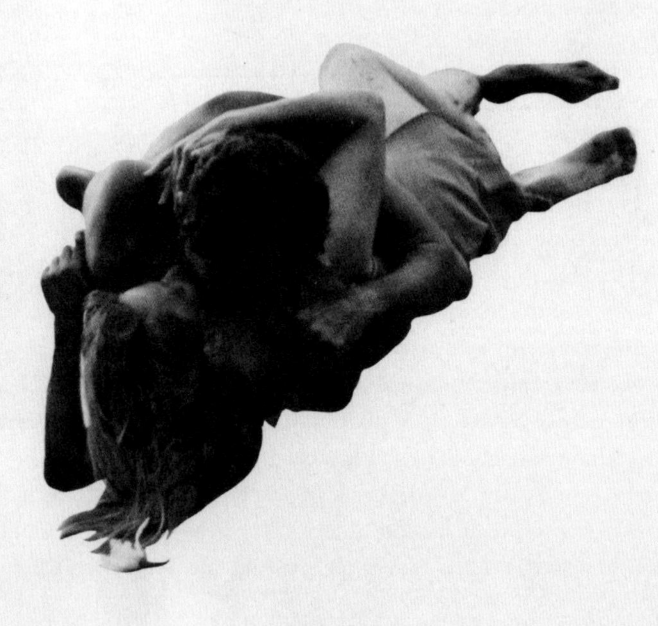

7.4

Thomas Lawson, *Afternoon TV*, 1980, *Real Life,* no. 3,
March 1980, cover. Courtesy of the artist.

When Lawson and Morgan first began to talk about publishing a magazine in 1978, the 1980s market boom had not yet begun, and postminimalist abstraction still reigned in the New York art world. "It seemed, at least to us at the time, the late 1970s, that the *Avalanche* generation had a lockdown in some ways, and *Art in America* and *Artforum* were solely focused on that work," Lawson recalled.[23] He and his friends rebelled against their minimalist and conceptualist predecessors—even as they remained indebted to this earlier generation of artists who were, in many instances, their teachers and mentors. With its return to narrative and recognizable figurative imagery, this new work by Lawson's generation was unfashionable and largely ignored by established critics and galleries. According to Lawson, "There was all this work beginning to be made, that I knew of, by people I knew of, that wasn't getting very much attention. And it seemed quite clear to me that it would never get attention if it wasn't made public—and it wouldn't grow. … And the major magazines were quite clearly not going to do that. … The little local magazines that had existed, like *Art-Rite*, seemed to be dying or dead! There was a real vacuum."[24] (Morgan remembers Edit deAk coming into the kitchen of a restaurant where she worked, carrying a picture of herself with a big *X* drawn across it and the caption, "No Longer Publicly Funded.")

Lawson's aspirations for the magazine were shaped by the frustrations he had encountered writing reviews for *Art in America* in the late 1970s—an experience that, he recalled, "forced me to think about what the point of writing would be and how you imagine your audience. And I began to realize that this was not the audience that I wanted to write for."[25] Rather than writing objective, descriptive accounts of work by established artists for a distant and anonymous public, he wanted to write about and for the local community of artists of which he was a part. A turning point occurred when he pitched an article on Cindy Sherman's work—an idea his editors promptly rejected because Sherman wasn't well known at the time. "Who's Cindy Sherman? She's just someone you know," he remembers them saying.[26] Lawson realized that this was precisely the point. The value of writing about Sherman and other artists he knew was his firsthand experience with the work, his ability, as he put it, to "understand it from the information of the studio, rather than a dispassionate dispatch coming from an older critic."[27] Lawson wanted to establish a more immediate connection to the artist's voice: "I had always imagined the magazine in the trajectory of surrealist journals; that it would be all about the voice from the inside. It would be the voice of a new beginning, providing primary information, something that art historians would look at in the future and say, 'This is what people were really thinking about,' not what someone observing them thinks they might be thinking about."[28]

As Richard Prince commented on Crimp's influential "Pictures" catalog essay, "I don't know who really ever read that essay. Those shows and essays are for other critics. … Critics tried to tell you what you were doing, and wanted you to make the kind of work that they were thinking about."[29] Indeed, within the polemics of the academic and commercial art press alike, critics were quick to draw lines in the sand, declaring heroes and villains, and historicizing the moment before it was even over. The term "postmodernism" itself implied such historicization, tidily positioning this new work in relationship to what came before it. And yet in their effort to pin things down, such critical and historical accounts sometimes overlooked the messiness of things as they were lived in the present. Lawson observed in his 1981 essay, "Last Exit: Painting": "At one extreme, René Ricard, writing in *Artforum* on Julian Schnabel, has offered petulant self-advertisement in the name of a reactionary expressionism. … On the other hand, *October* has been publishing swinging jeremiads condemning, at least by implication, all art produced since the late sixties, save what the editors consider to be permissible … and art itself is conveniently relegated to an insignificant position as background material serving only to peg the display of self or of theory."[30] By contrast, *Real Life* sought to create a discourse in which art was not a pawn in a critical argument but an equal player.

For the Pictures generation, as for the minimalist and conceptual artists who preceded them, critical writing remained a central component of artistic practice. As Levine recalled, "We didn't make a big distinction between artmaking, writing, and curating. Many people were engaged in more than one of these activities, none of them very financially lucrative at this point."[31] Lawson reflected on how the activities of writing, painting, and editing the magazine were for him intertwined, reciprocal activities, explaining, "The part of my work that takes the form of paintings is handled—represented—by a commercial gallery, Metro Pictures. Another part is criticism and appears in various magazines. … A third part, coming somewhere between the other two but perhaps less individualistic in appearance is the activity represented by *Real Life* magazine. … This refusal to settle down or be one thing or another is central to my activity as an artist."[32]

While this new generation of artists were well versed in the psychoanalytic and deconstructionist theories being introduced through academic journals such as *October* and *Screen*, they also sought to stake out a discursive space of their own. In the pages of *Real Life*, artists deftly crossed back and forth between the roles of artist and critic, writing about their own work and that of their peers. Allan McCollum wrote about Matt Mullican, and Paul McMahon in turn wrote about McCollum; Dan Graham and Jeff Wall wrote about one another's work. John Miller wrote on David Robbins's work. Publishing in the magazine was a way for artists to pay attention to one another's work, a way of establishing an artistic community. Accordingly, *Real Life* did not leave out the emotional and affective dimensions of human communication, but provided a place where artists could commiserate and empathize with one another, where they could vent their frustrations and joke around.

There is something speculative and exploratory about the artists' writings published in *Real Life*, as signaled by stylistic quirks and sudden shifts in tense and address—the way in which a distanced, passive narrative voice will suddenly erupt into the immediacy of the first-person singular, for example. Robbins's "Notes towards Film" combines quotations from Wittgenstein and V. S. Naipaul with images, newspaper headlines, and proverbs. Richard Prince contributed his manifesto-like "Primary Transfers," reflecting on his technique of rephotographing magazine advertisements, with vague yet urgent-sounding imperatives, such as "Transgression should be assumed, and desires and threats defined."[33] Several artists used pseudonyms to differentiate between and to play with various genres and identities. Prince, for example, published a stream-of-conscious fictional narrative, "Pissing on Ice," under the pseudonym Fulton Ryder, and Robbins published several articles and interviews, including a lengthy piece on Jenny Holzer, under the nom de plume Rex Reason (a play on "wrecks reason" and a reference to the lead character in the science fiction film *This Island Earth*).

The diversity of the contributions—which ranged from short playful apercus, inside jokes, and manifesto-like statements to dense historical and theoretical essays, as well as documents, notes, and found or appropriated texts—is striking in its contrast with the uniform, predictable contents of more mainstream magazines. *Real Life* had a light editorial hand, encouraging multiple voices, styles, and points of view. Lawson noted, "I remember getting one issue back and seeing voices that were so clearly not us."[34] Such inconsistency is echoed subtly in the magazine's layout, which had minor shifts and irregularities in font size and style. DeStaffan explained that she tried to capture the personality of each artist rather than thinking about the consistency of the magazine as a whole, remembering, "I felt like each message was very precious and important."[35]

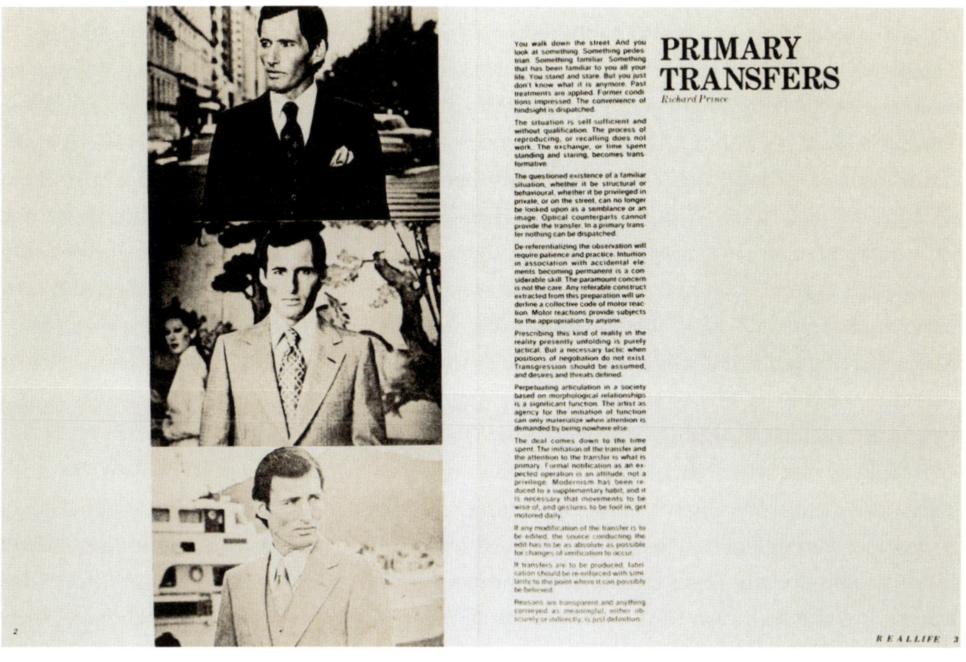

7.5

Richard Prince, "Primary Transfers," *Real Life*, no. 3, March 1980. ©Richard Prince. Courtesy Gagosian Gallery.

As Morgan observed, "there was an essential difference between us and the glossier, more mainstream, magazines that have an established format. … We wanted to get away from the way that everything had to sound resolved in regular art magazines. The people who contributed to *Real Life* were in transition. It was a place that encouraged questioning."[36] Many of the ideas originally discussed in *Real Life* did in fact eventually make their way into more mainstream publications. For example, in an essay for *Real Life* titled "Too Good to Be True," Lawson sketched out several of the concepts about painting's critical capacity within postmodernism that would culminate in his well-known essay "Last Exit: Painting," published in *Artforum* (where Barbara Kruger would also become a regular contributor). However, in contrast to the polished, carefully edited prose that characterized both the academic and the commercial art press, the writings in *Real Life* come across as less filtered and finished. As Lawson acknowledged of "Too Good to Be True," the essay functioned as "a collection of signposts indicating key points in an argument which has yet to be fully articulated, far less brought to a conclusion."[37]

Though the magazine's focus, especially in its first few years, was on the Pictures artists, it represented a much broader spectrum of related artistic and interdisciplinary practices than more authoritative accounts of the moment tend to admit, including the activities of collectives such as Colab and Group Material, and the interdisciplinary crossovers between downtown writers, artists, and musicians. It also published artists who, despite working at the same time and in a similar vein as the Pictures artists, have been omitted from dominant histories of this group for various reasons. For example, Philip Smith, who was included in Crimp's "Pictures" exhibition but was replaced by Cindy Sherman in the critic's revised catalog essay, was interviewed in the fourth issue of the magazine. Other such contributors included Steve Gianakos, Kathi Norklun, Jessica Diamond, Robin Winters, Ken Lum, Jennifer Bolande, Joan Wallace, Judith Barry, and Howard Singerman. The magazine "wasn't cliquey," Morgan insists, citing her interviews with artists such as Robert Moskowitz and Michael Hurson, who had been largely neglected by critics up to that point: "I remember Hurson saying, 'I thought nobody wanted to hear from us.'"[38] Also appearing in the magazine were interviews with an earlier generation of conceptual artists, including Ed Ruscha, Hans Haacke, William Wegman, and Lawrence Weiner, with whom this new generation felt an affinity.

Like earlier artists' magazines, *Real Life* sought to recalibrate the power balance between artists and critics, offering artists an opportunity for recourse against the critic's authority. In issue 17/18, Adrian Piper published an extended retort to the critic Donald Kuspit—a trenchant blow-by-blow account of his critical misdemeanors, including the critic's "disregard" for "what artists say about their own work," "his attempt to reduce one more artist to an inanimate object that doesn't talk back," and his tendency to "dehumanize artists and reduce their work to neurotic symptoms."[39] She further expressed her vexation at the critic by drawing him as a giant cockroach on the cover of the issue.

However, *Real Life* also provided a space for critics themselves to experiment. The curator Carol Squiers, writing under the pseudonym Elsa Bulgari, published a tongue-in-cheek review of an exhibition she had herself organized at P.S. 1 entitled "Women of Distinction: Photographs from Magazines 1930–1980"—one of several shows that she curated at the time consisting solely of magazine tearsheets she had collected and arranged on the gallery wall. Her unorthodox curatorial practice challenged received notions of both photography and curating by admitting mass-cultural representations into the realm of high art in ways that paralleled artistic investigations at the time, and even bordered on a kind of artistic practice itself.[40] Frustrated with the unfavorable (or sometimes nonexistent) critical response to her shows, Squiers lampooned baffled critics, feigning incomprehension in a heavy Slavic accent, writing "Vhat? Vhat vomen? Vhat distinction? Vhat is this??? Is she kidding?!!???"[41] Squiers later described the Elsa Bulgari piece as "a reaction to the traditional prejudices relative to photography as an art, which didn't recognize the ubiquity of photography and the fact that everything worthwhile couldn't be reduced to an Ansel Adams print. In part, the review was a response to trying to live in the worlds of both art and photography, which were very far apart at the time."[42]

In addition to artists' writings, *Real Life* published reproductions of works by artists including Sherrie Levine, Laurie Simmons, James Welling, and Paul McMahon—sometimes before they had been exhibited in a gallery, as was the case for Levine's *After Walker Evans* series. Other works were designed specifically for the page, such as Dara Birnbaum's video stills *Inserted Realities: Corner Insert* (1980) or Michael Smith's photographic comic strips. Yet others utilized advertising space. The Colab-associated mock corporation "The Offices of Fend, Fitzgibbon, Holzer, Nadin, Prince & Winters" announced its services as a consulting firm for artists in a full-page advertisement, and David Robbins (using the pseudonym J. Smith) created a fake IBM computer ad, "Fucked by Dracula," which appropriated a still from Charlie Chaplin's *Modern Times* to comment on corporate exploitation in the emerging information age.

As Robbins explained his experience with the magazine, "Since I hadn't gone to art school, I needed to educate myself about art. ... By interviewing artists and by thinking about art, I cobbled together my own approach to making art. *Real Life* gave me a place to put some of that stuff to promote my own undervalued heroes, and to make some experiments of my own with images and words."[43] Indeed, *Real Life* offered an opportunity for artists to try things out outside of the formal setting of a gallery. The magazine existed somewhere in between the privacy of the studio, where one might converse with close friends and acquaintances, and a more anonymous public space. This ability to mediate between the two realms was central to its artistic significance. Laurie Simmons published a pair of photographs entitled "Sam and Dottie Dance," in which she dressed her parents up in their old clothing and asked them to slow dance in their living room. As she later recalled about the pictures (which she never exhibited elsewhere), "Though they felt tangential to my thoughts at that moment, they relate way more to my future ideas than I ever imagined."[44]

THE ALTERNATIVE SPACE IN THE 1980S

The Pictures generation arose, quite literally, within the alternative, artist-run spaces that had cropped up throughout the 1970s, such as Artists Space, where the seminal "Pictures" exhibition was held. As Crimp himself observed of such spaces, they were central to the way this new work challenged modernist aesthetic criteria and exhibition spaces. "If we now have to look for aesthetic activities in so-called alternative spaces, outside the museum," he wrote, "that is because those activities, those *pictures*, pose questions that are postmodernist."[45] Alternative spaces not only offered valuable exhibition opportunities to these young, unestablished artists but also provided a vital support system and social network. At Artists Space, artists would often congregate informally on Friday afternoons in director Helene Winer's office. Winer later commented, "It's hard to imagine now, how inhospitable the art world was to young artists then. There were no young dealers with comfortable unintimidating galleries, like the ones artists started in the East Village and others which exist today. So if you didn't have a space like Artists Space to go to, you couldn't really go anywhere."[46] Several artists also worked at Artists Space: Paul McMahon was assistant director; David Salle worked in development; and Cindy Sherman was program coordinator—a position she once used as an opportunity for a performance in which she came to work dressed up as a 1950s secretary. Reviewed in the first issue of *Real Life*, Sherman's performance suggests the fluid boundaries between art making, day jobs, and socializing that characterized Artists Space at that time. As Lawson recalled, "The thing about Artists Space was that shows there rarely got reviewed, or even mentioned. This meant it was the perfect place to try out ideas for a small audience made up of mostly sympathetic colleagues who were usually willing to be supportive but tough—a place where you could risk failure."[47]

Like *Art-Rite* and other artists' magazines before it, *Real Life* was very much an extension of the artistic and social milieu of the alternative space. In fact, Artists Space helped to underwrite the first issue, contributing a few hundred dollars from its emergency materials fund to get the magazine off the ground, and Hallwalls Contemporary Arts Center in Buffalo provided free technical assistance. An unsigned review column in the first issue surveyed several artist-run alternative spaces, including Artists Space, 3 Mercer Street, P.S. 1, Franklin Furnace, Center for New Art Activities, the Clocktower, and the Kitchen, reflecting on their significance:

> New York can still boast more art activity than anywhere else, but anyone looking for innovative work had better steer clear of the commercial galleries, for in the current recession most dealers are playing an extremely safe game. As a result, younger artists look to the publicly funded spaces for support, or improvise and find their own means for getting the work out into some kind of public space. Unfortunately, little attention is paid any of this by the press and the audience tends to remain a small group of artists and friends who live in the neighborhood. A wider public, one interested in new art, never hears of anything until it receives the sanction of the establishment. By simply reporting on a cross section of these low-key events, this column will attempt to attract the attention of that wider public. At the same time, a record of things as they happen may help bring the range of current interests into focus. In the long run it ought to be possible to build a set of critical distinctions out of this information. Should that happen, this publication will have served its purpose.[48]

While this editorial statement expresses the magazine's goal to provide a critical perspective on current work, its provisional, even tentative, tone also hints at the challenges inherent in this endeavor, suggesting the difficulty of gaining distance from something that one is a part of. Perhaps because of this the column would never run again, as the editors realized that they "didn't want to be professional critics, but more quirky and personal."[49]

Even more significant, perhaps, was the fact that the role of the alternative space itself began to shift. Though *Real Life* was hatched in the context of Artists Space, and sought to provide a discursive space that would correspond to the noncommercial, artist-centered ethos of such spaces, the magazine soon witnessed a crisis in the very notion of the alternative space.

     ARTISTS' MAGAZINES IN THE 1980S

As the 1970s turned into the 1980s, the hope that art could remove itself from the aesthetic and economic conditions of the mainstream art world began to seem increasingly untenable—a shift that coincided with the conservative cultural climate ushered in by the Reagan administration. While alternative, artist-run spaces did not disappear altogether during the 1980s (despite initial attempts by the Reagan administration to eliminate them by dismantling public funding), the experimental, ad hoc character of these spaces was reined in, and they were encouraged to adopt more conventional business models under new NEA procedures.[50] This professionalization of alternative spaces curbed their antiestablishment character and inhibited the spontaneity that made them so vital in the 1970s.[51] Furthermore, as alternative spaces were increasingly forced to market themselves to fit government agendas, the artists they initially supported went on to achieve commercial success. Irving Sandler expressed misgivings about Artists Space, which he had helped to found in 1972: "We thought we might be able to set up a real alternative structure. That of course didn't happen. What we became was a foreign team for commercial galleries who recognized that we were in tune with what was liveliest in the art world."[52]

Meanwhile, overworked curatorial staff of alternative spaces found themselves increasingly inundated with bureaucratic paperwork and regulations. As Winer described her experience as director of Artists Space, "To satisfy funding agencies we had to have brochures, slides, documentation and publicity clippings. We had to look together, to plan in advance. All of which directed attention away from artists and into administration."[53] It was largely to escape such red tape that Winer left Artists Space in 1980 and, with her friend, former Castelli Gallery director Janelle Reiring, founded Metro Pictures, which included Lawson and many of the other Pictures artists in its stable.[54] As Metro Pictures and other new commercial galleries, such as Mary Boone, which represented painters such as Julian Schnabel, David Salle, and Matt Mullican, took over the role of supporting emerging artists in the 1980s, the relaxed, convivial atmosphere of the alternative spaces was replaced by a more businesslike, career-oriented environment. As Lawson later recollected: "The late 1970s, the years at Artists Space, were free in a way, meaning there was little enough at stake for everyone. We were young and enjoyed hanging out, making jokes, dissing shows we didn't like, getting excited about ones we did like. Things changed when Metro and Mary Boone opened. Suddenly there were careers to consider. Openings in the first years were still fun and party-like. Until they too became more controlled and collector-focused."[55] This transformation inevitably changed the role of artists' magazines, which had been so pivotal in supporting alternative spaces in the 1960s and 1970s. In some ways, however, such publications became even more crucial in fostering artistic communities. With Artists Space no longer a gathering place on Friday afternoons, *Real Life* and other artists' magazines continued to provide informal, communal spaces where artists could interact with one another and share ideas outside of the increasingly competitive, market-driven art world of the 1980s.

ANTI-ALTERNATIVE SPACES

As the alternative spaces of the 1970s began to appear increasingly institutionalized in the 1980s, artists sought out novel methods of making and exhibiting work in temporary, provisional, and unofficial spaces, outside of even the alternative gallery system.[56] As the collective Group Material insisted, "We never considered ourselves an 'alternative space.' In fact it seemed to us that the more prominent alternative spaces were actually, in appearance, character and exhibition policies, the children of the dominant commercial galleries."[57] Group Material, along with numerous other artists' collectives and spaces such as Colab, ABC No Rio, and Fashion Moda, challenged the sanctimonious attitude toward commerce that had characterized the 1970s alternative spaces and criticized the processes of gentrification in which the latter had so often unwittingly participated.

Dubbed an "anti-alternative space movement" by Colab member Walter Robinson, this new species of alternative practices borrowed from and exploited public and commercial venues such as billboards, magazines, the sides of buses, bars, and movie houses.[58] Colab's seminal Times Square show in 1980, for example, was held in a former massage parlor and had a gift shop where artists sold art for low prices. Other collectives of the 1980s, such as Political Art Documentation and Distribution (PAD/D), the Guerrilla Girls, Gran Fury, and the nationwide campaign Artists Call against U.S. Intervention in Central America, relied upon commercial forms and spaces to increase the political effectiveness of their activist-oriented practices. PAD/D protested Reagan's economic and military policies with events including "Death and Taxes" (1981) and "Not for Sale: A Project against Displacement" (1983–1984), which scattered art all over the city, from "public telephones and toilets to store windows, vacant lots and fire escapes to banks and tax centers."[59]

The newly complicated relationship between commercial and alternative spaces in the 1980s was exemplified by the East Village scene, where 124 galleries opened in small storefront spaces between 1981 and 1986. Many critics denounced the East Village as opportunistic, among them Craig Owens, who accused the East Village's "artist-entrepreneurs" of "surrendering to the means-ends rationality of the marketplace" and fueling the neighborhood's gentrification by marketing its "slum ambiance."[60] By contrast, Robinson, writing in the pages of *Real Life*, described the irreverent and often entertaining atmosphere of galleries such as Gracie Mansion, Fun, CASH, and Nature Morte as, at least partially, a parody of the market, maintaining that the East Village was "one big alternative space pretending to be a bunch of commercial galleries … and the idea was that we would fool the art world into paying attention to us and cutting us in on their action by giving it a kind of imaginary rag doll to play with, meanwhile keeping the real stuff to ourselves."[61] Such descriptions suggest the complex terrain of commercial and alternative practices during this period, one that was characterized by overlap, exchange, and mimicry, creating a situation in which it could be difficult to discern who was appropriating whom.

Whereas critics and art historians tended to neatly cordon off the Pictures generation, reading this work solely in terms of postmodernist aesthetics, *Real Life* portrayed the much broader and more eclectic cultural and social context in which this art existed alongside new artistic collectives as well as the graffiti, downtown poetry, and garage band, punk, and no-wave music scenes. In issue 3, Lawson interviewed Stefan Eins and Joe Lewis about Fashion Moda, their newly opened gallery in the South Bronx, best known for its support of graffiti artists, while Sonic Youth band member Kim Gordon discussed an experimental performance by Rhys Chatham, Wharton Tiers, Robert Longo, and Jules Baptiste in an essay entitled "Trash Drugs and Male Bonding." Graffiti art and street culture were highlighted in issue 8, one copy of which was itself "tagged" while on display on the newsstand, a playful assertion of the magazine's own integration within the urban context it portrayed.

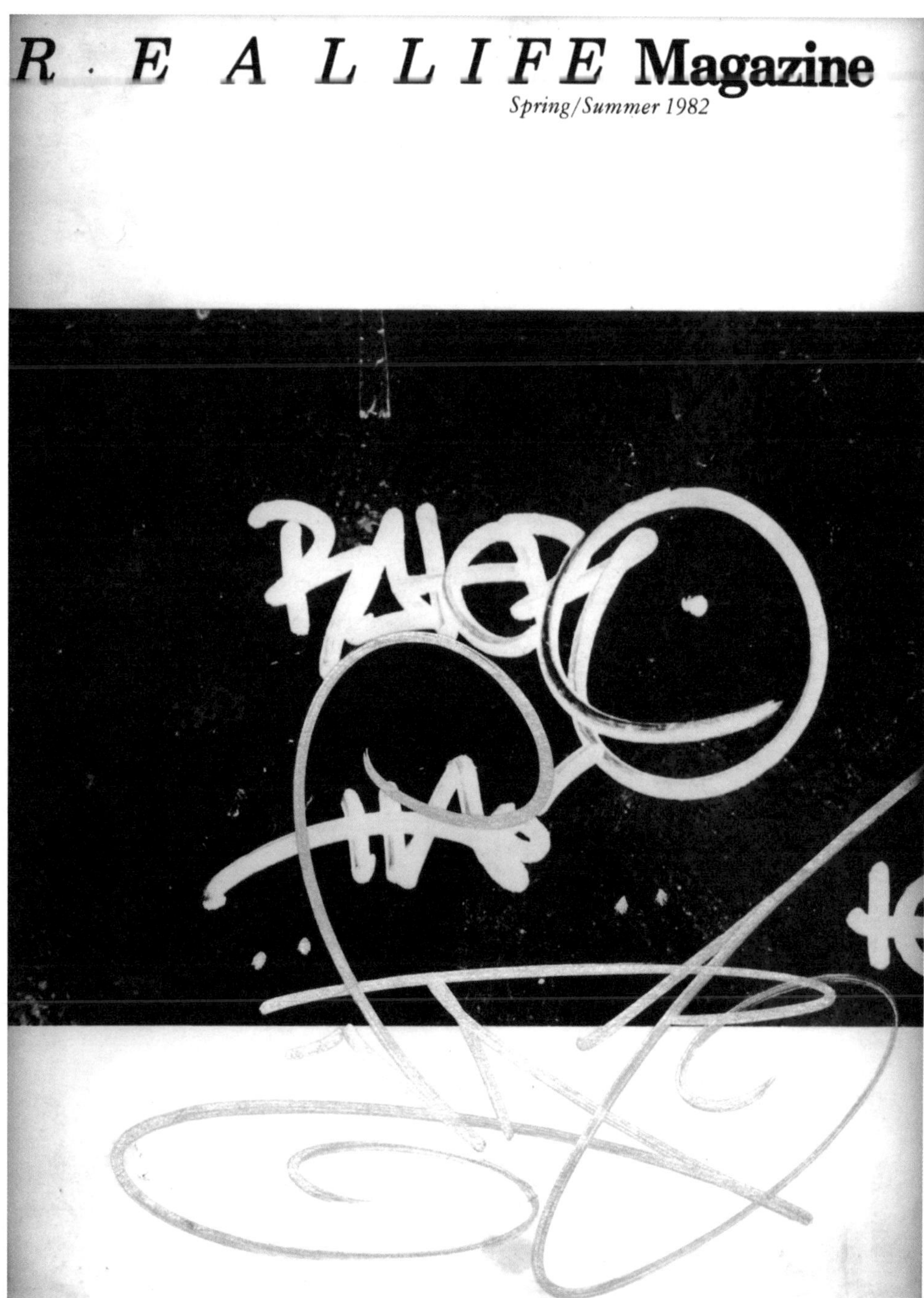

7.6
Tagged cover of *Real Life*, no. 8, Spring-
Summer 1982. Photograph by Thomas Lawson.
Courtesy of the artist.

As art in the late 1970s and early 1980s ventured outside of traditional gallery spaces, or sidestepped the art world altogether, artistic communities developed in the context of bands, parties, bars, and clubs, and other informal social interactions. The meaning of such communities—which depended on the unpredictable chemistry between individuals as well as more objective shared languages and interests—is difficult to quantify, never mind represent. As David Salle recalled, "What was really interesting about that moment if anything was something so ephemeral it could hardly be presented in any form. It was best presented at a party in the form of jokes … you had to have been there."[62] Reading *Real Life*, along with a flurry of new artists' magazines—including *Appearances, Bomb, Effects, Just Another Asshole, Blast, New Observations, Cover, Spanner, Upfront, Benzene, Raw, International Graffiti Times, East Village Eye,* ABC *No Rio, X Motion Picture, Spectacle, Aqui, Wedge, Tellus, Semiotexte,* and *Zone*—provides a glimpse of this moment that is itself partial, contingent, fragmented, and subjective. These publications not only documented the new alternative practices that were so often located in temporary, everyday spaces, outside of the art world; they helped to further disperse this work, participating in its transience and its evasion of the received categories and spaces of the art world.

As if mimicking the new breed of alternative practices of this decade, artists' magazines adopted malleable new formats and embraced more commercialized guises. *Just Another Asshole,* for example, published by Barbara Ess and Glenn Branca, evolved from a photocopied zine to a tabloid to an LP record to a book and an exhibition catalog. One issue was even published as a four-page section of the February 1980 issue of *Artforum.* Colab's *X Motion Picture* was a gritty, zinelike tabloid filled with artists' projects published for a mere three issues. The magazine *Aqui* took the form of artist-designed posters displayed on buildings around the city. Such publications were events as much as objects, like fluttering temporary spaces that arose momentarily, then disappeared.

In the face of the reactionary cultural policies of the Reagan era, including attacks on the NEA's grant procedures, alternative and activist artistic practices received increased, sometimes hostile scrutiny. In this environment, artists' magazines remained vital to supporting politically and socially concerned art of the 1980s, which addressed issues such as AIDS, homelessness, imperialism, and the identity politics of race, class, gender, and sexual orientation.[63] Issue 11/12 of *Real Life* (Winter 1983–1984) was devoted to critiquing the political situation. Published at the dawn of the culture wars, the issue ironically benefited from the Reagan administration's crackdown on controversial art, since, discouraged by rumors of the NEA's new conservatism, many artists did not even bother to apply for funding that year, resulting in especially large grants for those who did apply. The editors used their extra grant money to print the inside cover of the magazine in solid red, like a warning to signal the urgency of its contents. On the front and back cover were photographs of Joseph Stalin and Ronald Reagan thumbing their noses and making other juvenile gestures, while Pope John Paul II made googly eyes from inside the magazine. The issue included contributions by Group Material members Mundy McLaughlin, Tim Rollins, Doug Ashford, and Julie Ault; an interview with Komar and Melamid; an article by Coosje van Bruggen entitled "Repression and Resistance at the University of El Salvador, 1967–83"; an article about Adolf Hitler's paintings reprinted verbatim from a 1939 issue of *Life* magazine; and an ad for the PAD/D's Artists Call against U.S. Intervention in Central America. In its capacity to document the socially concerned art of the 1980s, the magazine constituted a form of what Lucy Lippard termed "archival activism," suggesting that the act of representing and recording alternative artistic activities—activities that were so often collaborative and fleeting in nature— was itself a central part of this art's political effectiveness.[64]

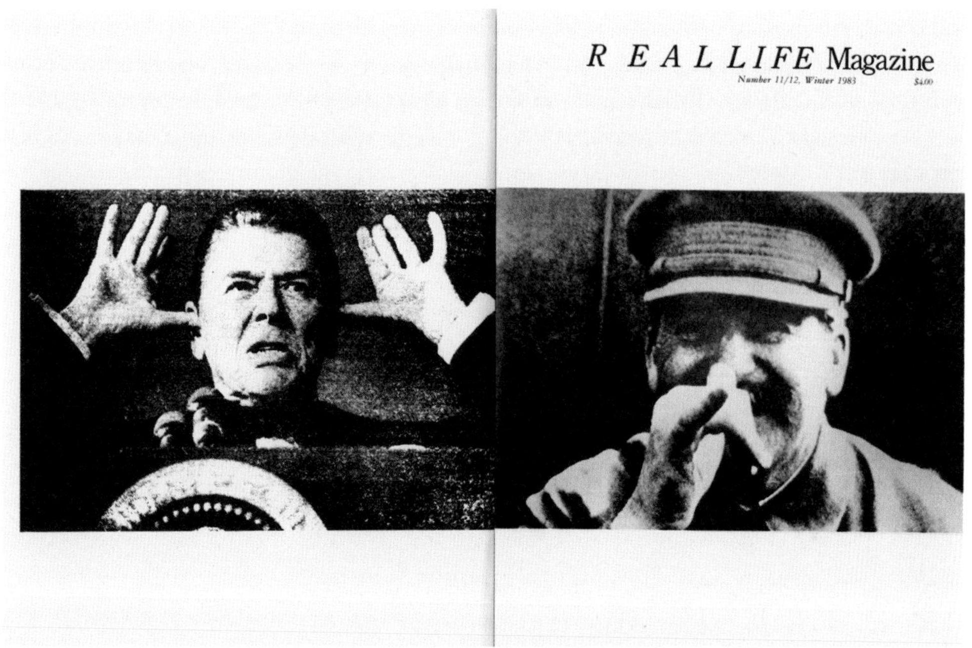

7.7

Real Life, no. 11/12, Winter 1983–1984, front and back covers. Courtesy of Thomas Lawson.

"It's true that we were interested in serious things like politics, but we were goofballs and irreverent, and it was important that the magazine reflect that," Lawson recalled of *Real Life*.[65] Indicative of the magazine's irreverence and sense of humor was a curious series of photographs of bunny rabbits made out of ice cream, published in issue 13. Attributed to one B. P. Gutfreund, these half-melted, slightly cross-eyed and lopsided creatures with gobs of frosting for ears and whiskers, and captions such as "Self-Portrait after Sherrie Levine," "Continued Success," "Who Luvs Ya Baby?" and "Here's Looking at You Kid," were a practical joke. While walking home late one night after a meeting of Artists Call against U.S. Intervention in Central America, Lawson and Morgan, along with Paul McMahon and Nancy Chunn, saw the bunnies displayed in a Chinatown ice cream parlor. On impulse they bought several and hand-delivered them to Julian Schnabel, Eric Fischl, and David Salle, with compliments from B. P. Gutfreund. "Those three had been very much part of our world," Morgan explained; however, as the art market skyrocketed, this close-knit social world had been polarized by fame and wealth. The abject desserts seemed the perfect antidote to the overdesigned loft spaces, openings with champagne and caviar, and other excesses of the 1980s art world. More than just an expression of sour grapes, the prank was a commentary on how commercial success had affected an artistic community.

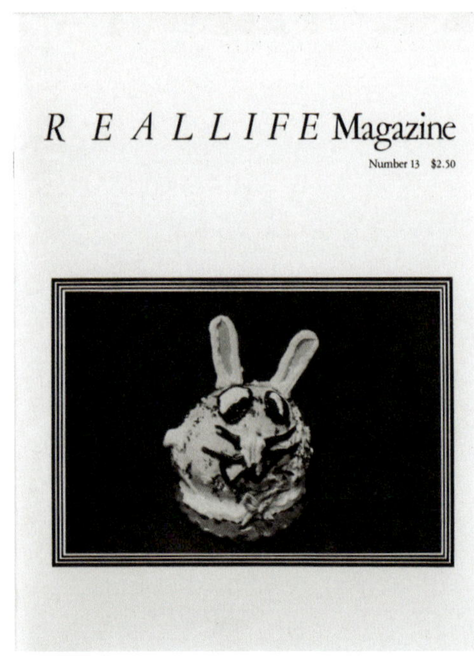

7.8

B. P. Gutfreund, "Self-Portrait after Sherrie Levine," *Real Life*, no. 13, Autumn 1984. Courtesy of Thomas Lawson.

In an interview with Rex Reason (a.k.a. David Robbins) in issue 11/12, Nature Morte gallery director Peter Nagy contemplated the changes that were reshaping the New York art world as the market soared, observing, "Due to massive hype and exposure, the art world is on the verge of becoming something it's never been before. More in the vein of popular culture, movies, television, fashion. It's competing for that segment of *Newsweek* magazine, that four-page color spread."[66] Indeed, glamorous photographs of artists such as Jean-Michel Basquiat and Julian Schnabel began to appear on the pages of *Vanity Fair* and other fashion magazines—a phenomenon that, while not altogether new, marked an unprecedented phase in the commodification of not only art but artist. As Karen Benson commented in *ZG* magazine, "This fascination for the artist-personality has not disappeared since Warhol's media antics in the '60s. But the more overt intrusion of the star system into the art world's more discrete space of commodities was resisted … only to erupt in the new constellation in the 1980s. … The newest art stars act themselves. They pander to the myth of the artist which the public wants rather than trying to disrupt the familiar forms of identification."[67]

Real Life provided a sharp counterpoint to this situation, denouncing the inflated art market and the role of mainstream media in encouraging it. Morgan satirized the self-made, media-fueled myths of artists such as George Baselitz and Jean Michel Basquiat in "Portraits of the Artists/Composite Drawings," which consisted entirely of appropriated excerpts from publications such as *Artforum, The Hollywood Reporter, House & Garden*, and *Vogue*. Even more blistering was an article on Schnabel entitled "Condensation and Dish-Placement," a bold indictment of Schnabel's self-aggrandizing perpetuation of the myth of artistic genius as well the complicity of his dealers, Mary Boone and Leo Castelli, in this process. The article was signed "the Holy Ghost Writers," a byline used by the curator and museum director Lisa Phillips and film critic/curator Berenice Reynaud, then students at the Whitney Independent Study Program.

Walter Robinson reflected on the vexed nature of success in the 1980s art world in his article "The Quest for Failure," noting that "the art world hungers for success like a vampire for blood, and it doesn't matter whose neck gets bitten, it's nothing personal."[68] Accompanied by pictures of Robinson's paintings of oversized aspirin and Tylenol bottles, the article ponders the overrated rewards of commercial success, and touts, only half-jokingly, the underappreciated virtues of failure: "With success becoming so common, the only way to remain unique is to fail. … Obviously, this takes more guts than being a success does, but it does have advantages—the IRS won't bother you, for instance, and you won't have to listen to rich people talk. … To fail is, of course, to be outside, and to be so is to suggest the possibility of preserving the vitality of the avant-garde."[69]

It was not only the painters associated with Mary Boone who were becoming commercially successful; many of the Pictures artists also started to gain a kind of celebrity status by the mid to late 1980s. Richard Bolton pointedly drew attention to this fact in the Winter 1988–1989 issue of *Real Life* by reproducing *Art News* covers featuring portraits of Sherman, Levine, Kruger, and Longo, alongside statistics about the income, gender, and educational level of *Art News* subscribers. As the artists it initially supported made their way into the mainstream, *Real Life* retrained its focus, seeking to "remain on that edge," as Lawson put it, explaining, "We operated out of a sense of curiosity. The magazine expanded, but it expanded on that principle. It was who we knew and who we ran into. Our first few issues are heavy on Sherrie and Barbara and Richard Prince, but after a few years we realized that the job of writing about them had been picked up by *Artforum*. They had sort of drifted into the mainstream, so there wasn't a necessity."[70] Meanwhile, *Real Life* went on to publish work by a new generation of emerging artists, including Critical Art Ensemble, David Hammons, Mark Dion, Felix Gonzalez-Torres, Gregg Bordowitz, and Andrea Fraser, while continuing to protest the effects of Reagan's policies both within the art world and outside of it. The cover of the Winter 1988–1989 issue, for example, featured Lawson's photograph of a homeless encampment near the Manhattan Bridge labeled "Reaganville, New York"—a reference to the Hoovervilles of the Great Depression.

While *Real Life* provided a critical perspective on commercial success within the art world, its editors also found themselves thinking about the magazine's own ambitions. As the publication became better known, they considered transforming it into a more profitable, self-sustaining business: "We had to make a decision about either really becoming magazine publishers, and clearing the necessary space in our lives to dedicate to producing four issues a year, buckling down and selling ads and having an office, or keeping it as this happily amateurish opportunity to publish whenever we felt like it. … It was an important moment for us."[71]

A little over a decade after *Real Life* began, the magazine published its twentieth issue (1990). The editors asked all those who had contributed to the magazine to submit something "to celebrate our survival and see how things have changed."[72] Lawson's editorial, entitled "No Bull," was accompanied by a photograph of three genetically identical bulls that he had clipped from the *New York Times*. He wrote, "I find myself looking at these bulls over and over again because the certainty of perfection they embody is so alarmingly ludicrous … that they seem to have that indistinct, yet definitely inflated sense of importance one associates with any number of 'successful' artists of the past decade."[73] The cover featured a photograph Lawson took of a giant light bulb marquee for a lighting store in Los Angeles—the classic symbol of originality rendered as a commercialized, kitschy roadside attraction. He and Morgan had started to spend more time in Los Angeles, where they would soon permanently relocate, and he recalled, "we hadn't decided to end the magazine, but we were, I guess, unconsciously, not sure if we would continue, so I went into that issue a little down, wondering if we'd somehow missed the point of the decade."[74] The magazine would only be published two more times—number 21/22 was guest-edited by Lane Relyea, and the final issue, no. 23 (1994), was published by California Institute of the Arts, where Lawson had accepted a position as dean.

7.9

Thomas Lawson, "No Bull," *Real Life,* no. 20, 1990.
Courtesy of the artist.

I have a clipping from the New York Times, a smudgy photograph of three genetically identical bulls. I keep it in my studio, part of the disordered pile of random images I regularly sift through looking for useful connections. I'm sure this picture holds a clue to something I've been looking for; it keeps returning to the surface, demanding attention yet never quite managing to translate into something useful. I find myself looking at these bulls over and over again because the certainty of perfection they embody is so alarmingly ludicrous. In this they seem of a piece with so many of the "success" manias of the eighties, great accomplishments that need never have happened.

Part of the fascination of the picture undoubtedly has to do with its grubby, nondescript rendering of a grandoise, yet pointless ambition. Just what is the benefit of having three identical bulls? And if there was a point wouldn't you want to show them off to better advantage? And if they are identical in every way, does that mean the bullshit is too? There is no end once the questions begin. Is this the same scientific approach to farming that improved cattle feed by adding sheep brains to the mix, thereby creating the new "mad cow disease" and terrifying the British public into giving up its beef habit? Or, to change the subject, is there a similarity between this and the desire to build three hugely vulgar casinos in Atlantic City where one would more than suffice? Or again, to bring it all closer to home, does the picture resonate because the three bulls make me think of that perfect marriage of theory and practice, the sculpture in edition? That they seem to have that indistinct, yet definitively inflated sense of importance one associates with any number of "successful" artists of the past decade?

When Susan and I first started publishing this magazine in 1979 the big issue in the art world was still originality, as now it is the supposed impossibility of the same. Both are essentially trumped up issues to mask a fear of the processes of history, which is to say the processes of aging. What Western culture craves is the stasis of perfect reproduction, an endless renewal of the same thing. With that comfortably in place it can then be declared that time is banished, communism defeated, and all the evils of the world put to rest. Fortunately for our safety and sanity this illusion of perfection constantly slips out of reach, proves as fugitive as my blurred picture of perfect bulls. But it is rarely art which accomplishes this, more often it is the brute realities of life; the inevitable intrusion of sickness, pain and death reconcile most of us to the realization that a craving for perpetual youthfulness is an unforgivably kitsch nostalgia. Yet the culture as a whole has such an investment in denying the realities of the body in favour of a fantasmagoria of untroubled sexuality and familial bliss that the requirement that artists work against the current manifestations of this ideology in the culture that enfolds them takes on a moral imperative.

As editors we have tried to follow that injunction, rejecting current platitudes as the arse-licking they invariably are. When we first started the magazine the pious rectitude of post minimalism held sway in the art world, and we confronted that with the shameless thievery and media fascination of appropriationist work. When that in turn became acceptable enough for the pages of *Artforum* and *Art in America* and the walls of the Whitney Museum, we went looking for other artists, other ways of working. We have managed never to be of the mainstream, but much of what we have published has gone on to find acceptance there temporarily. With luck and perseverence, we will continue on this path for the decade to come.

• • •

For this issue, to celebrate our survival and see how things have changed, we asked all those who have been part of our history to send in something new. We asked that contributions be short, taking up one or two pages. Some people went over, others never showed up at all. In the end we think it's a pretty good issue, a fair reflection of possiblities as we go into a period of continued battle over the direction of our shared culture, and the impact that culture has on our lives.

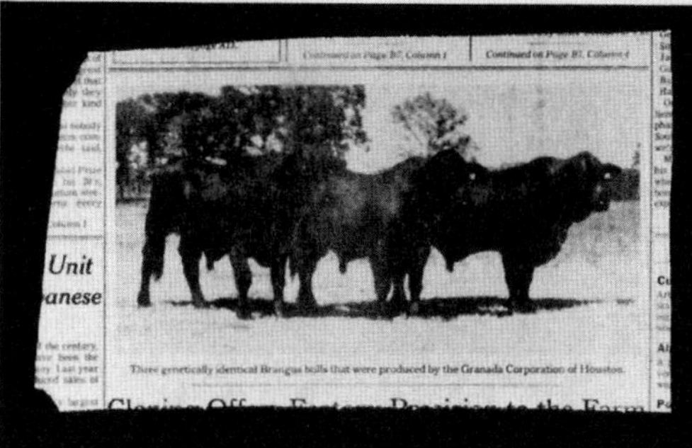

EPILOGUE: INTERNATIONAL ACTIVITY
INTERFUNKTIONEN, 1968–1975

One of the important things about the new dematerialized art is
that it provides a way of getting the power structure out of
New York and spreading it around to wherever an artist feels like
being at the time.

LUCY LIPPARD[1]

The vital role of independently published magazines in today's global art world was highlighted by the Magazines project, organized as part of Documenta 12 in 2007. The project continued the strategies of the previous Documenta 11, which, under the direction of Okwui Enwezor, had been dispersed over a number of discursive and geographical "platforms" as a way to undermine and decentralize its geopolitical power structure. Documenta 12 Magazines was likewise conceived as a critical intervention into the processes of globalization in which large-scale exhibitions have so conspicuously participated. Organized by Georg Schöllhammer, the Magazines project invited over ninety periodicals from more than fifty countries to produce essays, features, and artists' projects that considered the exhibition's themes and motifs from local perspectives. The participating magazines were then exhibited both at the exhibition proper and via an online archive, operating as decentralized, diverse sites of knowledge that might counter the exhibition's homogenizing tendencies and provide a "kaleidoscopic view of specific moments, configurations, and positions," as Schöllhammer wrote.[2]

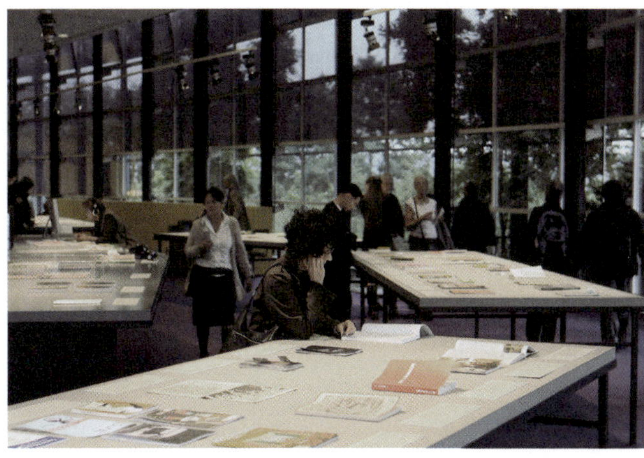

8.1
Documenta 12 Magazines, 2007.
Ryszard Kasiewicz/Documenta
Archiv.

While Documenta 12 Magazines highlighted magazines' function as local sites of knowledge production and reception, the project was also criticized for its attempt to capitalize on and co-opt this knowledge. Claire Bishop argued that the Magazines project "invite[d] the question of whether an initiative intended to give voice to local positions was ultimately instrumentalized as a 'research and development arm of the exhibition.'"[3] Especially emblematic of this instrumentalization, in Bishop's view, were three anthologies—themselves, oddly enough, called magazines—that compiled selections from the participating periodicals and that were sold at the exhibition. These three generic volumes had a homogenizing effect on their contents that went beyond their literal design: stripped of their materiality and temporality, their conditions of circulation and distribution, the publications were deprived of the very attributes that, this book has argued, makes the magazine such a distinct form of discourse and has made it such a compelling medium for artists.

This epilogue explores artists' magazines in relationship to the changing geographical conditions of the increasingly international art world of the 1960s and 1970s. Its main case study, the German artists' magazine *Interfunktionen*—founded in 1968 by Friedrich Heubach, and later taken over by Benjamin Buchloh—was born out of a dialog with the emerging global art world, and specifically to protest the conservative and U.S.-dominated curatorial program of Documenta 4. *Interfunktionen* provides an intriguing prelude to the 2007 Documenta Magazines project, shedding light on how the tensions between local and global cultural perspectives that marked the recent exhibition had played out in an earlier moment, while attesting to the important—and deeply ambivalent—role of magazines, then as now, in negotiating these tensions. Publishing writings and works by artists on both sides of the Atlantic, *Interfunktionen* exemplifies the important role of artists' magazines in both cultivating international exchange and fostering a sense of local, regional, and national identity for artists in the 1960s and 1970s—a role that was especially pivotal in Germany, given the country's struggle to overcome its postwar isolation and its difficulty in coming to terms with its own recent history.

While they have been at the center of this book, magazines in the United States and Canada represent only a fraction of the artists' periodicals published throughout the world since World War II. Conceptual art was itself a deeply decentralized and international phenomenon, and the proliferation of artists' magazines during the 1960s and 1970s was both a symptom and a catalyst of this unprecedented internationalization.[4] As affordable air travel and new communication technologies accelerated the circulation of people and ideas across the globe, magazines greatly enhanced such exchange, shuttling artistic ideas back and forth across oceans and borders and fostering contacts and friendships between artists, curators, editors, and critics in different geographical locations. Magazines provided opportunities for artists to correspond and collaborate over distances, and preserved traces of ephemeral meetings and conversations.

The magazine's emergence as a new kind of medium and distribution form for conceptual art was deeply tied to its communicative possibilities within this increasingly international art world. This was evident in the innovative exhibition practices of the dealer Seth Siegelaub, whose understanding of the printed page as a new kind of "primary information" was related to its capacity to transcend the limitations of geography. As he remarked in a 1969 interview: "I think that New York is beginning to break down as a center. Not that there will be another city to replace it, but rather that where any artist is will be the center. International activity."[5] Siegelaub's exhibition "July/August 1970," which, as discussed in chapter 1, took place solely in the pages of the July/ August 1970 issue of *Studio International*, suggests the magazine's potential as a site of such "international activity." Siegelaub invited six artists and curators from five different countries—Germano Celant from Italy, Michel Claura from France, Hans Strelow from the Netherlands, Charles Harrison from England, and David Antin and Lucy Lippard from the United States—to curate an eight-page section of the magazine by selecting artists to create works expressly for the mass-produced page. The 48-page exhibition was published in a special trilingual (English, French, and German) edition—a decision that Siegelaub elsewhere linked to his desire to internationalize the art world: "I am concerned with getting art out into the world and plan to continue publishing in multilingual editions to further this end. This is a very important communications consideration. American museums, with typical chauvinism, never publish in more than one language—just English."[6]

However, if "July/August 1970" epitomized Siegelaub's faith in the magazine as a transnational communicative space that might enable art to circulate freely around the globe—a model that echoed André Malraux's concept of the "museum without walls"—it also revealed the contradictions inherent in this model. As sincere as Siegelaub was in his desire to overcome the geographical hierarchies of the art world, "July/August 1970" did not approximate anything like a truly global space, and in some ways reinforced the dominant geopolitical (art) world order. Of the thirty-seven artists who participated, nearly half were from the United States, and all were working in North America and Western Europe (though the New York-based Japanese artist On Kawara and the London-based South African Roelof Louw were included among them). The choice to publish the magazine in English, French, and German implicitly marginalized other languages, countries, and even entire continents. Furthermore, the exhibition might be criticized for maintaining other kinds of inequalities—for example, it included only two women artists: Hanne Darboven and Eleanor Antin. Siegelaub's faith in the printed page as a neutral, universal space failed to account for the ways in which publications are themselves implicated in the same social and political relationships that structure actual places—in this case, manifesting the privileged position of a New York male art dealer and British commercial art magazine.[7] The shortcomings of "July/August 1970" were symptomatic of the larger problems with the internationalization of the art world during the postwar period: too often, it was tantamount to simply exporting American art—at least within mainstream exhibition venues and publications.

By contrast, even a cursory glance at the proliferation of artists' magazines published around the globe in the postwar period complicates the belief that publications transcend physical location; instead, we are prompted to consider how they register the specific national, regional, and local circumstances of their production and distribution. The importance of magazines in fostering artistic dialog between countries and continents is evident beginning with artists' periodicals of the 1950s and early 1960s, such as *Gutai, Boa, Zero, Gorgona, Revue Nul = o, Integration, Spirale, Azimuth, Diagonal Cero, El Corno Emplumado*, and *dé-coll/age*, which were often self-consciously international in orientation; they sought to give artistic movements a higher profile on the world stage, while opening up local artistic communities to influences from abroad—goals that were evidenced by their frequently polyglot pages. In the late 1960s and 1970s, numerous periodicals associated with conceptual art arose across the world, including,

Studio International

July/August 1970   Journal of modern art   Book Supplement   17/6 $2

David Antin
Dan Graham   1
Harold Cohen   2
John Baldessari   3
Richard Serra   4
Eleanor Antin   5
Fred Lonidier   6
George Nicolaidis   7
Keith Sonnier   8

Germano Celant
Giovanni Anselmo   9
Alighiero Boetti   10
Pier Paolo Calzolari   11
Mario Merz   12
Giuseppe Penone   13
Emilio Prini   14
Pistoletto   15
Gilberto Zorio   16

Michel Claura
Daniel Buren   17

Charles Harrison
Keith Arnatt   25
Terry Atkinson
David Bainbridge
Michael Baldwin
Harold Hurrell   26
Victor Burgin   28
Barry Flanagan   29
Joseph Kosuth   30
John Latham   31
Roelof Louw   32

Lucy R. Lippard
Robert Barry   33
Stephen Kaltenbach   34
Lawrence Weiner   35
On Kawara   36
Sol LeWitt   37
Douglas Huebler   38
N. E. Thing Co.   39
Frederick Barthelme   40

Hans Strelow
Jan Dibbets   41
Hannie Darboven   45

in addition to the North American publications already discussed, *Interfunktionen, +–o, Art-Language, Control, Black Phoenix, Salon, Robho, mela, Art & Project Bulletin, Der Löwe, Artitudes International, Schmuck, North, King Kong International, Die Schastrommel, VH 101, Bit, Data,* and *La Città di Riga* in Western Europe; *Hexágono, Malasartes, Paso de Peatones, Lacre, Artes Visuales,* and *Ovum* in Latin America; *Edition a, Signal, Rok, Maj 75, Artpool Letter,* and *bit International* in Eastern Europe; *Provoke, Bijutsu Shihyō,* and *Kirokutai* in Japan; and *Other Voices* and *Lip* in Australia. (The appendix contains a list of such magazines that is as comprehensive as possible.)

Artists' magazines demonstrate that artistic innovation did not proceed in a linear manner from center (New York) to periphery, spreading around the globe in a single homogeneous movement, but emerged unevenly and unexpectedly in different places and times, opening onto surprising constellations of artistic influences that go against the grain of teleological history and challenge the dominant logic of globalization. Thus it was that the performative and antiformalist activities of the Japanese Gutai group (themselves inspired by a strong misreading of Hans Namuth's photographs of Jackson Pollock painting) made their way across the world in the pages of the self-published magazine *Gutai* (1955–1965), foreshadowing later conceptual and performance-based practices as diverse as Allan Kaprow's Happenings, the activities of the Fluxus and Zero groups, and American process art of the late 1960s. Or that in the unlikely city of Zagreb, seven years before Lucy Lippard coined the term "dematerialization," the Gorgona group founded the "anti-magazine" *Gorgona* (1961–1966) as a conceptual medium for their ephemeral ideas and activities, anticipating the later explorations of American conceptual artists such as Dan Graham and Robert Smithson. Or that in the pages of the Parisian magazine *Robho* (1967–1971), edited by Jean Clay and Julien Blaine, the activities of the Brazilian artists Lygia Clark and Hélio Oiticica, as well as the Argentine *Tucumán arde* project, were broadcast alongside reports on the Art Workers' Coalition, the French BMPT Group, and the San Francisco Diggers, while soon-to-be *Avalanche* editor Willoughby Sharp wrote about kinetic art.

Artists' magazines provide a rich archive of conceptual art's deeply international character, tracking the interactions and cross-fertilizations among networks of artists from different countries. Like many of the North American publications discussed in previous chapters, artists' magazines published elsewhere during the 1960s and 1970s frequently served as radical alternatives to mainstream exhibition spaces and publications. However, while they reveal striking parallels between conceptual art practices internationally, artists' magazines also open onto national, regional, and local differences—differences that extend to the very meaning of the act of publishing a magazine to begin with.

In the countries of Eastern Europe, where artists were subject to varying levels of state supervision and censorship, independently published magazines served as a different kind of alternative space.[8] In the Soviet Union and in countries such as Hungary, Romania, Poland, and Czechoslovakia, artists' publications resonated with the dissident, underground practices of *samizdat*, literally meaning self-publishing, as opposed to state publishing (*gozidat*).[9] For example, *Metki* (Marks) was a handmade journal published in Moscow in 1975 with a circulation of only five to ten copies. *Artpool Letter* was an important vehicle for unofficial art, illegally published in Hungary during the early 1980s. Meanwhile, in the former Yugoslavia, magazines such as *Gorgona*, *bit International*, *Edition a*, *Signal*, *Rok*, and *Maj 75* were crucial sites through which artists participated in international avant-garde and neo-avant-garde practices, which were frequently suppressed or marginalized within local mainstream culture.

Likewise, in Latin America, artists' magazines were inflected by specific historical and political conditions, including the series of repressive dictatorships that swept across the region from the 1960s to the 1980s and the experience of U.S. imperialism.[10] Such conditions contributed to the critical and anti-imperialist approaches to the mass media witnessed in magazines such as *Malasartes*, published in Rio de Janeiro by Cildo Meireles and others, or the mail art magazine *Ovum*, published by Clemente Padin.[11] Artists' magazines in Latin America registered the political strife in this region; sometimes they ceased as a result of it, as did *El Corno Emplumado* in 1968 and *Hexágono* in 1975. Some magazines were published by artists in exile, such as *Schmuck*, published by the Mexican artists Martha Hellion and Felipe Ehrenberg in England in the late 1960s, or *Ephemera*, published by Ulises Carrión in Amsterdam.

Other examples, such as the Moroccan magazine *Souffles*, *Black Phoenix* (published in London by Rasheed Araeen), and the Paris-based *Présence Africaine*, suggest how the magazine's capacity to foster artistic communities and identities took on a special significance within a postcolonial context, providing a platform for artists to contest global conditions of cultural imperialism and domination. Yet other magazines have been important for maintaining connections between geographically dispersed artistic communities in an increasingly global art world. For example, *A/Ya*, illegally edited in Moscow and published in Paris between 1979 and 1986, and *Collective Farm*, published in New York during the 1980s, were crucial channels for the Russian art community in exile. More recently, Tania Bruguera's *Memoria de la Posguerra* (Postwar Memory) (1993–1994) provided a collective space, albeit short-lived, for Cuban artists living both inside and outside the country.

Such publications point to the complexity of magazines as sites of reception in an international context. They challenge the idea that a magazine is a universal, neutral space, and underscore the ways in which the magazine manifests geographical differences and specific cultural and historical circumstances. Indeed, if artists' magazines were crucial circuits in the increasingly international exchange of art in the 1960s and 1970s, they did not merely transmit artistic ideas and practices from one place to another, but, along the way, they provided opportunities for readers to reflect upon and transform these practices according to local experiences and conditions. At the same time, however, magazines counter traditional or essentialist notions of national, regional, or local artistic identity, insisting that such identities are themselves unstable, and always already informed by influences from elsewhere. While magazines have inevitably participated in processes of globalization, they also have the potential to be spaces of mediation that resist homogenization, assert local interests and identities, and complicate the very opposition between local and global, revealing them to be mutually constitutive.

"DOCUMENTA-DOCUMENTATION"

Interfunktionen sheds light on how the magazine's new status as a primary site for conceptual art in the 1960s was inflected by its capacity to mediate between local and international processes of reception. The magazine's title—literally meaning "in between functions"—referred primarily to the new intermedia and interdisciplinary artistic activities that it was founded to support in the wake of Documenta 4. However, the prefix "inter-" also strongly resonated with the internationalism that increasingly characterized postwar Germany. "'Inter' was in," Heubach recalled; "today one would call it 'global,' back then 'inter' was enough."[12]

The impulse to internationalize German art had been at the heart of Documenta itself. The first Documenta was staged in 1955 as part of Germany's effort to reclaim its ties with international modernism, which had been denounced as degenerate under the Nazi regime. But the internationalism of Documenta soon came to mean the hegemony of U.S. abstract expressionism, which masqueraded as a universal visual language that might transcend national identity, while actually serving as a vehicle for American cultural imperialism within the cultural politics of the Cold War.[13] *Interfunktionen* was born out of the controversy over the 1968 Documenta 4, which continued to support American abstraction, including post-painterly abstraction, color field painting, minimal art, and pop art, while neglecting new conceptual and performance-based practices that had emerged since, in Germany and elsewhere.[14] The work of important German Fluxus and conceptual artists such as Wolf Vostell, Joseph Beuys, and Jörg Immendorff, for example, was omitted from the exhibition; and adding insult to injury, a multimedia festival organized by Vostell had been canceled at the last minute. A series of artist-run protests ensued, including a "disturbance action" known as the Honey Blind Action, in which Immendorff, Chris Reinecke, Heubach, and others stormed a Documenta press conference, carrying out a series of guerrilla-style antics, including hugging and kissing exhibition officials, tossing handfuls of change at them, and pouring honey on the floor and furniture.

Billed as a "Documenta-Documentation," the first issue of *Interfunktionen* was 75 pages long and produced in an edition of 120—a fact that attests to its extremely local character. As Heubach explained in an editorial statement, the purpose of the publication was to create a more permanent record of the controversy surrounding Documenta 4 in order to prevent it from becoming merely "anecdotal."[15] On the cover was an enlarged newspaper photograph of Arnold Bode, the original founder of Documenta who had also organized Documenta 4, explaining the exhibition to German president Heinrich Lübke and two other men. The degraded image dissolves into halftone dots, emphasizing the magazine's status as a site of interference that aimed to disturb or disrupt official versions of the show. Yet this first issue documented not so much the actual events at Documenta as the extensive media coverage they generated—a fact that was fitting, given that these events had been so deliberately staged for the media to begin with. It published numerous press clippings from German and international newspapers reporting on the Honey Blind Action; correspondence between Reinecke and the city of Kassel concerning a

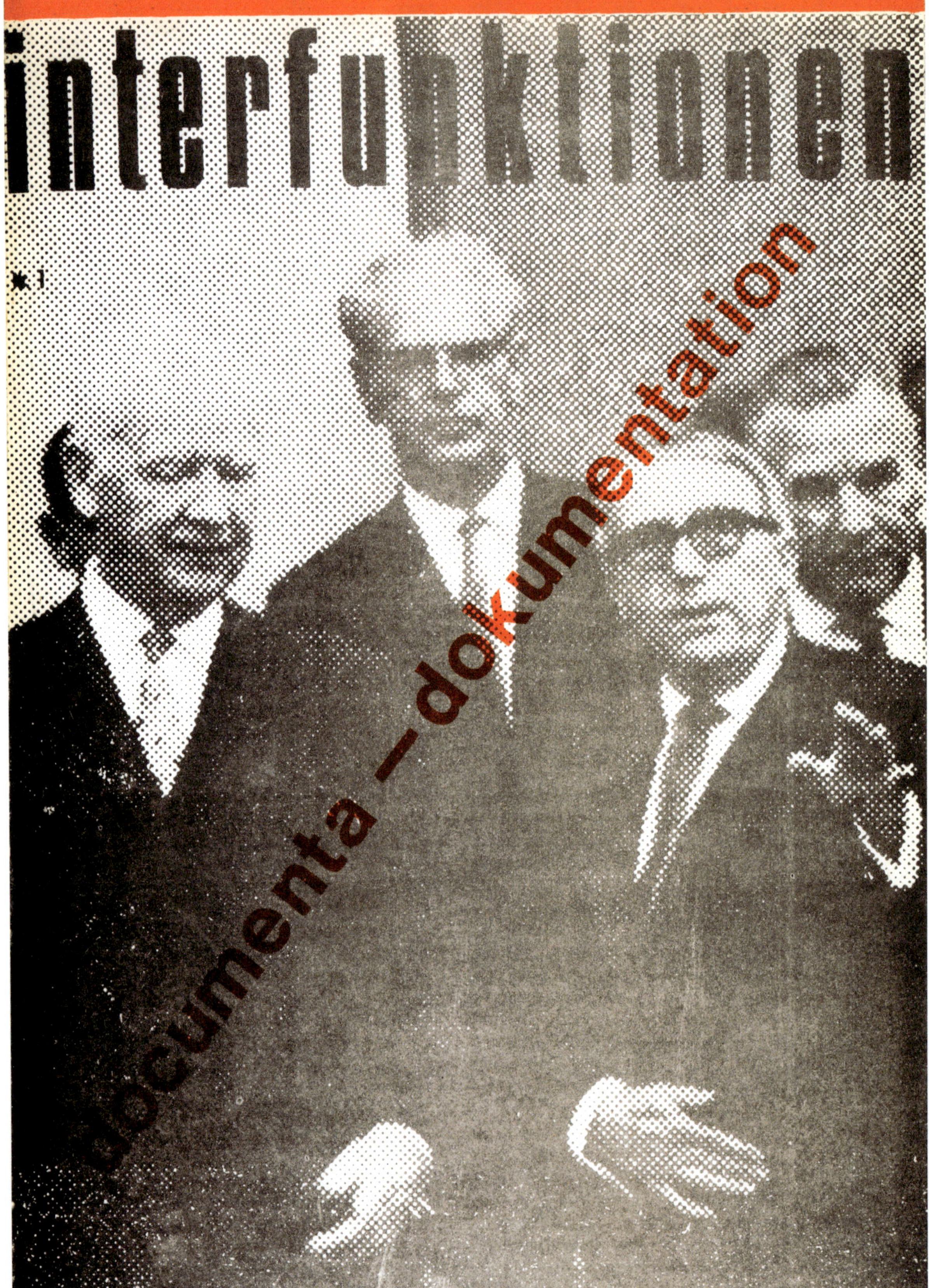

interfunktionen
*1
documenta – dokumentation

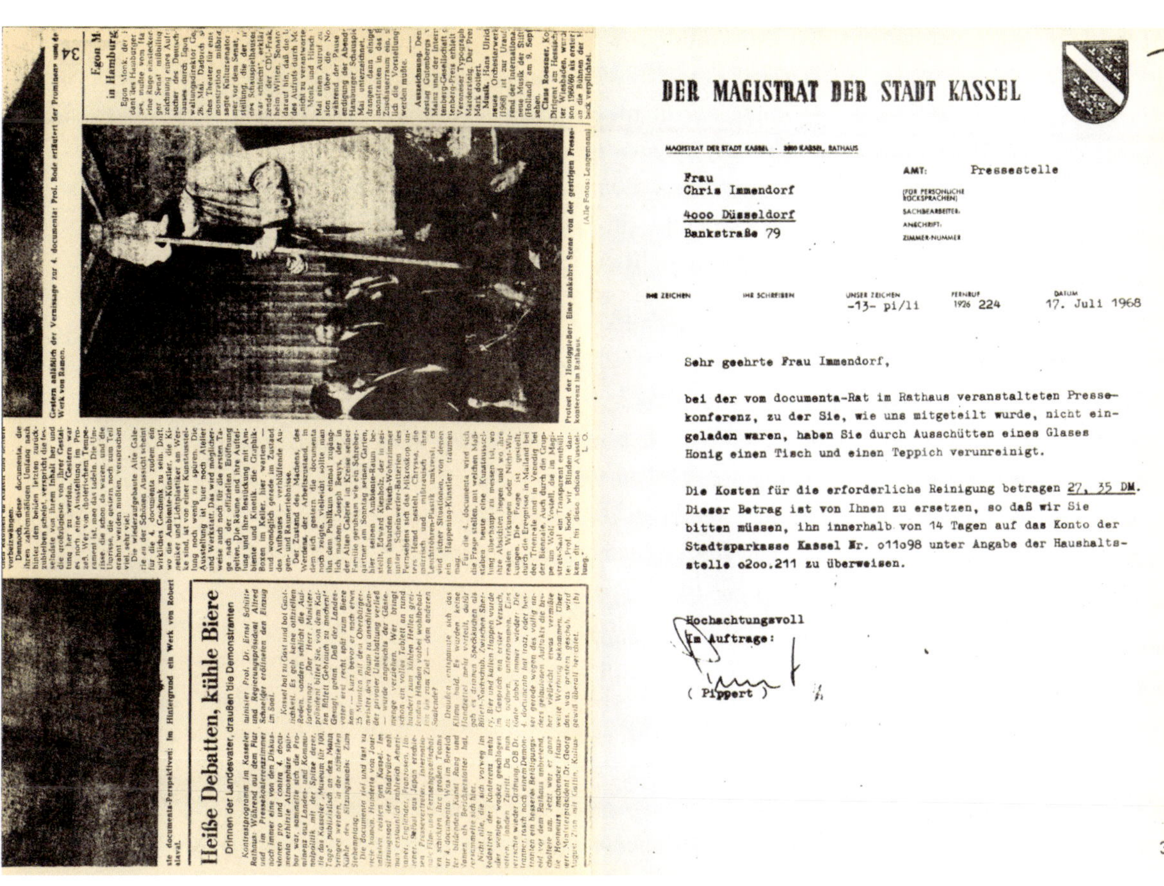

DER MAGISTRAT DER STADT KASSEL

MAGISTRAT DER STADT KASSEL · 3500 KASSEL, RATHAUS

Frau
Chris Immendorf

4000 Düsseldorf
Bankstraße 79

AMT: Pressestelle
(FÜR PERSÖNLICHE RÜCKSPRACHEN)
SACHBEARBEITER:
ANSCHRIFT:
ZIMMER-NUMMER:

IHR ZEICHEN   IHR SCHREIBEN   UNSER ZEICHEN FERNRUF   DATUM
                             -13- pi/li   1926 224   17. Juli 1968

Sehr geehrte Frau Immendorf,

bei der vom documenta-Rat im Rathaus veranstalteten Presse-
konferenz, zu der Sie, wie uns mitgeteilt wurde, nicht ein-
geladen waren, haben Sie durch Ausschütten eines Glases
Honig einen Tisch und einen Teppich verunreinigt.

Die Kosten für die erforderliche Reinigung betragen 27, 35 DM.
Dieser Betrag ist von Ihnen zu ersetzen, so daß wir Sie
bitten müssen, ihn innerhalb von 14 Tagen auf das Konto der
Stadtsparkasse Kassel Nr. o11o98 unter Angabe der Haushalts-
stelle o2oo.211 zu überweisen.

Hochachtungsvoll
Im Auftrage:

(Pippert)

8.3

Interfunktionen, no. 1, 1968, cover. Courtesy
of Friedrich Heubach. Research Library,
The Getty Research Institute, Los Angeles
(87-S406 no. 1).

8.4

Correspondence and news clippings related to the
demonstrations against Documenta 4, *Interfunktionen*,
no. 1, 1968, pages 34–35. Courtesy of Friedrich
Heubach. Research Library, The Getty Research Institute,
Los Angeles (87-S406 no. 1).

bill for the removal of the honey stains; notes and diagrams from Vostell's canceled multimedia event; plus a selection of original artist-signed flyers and postcards, which had been banned from being distributed at the exhibition proper. Many of these documents were facsimiled onto newsprint or stationary to mimic the originals, giving the magazine an authentic, handmade feeling, while signaling that the reproduced site of the magazine was being reconceived as a new kind of primary site at this time.

Thus, *Interfunktionen* came into being as a kind of *salon des refusés* for radical art that was marginalized by Germany's established exhibition spaces and media outlets, which, as Heubach observed in his editorial statement in the first issue, "no longer open up possibilities for art, but rather place terms and conditions on it," constituting "a restriction of art itself."[16] He elaborated upon such restrictions: "When museum, gallery, exhibition are the only possibilities for art to enter into a larger mode of communication, then art will necessarily orient itself according to the structures of these intermediaries, for the sake of communication. It stands to reason that any form of art that does not commit to the conditions of the established forms of communication, e.g. Happenings, will not get access to the market."[17] In fact, while there was perhaps no single publication in Europe with the kind of clout that *Artforum* had in the United States, the mainstream European art press of the late 1960s and 1970s was largely dominated by traditional forms of art and commercial interests. As Buchloh would observe of European art magazines, they "deal with (art) phenomena without participating in any way in the process of production ... their *raison d'être* is [the] culture industry"; he went on to criticize "the lack of historical perspective, of any aesthetic or political position, which characterizes most contemporary magazines and distinguishes them so strikingly from certain of their predecessors—Pfemfert's *Aktion*, for example, or Schwitters's *Merz*, van Doesburg's *Stijl*, or Breton's *Littérature*."[18]

Heubach, who was a doctoral student in psychology at the time, was an enthusiast of contemporary art, though he claimed to have a limited knowledge of it, at least in the sense of professional expertise. He had become involved in the German art scene in Cologne and nearby Düsseldorf through his friendship with artists, especially Vostell, and later recalled: "That my relationship to these innovative activities was at first not especially knowledgeable, and that we tended to agree more on what we were opposing than on the thing itself, did not bother either me or my artist friends."[19] Heubach's remove from the specialized field of professional art criticism in some ways made him an ideal spokesman for this new art: precisely because he had few preconceived notions of what art was or should be, he was (in direct contrast to modernist critics such as Michael Fried, for example) distinctly unconcerned with upholding traditional definitions of it. He was much more interested in the political possibilities of art, namely its capacity to question the status quo, explaining: "I preferred to avoid becoming involved in the art issue at all, but methodologically to suspend it ... I never asked myself the question, 'Is this art?' Primarily because, for me, nothing depended on the answer. As a reason for publication it was quite enough that a work promised an experience I felt was necessary—which to me meant any work that did not coincide with the general consensus on reality, any work in which this consensual construct presenting itself as 'reality' was attacked or demolished, or which took exclusion from this consensus as its theme."[20]

In his desire to create a magazine that would not merely report on experimental art but participate in its radicalism, Heubach was inspired by Vostell's journal *dé-coll/age* (1962–1967), which, he recalled, "was a model for me [of how] to present artists' work as directly as possible."[21] Vostell's journal, which promoted Fluxus and Happenings, both espoused and enacted the artist's concept of décollage—the construction of a new meaning through the destruction, fragmentation, or displacement of the original meaning—by encouraging readers to interact with the spatiotemporal form of the magazine through the inclusion of unbound sheets, serrated pages, and occasional three-dimensional objects. Likewise, Heubach attempted to wed the format of *Interfunktionen* with its aesthetic principles. To this end, he participated fully in the layout and printing of the magazine and encouraged artists to design their own contributions whenever possible, describing his desire "to do justice to the art itself rather than producing a tasteful, noble art review."[22] He also acknowledged, however, that economic considerations played a role in the magazine's appearance: "Although the design and print quality were shaped by an aesthetic agenda, they were in fact much more strongly dictated by our notoriously limited funds."[23]

Virtually free of advertisements, save for a few ads provided, often pro bono, to friends and other magazines, *Interfunktionen* was financed by subscriptions and sales, supplemented on occasion by Heubach's own research assistant salary. Additional income came from special artist-signed copies—in general, fifty to sixty copies per issue—which included original drawings and editioned multiples, such as Vostell's *Brotaktion*, a (very stale) piece of bread sealed in a plastic sleeve, included in issue 3. Yet the rejection of commercial motives was itself deeply ideological, and if the magazine's rudimentary format seemed to reflect this brute economic fact on a literal level, it simultaneously reinforced it on a symbolic level. As Buchloh would later point out, "Glossy color-reproductions and 'high standards of design,' apart from being economically unavailable, represent for us more the qualities of an independent magazine culture, serving aims of investment and capital interests more than the actual needs of artistic information."[24]

The second issue of *Interfunktionen*, published a few months after the first, in fall 1968, in many ways repeated the formula of the first issue. Increasing its circulation to 250, it covered another series of local, artist-led demonstrations, this time instigated by the experimental collective Labor (founded by Heubach, Vostell, the composer Mauricio Kagel, and the filmmaker Alfred Feussner as a "laboratory" for research of acoustic and visual phenomena). Labor staged a series of multimedia installations and performances known as the five-day race, designed to compete with and contest the internationalist, market-driven agenda of the second annual Cologne art fair, Kunstmarkt 68. Also included were writings by Beuys and Vostell on Die Ideale Akademie, the "Fluxus Expanded Arts Diagram," and correspondence and news clippings about the scandals at Immendorff's alternative LIDL school at the Staatliche Kunstakademie Düsseldorf. By the third issue, for which the magazine again doubled its circulation, to 500, *Interfunktionen* began to open its pages to international activity, focusing on conceptual art and new media, including earthworks, performance art, and video. Besides artist-designed contributions and documentation, the magazine added sections on "new work," "information" (which seemed to connote more abbreviated versions of artists' projects as well as other kinds of announcements), and "theory." In the theory section, Heubach published artists' writings and texts by Buckminster Fuller and the structural anthropologist Michael Oppitz, alongside his own speculative essays in which he attempted to apply his doctoral research in psychology to the artistic activities with which he had become so preoccupied.

While it would continue to publish German artists—including Sigmar Polke, Rebecca Horn, Dieter Roth, Lothar Baumgarten, A. R. Penck, Anselm Kiefer, Hans Haacke, and especially Joseph Beuys, whose lengthy contributions dominate several issues (the artist at one point even provided a subsidy to the magazine "when the extent of his contributions once again burst the bounds of my page calculation," according to Heubach)[25]—the magazine increasingly opened its pages to artists elsewhere on the continent and in the United States. Among them were Christo, Marcel Broodthaers, Daniel Buren, Arnulf Rainer, Günter Brus (whose magazine *Die Schastrommel* was actually published under *Interfunktionen*'s imprint for several issues), Valie Export, Jan Dibbets, Gilbert and George, Richard Long, Walter De Maria, Dennis Oppenheim, Michael Heizer, Robert Smithson, Vito Acconci, Bruce Nauman, Terry Fox, Nam June Paik, Keith Arnatt, John Baldessari, Peter Hutchinson, Carl Andre, Robert Morris, Philip Glass, Steve Reich, William Wegman, Maria Nordman, Yvonne Rainer, Hollis Frampton, and Dan Graham. Graham, to whom Heubach was introduced by the New York gallerist John Gibson, was an especially salient presence in *Interfunktionen*, and visited Heubach in Cologne several times, recommending other artists to him.[26]

INTERFUNKTIONEN AND THE INTERNATIONALIZATION OF GERMAN ART

Heubach insisted that *Interfunktionen*'s avid support of American art—an approach that would be continued by Buchloh when he took over the magazine in 1974—was not part of any systematic attempt to internationalize the German art scene but was simply due to his appreciation for the work itself: "I published whatever took my interest—if I am fond of bananas, than I am fond of bananas—and not concerned with the question of where they come from."[27] However, whether deliberately or not, the magazine, along with several other magazines founded in Germany during the period—including *Salon*, *Extra*, *Zweitschrift*, *Palazzo*, *Die Schastrommel*, and *Art Aktuell*—played a vital role in opening up the dialog between German artists and artists abroad during the late 1960s and early 1970s, a time when, Buchloh remembered, "German artists were desperate to transform and internationalize their situation with regards to contemporary art."[28] Contemporary American art in particular was ubiquitous in Germany, seen in museums, galleries such as Konrad Fischer and Heiner Friedrich, and private collections; in exhibitions such as "Konzeption/Conception" and "Live in Your Head: When Attitudes Become Form," both in 1969; as well as at the newly founded international art fairs in Cologne and Düsseldorf.[29]

And yet, while Germany's enthusiastic embrace of American art was a welcome corrective to the country's postwar isolationism, some began to wonder whether this international focus wasn't beginning to upstage Germany's own artists, hindering their ability to reflect upon their own history and identity, and thus exacerbating a kind of historical amnesia that, it has been argued, characterized cultural production in postwar Germany more generally. As Buchloh described the situation, "There was a very strange hiatus or discrepancy between the internationalization of the German art situation and the cultural reception processes, and the need to look at one's own conditions of cultural production right in front of one's door, by which we were surrounded and of which we were a part, and which, at that point, was rather uninteresting to the rest of the world or the American art world."[30] This tension between the internationalization of German art and the development of a local or regional artistic identity played out in the pages of *Interfunktionen* in a subtle yet telling way. While on the one hand the magazine participated in the Americanization of the German art world, it also provided a lens through which German artists could reframe this international activity in relationship to their own history and experience.

In its desire to encourage international dialog while supporting a local artistic community, *Interfunktionen* appears in some ways as the mirror image of *Avalanche*, founded two years after it in 1970. The striking similarities between the two magazines appear almost overdetermined, as they moved in lockstep, featuring many of the same artists on both sides of the Atlantic. The first issue of *Avalanche* (Fall 1970), for example, was nearly identical to issue 3 of *Interfunktionen* (1969): both featured Heizer, Smithson, De Maria, Long, Dibbets, and Beuys. Likewise, *Avalanche* 2 (Winter 1971) and *Interfunktionen* 6 (September 1971) both featured Bruce Nauman on the cover and were devoted to body art, with contributions by Fox, Acconci, Nauman, and Oppenheim. And yet, if such editorial overlap foreshadowed the homogenization often lamented in today's global art world, a close look at the two magazines also unearths particularities that express their distinct vantage points in New York and Cologne.

While both *Avalanche* and *Interfunktionen* sought to make the artist's voice more direct, the meaning and quality of this directness was not the same. As discussed in chapter 4, *Avalanche's* role in fostering the local SoHo art scene depended on the magazine's proximity to this neighborhood, expressed through its tone and form of address, its advertising section, and the informal, sociable quality of its interviews, which conveyed the immediacy of the spoken word. By contrast, *Interfunktionen's* view of American art feels decidedly more distanced, sifted through recirculated media accounts, retyped and translated publications, and poorly reproduced photographs, paralleling Germany's remove—or double or triple remove—from the New York art world.

Interfunktionen has the unfinished, fragmented quality of a scrapbook, in which photographs of works of art are interspersed with news clippings, poor-quality Courier-font typed sheets, and other kinds of documents. In issue 3, for example, an article by Lutz Schirmer entitled "Zur Land Art" is a kind of textual collage, in which the author's own text in German is punctuated by excerpts from published articles and artists' writings cut right out of their original sources, including Smithson's "Sedimentation of the Mind-Earth Projects" (initially published in *Artforum*); De Maria's "Art Yard," from La Monte Young and Jackson MacLow's 1963 *An Anthology*; an article clipped from the Parisian journal *Robho* on a land art project by Dibbets; and sections of Howard Junker's *Saturday Evening Post* column. The article engenders a deeply heterogeneous discursive space in which various types of documents, typefaces, and languages collide, and indicates the magazine's role in synthesizing such fragments and making them meaningful to a local audience. Indeed, if *Interfunktionen* attests to the newly important function of the magazine in disseminating the documents of conceptual art internationally, it also illustrates how such documents were filtered through local processes of reception.

Such processes were highlighted in an especially revealing way by the magazine works of Dan Graham—works that were designed specifically to appear within the reproduced medium of the magazine. Graham's *Homes for America*, initially published in the December 1966–January 1967 issue of *Arts Magazine*, was republished in *Interfunktionen* issue 7 (1971). Technically a reprint, perhaps, it calls into question that very term. The *Interfunktionen* version of *Homes for America* does not duplicate the original published article, but neither may it be considered an entirely new version of it; instead, the original *Arts* article has been cut up and rearranged to fit the dimensions of the two-page spread of *Interfunktionen*, accompanied by two of Graham's photographs that had been omitted from the initial published version.[31] The modified visual appearance of Graham's article coincides with the transformation of its meaning on a deeper level. For Graham's discussion of suburban American architecture presumably had a much different meaning within this limited-circulation German artists' magazine to a group of readers less well versed in the nuances of the "Cape Cod"-style house or "colonial red" and "sea foam green" as exterior paint colors. And yet, while this example emphasizes the mediated, secondhand quality of *Interfunktionen*'s presentation of American art, it also paradoxically opens onto the possibility of a new kind of immediacy, insisting on the magazine's own contingency with regard to the reception of art.

This was precisely the basis of Graham's site-specific approach to the magazine—an approach that is perhaps best exemplified by his *Schema (March 1966)*, first published in *Aspen* 5+6 in 1967. As discussed in chapter 2, *Schema* consists of a template of facts about its own grammatical form and typographical appearance, to be completed by the editor according to the specific design and layout of the magazine in which it is printed. In *Interfunktionen* 8 (1972), Graham presented a retrospective survey of all of the previously published versions of *Schema* alongside an "original," translated into German and based on the particular format of *Interfunktionen*. This opportunity to compare the various versions of the piece reveals a surprising number of inconsistencies, reflecting not only the typographical differences between magazines, but also the various ways in which editors have interpreted the template (in particular, there seems to be some discrepancy over what constitutes an adverb). In his accompanying text, Graham described the site-specific nature of the piece as follows: "It defines itself as place as it defines its limits and contingencies of placement. … It is a measure of itself—as place. It takes its own measure of itself as place, placed two-dimensionally on (as) a page."[32]

However, besides drawing attention to the two-dimensional "place" of the page, *Schema* also implicitly points to the actual places in which magazines themselves are produced and distributed. In its insistence that the magazine page is not merely a neutral or generic backdrop or the work of art, but a set of conditions that help to determine its significance, *Schema* dramatizes the magazine's contingency as a site of reception. With regard to *Interfunktionen*'s role within an increasingly international art world, this contingency suggests that the magazine went beyond merely importing artistic information from elsewhere into Germany, to enable an active process of reception which transformed and translated its meaning according to specific local conditions.

SITE SPECIFICITY IN THE MAGAZINE: DANIEL BUREN'S *INK ON PAPERS*

As *Interfunktionen*'s circulation rose to around 1,000, the magazine slowly began to gain a committed group of readers and a more professional veneer, signaled by the smaller digest-sized formats of issues 9 and 10. In issue 9 Heubach cast a rather melancholy look back at the magazine's origins, commemorating the protests against Documenta by reprinting a news clipping from issue 1, accompanied by the nostalgic caption, "These days are over now."[33] The magazine continued to challenge the art world status quo (for example, issue 10 published Hans Haacke's

EPILOGUE: INTERNATIONAL ACTIVITY

controversial work *Shapolsky et al. Manhattan Real Estate Holdings, A Real Time Social System, as of May 1, 1971* [1971], which had prompted the cancelation of the artist's one person show at the Guggenheim); and yet, with *Interfunktionen*'s rising reputation, Heubach began to feel pressure to satisfy various interests, which put a damper on his serendipitous and amateurish approach—one that had been guided by his travels, friendships, and above all, his own curiosity. He recalled, "As *Interfunktionen* got a certain public *renommée*, people would argue, 'You published that artist, why not this important artist too?' and reproach me for not presenting an unbiased 'objective' view of current artistic activity—a role that they saw as my obligation to fulfill as an editor of a contemporary art magazine."[34] Uninterested in brokering such art world micropolitics, and increasingly busy with his own university work, Heubach decided to end the publication with the tenth issue in 1973.

For Heubach's good friend Benjamin Buchloh, however, the magazine was too vital to be discontinued. "He—stressing my nerves—didn't stop arguing what a loss the end of *Interfunktionen* would be for our common cause of a radical art," Heubach remembered.[35] To quell these protests, he decided to transfer the rights to the magazine to Buchloh. For Buchloh, who had a background in literature and was working as assistant director of the Rudolf Zwirner Gallery, the political possibilities of the magazine as an alternative distribution form for conceptual art were paramount: "We were deeply convinced in all earnestness that the elimination of the commodity object from the work of art and the reduction of the work of art to linguistic proposition had a tremendous pedagogical and political potential and an egalitarian democratic implication that would have vast consequences in terms of the collectivization of aesthetic experience. That's really what drove the project."[36]

Buchloh explored these possibilities in issue 11 of *Interfunktionen* (1974), devoted to the topic of artists' books; he also changed the magazine's format back to its original larger size in order to better accommodate artists' projects. Issue 11 included several theoretical texts and resources: a foreword by Michel Claura, Germano Celant's catalog essay for the important 1972 exhibition "Book as Artwork," Dan Graham's "The Book as Object" (initially published in *Arts Magazine* in 1967), an essay by Roman Jakobson on the work of William Blake, and an extensive bibliography of artists' books from 1960 to 1974. The issue also contained artists' projects, including Marcel Broodthaers's *La séance,* a "film" structured by the form of the magazine; Jörg Immendorff's *Kritik entfalten!* consisting of portraits he painted of his working-class high school students alongside the students' own observations about their appearance; Bruce Nauman's *Instructions for a Mental Exercise,* a typed set of directions for achieving a meditative state while lying on the floor; Lawrence Weiner's *With an Advance Declined,* a series of phrases exploring different permutations of prepositions; and works by A. R. Penck, Italo Scanga, Bill Beckley, and Daniel Buren.

8.5 (following pages)

Dan Graham, *Schema (March 1966),* 1966–1967, as published in *Interfunktionen,* no. 8, 1972, pages 31–32. Courtesy of the artist and Marian Goodman Gallery. Research Library, The Getty Research Institute, Los Angeles (87-S406 no. 8).

POEM SCHEMA   DAN GRAHAM

```
              1   adjectives
              3   adverbs
1192½ sq. ems     area not occupied by type
 337½ sq. ems     area occupied by type
              1   columns
              0   conjunctions
            nil   depression of type into surface of page
              0   gerunds
              0   infinitives
            363   letters of alphabet
             27   lines
              2   mathematical symbols
             38   nouns
             52   numbers
              0   participles
         8½ x 5   page
      17½ x 22½   paper sheet
offset cartridge  paper stock
              5   prepositions
              0   pronouns
         10 pt.   size type
    Press Roman   typeface
             59   words
              2   words capitalized
              0   words italicized
             57   words not capitalized
             59   words not italicized
```

'Art and Language' (No 1, 1968)

Verschiedene Varianten von 'Schema'
different variants of 'Schema'

```
               35 adjectives
                7 adverbs
           35.52% area not occupied by type
           64.48% area occupied by type
                1 column
                1 conjunction
           0 mms. depression of type into surface of pa
                0 gerunds
                0 infinitives
              247 letters of alphabet
               28 lines
                6 mathematical symbols
               51 nouns
               29 numbers
                6 participles
          8" x 8" page
           80 lb. paper sheet
dull coated       paper stock
    .007" thin    paper stock
                3 prepositions
                0 pronouns
         10 point size type
      Univers  55 typeface
               61 words
                3 words capitalized
                0 words italicized
               58 words not capitalized
               61 words not italicized
```

'Aspen Magazin'

```
              3 adjectives
              3 adverbs
          62.1% area not occupied by type
          37.9% area occupied by type
              1 column
              0 conjunctions
             no depression of type into page's surface
              0 gerunds
              0 infinitives
            208 letters of alphabet
             27 lines
              2 mathematical symbols
             51 nouns
             23 numbers
              0 participles
        8' x 4' page
         50 lb. paper sheet
semi-gloss coated paper stock
              5 prepositions
              0 pronouns
       12 point size type
   Letter Gothic typeface
             53 words
              2 words capitalized
              0 words italized
```

'1966' (John Gibson, 1970)

```
               37 adjectives
                0 adverbs
           87.40% area not occupied by type
           12.60% area occupied by type
                2 columns
                0 conjunctions
           0 mms. depression of type into surface of page
                0 gerunds
                0 infinitives
               24 letters of alphabet
               28 lines
               11 mathematical symbols
               36 nouns
               49 numbers
                7 participles
        5¾" × 8" page
          Dondell paper sheet
 uncoated offset  paper stock
           .0039" paper stock
                6 prepositions
                0 pronouns
         10 point size type
            Aster typeface
               60 words
                2 words capitalized
                0 words italicized
               58 words not capitalized
               60 words not italicized
```

'Extensions' (No 1, 1968)

variant

       3   Adjektive

       o   Adverbien

      73 % unbedruckte Fläche

      27 % bedruckte Fläche

       1   Kolumne

       o   Konjunktionen

    keine Eindrucktiefe der Buchstaben in die Papierfläche

       o   Gerundien

       o   Infinitive

      32   Buchstaben

      23   Zeilen

       2   mathematische Symbole

      27   Hauptwörter

      21   Zahlen

       2   Partizipien

    9o gr. Papiergewicht

   Offset Papiertyp

       1   Präposition

       o   Pronomen

     3 mm Schriftgröße

  Quadrato Schriftart

      37   Worte

       o   versale Worte

       o   kursive Worte

(interfunktionen 8, 72)

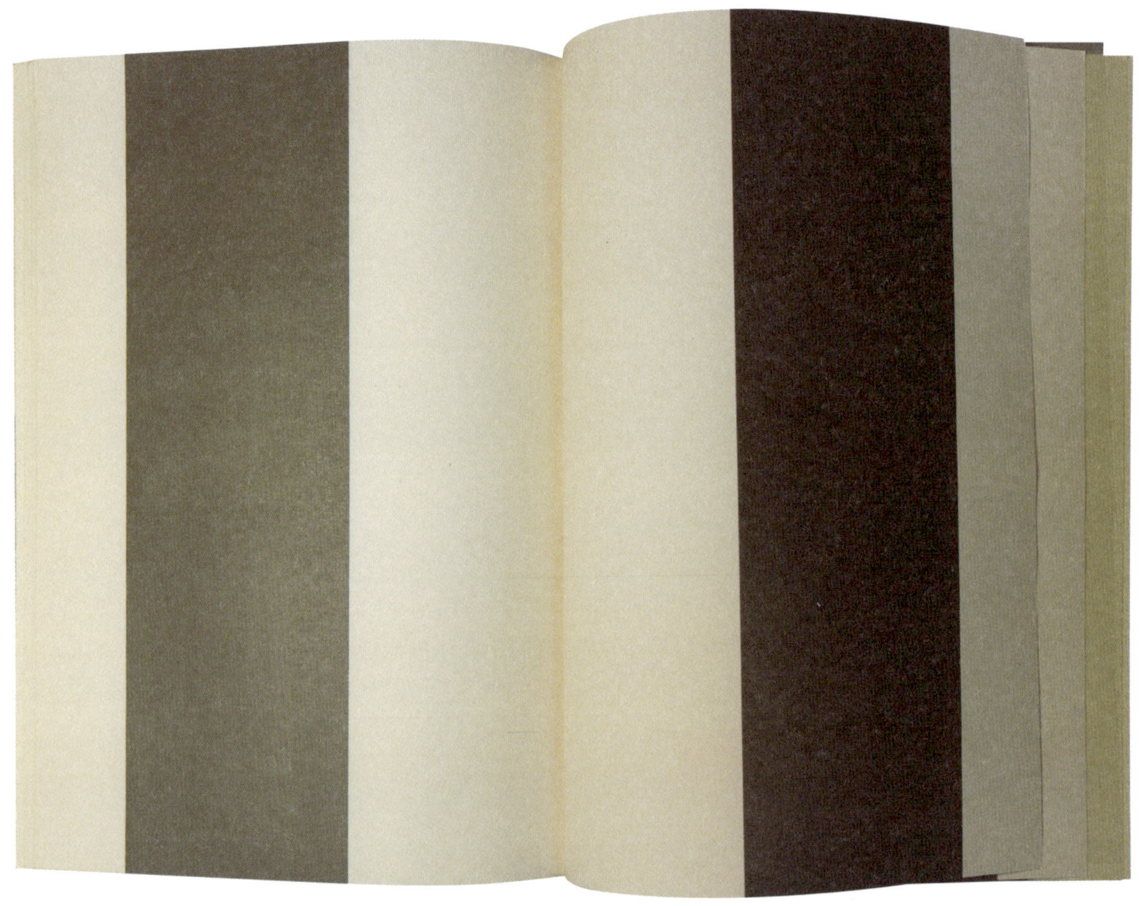

8.6

Daniel Buren, *Ink on Papers, Interfunktionen*,
no. 11, 1974. Courtesy of the artist and
Benjamin Buchloh.

Buren's *Encre sur papiers* (Ink on papers) dominated issue 11 visually. The work consisted of a series of vertical black stripes printed throughout the magazine, beginning with the cover and separating each of the articles, with the entire sequence repeated at the end. Printed on various kinds of paper from cardstock to newsprint to the thinnest glassine (Buren asked Buchloh to choose the widest possible range), the work drew attention to the materiality of the magazine page, emphasizing its different textures and finishes, its varying degrees of glossiness and absorbency, opacity and translucence, its pliability, and even the different sounds the pages made when turned—the crinkling of the glassine, for example. The striped motif clearly referenced the readymade posters and canvases that the artist was best known for at the time, such as his 1968 *affichages sauvages* (postering without permission), a set of striped posters pasted in over two hundred locations around Paris, including walls, shop windows, and advertising billboards. Seminal to the practices of site specificity and institutional critique, these works *in situ*, as Buren called them, explored how the site or context within which a work of art is encountered shapes its interpretation and aesthetic value. Buren addressed this idea extensively in his published writings, such as "Critical Limits," where he insisted that "art whatever it may be is exclusively political. What is called for is the analysis of formal and cultural limits (and not one or the other) within which art exists and struggles."[37]

Though Buren frequently used publications, such as exhibition catalogs and postcards, to document his temporary and context-bound *in situ* works, he was adamant that such publications, which he called photo-souvenirs, did not offer an authentic experience of the work itself, but were merely an ersatz supplement. In the catalog to the 1970 "Information" show, he explained: "The only possible information about my work is to really see it. … The photograph above [this caption] is taken in Montholon Square, Paris. It is given as information about my work rather than as photograph of my work itself."[38] And yet *Ink on Papers*—along with several similar works that Buren produced for newspapers, catalogs, and magazines at the time[39]—raises another possibility entirely: that the printed page might function as a medium or site, a place to "really see" the work. As the artist stated, "My idea was to use the format of the magazine as a place to show my work and not an image of my work."[40]

Stressing this distinction, Buren specified that the stripes used in *Ink on Papers* should be 8.7 cm wide, corresponding in a 1:1 ratio to the stripes of his readymade posters and canvases. Furthermore, the work self-reflexively referenced its context, since the number of articles in the magazine dictated the number of stripes. Underscoring the sequential nature of the codex form, it suggested the way in which publications—far from being dematerialized spaces—have a specific kind of objecthood or architecture, within which different positions (the cover, for example, as opposed to editorial pages or advertising) have different functions. By applying a model of site specificity to the magazine page, Buren demonstrated how art magazines function alongside other spaces and institutions to determine the meaning and aesthetic value of art. Like Graham, he revealed that the page is not a neutral or universal space—a "museum without walls"—but is shot through with various institutional and ideological forces.

Somewhat curiously, Buren was disappointed with the way that *Ink on Papers* turned out, explaining in an addendum published on the back cover of issue 11: "The editor of this magazine and myself think it is necessary to notify the reader that technical faults which had occurred during the realization of *Ink on Papers* have changed the intended sense of the work." The flaws to which the artist objected were relatively minor, having to do with slight irregularities in the layout of the striped pages in relationship to the other articles, as well as a few accidental smudges and smears of ink. For his part, Buchloh was surprised by Buren's dissatisfaction with the piece, since he felt that he had adhered to the basic idea of the artist's proposal if not to every last technicality. He agreed, however, to redo the piece in issue 12, this time using white ink (which, due to its quicker drying time, presented fewer technical challenges to the printer). While expensive to rectify, the mistake proved instructive, illustrating to Buchloh in a new, unequivocal way the transformed status of the magazine. "I didn't think I was doing an artists' magazine in *that* sense," he remembered. "I thought I was doing a magazine that propagated certain artistic positions."[41]

Buchloh's revelation that *Interfunktionen* was an artists' magazine "in *that* sense"—his realization that the magazine was the actual medium of the work of art and not merely a secondary reproduction or representation—was an idea that, as we have seen, echoed across a wide variety of artistic practices and artists' publications throughout the late 1960s and 1970s. Yet even as the magazine page was being reconceived as a new kind of primary site or medium for conceptual art, a distinction was usually maintained, however tenuously, between the work of art itself—whether the artist's idea, a documented event, or an original layout—and the material support of the magazine. It is precisely the tension or gulf between these two things—and the interplay between them—that gives so many of these projects their complexity and critical charge, since they highlight the contingency of the magazine page as a site of mediation or translation. By contrast, Buren's *Ink on Papers* appears to collapse this distinction entirely.

While Buren set out to question the institutional and economic context of the art magazine, *Ink on Papers* also risked aestheticizing this context itself as one more object to be consumed and fetishized within spectacular media culture—a fetishization that is hinted at by the artists' own bibliophilic finickiness regarding the execution of the work. Indeed, if conceptual art challenged the self-sufficiency and autonomy of art, this very loss of autonomy, it has since been pointed out, ironically rendered art even more susceptible to processes of reification and aestheticization.[42] Marcel Broodthaers reflected on this bleak prospect in his design for the flyleaf of *Interfunktionen* 11, consisting of the sentence: "View, according to which an artistic theory will function for the artistic product in the same way as the artistic product itself functions as advertising for the order under which it is produced. There will be no other space than this view, according to which etc. ... For copy conform"—a statement that captures, in its very grammatical structure, the self-perpetuating tautological nature of the spectacle.

The legacy of this collapse between the work of art and the promotional site of the magazine is evident today, as artists' pages and luxury printed editions no longer question or interrupt the institutional and economic conditions of the art world but appear to reinforce them, facilitating the integration of art and criticism alike within an increasingly global art market. At the same time, rather than pointing to some kind of lost innocence, the history of *Interfunktionen* and other artists' magazines of the 1960s and 1970s demonstrates that the radical potential of these publications was dialectically linked to their connection to the market from the beginning, raising the possibility that these two things are not necessarily mutually exclusive. Subsequent artists' magazines have embraced and even flaunted such contradictions for progressive ends, as did *Eau de Cologne* (1985–1993), in order to redress the gender imbalance in the art world.[43]

Looking back at the egalitarian possibilities of conceptual art that inspired *Interfunktionen*, Buchloh admitted, "In hindsight it looks unbelievably naïve and makes me blush when I think about the naïveté of people, including myself, who tried to make that a viable position, and in many ways it was, perhaps."[44] Yet even as Buchloh dismisses such beliefs as the delusions of a younger, more idealistic self, he raises the possibility, however faintly audible in the clause with which his sentence trails off, that conceptual art's radical possibilities, despite their many contradictions, were genuine and convincing to those who originally imagined them. While it is important not to romanticize the utopian aspirations of art of the 1960s and 1970s, it seems equally important to acknowledge and understand the very real historical context in which these aspirations arose, and in which they gained traction. *Interfunktionen* and other artists' magazines from the time provide compelling and concrete evidence of this context.

ENDINGS

While Buchloh continued Heubach's efforts to deprovincialize and internationalize the German art scene, he also began to think more about how the magazine might address the local, regional, and national specificity of German art—a prospect that implicitly contradicted his belief in the universal legibility of the page as an accessible form of distribution. As he recalled of his choice to publish German artists, it "made the magazine illegible to our American friends. I mean, nobody gave a damn about Richter or Polke or Kiefer or Immendorff in the early 1970s in the United States. You couldn't explain that work to an American conceptual artist easily."[45] In *Interfunktionen* 12, Buchloh published Anselm Kiefer's *Occupations* (1969), a series of photographs that show the artist, dressed in riding boots and jodhpurs and with his arm raised in a Hitler salute, posed in front of various historical monuments in France, Italy, and Switzerland, accompanied by the following laconic statement: "During the summer and fall of 1969, I occupied Switzerland, France, and Italy: a couple of photographs." This iconoclastic series has been read as a working through of German history by restaging this taboo historical moment in an ironic or absurd manner. The photographs articulate the artist's generational distance from the past, while at the same time enacting a mnemonic working through of the past—a productive mourning rather than a nostalgic melancholy, to use the psychoanalytic distinction that has frequently been employed with reference to German history.[46]

Buchloh had been impressed with Kiefer's work—especially with his early books, in which the *Occupations* photographs were originally published—since seeing the artist's first exhibition at Galerie Michael Werner in Cologne in 1973. He interpreted the *Occupations* series as a critical if deeply provocative work which, among other things, spoke to the historical specificity of contemporary German art within a wider international context. He was especially interested in how Kiefer's gesture might be read within the context of American performance art, such as that by Acconci, Wegman, and Nauman, which had been so prominently featured in the pages of *Interfunktionen*. Kiefer inflected performance art—up until then understood as a kind of "universal bodily language"—with "a regionally and nationally specific gesturality, and that was really quite politically appropriate for us, as a German magazine," Buchloh observed.[47]

AVIS
selon lequel

une théorie artistique fonctionne-rait comme publicité pour le pro-duit artistique, le produit artis-tique fonctionnant comme publi-cité pour le régime sous lequel il est né.
Il n'y aurait d'autre espace que cet avis selon lequel etc. ...

Pour copie conforme

ANSICHT
derzufolge

eine künstlerische Theorie letzt-lich als Werbung für das künstle-rische Produkt funktioniert, wie das künstlerische Produkt immer schon als Werbung für das Regime funktioniert, unter dem es ent-steht.
Es gibt keinen anderen Raum als diese Ansicht, derzufolge etc. ...

Für die Richtigkeit

Marcel Broodthaers

VIEW
according to which

an artistic theory will be func-tioning for the artistic product in the same way as the artistic product itself is functioning as ad-vertising for the rule under which it is produced
There will be no other space than this view, according to which etc. ...

For copy conform

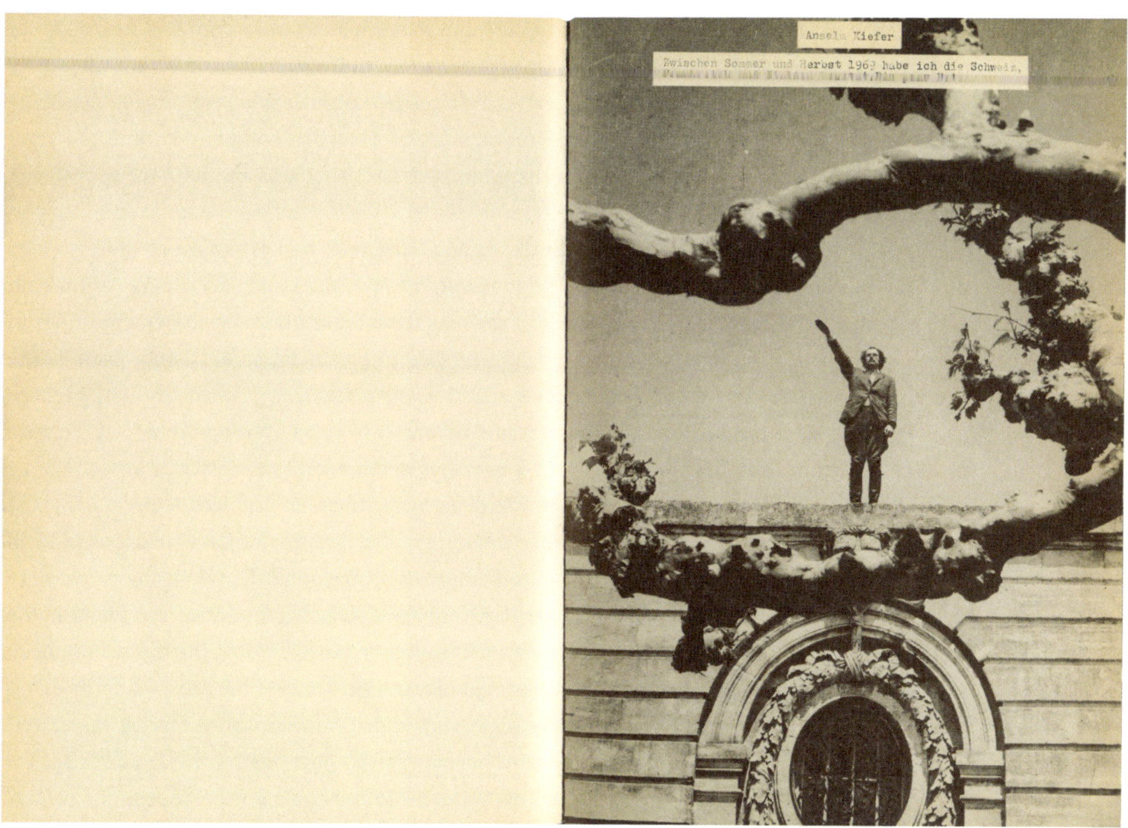

8.7

Marcel Broodthaers, "View according to which …," *Interfunktionen*, no. 12, 1975. Courtesy of Benjamin Buchloh.

8.8

Anselm Kiefer, *Occupations*, published in *Interfunktionen,* no. 12, 1975. © Anselm Kiefer. Courtesy of Gagosian Gallery. Research Library, The Getty Research Institute, Los Angeles (87-S406 no. 12).

The work, however, with its charged references to the history of fascism and its confrontation of this history at a moment when all overt references to it were repressed from the public sphere, prompted outrage among *Interfunktionen*'s readers both inside and outside Germany. Subscribers and advertisers boycotted the magazine, and Heubach condemned both the work and Buchloh's decision to publish it. Perhaps most devastating was the withering criticism Buchloh received from Marcel Broodthaers, who asked, "Who's this fascist who calls himself an antifascist?" and refused to go ahead with the signed edition he had promised in order to help fund the next issue of the magazine.[48] "No one would touch the issue," according to Buchloh, who recounted that boxes of unsold copies of the magazine sat in his sister's basement in Berlin for years.[49] He had neither the money nor the morale to produce another issue. Even as the controversy over Kiefer's *Occupations* series ended *Interfunktionen*, it affirmed—and perhaps even in some sense fully realized—the magazine's capacity to reflect on the problematic nature of German identity and history. Indeed, the magazine's demise might be seen as a measure of its success in prompting genuine, if painful, public debate over the taboo subject of Germany's past.

Though *Interfunktionen* ceased publication in 1975, the question of German art would still haunt it in 1980, when Buchloh published a scathing article on Joseph Beuys on the occasion of the artist's first major U.S. exhibition, prompting Heubach to legally withdraw from Buchloh the rights to the dormant magazine. In the article, which appeared in *Artforum*, Buchloh denounced Beuys's approach to the representation of German history. He accused the artist—and by extension his supporters—of glibly exploiting this history for shock value as well as market value, writing, "In the work and public myth of Beuys, the German spirit of the postwar period finds its new identity by pardoning and reconciling itself prematurely with its own reminiscences of a responsibility for one of the most cruel and devastating forms of collective political madness that history has known. … Speculators in Beuys's work did well: he was bound to become a national hero of the first order, having reinstalled and restored that sense of a—however deranged—national self and historic identity."[50]

Heubach's legal termination of Buchloh's rights to *Interfunktionen* was largely a symbolic gesture, since the magazine had been, for all practical purposes, defunct for five years by that point, and Buchloh, then living in the United States, had no intention of publishing another issue. This postscript is revealing, however, for its suggestion of magazines' capacity to register disagreement and conflict as much as to embody collective goals and ideals—even, in this case, long after they have ceased to be published. Heubach and Buchloh had never agreed on Beuys, and the artist's pervasive presence in *Interfunktionen* had ended abruptly once Buchloh took over. Heubach's dramatic reaction to Buchloh's harsh judgment of Beuys (and implicitly of *Interfunktionen*'s own role in the artists' recognition), and his choice to express his displeasure by terminating an already obsolete magazine, show how fundamental the question of the identity and evaluation of German art and history was to *Interfunktionen*.

If the January 1980 issue of *Artforum* in which Buchloh's article appeared marked the final dénouement of *Interfunktionen*, it also signaled the beginning of a new episode in *Artforum*'s own history, suggested by its new title, *Artforum International*, starting with that very issue. As then-publisher Amy Baker Sandback explained, "The art world had changed, and it was important to reflect a new focus: American artists showing in Europe, European artists showing in America, Japanese artists—everyone seemed to be traveling to or from some event. The art community had become the art world."[51] Indeed, the internationalization of the art world that *Interfunktionen* had helped to bring about in the 1960s and 1970s was well on its way to becoming the globalized arena of today.

NOTES ON THE APPENDIX: PARAMETERS, CRITERIA, AND APPROACH

This appendix was inspired in part by the classic 1946 study *The Little Magazine: A History and a Bibliography* by Frederick J. Hoffman, Charles Allen, and Carolyn F. Ulrich, as well as the more recent *A Secret Location on the Lower East Side: Adventures in Writing, 1960–1980* by Steven Clay and Rodney Phillips (1998), both of which include checklists and descriptions of magazines of experimental literature and poetry. Like these earlier studies, it is meant to serve as a useful resource, and one that I hope will prompt further research. More than providing a linear or chronological catalog, the appendix reveals unexpected resonances between different kinds of publications, demonstrating how they speak to one another across time and space.

In developing a set of criteria for the appendix, I was reminded of George Kubler's reflections upon the art historian's process of selection and categorization. Kubler wrote: "Unique cases and general cases form a gradient at whose extremes the possibility of history vanishes. The historian selects a median position on the gradient, in order to resolve the antithesis between a microstructure where no two actions are alike, and a macrostructure where all actions are alike. The position selected depends upon the historian's desire to represent activity as having purpose."[1] Indeed, my parameters for this appendix reflect my own "position on the gradient," determined according to my understanding of artists' magazines as having a specific historical meaning and purpose during the 1960s to 1980s, namely that of providing an alternative space for art, in the multiple senses of that term discussed in this book.

Thus, the appendix is most comprehensive when dealing with artists' magazines that were published around the world from the mid-1960s through the mid-1980s, which strongly echo the book's case studies in that they functioned as alternatives to the mainstream art press and gallery system. It also covers selected examples from the 1940s and 1950s, such as *The Tiger's Eye*, *Possibilities*, *Gutai*, *Phases*, *Cobra*, and *Boa*—historical precedents that demonstrate the magazine's important role in the artistic process and in fostering local and international artistic communities in this slightly earlier period. Additionally, it discusses magazines from the late 1950s and early 1960s that were influential precursors for conceptual art's exploration of the magazine as an alternative space. These include *Spirale*, *Zero*, *Gorgona*, *Nul = 0*, *Integration*, *Diagonal Cero*, *KWY*, *Revue Ou*, *material*, *dé-coll/age*, *V TRE*, and *Fluxus*, as well as Wallace Berman's *Semina*.

In general, the appendix covers independently published magazines which were produced by artists or to which artists were significant contributors. These magazines tend to eschew advertising and to reflect the opinions and interests of artists rather than those of critics or galleries. Though magazines such as *Parkett*, *Art Press*, *Flash Art*, *Arts Magazine*, and *Studio International* published artists' works and writings, they are more clearly art magazines, geared toward the professional art world, rather than artists' magazines, and are excluded on this principle. Conversely, publications such as *Macula*, *October*, and *Semiotext(e)* are included, even though they might be considered critical or art historical journals, because of their noncommercial aims and the way they privileged artists' contributions to art history and criticism.

As Kubler understood so well, the coherence of the art historian's categories is largely constructed and is riddled with exceptions, and this listing has its share of examples that reside at the outermost limits of its parameters. It includes the architectural magazine *Archigram*, the experimental film magazine *Film Culture*, music magazines such as *Source* and *Ear*, the design magazine *Dot Zero*, as well as numerous poetry magazines in which artists were important contributors, such as *Extensions*, *Some/thing*, *Caterpillar*, and *Unmuzzled Ox*. (Readers seeking a more complete guide to poetry magazines in the United States in the 1960s and 1970s should consult the previously mentioned *A Secret Location on the Lower East Side*.) This appendix also touches on publications such as Art Spiegelman and Françoise Mouly's *Raw* and Raymond Pettibon's *Tripping Corpse*, representing phenomena such as underground comix and punk zines which are largely outside the project's scope but which border on it in intriguing ways, pointing to contrasting and alternative narratives that may open up the topic in new directions.

There are a few areas in which the appendix is less comprehensive. While it considers key examples of visual poetry, mail, and stamp art magazines, and so-called assemblings—especially those that overlapped with conceptual art or that are directly related to the book's case studies, such as *VILE, BILE, SMILE*, and publications by the Bay Area Dadaists—it is by no means an exhaustive guide to these publications, which proliferated into the hundreds, maybe even thousands. In their extremely small circulations, handmade nature, and orientation toward personal correspondence rather than public communication, such publications suggest a slightly different publishing model from the one primarily explored by this book. Such phenomena have been covered more extensively in John Held Jr.'s *Mail Art: An Annotated Bibliography* (1991) and Géza Perneczky's *The Magazine Network* (1993), both written from their authors' perspectives as participants in mail art and alternative publishing. Perneczky's book is an especially rich resource for magazines related to correspondence art, concrete and visual poetry, rubber stamp, assemblings, xerography, and copy art, as well as several Eastern European *samizdat*-type artists' publications.

The choice to end the appendix with the year 1989 acknowledges that, while artists' magazines have continued to be published, their meaning and role as alternative spaces have changed since the late 1980s. There are probably many interlocking factors in this shift, including the rise of the Internet, decreases in public funding for the arts, and the intensification of processes of globalization that have transformed the possibilities of alternative publishing. The Internet has certainly not made artists' magazines obsolete. Publications such as *LTTR*, founded in 2004 by the collective LTTR (K8 Hardy, Ulrike Müller, Emily Roysdon, and Ginger Brooks Takahashi), and *Continuous Project*, founded in 2003 by Bettina Funcke, Wade Guyton, Joseph Logan, and Seth Price, attest to the ways in which contemporary artists have expanded the possibilities of artists' magazines, while at the same time self-consciously referencing magazines from the 1960s, 1970s, and 1980s. In doing so, they suggest that such publications are becoming historical and that, as they recede from our current moment, their meaning becomes available in new ways.

Most of the publications listed here were studied at one of three places: the Getty Research Library, the Museum of Modern Art Library, or the San Francisco Museum of Modern Art Library. Some were also seen in private collections. Because online catalogs are available, making it relatively easy for readers to check the holdings of individual institutions, I have not specified archives for individual publications (many are held by more than one).

The inherently ephemeral character of magazines thwarts bibliographic cataloging: they are irregularly issued and frequently have misnumbered, missing, or unpublished

issues, supplements, joint issues, and other types of inconsistencies. While I have tried
to be as consistent as possible in the format of notations and descriptions of magazines,
I have also tried to be flexible enough to accommodate their bibliographic quirkiness.
In general, the following information is provided in this order:

1. Title, as well as alternative titles and title changes.
2. Place of publication.
3. Publishing body. Because so many artists' magazines are self-published, the
publishing body is provided only when it is notable or different from the editor.
4. Dates. A question mark (i.e., 1968?) indicates that a definite date could not be
determined; the lack of an ending date (i.e., 1968–) indicates that the publication
is ongoing. Substantial gaps in between issues are also noted.
5. First and last issue numbers (and/or volumes, where appropriate). Misnumbered
and unpublished issues are also noted.
6. Publishers and editors. Because artists' magazines frequently challenge traditional
editorial hierarchies and roles, the designations "editor" and "publisher" are often
somewhat arbitrary. In general I have listed the person or persons responsible for
creating and producing the magazine, and used the titles "editor" or "publisher"
only in cases where it is clear that they performed only those tasks.
7. Editorial statements. Unless otherwise noted, editorial statements are taken from the
first issue. All quotes are in the langauge in which they were originally
published unless indicated otherwise (many non-English magazines provided English
translations).
8. Further reading. Books or articles about specific magazines as well as facsimile
reprints are noted.

+–0 (PLUS MOINS ZÉRO)
Genval, Belgium, 1973–1993 (1–84). Elisabeth Rona (publisher),
Stepháne Rona (editor), and Anne-Marie Rona.

+–0 was published by Madame Elisabeth Rona, founder of Galerie les Contemporains,
along with her son Stepháne and her daughter Anne-Marie. Inspired by Documenta 5,
organized by Harald Szeemann in 1972, the magazine sought to be "a new means for art
to freely express itself."[2] Deeply committed to fostering international dialog, the first issue
was created on the occasion of the Düsseldorf Art Fair in October 1973. Of the title, Anne-
Marie Rona recalled, "it was a bizarre title which we came up with spontaneously, three
mathematic signs. However, the idea was to find some sort of logo which could be read and
translated in all languages."[3] The Rona family produced the large-format, slender black-
and-white magazine themselves in the basement of their house, which was built around
the gallery, using a secondhand Heidelberg printing press. *+–0* published artists' writings,
interviews, criticism, and artists' projects with an emphasis on conceptual art in Europe
and the United States.

0 TO 9
New York, 1967–1969 (1–6; plus "Street Works"
supplement, sent out with no. 6). Vito Acconci and
Bernadette Mayer. See chapter 3.

Founded by Vito Acconci and Bernadette Mayer, the mimeographed poetry magazine *0 to 9*
witnessed the juncture between conceptual art and experimental poetry in lower Manhattan
in the late 1960s. Named after Jasper Johns's stencil paintings, the magazine was a vehicle for the visual, phonetic, and kinetic explorations of language by artists and poets,
including Ron Padgett, Clark Coolidge, Emmett Williams, Hannah Weiner, John Perreault,
Jerome Rothenberg, Sol LeWitt, Robert Smithson, Dan Graham, Adrian Piper, Yvonne Rainer,
Robert Barry, Douglas Huebler, Lee Lozano, and Lawrence Weiner. The final issue of the
magazine was accompanied by a supplement titled "Street Works," which documented
a series of public performances by artists and poets. 0 to 9 Press also published books,
including Aram Saroyan, *Coffee Coffee* (1967); Vito Acconci, *Four Book* (1968); Bernadette
Mayer, *Story* (1968); Adrian Piper, Untitled (1968); and Rosemary Mayer, *Book: 41 Fabric
Swatches* (1969).

    Facsimile reprint: Vito Acconci and Bernadette Mayer, *0 to 9: The Complete Magazine.*
New York: Ugly Ducking Presse, 2006.

4 TAXIS
Bordeaux, France, 1978–. Michel Aphesbero and
Danielle Colomine.

Originally subtitled "the magazine of the international boondocks," *4 Taxis* was, according
to its founders Michel Aphesbero and Danielle Colomine, "meant to be a place of gathering for artists' works specifically done for the magazine coming from four different cities:
Bordeaux, Barcelona, Rome, and New York."[4] Later this concept expanded to include other
cities, such as Los Angeles, Madrid, Berlin, São Paulo, Seville, and Oaxaca. Each issue has
a completely different layout and visual format, in an attempt to capture the character of
the city on which it is based. The magazine's title, with its reference to travel and transport,
suits the itinerant character of the magazine, which has more recently moved beyond the
printed form to inhabit a variety of nomadic practices including residencies, installations,
ephemeral interventions, and pedagogical workshops within various cities.

8 × 10 ART PORTFOLIO
New York, 1970–1973, nine unnumbered and
undated issues. Ely Raman.

This unbound assembling of visual poetry, mail art, conceptual art, stamp art, original woodcuts, drawings, paintings, collages, and photographs was housed in a paper folder. Contributors included Clemente Padin, Ken Friedman, Image Bank, Richard Kostelanetz, and Dana
Atchley. Readers were invited to pay whatever they wished for the publication—or even to
throw it away if they preferred, as editor Ely Raman suggested in the first issue:

> Enclosed is an issue of *8 × 10* art portfolio. If you like it, keep it. If you don't, throw it
> away and forget it. We won't bother you again. If you'd like to receive another
> issue of *8 × 10*, please write us. And if you'd like us to send *8 × 10* to friends of yours,
> send us names and addresses. What's the price of *8 × 10*? Pricing art, we feel, Is
> an artificial and arbitrary operation. Value, like love, is in the mind of the beholder.
> How valuable is this issue of *8 × 10* to you? How much pleasure, entertainment or
> intellectual stimulus did you get from it? In terms of your own income and bank account,
> how does this value translate into dollars and cents? That's the price of this issue of
> *8 × 10*. The next issue may be cheaper or more expensive … you determine that.

A (EDITION A)
Zagreb, 1962–1964 (1–7). Ivan Picelj.

Founded by the painter Ivan Picelj, *Edition a* represented the aesthetic and ideological
positions of the international art movement New Tendencies, which took root in Zagreb in
the early 1960s. Each issue of the slim, square magazine with a lowercase letter *a* on its
cover featured a different artist. In the first issue, Picelj published the text "For Active Art,"
a manifesto for the New Tendencies movement. Issue 4 was also by Picelj. Issue 2 was
by Victor Vasarely; issues 3 and 5 were by Vjenceslav Richter, and issue 6 included four
"no-stories" by Mangelos (Dimitrije Bašičević)—his first publicly presented work. Issue 7
was by Getulio Alviani.

ABC NO RIO MAGAZINE
New York: ABC No Rio, 1989–1990 (approximately 5 issues published).
Lou Acierno, Matthew Courtney, Sasha Forte.

ABC No Rio Magazine was a free magazine published by the alternative space ABC No Rio.
The photocopied, 8½-by-11-inch stapled magazine included poetry and collages by artists
and writers associated with the space (many of whom performed at Matthew Courtney's
weekly Open Cabaret). Copies were given away at the gallery, left in subway cars and bus
stops, and sent to selected bookstores.

AGENTZIA
Paris: Agentzia Éditions, 1967–1971 (1–31).
Jochen Gerz and Jean-François Bory.

According to editor Jochen Gerz, "*Agentzia* stressed agency—communication, information,
rapidity, news—rather than creativity."[5] With a circulation ranging from 12 to 10,000 copies,
the magazine published art, research, and visual poetry, with contributors including A. R.
Penck, Maurizio Nannucci, and Julien Blaine. In addition to the magazine, Agentzia Éditions
published objects, leaflets, stickers, posters, editions, books, and an artists' directory.

AGGIE WESTON'S
Belper, Derbyshire, England, 1973–1984 (1–21). Stuart Mills.

Aggie Weston's was an occasional magazine published by the poet Stuart Mills. In the first issue, he explained, "the name of the magazine comes indirectly from a work by Kurt Schwitters, 'A Small Home for Seamen.' I have been told that it was one Agnes Weston who founded the seamen's homes in this country and I hope that this magazine will likewise provide some sort of refuge." *Aggie Weston's* was a kind of sanctuary in its quiet, spare form, which ranged in length from six to twenty pages, and its focus on the English countryside. Issue 2 was devoted to photographs Mills took of Stonypath, the home of his friend Ian Hamilton Finlay, who contributed to the magazine, as did Simon Cutts and Thomas A. Clark. It also featured photographs by John Blakemore, Jonathon Williams, and Richard Long, to whom issue 16 was devoted.

AKTUAL ART
Prague, 1964–1965 (1–3). / *Aktual Newspaper.*
Prague, 1967–1968 (1–3). Milan Knížák.

Aktual Art was an illegal, mimeographed, *samizdat* magazine published by Milan Knížák to promote the conceptual and Fluxus-oriented activities of the Prague-based Aktual group. The magazine was published in an edition of 20 to 100 copies; the third issue of *Aktual Art* was titled *The Necessary Activity*. Subsequently, Knížák published three issues of the *Aktual Newspaper* between 1967 and 1968, in an edition of 10 to 200.

ALFABETA
Milan: Multhipla edizioni, 1975–1976 (1–7/8).
Editors: Pasquale Alferj, Giuseppe Galante, Carlo Romano,
and Gianbattista Troppmann.

Billing itself as a "laboratorio di critica della cultura visiva, della storia dell'arte," *alfabeta* published critical writings and artists' projects, with contributors including Jacques Lacan, Asger Jorn, Alison Knowles, George Brecht, Raoul Vaneigem, and Wolf Vostell.

AMAZON QUARTERLY: A LESBIAN FEMINIST ARTS JOURNAL
Oakland, California, 1972–1975 (vol. 1, no. 1–vol. 3, no. 2).
Gina Covina and Laurel Galana.

Named after the woman warriors of Greek mythology, *Amazon Quarterly* was one of the first art and literary magazines with a lesbian perspective. As the editors explained, "We are calling this an arts journal in the sense that art is communication. … We simply want the best of communication from lesbians who are consciously exploring new patterns in their lives."[6] Contributors included Adrienne Rich, Audre Lorde, Rita Mae Brown, and Louise Fishman.

AMERICAN LIVING
Allston, Massachussetts, 1982–1988 (1–25).
Angela Mark and Michael Shores.

Filled with line drawings and collages and devoid of text, *American Living* was representative of xerographic art and "graphzines" of the 1980s.

ANALYTICAL ART
Coventry, England: Analytical Art Press, 1971–1972 (1–2).
Graham Howard, Philip Pilkington, and Dave Rushton.

Produced by students at the Coventry School of Art, where several members of the Art-Language group taught, this short-lived journal stemmed out of the concerns of *Art-Language*, with which it officially merged in 1971.

AN ANTHOLOGY
New York, 1963. La Monte Young, George Maciunas,
and Jackson Mac Low.

While it might be classified as a book rather than a magazine, this seminal Fluxus publication was initially conceptualized as an issue of a magazine, and was an important jumping off point for George Maciunas's subsequent publications such as *Fluxus 1* and the *Flux Year Boxes*. Its full title was *An Anthology of Chance Operations Concept Art Anti-Art Indeterminacy Improvisation Meaningless Work Natural Disasters Plans of Action Stories Diagrams Music Dance Constructions Mathematics Poetry Essays Compositions*. The publication was begun in 1962 by La Monte Young as a special guest-edited issue of the magazine *Beatitude East,* which never came to fruition. George Maciunas took over as publisher; however, when he left for Germany, Jackson Mac Low stepped in. (On the masthead, Young and Mac Low are credited as copublishers, Young is listed as editor, and Maciunas as designer.) The almost square-format publication was printed on different colored pages with several tipped in sheets, some with tactile and/or performative components. Twenty-four artists participated, including George Brecht, John Cage, Walter De Maria, Dick Higgins, Ray Johnson, Jackson Mac Low, Robert Morris, Nam June Paik, Terry Riley, Dieter Roth, and La Monte Young. *An Anthology* published Henry Flynt's influential essay "Concept Art" for the first time.

APEÏROS
Paris and Vaduz, Lichtenstein: Centre d'Art et de Communication,
1971–1977 (1–9; 3 was never published). Roberto Altmann.

Billed as "apériodique utopique revue de la lettre et du signe," *Apeïros* published original works of art and writings associated with the lettrist movement, Fluxus, and conceptual art. Published in an edition of 1,000 to 3,000 copies, the magazine featured contributors such as Roberto Altmann, Jacques Villeglé, Annette Messager, William Burroughs, Dick Higgins, and Jean-François Bory. Each issue included twelve sheets of blank paper, with which the editor invited readers to experience the principle of "infinitesimal" reading.

APPEARANCES
New York, 1976–2001 (1–28); 2009– (28–). Bob Witz.

Published by the artist and writer Bob Witz—with help over the years from Vered Lieb, Hannah Wilke, Bill Mutter, Joe Lewis, Betty Tompkins, Ron Kolm, and Shelley Himmelstein—*Appearances* covered downtown New York artists and writers, especially the group of artists around the alternative South Bronx space Fashion Moda, which Lewis codirected. Calling itself "the friendly magazine," the 8½-by-11-inch, black-and-white publication featured short stories, poetry, and occasional interviews, alongside reproductions of works of art, which, as Witz noted, "were more effective on the pages of the magazine where they enhanced and were enhanced by the words around them."[7] He thought of the magazine as "architectural": some issues were more classical, others modernist. Wilke, who designed the logo, appeared on the first cover. Other contributors included Betty Tompkins, John Ahern, Ana Mendieta, Bruce Nauman, Barbara Kruger, Nancy Spero, Leon Golub, Chris Burden, Jackie Winsor, Richard Serra, Victor Burgin, Mierle Laderman Ukeles, Barbara Bloom, Robert Morris, David Wojnarowicz, and Keith Haring. Twenty-eight issues of *Appearances* were published between 1976 and 2001, along with several smaller chapbooks by individual artists and writers. The following handwritten note was sent out to subscribers with issue 28, a photocopied compilation of Witz's poems: "Dear People. *Appearances* is out of business. These 2 issues should square us away. Best Wishes. *Appearances*." After a seven-year hiatus, another issue (also numbered 28) was published in 2009. And it may appear yet again.

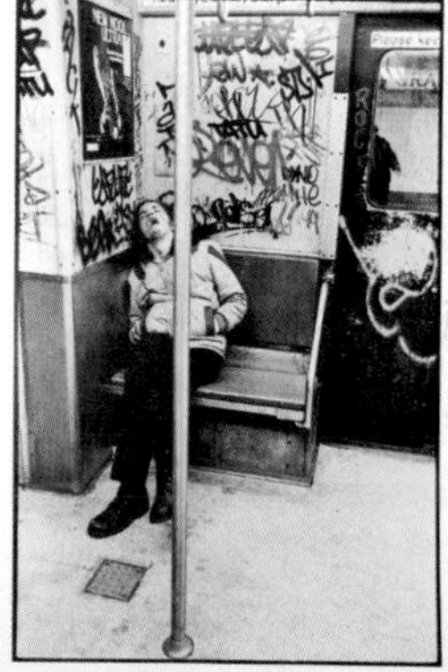

A.1

Appearances, no. 10, 1983. Cover photograph by Richard Sandler. Courtesy of Bob Witz and Richard Sandler.

DE APPEL
Amsterdam: The Appel Foundation, 1981–1987.
Editors: Wies Smals and Josine van Droffelaar (1981–1982);
Saskia Bros and Edna van Duyn (1984–1987).

De Appel was the quarterly bulletin of the Appel Foundation, an alternative gallery that opened in Amsterdam in 1975. The magazine published artist-designed contributions including "ideas/concepts to be realized in print, but also registrations/documentations of work whose features show affinities with De Appel's programme" (issue 1982/1). Collaborating with artists to develop formats that suited their needs, *de Appel* occasionally featured posters and flexi-disc records. Barbara Bloom designed the covers for all four issues published in 1982; other contributors included Louise Lawler, Lawrence Weiner, Barbara Kruger, and Marina Abramović and Ulay.

APPROCHES
Paris, 1966–1969 (1–4). Jean-François Bory and
Julien Blaine.

Approches published art and visual poetry, with contributions by Henri Chopin, Edgardo Antonio Vigo, and Richard Kostelanetz, among others. Issue 4 contained a flexi-disc 33 rpm record.

¡AQUI!
New York. 1984–1986 (1–10). Cliff Baldwin, Julie Bradrick,
and Davi Det Hompson.

¡Aqui! took the form of a series of silkscreened posters publicly displayed in downtown Manhattan and also sold at several New York bookstores. Named after the Spanish word for "here," *¡Aqui!* was described by Baldwin as "a portable, collapsible art space that existed wherever the viewer was at the time."[8] Each "issue" was a poster designed by a single artist, including the three editors, Davi Det Hompson, Cliff Baldwin, and Julie Bradrick, plus Les Levine, Barbara Kruger, Steve Gianakos, General Idea, and Gilbert and George.

ARCHIBRAS
Paris, Le Terrain Vague, 1967–1969 (1–7). Jean Schuster.

Continuing Andre Breton's *La Breche, Archibras* was the final surrealist periodical. Nos. 4 and 5 were published as political pamphlets in connection with the 1968 events in Paris and the Soviet takeover of Czechoslovakia.

ARCHIGRAM
London, 1961–1964 (1–9½). The Archigram group
(Warren Chalk, Peter Cook, Dennis Cromptom, David Greene,
Ron Herron, and Michael Webb).

Archigram was the newsletter of Archigram, a radical group of London-based architects who rebelled against the dominance of the International Style. Producing few actual buildings, Archigram's unorthodox practice largely took the form of blueprints, drawings, and writings, many of which were disseminated in their magazine. Thus *Archigram* was, in many ways, less a record of the group's activities than their starting point and intended format; as Cook explained:

> Why Archigram? It comes from the original desire not to put out a regularized and predictable "magazine" with lots of pages and a cover, but to push out, excrete (almost) a thing that would explode upon the oppressed assistants in London offices and the students in the shape of a large piece of poster, collage of images, or booklet …

whatever was necessary at the time. Hence the need for a name that was more analogous to a thing like a message or some abstract communication, telegram, aerogramme, etc.[9]

As Archigram explored its unconventional architectural ideas in the pages of *Archigram,* so too did they experiment with the printed form of the magazine itself, which published statements, drawings, plans, and collages in an evolving series of unusual formats. The first issue consisted of a few cheaply photocopied sheets, scrawled with handwritten poems and architectural sketches by Cook and Greene. Later issues were more professionally printed, with color, die-cut, and foldout pages, silk screens, pop-up pages (issue 4), and inserts such as an electronic resistor (in issue 7) and a packet of seeds (in issue 9).

ARK
London, 1950–1978 (1–54).

Ark was the student journal of the Royal College of Art. In the 1950s, the magazine became an important vehicle for the Independent Group under editor Roger Coleman, who produced three remarkable issues (nos. 18–20) in 1956 and 1957. Coleman and other contributors—including Alison and Peter Smithson, Reyner Banham, Lawrence Alloway, and Toni del Renzio—pioneered an innovative series of cover designs and articles, developing experimental layouts and printing techniques inspired by the visual abundance of American glossies.

ART AKTUELL
Cologne, 1971–1985 (vol. 1, no. 1–vol. 15, no. 7/8).
Dr. Willi Bongard.

Art Aktuell was a fortnightly newsletter, subtitled "Confidential Information about the Art Scene." As Bongard described it, "My newsletter—not a magazine—reflects my very personal interest in contemporary art and its market."[10] Published in an edition of 500 copies, including English and German versions, *Art Aktuell* consisted of four typed, unillustrated sheets that began with the salutation "Dear Art Lover," and were signed "Yours, Willi Bongard." Each year it ranked the market value of various contemporary artists according to the Kunst-Kompass, a pseudo-scientific method invented by Bongard, and still used in Germany today.

ART & PROJECT BULLETIN
Amsterdam: Art & Project Space, 1968–1989 (1–156).
Geert van Beijeren and Adriaan van Ravesteijn.

Brian O'Doherty described the pages of *Art & Project Bulletin* as "a floating artists' space."[11] Consisting of a single sheet of A3 paper folded in half, to make four pages, the *Art & Project Bulletin* served as a printed supplement to the experimental Art & Project gallery founded in Amsterdam in 1968 by Geert van Beijeren and Adriaan van Ravesteijn, who described their goals in the first issue: "Art & Project plans to bring you together with the ideas of artists, architects and technicians to discover an intelligent form for your living and working space. Art & Project invites you to participate in its exhibitions which will explore ways in which art, architecture, and technology can combine with your own ideas." A cross between an exhibition announcement and a traveling exhibition space, the *Art & Project Bulletin* was produced in an edition of 800 copies, of which 400 to 500 were sent out free to the gallery's mailing list, which extended across Europe and the United States; the rest were made available at the gallery itself.

Some artists used the bulletin to supplement their work inside the gallery, publishing photographs and other kinds of documentation. Others created stand-alone works for the

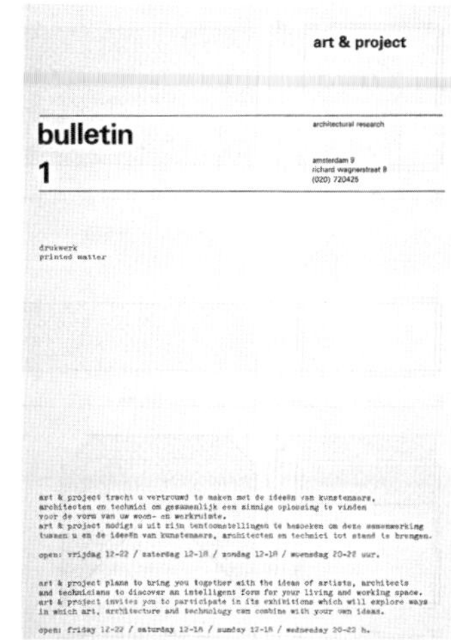

A.2

Art & Project Bulletin, no. 1. Courtesy of Twentieth Century Art Archives. Research Library, The Getty Research Institute, Los Angeles (86-S1343 no. 1).

page. Robert Barry printed the following sentence: "During the exhibition the gallery will be closed." Douglas Huebler sent the viewer on a treasure hunt for hidden photographs. Daniel Buren publicized his censored piece at the Guggenheim. Sol LeWitt folded his bulletin into forty-eight rectangles. Bas Jan Ader's bulletin featured a photograph of the artist in the sailboat in which he would soon attempt his fateful transatlantic voyage. Other artists who produced bulletins included Alighiero Boetti, Stanley Brouwn, Joseph Kosuth, Jan Dibbits, Gilbert and George, Keith Arnatt, Hanne Darboven, Ian Wilson, Allen Ruppersberg, Richard Long, Mel Bochner, John Baldessari, Hamish Fulton, and Lawrence Weiner.

ART COMMUNICATION EDITION (ACE) / STRIKE
Toronto: Centre for Experimental Art
and Communication, 1976–1979 (*ACE*, 1976–1977,
1–9; *Strike* 1978–1979, 1–3).

Published by the Toronto artists' space the Centre for Experimental Art and Communication, *Art Communication Edition* was a monthly tabloid that sought to be "a forum for neglected aspects of contemporary art activity," with a focus on media such as video and performance.[12] In 1978 the publication changed its name to *Strike*, suggesting its increasingly politicized editorial program. The second issue of *Strike* published court transcripts from the Red Brigade's trial and a photograph of Aldo Moro's murdered bodyguard on its cover, calling for artists to take a militant stance against the capitalist system. After issue 3, which heavily criticized the Canadian police, government funding was withdrawn from the CEAC and *Strike* .

ARTE POSTALE!
Forte dei Marmi, Italy, 1979–. Vittore Baroni.

The first fifty issues of Vittore Baroni's mail art magazine *Arte Postale!* were published in limited editions of 100, produced as assemblings with a completely open editorial policy explained very simply: "To be included in *Arte Postale!* send 100 pages." Later issues were produced by Baroni in photocopy or offset, with manual interventions, such as stamps and collage, in an edition ranging from 1 to 500. It was mostly exchanged free of charge for similar publications by other mail artists. As of 2009, 100 issues had been published.

ARTES VISUALES
Mexico City, 1973–1981 (1–29). Fernando Gamboa and
Carla Stellweg.

Published by the Museo de Arte Moderno under the legendary director and curator Fernando Gamboa, *Artes Visuales* was the most important and progressive art magazine in Mexico during the 1970s. *Artes Visuales* was edited by Carla Stellweg and designed by the artist Vicente Rojo; guest editors included Salvador Elizondo, Juan Acha, and Alfredo Joskovicz. The magazine focused on conceptual art and related practices, emphasizing the political nature of such work and featuring artists' projects and criticism associated with the alternative *grupos* movement, including No Grupo.

ARTITUDES INTERNATIONAL
Paris and Saint Jeannet, 1971–1977.
Editor: François Pluchart.

With a format reminiscent of *Avalanche*, though rectangular instead of square, *Artitudes* published artists' writings and documentation of works, focusing on conceptual art in Europe and the United States. An editorial statement in the first issue announced:

Artitudes International wishes, above all, to be a functional organ. We hope to be not merely a tool for analysis and for divulgation of innovative ideas and of creations which are more than simple estheticism, but also a junction between social conscience and that which one must continue to call "beauty." The magazine has adopted a more normal size (8" × 11½") in order to permit publication of most documents without size transformation, as no serious political attitude can exist without perfect organization and total clarity. Directed by people without prejudices, but with convictions, the magazine will not bother with the vain quarrels of a self-satisfactory avant-garde. We will make known creative impulses as soon as we are informed and will publish the works we receive. Thus we will be the vigilant echo of those whose prime thought is a principle of action.

ART-LANGUAGE

Coventry, England: Art & Language Press, 1969–1985. 19 issues (vol. 1, no. 1–vol. 5, no. 3). Terry Atkinson, David Bainbridge, Michael Baldwin, and Harold Hurrell (founding editors); Joseph Kosuth (American editor, vol. 1, nos. 2 and 3); Charles Harrison (general editor, 1971–1985); Philip Pilkington, Mel Ramsden, Ian Burn, David Rushton, Graham Howard, and Terry Smith.

Art-Language, published by the British Art & Language group, served as a vehicle for dialog about—and especially disagreement over—conceptual art within the Anglo-American art world. In the first issue, subtitled "The Journal of Conceptual Art" (a designation it would drop thereafter), the editors wrote: "Suppose the following hypothesis is advanced: that this editorial, in itself an attempt to evince some outlines as to what 'conceptual art' is, is held out as a 'conceptual art' work." The possibility that the magazine might be an artistic medium was demonstrated by Dan Graham's "Poem-Schema" *(Schema (March 1966))* and Lawrence Weiner's "Statements," both published in issue 1, as was Sol LeWitt's "Sentences on Conceptual Art." Densely printed in roman typeface, and unillustrated save for the occasional explanatory diagram, the black-and-white, digest-sized journal embodied in its very nondescriptness the "anti-retinal" propositions of the Art & Language group. The editors explained that "any decisions apart from this have been taken with a point of view to what it should not look like as a point of emphasis over what it should look like. These secondary decisions are aimed at eliminating as many appearance similarities to established art-objects as possible." *Art-Language* published theoretical, philosophical, and aesthetic articles by members of the Art & Language collective. In 1974 the entire contents of the journal to that point (including all published and unpublished submissions) were arranged in filing cabinets and exhibited as the *Art-Language Index* at Documenta 5—an arrangement that concretized the capacity of the journal to function as a site of collective communication and interaction. Like most collectives, the journal was defined by conflict and disagreement as much as consensus; the disagreements would eventually lead the New York wing of Art & Language to defect and found *The Fox,* a publication that was disavowed by *Art-Language*.

ART NOW: NEW YORK

New York: Profile Press, 1969–1972. Issued ten times a year, then quarterly starting in 1971. Publisher: Roger Peskin. Editor: Paul Katz.

Editorial Statement: "Each month *ART NOW: NEW YORK* will present a selection of the finest contemporary art from New York City's museums, galleries, and artists' studios. Along with the reproductions, each issue will include statements by the artists describing their methods

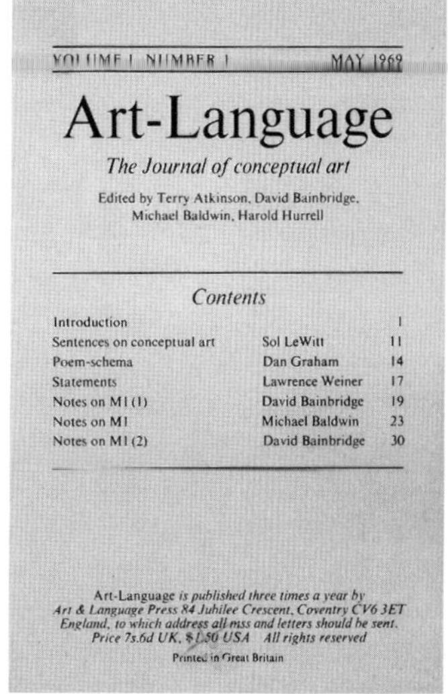

A.3

Art-Language, vol. 1, no. 1, May 1969. Courtesy of Art & Language.

and ideas. These color reproductions and artists' statements, published for the first time in *ART NOW: NEW YORK*, will be a unique source of primary material about advanced work being done today."

ART PAPERS
(Previously *Atlanta Art Workers Coalition Newsletter /
AAWC Newspaper / Atlanta Art Papers*). Atlanta, 1977–.
Julia Fenton, Dan Talley, and others.

Art Papers began as the newsletter of the Atlanta Art Workers Coalition Ltd., a nonprofit organization dedicated to the exchange of ideas and information among Atlanta-based artists. In 1978 Julia Fenton and Dan Talley expanded the newsletter into a bimonthly, tabloid-sized format called the *Atlanta Art Workers Coalition Newspaper* with the mission to cover art in the Southeast region within a broader national or international context. It included artist interviews, listings, and artists' pages. With the March-April 1980 issue, the publication became the *Atlanta Art Papers*, ending its affiliation with the AAWC, and the following year it merged with *Contemporary Arts Southeast*, changing its title to *Art Papers* with the subtitle "Covering the Arts in the Southeast."

ARTPOLICE
Minneapolis, 1974–1994 (69 issues). Frank Gaard.

Artpolice was started by art professor Frank Gaard in the midst of student and faculty protests at the Minneapolis College of Art and Design. The publication, which ranged from a single sheet of paper to a stapled booklet, featured line drawings in the provocative, counter-cultural tradition of underground comix by Gaard and his students, including Chris Woodward, Andrew Baird, Fritz Wolfmeyer, Robert Corbit, and Gregory Miller. According to Gaard, "I wanted to break all the rules, even the ones I didn't know existed, I fancied myself an artcriminal."[13] Financed by contributors and given away for free, *Artpolice* had a circulation of around 300 to 600. The following statement appeared in volume 3, no. 1:

> We are not for everybody. What we do is try to make something personal an art magazine for people who are turned off by the regular art journals. We share certain ideas and an approach to this endeavor. Our existence is marginal we are more a dream than reality. We've paid the freight for our collective illusion with minimal external support. … We have taken a position over the years that rejects much art being made today. Our purpose is to present a serious alternative (ironic and humorous) to all the pretensions filling current art activities. If we are excessive and enigmatic that's what makes us difficult to comprehend not our mixture of mirages and words. Some of us have more fun and it shows. We also approach each issue like a trip to the dentist. There is an inherent pain in trying to approach all this. We have a dream of an issue where everyone does their best work and it becomes unnecessary to continue. Being human prevents the end of *Artpolice*.[14]

ARTPOOL LETTER (AKTUÁLIS LEVÉL)
Budapest, 1983–1985 (1–11).
György Galántai and Júlia Klaniczay.

Artpool Letter was published by György Galántai and Júlia Klaniczay in association with Artpool, the alternative art institution they founded in 1979 to support and document non-official art in Hungary. As they described in issue 1, "Artpool is the only art archive and art space in Hungary with the objective to register changes in art, to present and document the latest art experiments, and to promote communication between artists in Hungary and abroad." An illegal *samizdat*, the booklet consisted of stapled, folded mimeographed sheets, with occasional hand stamps and stickers, and played on the personal correspondence theme implied by the magazine's title. The following editorial statement, translated into English by the editors, appeared in the first issue: "The aim of this letter is to present some untamed and unupdated ideas you usually do not bother to put down because writing needs strong concepts and much correction, and is thus less spontaneous. This letter is an improvisation in a field that is perhaps not just of my own interest. Therefore, it is a rare document at the same time. It does not [wish] to be either more or less than a letter." During a time when independent publishing was virtually nonexistent in Hungary, *Artpool Letter* played a vital role in supporting nonofficial art and establishing international contacts.

ART-RITE
New York, 1973–1978 (1–21; 16 was never published; 19 was a joint issue with *LAICA Journal*). Edit deAk, Joshua Cohn (nos. 1–7), and Walter Robinson. See chapter 5.

Art-Rite forged an iconoclastic, experimental style of criticism, focusing on younger, lesser-known artists in SoHo, whom the editors encouraged to write for the magazine and to use it as a medium. The magazine had a quaint, artless quality with its half-tabloid newsprint format, hand-stenciled logo, and do-it-yourself layout. It served as a rotating exhibition space for a series of artist-designed covers by artists, including Les Levine (no. 1), William Wegman (no. 2), Richard Tuttle (no. 3), Yuri (no. 4), Christo (no. 5), Dorothea Rockburne (no. 6), Vito Acconci (no. 7), Pat Steir (no. 8), Robert Ryman (no. 9), Joseph Beuys (no. 10), Ed Ruscha (no. 11/12), Carl Andre (no. 14), and Chris Burden (no. 19). In 1976, *Art-Rite* inaugurated its Dollar Art Series, in which entire issues of the magazine were given over to an artist or artists—including Alan Suicide (no. 13; two editions of this issue were produced—one with the cover logo in red and one in black, as well as other differences in the contents), Rosemary Mayer (no. 15), Kim MacConnel (no. 17), Image Bank (no. 18), Demi (no. 20), and Judy Rifka (no. 21)—to create a mass-produced work of art available for less than a gallon of milk.

ARTSCRIBE
London, 1976–1992 (1–90). James Faure Walker.

Published by the critic and painter James Faure Walker, *Artscribe* was intended to support British and American modernist abstract painting at a time when *Studio International* was heavily weighted toward conceptual art.

ART & TEXT
Prahran, Australia, 1981–2000 (1–67). Paul Taylor.

Art & Text was founded by Paul Taylor in 1981 as a vehicle to foster serious Australian art criticism, which, he wrote in the first issue, was "being underrated and neglected." The magazine's subdued format and editorial goals echoed those of the American journal *October*; an editorial statement explained:

> As the content of this first issue demonstrates, a wide variety of critical approaches is worthy of inclusion. Essays by and about Australian and, sometimes, overseas artists, theoretical and cultural analysis, enquiries into the relationships between the several arts and an avoidance of extensive interviewing, reviewing, and lavish illustration all aim to establish *Art & Text* as a forum for critical and artistic re-examination and experimentation. By means of such a forum Australian artists and critics may gain a progressive understanding of their role and practical potential.

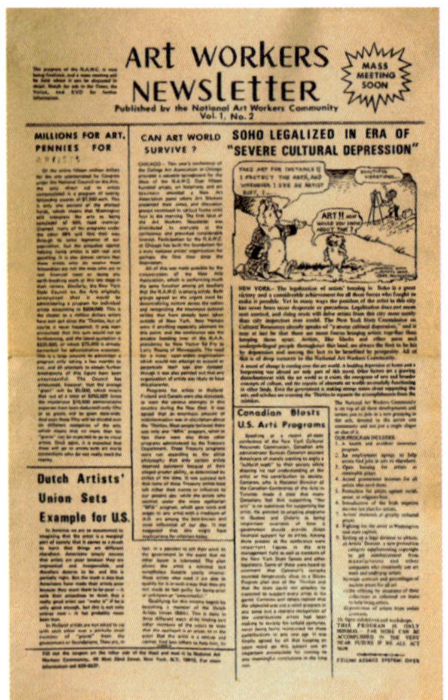

A.4

Art Workers Newsletter, vol. 1, no. 2, 1971. Courtesy of Elliott Barowitz.

ART WORKERS NEWSLETTER / ARTWORKERS NEWS / ART & ARTISTS

New York: National Art Workers Community / Foundation for the Community of Artists, 1971–1989. Editors: Laurin Raiken, Bernie Brown, Saunders Ellis, Pamela Bickart, Alex Gross, and others (1971–1975); Peter Leggieri (1975–1978); Daniel Grant (1979–1980); Elliott Barowitz (1981–1989).

"*Artworkers News* lobbies for artists against all comers," Edit deAk and Walter Robinson wrote about *Artworkers News,* which was the first artists' publication to focus sustained attention on artists' rights.[15] Founded by the National Art Workers Community (a splinter group of the Art Workers' Coalition) in 1971, the *Art Workers Newsletter* began as a four-page broadsheet, reporting on artists' housing, the possibility of an artists' union, health insurance, and copyright and censorship issues. Despite several format and title changes, these concerns formed the core of the publication's editorial mission over the course of its eighteen-year existence.

Notable editors and contributors included the eminent sociologist and historian of art Laurin Raiken, *New York Post* journalist Bernie Brown, *East Village Other* founder Peter Leggieri, Gerald Marzorati, Lawrence Alloway, Eva Cockcroft, Adam Gopnick, Gregory Battcock (whose byline was Dr. Lawn Mower), Daniel Grant, Lucy Lippard, Donald Kuspit, Irving Sander, Dore Ashton, Leon Golub, Jimmie Durham, and the artist Elliott Barowitz, chair of the board and president of the Foundation for the Community of Artists (FCA), who was executive editor for the last eight years. Barbara Nessim, Marc Kostabi, and former Fugs band member Tuli Kupferberg worked as cartoonists.

Published monthly, then bimonthly starting in 1982, it retained the look and function of an underground newspaper for the art world, with bold headlines and graphics designed not to foster aesthetic appreciation, but to inform and incite readers to action. In lieu of traditional art criticism, it published articles on health hazards, education, race and gender equality within the art world, and socially and politically engaged forms of art, as well as listings of artists' resources, events, and opportunities. Special issues covered Richard Serra's *Tilted Arc* controversy, Artists against Apartheid, and Artists Call against U.S. Intervention in Central America. In addition to the magazine, the Foundation for the Community of Artists published important resource books for artists, such as *The Legal Guide for the Visual Artist* by Tad Crawford, *Health Hazards Manual for Artists* by Dr. Michael McCann, and *The Art Law Primer* by Caryn Leland, and offered health insurance, including mental health coverage, for artists.

ARTZIEN

Amsterdam, 1978–1982 (1–28). Michael Gibbs.

Edited by Michael Gibbs (who previously published *Kontexts*), *Artzien* supported alternative art in Amsterdam during the late 1970s and early 1980s.

ASPEN

New York: Roaring Fork Press, 1965–1971 (1–10). Phyllis Johnson, plus numerous guest editors and designers. See chapter 2.

Aspen: The Magazine in a Box was a multimedia magazine in a cardboard box that included unbound pamphlets, posters, Super 8 films, and flexi-disc records. Named after Aspen, Colorado, it initially highlighted the town's rich cultural and recreational offerings, including events at the Aspen Institute, cross-country skiing, Colorado wildlife, and regional architecture, accompanied by jazz and classical records. Starting with issue 3, designed by Andy

Warhol and David Dalton in the form of a box of Fab laundry detergent, *Aspen* became an experimental artists' magazine. Each subsequent issue of the magazine was sui generis: issue 4, designed by Quentin Fiore, focused on the ideas of Marshall McLuhan; issue 5+6, edited by Brian O'Doherty, highlighted minimalism and conceptual art; issue 6A was a reprint of the Judson Church Gallery magazine *Manipulations*; issue 7 was a game-filled "British Box" edited by Mario Amaya; Dan Graham edited issue 8, titled "Art/Information/Science"; issue 9 was a psychedelic "Dream Weapon" issue edited by musicians Angus and Hetty MacLise; and issue 10 (which did not have editorial credits) was an incense-scented "Far East" issue.

ASSEMBLING

New York, 1970–1987 (1–13.2). Richard Kostelanetz (1–11),
Henry Korn (1–8), Mike Metz (2–8), and Charles Doria (12–13.2).

"A cooperative annual magazine of the unpublished and the unpublishable," *Assembling* vowed to publish works "too eccentric to be published elsewhere." Frustrated by the limited possibilities of the "editorial/industrial complex," as they called mainstream publishing, Richard Kostelanetz and Henry Korn founded *Assembling* to expand the possibilities of collective self-publication and to challenge traditional hierarchies between publishers, editors, and authors. Contributors were invited to submit 1,000 copies of up to four 8½-by-11-inch pages. No manuscript was refused. Removing the authority of the editor to filter content, the editors merely collated the submissions alphabetically and distributed the magazine, sending out three copies to each contributor, and selling the rest. While it was not the first magazine to be published in this way (Kostelanetz was inspired by the German magazine *Omnibus News* [1969], in particular), *Assembling* coined the term "assembling," and established an important new do-it-yourself publishing model.

Reflecting its antiauthoritarian editorial structure, *Assembling* appears as a chaotic and uneven (in every sense of the word) mix of art, poetry, and other kinds of texts and documents with inconsistent margins, fonts, and layouts, printed on a heterogeneous range of papers, from colored construction paper to college-ruled notebook paper. The first issue contained Vito Acconci's "Notebook Excerpts," Dan Graham's "Ecological Rock," and Ed Ruscha's "Chocolate" (a sheet of paper marked with a faint smudge of chocolate), alongside works by Arakawa, Tom Ahern, Michael Metz, Madeline Gins, and Alan Sondheim. Subsequent contributors included Dana Atchley, Ken Friedman, Clemente Padin, and John Baldessari. Kostelanetz explained in the first issue, "the long range goal of *Assembling* is to open the editorial/industrial complex to alternatives and possibilities," observing that the fulfillment of this goal would ultimately make the magazine redundant: "In the end, of course, we should like to find the dissemination of experimental writing changed so radically that *Assembling* would have no further need to exist."

AUDIO ARTS

London, 1973–2006 (vol. 1, no. 1–vol. 25, no. 4). William Furlong.

Artist William Furlong founded the "spoken magazine" *Audio Arts* in 1973. Each issue consisted of a cassette tape that documented artists' voices in the context of interviews, readings, symposia, and other situations. Contributors included Art & Language, Wyndham Lewis, Joseph Beuys, Buckminster Fuller, Carl Andre, Marcel Duchamp, Lucy Lippard, Les Levine, Willoughby Sharp, Richard Hamilton, Glen Branca, Philip Glass, Andy Warhol, Gerhard Richter, Nam June Paik, Ilya Kabakov, and Jeff Koons.

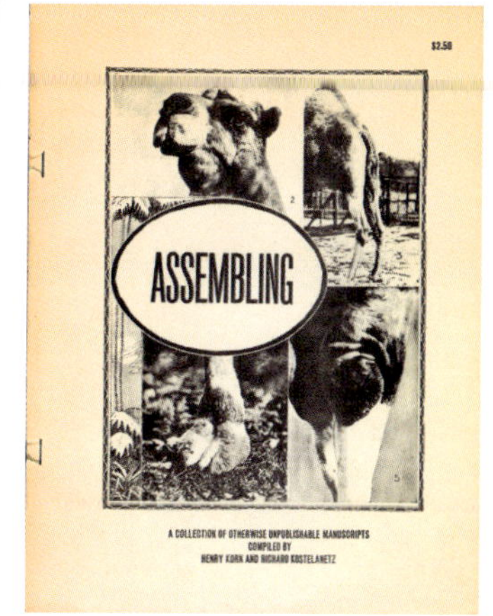

A.5

Assembling, no. 1, 1970. Courtesy of Richard Kostelanetz. Research Library, The Getty Research Institute, Los Angeles (86-S1149 no. 1).

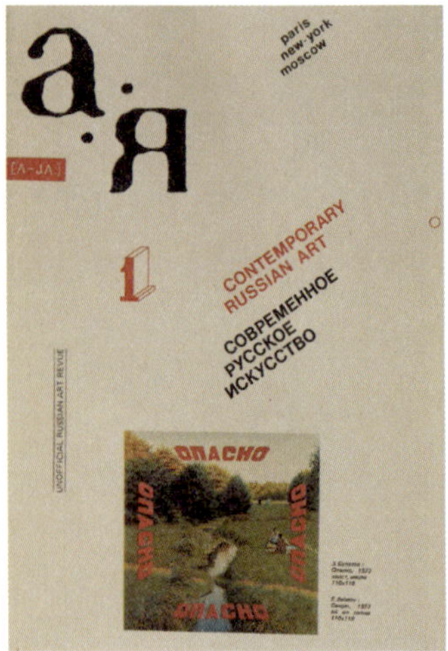

A.6

A/Ya, no. 1, 1979. Courtesy of Igor Shelkovsky.

AUSGABE

Berlin, 1976–1983 (1–7). Armin Hundertmark.

Ausgabe, meaning "distribution," published conceptual art, poetry, Fluxus scores, and other documents by contributors including Günter Brus, Henry Flynt, Dick Higgins, Dieter Roth, George Brecht, Philip Corner, Alison Knowles, Herman Nitsch, and Henri Chopin.

AVALANCHE

New York: Kineticism Press, 1970–1976 (1–13).
Liza Béar and Willoughby Sharp. See chapter 4.

By eliminating art criticism and exhibition reviews in favor of interviews and documentation of works, *Avalanche* provided a more direct channel for the artist's voice. From its vantage point in SoHo, *Avalanche* surveyed the new media art of the late 1960s and early 1970s, including conceptual art, performance, video, dance, and music. Both chronicle and agent for these newly minted forms, *Avalanche* sought to put the media into the hands of artists—who, in turn, not only used the magazine to promote themselves and publicize their work but tapped its potential as a medium in and of itself. The first eight issues were in the form of a square magazine with coated pages, featuring brooding portraits of artists on each cover: Joseph Beuys (no. 1), Bruce Nauman (no. 2), Barry Le Va (no. 3), Lawrence Weiner (no. 4), Yvonne Rainer (no. 5), Vito Acconci (no. 6), William Wegman (represented by his dog and frequent artistic collaborator, Man Ray) (no. 7), and Robert Smithson (no. 8). When printing costs skyrocketed in 1974, *Avalanche* switched to a newspaper format. Its circulation ranged from 4,000 to 6,250.

Facsimile reprint: *Avalanche: The Complete Thirteen Issues, 1970–1976.* New York: Primary Information, 2010.

AXE

Antwerp, 1975–1976 (1–3). Guy Schraenen.

Axe comprised unbound pages of original prints and multiples, written works, embossed pages, and a seven-inch vinyl record in a folder. Among its contributors were Henri Chopin, Brion Gysin, Sten Hanson, and François Dufrêne. Printed in an edition of 500.

A/YA

Moscow and Elancourt, France: Boris Karmashov, 1979–1986 (1–7).
Alexander Sidorov (under the pseudonym Alexej Alexejev),
Igor Shelkovsky, and Alexander Kosolapov.

A/Ya, subtitled "the unofficial Russian art revue," was founded in Paris by the Russian expatriate artist Igor Shelkovsky; it was illegally edited from Moscow by Alexander Sidorov, under the pseudonym Alexej Alexejev, and was edited and distributed in New York by Alexander Kosolapov. Printed in an edition of 7,000 copies for the first issue and 3,000 thereafter, the magazine was published seven times in seven years. It set out the following editorial goals in the first issue:

> To acquaint Russian artists—in and outside Russia—with each other's work; to inform the reader about the artistic creativity and developments in contemporary Russian art; [and] to provide a forum where writers on art can express their opinions on artists or artistic phenomena. This review does not represent any particular group of persons. Its pages are open to all independent thought and new ideas.

Printed in English and Russian, and partially funded by the art collector Jack Mikonian, the magazine was a crucial vehicle for critical discourse within the international Russian art community, with contributors including Boris Groys, Margarita Tupitsyn, Viktor Tupitsyn,

Rimma Gerlovina, and Valeriy Gerlovin. It introduced Western audiences to Russian artists such as Eric Bulatov, Ilya Kabakov, and Dmitry Prigov.

The magazine's title, composed of the first and last letters of the Cyrillic alphabet—*A* (which corresponds to the Latin letter *A*) and *Ya* (for which there is no exact Latin equivalent)—signaled both the promise and perils of translation. Glossy and professional-looking, with a full-color cover, *A/Ya* represented the new possibilities of the Western commercial art magazine for Russian artists. In the words of Moscow artist Igor Makarevich,

> It was the first time we could read analytical texts about our work. Before that there were only ethnographic texts by Western journalists or slander in the Soviet official press. Before *A/Ya* Russian intellectual art was based on kitchen conversation and discussion clubs in studios and in private spaces. … It was like magic, a miracle to see your own work printed on glossy paper. Because only Western artworks could be seen in reproduction, seeing our own work in *A/Ya* made us associate ourselves with the West. It was a new step in our self-esteem and recognition; the birth of *A/Ya* transformed its participants and brought a new status to them and their creative work.[16]

AZIMUTH
Milan, 1959–1960 (1–2). Enrico Castellani and Piero Manzoni.

Azimuth was published by Enrico Castellani and Piero Manzoni to support the activities of the Nouveaux Réalistes centered around the Azimuth Gallery, which they opened in Milan in December 1959. Both gallery and magazine took their name from the mathematical concept "azimuth," which refers to the angle between the apparent position of an object and a specific observation point—a concept that suggests the concern with the relationship between viewer and object that would characterize Nouveau Réalisme. In the first issue, they collaborated with the Leo Castelli Gallery and the Iris Clert Gallery, publishing reproductions of Jasper Johns's *Target with Casts*, Robert Rauschenberg's *Monogram*, an unbound Jean Tinguely *Metamatic* drawing, a sheet of solid blue by Yves Klein, plus works by Manzoni, Kurt Schwitters, Francis Picabia, Lucio Fontana, Heinz Mack, and Samuel Beckett. The second (and last) issue of *Azimuth* was published the next month, in January 1960, on the occasion of a seminal exhibition at the Azimuth Gallery that showed the work of Manzoni, Kilian Breier, Enrico Castellani, Oskar Holweck, Yves Klein, Heinz Mack, and Almir Mavignier. The issue functioned as the catalog of the exhibition, and published Manzoni's important essay "Free Dimension."

THE BALLOON NEWSPAPER
Santa Cruz, California, 1969–1972 (1–13). Bruce Kleinsmith
(Futzie Nutzle), Victor Harlow (Spinny Walker), and
Phil Sievert (henry humble).

The Balloon Newspaper was a vehicle for the collaborative drawings and cartoons of three pseudonymous artists: Futzie Nutzle (who later contributed drawings to *Rolling Stone*), Spinny Walker, and henry humble. The publication was named after the Balloon, a makeshift compound on a plot of farmland in Santa Cruz where the three lived and worked.

BENZENE
New York, 1980–1985 (1–10). Allan Bealy and Sheila Keenan.

Benzene published downtown art, music, performance, and poetry in a large tabloid format (some issues also came with flexi-disc records). Contributors included Peter Cherches, Tom Ahern, Richard Kostelanetz, Bruce Benderson, Ursule Molinaro, David Wojnarowicz, and Mike Bidlo. Issue 10 was combined with the final issue of *Zone*.

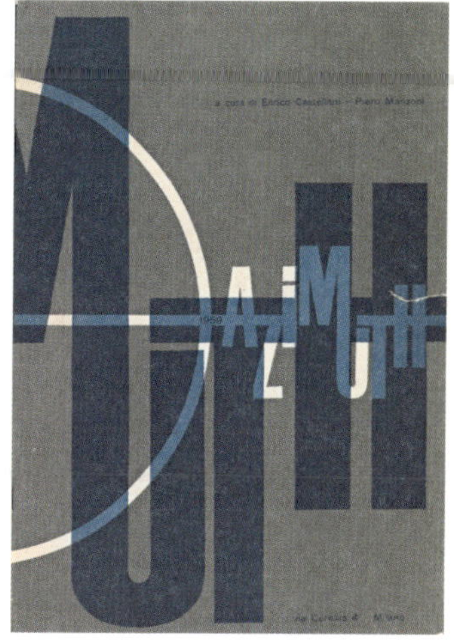

A.7

Azimuth, no. 1, 1959. Edited by Enrico Castellani and Piero Manzoni. © 2009 Artists Rights Society (ARS), New York/SIAE, Rome. Research Library, The Getty Research Institute, Los Angeles (87-S87 v. 1).

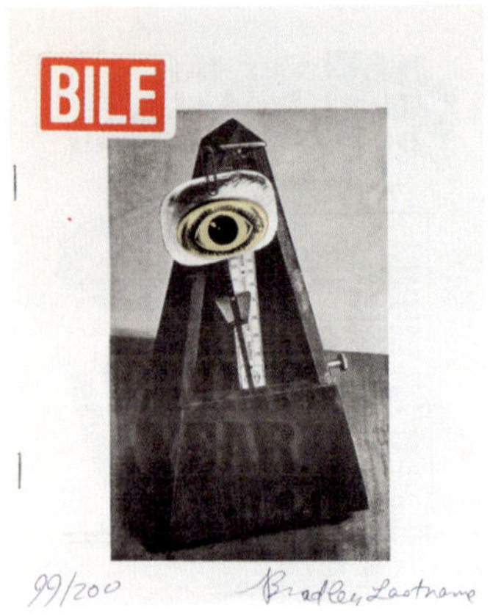

A.8

BILE, unnumbered, undated issue.
Courtesy of Bradley Lastname.
Research Library, The Getty Research
Institute, Los Angeles (93-S266 no. 99).

BIG DEAL

New York, 1973–1977 (1–5). Barbara Baracks.

The writer Barbara Baracks published five issues (approximately one per year) of the sarcastically titled art and literature magazine *Big Deal*. She did the printing, layout, and typesetting herself. Mike Metz did photography, and Jackson Mac Low assisted with pasteup. Among the contributors were Lucy Lippard, Kathy Acker, Bernadette Mayer, Dick Higgins, Alison Knowles, Alan Sondheim, Carl Andre, Jasper Johns, Dan Graham, David Antin, John Cage, Maureen Owen, and Robert Smithson, whose essay "The Spiral Jetty" appeared in issue 3.

BIJUTSU SHIHYŌ

Tokyo, 1971–1978 (1–9). Naoyoshi Hikosaka

Bijutsu Shihyō (Art history and criticism) was published by Naoyoshi Hikosaka and other members of the radical artists' group Bikyoto (Artists' Joint-Struggle Council), which came out of the student protests of the late 1960s. The magazine was founded in the aftermath of Bikyoto's protest of mainstream Japanese art venues, including its effort to abolish the important annual exhibition, the Nitten. According to Hikosaka, it came out of the realization that "we have to reevaluate art history in Japan."[17] The small, subdued black-and-white magazine with red lettering on its cover published texts and works by the Bikyoto collective and its subsequent subgroups, such as the Bikyoto Revolution Committee, which organized a series of exhibitions outside of art world institutions and abstained from making and exhibiting art during 1974. Also see *Kirokutai*.

BILE

Chicago: No Tickee / No Washee Enterprises, 1978–1984
(1–25; all issues unnumbered and undated).
Bradley Lastname.

BILE, a photocopied, rubberstamped magazine published by Bradley Lastname, was a takeoff on the mail art magazines *VILE* and *FILE*. Typical of the magazine's facetious and absurdist character was the following editorial statement, published in issue 1:

> The *FILE-VILE-BILE* dialectic: Four Fallacious Causal Structures and a True One. (a) *Bile* is not causally connected to either *File* or *Vile*. (b) *File* is a cause of *Bile*, but not of *Vile*. (c) *File* is a cause of both *Vile* and *Bile*, but the effect of *File* on *Bile* is completely contained in *Vile* or mediated by *Vile*. (d) The covariation between *Vile* and *Bile* is totally due to their direct common dependence upon an outside cause. (e) The covariation between *Vile* and *Bile* is due in part to the causal dependence of *Bile* on *Vile*, and due in part to their direct sharing of a common cause. Note also that this is the only causal structure that crystallizes into a dadagorean triangle.

Like its predecessors, *BILE* appropriated *Life* magazine's red and white logo. However, published in a numbered edition of 200 copies, it had a much more handmade feeling: a safety pin was attached to the page of one issue; another had scratch 'n sniff covers; yet another featured a drawing of Man Ray's *Object to Be Destroyed* (1923), with a venticular eye glued to the page that blinked open and closed as the reader wiggled the page. Contributors included Jeff Twiss, Steve Spera, Brooke Rothwell, and Kevin Riordan, among many others.

BIT

Milan, 1967–1968 (no. 1–vol. 2, no. 4).
Editor: Daniela Palazzoli. Editorial board: Germano Celant,
Mario Diacono, Daniea Palazzoli, Tommaso Trini.

Bit, subtitled "Art: What's Happening in Italy Today," published art and writings by the Arte Povera group, including Gianni Emilio Simonetti, Michelangelo Pistoletto, Jannis Kounellis, and Alighiero Boetti, alongside international conceptual artists including Dan Flavin, Arakawa, George Brecht, Öyvind Fahlström, and Dieter Roth, and critics such as Gillo Dorfles and Germano Celant, who published his essay "Arte Povera" here. Billing itself as "the most aggressive art magazine," *Bit* had a countercultural vibe in both form and content. The digest-sized magazine contained inserts and die-cut and foldout pages, and grew increasingly psychedelic over time, using split fountain, multicolor printing; one issue even included a pair of 3-D glasses. *Bit* stressed the connections between radical art and antiestablishment politics in the late 1960s, publishing *Interfunktionen*'s "Anti-Documenta Hearing," an anti-Coca Cola advertisement, and a reproduction of the *Berkeley Barb*, an underground newspaper.

BIT INTERNATIONAL

Zagreb: Gallery of Contemporary Art Zagreb, 1968–1972 (1–9).
Editorial Board: Božo Bek, Dimitrije Bašičević (Mangelos),
Vera Horvat-Pintarić, Boris Kelemen, Matko Meštrović, Vatroslav Mimica,
Ivan Picelj, Radoslav Putar, and Vjenceslav Richter.

bit International stemmed out of the rich dialog between art and technology that arose around the influential New Tendencies movement, which staged its fourth exhibition, "Tendencije 4," in Zagreb in 1968, showcasing computers and visual research. Published under the auspices of the Gallery of Contemporary Art in Zagreb, *bit International* was named after the abbreviation for the most basic unit of computing: the binary digit. The first issue was a substantial-looking volume, printed in English and Croatian. The magazine's cover featured a background of graph paper—the color of which changed from issue to issue— upon which its title was printed in a lowercase techno typeface, along with the subtitle "the theory of informations and the new aesthetics." The first issue, edited by Dimitrije Bašičević (known as Mangelos) and Ivan Picelj, contained writings by Max Bense and Abraham Moles as well as a review of the "Cybernetic Serendipity" exhibition at the ICA in London. The editorial statement explained the magazine's goals:

> To present the theory of information, exact aesthetics, design, communication mass media, visual and related subjects; and to be an instrument of international cooperation in a field that is becoming daily less divisible into strict compartments. … The pages of *bit* are equally open to research and to reports on current experience and newly developed methods that are being worked out in workrooms, laboratories, factories, and institutes; individual and particularly collective works are also hoped for. News of finished and classified results and of exploratory action begun are equally welcome. *bit* is not a medium for showing off and the capitalization of intellectual gains, it is first and foremost a vehicle for continuous effort to develop the theory and practice of communications. … It will present various opinions and approaches. There will also be no conventional limits to expression in the pages of *bit*.

Published nine times between 1968 and 1972, *bit* was continued by *Spot* magazine (1972 to 1978), dedicated to experimental photography, video, and the media.

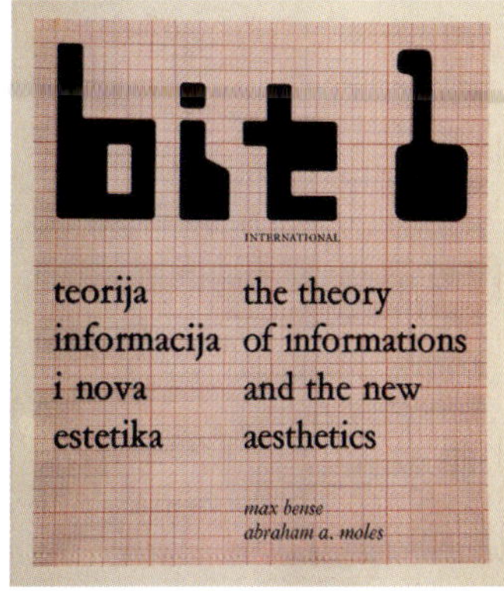

A.9

bit International, no. 1, 1968.
Courtesy of the Museum of
Contemporary Art, Zagreb.

BLACK ART
Jamaica, New York, 1976–1982 (vol. 1–vol. 5). Later continued
by *The International Review of African American Art*,
Santa Monica, California, 1984– (vol. 6–). Founding editor-in-chief:
Val Spaulding; founding art editor: Samella Lewis.

Black Art: An International Quarterly published contributions by and about contemporary African diaspora and African American artists, including Betye Saar, Elizabeth Catlett, Justo Susana, George Smith, Wifredo Lam, Souleymane Keita, Ruth Lucetty Bell, Howard Smith, Carroll Parrott Blue, and Camille Billops. Though advertising was kept to a minimum, the publication resembled more mainstream art magazines with its coated pages and color reproductions. An editorial statement in the first issue described the magazine's goals: "A living approach to art entails a composition of experiences rich in vibrant, personal relationships and communal interactions. … Black peoples are especially fortunate in that theirs has always been a living art. The profusion of cultural experiences permeates the whole of life. In bringing you *Black Art: An International Quarterly*, we will chronicle the heritage of our ancestors, encourage the participation of our contemporaries and enrich this heritage for our descendents."

BLACK ON WHITE (CERNÉ NA BÍLÉM / SCHWARZ AUF WEISS /
BLACK ON WHITE / NOIR SUR BLANC)
Düsseldorf, 1974–1980 (1–6). F. Kyncl and E. Spitmann.

The cover of *Black on White* displayed its title in Czech, German, English, and French. The purpose of the magazine, its editor wrote in the first issue, was to "draw the attention of specialists, particularly those in the Federal Republic of Germany, to a number of artists, mainly Czechoslovakian, who live in their homeland but for various reasons are not willing or are not permitted to exhibit in Czechoslovakia; and also to those Czechoslovakian artists who live outside their own country." Subtitled "Documentation of visual operations," the magazine included contributors such as Milos Laky, Jan Kotik, Joseph Beuys, Bridget Riley, and Vassilakis Takis. The first 300 copies of each issue included a signed and numbered original work.

BLACK PHOENIX
London, 1978–1979 (1–3). Rasheed Araeen and Mahmood Jamal.

According to editor Rasheed Araeen, *Black Phoenix: Journal of Contemporary Art & Culture in the Third World* was "not an art journal in the conventional sense, in order merely to support art or artistic activity, but a collaborative textual artwork in its own right."[18] An editorial in the first issue explained the magazine's impetus:

> *Black Phoenix* is the result of a realization that we who are concerned with the cultural predicament of the Third World must stand on our own feet and speak with a unified voice, that we must collectively confront, on an international level, those forces which in the name of "universal freedom of man" are actually causing enslavement of men and women. No matter how inarticulate some of our first attempts may appear, this should not prevent us from speaking up. We can only learn from our own efforts and develop the precision of thought and action. … *Black Phoenix* is not a journal merely for professional writers or critics (to perpetuate their self-interests) but a platform for discussion, a channel for the exchange of ideas relating to the cultural predicament of mankind in the era of advanced capitalism and imperialism. It represents a commitment to the struggle against cultural domination and hegemony; and all those who are engaged in this struggle—irrespective of their race, colour, or creed—are invited to participate in this dialogue.

A pioneer of minimalist sculpture in England in the 1960s, Araeen found himself disillusioned with the humanism of the West's liberal institutions, and especially the Eurocentrism of the art world (a bias that he had experienced firsthand, as a Pakistani artist living and working in London). Inspired by the writings of Frantz Fanon, he increasingly turned from traditional artistic activities to politics, joining the Black Panthers in London—a shift that led him to produce what he considers his first textual work, "Preliminary Notes for a Black Manifesto," in 1975–1976.[19] When this seemed unlikely to find a publisher, the idea for *Black Phoenix* arose.

With little previous publishing experience aside from helping with the Black Panthers' weekly newsletter, Araeen asked his friend the Indian poet Mahmood Jamal to help edit the magazine. As they later described, "we started this magazine in very difficult conditions. Everything seemed to be against us: lack of proper expertise, lack of experience of professional writing, lack of material resources and money, etc. It was only the will to survive and struggle that enabled us to take the plunge."[20] Araeen did the layout for *Black Phoenix* himself, and found a sympathetic Bangladeshi printer who agreed to do the job inexpensively. The first issue of *Black Phoenix* came out in 1978, six months prior to Edward Said's *Orientalism.*The magazine introduced postcolonial discourse into the British art world, with contributors including Guy Brett, Arial Dorfman, Kenneth Coutts-Smith, Ayyub Malik, and Eduardo Galeano. While *Black Phoenix* folded after just three issues, it remained true to its mythological eponym when it was resurrected by Araeen as *Third Text* in 1987.

BLAST
New York: Colab, 1986 –1988 (May 1986–February 1988;
approximately 10 issues published). Mitch Corber.

Blast: A Monthly Publication of Collaborative Projects / COLAB was published and edited by Mitch Corber, who also did layout, with help from Baird Jones. Corber wrote in the first issue: "The new monthly Colab Newsletter is a hopeful tonic for the group. At once, members (past, present, & future) may (re)establish contact and familiarize themselves with facts & faces. Key phone numbers. Key shows. Artist/club nites. One-nite-only performances. A spate of data." Xeroxed on 8½-by-14-inch colored paper, folded in half and stapled, in a run of 500, and crammed with found and hand-drawn imagery, news clippings, and appropriated headlines, *Blast* resembled a punk zine. It published listings of local events, Colab meetings, films, exhibitions, an artists' cross-referenced directory with Colab members' names and addresses, as well as poetry, news briefs, and artists' statements. Artists contributed cover art, hand-painted pages, and original collages. According to Corber, there was no connection between his magazine and Wyndham Lewis's *Blast*, though there may have been a subliminal association with the contemporaneous *Bomb* magazine.

BLOK
Brno, 1947–1949 (1–10). František Kaláb.

Blok, subtitled "Information on cultural work," was an important avant-garde periodical published by Czech artist František Kaláb. It focused on architecture, literature, film, and art with contributors including Asger Jorn, Karel Teige, Max Bill, Jiří Kroha, and Bohuslav Fuchs.

BOA
Buenos Aires, 1958 (1–3). Julio Llinás. ·

Subtitled "International notebooks for the documentation of avant-garde poetry and art," *Boa* was founded by poet Julio Llinás as a vehicle for Argentine surrealism. The magazine was inspired by *Phases* and *Cobra* (which its title played on).

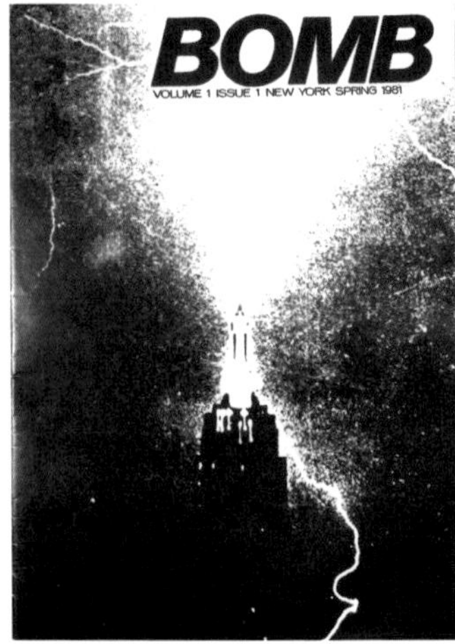

A.10

Bomb, vol. 1, no. 1, Spring 1981.
Cover image by Sarah Charlesworth.
Courtesy of the artist and *Bomb*.

BOMB

New York: X Motion Picture and Center for New Art Activities,
1981– (vol. 1, no. 1–). Betsy Sussler.

Billed as "the only authorized successor to *Avalanche*," *Bomb* grew out of the interdisciplinary downtown art scene of the late 1970s as a publication that would foster conversation about the creative process, focusing on film, fiction, theater, television, photography, and painting.[21] According to founder Betsy Sussler, who had been involved in the short-lived *X Magazine* and was working with the ensemble theater group Night Shift at the time *Bomb* was launched, the title referenced the possibility that the magazine might not last: "I thought that this magazine would be this ephemeral moment in time, and that perhaps it would not last. It might bomb, just like a play bombs."[22] The title also alluded to Wyndham Lewis's seminal literary magazine *Blast*, two issues of which were published in England from 1914 to 1915. Among those on the masthead in the first several years were Liza Béar, Michael McClard, Glenn O'Brian, Cookie Mueller, Mary Heilmann, Sarah Charlesworth, Barbara Kruger, and Saul Ostrow. The cover of the first issue, designed by Charlesworth (who was Sussler's roommate at the time), was a grainy, high-contrast photograph of the Empire State Building lit up at night, evoking an electrical charge that suggested the kind of creative energy the magazine hoped to spark. The large-format magazine, initially printed on newsprint with a coated cover, published artists' projects, interviews, and texts by Kathy Acker, Joan Jonas, Gary Indiana, Barbara Bloom, Keith Haring, William Wegman, Richard Prince, Nan Goldin, Nancy Spero, Carolee Schneemann, Walter Robinson, Robert Mapplethorpe, Joseph Kosuth, and Charlie Ahern. Inheriting *Avalanche*'s redefinition of the artists' interview, *Bomb* frequently published interviews consisting of conversations between two artists. In spite of its title, the magazine did not "bomb," but endured, moving gradually toward a more commercially viable model of publishing—a shift that was necessitated in part by the increasingly precarious nature of public funding during the 1980s. This change is evidenced by its increasing reliance on advertising, including the Absolut Vodka ads by artists such as Keith Haring, Andy Warhol, and Kenny Scharf, which began to appear in the magazine in 1987.

BRUMES BLONDES

Amsterdam: Bureau de recherches surréalistes,
1968–1972 (1–4). Editors: Herman de Vries
and Laurens Vancrevel.

Brumes Blondes: Actualité surréaliste was an important surrealist journal in Amsterdam.

BULLETIN FROM NOTHING

San Francisco, 1965 (1–2). Editor: Claude Pelieu.

Bulletin from Nothing included contributions by Antonin Artaud, Ed Sanders, Lawrence Ferlinghetti, William S. Burroughs, and Bob Kaufman.

CATERPILLAR

New York / Sherman Oaks, California, 1967–1973 (1–20).
Publisher and Editor: Clayton Eshleman.

Caterpillar, "a magazine of the leaf, a gathering of the tribes," was edited and published by Clayton Eshleman. The magazine's title was taken from William Blake's couplet, "The Caterpillar on the Leaf / Repeats to thee thy Mother's grief." On the cover of the first issue was Nancy Spero's *The Bomb* (1966) from her *The War Series* (1966–1970), and on the title page the editor wrote: "Don't kill; everyone alive, here & now." In addition to poets such as Robert Duncan, Jerome Rothenberg, Allen Ginsberg, David Antin, Robert Creeley, and Jackson Mac Low, *Caterpillar* published visual artists and filmmakers, including Jess

Collins (whose work appeared on several covers), Carolee Schneemann, Leon Golub, Stan Brakhage, and Wallace Berman. In addition to *The War Series*, Spero contributed her *Codex Artaud* (1969) to issue 8/9 and *Torture of Women* (1972) to issue 18.

CENTERFOLD / FUSE
Centerfold, Toronto, 1976–1979. Founding editors: Clive Robertson and
Marcella Bienvenue. Continued as *Fuse*. 1979–. Founding editors:
Clive Robertson, Lisa Steele, and Tom Sherman.

Centerfold began as a newsprint magazine covering alternative arts in Canada. After the November 1979 issue, the publication changed its name to *Fuse*. Clive Robertson also published the audiocassette magazine *Voicespondence* in Calgary from 1974 to 1978, which he later turned into a record label.

CHEVAL D'ATTAQUE
Paris, 1968–1978(?) (0–19?). Didier Paschal-Lejeune.

Subtitled "Revue internationale d'expression ludique," *Cheval d'Attaque* published avant-garde art and poetry by André Breton, Henri Chopin, and others.

CHOKE
Los Angeles, 1976 (1). Barbara Burden and Jeffrey Gubbins.

A single issue of *Choke* was published in Fall 1976. The magazine's title—a reference to the air quality in Los Angeles—was a wry comment on the way West Coast artists felt suffocated by the East Coast art world. The title was printed in red block letters on the otherwise white cover of the small, horizontal-format magazine. It published original works and writings by Bruce Nauman, Chris Burden, Guy de Cointet, and Billy Adler. An editorial statement explained: "*Choke* is a magazine format providing possibilities for expression not usually available to artists. ... With few exceptions, artists have very little control over information about their work appearing in printed media. Art magazines whose subject matter is largely criticism are supported by a system of galleries and critics. Their content is determined by the art that is commercially successful, and review of a show often depends on purchase of advertising space." Rejecting paid advertising entirely, the editors pledged economic transparency, vowing to publish a cost breakdown for each issue. Unfortunately, funding ran out before they could publish a second issue.

CHORUS
Paris, 1968–1974 (1–11/12). Franck Venaille.

Chorus published poetry and art, including original silkscreens; Christian Boltanski and Annette Messager were among its contributors. Editor Franck Vanaille went on to publish *Monsieur Bloom* (1978–1981).

CHRYSALIS
Los Angeles, 1977–1980 (1–10). Kirsten Grimstad,
Arlene Raven, Sheila Levrant de Bretteville,
Ruth Iskin, and Susan Rennie.

Published by women and for women, *Chrysalis: A Magazine of Women's Culture* took its name from an 1882 essay by Angelina Grimke, who wrote: "When an insect emerges with struggles from its chrysalis state, ... this illustrates the present condition of Woman. She is just emerging from the darkness and ignorance by which she has been shrouded."[23] *Chrysalis* published interviews, essays, fiction, and poetry, as well as a resource catalog. Among the magazine's contributors were Lucy Lippard, Michelle Wallace, Linda Nochlin, Judy Chicago, Carol Duncan, Arlene Raven, and Mary Beth Edelson.

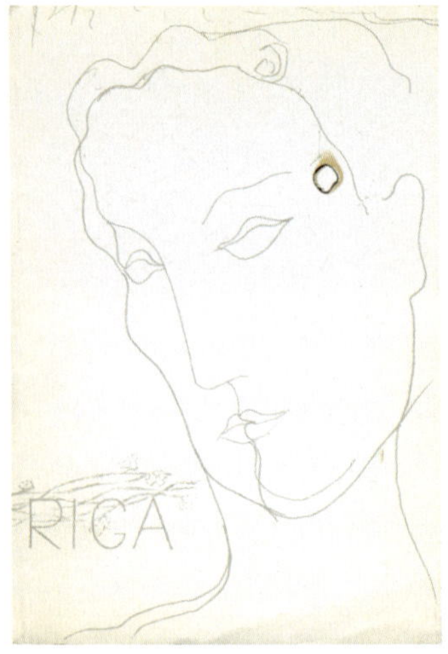

A.11

La Città di Riga, no. 1, 1976. Cover image by Jannis Kounellis. Courtesy of the artist.

CIRCOLARE SINISTRA

Torino, 1955–1956 (1–6). Editors: Italo Cremona and Mino Maccari.

Circolare Sinistra was an idiosyncratic, satirical magazine billed as "Rivista bimestrale d'Arte e Letteratura," with contributors including Yves Tanguy, Salvador Dalí, and others.

LA CITTÀ DI RIGA

Pollenza, Italy, 1976–1977 (1–2). Jannis Kounellis, Fabio Mauri, Umberto Silva, Alberto Boatto, Maurizio Calvesi, and Elisabetta Rasy.

La Città di Riga published Arte Povera artists, including Jannis Kounellis, Michelangelo Pistoletto, Giovanni Anselmo, and Alighiero Boetti, alongside American conceptualist artists such as Bruce Nauman and Vito Acconci. It focused on artists' works and writings with occasional theoretical texts, such as an essay by Giorgio Agamben in the second issue. The following editorial statement appeared in the first issue (my translation):

> *La Città di Riga*, which is not *explicitly* an art magazine, shall encompass everything art *implies*, and it shall do so by way of research rather than on preexisting foundations. It shall cover the more expansive area of the implicit and that which can be implied, using this area as a platform. It shall also eliminate, within the latitude of implications, the "diversity" of painters and writers, artists and critics. Offering these lines as a succinct evaluation as we are about to go to press, we note however that, notably through our exchanges of ideas, "diversity" remains as a tension, and hopefully as a dialectic between defined and indefinite utterances, between, perhaps, the explicit and the implicit, the closed, the built, and the open. Will such diversity pertain only to instruments? In truth, we are united by our particular trust in the poison of the ousted and the revolutionary practice of signification—and therefore by a few goals. We are now to submit the product of this first volume to a vast debate, which will be the object of our second issue.

COBRA

Brussels, Amsterdam, and Hannover, 1948 or 1949–1951 (1–10; no. 8/9 not published but appears, reproduced from proofs, in the 1980 reprint). Editor: Christian Dotremont.

Cobra: Bulletin pour la coordination des investigations artistiques was the official organ of the Cobra group. Some issues contain original lithographs by Pierre Alechinsky, Asger Jorn, Carl-Henning Pedersen, and others. Issue 4 served as the catalog for the first Cobra exhibition, the "International Exhibition of Experimental Art," in Amsterdam in 1949.

COLLECTIVE-COPY

Kassel, 1977–1985? Jürgen Olbrich.

Compiled solely out of found photocopies and test prints salvaged mainly from waste bins, this collection of found photocopies was influential on later xerographic art and publications. A supplement, titled *Test-Copy* or *Copy-Test*, was sent out with some issues.

COLLECTIVE FARM

New York, 1982–1987 (1–6). Rimma Gerlovina, Valeriy Gerlovin, Vagrich Bakhchanyan, and Victor Tupitsyn (no. 1).

Drawing on the tradition of *samizdat* art in their native Moscow, Rimma and Valeriy Gerlovin published *Collective Farm* after emigrating to New York in 1979. The title *Collective Farm* (or *Kolkhoz* in Russian) was, according to the editors, "an ironical synonym of collective effort in the former USSR."[24] Instead of pages, the magazine, which was published in an edition of 50 to 100 copies, consisted of a series of envelopes bound together, each of which contained work by a different artist. The editors described the origins of the magazine: "The idea of the design came to us when we found a huge container of boxes of new envelopes across from our loft on Spring Street in SoHo. The printing company was getting rid of its overstock. So we utilized the famous 'overproduction' in capitalist society for creative purposes."[25] *Collective Farm* included a diverse range of media, including silkscreens, monoprints with the aid of Russian color carbon paper, Xerox copies, original drawings, rubber stamps, and collages. Each of the six issues was centered on a different theme: Russian Artists (no. 1); Letters to the U.S.S.R. (no. 2); Post-Office Dinner (no. 3); Wonderkids, which included drawings by children who were inspired by famous artists who were inspired by children, e.g., an eight-year-old paints Pollock (no. 4), Five Year Plan (no. 5), and Stalin Test (no. 6). Contributors included Carlo Pittore, Vittore Baroni, Klaus Groh, Ken Friedman, Komar and Melamid, Guerrilla Art Action Group, and Tehching Hsieh.

COMMONPRESS
Eblag, Poland, and other cities, 1977–1992 (1–100). Pawel Petasz.

Commonpress was a decentralized, traveling mail art magazine launched by the Polish artist Pawel Petasz. While Petasz coordinated the issues, each was edited and printed by a different artist in a different location (among them Ulises Carrión in Amsterdam, Robin Crozier in the United Kingdom, Vittore Baroni in Italy, György and Julia Galántai in Hungary, and John Held in Texas).

CONTROL
London, 1965– (1–). Stephen Willats.

Control, founded by artist Stephen Willats, took its name from the cybernetic concept of self-determinism. It was the magazine's mission to explore this concept within the realm of art. According to the editorial statement in the inaugural issue, "*Control*'s main function will be to publish articles by the personalities which make up the new attitude in visual communication." The large-format magazine published artists' writings and projects, initially focusing on British artists who were working in the field of cybernetics, such as Willats, Roy Ascot, Peter Cook, Victor Burgin, John Latham, John Sharkey, and Logie Barrow, and later expanding to include contributors such as Dan Graham, Herve Fischer, Alan Sondheim, Mary Kelly, Jenny Holzer, Tony Cragg, Anish Kapoor, Lawrence Weiner, Martha Rosler, Christian Philipp Müller, and Thomas Hirschhorn. The stylized techno typeface of the original logo and the large purple screenprinted dot that appeared on the first cover were created by Dean Bradley of the Pushpin Agency in New York and Design Communications in the U.K. The dot represented the concept of the node—a point of connection within a communication network—and was repeated as a centerfold poster within the issue. The first several issues repeated variations on this colored shape motif: a large yellow square, a large blue dot, a large orange square, and so on.

Though *Control* was founded to explore the concept of self-determination within art, the magazine also became a vehicle of self-determination for artists themselves. Indeed, as Willats observed, the magazine held out the possibility "that the artist might himself determine the resources for his activity as extensions of the work. The magazine is intended to function as an agent of reform within the preoccupations of the art community. … The theoretical foundations of art will need to be self-determined by the artist, rather than being left, as in the past, to others. For example: the Art Historian."[26] Willats addressed the

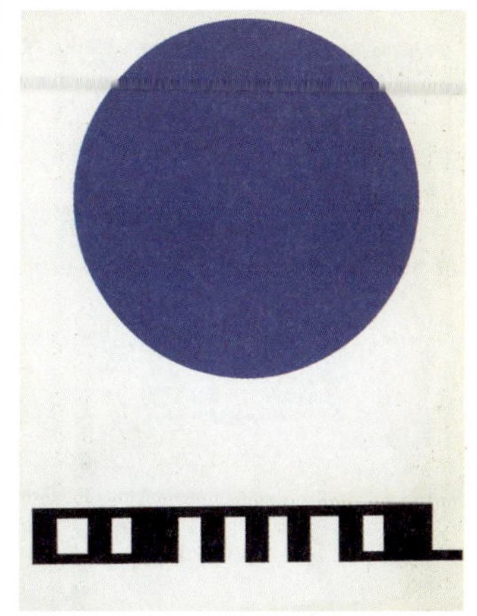

A.12
Control, no. 1, 1965. Edited by Stephen Willats. Research Library, The Getty Research Institute, Los Angeles (87-S1275).

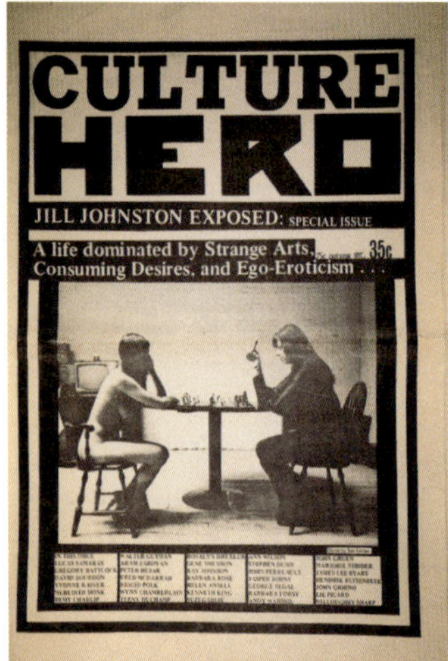

A.13

Culture Hero, no. 3, February 1970. Edited by Les Levine. Courtesy of the artist. Collection of Steven Leiber, San Francisco.

implications of artists' ability to control the discourse about their work even more explicitly in the fifth issue of the magazine, where he wrote in an editorial: "The concepts that *Control* Magazine is proposing are directly opposed to the art establishment structure as it stands at the moment."[27] The magazine was published every year or so until 1982 and has been published sporadically since. Issue 18 appeared in 2009.

COVER
New York, 1979–1983 (1–7). Judith Aminoff.

Following on the heels of magazines such as *Avalanche* and *Art-Rite*, *Cover* "covered" the downtown New York art scene in the late 1970s and early 1980s, publishing "artists' contributions in all forms to the current- and future-discourse." Aspiring to be "a catalyst in magazine format," the magazine presented interviews, artists' writings, and artists' projects, while a column called "circuits" offered news and information. Among its contributors were Thomas Lawson, Edit deAk, Walter Robinson, Liza Béar, Betsy Sussler, Sarah Charlesworth, Richard Serra, Vito Acconci, Barbara Kruger, Jenny Holzer, Richard Prince, Kathy Acker, and David Salle.

CRISS-CROSS COMMUNICATIONS / CRISS-CROSS ART COMMUNICATIONS
Boulder, Colorado: Criss-Cross Foundation, 1974–1981 (1–14).
Fred Worden, Charlie DiJulio, Clark Richert, Richard Kallweit, and others.

Criss-Cross Communications began as the mouthpiece of Criss-Cross, an artists' cooperative in Colorado that had connections with the 1960s alternative community of Drop City, Colorado. The magazine was a vehicle to support art regionally, especially the Pattern and Decoration movement, through interviews, articles, and artists' projects. Named for its connotation of "cross-fertilization by interaction," the magazine intended, according to an editorial statement in the first issue, "to support and provide exposure to the best serious art being done in a region of the United States, roughly between Chicago and Los Angeles, which is virtually isolated geographically from attention given to mainstream activity in urban centers—a vacuum inconsistent with the pervasiveness of modern communications technology. ... *Criss-Cross* intends to be a part of the ongoing process of the decentralization of the art world—a situation in which everything is possible, but only if it is worked for." One of the more idiosyncratic aspects of the magazine was that it published the editors' brainstorming sessions—lists of ideas, logistics, and the occasional non sequitur: "Who are some of the people we want to include in the next issue? ... Interview with an alien ... distribute mags in NY ... find out when to apply for next NEA grant ... Find Daniel Buren today ... no short articles ... more sex."

CRISS CROSS DOUBLE CROSS
Los Angeles, 1976 (1). Paul McCarthy.

Paul McCarthy published a single issue of the newsprint tabloid *Criss Cross Double Cross* in 1976, inviting artists living in California to contribute. The issue featured, among others, Douglas Huebler, Chris Burden, Eleanor Antin, Bruce Nauman, Allan Kaprow, Barbara Smith, and Ron Benom. McCarthy's own contribution consisted of two Max Factor perfume advertisements, appropriated with the company's permission.

CULTURE HERO
New York: 1969–1970 (1–5). Publisher: Les Levine. Editor: Claudia Dreifus.

Les Levine, who called himself a "media sculptor," published the art world tabloid *Culture Hero: A Fanzine of Stars of the Super World* in order to expose the reality of the media's role in branding the artist. A cross between Andy Warhol's *Interview* (founded the same year) and John Wilcock's countercultural paper *Other Scenes*, *Culture Hero* anticipated magazines such as *FILE* and *Avalanche* in its frank, satirical approach to promotional publicity. With a print run of 3,000 to 4,000 copies, *Culture Hero* was less about art itself than about the social world surrounding it, and announced its goal of "checking out art in fashion, commercial design, poetry, journalism, food, classical music, rock, t.v., theater, movies, and a few other things." Among those on the masthead were Claudia Dreifus, John Giorno, Anne Waldman, Gerard Melanga, Peter Schjeldahl, Lil Picard, John Perreault, and Carter Ratcliff. Other contributors included Andy Warhol, Willoughby Sharp, Van Schley, Ray Johnson, and Gregory Battcock. A column called "What's It Worth?" aimed "to give a clear picture of the prices and practices of the art market today." Meanwhile, Giorno's gossip column "Vitamin G" provided grist for the art world rumor mill with exclusive dispatches from "informed sources," such as "Anne Waldman and Lewis Warsh are on the rocks," "Does Dan Flavin have a girlfriend in Canada?" and "Is Lucy Lippard making it conceptually with Seth Siegelaub?" As one reviewer observed about *Culture Hero*, "Some of the talk is very good, some shrill and bitchy, some too deadly earnest, some just deadly, burnt out, some of it heavy-breathing sexy (both male and female). All of it is reflexive; there has surely not been a group so eager to render each other's portraits in public among American artists since the 1920s."[28] A special issue on *Village Voice* dance critic Jill Johnston entitled "Jill Johnston Exposed: A Life Dominated by Strange Arts, Consuming Desires and Ego-Eroticism" was reissued in 1970 as Levine's *Master Print*, a large-format portfolio of photo-offset lithographs, produced using a split fountain technique that evoked rainbow-colored psychedelic underground papers such as the San Francisco *Oracle*.

D.P.V. DER POLITISCHE VENTILATOR
Milan, 1973 (1). Fabio Mauri and Achille Mauri.

D.P.V. was a politically oriented Italian artists' periodical addressing issues such as the legacy of World War II, fascism, and anti-Semitism.

DADAZINE
San Francisco, 1970–1975 (approximately 10 issues). Bill Gaglione.

Dadazine focused on the Bay Area Dadaist scene, publishing mail art, stamp art, and visual poetry in a photocopied format.

DAILY BÛL
La Louvière, Belgium, 1957–1967 (1–13); 1983 (14).
André Balthazar and Pol Bury.

Daily Bûl was founded by Pol Bury and André Balthazar to document the Academy of Montbliart, which they founded in 1954. It published contributions by artists such as Dieter Roth, David Antin, Robert Filliou, Daniel Spoerri, Christo, John Cage, Jacqueline de Jong, and Dick Higgins.

DATA
Milan, 1971–1978 (1–32). Tommaso Trini.

Focusing on Arte Povera and conceptual art, *Data* published theoretical and critical writings alongside artists' documents, writings, and interviews, with texts in both Italian and English. The magazine was originally subtitled "International Art Data," then, starting with issue 3, "Practice and Theory of Art." Contributors included Tommaso Trini, Germano Celant, Michel Claura, Giovanni Anselmo, Daniel Buren, Joseph Kosuth, Hans Haacke, Seth Siegelaub, Lucy Lippard, James Coleman, Vito Acconci, Chris Burden, Douglas Crimp, and Mel Bochner.

décoll|age

Bulletin aktueller Ideen NO 1/1962

Arthur Köpcke   George Maciunas   Benjamin Patterson   Braun
Name June Paik   Pera   Wolf Vostell   La Monte Young

A.14

dé-coll/age, no. 1, 1962. Edited by
Wolf Vostell. © 2009 Estate of
Wolf Vostell / Artists Rights Society
(ARS), New York / VG Bild-Kunst,
Bonn. Research Library, The Getty
Research Institute, Los Angeles
(87-S769 no. 1).

DÉ-COLL/AGE
Cologne, 1962–1969 (1–7). Wolf Vostell.

Initially subtitled "Bulletin aktueller ideen," the journal *dé-coll/age* both espoused and enacted Wolf Vostell's concept of décollage: the construction of a new meaning through the destruction—fragmentation or displacement—of an original meaning. Promoting Fluxus and Happenings, the magazine published documentation, scores, and writings including Nam June Paik's *Zen for Head* and *Violin Solo,* Allan Kaprow's *Yard,* Dick Higgins's "Statement on Intermedia," and Alison Knowles's *The Big Book.* It also published works by Vostell, George Brecht, Claes Oldenburg, Al Hanson, George Maciunas, La Monte Young, Stanley Brouwn, Charlotte Moorman, and Jean Tinguely. The magazine encouraged readers to interact with it by including tactile objects, along with serrated, foldout, and unbound sheets and participatory projects. For example, in the first issue, Ben Patterson's *collected poem No. 35* was accompanied by the following instructions: "1. Tear along perforations, 2. shuffel [*sic*] pieces, 3. reassemble." The magazine's format varied from the spare modern design of issue 1 to the boxed format of issue 5, produced in an edition of 500, which included unbound sheets, original works, and three-dimensional objects such as a plastic hook attached to a sheet of cardboard. The final issue, number 7, was a more professionally produced book documenting Vostell's *Elektronischer de-coll/age Happening raum* (1959–1968), with an introduction by *Interfunktionen* editor Friedrich Heubach.

DIAGONAL CERO
La Plata, Argentina, 1962–1968 (1–28; number 25 never published).
Edgardo Antonio Vigo.

Founded by the artist and visual poet Edgardo Antonio Vigo (who had previously edited the magazines *WC* [1958], and *DRKW* [1960]), *Diagonal Cero* published art and concrete poetry by a group of poets who would become known as the Diagonal Cero group: Calvo Perotti, Lucio Loubet, Omar Gancedo, Néstor Reinaldo Morales, and Alberto Piergiácomi; it also published work by European poets and artists such as Eugen Gomringer, Henri Chopin, Julien Blaine, Max Bense, Francis Picabia, and Kurt Schwitters. The magazine's title was taken from the numbered streets or "diagonals" that cut across the street grid of the city of La Plata. While there is no actual street named Diagonal 0, the name suggests a kind of theoretical starting from scratch (analogous, perhaps, to the contemporaneous German Zero group and the Dutch Nul group). Describing the intermedia nature of the activities the magazine supported, Vigo voiced his desire to realize "the natural integration [that] brings us toward a substance with sounds, towards a music of plastic forms, to one poetry to see and another to hear, to a cinema filmed in real time."[29] *Diagonal Cero* manifested this goal not only in its contents but in its self-reflexive experimentation with the format of the magazine, which consisted of unbound sheets of translucent, colored, and die-cut pages, as well as woodcuts. The final issue included a blank page with a die-cut hole, through which readers were encouraged to take flight from the two-dimensional limits of the magazine and produce their own work.

DIMANCHE
Paris, 1960. Yves Klein.

Dimanche: Le Journal d'un Seul Jour (Sunday: The newspaper for only one day) was a four-page newspaper published a single time by Yves Klein on Sunday, November 27, 1960. Among other things, *Dimanche* contained Klein's well-known photomontage *Leap into the Void,* which shows the artist leaping out of a second-story window.

DOC(K)S

Ventabren, France, 1976–1985 (1–75). Julien Blaine.

Doc(k)s published concrete poetry and mail art with different issues temporarily stationed in various parts of the world, including Japan, Yugoslavia, Poland, China, and Spain.

DOCUMENTS I

New York, 1969. Art Workers' Coalition.

Published in April 1969, *Documents I* was published by the artist-activist group the Art Workers' Coalition. Produced in an ad hoc fashion, though with the expectation that there would be subsequent issues, the Xeroxed booklet contained little in the way of an editorial statement, simply announcing: "Other groups with goals similar to those of the AWC are invited to make free use of the contents of this publication for the purpose of realizing our common aims." Its cover was illustrated with a stack of four Museum of Modern Art annual passes stamped "AWC," suggesting the challenge to the museum which initially prompted the group's formation, when artists and museum officials clashed over the removal of Vassilakis Takis's scultpure from the Museum of Modern Art in January 1969. *Documents I* chronicled this event through the inclusion of numerous news clippings, a statement by Takis, correspondence between museum officials and the AWC, memos, and the "Thirteen Demands" that would define the AWC's activist program. Though a second issue of *Documents* did not materialize, the AWC subsequently published the booklet *An Open Public Hearing on the Subject: What Should Be the Program of the Art Workers Regarding Museum Reform and to Establish the Program of An Open Art Workers' Coalition.*

DOT ZERO

New York, 1966–1968 (1–5). Edited by Robert Malone.
Designed by Massimo Vignelli.

The groundbreaking design journal *Dot Zero*, edited by Robert Malone and designed by Massimo Vignelli, set out its goals in the first issue: "It is an interdisciplinary quarterly covering a network of design topics on an international scale. It will deal with the theory and practices of visual communication from varied points of reference, breaking down constantly what used to be thought of as barriers, and are now seen as points of contact." Each subsequent issue was focused on a specific theme: Corporate Identity (no. 2); Mass Communications (no. 3); World's Fairs (no. 4); and Transportation Graphics (no. 5). The magazine's title, which evoked a conceptual "starting over," referenced the Colorado town Dotsero, named after its position (0.0) as the starting point for an 1885 survey of the Colorado River. (Perhaps it was also a subtle—or even subconscious—tribute to another innovative art and design magazine, likewise named after a Colorado town: *Aspen.*) In the first issue Herbert Bayer praised *Dot Zero* for its aspiration "to assume an unattached attitude by starting from naught and freeing itself from the impediments of taking sides." In keeping with its editorial mission, the magazine, which was sponsored by the paper company Finch Pruyn, was elegantly designed and printed with a spare modernist layout and embossed covers. It had a circulation of 8,000 and published contributors such as Mildred Constantine, Marshall McLuhan, Reyner Banham, Umberto Eco, Ivan Chermayeff, John Szarkowski, and John Kenneth Galbraith.

THE DUMB OX
Los Angeles, 1976–1980 (1–10/11). James Hugunin, Leslie Hugunin,
Theron Kelley, and Mary Kenon Breazeale. Guest editors:
Lew Thomas, Allan Kaprow, and Paul McCarthy.

The Dumb Ox, "an intermittently published paper of the arts," was founded by James Hugunin and Theron Kelley. Fresh out of graduate school, the two editors were "very dissatisfied with the Los Angeles art/photography scene and wanted to put forth an alternative critical voice that would also provide exposure for many artists we felt were being marginalized (especially conceptually oriented artists) by the art establishment in LA."[30] The magazine's title referred to the nickname of St. Thomas Aquinas, whose large, slow demeanor belied his genius (it was also a nod to Michael Andre's important art and poetry journal *Unmuzzled Ox*, discussed below). The editors wrote in the first issue, "Why *The Dumb Ox*? We have no axe to grind, only an ox to feed. We are looking for contributions from all varieties of talents. Send us articles and/or artworks so we may satisfy the hunger of our ravenous beast. *The Dumb Ox* enjoys grazing on a myriad of disciplines, loves to ruminate on problems tangential to the various arts. He has been known to severely gore all the ineptitudes found in the status quo!" The magazine published articles, reviews, and interviews, and maintained a humorous, irreverent tone; when the curator Maurice Tuchman was too busy to grant an interview, the editors published a "Do-It-Yourself Interview" consisting of the questions they had wanted to ask him with spaces where readers could fill in their own answers. *The Dumb Ox*, which had a print run of 1,500 at its peak, began as a tabloid and changed to a magazine format with issue 4. Notable issues included no. 4 on artists' books and no. 10/11, which was guest-edited and designed by Paul McCarthy and Allan Kaprow, with contributions from McCarthy, Kaprow, Max Neuhaus, Carolee Schneemann, Wolf Vostell, Michael Kirby, Otto Muehl, Mierle Laderman Ukeles, and Linda Burnham.

THE DUPLEX PLANET
Brookline, Massachusetts, 1979– (1–). David Greenberger.

Artist David Greenberger started *The Duplex Planet* while working as activities director at the Duplex Nursing Home in Brookline, Massachusetts. The small, newsletter-like publication compiled quotes from residents on a variety of topics from the mundane to the occult, including parking tickets, embarrassment, sleep, life on other planets, and vampires. According to Greenberger, *The Duplex Planet* is "an ongoing work designed to portray a wide variety of real characters who are old or in decline." While often humorous, the magazine is not ironic but decidedly sincere in its portrayal of old age, seeking "to offer a range of characters who are already old, so that we can get to know them as they are in the present, without celebrating or mourning who they were before."[31]

EAR
San Francisco and New York, 1973–1991 (no. 1–vol. 16, no. 2).
Published by the New Wilderness Foundation from 1976 to 1987.
Anne Kish, Charles Shere, and Beth Anderson.

Ear: A Magazine for New Music was founded in 1973 in San Francisco by Anne Kish and Charles Shere as an alternative tabloid for musicians. Beth Anderson took over as editor soon after; when she moved to New York in 1975, she published an East Coast edition of the magazine, which was taken over by the New Wilderness Foundation in 1976. From 1973 until the early 1980s a West Coast and an East Coast edition of *Ear* existed, which were at times referred to as *Ear Magazine West* and *Ear Magazine East*. The following editorial statement appeared in the first issue:

What is *Ear*? *Ear* is a new place to read about what's happening on the music front. What the MUSICIANS are saying about their jobs; RECTIFIED REVIEWS of past events: PROGRAM HANDICAPS for the next few weeks. Articles for the layman and for the musician. WHY *EAR*? Currently appearing publications ignore too much of the music scene. Reviews of the musical establishment aren't enough. What about the musical establishment and TV, what about benefit concerts, what about the small recitals of new music, of young artists? What about the real problems facing musicians, composers, audiences? What good are boards of directors, critics, publicists? The answers aren't inside. But maybe we can make a start towards finding them.

EAST VILLAGE EYE
New York, 1979–1987 (1–72). Leonard Abrams.

With a colored tabloid format that was equally indebted to underground papers of the 1960s and to the crude, clashing aesthetic of punk, *East Village Eye* covered the interdisciplinary downtown arts scene in the 1980s, documenting the crossover between art and new subcultural forms such as hip-hop, break dancing, and graffiti. An editorial note in the second issue announced: "*East Village Eye* is a new newspaper for culture. Enjoying a mutually parasitic relationship with the East Village and surrounding areas, the *Eye* serves and guides its readership and community, and promotes the new mutations of positivist futurism, put forth in the watchwords: 'It's all true.' As it becomes clear the future of Western culture is in the hands of artists, the influx of creators from all parts of the world to this vicinity takes on new significance." According to publisher Leonard Abrams, "my idea was to create a community in print, a free space, a liberated zone."[32] To this end, the publication encouraged experimentation, both with genres of writing, and with the format of the magazine itself. Former *Art-Rite* editor Walter Robinson served as the *Eye*'s art editor, encouraging artists such as Futura 2000, Josef Nechvatal, and Jane Dickson to design covers and centerfold posters. The actress Cookie Mueller doled out medical advice in her column "Dr. Mueller." Richard Hell chronicled the punk movement in his "Slum Journal." Even *Avalanche* publisher Willoughby Sharp wrote a column, "The Electronic Eye," on computers and new media. Others who contributed to or were featured in the paper included David Wojnarowicz, Christof Kohlhofer (who served as art director), Barbara Kruger, Jenny Holzer, Diamanda Galas, and Steven Parrino. The *East Village Eye* also distributed promotional EPs for Shake Records (including Richard Hell's "Time" and "Don't Die") and cassettes for Neil Cooper's cassette-only label, Reachout International Records (ROIR).

E.A.T. NEWS
New York: Experiments in Art and Technology,
1967–1968 (vol. 1, no. 1–vol. 2, no. 1).
Editor: Julie Martin.

E.A.T. News was the newsletter of Experiments in Art and Technology, Inc. (E.A.T.), which arose from the collaboration between artists and engineers that resulted in "9 Evenings of Theater and Engineering" in New York in October 1966. Consisting of four 8½-by-11-inch sheets of paper stapled together, the publication reported on E.A.T. activities, including mission statements and diagrams of the organization's goals and structure, and minutes from meetings. It also distributed a questionnaire through which the organization hoped to match up artists and engineers. Logistical, matter-of-fact information was published alongside descriptions and documents of "9 Evenings" and Robert Rauschenberg and Billy Klüver's statement about E.A.T. *E.A.T. News* was continued by *Techne*.

EAU DE COLOGNE
Cologne, 1985–1993 (1–3). Monica Sprüth.

Eau de Cologne was published by the Cologne art dealer Monica Sprüth to promote her gallery program and especially to champion women artists and redress the gender imbalance within the art world. The first two issues of the magazine coincided with the first two in a series of three all-women exhibitions (also titled "Eau de Cologne") that took place at the Monica Sprüth Gallery between 1985 and 1993. The magazine published artworks, interviews, and writings by artists in the shows, including Cindy Sherman, Barbara Kruger, Rosemarie Trockel, Jenny Holzer, Ina Barfuss, Anne Loch, Louise Lawler, Katharina Fritsch, Gretchen Bender, Nancy Dwyer, Barbara Bloom, and Andrea Fraser. Interviews with notable female editors, curators, and gallerists, such as Ingrid Sischy, Ileana Sonnabend, Edit deAk, Mary Jane Jacob, and Rosetta Brooks, were also included. Recalling various earlier artists' magazines, from *Azimuth* to *Avalanche* to *Interfunktionen* (and not least Warhol's *Interview*, which it explicitly cited in its format and design), *Eau de Cologne* appropriated these models specifically to promote women artists. The third and final issue was guest-edited by the American art historian Karen Marta (then editor of *Parkett*) and the German artist Jutta Koether, and signaled a shift in format and intention, manifesting a more self-reflexive and less essentializing investigation of gender categories and subjectivities.

Further reading: Johanna Burton, "A Will to Representation: *Eau de Cologne*, 1985–1993," in Rhea Anastas and Michael Brenson, eds., *Witness to Her Art* (New York: Bard College Center for Curatorial Studies, 2006).

EDDA
Brussells, 1958–1964 (1–5). Jaques Lacomblez.

Edda: Cahier international de documentation sur la poésie et l'art d'avant-garde published contributions by Marcel Broodthaers, Edouard Jaquer, Raoul Hausmann, Wilfredo Lam, and others.

EDITION AFTER HAND.
Ringkobing, Denmark 1973–1985 (1–25).
Henry Garden and Peter Laugesen.

This Danish artists' periodical was published in various formats, from folders containing unbound texts and works to pamphlets.

EFFECTS
New York, 1983–1986 (1–3). Tricia Collins and Richard Milazzo.

Effects: Magazine for New Art Theory was published by Collins & Milazzo, the collective signature used by curators Tricia Collins and Richard Milazzo. The idea for the magazine emerged out of a series of informal gatherings of artists at their apartment on Second Avenue and Saint Mark's Place in the heart of the East Village gallery scene. Peter Nagy and Alan Belcher, who ran Nature Morte gallery, did typesetting and layout, and contributors included David Salle, Robert Longo, Barbara Kruger, Richard Prince, Jack Goldstein, Ross Bleckner, Allan McCollum, Louise Lawler, James Welling, and Sarah Charlesworth.

EPHEMERA
Amsterdam: 1977–1978 (1–12). Ulises Carrión.

This mail art magazine was published by the Mexican expatriate artist Ulises Carrión, who founded Other Books & So, an important bookstore and distribution center for artists' publications in Amsterdam.

L'ESPERIENZA MODERNA
Rome, 1957–1959 (1–5). Achille Perilli.

L'Esperienza Moderna: Rivista di cultura contemporanea was considered to be the Italian counterpart to *Phases*.

EXTENSIONS
New York: 1968–1974 (1–8). Suzanne Zavrian and Joachim Neugroschel.

Suzanne Zavrian and Joachim Neugroschel named their experimental poetry magazine *Extensions* after Marshall McLuhan's 1964 book *Understanding Media: Extensions of Man*. They were interested in how the magazine itself was a medium capable of extending language into other realms. The first issue of *Extensions* published poetry by Vito Acconci, conceptual art by Dan Graham, and photographs of student graffiti on the walls of the Sorbonne during the uprisings of May 1968. The digest-sized magazine, with a cardstock cover and a no-frills feeling, published poetry by John Perreault, Hannah Weiner, Richard Kostelanetz, Dianne Di Prima, Shusaku Arakawa, Madeline Gins, and Paul Celan, as well as contributions from Norway, Yugoslavia, France, Italy, Brazil, Germany, Austria, Japan, and Switzerland. The final issue was largely devoted to a public art piece by the Brazilian designer Aloisio Magalhães accompanied by an essay by Max Bense.

EXTRA
Cologne, 1974–1975 (1–5). Werner Lippert.

Coming on the heels of magazines such as *Interfunktionen* and *Avalanche*, *Extra* published artists' writings and contributions, focusing on conceptual art from around the world. Hans Haacke wrote about the censorship of his *Manet-PROJECT '74*; Daniel Buren contributed an in situ work: two pages with vertical yellow stripes printed on vellum; Sol LeWitt provided *Drawings* (1974); and Hanne Darboven contributed "Manuscript for a Film." Other contributors included Lynda Benglis, Terry Atkinson, Robert Barry, Joseph Kosuth, Duane Michals, Art & Language, Bernar Venet, and Karl Blossfeld. Issue 4 (April 1975) was devoted to documenting the works of David Askevold.

FACTOTUM ART
Calaone-Baone, Italy, 1977–1979 (1–7).
Paul de Vree and Sarenco.

Factotum Art published visual poetry, mail art, and Fluxus activities.

FANDANGOS
Maastrict, 1971–1987. Raul Marroquin.

Fandangos, founded by the Columbian artist Raul Marroquin in 1971, evolved from a large bulletin board in the artist's studio at the Jan van Eijck Akademie, where he was an M.F.A. student at the time. Using pushpins, he would post photographs, texts, drawings, and newspaper clippings; he also invited fellow students, visiting lecturers, and art historians to post to the board. The printed form of *Fandangos* began as a large-format silkscreened publication that resembled a bulletin board in its layout. The title, which is the name of a type of flamenco dance, was also used as slang in Marroquin's native Bogota to describe a wild party; he would occasionally play with variations of the name, including *Phandangos*, *Vandangos*, and *Fundangos*. By the fourth issue, the magazine had evolved into a tabloid newspaper format printed on offset; it changed again in 1973, to a magazine format. Most issues incorporated hand-pasted collages, stencils, rubber stamps, or hand coloring, as well as postcards and foldout pages, and editions generally ranged from 1,000 to 3,000 copies per issue. After

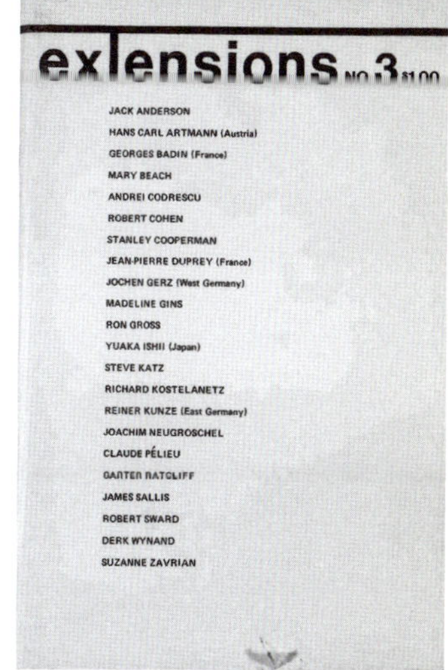

A.15
Extensions, no. 3, 1969. Courtesy of Suzanne Ostro.

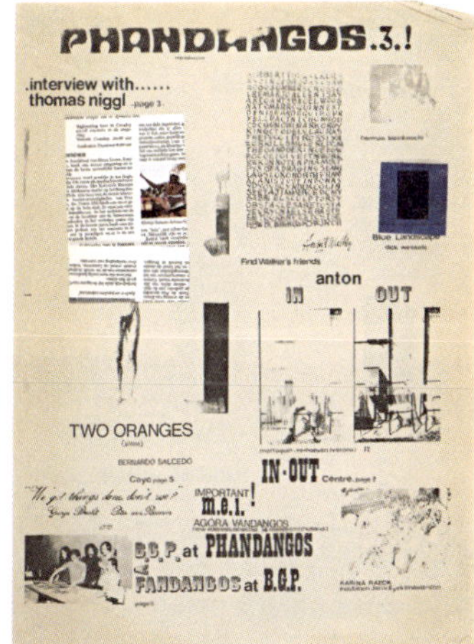

A.16
Fandangos, no. 3, 1974. Courtesy of Raul Marroquin. Research Library, The Getty Research Institute, Los Angeles (89-S191 no. 3).

1974 *Fandangos* was published in a wide array of formats. Among its contributors were Vito Acconci, Marina Abramović, Laurie Anderson, Felipe Ehrenberg, Philip Glass, General Idea, Nam June Paik, and Dieter Roth.

FILE
Toronto, 1972–1989 (vol. 1, no. 1–no. 28).
General Idea (AA Bronson, Felix Partz, and Jorge Zontal).
See chapter 6.

FILE magazine—or megazine, as it was frequently called—was published by the Canadian collective General Idea. It served as a vehicle for the group's eclectic, evolving interests and activities, from the Canadian mail art scene to elaborate preparations for a campy "fake" beauty contest known as the 1984 Miss General Idea Pageant, to new wave and punk music. Appropriating *Life* magazine's red and white logo—an act of cultural piracy for which Time Inc. later threatened to sue—the magazine denaturalized dominant cultural categories of gender, class, beauty, and artistic production—and questioned the role of the media in upholding such categories.

Facsimile reprint: General Idea, *FILE Megazine.* Ed. Beatrix Ruf. Zurich: JRP Ringier, 2008.

FILM CULTURE
New York, 1955–1999 (1–80). Jonas Mekas and Adolfas Mekas.

The seminal avant-garde cinema magazine *Film Culture* was founded by Jonas Mekas and his brother Adolfas. Fluxus artist and fellow Lithuanian George Maciunas helped to do the layout and typography for the magazine, designing the following issues completely: 14–18, 30, and 43–45.[33] *Film Culture* helped to define new American cinema, publishing important essays on film history and theory such as P. Adams Sitney's "Some Comments on Structural Film" and Stan Brakhage's "Metaphors on Vision."

THE FLUE
New York: Franklin Furnace, 1980–1989 (vol. 1, no. 1–vol. 6, no. 2).
Martha Wilson.

The Flue was the newsletter of the Franklin Furnace, founded by Martha Wilson in 1976 as an archive and alternative space devoted to artists' books. As Wilson wrote, "If 'Furnace' connotes an organization dedicated to preserving ephemeral art, *Flue* suggests the ephemeral art itself." The tabloid-format magazine documented activities and exhibitions at the Franklin Furnace, published information and articles on artists' books, and also served as an artists' publication in its own right, with issues that were designed by various artists including Louise Lawler, Barbara Kruger, and Sherrie Levine.

FLUXUS
Fluxus 1 (circa 1964–1979) / *Flux Year Box 2* (1966–1968/1976) / *Fluxpack 3* (1973–1975). New York. George Maciunas.

George Maciunas initially conceived of the word "fluxus" as the name of a publication, and publishing remained central to the diverse activities associated with the Fluxus movement.[34] After working with La Monte Young on the first and only issue of *An Anthology* (1963), Maciunas was eager to produce a second issue. This evolved into an unorthodox serialized publication containing printed matter alongside various kinds of multiples and objects. Seven issues were mapped out, but only three materialized: *Fluxus 1, Flux Year Box 2*, and *Fluxpack 3. Fluxus 1* consisted of manila envelopes containing loose leaves, texts, images, and objects—including a rubber glove, a cocktail napkin, stamps, and mirrors—bolted together with three steel screws, and housed in a wooden box that also served as its shipping crate. Though Maciunas printed some portions of it in 1962, the first issue was not assembled until 1964, and various permutations would continue to be produced until around 1979, with a changing roster of contributors, including Maciunas, George Brecht, Christo, Willem de Ridder, Alison Knowles, Shigeko Kubota, Jackson Mac Low, Yoko Ono, Benjamin Patterson, Ben Vautier, Emmett Williams, and La Monte Young. It is estimated that Maciunas put together about 100 copies in New York and that de Ridder also assembled around 100 copies in Amsterdam. *Fluxus Year Box 2* consisted of flip books and 8-millimeter film loops, a handheld viewer, printed works, and scores contained in a box. It was planned as an edition of 100 copies, of which only 50 were assembled. Maciunas proposed to make 1,000 copies of *Fluxpack 3* (1973–1975), but only a handful of copies, consisting of works on vinyl and paper in poster tubes, were assembled. In addition to this serial publication, Maciunas created numerous other publications, including the *Fluxus Preview Review*, the *Fluxcabinet*, the *Flux Post Kit*, fluxfilms, and various fluxkits. He also produced *V TRE*, and designed *Film Culture*.

FORM
Cambridge, England, 1966–1968 (1–10). Philip Steadman, Mike Weaver, and Stephen Bann.

Published by the architect Philip Steadman, the art historian Mike Weaver, and the translator and poet Stephen Bann, *Form: A Quarterly Magazine of the Arts* aimed "to publish and provoke discussion of the relations of form to structure in the work of art, and of correspondence between the arts." The magazine published writings (many of which were translated here for the first time) and works of art by Theo van Doesburg, Kurt Schwitters, Guillaume Apollinaire, Aleksandr Rodchenko, Gertrude Stein, William Carlos Williams, Roland Barthes, Frank Popper, Gillo Dorfles, and Ian Hamilton Finlay. *Form* reevaluated earlier twentieth-century avant-garde movements, such as de Stijl, Bauhaus, and Dada, at the very moment that these practices were becoming historical—a fact made poignant in the ninth issue by Hans Richter's obituary of Marcel Duchamp. Among the practices *Form* emphasized and reassessed was the artists' magazine itself. A column called "Great Little Magazines" surveyed publications such as *Blues, G, De Stijl, Die Form, Mecano, LEF, Secession, Ray,* and *Kulchur*, providing detailed descriptions, translated excerpts, author indexes, and recommended library holdings. *Form* clearly understood itself in relationship to this lineage, and the very act of publishing the magazine was a way to retrieve for current practice the significance of the periodical in the historical avant-garde. Designed by Steadman, the magazine announced its modernist agenda through its square format and Helvetica font, clearly rooted in Swiss design. Steadman initially intended to keep publishing the magazine until the issues, when stacked, would produce a perfect cube.

THE FOX
New York, 1975–1976 (1–3). Sarah Charlesworth, Michael Corris, Preston Heller, Joseph Kosuth, Andrew Menard, Mel Ramsden, and Ian Burn.

The Fox was started by several members of the New York faction of Art & Language, who announced in the first issue: "It is the purpose of our journal to try to establish some kind of community practice. Those who are interested, curious, or have something to add (be it pro or con) to the editorial thrust … the revaluation of ideology … of this first issue are encouraged, even urged, to contribute to following issues." The magazine's title was an allusion to a line by the Greek poet Archilochus ("the fox knows many things, but the hedgehog knows one big thing"), which, as the philosopher Isaiah Berlin argued in a 1953 essay, suggests two forms of knowledge: one systematic and narrow and the other more broad and varied. Funded by NEA and NYSCA grants and distributed by the New York bookseller Jaap Reitman,

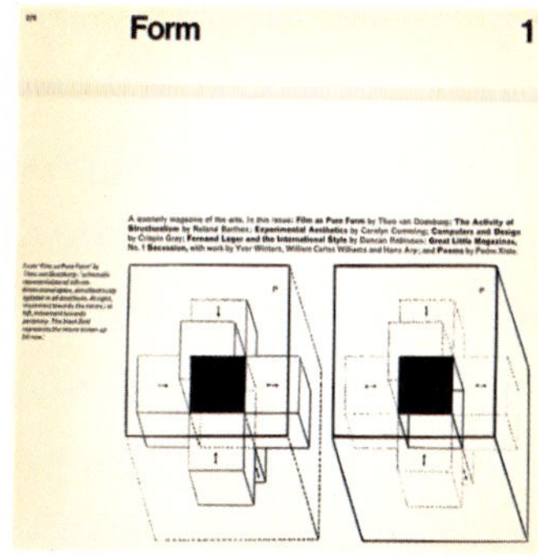

A.17

Form, no. 1, 1966. Drawing by Theo van Doesburg. Research Library, The Getty Research Institute, Los Angeles (86-S1525 no. 1).

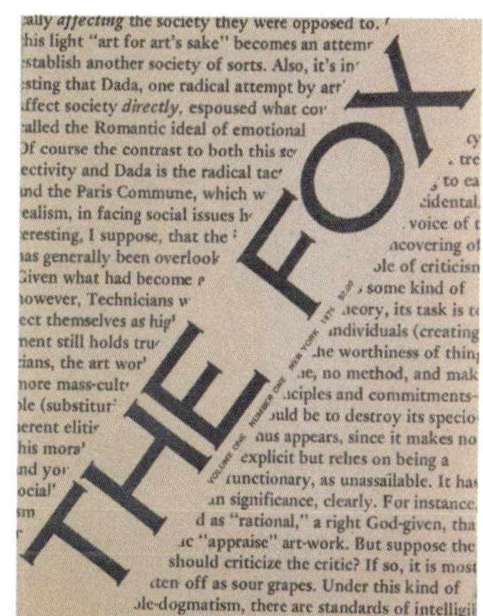

A.18

The Fox, no. 1, 1975. Courtesy of Sarah Charlesworth.

The Fox arose out of "frustration … with the extremely oppressive nature of a very elitist and rather irrelevant (in terms of effective practice) theoretical debating society which was Art & Language," according to Sarah Charlesworth's "Memo for *The Fox*" in issue 2.

Printed on newsprint with uncoated cardboard covers, the short-lived magazine had a self-consciously crude, unfinished look that corresponded to its Marxist agenda. In addition to polemical articles by the editors, *The Fox* published papers developed out of the Artists Meeting for Cultural Change and other politically oriented articles and criticism. Adrian Piper contributed "To Art (Reg. Intrans. v.)," a philosophical and semantic investigation of the act of making art (no.1). In the second issue, Lizzie Borden took the journal to task for burying practical problems in "heavy theory," in her article "Dear *Fox*." Martha Rosler wrote "Review under the Rug," a critical discussion of art and craft (no. 3). *The Fox* was poorly received by Art & Language in England, as witnessed by the derisive review published in *Art-Language* 3, no. 2. In the third and final issue of *The Fox*, a transcript of discussions entitled "The Lumpen-Headache" aired some of the tensions between the two groups, and chronicled the developing discord within the American faction of Art & Language itself— problems that would soon cause the American group to disband, and *The Fox* to end. *Art-Language* 3, no. 4 (October 1977), sarcastically designated as "The Fox 4," recounted this history from the perspective of the English group. Subsequently, the magazine *Red-Herring* was published by several of the former editors of *The Fox*.

FRAMEWORKS
London, 1972–1973 (vol. 1, no. 1–vol. 1, no. 2).
Editor: Coston Sanger. Contributing editors:
Michael Baldwin and John Stetzaker.

In *Frameworks* 1, no. 2, the editors explained: "The policy of *Frameworks* journal is to publish the theoretical work of artists together with contributions by philosophers and others whose work includes a study of art in a variety of conceptual frameworks."

FUCK YOU
New York, 1962–1965 (1–13). Ed Sanders.

Fuck You: A Magazine of the Arts was a poetry journal published by Ed Sanders, a poet, peace activist, and member of the band The Fugs. Printed on a hand-cranked mimeograph machine in an edition of 500 copies which Sanders distributed for free, the magazine included contributions by Tuli Kupferberg, Allen Ginsberg, Frank O'Hara, Diane Di Prima, William Burroughs, Robert Creeley, Michael McClure, Ted Berrigan, Joe Brainard, and Andy Warhol.

FUTURA
Stuttgart, 1965–1968 (1–26). Hansjörg Mayer.

Each issue of this concrete poetry broadsheet, consisting of a single sheet of folded paper, was devoted to the work of a single artist or poet, including Max Bense, Ian Hamilton Finlay, Augusto de Campos, Edward Lucie Smith, Dieter Roth, and Emmett Williams.

GEIGER
Torino, 1967–1982 (1–9); 1996 (10). Maurizio Spatola and Adriano Spatola.

This visual poetry periodical, published in a limited edition of 300 copies, contained embossed and die-cut pages and original works of art. Contributors included Marina Abramović, Ian Hamilton Finlay, Dick Higgins, and Wolf Vostell.

IL GESTO
Milan, 1955–1958.

Il Gesto was the journal of the group Movimento Arte Nucleare. Both Enrico Castellani and Piero Manzoni worked on *Il Gesto* before founding *Azimuth*.

GORGONA
Zagreb, 1961–1966 (1–11). Editor: Josip Vaništa.

The "anti-magazine" *Gorgona,* published by the Zagreb-based Gorgona group between 1961 and 1966, manifested a new understanding of the magazine as an artistic medium, presciently anticipating conceptual art's later investigations. Nearly a decade before the American critic Lucy Lippard coined the term "dematerialization," the Gorgona group, loosely associated with the New Tendencies movement, as well as the Zero and Azimuth artists, developed a non-object-based practice, claiming, "Gorgona is for the absolute ephemeral in art. Gorgona does not seek results or works in art."[35] The magazine, *Gorgona*, published in an edition of 65 to 300, remains the most important vestige of the group's activities, not only as an artistic document, but as itself a work of art that self-reflexively explores the magazine's serialized, sequential, reproducible form. Josip Vaništa, who edited the magazine, designed the first issue, which consisted of the same photograph of a shop window in Zagreb repeated nine times on each page of the magazine—an image Vaništa described as follows:

> In the winter of 1960 I passed a second-hand shop in Vlaška Street, facing the Studio Cinema, and in the shop window I saw an unknown object: a vertical board connecting four horizontal ones. A meaningless spatial structure offered for sale. The winter light fell perpendicular on the shop window and the object cast its shadow on the pale background. I stopped, fascinated, probably because the scene I was looking at was so similar to the still lives I had painted in the fifties, in which I had separated the interior from the exterior by vertical dividing lines. I asked my friend Pavao Cajzek for help, and next morning we photographed the shop window. I decided to repeat the photograph nine times, made a model, had it printed, and the first number of *Gorgona* appeared in Holy Week 1961. ... This was the beginning of *Gorgona* magazine.[36]

Gorgona magazine was thus established as a medium—like the shop window itself—with the capacity to frame the fleeting, everyday experiences of modern life, while wresting from these commodified forms new kinds of aesthetic meaning. Subsequent issues included Julije Knifer's no. 2, a "continous meander" drawing in which the pages of the magazine, instead of being bound in sequence, were connected to produce an unbroken circle; Ivan Kožarić's no. 5, consisting of photographs of the front and back of his sculpture; and Vaništa's no. 6, a reproduction of the *Mona Lisa*, which he described as "the most senseless thing to print in a magazine because reproducing the *Mona Lisa* is the same thing as leaving the page blank"[37]—an idea he would subsequently realize in issue 10, which consisted of completely empty pages. Vaništa's final issue, no. 11, opened to reveal a photograph of the cover—an emblem of the magazine's self-reflexivity. Other issues were designed by Marijan Jevšovar (no. 3), Victor Vasarely (no. 4), Miljenko Horvat (no. 7), Harold Pinter (no. 8), and Dieter Roth (no. 9). Additionally, several unrealized proposals for the magazine exist: Piero Manzoni wanted to produce an issue with his fingerprints stamped down the middle of each page, and Ivo Gattin proposed sealing sixteen pages together with wax, to be ripped apart by the reader. In what was perhaps the ultimate expression of the "anti-magazine," Dimitrije Bašičević (Mangelos) designated an issue that was not to be published.

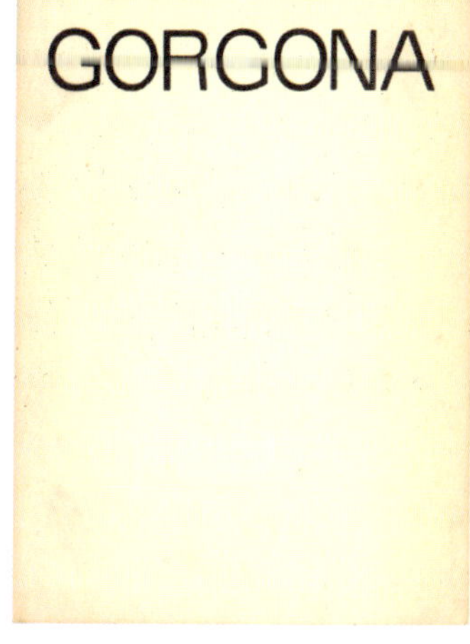

A.19

Gorgona, no. 9, 1966. Edited by Josip Vaništa. Issue by Dieter Rot. Collection of Roger Conover.

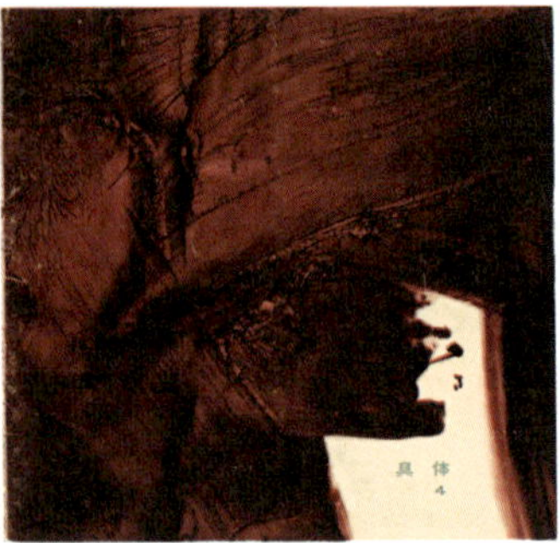

A.20

Gutai, no. 4, 1956. Special Edition of the First Gutai Art Exhibition, 1955. Shows part of work by Kazuo Syiraga. Edited by Syozo Shimamoto and Jiro Yoshihara. Courtesy of the Ashiya City Museum of Art and History. Research Library, The Getty Research Institute, Los Angeles (2595-157 no. 4).

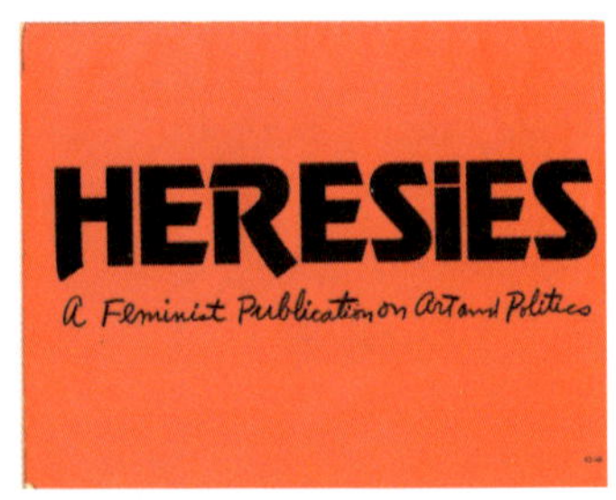

A.21

Heresies, no. 1, January 1977. Courtesy of Joan Braderman.

GUTAI

Nishinomiya, Japan, 1955–1965 (1–14; nos. 10 and 13 were not published). Syozo Shimamoto and Jiro Yoshihara.

The self-published journal *Gutai* (translated as "concreteness") documented the highly performative and process-based art of the Japanese Gutai group, which was influenced by Hans Namuth's photographs of Jackson Pollock painting. In the first issue—a square, slender volume, which contained black-and-white reproductions of several Gutai works—an editorial statement appeared in both Japanese and the following English translation:

> This pamphlet is made by seventeen modern artists who are living between Osaka and Kobe of Japan, to ask their works to the world. Each of them has spent their expences and by borrowing a printing machine they have printed their works by their own hands. Many of them are the twenty agers of young artists. They have spared the time and by encouraging each other this pamphlet has been completed. Therefore, this may be said not a skillful and a beautiful printing, or there maybe some dirts of their fingers seen on the papers. Moreover, they have experienced that by using an incomplete machine they had to spent more efforts and was a very difficult work by amateur techniques. But these people are firmly believing that now is the chance to call oversea people's deep impression through their each works.

Subsequent issues grew more professional, documenting in black and white, or occasionally in color plates, the Gutai exhibitions and works such as Kazuo Shiraga's "foot paintings" and his *Challenge to the Mud* (1955), in which he flung himself into a pile of mud, and Saburo Murakami's *Passage* (1956), in which the artist plowed through a row of paper screens.

HERESIES

1977–1993 (1–27). Edited by the Heresies Collective: Patsy Beckert, Joan Braderman, Mary Beth Edelson, Harmony Hammond, Elizabeth Hess, Joyce Kozloff, Arlene Ladden, Lucy Lippard, Mary Miss, Marty Pottenger, Miriam Shapiro, Joan Snyder, Elke Solomon, Pat Steir, May Stevens, Michelle Stuart, Susana Torre, Elizabeth Weatherford, Sally Webster, and Nina Yankowitz.

Heresies: A Feminist Publication on Art and Politics was founded by the Heresies Collective as "an idea-oriented journal devoted to the examination of art and politics from a feminist perspective," according to an editorial statement in the first issue. The magazine's bright red cover, with its title printed horizontally in black, seemed to signal the urgency of its mission. Its title was inspired by Susan Sontag's phrase: "New truths begin as heresies." The editors wrote, "We believe that what is commonly called art can have a political impact, and that in the making of art and of all cultural artifacts our identities of women play a distinct role. We hope that *Heresies* will stimulate dialogue around radical political and esthetic theory, encourage the writing of the history of *femina sapiens*, and generate new creative energies among women." Among other things, *Heresies*, which carried few advertisements, and those mainly for other feminist publications such as *Off Our Backs* and *Chrysalis*, sought to challenge the art market and the promotional aspect of criticism: "As a step toward the demystification of art, we reject the standard relationship of criticism to art within the present system, which has often become the relationship of advertiser to product. We will not advertise a new set of genius-products just because they are made by women." The editors insisted that text and image, artists and critics, occupy equal footing: "As material for the first issue came to us, we found that no hard line could be drawn between texts and visual material. There are, therefore, few 'illustrations' here, but independent statements expressed visually, verbally, or in combination, sharing the same power and the same intent, and indicating that word and image can be equal ingredients in politically effective art." Members of the Heresies Collective took turns editing the magazine; other contributors included Martha Rosler, Carol Duncan, Nancy Spero, Eva Cockcroft, Louise Bourgeois, Marisol, Frida Kahlo, Yvonne Rainer, and Howardena Pindell.

HEXÁGONO
La Plata, Argentina, 1971–1975. Edgardo Antonio Vigo.

Like Vigo's previous magazine, *Diagonal Cero, Hexágono* (sometimes referred to as *Hexágono '71*) published visual poetry and art. *Hexágono* registered the increasingly fraught political situation in Argentina during the 1970s, announcing itself as "the most dangerous" magazine. One issue was self-censored, sealed by a paper band that prevented it from being opened.

HIGH PERFORMANCE
Los Angeles, 1978–1997 (1–76). Linda Frye Burnham.

A crucial archive of performance art, *High Performance* was founded to foster performance art as its own medium, apart from dance, theater, and music. At the magazine's core was a section known as the "Artists' Chronicle," which consisted of documentation of specific performances with photographs and artists' texts. Issued quarterly, the magazine also published interviews, reviews, articles, and occasional fiction and poetry. Until 1982 *High Performance* had an open submissions policy. It focused especially on Los Angeles-based artists, with contributors including Susan Lacy, Linda Montano, Carolee Schneemann, Rachel Rosenthal, the feminist collective The Lesbian Art Project, Paul McCarthy, and Chris Burden. When the magazine's printer refused to print issue 8 because it contained an explicit photograph of oral sex submitted by The Lesbian Art Project, Burnham found a new printer and defiantly repeated the image six times in the issue.

Further reading: Jenni Sorkin, "Envisioning *High Performance*," *Art Journal*, Summer 2003.

L'HUMIDITÉ
Paris, 1970–1977 (1–24). Jean-François Bory, Janusz Chodorowicz, Georges Unglik, and Leonardo Numez.

Though it was largely devoted to visual poetry, *L'Humidité* published contributions by artists including John Cage, Vito Acconci, Christian Boltanski, and Gina Pane.

IAC INFO / INTERNATIONAL ARTISTS COOPERATION INFO
Edewecht, Germany, 1972–1977. Klaus Groh.

Consisting of a single sheet of paper folded in half, *IAC Info* served as a point of exchange between mail artists internationally and especially between those in Eastern and Western Europe, publishing artists' address lists, news, and calls for participation by mail artists and mail art groups.

IMAGE NATION
Toronto: Coach House Press, 1969–1982 (1–26). Fletcher Starbuck and David Hlynsky.

The experimental photography magazine *Image Nation* began as a biweekly literary magazine and newsletter for the radical free university Rochdale College. Fletcher Starbuck edited several issues of the magazine before David Hlynsky took over with issue 12 in 1973. Hlynsky, who moved to Toronto from the United States in 1971 out of solidarity with draft resistors, radically expanded its editorial criteria, focusing on emerging Canadian artists

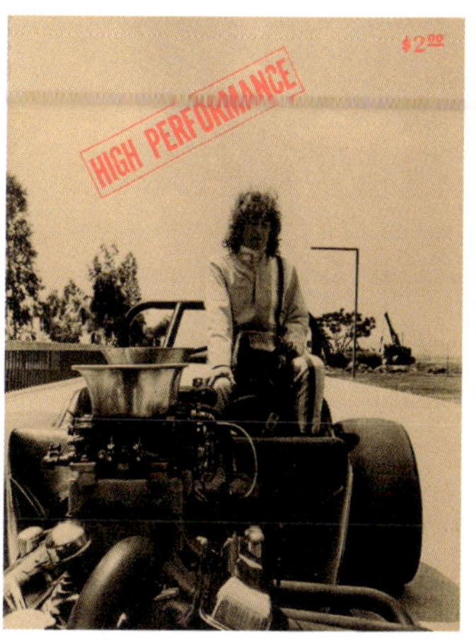

A.22
High Performance, no. 1, 1978.
Courtesy of Linda Burnham.

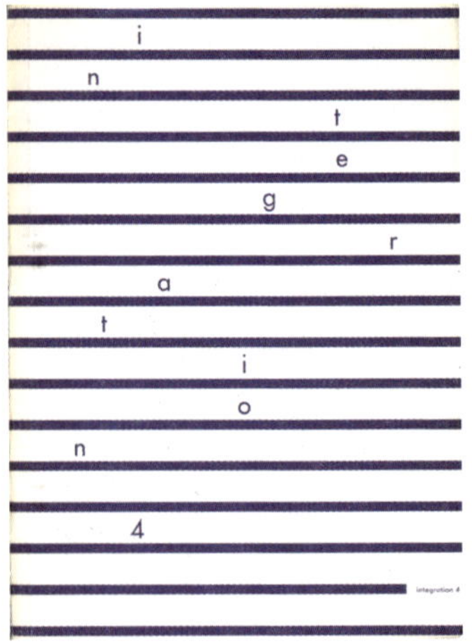

A.23

Revue Integration, no. 4, 1965.
Courtesy of Herman de Vries.
Research Library, The Getty Research
Institute, Los Angeles (86-S1545
no. 4).

such as Ken Doll, Sharon Smith, General Idea, Eldon Garnet, Marion Lewis, and Michael Sowdon. No. 13 was compiled from a garbage bag full of rejected snapshots found behind a photo printing lab; no. 19–20 was a catalog for "The Rolling Landscape," held in a Toronto subway car in full service; no. 22 was devoted to artists who used stereoscopic cameras and included a plastic stereo viewer; and no. 23 featured artists who mutilated, scratched, or altered their photographs. The magazine had a circulation of around 1,000 and was a labor of love, according to Hlynsky.

IMPULSE
Mississauga and Toronto, 1971–1991 (vol. 1, no. 1–vol. 16, no. 1).

Edited by Eldon Garnet from 1975 to 1990, *Impulse: Canada's Creative Quarterly* published artists including Michael Gibbs, Michael Snow, David Hlynsky, Willoughby Sharp, Victor Coleman, Dennis Oppenheim, Les Levine, and David Gilhooly.

INTEGRATION
Arnhem, Holland, 1965–1972 (1–13/14). Herman de Vries.

Herman de Vries founded *Revue Integration* as a continuation of his earlier journal *Revue Nul = 0* (1963–1965). Whereas the latter had focused on the Dutch Nul group, *Revue Integration* encompassed a wider range of experimental art and poetry. In the first issue, De Vries listed an international roster of editorial collaborators including Wybrand Ganzevoort (Antwerp); Herman Goepfert (Frankfurt); Mathias Goeritz (Mexico); Nanda Vigo (Milan); Dietrich Sauerbier (Berlin); Peter K. Iden (Frankfurt); and Christian Megert (Bern). Issue 1, published to coincide with the exhibition "Aktuell 65: Nouvelle Tendance—recherche continuele" at the Galerie Aktuell in Bern, contained a large foldout poster of the exhibition, along with de Vries's essay "Visual Information: Aktuell '65" (printed in German, Dutch, English, and French) in which he discussed the new participatory and avant-garde forms of art associated with the international New Tendencies movement, born in Zagreb in 1961. The magazine's title was a reference to "the integration in all conceivable domains of life" associated with New Tendencies, which might "bring together poets, writers, cinematographers, plastic arts, composers and philosophers in a unified manifesto of the spirit of these days."[38] The offset and mimeographed, stapled magazine, printed in an edition of around 300 (most issues also included ten hand-numbered and signed copies), published writings, poetry, documentation, and works of art. *Revue Integration* revealed various kinds of formal and conceptual experimentation with the magazine page, occasionally including objects affixed to its pages, such as sugar packets and shards of mirror. Dieter Roth's "Sample Pages from a Prepared Webster for John Cage" consisted of photocopied dictionary pages in which each word has been replaced with "music"; Bernard Aubertin glued three matches to the page and lit them, leaving three singed plumes; and Lucio Fontana ripped a page down the middle. De Vries, Mathias Goeritz, and Ad Reinhardt collaborated on issue 9, made up of thirteen black pages, followed by two metallic gold ones, and then thirteen white pages, with no text.

INTERFUNKTIONEN
Cologne, 1968–1975 (1–12). Editors: Friedrich Heubach (nos. 1–10) and Benjamin Buchloh (nos. 11–12). See chapter 8.

Interfunktionen was founded to protest the conservative curatorial agenda of Documenta 4, and soon evolved into a vehicle for conceptual art on both sides of the Atlantic. The magazine, which began in an edition of 120 and increased to 1,000, featured documentation of works and artist-designed pages, fostering a new kind of exchange between American and

European artists. Special editions of approximately 50 copies per issue included signed originals and multiples. Contributors included Joseph Beuys, Sigmar Polke, Rebecca Horn, Anselm Kiefer, Hans Haacke, Christo, Marcel Broodthaers, Daniel Buren, Valie Export, Jan Dibbets, Richard Long, Walter De Maria, Dennis Oppenheim, Michael Heizer, Robert Smithson, Vito Acconci, Bruce Nauman, Terry Fox, Carl Andre, Robert Morris, Philip Glass, Yvonne Rainer, Hollis Frampton, and Dan Graham.

INTERMEDIA

Los Angeles and San Francisco, 1974–1979 (1–7). Editor: Harley Lond.

Intermedia, "an Interdisciplinary Journal of the Arts, Resources & Communications, by and for the Communicator/Artist," was started by Harley Lond as a kind of yellow pages for artists, writers, and musicians in the Los Angeles area and beyond. Lond wrote in the first issue:

> The vacuum in which artists have struggled for years is now being filled by a host of political and economic organizations striving to create a stronger representation and voice for artists everywhere. There is almost a grassroots movement amongst artist to take control over their destinies in the econo/political facets of capitalist society. … One of the goals of *Intermedia* is to link the new art movement with these other alternative movements—to create a unified alternative force of artists, writers, workers, and radicals. … We want *Intermedia* to be by and for artists, to be a forum for artists' concerns and needs, to be a mode of interdisciplinary communications between the artist and the alternative learning people, radicals, communicators, and especially a mode of communication between artists of different media.

Inspired by Dick Higgins's Something Else Press, Lond borrowed the magazine's title from Higgins's "Statement on Intermedia" (he got the artist's permission first). Lond, who started the magazine with his savings and donations from family and friends, did all of the layout and typesetting himself, financing the magazine largely through small grants. After moving to San Francisco in 1977, he worked at the counter of an auto supply store, saving money, and then periodically taking time off to publish the magazine. The first three issues were 8½-by-11-inch magazines that included artists' contributions and writings plus a listing of art services, organizations, small presses, and free artists' classifieds. The magazine expanded as Lond began to realize the magazine's potential as an artistic medium: issue 4 was a "Special Literary Issue," printed as a tabloid newspaper (48 newsprint pages) of experimental art and literature; issue 5 was a tabloid compendium of 17-by-22-inch posters by artists; and issue 6 was a box containing artist-designed postcards, broadsides, folders, and posters. Among its contributors were Martha Rosler, Clemente Padin, Richard Kostelanetz, Opal Nations, Dick Higgins, Anna Banana, and Lew Thomas.

INTERNATIONALE SITUATIONNISTE

Paris, 1958–1969 (1–12). Guy Debord.

The *Internationale Situationniste* was the house organ of the Situationist International and was published and edited by its members, including Michèle Bernstein, Guy Debord, Theo Frey, Asger Jorn, Mustapha Kayati, Attila Kotanyi, Constant Nieuwenhuys, and Raoul Vaneigem, among others. In the pages of the journal the group forwarded their radical critique of spectacular media culture, architecture, and urbanism, and articulated practices such as the *dérive* and *détournement*. The magazine's reflective metallic covers, which Debord once compared to "a deforming mirror," both literalized and warped the tautological character of the spectacle that the Situationist International theorized.[39] The editors stated

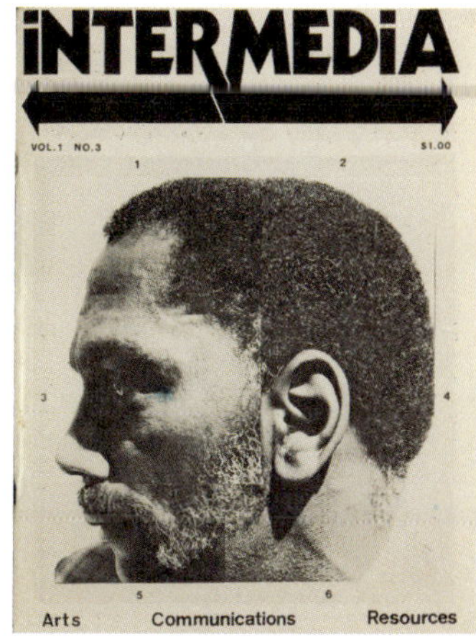

A.24

Intermedia, no. 3, 1975. Cover image: Lew Thomas, *Arithmetical Portrait 1973*. Courtesy of Harley Lond and Lew Thomas.

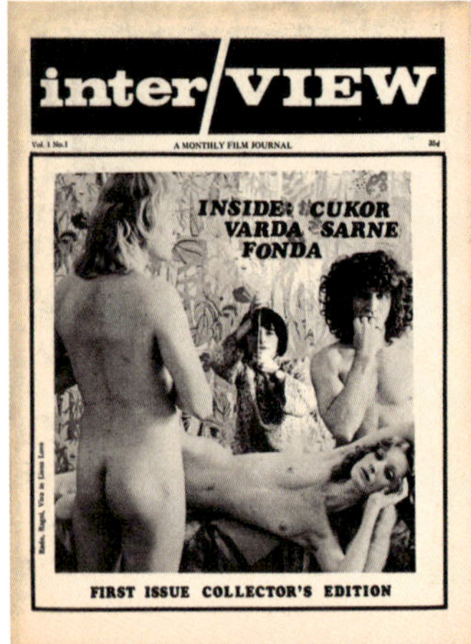

A.25

Interview Magazine, vol. 1, no. 1, Winter 1969, featuring James Rado, Viva, and Gerome Ragni. Courtesy of Interview, Inc.

in the first issue (my translation): "As a rule, this newsletter is edited collectively. The few articles written individually and signed must also be regarded as affecting all of our comrades, and as particular points of their joint research. We are opposed to the survival of such forms as the literary review or art magazine. All texts published in *Internationale Situationniste* may be freely reproduced, translated and adapted, even without indication of origin."

INTERNATIONAL GRAFFITI TIMES
(alternate titles: *IG Times* / *International Get Hip Times* / *Tight*)
New York, 1984–1994 (1–15). David Schmidlapp and Phase 2.

One of the first graffiti zines, *International Graffiti Times* published interviews with and contributions by graffiti writers, including collages and photographic documentation of graffiti writing. It started off as a single broadsheet, which was folded four times, like the free maps of the New York subway system, starting with issue 2. Later issues were printed on glossy stock with color photographs. Contributors included Phase 2 (who was the magazine's art director) and Vulcan. The following editorial statement appeared in the first issue:

> Graffiti is an exercise of global citizenship. As an anarcho-architectural manifestation of free speech, graffiti bucks the bondage of propriety. An armed elite has controlled and manipulated the word plus image from parchment to the associated press, leaving the prophets to the walls to write on. In some places, like Latin America, graffiti is an informational weapon in surviving omnipresent disappearances of citizens. This publication will put forth an international perspective on graffiti.

INTERVIEW
New York, 1969– (vo1. 1, no. 1–). Andy Warhol.

"Like *Rolling Stone* but on movies" is how Andy Warhol described his new magazine *Interview: A Monthly Film Journal* in the first issue.[40] In 1969, when *Interview* began as a quarter-fold tabloid, *Rolling Stone* was itself a countercultural alternative to mainstream music journalism. Warhol's studio assistant David Dalton was a founding editor of *Rolling Stone*, and the two had worked closely together on issue 3 of *Aspen* (1966), designed in the form of a box of Fab laundry detergent. Another clear influence on *Interview* was the underground press. John Wilcock, founder of the seminal underground paper the *East Village Other*, was listed on the first masthead, as were the film director Paul Morrisey and the poet Gerard Malanga. However, though *Interview*'s pedigree included such alternative and underground precedents, like much of Warhol's practice it also had one foot firmly planted in the culture industry. Indeed, the first issue was billed, not altogether ironically, as a "collectors' item." While most artists' magazines were staunchly noncommercial, Warhol shrewdly borrowed promotional and marketing techniques, giving complimentary copies to celebrities and potential advertisers. Asked about the magazine's funding, he blithely answered, "All income is derived from advertising and circulation."[41]

From the beginning, the magazine sought to shake up the rigid question-and-answer format of the interview, in ways that anticipated the spontaneous character of the artist interviews in *Avalanche*, founded the following year. A conversation with Agnes Varda in the first issue was prefaced: "The interviewer, Soren Agenoux, does not like the form of the interview and the implication of the form that the person has information to be given to the interviewer which the interviewer does not have and can not get except by asking." Agenoux then began the interview by admitting to Varda, "I don't know what kind of questions to ask you." Other interviews had the unscripted character of Warhol's own movies. Halfway through Amy Sullivan's interview with Mark Frechette and Daria

Halprin in the first issue, Warhol himself wanders in with a Polaroid camera and asks them to take their clothes off. While *Interview* started off by juxtaposing the art world with the worlds of celebrity, entertainment, and fashion, its history attests to the increasingly blurred lines between these worlds. Since shortly after Warhol's death in 1987, *Interview* has been published by Brant Publications, Inc.; it was edited by former *Artforum* editor Ingrid Sischy from 1990 to 2008.

IS.
Toronto: Coach House Press, 1966–1976 (1–19/20). Victor Coleman.

Is. magazine (pronounced "eyes") was an experimental art and literary magazine edited by Victor Coleman that served as the house organ of the renowned Coach House Press. It evolved out of an earlier poetry magazine called *Island*, which Coleman founded in 1964 while living on Toronto's Ward Island. No two issues were alike, and many were guest-edited and guest-designed by artists, including AA Bronson, Ken Doll, Michael Sowden, John Oughton, Ted Whitaker, Michael Morris, and Stan Bevington.

IT IS
New York, 1958–1965 (1–6). Philip Pavia and Natalie Edgar.

It Is: A Magazine for Abstract Art was an important abstract expressionist periodical, publishing artists' writings and reproductions of works in half-tone and color plates. Among its contributors were Hans Hoffman, Allen Ginsberg, Elaine de Kooning, Robert Motherwell, Ad Reinhardt, John Cage, Allan Kaprow, David Smith, Adolph Gottlieb, Grace Hartigan, Helen Frankenthaler, Louise Nevelson, and Isamu Noguchi.

JUST ANOTHER ASSHOLE
New York, 1978–1987 (1–7). Barbara Ess, with Jane M. Sherry (nos. 3–4) and Glenn Branca (nos. 5–7).

Just Another Asshole published artists, writers, and musicians from downtown Manhattan in an ever-changing format—from photocopied zine, to large-format tabloid, to commercial magazine, to LP record, paperback book, and exhibition catalog. Barbara Ess started the magazine in 1978 as a personal zine: a crudely photocopied compilation of her collages in a makeshift transparency cover on which the title was painted in bright red nail polish. Produced in an edition of around 20, the first two issues were peppered with appropriated newspaper headlines and détourned news clippings, many of them about banal and tragic happenings: fluke accidents, random murders, pedestrians killed by falling debris, television hypochondriacs, and botched suicides. Ess came up with the magazine's title after reading a *New York Post* article about a deaf-mute boy killed by an intruder he couldn't hear: "There was a picture of the boy, and he looked so sweet. I made a color Xerox of it, and I wrote on it, 'just another asshole,'" she recalled.[42] Yet if the publication started as response to the alienating and dehumanizing effect of the media, which exploited such events for their shock and entertainment value, it evolved into an exploration of the media's potential to foster community and collectivity among artists. The third issue, a larger tabloid-format magazine (coedited with J. M. Sherry), was an "open issue" in which "anything submitted will be accepted, no matter what, no matter by whom," produced to accompany the "Library Show" exhibition organized at Colleen Fitzgibbon's East Village gallery. The fourth issue consisted of a four-page spread published in the February 1980 issue of *Artforum*. Issue 5 was a compilation LP, produced with the assistance of White Columns, of short, experimental music and spoken word recordings by eighty-four artists and musicians. Issue 6 was a paperback anthology of writings by sixty artists and writers. The seventh and

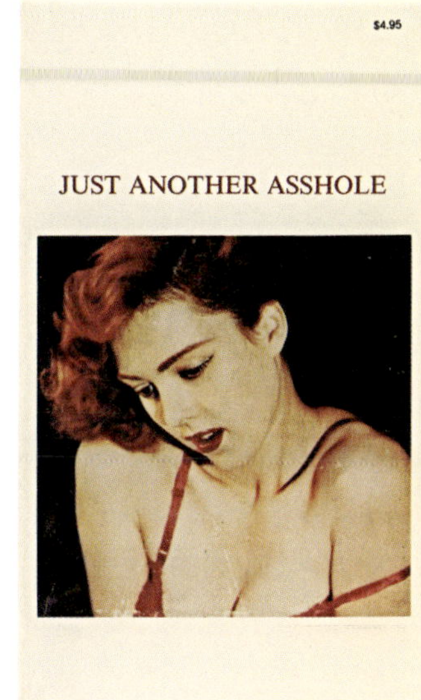

A.26
Just Another Asshole, no. 6, 1983. Courtesy of Barbara Ess. Research Library, The Getty Research Institute, Los Angeles (93-S10916 no. 6).

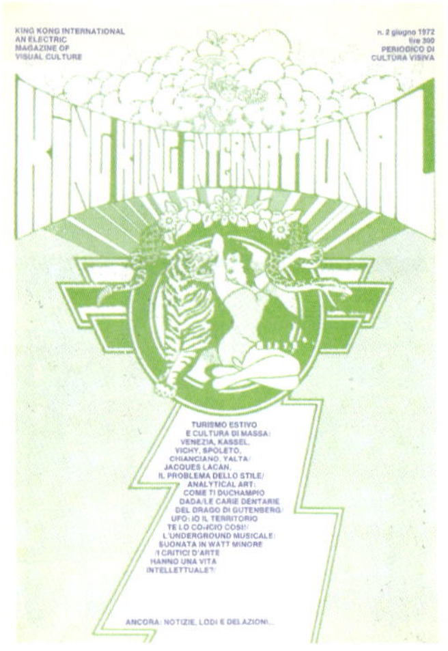

A.27

King Kong International, no. 2, 1972. Research Library, The Getty Research Institute, Los Angeles (87-S596, no. 2).

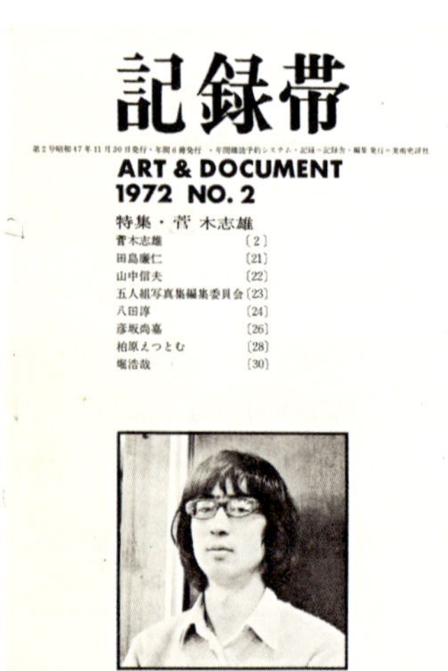

A.28

Kirokutai, no. 2, 1972. Research Library, The Getty Research Institute, Los Angeles (2006.M.2).

final issue, entitled "Thought Objects," was an exhibition catalog for a show of photography at the Cash/Newhouse Gallery. Contributors to *Just Another Asshole* included Dara Birnbaum, Jenny Holzer, Dan Graham, Thurston Moore, Barbara Kruger, Paul McMahon, Kiki Smith, Thomas Lawson, Rhys Chatham, Kim Gordon, Joseph Nechvatal, Martha Wilson, Jeff Koons, Christy Rupp, Kathy Acker, Jack Goldstein, David Wojnarowicz, and Richard Prince.

KALDRON

Shell Beach, California, 1976–1990; continues as an online magazine. Karl Kempton.

Named after hexagram 50 of the *I Ching, Kaldron* was an important visual poetry journal in the United States. Published in an edition of 1,000, it was distributed for free, largely through the mail art network.

KALEJDOSKOP

Lund, Sweden, 1975–1985. Sune Nordgren.

Citing the earlier Swedish artists' magazine *Salamander* as an important precedent and source of inspiration, editor Sune Nordgren published about six issues per year of *Kalejdoskop* over a decade. The magazine, with its subdued digest-sized format, focused on Scandinavian conceptual art and poetry, with contributions from abroad by artists and writers such as Richard Long, Richard Kostelanetz, Ulises Carrión, Michel Foucault, Felipe Ehrenberg, George Maciunas, Dick Higgins, and Nam June Paik. In addition to the magazine, Nordgren published monographs and artists' books under the Kalejdoskop imprint.

KING KONG INTERNATIONAL

Milan, 1972 (1–2). Editors: Rara Bloom, Dante Goffetri, Bruno Sanguanini, Riccardo Sgarbi, and Mizio Turchet.

Published just two times in 1972, *King Kong International* was a tabloid-format magazine that focused on conceptual and new media art in Italy and elsewhere. It had a countercultural vibe, expressed through colored ink (indigo, bright green, purple), psychedelic fonts and graphics, and kaleidoscopic superoverlays. Issue 2 contained Jacques Lacan's "Il problema dello stile e la concezione psichiatrica delle forme paranoiche dell'esperienza" (The Problem of Style and the Psychiatric Conception of Paranoiac Forms of Experience), first published in *Minotaure* in 1933, alongside an article by conceptual artist Philip Pilkington. Other artists who contributed to or were featured in the magazine included Dan Graham, Steve Reich, Terry Riley, John Cage, and Joseph Beuys.

KIROKU

Tokyo, 1972–1973 (1–5); 2006– (6–). Daido Moriyama.

Originally part of the Provoke group, Moriyama later published *Kiroku,* in which he presented his own photographs accompanied by texts by Kazuo Nishii. Issue 5, based on the theme of a baseball game, was anomalous in that it had multiple other contributors as well. After a thirty-three-year gap, Moriyama began publishing the magazine again in 2006.

KIROKUTAI

Tokyo, 1972–1977 (1–5). Editor: Naoyoshi Hikosaka; no. 1 edited by Hori Kosai.

Published by Naoyoshi Hikosaka and other members of the radical artists' group Bikyoto, *Kirokutai* (Document zone) was founded to document the exhibitions and activities of Bikyoto, which included conceptual art performance, sound art, photography, and film.

According to Hikosaka, the magazine was founded when the art magazine *Bijutsu techō* stopped publishing a column for exhibition reviews, "causing the artists to fear that they would lose a place to record their exhibition histories."[43] The slim black-and-white magazine featured writings and photographs by artists such as Hikosaka, Kishio Suga, Kenji Inumaki, Shigehide Yonezu, Yoshio Kitatsuji, Tetsuya Watanabe, Hitoshi Nimura, and Hori Kosai.

KONTEXTS
Coventry, England, and Amsterdam, 1969–1977 (1–9/10). Michael Gibbs and Paul Merchant.

"An occasional review of concrete/experimental/visual poetry." *Kontexts* published conceptual artists including Dan Graham and Lawrence Weiner.

KULCHUR
New York, 1960–1965 (1–20). Marc Schleifer, Lita Hornick, and others.

Kulchur was an influential, eclectic magazine of poetry, literature, film, theater, music, and art. Among the contributors were LeRoi Jones, Frank O'Hara, David Antin, Bill Berkson, Charles Olson, Diane Di Prima, and Robert Duncan. Covers were contributed by artists including Franz Kline, Robert Indiana, and Joe Brainard.

KUNSTSTOFF
Cologne, 1975–1977 (1–6). Jürgen Klauke and Rudolf Bonvie.

Kunststoff published photography and conceptual art, with contributions by Klauke, Bonvie, Ulay, and others.

KWY
Paris, 1958–1963 (1–12). René Bertholo, Christo, Lourdes Castro, Jan Voss, and others.

KWY was founded by the artists René Bertholo and Lourdes Castro as a vehicle for the Portuguese avant-garde in exile. The letters *K*, *W*, and *Y* were so rarely used in Portuguese that they were officially banished from the language in 1943, serving as a metaphor for the artists' own feelings of marginalization from their native country. The magazine began as eight pages of small handmade abstract silkscreens that the artists produced in their Paris apartment in an edition of 60 and sent out to friends across Europe. The magazine grew to include contributors such as Maria Helena Vieira da Silva, Gonçalo Duarte, Costa Pinheiro, José Escada, Christo, and Pol Bury. Several of the contributors exhibited together between 1960 and 1967, becoming known as the KWY group. Christo edited issue 11 (Spring 1963), which featured a portrait of Jean-Claude on the cover and was dedicated to Yves Klein, with contributions by Klein, Nikki de Saint Phalle, Jacques Villeglé, Jean Tinguely, Daniel Spoerri, Arman, Emmett Williams, and Ben Vautier, as well as a vinyl record of sound poetry by Bernard Heidsieck.

L.A. ARTISTS' PUBLICATION
Los Angeles 1972–1973 (vol. 1, no. 1–vol. 1, no. 4½). Fidel Danieli.

This unbound assembling was started as "a communication exchange between Southern California artists and their friends," editor Fidel Danieli wrote in the first issue. Contributing artists were responsible for printing their works and for providing a mailing list of twenty-five people. The generic title was meant to be temporary, until readers voted on a more permanent title; however, the name *L.A. Artists' Publication* stuck. Contributors included Betye Saar, Eleanor Antin, and John Beckman.

LAICA JOURNAL

Los Angeles: Los Angeles Institute of Contemporary Art,
1974–1987 (1–48). Editor: Fidel Danieli;
later Peter Clothier.

The *LAICA Journal*, sometimes simply called the *Journal*, was the magazine of the Los Angeles Institute of Contemporary Art. It covered the Southern Calfornia alternative art scene and published original artists' contributions. Issue 19 was a joint issue with *Art-Rite*.

LACRE

Mexico City: La Tinta Morada, 1983 (1–2).

Lacre, subtitled "Revista de comunicación alternativa," was a handmade artists' magazine published in a limited edition of approximately 100. The magazine consisted of unbound sheets tied with a ribbon, and was contained in a brown paper bag sealed with wax—hence the title *Lacre*, which means "sealing wax." *Lacre* published a wide variety of media including prints, drawings, collage, hand-stitching, watercolor, and rubber stamps. The editorial board was composed of María Teresa Cervantes, Alicia García Bergua, Ana García Bergua, Alonso Leaf Güemes, Gertrudis Martínez de Hoyos Delamain, Francisco Pellicer Graham, Alejandra Queredo Runne, and Armando Sáenz Carrillo.

LANDSLIDE

Los Angeles, 1969–1970 (1–7). Bas Jan Ader and William Leavitt.

Billed as "the Quarterly Journal of Underground Art," *Landslide* was published anonymously in Los Angeles by the artists William Leavitt and Bas Jan Ader. The mimeographed and hand-stapled magazine, which the publishers sent out to a mailing list of about forty artists, curators, and critics, caricatured the art world by featuring contributors named Brian Shitart and Dove Feeler and fake interviews. One such interview was with the fictive artist John Grover, a carpenter turned minimalist sculptor whose comparison between his work and the mass-produced forms of suburban architecture reads as a parody of Dan Graham's *Homes for America* (1966–1967). The magazine's title, according to Leavitt, referred to "the southern California hillsides and their problems," and, like the better-known magazine *Avalanche*, founded in 1970, alluded to earth art.[44] However, while *Avalanche* expressed faith in the revolutionary ambitions of 1960s art, *Landslide* was a kind of ironic, slacker West Coast cousin, conveying a sense of entropic collapse. Issue 3 was an "expandable sculpture," consisting of several packing peanuts in an envelope, and issue 6 was allegedly an actual McDonald's hamburger mailed out in a cardboard box. If *Landslide* was a spoof on conceptual art, it was also itself a work of conceptual art; and it wasn't always clear where one ended and the other began.

Further reading: Eric Bluhm, "Minimalism's Rubble: On William Leavitt's and Bas Jan Ader's *Landslide* (1969–1970)," *Art US*, no. 10, October-November 2005, 14–17.

A.29

Landslide, nos. 1–7, 1969–1970.
Courtesy of William Leavitt. Collection of Steven Leiber, San Francisco.

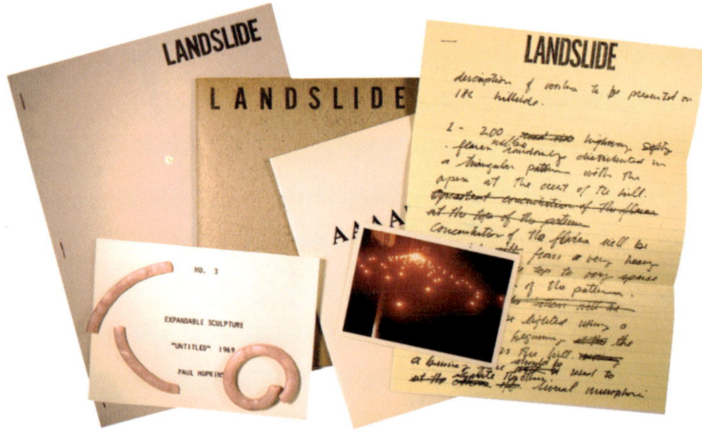

LEFT CURVE

San Francisco, 1974– (1–). Founding editors: Richard Olsen
and Csaba Polony.

An editorial in the first issue of *Left Curve: Art & Revolution* announced: "This magazine should be looked at as somewhat of an experiment. It's experimental because of (1) its open format—in terms of styles and positions—and (2) its future direction is not determined before the fact. It does, however, have a basic orientation centering around issues concerning art and revolution. For the editors, the magazine form seemed to be one of many needed extensions of our own works, works that though often different, equally ran into confrontations with the art-monopoly and its capitalist base. Hopefully it will give you (and us) a chance to voice such confrontations, solutions, art-works, etc." Contributors to *Left Curve* included Ian Burn, Terry Smith, Eva Cockcroft, and the Guerrilla Art Action Group.

LIGHTWORKS

Ann Arbor, 1975–2000 (1–22). Publisher: Bob Hoot;
Editor: Deborah Schwarz; Designer: Eric Keller.

Lightworks began as a broadside newspaper covering alternative and new media art in the Detroit and Ann Arbor area.

LIP

Carlton, Australia, 1976–1984 (1–8). The Lip Collective: Janine Burke,
Mary Callaghan, Suzanne Davies, Folly Gleeson, Carolyn Howard,
Christine Johnston, Sue Johnston, Pat Longmore, Suzanne Spunner,
Ann Stephen, Toni Wilkinson.

The Melbourne-based feminist collective Lip—a word chosen for its anatomical and gendered definitions but also meaning to speak, utter, or sing, and to be self-reliant (as in "a stiff upper lip")—published a magazine with the same name. An editorial statement in the first issue explained:

> Lip's fundamental concern is with the cultural conditions and lives of Australian women, in order to define and shape our national identity. We shall be responsive to and in contact with the international feminist community. We want the Lip collective to remain open and we encourage women to participate in the editorial collective and contribute to the magazine—both in its content and production. Each issue will reflect and explore the interests of the women involved. An open evaluation meeting will be held after the publication of each issue to generate critical discussion, to explore themes for the subsequent issues, and to make Lip as accessible as possible. … In opposing the prevailing bias of patriarchal art, in dismantling the myth of individual genius, and in breaking-down the barriers between the fine and decorative arts, Lip does not seek to replace them with new 'female' commodities, endorsing the competitive mentality of the art market. Nor do we espouse a feminist orthodoxy or the establishment of a particular style.

LOTTA POETICA

Milan. Series 1: 1971–1975 (1–50); Series 2: 1982–1984 (1–24);
Series 3: 1987 (1–2). Paul de Vree, Sarenco,
and Gianni Bertini.

Lotta Poetica was a visual poetry magazine founded by the Belgian artist Paul de Vree (who also published *Tafelronde*) and the Italians Sarenco and Gianni Bertini. Meaning "poetic struggle," the magazine's title implied its "commitment, as poets and artists in general, to

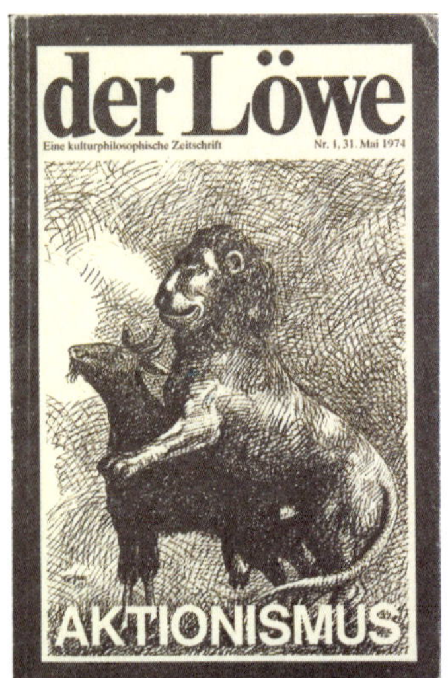

A.30

Der Löwe, no. 1, May 1974. Courtesy
of Gerhard Johann Lischka.

waging a continuous battle."[45] The magazine's militant stance toward the mainstream art world and market was further emphasized by its cover, which for the first twelve issues featured a photograph of Bertini pointing a gun directly at the reader. The editors stated as their goal "to create a medium for information and the exchange of ideas at the international level" and to "speak more directly and more deeply to all social classes."[46] They also called for "a total conceptual reform (collective emotion, involvement of the reader, reworking of language, merging of disciplines)."[47] After the magazine ended in 1975 due to funding problems, Sarenco edited two subsequent series of it in the 1980s, as a more glossy, standard art magazine. Contributors included Sarenco, De Vree, Klaus Staeck, Bernard Aubertin, Joseph Beuys, and Jean-François Bory.

DER LÖWE
Bern, 1974–1977 (1–9). Dr. Gerhard Johann Lischka.

The Swiss art historian and critic Gerhard Johann Lischka named his magazine *Der Löwe* (The lion) after his own long hair, which people often compared to a lion's mane. The digest-sized magazine, published in an edition of 1,200 to 3,500, featured international conceptual art, publishing writings and works by artists such as Hermann Nitsch, Otto Muehl, Arnulf Rainer, Chris Burden, Terry Fox, Tom Marioni, John Cage, Vito Acconci, Willoughby Sharp, Carl Andre, Andy Warhol, Gerhard Richter, and Claes Oldenburg. Issue 6 (December 1975), called *Die Löwin* (The lionness), featured women artists including Valie Export, Rebecca Horn, Charlotte Moorman, Gina Pane, Carolee Schneemann, and Lynda Benglis. Lischka ended the magazine after the ninth issue in 1977, recalling, "It was enough, it would have become a business."[48]

LUNA-PARK
Brussels, 1974–1985 (1–8/9). Marc Dachy.

Luna-Park published experimental art and literature. Among its contributors were Alain Arias-Mission, Christian Dotremont, Roberto Altmann, and Henri Lefebvre.

MACULA
Paris, 1976–1979 (1–5/6). Editors: Yve-Alain Bois
and Jean Clay.

Macula was founded by the art critic Jean Clay and the art historian Yve-Alain Bois, then a student at the École des Hautes Études en Sciences Sociales, where he studied with Roland Barthes, Hubert Damisch, and Jacques Derrida. In "Extracts from the Editorial," published in the first issue, the editors described the magazine's goals in a kind of textual collage, punctuated by ellipses—a breathless rush of ideas that captured the intellectual energies out of which the journal sprang. Against a traditional art history that sought to "go over the roll-call of the 'great figures'" and "index all the productions of culture in accordance with the mythical unity of an age," they wished to consider the institutional and political conditions of artistic production and reception: "What sort of power—and for whose benefit—is created by the present-day output of painting, and by the conditions under which it is produced?"[49] The elegant-looking journal with few illustrations and no advertisements vowed to publish contemporary criticism as well as "concealed or confiscated texts of/on art, in order to renew the tissue of documentation, to create new opportunities for research." Contributions by artists including Kazimir Malevich, Josef Albers, Piet Mondrian, Max Bill, Lygia Clark, Christian Bonnefoi, Barnett Newman, and Robert Ryman were juxtaposed with criticism by Bois, Clay, Rosalind Krauss, Walter Benjamin, Erwin Panofsky, and Clement Greenberg. Damisch published a lengthy essay that would become the basis for his book *The Origin of Perspective* in issue 5–6. Issue 3–4 contained Derrida's "Restitutions of the Truth in

Pointing," alongside Heidegger's original essay "The Origin of the Work of Art" and Meyer Schapiro's "The Still Life as a Personal Object—A Note on Heidegger and van Gogh," which led, Bois recalled, to "a complicated diplomatic dance between two writers we equally, but differently, admired."[50] *Macula* had an influence far beyond its circulation of 1,000.

MAIL ORDER ART
Oakland, California, 1971–1972 (1–4). Patricia Tavenner.

Riding on the wave of correspondence art, artist Patricia Tavenner founded *Mail Order Art* as a kind of Sears catalog for artists, who advertised wares, such as decals, stickers, toys, and other kinds of multiples. Contributing artists chipped in to help print the tabloid-format magazine, which ranged from 500 to 5,000 copies per issue.

MAJ 75
Zagreb, 1975–1984 (A–Lj). The Group of Six.

Maj 75 was published by a group of artists known as the Group of Six—painter Boris Demur; photographers Željko Jerman, Sven Stilinović, and Fedor Vučemilović; poet Vlado Martek; and filmmaker Mladen Stilinović. An editorial statement described the magazine as "an effort to show work and add verbal support during the presentation. An alternative to the contemporary trend of shaping works of art through the compartmentalization of media and presenting it exclusively through institutions."[51] It was named after the date of their first public exhibition (May 1975), on a beach on the Sava River. Subsequent exhibition-actions were similarly held outside of the traditional gallery space, dispersed throughout public and private spaces (streets, city squares, homes). The pages of *Maj 75* were another alternative exhibition space that the group explored. It was an unofficially published and collectively produced assembling in which each artist contributed 100 to 200 copies of his or her work, including drawings, photographs, texts, manifestos, visual poetry, and collages, which were collated and bound within silkscreened covers. Seventeen issues were produced in all, identified by the letters of the Croatian alphabet. Copies of *Maj 75* were handed out at the group's exhibition-actions, and a few were sold in galleries. Issue F, edited by Vlasta Delimar in 1981, was a women-only issue.

MALASARTES
Rio de Janeiro, 1975 (1–3). Cildo Meireles, Bernardo de Vilhena, Carlos Vergara, Carlos Zilio, José Resende, Luiz Paulo Baravelli, Ronaldo Brito, Rubens Gerchman, and Waltércio Caldas.

Published only three times, *Malasartes* was an important critical vehicle for Brazilian art, published by a group of artists and critics from Rio de Janeiro and São Paulo. The editorial statement in the first issue explained (my translation):

> The central concern of *Malasartes* is the visual arts, but we will pay attention to all cultural fields in general. More than art objects, we will focus on studying the processes of art production, its promotion and the mechanisms that feed it. Traditionally, the magazines in which artists are the majority have defended an artistic movement, an "ism." Coming from different backgrounds, but with similar artwork, what unites us is a consensus on the role that art plays in our cultural environment and what it could play. *Malasartes* is therefore a magazine about the politics of the arts. Among the apparent options of editing a publication that treats art as an object of consumption and another that follows the fashion of enigmatic magazines, *Malasartes* preferred, boldly, to take upon itself the task of analyzing the contemporary reality of Brazilian art and pointing out alternative solutions.

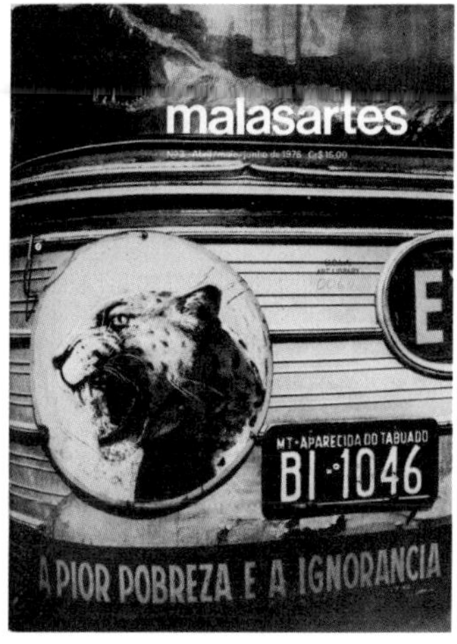

A.31
Malasartes, no. 3, 1975.

Published in Portuguese in an edition of 5,000, *Malasartes* published articles, poetry, and works of art by Brazilian artists alongside translated materials. Contributors included Cildo Meireles, Waltércio Caldas, Terry Smith, Joseph Kosuth, Lygia Pape, Allan Kaprow, Carlos Vergara, Tunga, Ronaldo Brito, Ferreira Gullar, and Mário Pedrosa.

LA MAMELLE / ART CONTEMPORARY / ARTCOM
San Francisco, 1975–1984 (1–25; continued as an
electronic journal on the Art Com Electronic Network
from 1986 to 1992). Carl Loeffler.

The magazine *La Mamelle* was published by Carl Loeffler as an adjunct to La Mamelle, the nonprofit alternative space and artists' bookstore he founded in San Francisco in 1975. The title *La Mamelle*, meaning breast or udder in French, implied a nourishing source for both artists and audiences. Both exhibition space and publication supported alternative art forms, especially video, performance, artists' publications, and mail art. *La Mamelle* evolved from a tabloid-format newspaper to a standard 8½-by-11-inch magazine, and its title changed to *Art Contemporary* and then to *Art Com*. In addition to articles, artists' documentation, and artists' pages, it contained artists' resources and listings for other nonprofits. Issue 12 (1978) was a special joint issue with the Toronto-based *Only Paper Today,* a "Special Trans-mittable Booklet Issue" designed to be reassembled into individual artists' books. Loeffler also published other magazines under the La Mamelle banner: *Audiozine*, an audio-cassette magazine, 1977–1978 (1–8); *Videozine*, a video-cassette magazine, 1977–1978 (1–6); and *Imagezine*, a magazine in the form of a rubber stamp, 1977–1978 (1–4), with which the editor encouraged all readers to "be an art publisher!"

MANIPULATIONS
New York: Judson Publications, 1967 (1 issue).
Ralph Ortiz, Jon Hendricks, Jean Toche, Al Hansen, Lil Picard.

A single issue of *Manipulations* was published by the Judson Church Gallery in 1967, in conjunction with "Twelve Evenings of Manipulations," a Judson performance event with participants including Ralph Ortiz, Jean Toche, Allan Kaprow, Al Hansen, Geoffrey Hendricks, Carolee Schneemann, Lil Picard, Nam June Paik, Bici Hendricks, Malcolm Goldstein, Steve Rose, and Kate Millet. Printed on a small press in the church in an edition of 500, the publication documented each performance, through photographs, descriptions, and notes, which were photocopied onto sheets of colored sheets of paper and collected, unbound, in an envelope. Some incorporated handmade objects and original works: Picard's *Peace Object* consisted of a plastic bag containing ashes of burnt newspaper clippings about the Vietnam war sealed with green DayGlo paint; Ortiz's *Explode This War in Vietnam Bag* was a paper bag covered with media images of the war, meant to be blown up and violently burst by the reader. A handwritten editorial statement described the publication's role in the political goals of the Judson Gallery during this time:

> Judson Publications is intent on filling a vacuum bridging a gap left by the profiteering proselytizers of culture. We are anti-profit. No one gets paid for anything, anytime—we do not advertise anything for anyone anytime. We will send a copy of the Judson Publications to whom-so-ever requests it (as long as copies are available). The Judson Publication is a unique communiqué to you from artists who are concerned with the corruption of culture by profit. We believe the function of the artist is to subvert culture, since our culture is trivial. We are intent on giving a voice to the artist who shouts fire when there is a fire; robbery when there is a robbery; murder when there is a murder; rape when there is a rape. Judson Publications will attempt to serve the public for as long as the trivial culture of the establishment distracts us from the screams of crisis.

Manipulations was reissued as issue 6A of *Aspen* (Winter 1968–1969), which was nearly identical to the original publication, minus the handmade works. Other Judson Church publications included *Exodus* and *The Judson Review*.[52]

MANIPULATOR
Düsseldorf, 1984–1987 (1–10). Editors: David Colby and Wilhelm Moser.

Manipulator was an oversized tabloid (27½ by 19¾ inches) that declared its editorial purview as "Film, Fashion, Music, Design with a strong interest in Art!"

MATERIAL
Darmstadt and Paris, 1958–1959 (1–5, plus supplement; no. 4 never published). Daniel Spoerri.

Inspired by the art and concrete poetry magazine *Spirale*, the dancer and artist Daniel Spoerri founded *material* in 1958. The magazine's participatory aims were reflected in its format. The first issue, which included contributions by Dieter Roth, Eugen Gomringer, and Josef Albers, was assembled at random with pages arranged in various sequences and orientation so that no two copies were alike, as was issue 2, devoted solely to Roth's work. Issue 3 consisted of a text by Emmett Williams with a die-cut cover and pages. Issue 5 was a paper machine by Pol Bury in which pieces of paper fluttered around in a shallow paper container, accompanied by poems by Gherasim Luca. (The fourth issue was never published due to editorial and financial difficulties.) Spoerri went on to publish *Le Petit Colosse de Symi*.

ME
New York, 1980–1985 (1–7). Carlo Pittore.

Carlo Pittore named his mail art magazine *ME* after the abbreviation for the state of Maine, where he lived and worked for much of his life.

M/E/A/N/I/N/G
New York, 1986–1996 (1–19/20). Susan Bee and Mira Schor.

M/E/A/N/I/N/G was founded as an outlet for poststructuralist and feminist criticism that sought to escape the "sobriety and tonal deadliness" of scholarly journals.[53]

MEC
Milan, 1970–1971. Gianni Bertini.

Mec was an influential visual poetry magazine, named after the Mec-art movement (short for "mechanical art").

MENTALNI PROSTOR
Belgrade, 1983–1987. Association for Space Research.

Four issues of *Mentalni Prostor* (Mental space) were published by the artistic collective Association for Space Research (Zoran Belić Weiss, Dubravka Djurić, Miško Šuvaković, Mirko Radojičić, Marko Pogačnik, and Nenad Petrović). Directed toward developing critical and theoretical discourse, the magazine published articles, interviews, and works by the editorial collective as well as by international contributors including Joseph Beuys, Marina Abramović, Ulay, Hamish Fulton, Herman de Vries, Wolfgang Laib, Kathy Acker, Art & Language, Gilles Deleuze and Félix Guattari, Lawrence Weiner, Ian Wilson, and Ludwig Wittgenstein.

METKI
Moscow, 1975 (1–3). V.G. (Vitaly Gribkov).

Metki (Marks) was a handmade *samizdat* journal/art object illegally published by the Russian artist Vitaly Gribkov, listed as simply V.G. The magazine, which had a circulation of 5 to 10 copies, published articles, interviews, drawings, poetry, and photographs by Moscow-based artists. The third issue was prepared by Rimma Gerlovina and Valeriy Gerlovin, with contributions by Komar and Melamid, Yuri Sobolev, and the composer V. Artyomov.

MW
Noordwijk, The Netherlands, 1982–1989 (1–10). Martina Wagener.

This newsprint artists' tabloid published work by Richard Long, Robert Filliou, Dieter Roth, Robert Smithson, Barry Flanagan, and Ian Hamilton Finlay.

NADADA
New York, 1964–1965 (1–2). Editors: Timothy Baum and
Gerard Malanga.

Nadada published contributions by Andy Warhol, Allen Ginsberg, and Charles Bukowski.

NEON DE SURO
Mallorca, Baleares, Spain, 1975–1982 (1–21).

Neon de Suro was published by the Taller Lunatic group of conceptual artists, which included Sara Gilbert, Tomeu Cabot, Steva Terrades, Miquel Barceló, Muntadas, and Julien Blaine. Each issue of the small, eight-page journal was edited by a different artist and distributed for free.

NERVENKRITIK
Vienna, 1976 (1–4). Editor: Dominik Steiger.

Nervenkritik published contributions by Arnulf Rainer, Deiter Roth, Oswald Wiener, Hermann Nitsch, Günter Brus, and others.

NERVO ÓPTICO
Porto Alegre, Brazil, 1977–1978 (1–12).

Nervo Óptico: Publicacão aberta a divulgacão de novas poéticas visuais documented the activities of Nervo Óptico (Ana Alegria, Carlos Asp, Carlos Pasquetti, Clovis Dariano, Elton Manganelli, and others), an artistic collective founded to protest the commercial art market and the government's cultural policies.

NEW OBSERVATIONS
New York, 1981–2001 (1–128). Lucio Pozzi and
Diane Karp (nos. 70–128).

After a very short stint as a founding editor of *October*, from which he resigned before the first issue was published, the artist Lucio Pozzi created the idiosyncratic journal *New Observations*, which he conceived as a "collaborative work of art" which would be edited by a series of guest editors.[54] Published on a shoestring, the magazine began as a makeshift photocopied compilation of criticism and artists' writings and projects. Diane Karp took over as editor in 1988, continuing the magazine's mission of providing an independent, noncommercial forum for artists. Of choosing the title, Pozzi recalled, "I sought the most banal. New or underground magazines had flashy titles, dense with innuendo or intention. I thought that since in the rushed consumer society one factor that is ignored is that of observing with attention, the word 'observations' could be appropriate for my masthead. ...I added 'new' almost as a tease. The last thing I was concerned with was being new."[55] Guest editors included: Tricia Collins and Richard Milazzo (nos. 20 and 51); Maurice Berger (no. 35); Shirin Neshat (no. 62); The Guerrilla Girls (no. 70); Tim Rollins and K.O.S. (no. 78); Adrian Piper (no. 97); and Martha Wilson (no. 95). Among the magazine's contributors were Jeremy Gilbert-Rolfe, Peter Lichte, Barbara Kruger, Sol LeWitt, Walter Robinson, Cindy Sherman, Judy Rifka, Betsy Sussler, Louise Lawler, Allan McCollum, Robin Winters, Sarah Charlesworth, Vito Acconci, Andrea Fraser, Krzysztof Wodiczko, Nancy Spero, Leon Golub, David Wojnarowicz, Jimmy Durham, Barbara Bloom, Julia Kristeva, and Umberto Eco.

NEW YORK CORRESPONDENCE SCHOOL WEEKLY BREEDER
New York and San Francisco, 1971–1974.
Ken Friedman, Stu Horn, Tim Mancusi,
and Bill Gaglione.

The *N.Y.C.S. Weekly Breeder* was started by Ken Friedman in homage to Ray Johnson's New York Correspondence School as a single Xeroxed sheet of collaged newsclippings and short, Fluxus-inspired articles sent out weekly. Mail artist Stu Horn took over the magazine briefly, before passing it along to Tim Mancusi and Bill Gaglione in San Francisco, who expanded it into a "dadazine" for the Bay Area Dadaists and their mail art activities. They published seven issues in an edition of 200 copies, distributed for free, with contributors such as General Idea, Lowell Darling, Robert Cumming, Futzie Nutzle, Monte Cazazza, and Ray Johnson.

DE NIEUWE STIJL
Amsterdam, 1965 (1–2). Armando, Henk Peeters,
Hans Sleutelaar, Cornelis Bastiaan Vaandrager,
Hans Verhagen.

Continuing the experimental poetry magazine *Gard Sivik, De Nieuwe Stijl: Werk van de internationale avant-garde* was devoted to the "New Style," connected to the German Zero and Dutch Nul groups. Contributors included Yves Klein, Heinz Mack, and Yayoi Kusama.

NORTH AND NORTH-INFORMATION
Copenhagen, 1976–1995. Poul Henning Nielsen and Bent Petersen.

According to the editors' statement in issue 1, "*NORTH* and *NORTH-Information* bring news of Scandinavian art and artistic activities. Besides being published in the original language, the magazine gives the full text in English. *NORTH* will primarily bring original contributions by Scandinavian artists and also interviews and informative articles on artistic theory and [the] history of art. *NORTH-Information* is a newsletter bringing documentation or background information about current exhibitions, publications, and other activities of Scandinavian artists."

NOTA
Munich, 1959–1960 (1–4). Gerhard von Graevenitz
and Jürgen Morschel.

The international avant-garde journal *nota: studentische zeitschrift für bildende kunst und kichtung* published contributions by Hans Mack, Otto Piene, Piero Manzoni, John Cage, Dieter Roth, Marcel Duchamp, and Yves Klein.

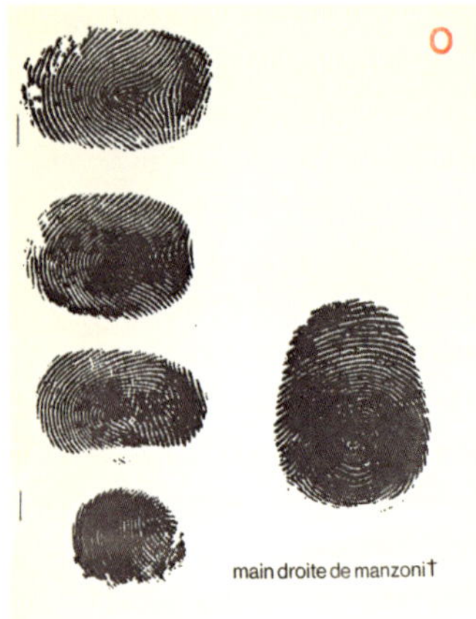

A.32

Revue Nul = 0, no. 2, 1963. Courtesy of Herman de Vries. Research Library, The Getty Research Institute, Los Angeles (87-S917 no. 2).

NOVE

Rio de Janeiro, 1969–1970? (1–3?).
Tunga, Paulo Ramos Filho, Gerardo Mello Mourão, and Gonçalo de Mello Mourão.

Nove was an unbound periodical publishing original works by the artist Tunga alongside texts by Brazilian writers.

NUL = 0

Arnhem, The Netherlands, 1961–1964 (1–4).
Herman de Vries, Henk Peeters (1–2), and Armando (1).

Billed as a "review for new artistic concepts," *Revue Nul = 0* was founded to support the artistic activities of the Dutch Nul group, which had strong affinities with the German Zero group (which published its own magazine, *Zero*, 1958–1959). Stressing international dialog, *Revue Nul = 0* published contributions in French, German, and English by artists including Yves Klein, Piero Manzoni (issue 2 was published in homage to the recently deceased artist), Yayoi Kusama, Daniel Spoerri, Hans Haacke, Heinz Mack, Otto Piene, and the three founding editors, Herman de Vries, Henk Peeters, and Armando. Published in an edition of 300 to 500, *Revue Nul = 0* included die-cut, embossed, and hand-collaged pages (including a glittery, sandlike substance glued to the page in one case), suggesting how the magazine was being reconceived as a new kind of primary site—a tactile, temporal medium through which to express artistic concepts. Like the Dutch Nul group itself, the magazine split over conflicting ideas of artistic identity: according to De Vries, Peeters "tried to build up an image of the Nul group as orderly, well-dressed persons with polished shoes and ties"[56]—a concept that De Vries, with his unkempt beard and preference for wearing socks with sandals, did not adhere to. Peeters left after issue 2, and De Vries continued publishing the magazine for two more issues until a legal battle with Peeters over the rights to the title forced him to end *Revue Nul = 0* and begin a new journal, *Revue Integration*.

NUMBERED BOOKS (5 NUMBERED BOOKS)

Budapest, 1970 (1–5). Géza Perneczky.

Published in an edition of 50 to 100, this *samizdat* artists' magazine incorporated handmade prints, collage, photos, and drawings, focusing on mail art and conceptual art.

NUMMER

Cologne, 1971–1972 (1–4).
Eberhard Prangenberg and Heinz Breloh.

Nummer published conceptual art, mainly in the form of photo documentation, with contributions by Gordon Matta-Clark, Géza Perneczky, Christian Boltanski, David Troy, Peter Pick, Arnulf Rainer, and others.

OCTOBER

New York and Cambridge, 1976– (1–).
Founding editors: Rosalind Krauss, Annette Michelson, and Jeremy Rolfe-Gilbert (nos. 1–3). See chapter 1.

October was founded by several former *Artforum* editors who were disillusioned by the commercialism of the mainstream art press. As they confessed in the first issue, "long working experience with major art journals has convinced us of the need to restore to the criticism of painting and sculpture, as to that of the other arts, an intellectual autonomy seriously undermined by emphasis on extensive reviewing and lavish illustration." Against the visual excess of the mainstream art press, *October* carried no gallery advertisements and vowed to be "plain of aspect, its illustrations determined by considerations of textual clarity." Named after Sergei Eisenstein's 1927–1928 film, *October* harked back to "that moment in our century when revolutionary practice, theoretical inquiry and artistic innovation were joined in a manner exemplary and unique." The magazine has encouraged the intersection between theory and practice, with texts by art historians, critics, and theorists including Jacques Derrida, Michel Foucault, Julia Kristeva, Douglas Crimp, Craig Owens, Daniel Buren, Tricia Brown, Laurie Anderson, Hollis Frampton, Michael Snow, Samuel Beckett, Yvonne Rainer, Robert Morris, and Carl Andre. Initially published by the Institute for Architecture and Urban Studies, it has been published by the MIT Press since the fifth issue.

OMNIBUS NEWS
Munich, 1969 (1). Thomas Niggl, Christian d'Orville, and Heimrad Prem.

Omnibus News was one of the first assemblings in which contributors submitted 1,500 copies of their work to be collated by the editors. As Christian d'Orville wrote in the editorial statement in the first issue, "Everybody can be their own editor." A hodgepodge of different kinds of documents—texts and images printed on various kinds of paper and arranged alphabetically—*Omnibus News* inspired many subsequent publications, including Richard Kostelanetz's own *Assembling.* Punning on the double meaning of "omnibus," the front and back cover of the first issue contained a photograph of a crash between a bus and a train. Contributors included Jochen Gerz, Dick Higgins, the Bread and Puppet Theater, Stanley Brouwn, Jörg Immendorff, Milan Knížák, Arnulf Rainer, Hermann Nitsch, and Wolf Vostell.

ONLY PAPER TODAY / PROOF ONLY
Toronto, 1974–1980 (issued monthly). Victor Coleman.

Only Paper Today, originally called *Proof Only,* was associated with the Toronto alternative space or "parallel gallery" A Space. Edited and designed by Victor Coleman (who sometimes went by the pseudonym Vic d'Or), the tabloid newspaper was distributed free in an edition of 1,500 copies, and published articles and artists' projects. Also on the masthead were Rodney Werden, Jennifer Oille, and Opal Nations. An editorial statement explained, "*OPT* is designed as a tabloid newspaper specifically to avoid the glossy, precious, pretentious qualities of art magazines."[57]

ON SITE
New York: Site, Inc., 1972–1976 (1–5/6). Alison Sky.

According to the editorial statement in issue 1, "*On Site* will be published as a line of communication dealing with the environmental arts. Appearing quarterly, it will cover the problems of metropolitan blight and the role of the artist as a contributor to urban visual standards. Editorials will explore the subjects of visual pollution, perceptual habits, the development of urban space, participatory art, and the projection of fantasy over function on environmental terms." *On Site* blurred lines between disciplines, among them art, architecture, and ecology. Issue 4 was devoted to the topic of the dematerialization of art, with works by Robert Smithson, Nancy Holt, Les Levine, Yves Klein, Jean Tinguely, Charles Simonds, and others.

OPEN LETTER
Toronto: Coach House Press, 1966– (1–). Frank Davey.

Billed as "A Canadian tri-quarterly review of writing and sources," *Open Letter* has functioned as an important vehicle for alternative art and poetry as well as critical writing in Canada.

OTHER VOICES
Sydney, 1970 (1–3). Terry Smith and Paul McGillick.

The editorial statement in issue 1 describes the magazine's goals: "*Other Voices* is a critical journal concerned with seeking an informed and discriminating assessment of contemporary Australian art. The magazine is oriented towards painting and sculpture and the teaching of these subjects at the secondary and tertiary level. However, the editors feel that painting and sculpture cannot be adequately appreciated in isolation from the concerns and directions of theatre, music, literature, film, dance, architecture and television in Australia, and therefore, where possible and appropriate, in-depth articles on those areas will be available in the magazine. ... *Other Voices* is ... an Australian magazine devoted primarily to the discussion of Australian art by Australian critics. ... Any artistic activity requires virile and intensive dialogue if it is to remain healthy, and continue to make a contribution to its culture. This magazine is intended to be the vehicle for such a dialogue. Editorially, therefore, it is strictly non-partisan; its only commitment is to the contemporary and to the reassessment of the past in terms of the contemporary. *Other Voices*, it is hoped, will be a documentation of the quest within contemporary Australian art to be significant, relevant, and of quality."

OU / CINQUIÈME SAISON
Paris, 1958–1974 (1–44). Henri Chopin.

Henri Chopin published concrete and visual poetry along with sound poetry in *Revue Ou*. He later designated the first nineteen issues of the magazine as *Cinquième Saison* to distinguish it from the second phase of the publication, which he called *Nouveau Saison*. During this later period, from 1964 to 1974, the magazine often used a *pochette* (pocket) format, containing LP records, unbound pages, posters, and art objects. Contributors included Chopin, Bernard Heidsieck, Brion Gysin, Raoul Hausmann, Paul de Vree, William S. Burroughs, François Dufrêne, Bob Cobbing, Paul Armand Gette, and Hugh Davies.

A.33

Revue Ou, no. 38–39, 1971. Research Library, The Getty Research Institute, Los Angeles (86-S1636).

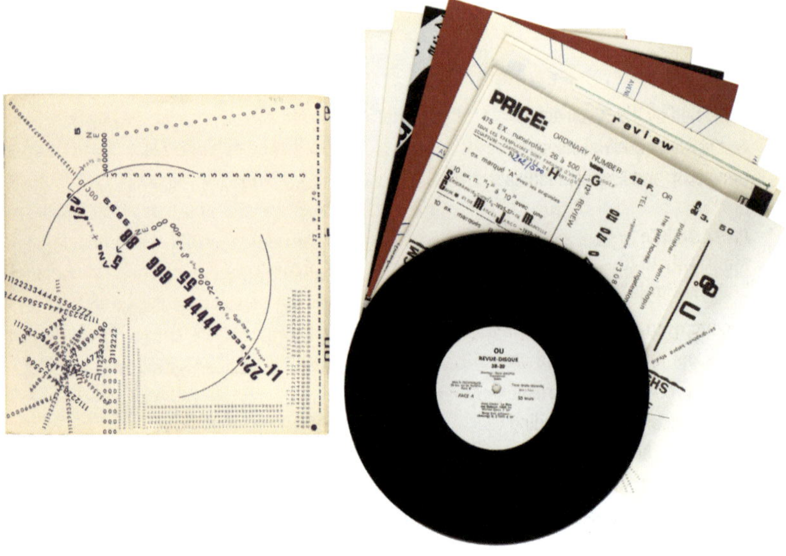

OVUM / OVUM 10 / OVUM 2A
Montevideo, Uruguay, 1969–1974. Ovum (1–10)/Ovum 2A (1–6).
Clemente Padin.

Ovum was an important experimental magazine of conceptual art, visual poetry, and mail art, published by Clemente Padin, who had previously published *Los Huevos del Plata* (1965–1969). Ten issues of *Ovum* (also sometimes called *Ovum 10*) were published between 1969 and 1974, and a separate but related magazine, *Ovum 2A* was published in 1973–1974. Most of the magazine's contributors were from Latin America and Europe. *Ovum* exemplifies the more explicitly politicized nature of mail art in Latin America. Issue 9 (December 1971) was devoted to the *Tucumán arde* project in Argentina. In 1977, Padin was imprisoned as a result of his artistic activities.

PAGES
Hertfordshire, England: HRS Graphics Ltd.,
1970–1972 (1–3). David Briers.

Pages published concrete poetry and artists' writings and projects by contributors such as Dieter Roth, Emmett Williams, Tom Phillips, Jochen Gertz, Richard Hamilton, and Robert Filliou. Editor David Briers explained in issue 1: "The aim of *Pages* is to publicize the avant-garde, and by doing so to prove that it does not exist, except as a name. … *Pages* will inform on the changing forms of art at the moment, most importantly those which are reproducible in as many copies as there exists a demand for them (one to millions), and whose price is directly related to the cost of their manufacture, and not only to the reputation of the artist. … The specific intention of *Pages* is to inform, and not to worry about whether art is necessary, for as John Cage has pointed out, we should by now have disposed of the Germanic concept of doing only what is necessary."

PALAZZO
Cologne, 1978–1983 (1–5). Heinz Zolper.

The painter Heinz Zoppler published the newspaper *Palazzo* once a year as a work of art "which had the goal of crossing, questioning, and dissolving many borders and boundaries through the means of subversion."[58] When Andy Warhol discovered the magazine, he invited Zoppler to New York; their collaborations from this trip appeared in issue 3.

PANDERMA
Basel, 1958–1977 (1–13). Carl László.

Published by the Basel art collector Carl László, *Panderma: Revue de la fin du monde* printed writings and original silkscreens by artists including Victor Vasarely, Man Ray, Jean Cocteau, Hugo Ball, and Francis Picabia. Later, László published the magazine *Radar*.

PARACHUTE
Montreal, 1975–. Founding Editors: France Morin and
Chantal Pontbriand.

According to an editorial statement in the first issue, the Canadian magazine *Parachute* "offers the reader in-depth articles on the practice and theory of art, interviews, texts and works as conceived by artists themselves as well as information relative to different aspects of contemporary art, including visual arts, music, film, and video." *Parachute*'s simple format and rough, brown paper cover signaled its noncommercial aims. Contributors included Tina Girouard, Keith Sonnier, Simone Forti, Gerhard Richter, Yvonne Rainer, Jonas Mekas, Alison Knowles, Liza Béar, and Michael Snow.

PARALLELOGRAMME
Vancouver: Canadian Association of Non-Profit Artist Centres, 1976–1995.

"*Parallelogramme* compiles monthly information on programmes of the member galleries within the Canadian Association of Non-Profit Artist Centres. It establishes a communication service to assist in the exchange of information on exhibitions, multi-disciplinary events, tours, and artists, not only amongst the Parallel Galleries, but amongst a broad art community."

PARENTHÈSE
New York, 1975–1979 (vol. 1, no. 1–vol. 2, no. 3/4). John Bernard Myers.

Parenthèse: A Magazine of Words and Pictures published contributions by Mary Frank, Al Held, Rudi Burckhardt, Paul Auster, Red Grooms, Cecil Beaton, Robert Rauschenberg, and Guy Davenport. The following editorial appeared in the first issue: "PARENTITHEMI: I-put-in-beside, and thereby besides. Between the curving lines like thin angels of rhetoric come our after-thoughts, sidelights and nervous disclaimers; the hedges that guard the truth; the necessary appositives too frail to stand unpropped; the logical friendships that banish the monster hidden in (mock) (turtle soup). But in the end, between these cupped hands upheld, the special radiance of the in-between."

PASO DE PEATONES
Mexico City: La Cocina Ediciones, 1978–1980.
Gabriel Macotela, Yani Pecanins, and Walter Doehner.

Paso de Peatones (meaning "pedestrian way") was an art and visual poetry magazine published in an edition of 350 by Gabriel Macotela, Yani Pecanins, and Walter Doehner under the imprint of La Cocina Ediciones, an important small press in Mexico City. Among its contributors were Guinovart, Michael Tracy, René Freire, Manuel Marin, Magali Lara, Ana Checchi, and Mario Rangel. In 1985, Macotela and Pecanins helped to found El Archivero, an important center for artists' publications in Mexico, along the lines of Printed Matter in the United States.

PERFORMANCE ART / LIVE
New York, 1979–1982 (1–6/7). Editors: Bonnie Marranca
and John Howell.

Performance Art (the title of which changed to *Live* in 1980 with issue 3) was published by the *Performing Arts Journal* "with the intention of offering the broadest possible coverage of 'performance art' which we recognize as an art world, as distinct from a theatre world, phenomenon." Edited by Bonnie Marranca and John Howell, it focused specifically on performance art with interviews, documentation, artists' writings, and articles by Carolee Schneemann, Ken Friedman, Robert Wilson, Richard Foreman, Yvonne Rainer, Meredith Monk, and others.

PERIODICAL
Los Angeles, 1969–1972 (1–10). Robert Heinecken.

In the late 1960s the artist Robert Heinecken began to alter magazines such as *Newsweek*, *Good Housekeeping*, and *Glamour.* He disassembled the magazines and used offset lithography or rubber stamps to overprint subversive found imagery on top of their smiling faces and anodyne scenes, then reassembled and bound them. In other magazines he cut out shapes to reveal portions of the pages underneath. These détourned magazines constituted his publication *Periodical*, of which he produced ten issues (the first of which was called *Periodical Pain*) in editions of 3–23. Heinecken sold the magazines cheaply and also occasionally left them in doctors' and dentists' offices and newsstands, to catch unsuspecting readers off guard.

LE PETIT COLOSSE DE SYMI
Basel and Zurich, 1966–1967 (1–4). Daniel Spoerri.

Le Petit Colosse de Symi: The Nothing Else Review was edited by Daniel Spoerri from the Greek island of Symi, with contributions by Dieter Roth, Jean Tinguely, Emmett Williams, and George Brecht.

PHASES
Paris, 1954–1965 (1–10). Edouard Jaguer.

Phases, subtitled "International notebooks for the documentation of avant-garde poetry and art," was the vehicle of the influential post-surrealist Phases group.

THE PLUMED HORN / EL CORNO EMPLUMADO
Mexico City, 1962–1968 (1–31).
Margaret Randall, Sergio Mondragón,
and Harvey Wolin (nos. 1–2).

Margaret Randall started *El Corno Emplumado* (simultaneously called *The Plumed Horn*) with her husband, Sergio Mondragón, and Harvey Wolin, who left the project shortly after the second issue. The magazine, published bilingually in Spanish and English, presented poetry and art from both hemispheres of the Americas. Its title was a dual reference to the Mesoamerican deity Quetzalcoatl (the plumed serpent) and a jazz horn, symbolizing the cultural confluence the magazine sought to facilitate. In the first issue, the editors wrote that the magazine was published "out of the need for a NEW MAGAZINE ... whose pages conform to the word instead of whose words conform to the pages ... now, when relations between the Americas have never been worse ... a showcase (outside politics) for the fact that WE ARE ALL BROTHERS." Contributors included Robert Creeley, Felipe Ehrenberg, Clayton Eshleman, Allen Ginsberg, Haroldo de Campos, Julio Cortázar, Heberto Padilla, Mark di Suvero, Bruce Conner, Hermann Hesse, Charles Bukowski, Lawrence Ferlinghetti, Jackson Mac Low, Marisol, Octavio Paz, Ulises Carrión, David Antin, Elaine de Kooning, Philip Guston, Roberto Fernández Retamar, and Mario Benedetti. After *The Plumed Horn* supported the Mexican student movement in 1968, its editors faced political reprisal, losing advertisers and subscribers, a situation that forced them to flee the country in 1969, ending the magazine.

PLURAL
Mexico City, 1971–1976 [1994] (1–58).
Octavio Paz.

Plural was a literary and cultural journal founded by Octavio Paz to support Mexican writers and artists and to increase their profile abroad. Contributors included Mario Vargas Llosa, Umberto Eco, Dore Ashton, Georges Bataille, Roland Barthes, Roman Jakobson, Norman O. Brown, Harold Rosenberg, Claude Lévi-Strauss, Susan Sontag, Augusto and Haroldo de Campos, José Luis Cuevas, Gillo Dorfles, Juan Acha, Damian Bayon, and Alberto Manrique. The newsprint magazine was designed by Vincente Rojo, then by Kazuya Sakai. It included a regular artistic supplement in color with works by Mexican and Latin American artists. Paz left *Plural* in 1976 when its publisher, the Excelsior Newspaper Cooperative, was taken over by the government in response to its refusal to support the ruling party. He went on to found *Vuelta* (Back) later that year, proclaiming in the first issue, "We are back." Though *Plural* continued to be published until 1994, it was disavowed by Paz after 1976.

POETRIE
(alternate titles: *Poesy, Poeting, Poeterei, Poemetry*)
Stuttgart: Hansjörg Mayer, 1966–1969/70
(1–5; issue 3/4 was followed by issue 4). Dieter Roth.

Having previously published the important art and concrete poetry magazine *Spirale,* Dieter Roth pushed the materiality of language even further in his "semiannual poetry journal" *Poetrie: der Halbjahresschrift für Poesie.* Produced in runs of 130–230, with numerous hand-altered copies, special editions, and title changes, the magazine is challenging to catalog. *Poesy* 1 was printed on letterpress with some copies hand-painted; it included a special edition of 7 on embossed colored leather. Several issues of *Poeting* 3/4 were covered in goat embryo skin with original collages; a special edition of 7 consisted of letterpress on tin foil bags filled with lamb cutlets, sauerkraut, sausages, and cheese, contained in a wooden box. *Poemetry* 4 was made of 19 transparent plastic bags filled with minced mutton, or alternately, urine and vanilla pudding. Issue 5, *Poesy 5 bis 1: Zeitschrift für Posiererei Pometrie Poeterei und Poesie,* consisted of a reprint of all 4 previous issues.

POOR. OLD. TIRED. HORSE.
Edinburgh: Wild Hawthorn Press, 1962–1967 (1–25). Ian Hamilton Finlay.

Ian Hamilton Finlay's lightweight, unpretentious poetry magazine *Poor. Old. Tired. Horse.* resembled a newsletter more than a periodical, starting off as a single folded sheet of paper. Jessie McGuffie and Paul Pond helped edit the first issue. Pond dropped off after issue 1, and McGuffie left in 1964. The title is a line in Robert Creeley's poem "Please" (1959). The magazine, which had a circulation of 300 to 750, was received unfavorably in Scotland due to the unconventional nature of the concrete and visual poetry it published. Among its contributors were Finlay, McGuffie, Jerome Rothenberg, Lawrence Ferlinghetti, Kurt Schwitters, Paul de Vree, Mary Ellen Solt, and Eugen Gomringer. Bridget Riley and Ad Reinhardt collaborated on issue 18.

POSSIBILITIES
New York, 1947–1948 (1). Editors: Robert Motherwell,
Harold Rosenberg, John Cage, and Pierre Chareau.

Possibilities: An Occasional Review was published just once, in Winter 1947–1948. In their editorial statement, Robert Motherwell and Harold Rosenberg argued for the value of indeterminacy against the instrumentalization of artistic process for political ends during the Cold War:

> This is a magazine of artists and writers who "practice" in their work their own experience without seeking to transcend it in academic, group or political formulas. Such practice implies the belief that through conversion of energy something valid may come out, whatever the situation one is forced to begin with. The question of what will emerge is left open. One functions in an attitude of expectancy. As Juan Gris said: "You are lost the instant you know what the result will be." … If one is to continue to paint or write as the political trap seems to close upon him he must perhaps have the extremist faith in sheer possibility.

POTLATCH
Paris, 1954–1959 (1–30). Andre-Frank Conord, Mohamed Dahou,
Gil J. Wolman, and Jacques Fillon.

Published in an edition of 50 to 500, the mimeographed leaflet *Potlatch,* subtitled "Information bulletin of the French section of the Lettrist International," was one the most important lettrist publications. Others included *Jerimadeth, Ur,* and *Internationale Lettriste.*

PRAXIS

Berkeley, California, 1975–1978 (1–4). Editor: Ronald Reimers.

Praxis: A Journal of Radical Perspectives on the Arts published critical articles, translations, and occasionally artists' writings.

PRÉSENCE AFRICAINE

Paris: Editions du Seuil, 1947– (1–). Founding editor: Alioune Diop.

Présence Africaine, subtitled "Revue culturelle du monde noir," was founded by the Senegalese-born professor of philosophy Alioune Diop. He described the magazine's editorial mission in the first issue: "to help define African originality and to hasten its introduction into the modern world." The digest-sized magazine featured an illustration of a Dogon mask on its cover. The magazine's ideological and intellectual program was further articulated in 1955: "All articles will be published, provided … they are concerned with Africa, and are faithful to our anti-racialist and anti-colonialist policy, and to the solidarity of colonized peoples."[59] *Présence Africaine* published contributions by African, European, and American intellectuals, writers, and social scientists, including Aimé Césaire, Léopold Sédar Senghor, Jean-Paul Sartre, André Gide, Richard Wright, and Albert Camus. The art historian William Fagg and the art dealer Charles Ratton also wrote for the magazine, and in 1956, *Présence Africaine* organized the First International Congress of Black Writers and Artists in Paris. It also helped finance Alain Resnais and Chris Marker's 1953 film *Statues Also Die*, which was censored in France because of its anticolonialist stance.

Further Reading: Valentin Y. Mudimbe, ed., *The Surreptitious Speech: "Présence Africaine" and the Politics of Otherness, 1947–1987* (Chicago: University of Chicago Press, 1992).

PROFILE

Chicago: Video Data Bank, 1981–1985 (vol. 1, no. 1–vol. 5, no. 4).
Editors: Lyn Blumenthal and Kate Horsfield.

Profile, published by Video Data Bank, announced itself as "an idea-oriented publication devoted to an exploration of artists' ideas by the artists themselves." Each issue profiled a single artist with a transcript of an in-depth videotaped interview (also available on videotape cassette). The magazine's cover featured a tightly cropped still from the interview. Artists interviewed included Joseph Beuys, Agnes Martin, Lucy Lippard, Eleanor Antin, Allan Kaprow, Pat Steir, Nancy Spero, Michelle Stuart, Shigeko Kubota, Thomas Lawson, Vito Acconci, Linda Montano, Martha Rosler, and Yvonne Rainer.

PROP

Albany, New York: Workspace Loft, 1979–1986 (1–13).
Editors: Jessica Lawrence and Bob Durlak.

Prop was an irreverent zine-like booklet of mail art with contributions by Anna Banana, Carlo Pittore, Vittore Baroni, and Opal Nations.

PROVOKE

Tokyo, 1968–1968 (1–3). Takuma Nakahira, Yutaka Takanashi,
Daido Moriyama (2–3), Takahiko Okada, and Koji Taki.

Provoke: Provocative Materials for Thought was published by a group of Japanese photographers, poets, and critics who promoted a new photographic style known as *are/bure/boke* (grainy/blurry/out-of-focus). A manifesto in the first issue described the group's aesthetic principles:

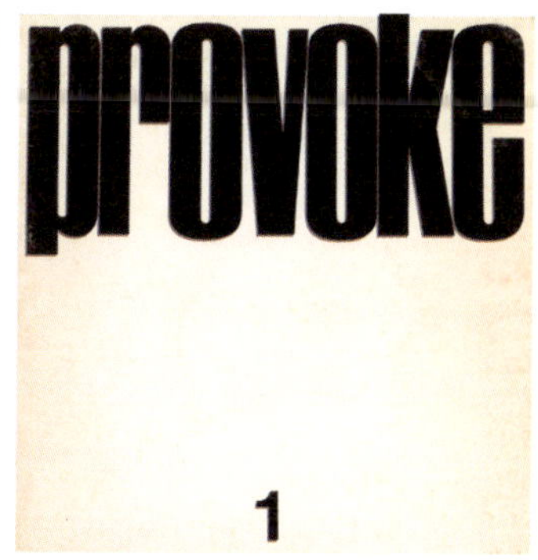

A.34
Provoke, no. 1, 1968. Research Library, The Getty Research Institute, Los Angeles (2604-874 no. 1).

Visual images are not ideological themselves. They cannot represent the totality of an idea, nor are they interchangeable like words. However, their irreversible materiality—reality cut out by the camera—belongs to the reverse side of the word of language. Photographic images, therefore, often unexpectedly stimulate language and ideas. Thus, petrified language can transcend itself and become an idea, resulting in a new language and in new ideas. Today, when words have lost their material base—in other words, their reality—and seem suspended in midair, a photographer's eye can capture fragments of reality that cannot be expressed in language as it is. He can submit those images as documents to be considered alongside language and ideology. This is why, brash as it may seem, *Provoke* has the subtitle "provocative documents for the pursuit of ideas."[60]

While it broke with traditional notions of photojournalistic objectivity, *Provoke* did not conceive of the photograph as a purely subjective expression, but rather as an accurate record of the contingency of human vision itself. For, Nakahira wrote, "Even human vision is out of focus and blurry."[61] As the group explored the magazine's potential as a distribution form, they experimented with its format to enhance their aesthetic aims, frequently printing photographs horizontally as full-bleed double-page spreads, or repeating photographs as mirror images. Texts were relegated to the front and back of the magazine. The paper quality became increasingly rough and unrefined over the three issues, as if mimicking or exaggerating the graininess of the photographs themselves. *Provoke* ended with the publication of the book *First, Abandon the World of Seeming Certainty,* edited by Koji Taki and Takuma Nakahira in 1970, often considered to be the magazine's fourth issue.

Further reading: Christoph Schifferli, ed., *The Japanese Box: Facsimile Reprint of Six Rare Photographic Publications of the Provoke Era* (Paris: Edition 7L, 2001).

PUBLIC ILLUMINATION
New York, 1979– (1–). Zagreus Bowery
(pseudonym for Jeffrey Isaac).

Public Illumination is a miniature (7-by-11-centimeter) magazine publishing strictly pseudonymous contributions. Originally billed as a "non-weekly" featuring "Politics, Gossip, Sports, Violence, Sex, and More!" the magazine published quirky text and image contributions on topics such as Telephones, Virulence, Mass Transit, and Cosmetic Mutilations. Contributors have allegedly included Kathy Acker, John Ashbery, Jean-Michel Basquiat, Keith Haring, and David Wojnarowicz.

QUEEN STREET MAGAZINE
Toronto: Goathair Press, 1973–1977
(vol. 1, no. 1–no. 10/11/12/13).
Angelo Sgabellone.

Queen Street Magazine covered alternative and unknown artists in Toronto's historic Queen Street West neighborhood, which grew into a vibrant arts district in the 1970s.

RADAR
Basel and New York, 1982–1988 (1–5/6). Carl László.

Radar was published by Basel-based art collector Carl László, who previously published *Panderma*. Contributors included Robert Mapplethorpe, Gerard Malanga, William S. Burroughs, Allen Ginsberg, Les Levine, and Andy Warhol.

RADICAL SOFTWARE

New York: Raindance Corporation, 1970–1974
(vol. 1, no. 1–vol. 2, no. 6). Beryl Korot, Ira Schneider,
Phyllis Gershuny, Michael Shamberg, and others.

Originally meant to be called *The Video Newsletter*, *Radical Software* was founded by a
group of artists and radical media activists who were interested in the artistic and social
potential of video. The following editorial statement appeared in the first issue:

> As problem solvers we are a nation of hardware freaks. Some are into seizing prop-
> erty or destroying it. Others believe in protecting property at any cost—including
> life—or at least guarding it against spontaneous use. Meanwhile, unseen systems
> shape our lives. Power is no longer measured in land, labor, or capital, but by access
> to information and the means to disseminate it. As long as the most powerful tools
> (not weapons) are in the hands of those who would hoard them, no alternative cultural
> vision can succeed. Unless we design and implement alternate information struc-
> tures which transcend and reconfigure the existing ones, other alternate systems and
> lifestyles will be no more than products of the existing process. … So six months
> ago some of us who have been working in videotape got the idea for an information
> source which would bring together people who were already making their own televi-
> sion, attempt to turn on others to the idea as a means of social change and exchange,
> and serve as an introduction to an evolving handbook of technology.

The first issue, a quarter-fold tabloid printed in blue ink, showed on its cover a diagram
of a hodological space, theorized by the psychologist Kurt Lewin as a kind of topology in
which psychological and geometrical forces interact. The image reinforced an understanding of the media (including the magazine itself) as a kind of interactive force field of the
type that Lewin theorized. In addition to articles and interviews, the magazine published a
column called "Feedback," where snippets sent in by various video groups or individuals
were printed on a lopsided matrix, visually embodying the chatter of multiple voices and
points of view. In other ways as well, the magazine's layout visualized the new forms of
information it reported on, arranging text nonlinearly in bubbles and boxes linked by arrows,
allowing readers to determine the sequence. The magazine replaced its copyright symbol
with an *x*, explaining: "To encourage dissemination of the information in *Radical Software*
we have created our own symbol of an *x* within a circle. This is a Xerox mark, the antithesis
of Copyright, which means DO copy." Contributors included Gregory Bateson, Dan Graham,
David Ross, Gene Youngblood, Nam June Paik, Buckminster Fuller, and the collective Ant
Farm, which designed the cover of issue 4. *Radical Software* was initially published by the
Raindance Corporation, a radical media think tank (its name was a send up of the Rand
Corporation) founded by Frank Gillette. Later, when Gordon and Breach Publishing took over,
it switched to a 9-by-12-inch magazine format. Eleven issues were published in four years
(plus the 1971 book *Guerrilla Television*, which was designated as vol. 1, no. 6), and its
print run increased from 2,000 to 10,000. Disagreements between Gordon and Breach and
Raindance over the frequency of issues and the quality of print production brought *Radical
Software* to an end.

RAMPIKE

Toronto, 1979– (vol. 1, no. 1–). Karl Jirgens.

Published and edited by Karl Jirgens and printed by Toronto's renowned Coach House Press,
Rampike has been an important vehicle for innovative art and writings within and outside
Canada, with a strong focus on Canadian expression. As Jirgens explained in an editorial,

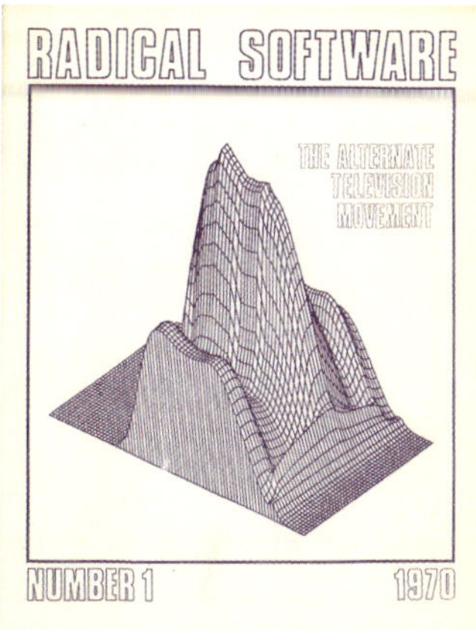

A.35

Radical Software, vol.1, no. 1, 1970.
Courtesy of Ira Schneider.

"the name 'Rampike' stands fro the skeleton of a tree that has been ravaged by lightening or forest fire. There is a tree that grows in Canada known as the lodge-pole pine. When threatened by fire, its cones release winged seedlings which hover in the heat above the flames, and when the danger has passed they spin to the ground and settle in the fertile ash so that a new generation can emerge. This image represents the on-going cycle of death and re-birth evident in any vital culture."[62] Contributors have included Marshall McLuhan, Northrop Frye, Victor Coleman, Eli Mandel, Dennis Oppenheim, Joseph Beuys, Vito Acconci, Chris Burden, Julia Kristeva, Jacques Derrida, and William Burroughs.

RAW
New York, 1980–1991 (vol. 1, no. 1–vol. 2, no. 3).
Art Spiegelman and Françoise Mouly;
Paul Karasik joined the staff as an associate editor
starting with no. 4.

When Art Spiegelman and Françoise Mouly decided to publish a new comic magazine on New Year's Eve 1980, they wanted, according to Mouly, "to force people to see how beautiful, and how moving, and how powerful the work could be … to fight the prejudice against comics as toilet literature, that they should be printed only on newsprint and be disposable."[63] A French expatriate who had abandoned her studies in architecture at the Beaux-Arts for a more bohemian life in New York (where, among other things, she acted in a play by Richard Foreman), Mouly printed the magazine on a secondhand press she had set up in the couple's SoHo loft.[64] *Raw*'s large and "luxurious" format signaled its editors' aspirations to elevate comics to a respectable art form.[65] While mostly black and white, the first issue had a tipped-in color sheet on the cover and contained Spiegelman's *Two Fisted Painter*, a small color insert booklet. Hand-collated by the editors and their friends, subsequent issues included various kinds of special inserts and handmade interventions, including die-cut pages, a flexi-disc recording (no. 4), a hand-ripped cover (no. 7), and bubblegum cards and an actual piece of chewing gum in a plastic bag stapled into the centerfold (no. 2). Starting with the second issue, each issue of *Raw* published a chapter of *Maus*, Spiegelman's graphic novel about his parents' experience in Auschwitz, in the form of an insert booklet. Other contributors included American and European comic artists including Heinz Emigholz, Patricia Caire, Mark Beyer, Joost Swarte, Gary Panter, Charles Burns, Yoshiharu Tsuge, Robert Crumb, Sue Coe, and Chris Ware. *Raw* introduced comic art into the interdisciplinary mix that characterized the downtown art scene of the 1980s.

REAKTION
Düsseldorf, 1975–1983 (1–7). Milan Molzer.

Published annually by the Verlaggalerie Leaman, *Reaktion* was a two-ring binder containing photocopies and multimedia works including mirrors and other objects in plastic slipcases.

REALITY
New York, 1953–1955 (1–3). Isabel Bishop, Edward Hopper,
Jack Levine, and others.

Reality: A Journal of Artists' Opinions was a free, newsletter-like publication founded by a group of artists who felt marginalized by the dominance of modernist abstraction in New York in the 1950s. A statement in the first issue explained: "A group of artists have joined together to discuss their problems. … We believe that art cannot become the property of an esoteric cult. We reaffirm the right of the artist to the control of his profession. We will work to restore to art its freedom and dignity as a living language." Among those who signed the statement were Milton Avery, Robert Gwathmey, Edward Hopper, Reginald Marsh, Jacob Lawrence, Jack Levine, and Anton Refregier.

REAL LIFE

New York, 1979–1994 (1–22). Thomas Lawson and
Susan Morgan. See chapter 7.

Perhaps more than any other publication, *Real Life* crystallized the sensibilities and interests of the Pictures generation, publishing a diverse range of material including artists' writings and projects, criticism, working notes, reproductions, and interviews. With a circulation of 1,000 to 2,000 and just a handful of ads, mainly for emerging galleries and nonprofit spaces such as Artists Space, Metro Pictures, and the Kitchen, the magazine offered a different view onto this moment than more canonical accounts of its market- and media-fueled hype. Contributors included Thomas Lawson, Susan Morgan, Sherrie Levine, Richard Prince, David Robbins, Louise Lawler, Allan McCollum, and Barbara Kruger, among many others.

Further reading: Miriam Katzeff, Thomas Lawson, and Susan Morgan, eds., *Real Life Magazine: Selected Projects and Writings, 1979–1994* (New York: Primary Information, 2007).

RED-HERRING

New York, 1977–1978 (1–2). Editors: Karl Beveridge,
Jill Breakstone, Ian Burn, Carole Conde, Michael Corris,
Preston Heller, and Andrew Menard.

Red-Herring was a tabloid newspaper published by several former editors of *The Fox*, which had dissolved after three issues due to editorial infighting. *Red-Herring* referenced the earlier magazine on the front page of the first issue, which showed a man sitting at a desk with a gun, a pack of cigarettes, and a mock-up of the nonexistent issue 5 of *The Fox*. An editorial statement explained:

> This is the first issue of a magazine being edited and published by some of the former editors of *The Fox*. Why are we publishing another magazine? While it is true to say that most of our production and history is appropriated, this process is certainly never air-tight. In any struggle against such appropriation, progressive forces emerge and coalesce. There may be little we can do to stop this magazine from becoming another coffee-table class diversion; there is much we can do to make sure that isn't all it becomes. Of course the forms that this struggle takes are of necessity transitional, as *Red-Herring* is transitional. … We clearly recognize that what we are doing should, like everything else "made-in-New York," be regarded in many ways as yet another red-herring.

Articles were unsigned in order to stress collective rather individual authorship. Advertisements for *Heresies* and *Left Curve* suggested the partisan editorial agenda of *Red-Herring*, which criticized state and corporate involvement in culture and advocated for artists' rights and organizing. An article entitled "Salami Tactics: How to Write an Article for a 'Radical' Art-Magazine" parodied the widely perceived careerism of certain "radical" artists that had fueled the editorial discord of *The Fox*: "Yes, you too can write your own radical article! You never need to fear the power of other's verbiage. … Such writing has proven invaluable for decimating uncountable déjà-vu artists, been simply super for bowling over all sorts of art-world forgettables, not to mention the amazing potential for endless pettifogging careers." *Red-Herring* ended after two issues.

RED LETTER DAYS

New York: Political Art Documentation/Distribution,
1983–1984 (vol. 1, no. 1–vol. 2, no. 8).

Red Letter Days: A Monthly Listing of Left Cultural Events was sponsored by the artists' collective Political Art Documentation/Distribution (which also published *Upfront*). According to an editorial statement, the publication "intended to fill a gap in N.Y.'s info about socially relevant cultural events." Photocopied on a single sheet of paper and distributed freely at Printed Matter, Franklin Furnace, and other venues, *Red Letter Days* listed alternative venues, films, performances, and protests. A calendar circled in red marker appeared on the front of each issue.

REDTAPE

New York, 1982–1992 (1–7). Michael Carter.

Redtape featured artists and writers who were part of the Lower East Side scene in the 1980s, including Kathy Acker, Constance DeJong, Lynne Tillman, and David Wojnarowicz.

REFLEX

Amsterdam, 1948–1949. Edited by the Experimental Group in Holland.

Reflex: Orgaan van de experimentele groep in Holland was the first periodical published by the Cobra group. It contained contributions and original lithographs by Constant Nieuwenhuys, Corneille, Karel Appel, Anton Rooskens, Jan Nieuwenhuys, Theo Wolvecamp, and Eugene Brands.

REVIEW FOR EVERYTHING

Stuttgart, 1975–1986 (1–10, plus 10B). Dieter Roth
(nos. 1–7) and Barbara Wien (nos. 8–10B*).

Dieter Roth promised to publish everything submitted to his *Review for Everything*. In a handwritten editorial note in the second issue he explained, "The *Review for Everything*, where everybody (Everybody), every man (everyman) can appear [where contributions of anybody who can write or draw (or not) may (can) appear], if she (he) likes to (do so); she (he) should send her (his) contribution (stuff)." Submissions—which he specified should be no longer than four A4 pages—were printed in alphabetical order, and in return contributors received five copies each. The magazine's covers were designed by the graphic artist Uwe Lohrer, and the first three issues were copublished with Hansjörg Mayer. Roth announced the ending of the magazine with issue 7, but it continued under the direction of Barbara Wien in Berlin for another three issues. True to its original editorial policy, the magazine grew to include 300 contributors and 1,396 pages. Issue 10B was a supplement consisting of manuscripts received after the cutoff of the final issue.

RHINOZEROS

Berlin, 1960–1965 (1–10). Rolf-Gunter Dienst and
Klaus-Peter Dienst.

Edited by the brothers Rolf-Gunter and Klaus-Peter Dienst, *Rhinozeros* published art and poetry by William S. Burroughs, Hans Arp, Brion Gysin, Jean Cocteau, and Raoul Hausmann.

RIXES

Paris, 1950–1951 (1–2). Max Clarac-Sérou, Édouard Jaguer,
and Iaroslav Serpan.

Rixes was related to the magazines *Cobra* and *Phases*. Contributors included Asger Jorn, Michel Butor, Öyvind Fahlström, and Richard Huelsenbeck.

ROBHO

Paris, 1967–1971 (1–5/6; unnumbered November–December 1967
issue constitutes no. 2). Julien Blaine and Jean Clay.

Robho was founded by the art critic Jean Clay and the poet and artist Julien Blaine as a
way to trigger dialog between their different interests in kinetic art and guerrilla theater,
respectively. Reflecting Clay's interest in kinetic art, the title was an intentional misspelling
of the word "robot," reflecting its phonetic spelling when pronounced in French. As Blaine
recalled, it wasn't "'robot' but 'robho': so a word about a sort of human mechanical thing
but upset, wrong, broken, put out of order."[66] Published in an edition between 1,000 and
1,500, *Robho* was a large-format magazine, each issue of which was printed in a different
color ink: maroon, dark blue, etc. It contained criticism, interviews, and artists' writings
covering an international range of activities by artists' groups such as the Parisian BMPT
group, the neoconcretists in Brazil, the Gutai group in Japan, the *Tucumán arde* project in
Argentina, and the Art Workers' Coalition in New York. It included a "guerrilla theater" section that reported on the San Francisco Mime Troupe, the Bread and Puppet Theater, and
the Diggers. Contributors included Willoughby Sharp, Yve-Alain Bois, Jack Burnham, Hans
Haacke, Christo, and Vassilakis Takis. Notably it published an extensive dossier of writings
by Lygia Clark in issues 4 and 5/6.

ROK

Belgrade, 1969–1970 (1–2). Bora Ćosić.

Rok, subtitled "A periodical for literature and the aesthetic study of reality," was published
in Belgrade by the blacklisted author Bora Ćosić, who announced that the magazine would
"fight against writing that increasingly 'took the wrong tack' … by pleasing individuals and
making them 'happy.'"[67] The first issue had a blue vinyl cover and was dedicated to the
activities of the Slovenian neo-avant-garde, including the OHO group, as well as to Fluxus
activities. Contributors included Ćosić, Mica Danojlić, Mirko Klarin, Vladan Radovanović,
and Mirjana Stefanović.

SALAMANDER

Malmö, Sweden, 1955 (1–3). I. Gustafson, C. O. Hultén, I. Laaban,
and G. Printz-Påhlson.

The Swedish art and poetry magazine *Salamander* was related to publications such as
Phases, Cobra, and *Boa,* adding an amphibian to the reptile-themed titles that had begun
to proliferate in this cluster of magazines.

SALON

Cologne, 1977–1983 (1–11; no. 12 produced as a
retrospective issue in 1992). Gerhard Theewen.

Gerhard Theewen published the idiosyncratic artists' magazine *Salon* eleven times between
1977 and 1983. In addition to publishing contributions by artists from Germany and abroad,
the magazine was an opportunity for Theewen to indulge his own personal obsessions with
ephemera, 1950s rock 'n' roll and fashion (he started dressing like a teddy boy in 1979),
and kitschy nudes. He chose the title for its references to both high art (the Salon d'art
moderne) and mass culture (hair salon, auto salon, and *Waschsalon* [laundromat]). The
magazine's cursive logo was hand-painted by a man who painted shop windows for a living.
Artist Hans-Peter Feldmann designed *Salon*'s covers: a series of appropriated photographs,
including a starlet, a robot, two flamingos, a car, an old radio. Theewen observed, "You have
a very broad range of visual information but no idea of what could be inside. If you open the

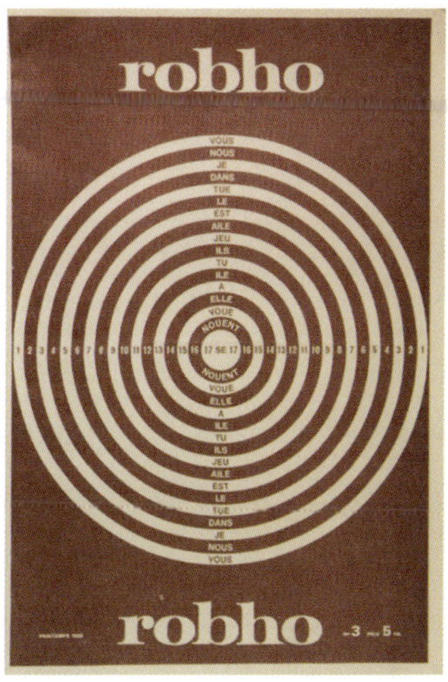

A.36
Robho, no. 3, Spring 1968. Courtesy
of Julien Blaine.

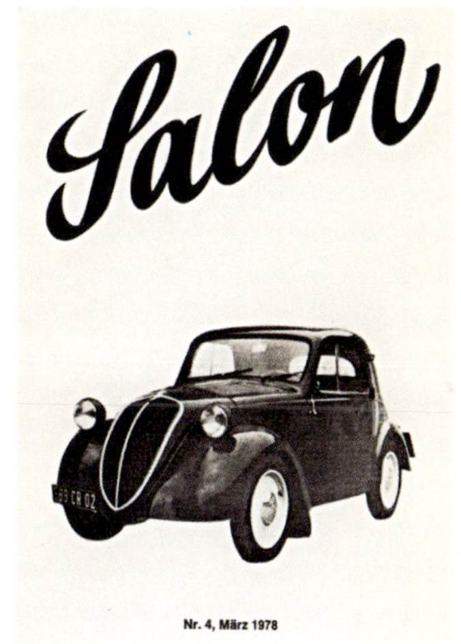

A.37
Salon, no. 4, 1978. Courtesy of
Gerhard Theewen. Research Library,
The Getty Research Institute,
Los Angeles (87-S95).

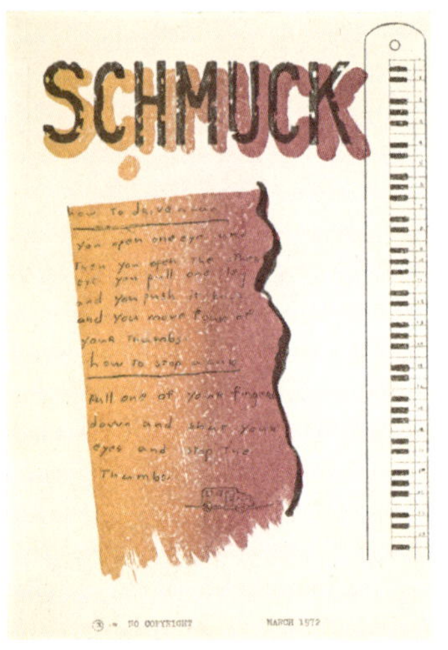

A.38

Schmuck, no. 5, 1975. Courtesy of
Felipe Ehrenberg. Research Library,
The Getty Research Institute,
Los Angeles (91-S582).

magazine you will find conceptual art, naturalistic drawings, photography. This was, for me, a chance to collect art. For all the contributions were made especially for *Salon*. So one can describe the project as a private collection made public."[68] Contributors included Jochen Gerz, Geoffrey Hendricks, Maurizio Nannucci, Raul Marroquin, David Askevold, Robert Barry, Chris Burden, Italo Scanga, Robert Cumming, and Lawrence Weiner.

SAN FRANCISCO EARTHQUAKE
San Francisco: Nova Broadcast Press, 1967–1967 (1–5).
Jan Herman.

The *San Francisco Earthquake* was a poetry magazine published by Jan Herman (who also published the important Nova Broadcast series of pamphlets) featuring Beat generation poets and artists.

DIE SCHASTROMMEL / DIE DROSSEL
Berlin, 1969–1977 (1–17). Günter Brus.

Die Schastrommel was a Viennese actionist magazine published by Günter Brus in Berlin, where he moved in 1969 after being arrested for his 1968 performance in which he sang the Austrian national anthem while masturbating. Ironically subtitled "The organ of the Austrian Government in Exile," the magazine published writings and documentation of performances by Brus, Valie Export, Hermann Nitsch, Arnold Schwarzkogler, Otto Muehl, Gerhard Rühm, and Oswald Weiner. The magazine's title, literally meaning "fart drum," but also slang for a gossipmonger, suggested the scatological tendency of some of the group's performances. *Die Schastrommel* began as a limited-edition stapled photocopy. Issues 3 through 5 were published under *Interfunktionen*'s imprint, which increased the production value and circulation to around 500; several issues had special editions with signed original works. Issue 8 was produced in three volumes (a, b, and c) as an attempt to comprehensively archive actionist works. With issue 13, Brus changed the magazine's title to *Die Drossel* (the thrush), which also suggested the word *Schimpfdrossel* (whiner). Brus ended the magazine in 1977 when he was pardoned by the Austrian government and moved back to Vienna.

SCHMUCK
Cullompton, Devon, England: Beau Geste Press,
1972–1978 (1–8). Editors: Martha Hellion, Felipe Ehrenberg,
and David Mayor.

Schmuck was published by the Mexican artists Martha Hellion and Felipe Ehrenberg, who moved to England in the wake of the 1968 student movement in Mexico. Inspired by the magazine *The Plumed Horn / El Corno Emplumado*, they founded the Beau Geste Press on a farm in Devon, England, with David Mayor, and published *Schmuck*, along with numerous artists' books, to foster communication between artists internationally. The magazine, published in an edition of around 550 copies, focused on Fluxus and mail art, with special issues dedicated to art in Czechoslovakia, France, Germany, Hungary, Japan, and Iceland.

SCRAP
New York, 1960–1962 (1–8). Sidney Geist and Anita Ventura.

Scrap was an irreverent alternative to mainstream criticism published by sculptor and writer Sidney Geist and curator Anita Ventura. Geist explained the magazine's editorial mission and title as follows: "a lot of art is very serious, and criticism is very serious, and the whole thing gets kind of heavy. We thought it would be good to take an attitude toward it that would be irreverent in its seriousness. Art is more important than criticism anyway, and we got that idea out quickly in the title."[69] Printed on newsprint, in Courier font, with a crowded, chaotic layout, the magazine had an appropriately "scrappy" do-it-yourself feel, publishing criticism and artists' writings. Artists such as Robert Rauschenberg and Ad Reinhardt contributed letters to the editor. Folded into issue 2 was an issue of *Pandemonium*, a sheaf of poetry by artists published by Bob Hauge and Pat Passlof.

SEMINA

Los Angeles, San Francisco, and Larkspur, California, 1955–1964 (1–9). Wallace Berman.

Semina was an idiosyncratic, personal, handmade magazine, published by Wallace Berman, an artist associated with California assemblage and the Beats. It served as a traveling exhibition space, containing unbound collages, photographs, drawings, and texts by Berman, his friends, and those he admired. He printed the magazine on a mail order Kelsey tabletop platen handpress in an edition of 150 to 350 copies, sent to a private mailing list. (At least one issue, no. 3, was also sold at the City Lights bookstore.) Some issues had just a few contributors, while others had over twenty, among them Berman (who sometimes used the pseudonym Pantale Xantos), William Blake, Lewis Carroll, Jean Cocteau, Herman Hesse, Walter Hopps, Paul Éluard, Charles Bukowski, William Burroughs, Allen Ginsberg, Antonin Artaud, and Jess Collins, who submitted an unsigned collage to issue 8. The first issue of *Semina* was confiscated during the artist's exhibition at the Ferus Gallery because it contained an erotic ink drawing based on a peyote vision by an artist who went by the name Cameron. Issue 7, titled "Aleph," was devoted solely to Berman's work. The final issue was a single sheet containing an altered news photograph of Jack Ruby shooting Lee Harvey Oswald, accompanied by a Michael McLure poem. The sixties had begun.

Further reading: Michael Duncan and Kristine McKenna, *Semina Culture: Wallace Berman & His Circle* (New York: D.A.P./Distributed Art Publishers, 2005).

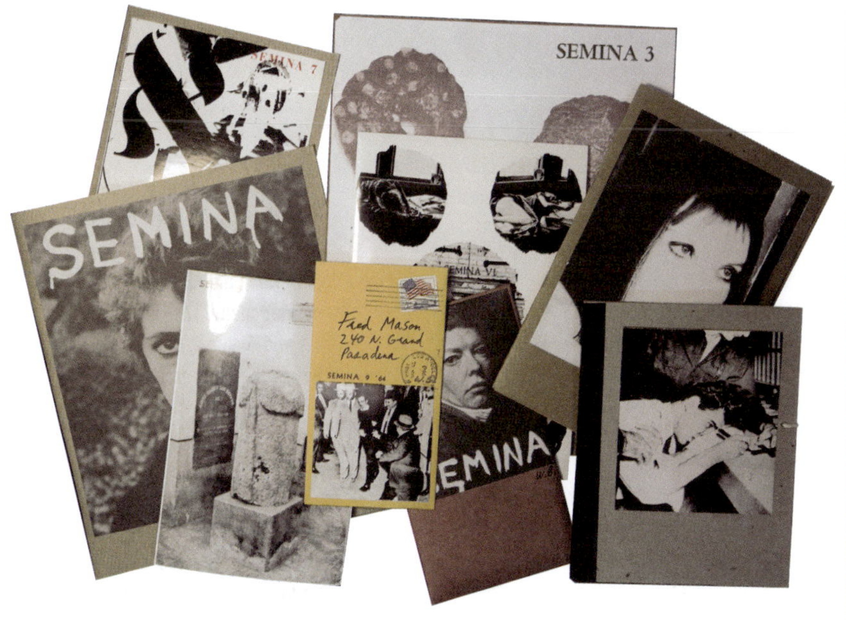

A.39

Semina, 1955–1964. Courtesy of Shirley Berman.

SEMIOTEXT(E)
New York, 1974–1984 (vol. 1, no. 1–vol. 4, no. 3).
Sylvère Lotringer.

Semiotext(e) was founded by the French literary critic Sylvère Lotringer, along with several of his graduate students at Columbia University, who chipped in fifty dollars apiece to get the journal started. *Semiotext(e)* introduced writers such as Michel Foucault, Gilles Deleuze and Félix Guattari, and Jacques Derrida to an American audience, and soon began to reach outside of the academic world, publishing interviews with downtown artists, such as Jack Smith, Philip Glass, Steve Reich, Robert Wilson, and John Cage. In 1983 Semiotext(e) began publishing the Foreign Agents series, compact black books of theory, presented in an irreverently unacademic format, by Deleuze and Guattari, Paul Virilio, and Jean Baudrillard (whose *Simulations* appeared in 1983). Later it published fiction in its Native Agents series and, most recently, has published an Intervention series and the magazine *Animal Shelter.*

SIGNAL
Belgrade, 1970–1973 (1–8/9). Miroljub Todorović.

Signal was founded to support signalism, described in the first issue as "an avant-garde creative movement whose aim it is to affect and revolutionize all of the arts, introducing the kind of thinking that is common to exact science and initiating new processes and methods within a permanent creative revolution influenced particularly by the technological civilization, the sign civilization, the increasing use of science and scientific methods, and the emergence of the computer." Contributors included Paul de Vree, Marina Abramović, Jochen Gerz, On Kawara, Sol LeWitt, and Julien Blaine.

SIGNALS
London: Centre for Advanced Creative Study,
1964–1966 (1–11). Paul Keeler (director) and
David Medalla (editor).

Signals (spelled *Signalz* in the first issue) was published by the Centre for Advanced Creative Study, which would become the legendary Signals Gallery, a vital center for kinetic and experimental art. Both magazine and gallery featured avant-garde European and Latin American artists, including Jesús Rafael Soto, Takis, Lygia Clark, Sergio de Camargo, Carlos Cruz-Díaz, Li Yuan-chia, Gerhard von Graevenitz, Eduardo Chillida, and Marcela Salvadori. Named after a series of tensile sculptures by Takis, *Signals* published artists' writings, documentation, poetry, critical writings, and news in a large-format tabloid. The following editorial statement appeared in the first issue:

> This is the first number of *Signalz,* the montly news bulletin of the Centre for Advanced Creative Study. *Signalz* will contain news items on the activities of the Centre, documentation and critical studies on the Centre's artists, as well as original writings by the artists themselves. … *Signalz* shall bring to the attention of the artist new developments in technology and science which might be of assistance in the formation of the artist's discipline, in the choice of his materials and the improvement of his technique. We hope to provide a forum for all those who believe in the correlation of the arts and Art's *imaginative* integration with technology, science, architecture, and our entire environment. We believe that such an integration can only be accomplished by more rigorous means: by the exercise of the highest aesthetic standards, and when society gives to the artist its available materials, its support—and complete freedom in the pursuit of his (the artist's) art.

SITES

New York: Lumen, Inc., 1979–1995 (1–26). Dennis L. Dollens.

Sites was billed as "a literary-architectural magazine" that provided "a rare blend of literature with architecture, sculpture, and urban design." Each issue featured a little-known or
neglected building, monument, or public place, providing historic and contemporary photographs, maps, visitors' information and walking tours, as well as essays, interviews, poems,
and criticism. Among its contributors were Dore Ashton, Antonio Muntadas, Paul West, and
Diane Ackerman. Special issues were published on the Big Duck (a duck-shaped building
on eastern Long Island), Mies van der Rohe's Barcelona Pavilion, and Portland, Maine's
Breakwater Lighthouse, which included a paper model of the lighthouse to cut out and
assemble. Krzysztof Wodiczko and Rudolph Luria published their *Homeless Vehicle Project*
in issue 20.

THE SITUATIONIST TIMES

Paris, 1962–1967 (1–6). Jacqueline de Jong.

Published by Jacqueline de Jong with assistance from Asger Jorn and Noël Arnaud, *The
Situationist Times* was filled with found and détourned imagery, collages, drawings, and
original lithographs.

SMILE

London, 1984–1989. Editor: Stewart Home.

Founded by Stewart Home, *SMILE* stemmed out of the lineage of *FILE*, *VILE*, and *BILE*.
Embracing plagiarism and mistaken identities, and pushing the egalitarian premise of mail
art to its limit, Home suggested that all magazines be called *SMILE* and encouraged readers to publish their own issues of *SMILE*. Home produced eleven issues of *SMILE* between
1984 and 1989; however, countless issues have been produced by others around the world,
making it impossible to know how many issues have actually been published.

S.M.S.

New York: Letter Edged in Black Press,
February-December 1968 (1–6). William Copley.

Published by the American surrealist painter and art dealer William Copley, *S.M.S.* consisted of a series of portfolios containing intricate, artist-designed multiples. The publication's
initials stood for "Shit Must Stop," suggesting the countercultural ethos that guided its
attempt to liberate artists from the restrictions of the gallery space. Copley's Letter Edged
in Black Press, on Manhattan's Upper West Side, was a bohemian gathering spot for artists
featuring "a buffet perpetually replenished by nearby Zabar's Delicatessen, an open bar,
and a pay phone with a cigar box filled with dimes."[70] *S.M.S.* was published bimonthly in
an edition of 2,500 copies and was available by subscription for $125. In addition to various
kinds of printed projects including booklets, postcards, and decals, it included cassette tapes
and three-dimensional objects. Yoko Ono contributed a smashed tea cup with a tube of
glue. Lil Picard produced a miniature bow tie that had been partially scorched. Julien Levy's
Metamedics prescription pad came with brightly colored pharmaceutical capsules; Hollis
Frampton created a phenakistoscope. Other contributors included Marcel Duchamp, Meret
Oppenheim, Joseph Kosuth, Dick Higgins, Dieter Roth, Terry Riley, La Monte Young, Bruce
Nauman, Lawrence Weiner, Lee Lozano, Roy Lichtenstein, On Kawara, Bruce Conner, Christo,
Walter De Maria, Richard Hamilton, and Congo the chimpanzee. About publishing *S.M.S.,*
Copley observed, "It's a vacation from painting for me. But then it's like making a painting
putting this thing together. Art has left the canvas. It's expanded its activity and every kind
of activity has become art."[71]

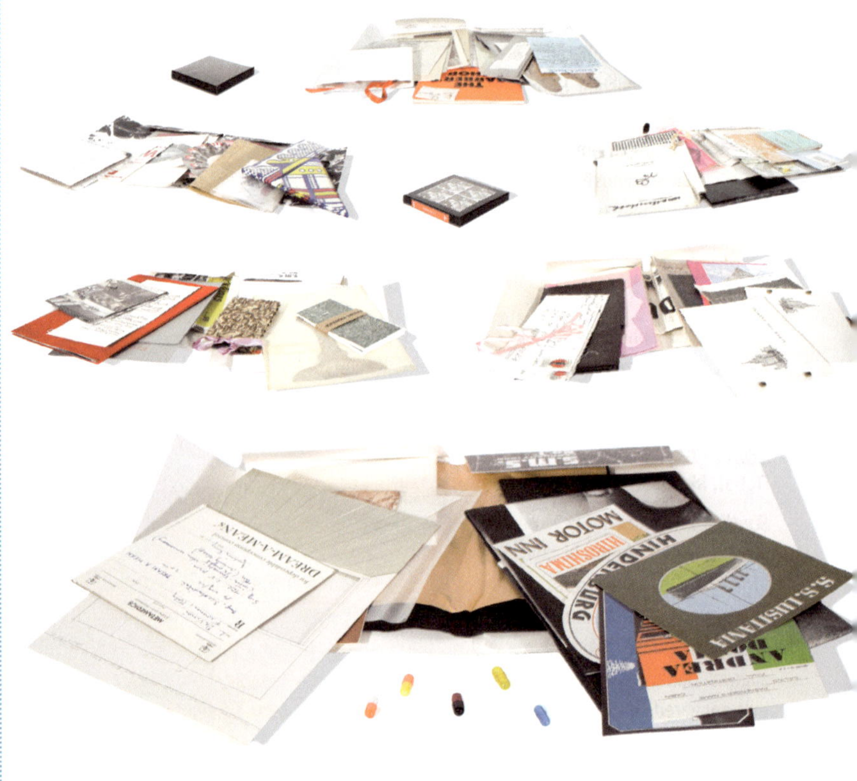

SNORE COMIX
Toronto: Coach House Press, 1969–1970 (1–3).

Artists including Greg Curnoe, Victor Coleman, and Michael Tims (AA Bronson of General Idea) edited and contributed to *Snore Comix*.

SOFT ART PRESS
Lausanne, Switzerland, 1975–1979 (1–18).
Max Bucher and Noémi Maiden.

Published by the Soft Art Galerie, *Soft Art Press* supported conceptual and mail art, and contained original artists' contributions in the form of offset, silkscreen, and rubber stamps.

SOME/THING
New York, 1965–1968 (1–4/5). Jerome Rothenberg and David Antin.

Some/thing provided a nexus for the worlds of art and poetry, publishing poetry by Diane Wakoski, Jerome Rothenberg, and David Antin alongside works by the Judson Dancers, Carolee Schneemann, Robert Morris, Jackson Mac Low, George Maciunas, and Andy Warhol, who designed a perforated sticker cover for issue 3.

SOMETHING ELSE PRESS NEWSLETTER
1966–1973 (vol. 1, no. 1–vol. 2, no. 7). Dick Higgins.

Dick Higgins published *Something Else Press Newsletter* to publicize information about his Something Else Press, as well as to spread news about authors and friends. Higgins published his important essay "Intermedia" in the first issue.

Further reading: Peter Frank, *Something Else Press: An Annotated Bibliography* (New York: McPherson & Company, 1983).

SONDERN
Berlin / Zurich, 1976–1986 (1–7). Dieter Schwarz.

Sondern published artists' contributions, focusing on conceptual art, in a digest-sized format. Contributors included Arnulf Rainer, Günter Brus, Marcel Broodthaers, Robert Filliou, Emmett Williams, Dieter Roth, Richard Hamilton, and Ed Ruscha.

SOUFFLES
Rabat, Morocco, 1966–1971 (1–22). Abdellatif Laâbi.

Souffles was founded by Moroccan poet and writer Abdellatif Laâbi to foster experimental Moroccan and Maghrebi culture in a postcolonial context. The magazine featured North African poets, filmmakers, artists, and intellectuals, including the influential Casablanca group of artists (Mohamed Melehi, Farid Belkahia, and Mohamed Chebaa). Published in French and Arabic, *Souffles* was committed to creating a new independent national and cultural identity in Morocco. The painter Mohamed Melehi designed the blazing black sun that appeared on the magazine's cover. Starting with issue 16, the magazine's cover and format changed to reflect its new, more explicitly political editorial program, which was dedicated to a Marxist-Leninist critique of colonialism. In 1972 the magazine was banned and its editor imprisoned until 1980.

SOURCE
Sacramento: Composer / Performer Editions,
1967–1972 (1–11). Larry Austin.

Source was published by Larry Austin, a "new music" composer who taught at the University of California-Davis and directed its improvisational New Music Ensemble. In his editorial in the first issue, Austin wrote: "Next to actual performance—recorded or live—the score remains to date the most reliable means of circulating and evaluating new music. *Source,* a chronicle of the most recent and often the most controversial scores, serves as a medium of communication for the composer, the performer, and the student of the avant-garde." The large, horizontal-format, spiral-bound magazine was graphically striking, with colored paper and abundant photographs. It published scores, articles, interviews, manifestos, poems, and occasional LP recordings. Austin explained, "Our idea of a 'score' is broad. To us it is transcribed information about the composer's music-making process and contains a way of imparting this information to others who might recreate the composition." Among the scores published in the magazine were John Cage's *4'33"* in issue 2, consisting of a space-time notation known as the "Kremen manuscript," accompanied by the composer's correspondence with Irwin Kremen and the editor. Cage guest-edited issue 7, in which he published "Plexigram IV," a series of printed transparent sheets printed with colored letters. In issue 9 Nelson Howe published "Fur Music," consisting of actual swatches of synthetic fur pasted to the page, with the instructions to rub the fingers gently across the fur "to focus attention on the exploration of the tactile qualities of fur, but with the added require-ment that the tactile sensation be *heard*." Other contributors included Alvin Lucier, Stanley

Lunetta, Arthur Woodbury, Morton Feldman, Karlheinz Stockhausen, Dick Higgins, Philip Corner, and Steve Reich. The final issue, subtitled "International Source," was guest-edited by Ken Friedman along with Lunetta, and contained contributions by Milan Knížák, Allan Kaprow, Image Bank, and Christo.

SPANNER / NEW YORK SPANNER
1978–1980 (1–3). Dick Miller and Terise Slotkin.

Spanner was published by Colab members Dick Miller and Terise Slotkin to provide an alternative space for artists at a moment when such spaces were becoming increasingly rare in New York, as described in an editorial statement in the first issue:

> The features that appear in this magazine are here because I found them interesting. I quickly realized that if the magazine was going to have a concentrated purpose it was to try to convey the energies and motivations of the cultural phenomena in New York City of which I am a part. … There are an increasing number of artists whose disciplines are not easily described. This is a magazine of those people. … Some of the artists in this magazine I met in a bar, some at gallery openings. Most I have forgotten exactly where except it was below 14th Street in Manhattan. Some I have known for several years; others I met only recently through the making of this magazine. … Financially in its present form, New York City feels lost—as depressing as a dying mill town in the north of England. For many years the availability of unviable manufacturing real estate in several parts of the city resulted in an environment where interactions could happen: low rent and the minimum of restrictions meant that experimentation in all manner of forms and media could happen. This is the New York myth, the light that draws people here to NYC. The fact is that low rents are a faded memory. To live in a loft is now expensive. Realtors discovered rapidly that white walls and a urethaned floor provide a desirable dwelling for the middle classes. New York art has a bitterness and an irony of loft existence viewed from a small room. Yet art is created here, and the social reality of everyday is in it.

The magazine's title referenced the British word for wrench, as in the expression "throw a spanner in the works," suggesting the editors' desire to challenge the art world status quo. It was sometimes called *New York Spanner* to distinguish it from the other London-based *Spanner,* a poetry magazine that Miller had founded with Allen Fisher in 1974 before moving to New York. The magazine was not numbered; instead each issue had a different colored wrench on the cover: red, green, and blue, respectively. Printed in an edition of 500 to 1000, *Spanner* published works and writings by artists including Cindy Sherman, Robin Winters, Paul McMahon, Judy Rifka, Kathy Acker, Tom Otterness, Terry Fox, Kiki Smith, Diego Cortez, Jenny Holzer, Peter Nadin, Willoughby Sharp, Walter Robinson, and Christy Rupp.

SPECTACLE
Los Angeles, 1984–1886 (1–5/6). Kathi Norklun.

Spectacle: A Field Journal from Los Angeles published artists' writings and works located in the intersection between art and media. Editor Kathi Norklun wrote in the first issue: "Los Angeles is hard to know. It looks familiar: it's a town we all grew up in, right there on the television set. … If it is true that everything that was directly lived has moved away into a representation, then Los Angeles is the site of that process. … There is power here. This magazine offers Angelenos a forum for the critical appraisal of the industry of media representation. We are practitioners. It is not enough to be visually astute, critically naive. It is necessary to consider the use, the power, of the image." Among *Spectacle*'s contributors were Lane Relyea, Joseph Nechvatal, Christy Rupp, Alan McCollum, Bruce and Norman Yonemoto, Laurie Simmons, Jim Pomeroy, James Turrell, and Mike Kelley.

SPIRALE
Bern, 1953–1964 (1–9). Eugen Gomringer,
Dieter Roth (1–4), Marcel Wyss (2–9), and
Karl Gerstner (5–9).

Initially subtitled "International review for young art," *Spirale* was founded by the poet Eugen Gomringer and the artist Dieter Roth. Marcel Wyss joined as an additional editor starting with issue 2, and Karl Gerstner with no. 5. The magazine was a vital site for the cross-fertilization of art and concrete poetry, with contributors including, in addition to the four editors, Hans Arp, Paul Celan, Paul Klee, Federico García Lorca, Hans Hoffman, Max Bill, Piet Mondrian, Wallace Stevens, William Carlos Williams, Wassily Kandinsky, and Kurt Wirth. The first four issues, produced in an edition of 300 to 600, contained original woodcuts, writings, poetry, and reproductions, within large (19½-by-13¾-inch) colored paper folders. Despite its small print run, the magazine had worldwide distribution and was available in major European cities as well as New York, Melbourne, Johannesburg, Rio de Janeiro, and Mexico City. Issue 8 reflected the influence of Swiss design in its square format, grid-based layout, and sans serif font. *Spirale* witnessed not only new understandings of visual art and language, but also new understandings of the role of the magazine itself. This was most explicit in issue 9, which contained Wyss's *Trans-variations*: five transparent plastic sheets, printed with a series of geometrical lines, to be superimposed on top of one another so that "you become your own designer." Gerstner described the work's radical implications: "Attention: first read this before going on. This issue of the spiral is like none that has gone before. It does not contain copies of pictures. It contains a picture in itself."[72]

SPUR
Munich, 1960–1961 (1–7). Gruppe Spur (Heimrad Prem, Helmut Sturm,
Lothar Fischer, and Hans Peter Zimmer).

Spur, published by the Spur group, was a mouthpiece for the Situationist International in Germany.

STEREO HEADPHONES
Kersey, England, 1969–1982 (1–8/10). Nicholas Zurbrugg.

Stereo Headphones: An Occasional Magazine of the New Poetries was an important visual and sound poetry magazine that also published visual artists. Printed in an edition of 500, the magazine featured inserts, collages, objects, and original prints. The last issue, in an edition of 1,000, featured a record. Contributors included Dick Higgins, Julien Blaine, Jochen Gerz, Henri Chopin, Eugen Gomringer, Edgardo Antonio Vigo, Bob Cobbing, Paul de Vree, Ian Hamilton Finlay, Ed Ruscha, Lawrence Weiner, Tom Phillips, Hannah Höch, Brion Gysin, Samuel Beckett, and Lourdes Castro.

STRAIGHT
New York, 1968 (1). Joseph Kosuth.

Joseph Kosuth published a single issue of *Straight: Audio Visual Arts Newsreview* in April 1968, under the auspices of the School of Visual Arts in New York, where he had been a student. The publication consisted of a single 27-by-18-inch sheet of coated paper, folded to create a nine-inch square. One side was laid out like a newspaper and the other side was a poster. For his editorial, Kosuth listed quotes by artists and historical figures including Donald Judd, Albert Einstein, and Oscar Wilde. Other contributors included Dan Graham, Jerome Rothenberg, and Robert Mangold.

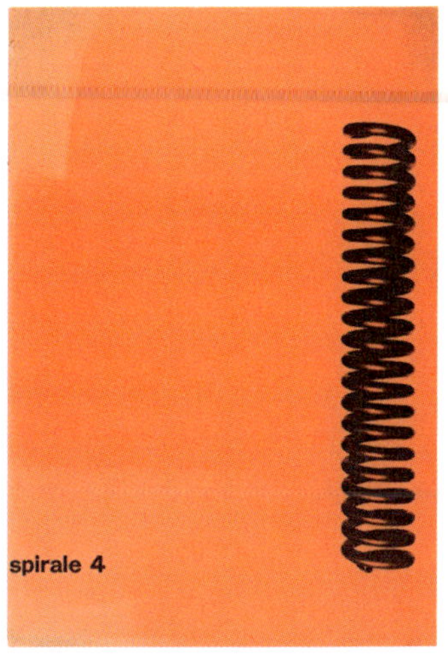

A.41

Spirale, no. 4, 1958. Cover illustration by Kurt Blum. Research Library, The Getty Research Institute, Los Angeles (94-S414).

STRAIGHT TURKEY
Los Angeles, 1974 (1–3). Timothy Silverlake.

The short-lived magazine *Straight Turkey,* published by artist Timothy Silverlake, was a bit like a West Coast *Avalanche.* Silverlake explained, "Editorially, my goal was to record and present content and correspondence in as unfiltered a manner as possible. We interviewed local artists who seemed to have international sensibilities and who were plugged into the art world at the time. Our format was to sit for an hour or two, turn on a tape recorder and chat."[73] The magazine's title, meant with a wink, referred to an expression at the time loosely meaning "genuine article." The actual name of the magazine evolved from issue to issue, and sometimes it was left untitled. Among the magazine's contributors were John Baldessari, Peter Plagens, Claire Copley, Barbara Munger, Walter Gabrielson, and Theron Kelley.

STRANGE FAECES
London, 1970–1975 (1–20). Opal Louis Nations.

This experimental poetry and art journal featured contributors such as Aram Saroyan, Vito Acconci, Kathy Acker, Bernadette Mayer, Dieter Roth, and Felipe Ehrenberg.

STROLL
New York, 1985–1988 (1–6/7). Melissa Feldman.

The following editorial statement appeared in the first issue of *Stroll: The Magazine of Outdoor Art and Street Culture:*

> *Stroll* magazine will document street imagery and analyze the issues which confront us in the great "urban" outdoors. The aesthetic and socio-political critique which characterizes much of today's contemporary art has overflowed from the galleries into the streets. *Stroll* will attempt to capture this haphazard media. Traditional outdoor advertising and informational messages no longer monopolize the avenue. Many artists have utilized these outdoor techniques to display their personal messages and aesthetics. Street art has a renewed and forceful presence, which for the moment is in the hands of these fugitive artists. Each issue of *Stroll* will present this raw and tentative roadway subversion to our readers.

David Wojnarowicz designed the hand-silkscreened cover of the first issue. Other contributors included Dennis Adams, Mierle Laderman Ukeles, Sophie Calle, and the Guerrilla Girls.

SUBVERS
Ijmuiden, Holland, 1970–1976 (1–12). Hans Clavin.

Subvers: Tidschrift voor (onder meer) konkrete poezie published concrete poetry and art in various unbound formats, including posters and records, by contributors such as Paul de Vree, Clemente Padin, Edgardo Antonio Vigo, Herman de Vries, and Genesis P-Orridge.

SUN & MOON
College Park, Maryland, and Los Angeles, 1976–1986 (1–17/18). Douglas Messerli and Howard Fox.

Sun & Moon was an art and literature magazine with contributors including Bernadette Mayer, Allan Kaprow, Dick Higgins, and Moira Roth. Messerli also published the mimeographed poetry newsletter *Là-bas.*

SUNDAY CLOTHES
Hermosa, South Dakota: Lame Johnny Press,
1972–1976 (vol. 1, no. 1–vol. 5, no. 4).
Linda M. Hasselstrom.

Sunday Clothes: A Magazine of the Fine Arts was founded by South Dakotan writer Linda M. Hasselstrom, who explained the magazine's title: "Folks who grew up in the rural Midwest were in the habit of saving their best clothes for Sunday—often for church-going, but also for visiting family and friends. Your Sunday clothes were the best you had, no matter what that was. So our idea was that we would showcase the best of writing and art available from the artists in this region."[74] The first issue of the magazine was destroyed in the June 9, 1972, flood that devastated Rapid City. All 1,000 printed copies along with the original copy and negatives were lost. (The issue was partially reconstructed from salvaged flats.) Published quarterly, first in an 8½-by-11-inch magazine format, then as a newsprint tabloid, *Sunday Clothes* featured local artists in South Dakota and neighboring states, including R. C. Gorman, Frank Stack, Dave Huebner, RaVae Marsh, Don Boyd.

SVART Á HVÍTU
Reykjavik, 1977–1980.

Svart á Hvítu was an important magazine for Icelandic avant-garde and experimental art, music, literature, and film, published by Suðurgata 7, an artist-run exhibition space in an old corner house in Reykjavik.

TA' / TA' BOX
Copenhagen, Denmark, 1967–1970. Erik Thygesen.

Ta' was a Danish conceptual art magazine published in two issues between 1967 and 1968. It was continued by *Ta' Box* from 1969 to 1970 (1–4), which was an array of unbound works of art, ephemera, and objects including a pinecone, a little plastic flower, pieces of cloth, collages, pamphlets, a green wooden stick, a match in a plastic bag, a fake silver coin, a crumpled sheet of typing paper, and a bag of sand.

TAFELRONDE
Antwerp, 1953–1981 (1–24). Andries Dhoeve, Peter Dietrich,
Rudo Durant, and Henri Chopin.

Tafelronde, which means "roundtable," was an important Dutch visual poetry and sound poetry magazine.

TECHNE
New York: Experiments in Art and Technology,
1969–1970 (vol. 1, no. 1–vol. 1, no. 2).
Publisher: Billy Klüver. Editors: Julie Martin,
Ritty Burchfield, and Elisabeth Joyce.

Continuing *E.A.T. News*, *Techne: A Projects and Process Paper* reported on the activities of Experiments in Art and Technology. Expanded into a large-format tabloid, *Techne* documented specific E.A.T. projects, such as Billy Klüver's Pepsi Pavilion.

TECHNÉ
Florence, 1969–1976 (1–19). Gianni Broi, Egidio Mucci, and Pier Luigi Tozzi.

Like *Geiger*, *Techné* published artists' submissions and concrete poetry in a handmade format with die-cut pages, orignal prints, and posters. Contributors included Sarenco, John Cage, Bernard Aubertin, and the OHO Group.

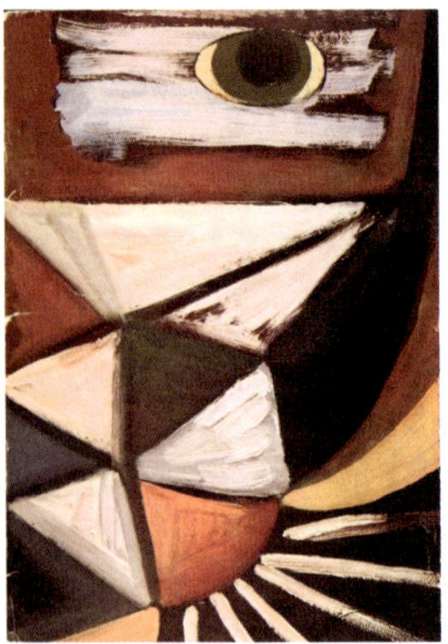

A.42

The Tiger's Eye, no. 1, 1947, cover.
Untitled painting by John Stephan.
Courtesy of John J. Stephan.

TELLUS
New York, 1983–1993 (1–27).
Joseph Nechvatal, Claudia Gould,
and Carol Parkinson.

Tellus was a magazine of audiocassette tapes that published experimental and No Wave music, sound poetry, audio art, and sound collage, including works such as Louise Lawler's *Birdcalls* (no. 5–6), Christian Marclay's *Groove* (no. 8), and Lee Ranaldo's *The Bridge* (no. 10). Other contributors included Kiki Smith, Sonic Youth, Richard Prince, Rhys Chatham, Glenn Branca, Lydia Lunch, Mike Kelley, Alison Knowles, David Wojnarowicz, and Joan Jonas. Many artists also contributed cover art, including Cindy Sherman, Vito Acconci, Walter Robinson, and Matt Mullican.

THE TIGER'S EYE
New York, October 1947–October 1949 (1–9).
John Stephan and Ruth Stephan.

The Tiger's Eye was an important abstract expressionist periodical published by the painter John Stephan and his wife, Ruth. The magazine was named after William Blake's poem "The Tyger" in which the sublime forces of creativity are figured as a fierce yet beautiful beast in a dark forest. Barnett Newman was the art director for issue nos. 2 and 3. The magazine's cover featured a painting of an abstracted tiger's face by John Stephan that wrapped around both front and back covers, its large yellow eyes gazing out, suggesting the faith in observation that was key to the magazine's editorial program. "The critic, if he is to be respected, must prove his value as a wise observer," the editors wrote.[75] Condemning critics who wield art "as a sword," they advocated a sympathetic, supportive criticism such as that described by Henry James, whose essay "Criticism" was published in the first issue.[76] Rejecting traditional exhibition reviews, the editors insisted that "any text on art will be handled as literature."[77] By printing artists' words alongside their art, *The Tiger's Eye* stressed artistic process. It published artists' writings, poetry, essays, fiction, drawings, and reproductions of paintings. Printed in an edition of 3,000 to 5,000 with international distribution, it was distinguished by its lively visual form: color covers; heavyweight, tinted papers; and occasional color plates. One of the magazine's hallmarks was its isolation of images and texts from artist's and author's names, which were printed separately in the table of contents in the center of the magazine "because each piece is chosen for its own sake and always should be approached as such, regardless of who designed or wrote it," the editors explained.[78] The magazine's attempt to cultivate an innocent eye was tied to its desire to foster the reader's own critical capability: *The Tiger's Eye*, its editors wrote, "is Looking for Readers who wish to be their own Critics."[79]

Further reading: Pamela Franks, *The Tiger's Eye: The Art of a Magazine* (New Haven: Yale University Art Gallery, 2002).

TOOTHPICK, LISBON, AND THE ORCAS ISLANDS
Seattle, 1971–1973 (1–5). Editor: Michael Wiater.
Guest editor: Bruce Andrews (no. 5, Fall 1973).

Issue 5 of Michael Wiater's poetry journal was guest-edited by Bruce Andrews, who based it on the model of Vito Acconci and Bernadette Mayer's *0 to 9*. It included contributions by language poets and conceptual artists including Arakawa, Sol LeWitt, Vito Acconci, and Lawrence Weiner.

TOP STORIES
Buffalo, New York: HallWalls, 1979–1990 (1–29).
Anne Turyn.

Top Stories was an experimental art and literary journal founded by Anne Turyn and published by HallWalls starting with issue 3. Each issue was a small book devoted to a single author or artist, including Kathy Acker, Laurie Anderson, Constance DeJong, Pati Hill, Richard Prince, Cookie Mueller, and Ursule Molinaro.

TRACKS
New York, 1974–1977 (vol. 1, no. 1–vol. 3, no. 3).
Herbert George.

In the second issue of *Tracks: A Journal of Artists' Writings*, editor Herbert George stated, "*Tracks* is a magazine devoted to presenting the writings of painters and sculptors in a neutral format. It has no particular aesthetic to promote and will not accept advertising." Unlike magazines such as *Art-Rite*, in which its first issue was advertised, *Tracks* did not encourage artists to use the magazine itself as a work of art, but rather saw artists' writing as a means to prompt dialog about the creative process. George, himself a sculptor, observed, "Finished art objects were far too limiting. There was a rich and fascinating process of thought that silently radiated from each object—a process of thought that was at least as compelling as the material work."[80] Inspired by Barnett Newman's description of the New York art world of the 1940s and 1950s as a place in which "ideas were argued and discussed openly in an informal, unstructured environment," the editor also sought to foster a different kind of artistic community.[81] He explained: "What I saw in the New York art world was a power structure wherein the artist was last on the list. We made work, but after it left the studio it fell into a closed commercial circle that did not include the artist. There was no opportunity to have a conversation that was inclusive with respect to alternative approaches and ideas. There was little free space for open discussions to take place."[82]

Tracks was a digest-sized black-and-white magazine. It published only texts that had never been published before or that had never been translated into English. Among its contributors were Alberto Giacometti, Robert Indiana, Sol LeWitt, Robert Motherwell, Barnett Newman, Ad Reinhardt, Joseph Cornell, Öyvind Fahlström, Barbara Kruger, Lucio Pozzi, Claes Oldenburg, Vito Acconci, Carl Andre, Dan Graham, Piet Mondrian, Hans Haacke, Shigeko Kubota, Victor Burgin, Arakawa, Nam June Paik, and Rosemary Mayer. George insisted that manuscripts be mailed in the exact format in which they were to appear, and did not alter or edit texts in any way, aside from occasional grammatical suggestions, which the author was free to ignore. The magazine underscored the materiality of contributions, printing handwritten texts and preserving the physicality and texture of paper by reproducing, for example, Ad Reinhardt's postcards and Mondrian's scribbled statement on a torn scrap of paper. George ended the magazine after the eighth issue, by which point the circulation had risen to around 2,000, because "I saw then that I had the opportunity to … take the magazine to the next level, making it into a real commercial publication. But to do this I would have had to accept advertising, hire additional people, etc. All things I didn't want to do, in part because these things went against what I thought the magazine was about."[83]

Further reading: Jo Melvin, "Tracing the Way to Work: *Tracks:* A Journal of Artists' Writings, New York 1974–1977," *Sculpture Journal*, Spring 2008, 89–93.

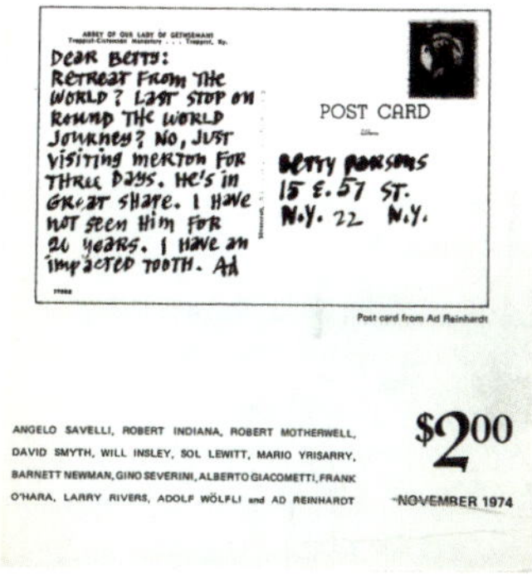

A.43

Tracks, vol. 1, no. 1, 1974. Courtesy of Herbert George.

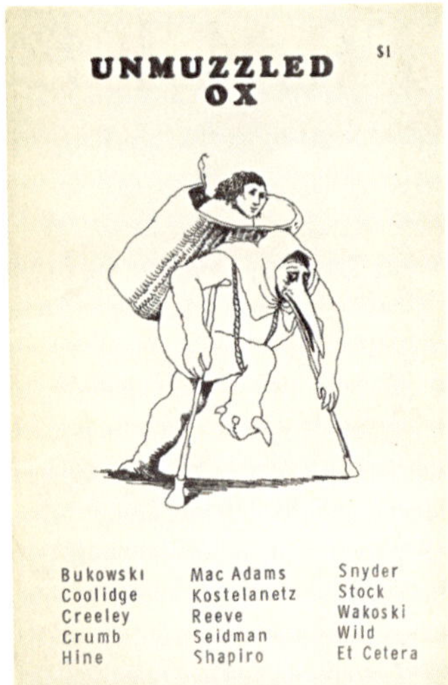

A.44

Unmuzzled Ox, no. 1, 1971. Drawing
by Robert Crumb. Courtesy of Michael
Andre. Research Library, The Getty
Research Institute, Los Angeles
(87-S1620).

TRANS/FORMATION

New York, 1950–1952 (1–3). Editor: Harry Holtzman.

Trans/Formation: Arts, Communication, Environment published contributions by artists, architects, and writers including Oscar Wilde, Sigfried Giedion, Alfred H. Barr Jr., Buckminster Fuller, Ad Reinhardt, Piet Mondrian, Nicolas Calas, Siegfried Kracauer, György Kepes, Willem de Kooning, Kurt Seligmann, Merce Cunningham, Alberto Giacometti, and Albert Einstein. An editorial in the first issue stated, "*trans/formation* affirms that art, science, technology are interacting components of the total human enterprise … but today they are too often treated as if they were cultural isolates and mutually antagonistic. Lack of time, misinformation, specialized terminology makes it hard to keep pace with advances in all fields."

TRIPPING CORPSE

Los Angeles: SST, 1981–1990 (1–12). Raymond Pettibon.

One of several self-published zines that Raymond Pettibon produced beginning in the late 1970s, *Tripping Corpse* was notable for its serialized nature. In it the artist combines the dystopic 1960s spirit of Charles Manson with the L.A. punk scene of the 1980s, presenting his drawings along with articles and interviews with bands such as Black Flag. Initially printed offset in an edition of 500 (many copies of which the artist later destroyed), the magazine switched after issue 8 to a photocopied format produced in an edition of 50.

TRI-QUARTERLY

Evanston, Illinois: Northwestern University, 1958–.

Tri-Quarterly no. 32 (Winter 1975) was guest-edited by Lawrence Levy and John Perreault, and was devoted to "Anti-Object Art." The issue included artists' projects by Lawrence Weiner, Joseph Beuys, Christo, Douglas Huebler, John Baldessari, Gilbert and George, Vito Acconci, Hans Haacke, Richard Serra, Eleanor Antin, Nancy Holt, Adrian Piper, Robert Barry, Sol LeWitt, Richard Long, Robert Smithson, Joseph Kosuth, Daniel Buren, and Les Levine.

UMBRELLA

Glendale, California, 1978–2005 (vol. 1–vol. 28; continued online).
Judith Hoffberg.

Founded by Judith Hoffberg, an important supporter of artists' publications who worked as an art librarian at the University of California at San Diego, *Umbrella* is a crucial information source and network for artists' publications. Starting as a black-and-white newsletter, it published articles, reviews, and artists' pages by contributors including Richard Kostelanetz, Anna Banana, Ulises Carrión, Wolf Vostell, Dick Higgins, and Maurizio Nannucci.

UNMUZZLED OX

New York, 1971– (1–). Michael Andre.

In 1976, Michael Andre described his magazine as follows: "There's nothing mysterious in *Unmuzzled Ox*. The poets, painters and editors all seek common places where their statements might exist in truth. The magazine has the aspect of a community."[84] A Canadian expatriate, Andre was working on his doctorate in English at Columbia University and working for a little magazine called *The Little Magazine* when he started *Unmuzzled Ox* in 1971. In the first issue he wrote, "*Unmuzzled Ox* is not a neighborhood magazine; not a New York magazine; and certainly not a Kingston, Ontario, magazine. We will print the best writers we can. Some of the writers we print, if we met them, we would dislike; some, we suspect, may dislike us; and some clearly dislike one another. None of which matters." The magazine's title alludes to a verse in Deuteronomy, "Thou shalt not muzzle the ox that treadeth out thy corn on the floor." It also had a countercultural ring, for The Unmuzzled Ox was also the name of a radical coffeehouse in Ithaca, New York, in the 1970s.

While it started as a poetry magazine, visual art was part of *Unmuzzled Ox* from the beginning. Robert Crumb did the first cover; Laurie Anderson, who was the roommate of Andre's girlfriend at the time, contributed to issue 3. While writing for *Art News*, Andre met other artists, including Jack Wesley. Especially notable was the magazine's publication of conceptual artists. In issue 13 (1976), Lucy Lippard and Sol LeWitt collaborated on a series of "page drawings" alongside contributions by John Baldessari, Robert Mapplethorpe, Romare Bearden, Ray Johnson, William T. Wiley, and General Idea. Issue 14 included work by Claes Oldenburg, Andy Warhol, and Hannah Wilke. Andre's poem "John Cage Shoes," about Ray Johnson's footwear, inspired responses from both Cage and Johnson in issue 15. (Later Johnson made a sculpture of two shoes, named John and Cage.) *Unmuzzled Ox* published poetry by Kathy Acker, Carolee Schneemann, Roger Conover, John Unterecker (who had been Andre's doctoral thesis advisor), Allen Ginsberg, Gerard Malanga, Dick Higgins, and Lou Reed. In 1979 "The Poet's Encyclopedia" issue was published, in which 225 poets and artists created an alphabetical compendium of offbeat and humorous entries. The format changed over time from a digest-sized paperback to a newsprint tabloid, and circulation ranged from 1,000 for the first few issues to 25,000 for the newspaper version.

UPFRONT
New York, 1981–1988 (1–14/15).
Political Art Documentation/Distribution.

Upfront was the newsletter of Political Art Documentation/Distribution (PAD/D), an artists' resource and networking organization founded in 1980 by Lucy Lippard, Gregory Sholette, Herb Perr, Irving Wexler, Elizabeth Kulas, and Jerry Kearns. The first two issues were simply entitled *1st Issue*, a play on the social "issues" the group sought to address. Lippard and Kearns described the organization's mission as follows: "Our main goal is to provide artists with an organized relationship to society; one way we are doing this is by building a collection of documentation of international socially concerned art. PAD/D defines 'social concern' in the broadest sense, as any work that deals with issues—ranging from sexism and racism to ecological damage or other forms of human oppression. We document all kinds of work from movement posters to the most personal of individual statements. Art comes from art as well as from life. … The development of an effective oppositional culture depends on communication." The publication, which evolved from a single folded sheet of paper into a more substantial magazine format, documented the organization's activist activities, along with those of likeminded practitioners such as Group Material and the Guerrilla Girls. It also published listings for alternative spaces and collectives, selections from its extensive archive of socially concerned art, and artist-designed pages and covers.

VARGEN
Hägersten, *Sweden*, 1974–1975 (1–8).
Rolf Börjlind, Ann-Marie Regild,
and Carsten Regild.

Vargen (The wolf) was an experimental Swedish artists' magazine published in an edition of 500 to 2,000 copies, with international distribution.

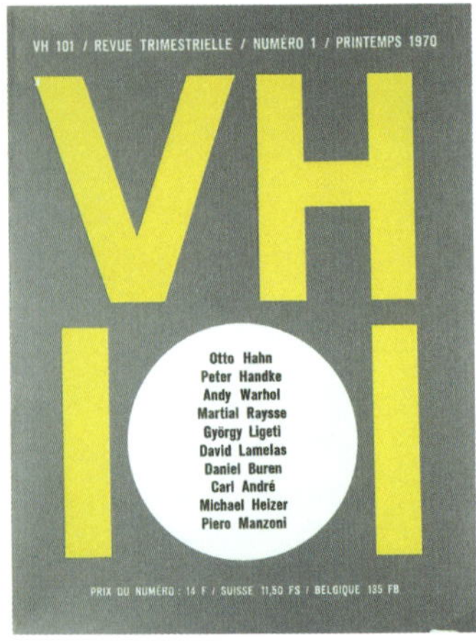

A.45

VH 101, no. 1, Spring 1970. Cover design by Yvaral.

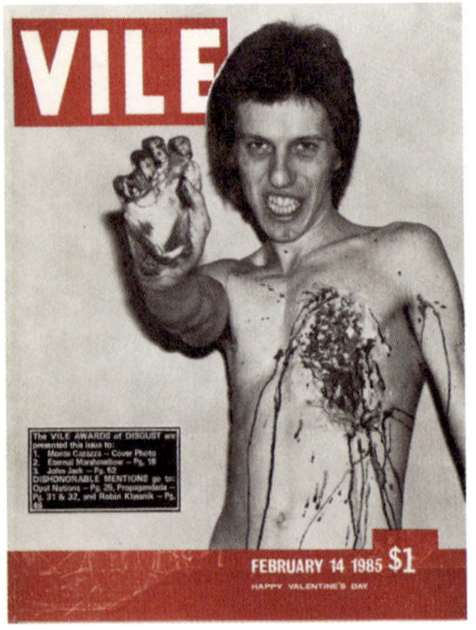

A.46

VILE, no. 1, 1974. Courtesy of Anna Banana. Research Library, The Getty Research Institute, Los Angeles (87-S1624 no. 1).

VH 101

Zurich and Paris, 1970–1972 (1–10). Editors: Otto Hahn and Françoise Karshan-Essellier.

Founded by Otto Hahn and Françoise Essellier, *VH 101* published artists' writings, projects, and documents, interviews, and theoretical texts, focusing on conceptual art and new media. Among its contributors were Roland Barthes, Pierre Bourdieu, Claude Lévi-Strauss, Alain Robbe-Grillet, Catherine Millet, Robert Barry, Sol LeWitt, Daniel Buren, Douglas Huebler, Lawrence Weiner, Mel Bochner, Joseph Kosuth, Marcel Duchamp, Yve-Alain Bois, Jasper Johns, John Cage, Morton Feldman, Philip Glass, La Monte Young, Steve Reich, Karlheinz Stockhausen, Christian Wolff, and Manfredo Tafuri. The magazine was glossy and substantial. The op and kinetic artist Yvaral (Jean-Pierre Vasarely) designed the cover: a bold modern design with striking color combinations that changed from issue to issue: yellow and gray, hot pink and green, orange and blue, yellow and purple.

VIEW

Oakland, California: Point Publications, 1978–1994 (vol. 1, no. 1–vol. 8, no. 2).

Each issue of *View* consisted of an interview with an individual artist, including John Cage, Robert Barry, Jannis Kounellis, Chris Burden, Tom Marioni, Hans Haacke, Vito Acconci, and Howard Fried. Interviews were conducted at Crown Point Press by Robin White, and, in later issues, by Constance Lewallen.

VILE

San Francisco, 1974–1983 (1–8). Anna Banana and Bill Gaglione (4, 6, and 7*).*

VILE was founded by artist Anna Banana in response to "*FILE* Magazine's growing disdain for mail-art."[85] While acknowledging the "uneven aesthetic" of the mail art network, she believed "that the process of communication and exchange is important regardless of the aesthetics and skills of the sender."[86] *VILE* appropriated *FILE*'s already appropriated red-and-white *Life* magazine logo. According to Banana, "I visualized a magazine that would look like *LIFE* but on close examination would reveal its true nature; subtle put-downs of the mass culture with nasty, dada, 'up-yours' type messages."[87] The first cover featured a suitably depraved image of the industrial musician Monte Cazazza tearing his heart out—a reference to the provocations of Dada, which also strongly resonated with punk. (*VILE*'s do-it-yourself format anticipated later punk zines.) *VILE* compiled examples of mail art and address lists of artists, and included editorial copy and détourned clippings that parodied early issues of *Life* magazine. The first two issues had editions of 200 copies, distributed through the mail art network; later the circulation grew to 1,000, and Bill Gaglione edited several issues. Contributors included Felipe Ehrenberg, Judith Hoffberg, Genesis P-Orridge/ Throbbing Gristle, Image Bank, David Mayer, Alison Knowles, Ray Johnson, Gary Lee Nova, Yoko Ono, Ken Friedman, Klaus Groh, Raul Marroquin, Clemente Padin, and Martha Wilson. Issue 6, subtitled "Fe-Mail Art," was a collection of mail art works by over 100 women. Issue 7 was an assembling of rubber stamp art. No. 8 was a retrospective, "About *VILE*."

VISION

San Francisco: Crown Point Press, 1975–1981 (1–5). Publisher: Kathan Brown; editor: Tom Marioni.

Vision in some sense came out of Tom Marioni's Museum of Conceptual Art, which he conceived of as itself a conceptual art practice. *Vision* extended the practice of curating to the printed page. According to Marioni, the magazine's title implied both senses of the word "vision": "having to do with sight but also having to do with ideas, as in having a vision of something."[88] Published by Crown Point Press in an edition of 1,000, *Vision* could not have been further from the throwaway materiality of magazines like *Art-Rite*. It sold for ten dollars and had a substantial, polished feeling—a higher production value which allowed for a different kind of artistic experimentation with the page. Michael Asher, for example, glued two pages together as his contribution to issue 1. Inspired by the Swiss magazine *Der Löwe*, Marioni sought to foster exchange between artists on local, national, and international levels, including Vito Acconci, Larry Bell, Eleanor Antin, Bruce Conner, Chris Burden, Robert Irwin, Bruce Nauman, Claes Oldenburg, and Ed Ruscha. The first issue focused on California, the second on New York, and the third on Eastern Europe. As the magazine expanded its purview overseas, it became increasingly difficult to coordinate. An issue on Italy never materialized, and Marioni changed course. Issue 4 was an LP record that documented an artistic retreat the magazine had sponsored on the Pacific island of Ponape, with participants including Joan Jonas, Marina Abramović, Ulay, Laurie Anderson, Chris Burden, Daniel Buren, Pat Steir, and William Wiley. The fifth and final issue was a portfolio of fifty-six photographic prints in a box, which lent itself to being staged as an actual exhibition, bringing the magazine full circle.

V TRE
New York, 1964–1979 (1–11; no. 9, 1970,
is misnumbered as no. 8). George Maciunas.

George Brecht originally published a single broadside called *V TRE* to accompany his 1963 Yam Festival. In 1964 George Maciunas appropriated the title for a series of newspapers, which he initially designated as *cc V TRE* to signify that the publication was a copy of Brecht's original version. Mimicking a newspaper in its size and layout, *V TRE* was a promotional house organ for Fluxus, publicizing events, publishing scores, and advertising Fluxus multiples and Fluxkits. Actual announcements and works were interspersed with appropriated headlines and satirical ads. The title, taken from a faulty neon sign that Brecht saw in New Jersey in which all the letters had been blanked out except for V TRE, changed from issue to issue: *Fluxus cc Valise e TRanglE* (no. 3), *Fluxus Vacuum TRapEzoid* (no. 5), *Fluxus Vaseline sTREet* (no. 8). Maciunas published nine issues of *V TRE* between 1964 and 1970. No. 10 was a festschrift published in 1976, and no. 11 was a posthumous tribute to Maciunas, published in 1979.

WEDGE
New York, 1982–1987 (1–9/10). Brian Wallis and Phil Mariani.

Wedge: An Aesthetic Inquiry published poststructuralist theory, criticism, and artists' writings and projects. According to Brian Wallis, who edited the magazine along with Phil Mariani, the title alluded to Lissitzky's *Beat the Whites with the Red Wedge* and Duchamp's *Wedge of Chastity,* and also "suggested the political concept of inserting the leading edge of a wedge of critical discourse to open a wider and more challenging debate."[89] The neutral, understated academic-looking cover of the first issue—reminiscent of *October* with its red title on light-gray matte paper—was, according to Wallis, "a deliberate joke to make it appear elegant and snoozy and to play on the anesthetic aspect of aesthetics."[90] By contrast, the content of the publication was anything but snoozy: theoretical writings such as Guy Debord's "Society of the Spectacle" and Gayatri Chakravorty Spivak's "Can the Subaltern Speak? Speculations on Widow-Sacrifice" appeared alongside artists' writings such as Martha Rosler's "Notes on Quotes," Mary Kelly's "Desiring Images/Imaging Desire," and projects such as Louise Lawler and Sherrie Levine's *A Picture Is*

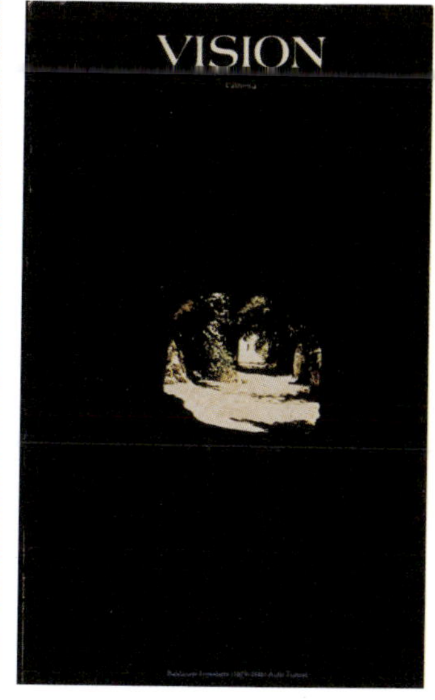

A.47
Vision, no. 1, 1975. Courtesy of Tom Marioni.

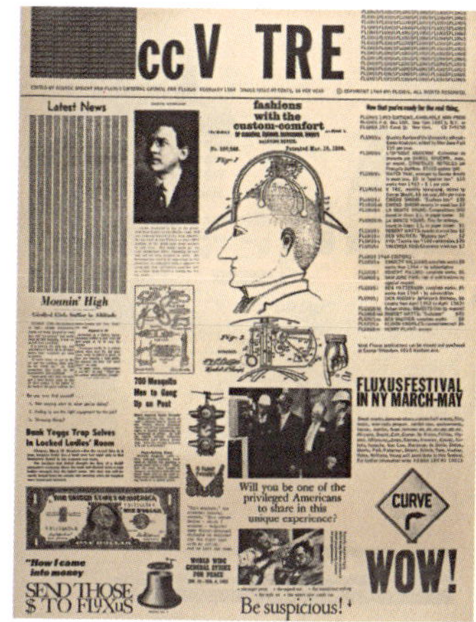

A.48
V TRE, no. 2, February 1964. Research Library, The Getty Research Institute, Los Angeles (87-S1082 no. 2).

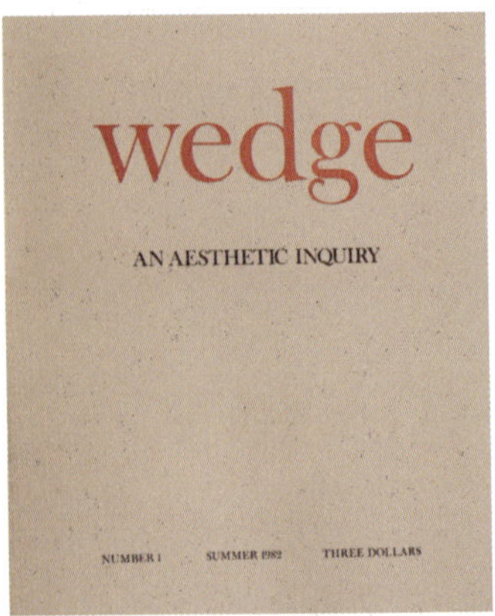

A.49

Wedge, no. 1, 1982. Courtesy of Brian Wallis.

No Substitute for Anything. Other contributors included Joseph Beuys, Jonathan Crary, Kathy Acker, Jenny Holzer, Öyvind Fahlström, Robert Longo, the Guerrilla Art Action Group, Hans Haacke, Barbara Kruger, Silvia Kolbowski, Richard Milazzo, Theresa Hak Kyung Cha, Sarah Charlesworth, Connie Hatch, Jean-François Lyotard, Victor Burgin, Carol Squiers, Judith Barry, and Edward Said. Issue 2 was dedicated to the spectacle; no. 3/4/5 consisted of several individual pamphlets and booklets contained within a special boxlike container; no. 6, guest-edited by Silvia Kolbowski, was subtitled "Sexuality: Re/Positions"; no. 7/8 was on "The Imperialism of Representation/The Representation of Imperialism"; no. 9/10 was a book titled *Global Television,* published by the MIT Press. *Wedge* ended, as planned, after 10 issues—"long enough for any such project," according to Wallis.[91]

WEST BAY DADAIST / QUOZ?
San Francisco, 1973–1976. Arthur Cravan
(pseudonym for Charles Chickadel).

West Bay Dadaist, later renamed *Quoz?*, was a pocket-sized, Xeroxed and stapled publication focusing on mail art and the Bay Area Dadaist movement. It featured collages, détourned newsclippings, and drawings by Genesis P-Orridge, Monte Cazazza, Tim Mancusi, Bill Gaglione, Opal L. Nations, Anna Banana, General Idea, and others.

WET
Venice and Santa Monica, California, 1976–1981 (1–34).
Leonard Koren.

Wet: The Magazine of Gourmet Bathing covered an offbeat mix of art, music, and fashion (everything from necrophiliac performance art to the work of Ed Ruscha) in an innovative and influential visual format that helped to define the Los Angeles New Wave aesthetic. In the first issue, editor Leonard Koren wrote: "*Wet* is a magazine devoted to upgrading the quality of your bathing experience. Hopefully, in the great American tradition of Coca Cola, doggie diapers and Pet Rocks, *Wet* will become one of those things you never imagined you needed until you find you can't live without it." The concept for the magazine evolved out of Koren's "bath art" phase, in which he produced works such as the silkscreen print 23 *Beautiful Women* and the book 17 *Beautiful Men Taking a Shower. Wet* broadened the definition of bathing to include other water-related phenomena such as hot tubs, rolfing, drinking water ("bathing from the inside"), and waterbeds. Gradually the magazine grew to encompass "'gourmet *bathing*' in a metaphorical sense: an eclectic lifestyle grounded in a boundless appreciation of absurdity."[92] Starting as a four-page black-and-white zine, it went through numerous format changes, adding color covers and developing a distinctive graphic style that exploded the modernist grid with asymmetrical, clashing layouts. Koren described the magazine as "an eclectic collage; virtually any visual or written piece can be given a *WET* slant. The pictorial and graphical is more important than the textual. (Legibility and readability are of minor concern.)"[93] *Wet*'s influential look was said to inform, among other things, the changing style of *Artforum*, which earned the epithet "Wetforum" in the 1980s.[94] Notable *Wet* contributors included Matt Groening, Matthew Ralston, and April Greiman. Published bimonthly and selling 15,000 to 25,000 per issue, the magazine became a sustainable if not exactly profitable enterprise. Growing restless with the increasingly routine nature of running the publication, Koren thought about trying to sell it, but in the end decided, "No thanks. I felt better about dumping the magazine altogether and letting its memory live on undefiled."[95]

WHITEWALLS

Chicago, 1978–2002 (1–45). Founding editors:
Buzz Spector, Regan Upshaw, and Roberta Upshaw.

WhiteWalls: A Magazine of Writings by Artists was founded in 1978 by the artist Buzz Spector along with the writers Regan and Roberta Upshaw. Spector wrote in the first issue, "*WhiteWalls* is an experiment in synthesizing word-related interests of artists and poets, focusing on that interface where poetic metaphor merges with the more iconographic structure used in written conceptual art texts." Among its contributors were Dick Higgins, Richard Kostelanetz, Richard Prince, Rosemary Mayer, Lucio Pozzi, Dotty Attie, Ed Ruscha, Michelle Stuart, Arakawa, Barbara Kruger, Mary Kelly, Jenny Holzer, and Gregg Bordowitz.

WOMEN ARTISTS NEWSLETTER / WOMEN ARTISTS NEWS

New York, 1975–1992 (vol. 1, no. 1–vol. 17).
Cynthia Navaretta.

Women Artists Newsletter grew out of an earlier periodical that Cynthia Navaretta published to report on Women in the Arts, an organization she helped to found in 1971. Navaretta published *Women Artists Newsletter* with many volunteer writers and photographers and freelance designers, including Judy Siegel and Sylvia Moore who helped with copy editing. The magazine functioned as "an information exchange for artists" and "a vehicle for artists to talk about art—[we] see ourselves as an advocate and voice for artists, and specifically women artists."[96] It published book reviews and articles on topics such as sexism in the art world and balancing work and motherhood. The magazine's name changed to *Women Artists News* with vol. 3, no. 7 (January 1978). Its circulation hovered around 6,000 to 7,000, reaching 10,000 at one point. Contributors included Joyce Kozloff, Lil Picard, Miriam Schapiro, Sylvia Sleigh, Joan Snyder, Nancy Spero, and May Stevens. Asked about the significance of the magazine, Navaretta responded, "Significance? I remember demonstrating in front of the Museum of Modern Art and the Whitney, where we were trying to educate the public as to the absence of women artists in the museum's collections and exhibitions, and being asked, 'Are there women artists?' We've come a long way."[97]

X MOTION PICTURE / X

New York, 1977–1978 (1–3). Betsy Sussler,
Eric Mitchell, and Michael McClard.

Published in connection with the artists' group Colab, the short-lived *X Motion Picture* magazine (later shorted to *X*) was an ad hoc, do-it-yourself, collective publishing venture featuring writings and projects by Kathy Acker, Jackie Ochs, Charlie Ahern, Liza Béar, Robin Winters, Tom Otterness, Judy Rifka, Allan Moore, Diego Cortez, and Coleen Fitzgibbon. Its founders, Betsy Sussler (who would soon go on to found *Bomb*), Eric Mitchell, and Michael McClard, assembled the first issue by hand. Each artist financed and designed his or her own contribution, resulting in a heterogeneous array of layouts and typefaces. The publication's crude tabloid format and title ("appropriately brutish and raw for the provocative rag we had in mind," according to McClard)[98] captured the edginess of the late 1970s downtown scene. The magazine's themes included French New Wave cinema, the Baader-Meinhof group, and punk music. The cover of the first issue consisted of three stills from Godard's 1976 film *Ici et ailleurs*, in which he appropriated footage from his own 1970 pro-Palestinian political film *Jusqu'à la victoire* (made with Jean-Pierre Gorin)—a reference that suggested the magazine's own interest in the capacity of the media to be a site for self-critical reflection as well as manipulation. The second cover featured a found photograph of a man holding two swords in the shape of an *X*. The final cover referenced the Baader-Meinhof group, which would be discussed in the issue, with the phrase "ed brigade" scrawled on a brick wall. Then the magazine ended as abruptly as it had begun.

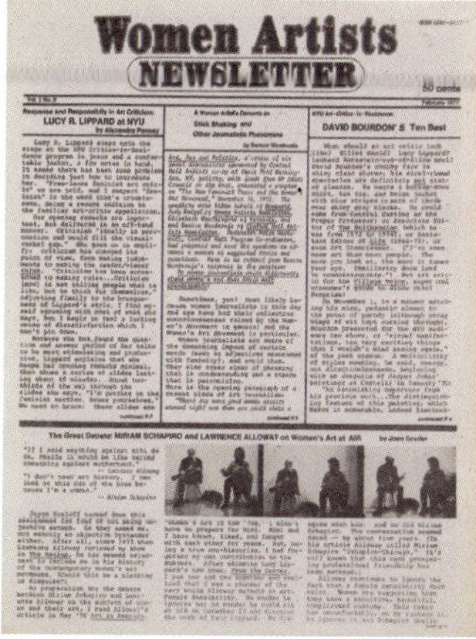

A.50

Women Artists Newsletter, vol. 2, no. 8, February 1977. Courtesy of Cynthia Navaretta.

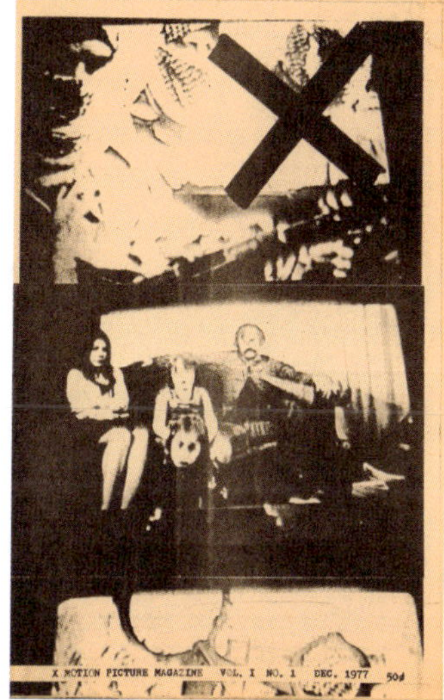

A.51

X Motion Picture, no. 1, 1977. Courtesy of Michael McClard.

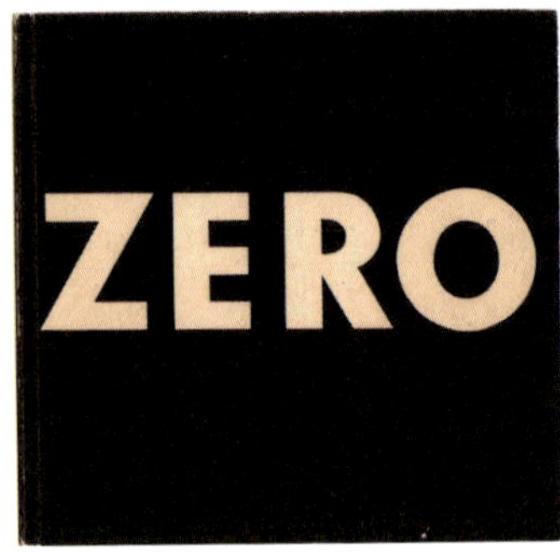

A.52

Zero, no. 3, 1959. Courtesy of Otto Piene.

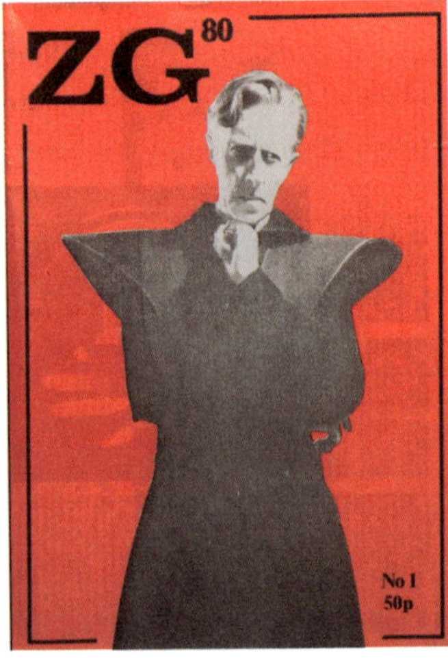

A.53

ZG, no. 1, 1980. Courtesy of Rosetta Brooks.

ZERO

Düsseldorf, 1958–1959 (1–3). Otto Piene and Heinz Mack.

Zero was a vehicle for the activities of the Düsseldorf-based Zero group. As Otto Piene explained of the group's name, it was "not as an expression of nihilism—or a dada-like gag, but as a word indicating a zone of silence and of pure possibilities for a new beginning as at the count-down when rockets take off—zero is the incommensurable zone in which the old state turns into the new."[99] The first two issues of *Zero* were catalog-magazines, corresponding to the seventh and eighth "Night Exhibitions" organized by the Zero group—each staged for a single evening. Issue 1, devoted to the exhibition "The Red Painting," based on monochrome paintings, featured articles and statements by Piene, Heinz Mack, and Yves Klein, along with responses by several artists to the question: "Does contemporary painting influence the shape of the world?" Issue 2 was based on an exhibition entitled "Vibration" and contained texts by Max Bense, Adolf Zillmann, and the two editors.

The third issue of *Zero,* a more substantial, book-sized volume, was characterized by a new kind of typographical experimentation, inaugurating a shift in the approach to the magazine page, from secondary document to primary site of artistic activity. It chronicled Jean Tinguely's *Homage to New York* and included a reprint of the front page of Klein's self-published broadsheet *Dimanche*, reproducing his *Leap into the Void* (1960). It also contained several pages of photographs arranged in a grid that juxtaposed works by the Zero group alongside images of a water tower, night sky, sand dunes, and other phenomena, suggesting a realm in which works of art might interact with natural and technological forms. Most innovative of all were several contributions that explored the spatiotemporal form of the magazine itself: Klein published one article that ends midsentence where the page is burnt, and another that ceased with the page being torn; Tinguely pasted an actual sunflower seed to the page, encouraging the reader to plant it in soil; and Daniel Spoerri attached a book of matches to the page, accompanied by "pyromaniac instructions" to burn the entire magazine. *Zero* 3 also contained a series of pages that count down from 10 to 1, ending with the word "zero" pictured as a rocket blasting off. According to Piene, the magazine ended because "its mission had been fulfilled."[100]

Facsimile reprint: Otto Piene and Heinz Mack, *Zero* (Cambridge: MIT Press, 1973).

ZG

London, 1980–1988 (1–15; issue 3 labeled no. I; issue 4 labeled no. 2; and issue 5 labeled no. 3). Rosetta Brooks.

Rosetta Brooks described the goals of *ZG* magazine in the first issue:

> Trends in the '70s make the prospects seem gloomy for a magazine which intends to deal with diverse areas of cultural activity. … The loss of mainstream has given the impression of a culture of ghettos. This has meant the erection of false barriers between the different worlds of cultural experience and a return to the safety of traditional ideas. The consolidating of traditions is nowhere more dramatically reflected than in art which has become increasingly isolated as one amongst many minority cultures. Its privileged position has been challenged. What has been seen in the galleries has tended to look more and more like the products of a cottage industry protected by a minority group of conservationists. However, while entrenchment has been the dominant trend, other ascendant tendencies refuse to accept the self-imposed limits. … In some of the most recent art, the rediscovery of the image as a reality of broad cultural experiences threatens the purism of art fed only on its own history. Whatever these tendencies mean, they are the ones which challenge our most deep-rooted orientation to the world whether they are in terms of art/culture, elite/popular or male/female.

ZG published critical writings and artists' projects, approaching visual art as one facet of a wider arena of cultural production including fashion, punk music, and television. It juxtaposed work by the Pictures generation with British subcultural activities, focusing on "self-consciously borderline activities."[101] Issues were organized around themes which included Sadomasochism (no. 2), Image Culture (no. 3), Future Dread (no. 4), New York (no. 5), Street Vision (no. 6), Desire (no. 7), Heroes (no. 8), Breakdown (no. 9), The Body (no. 10), Double Trouble (no. 11), Religion (no. 12), Political Fictions (no. 13), Icons and Idols (no. 14), and Altered States (no. 15). Among *ZG*'s contributors were Peter Halley, Glenn O'Brien, Dick Hebdige, Carlo McCormick, Silvia Kolbowski, Jenny Holzer, Gilbert and George, Dara Birnbaum, Richard Prince, Malcolm McLaren, Kim Gordon, Cindy Sherman, Vivienne Westwood, Thomas Lawson, Robert Longo, Jack Goldstein, Glenn Branca, and Edit deAk.

Further reading: Mathew Higgs, "'Zines for a Day," *Artforum,* March 2003.

ZIPPER

New York, 1980 (1). Judith Wong and Sally Beers.

Judith Wong and Sally Beers published just one issue of *Zipper,* a tabloid "anti-fashion" magazine with artists' contributions by Demi, Peter Grass, Kiki Smith, Teri Slotkin, Jorge Zontal, and Christy Rupp. The cover showed an altered photograph of a woman's back as she zips her tight black leather dress against a red background (the model was Zoe Leonard; Wong took the photograph, and the artist Scott Gillies painted over it). The magazine was a crossover fashion/art magazine that parodied both worlds, with an advertisement for "Boomingsales" and a fashion hotline with instructions on how to tie your shoes, underwear etiquette, and regulation sock folding. At the time, Beers was designing experimental collections of leather and vinyl clothing with embedded LEDs having dropped out of Parsons, and Wong was photographing the punk and rock music scene, playing in bands, creating art, and designing jewelry. According to Wong, the magazine "was a natural extension of the fun that we were having to produce this art/fashion/design magazine as a synthesis of our activities and the people around us."[102] They funded *Zipper* with a grant from the Committee for the Visual Arts and distributed it by taxi since they didn't have a car.

ZONE

Brooklyn, 1977–1985 (1–10). Peter Cherches, Dennis DeForge,
Jay Heller, and Steve Lackow.

Zone began as an art and poetry magazine in a subdued, digest-sized format, with contributors including David Wojnarowicz, Christian Marclay, and Spalding Gray. Its format morphed over time, becoming a newspaper tabloid and an LP record (no. 9). Issue 10 was a joint issue with *Benzene,* called "The Nothing Issue," with contributions by John Cage, Ray Johnson, Dick Higgins, and Eleanor Antin.

ZWEITSCHRIFT

Hannover, Germany, 1975–1982 (1–10).
Uta Brandes-Erlhoff and Michael Erlhoff.

Zweitschrift published works, documentation, and writings by Friedrich Heubach, Christo, Peter Cook, Bernd and Hilla Becher, Jan Voss, Dennis Oppenheim, Jackson Mac Low, Krzysztof Wodiczko, On Kawara, Valie Export, Dan Graham, Lawrence Weiner, Braco Dimitrijević, Sigmar Polke, Ulises Carrión, Daniel Buren, Alison Knowles, George Brecht, Allan Kaprow, La Monte Young, Henry Flynt, and John Cage.

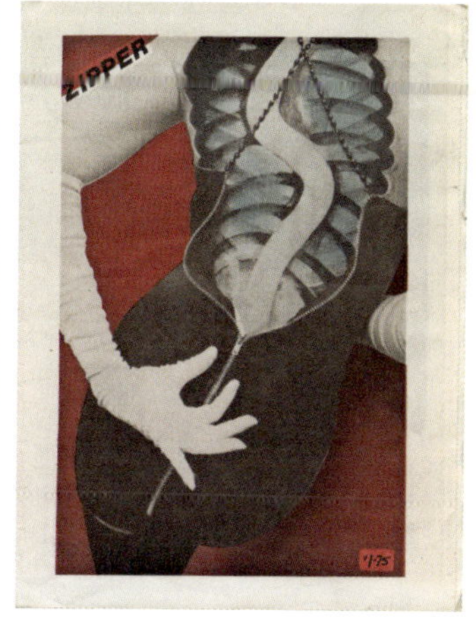

A.54
Zipper, no. 1, 1980. Courtesy of Judith Wong and Sally Beers.

Introduction

1. Noah Webster, "Acknowledgements," *The American Magazine*, February 1788, 130; quoted in Frank Luther Mott, *A History of American Magazines, 1741–1850* (New York: D. Appleton, 1930), 13.

2. Mott, *A History of American Magazines, 1741–1850*, 21.

3. David Rosand, interview by Amy Newman, in Amy Newman, *Challenging Art: Artforum 1962–1974* (New York: SoHo Press, 2000), 140.

4. Clive Phillpot coined the term "magazine art," defining it as "art conceived specifically for a magazine context, and therefore, art which is realized only when the magazine itself has been composed and printed." Clive Phillpot, "Art Magazines and Magazine Art," *Artforum*, February 1980, 52. Also see Anne Rorimer, "Siting the Page: Exhibiting Works in Publications—Some Examples of Conceptual Art in the USA," in Michael Newman and Jon Bird, eds., *Rewriting Conceptual Art* (London: Reaktion Books, 1999), 11–26; and May Castleberry, "The Magazine Rack," *Afterimage*, March 1988, 11–13.

5. Joseph Kosuth, interview with Patsy Norvell, April 10, 1969, quoted in Alexander Alberro, *Conceptual Art and the Politics of Publicity* (Cambridge: MIT Press, 2003), 49.

6. Benjamin Buchloh, interview with the author, May 29, 2008.

7. Walter Benjamin, "The Work of Art in the Age of Mechanical Reproduction," in *Illuminations*, ed. Hannah Arendt (New York: Schocken Books, 1986), 234.

8. See Peter Uwe Hohendahl, *The Institution of Criticism* (Ithaca: Cornell University Press, 1982), 25.

9. Johann Wolfgang von Goethe, "Introduction to the *Propyläen*," in Charles Harrison, Paul J. Wood, and Jason Gaiger, eds., *Art in Theory 1648–1815: An Anthology of Changing Ideas* (Oxford: Blackwell, 2000), 1044.

10. For a survey of avant-garde periodicals, see Steven Heller, *Merz to Emigre and Beyond: Avant-Garde Magazine Design of the Twentieth Century* (London: Phaidon Press, 2003). For an excellent history of abstract expressionist periodicals, see Ann Eden Gibson, *Issues in Abstract Expressionism: The Artist-Run Periodicals* (Ann Arbor, Mich.: UMI Research Press, 1989). Also see Pamela Franks, *The Tiger's Eye: The Art of a Magazine* (New Haven: Yale University Art Museum, 2002).

11. Phillpot, "Art Magazines and Magazine Art," 52.

12. Ibid.

13. In a set of unpublished notes, Robert Smithson wrote, "The Magazine as a quasi-Object; If we consider a magazine in terms of space and form, we discover rectangular sheets composed of strata." Robert Smithson, Notebook 3 [Microfilm reel 3], Robert Smithson and Nancy Holt papers, 1905–1987, Archives of American Art, Smithsonian Institution. Sol LeWitt, "Page Drawings," *Avalanche* no. 4 (Spring 1972): 18–19. See chapter 3 below for a discussion of Acconci's performative understanding of the printed page. Dan Graham, interview by Mike Metz, *Bomb*, Winter 1994, 24.

14. Guy Debord, *The Society of the Spectacle* (Detroit: Black & Red, 1977), n.p. This shift, located around 1968 in various accounts, designates the change from an industrial capitalist society to what has variously been called a postindustrial, post-Fordist, postmodern, spectacular, or information society. All of these terms point to how communication has superseded the factory not only or even primarily as a site of production, but more significantly as a model for productive processes of all

kinds. See Daniel Bell, *The Coming of Post-Industrial Society: A Venture in Social Forecasting* (New York: Basic Books, 1976); Manuel Castells, *The Rise of Network Society*, vol. 1 (Oxford: Blackwell Publishers, 1996); Fredric Jameson, *Postmodernism, or, The Logic of Late Capitalism* (Durham: Duke University Press, 1991); and Michael Hardt and Antonio Negri, *Empire* (Cambridge: Harvard University Press, 2000).

15. See, for example, David Joselit, *Feedback: Television against Democracy* (Cambridge: MIT Press, 2007); Carrie Lambert-Beatty, *Being Watched: Yvonne Rainer and the 1960s* (Cambridge, MIT Press, 2008); and Pamela M. Lee, *Chronophobia: On Time in the Art of the 1960s* (Cambridge: MIT Press, 2004).

16. For important previous accounts of the political significance of conceptual art's use of language, documentation, and publicity, see Alberro, *Conceptual Art and the Politics of Publicity*; Julia Bryan-Wilson, *Art Workers: Radical Practice in the Vietnam War Era* (Berkeley: University of California Press, 2009); Benjamin H. D. Buchloh, "Conceptual Art 1962–1969: From the Aesthetic of Administration to the Critique of Institutions," *October* 55 (Winter 1990); Lucy R. Lippard, *Six Years: The Dematerialization of the Art Object from 1966 to 1972* (1973; repr., Berkeley: University of California Press, 1997); and Frazer Ward, "The Haunted Museum: Institutional Critique and Publicity," *October* 73 (Summer 1995).

17. Howardena Pindell first identified the artists' magazine as an alternative space in her important 1977 article, "Alternative Space: Artists' Periodicals," *Print Collectors Newsletter* 4 (September– October 1977): 96–110.

18. For an account of the rise of the alternative space in the United States, see Julie Ault, ed., *Alternative Art New York, 1965–1985* (Minneapolis: University of Minnesota Press, 2002).

19. For accounts that consider the importance of publications in general to conceptual art, see Ursula Meyer, *Conceptual Art* (New York: E. P. Dutton, 1972); Lippard, *Six Years*; Gregory Battcock, ed., *Idea Art: A Critical Anthology* (New York: E. P. Dutton, 1973); and Alberro, *Conceptual Art and the Politics of Publicity*.

20. Arjun Appadurai, *The Social Life of Things: Commodities in Cultural Perspective* (Cambridge: Cambridge University Press, 1986).

Chapter 1

1. "Art as News," *Newsweek*, September 18, 1972.

2. John Walker, "Internal Memorandum," *Studio International*, September-October 1976, 113.

3. Lucy Lippard and John Chandler, "The Dematerialization of Art," *Art International*, February 1968, 31.

4. Lucy R. Lippard, interview by Ursula Meyer, December 1969, in Lippard, *Six Years: The Dematerialization of the Art Object from 1966 to 1972* (1973; repr., Berkeley: University of California Press, 1997), 8.

5. Lippard, *Six Years: The Dematerialization of the Art Object*, xviii.

6. Charles Harrison and Seth Siegelaub, "On Exhibitions and the World at Large," in Alexander Alberro and Blake Stimson, eds., *Conceptual Art: A Critical Anthology* (Cambridge: MIT Press, 1999), 199.

7. For an excellent account of these contradictions in the context of Siegelaub's activities and publications, see Alexander Alberro, *Conceptual Art and the Politics of Publicity* (Cambridge: MIT Press, 2003).

8. Gregory Battcock, "Documentation in Conceptual Art," *Arts Magazine*, April 1970, 42.

9. Jürgen Habermas, *The Structural Transformation of the Public Sphere*, trans. Thomas Burger (Cambridge: MIT Press, 1989), 41–42.

10. See Thomas Crow, *Painters and Public Life in Eighteenth-Century Paris* (New Haven: Yale University Press, 1987), 1–22.

11. Habermas, *The Structural Transformation of the Public Sphere*, 40.

12. Ibid., 42.

13. Ibid.

14. Charles-Nicolas Cochin, quoted in Crow, *Painters and Public Life in Eighteenth-Century Paris*, 9.

15. See Thomas Crow, "Diderot's Salons: Public Art and the Mind of the Private Critic," in *Diderot on Art*, vol. 1, *The Salon of 1765 and Notes on Painting*, ed. John Goodman (New Haven: Yale University Press, 1995), ix–xix.

16. See Anthony Burton, "Nineteenth Century Periodicals," in Trevor Fawcett and Clive Phillpot, *The Art Press: Two Centuries of Art Magazines* (London: Art Book Company, 1976), 3–10. According to Burton, the first art magazine was the German periodical *Die reisende und correspondirende Pallas oder Kunstzeitung* (1755–1756), a weekly magazine produced by the Kaiserliche Akademie der freien Kunste und Wissenschaften at Augsburg, and edited by Daniel Herz, son of the founder of the academy. For information on art periodicals in the United States during the eighteenth and nineteenth centuries, see Frank Luther Mott, *A History of American Magazines, 1741–1930*, 5 vols. (New York: D. Appleton, 1930; repr., Cambridge: Harvard University Press, 1938–1968).

17. Burton, "Nineteenth Century Periodicals," 9.

18. Carl Bücher, *Gesammelte Aufsätze zur Zeitungskunde* (Tübingen: H. Laupp'sche Buchhandlung, 1926), 21, quoted in Habermas, *The Structural Transformation of the Public Sphere*, 184.

19. For a detailed oral history of *Artforum* in this period, see Amy Newman, *Challenging Art: Artforum 1962–1974* (New York: SoHo Press, 2000). What follows draws heavily on this important primary source.

20. Charles Cowles, interview by Amy Newman, in Newman, *Challenging Art*, 91.

21. John Coplans, quoted in "Art as News," *Newsweek*, September 18, 1972.

22. Editorial note, *Artforum*, June 1962.

23. Philip Leider, interview by Amy Newman, in Newman, *Challenging Art*, 92.

24. Max Kozloff, interview by Amy Newman, in Newman, *Challenging Art*, 56.

25. Philip Leider, letter to Michael Fried, November 7, 1966, quoted in Newman, *Challenging Art*, 209. Leider's proposal that *Artforum* be free of advertisements is recounted by Walter Hopps in "No Phil, No Forum," *Artforum*, September 1993, 118.

26. Donald Judd, "Complaints I," *Studio International*, April 1969, 184.

27. Clement Greenberg, "How Art Writing Earns Its Bad Name," *The Second Coming*, March 1962, 62.

28. Leider, interview in Newman, *Challenging Art*, 227.

29. Michael Fried, interview by Amy Newman, in Newman, *Challenging Art*, 436. Fried added: "I'm being ironic, but only up to a point. That was thrilling, it remains thrilling to me, I wouldn't have missed it for anything."

30. Thomas Crow, "The Birth and Death of the Viewer: On the Public Function of Art," in Hal Foster, ed., *Dia Art Foundation Discussions in Contemporary Culture* (New York: New Press, 1987), 7. Also see Hal Foster, "Art Critics in Extremis," in *Design and Crime* (New York: Verso, 2002).

31. Clement Greenberg, "Problems of Criticism, II: Complaints of an Art Critic," *Artforum*, October 1967, 38.

32. Barbara Rose, "Problems of Criticism, VI: The Politics of Art, Part III," *Artforum*, May 1969, 46.

33. Philip Leider, "How I Spent My Summer Vacation, or, Art and Politics in Nevada, Berkeley, San Francisco and Utah (Read about It in *Artforum!*)," *Artforum*, September 1970, 42.

34. Stanley T. Lewis, "Periodicals in the Visual Arts," *Library Trends* 10, no. 3 (January 1962): 330.

35. *Artforum*'s original design was created by a young graphic designer named James Robertson, who was teaching at the San Francisco Art Institute at the time and who was part of the design firm Robertson-Montgomery. Robertson's original design for *Artforum* was described by Bruce Montgomery, who was a partner in the firm, in a telephone conversation with the author in August 2002. Additional information, including other examples of Robertson's work at that time, was found in archives at the San Francisco Art Institute.

36. Rosalind Krauss, interview by Amy Newman, in Newman, *Challenging Art*, 77.

37. Leo Castelli recounts this story in his foreword to *Jasper Johns* (New York: Universe/Vendome, 2007). According to Castelli, the editor of *Art News*, Tom Hess, stopped by the gallery before the show was installed, and on seeing *Target with Four Faces* made off with the painting in a taxi to be photographed for the magazine. The painting appeared on the cover of the January 1958 issue of *Art News*, the same month the Castelli show opened. Castelli himself attributed the extraordinary success of the show to the fortuitous magazine cover. While Alfred Barr's assessment of Johns may well have been influenced by the *Art News* cover, his purchase of that particular work was not a direct result of it (according to Castelli, Barr initially wanted to buy *Target with Plaster Casts* but was worried that the Museum's Acquisitions Committee might object to the green plaster penis included in that work, and settled for *Target with Four Faces* instead).

38. This adage is quoted in John Walker, "Periodicals since 1945," in Fawcett and Phillpot, *The Art Press*, 51.

39. Clement Greenberg, "Recentness of Sculpture," in Gregory Battcock, ed., *Minimal Art: A Critical Anthology* (New York: E. P. Dutton, 1968), 184.

40. James Meyer, *Minimalism: Art and Polemics in the Sixties* (New Haven: Yale University Press, 2001), 211–221.

41. Dan Graham, "My Works for Magazine Pages: 'A History of Conceptual Art,'" in *Two-Way Mirror Power: Selected Writings by Dan Graham on His Art*, ed. Alexander Alberro (Cambridge: MIT Press, 1999), 12.

42. See "Round Table: The Present Conditions of Art Criticism," *October*, no. 100 (Spring 2002): 200–228. Participants were George Baker, Benjamin Buchloh, Hal Foster, Andrea Fraser, David Joselit, Rosalind Krauss, James Meyer, John Miller, Helen Molesworth, and Robert Storr.

43. *Artforum*'s advertising space increased from 6 pages in its first issue (June 1962) to an average of 43 pages per issue in 1970. As Jennifer Wells has pointed out in her study of the New York art market of the 1960s, "the impact of mass media and its excited exposure of the ecstatic art scene combined with new market patterns to effect a near total reversal of the traditional processes by which artists were recognized. … Those collecting works by Color-Field artists were likely to have had an association with a critic rather than with a particular dealer." Jennifer Wells, "The Sixties: Pop Goes the Market," in Kermit Champa, ed., *Definitive Statements: American Art 1964–66* (Providence: Brown University Press, 1986), 53, 59.

44. Rosalind Krauss, interview in Newman, *Challenging Art*, 414–415.

45. This episode is recounted in Newman, *Challenging Art*, 315–321.

46. Lynda Benglis, quoted in Susan Krane, *Lynda Benglis: Dual Natures* (Atlanta: High Museum of Art, 1990), 41.

47. Lawrence Alloway et al., letter to the editor, *Artforum*, December 1974, 9.

48. Annette Michelson, interview by Amy Newman, in Newman, *Challenging Art*, 417.

49. For an excellent discussion of the gender politics of art criticism in the 1960s and 1970s, see the chapter "Lucy Lippard's Feminist Labor" in Julia Bryan-Wilson, *Art Workers: Radical Practice in the Vietnam War Era* (Berkeley: University of California Press, 2009). Bryan-Wilson spoke specifically about Benglis's *Artforum* ad in this context in her paper "Artists, Dealers, Pimps, and Whores," delivered at the College Art Association Conference in Boston in February 2006.

50. Lynda Benglis, interview by Amy Newman, in Newman, *Challenging Art*, 391.

51. Richard Meyer, "Bone of Contention," *Artforum*, November 2004, 73.

52. Rosalind Krauss, interview in Newman, *Challenging Art*, 414.

53. See Newman, *Challenging Art*, 360–365.

54. Editors, "About *October*," *October*, no. 1 (1976): 5.

55. Ibid.

56. Ibid. 3.

57. Ibid., 3–4.

58. Pozzi realized he wasn't interested in something as serious and professional as *October*, and went on to found *New Observations*.

59. Jeremy Gilbert-Rolfe, email to the author, September 28, 2009.

60. See Roger Conover, "1–100: Some Particulars," *October*, no. 100 (Spring 2002): 229–230.

61. Irena von Zahn, "Jaap Rietman, the Reigning Art Book Dealer," *Art-Rite*, no. 14 (Winter 1976–1977): 50.

62. Ibid.

63. Sol LeWitt, "Paragraphs on Conceptual Art," *Artforum*, Summer 1967, 76.

64. Ibid., 77.

65. Philip Leider, email to the author, March 19, 2001.

66. See Meyer, *Minimalism*, 155.

67. Robert Smithson, "A Museum of Language in the Vicinity of Art," in *Robert Smithson: The Collected Writings*, ed. Jack Flam (Berkeley: University of California Press, 1996), 78.

68. Ibid., 79.

69. Ibid.

70. Ibid.

71. Ibid., 79–80.

72. Philip Leider, introduction to *The Writings of Robert Smithson*, ed. Nancy Holt (New York: New York University Press, 1979), 12.

73. Robert Smithson, "Incidents of Mirror-Travel in the Yucatan," in *Robert Smithson: The Collected Writings*, 133.

74. Ibid., 129–130.

75. Ibid., 130.

76. Ibid.

77. For a formative account of Dan Graham's magazine articles, see Benjamin H. D. Buchloh, "Moments of History in the Work of Dan Graham" (1978), in his *Neo-Avantgarde and Culture Industry: Essays on European and American Art from 1955 to 1975* (Cambridge: MIT Press, 2000); for a discussion of Smithson's "Quasi-Infinities and the Waning of Space," see Pamela M. Lee, "Ultramoderne: Or, How George Kubler Stole the Time in Sixties Art," in Lee, *Chronophobia: On Time in Art of the 1960s* (Cambridge: MIT Press, 2004); for a discussion of artists' writings published in *Harper's Bazaar* under editor Dale McConathy in the late 1960s, see James Meyer, "The Mirror of Fashion," *Artforum*, May 2001.

78. Dan Graham, "Homes for America," *Arts Magazine*, December 1966–January 1967, 22.

79. Donald Judd, "Specific Objects," *Arts Yearbook* 8 (1965), 82.

80. Dan Graham, interview with the author, June 4, 2009.

81. Dan Graham, "My Works for Magazine Pages: A History of Conceptual Art," in *Dan Graham*, exh. cat. (Perth: Art Gallery of Western Australia, 1985), 12, quoted in Marianne Brouwer, ed., *Dan Graham: Works 1965–2000* (Düsseldorf: Richter Verlag, 2001), 104.

82. Mel Bochner, interview with the author, October 2001.

83. Donald Judd, introduction to *Donald Judd: The Complete Writings 1959–1975* (Halifax: Press of Nova Scotia College of Art and Design, 1975), vii.

84. Sam Edwards published the *New York Review of Sex* and the *New York Free Press*.

85. Bochner, interview with the author, October 2001.

86. Lee Lozano, letter to Joseph Kosuth (March 4, 1968), quoted in Alberro, *Conceptual Art and the Politics of Publicity*, 184, note 67.

87. Dan Graham, interview with the author, New York, June 7, 2007.

88. The ads are "Art Works," November 1968; "Johnny Appleseed," December 1968; "Art," January 1969; "Tell a Lie," February 1969; "Start a Rumor," March 1969; "Perpetrate a Hoax," April 1969; "Build a Reputation," May 1969; "Become a Legend," Summer 1969; "Teach Art," September 1969; "Smoke," October 1969; "Trip," November 1969; and "You Are Me," December 1969.

89. Stephen Kaltenbach, interview by Patricia Norvell, in Alexander Alberro and Patricia Norvell, *Recording Conceptual Art* (Berkeley: University of California Press, 2001), 83.

90. Ibid.

91. Ibid.

92. Robert Smithson, "Hidden Trails in Art," in *Robert Smithson: The Collected Writings*, 366.

93. Ibid.

94. Nancy Fraser, "Rethinking the Public Sphere: A Contribution to the Critique of Actually Existing Democracy," in Craig Calhoun, ed., *Habermas and the Public Sphere* (Cambridge: MIT Press, 1992), 123.

95. Oskar Negt and Alexander Kluge, *Public Sphere and Experience: Toward an Analysis of the Bourgeois and Proletarian Public Sphere*, trans. Peter Labanyi, Jamie Owen Daniel, and Assenka Oksiloff (Minneapolis: University of Minnesota Press, 1993).

96. For an excellent critical account of activist groups such as the Art Workers' Coalition and the New York Art Strike at this moment, see Bryan-Wilson, *Art Workers: Radical Practice in the Vietnam War Era*.

97. Lee Lozano, "Statement for Open Public Hearing, Art Worker Coalition," in *An Open Public Hearing on the Subject: What Should Be the Program of the Art Workers Regarding Museum Reform and to Establish the Program of an Open Art Workers Coalition* (New York: Art Workers' Coalition, 1969), 32.

98. Dan Graham, "Art Workers' Coalition Open Hearing Presentation," 10 April 1969, in Alberro and Stimson, eds., *Conceptual Art: A Critical Anthology*, 92–93.

99. Carl Andre, "A Reasonable and Practical Proposal for Artists Who Wish to Remain Free Men in These Terrible Times," in *An Open Public Hearing on the Subject*, 32.

100. Andrew Menard and Ron White, "Media Madness," *The Fox*, no. 2 (1975): 114.

Chapter 2

1. Phyllis Johnson, "Letter from the Editor," *Aspen*, no. 1 (1965): n.p.

2. Ibid.

3. Advertisement for *Aspen*, published in the *Evergreen Review*, no. 76 (March 1970).

4. For a recent account of Aspen's important cultural history, see Dean Sobel, *One Hour Ahead: The Avant-Garde in Aspen, 1945–2004* (Aspen: Aspen Art Museum, 2004).

5. Advertisement for *Aspen*, from *Evergreen Review*, no. 46 (April 1967).

6. George Lois, telephone conversation with the author, June 2007.

7. Phyllis Johnson, quoted in unsigned review of *Aspen*, *Time*, June 7, 1968, 66.

8. Johnson, "Letter from the Editor."

9. It is interesting to note that Warhol cited *Rolling Stone* magazine as an inspiration for his own *Interview*, founded in 1969. Andy Warhol, quoted in Amy Sullivan, interview with Mark Frechette and Daria Halprin, *Interview* 1, no. 1 (1969): 34.

10. For an excellent account of the Exploding Plastic Inevitable and its implications for 1960s art and media culture, see Branden W. Joseph, "'My Mind Split Open': Andy Warhol's Exploding Plastic Inevitable," *Grey Room*, no. 8 (Summer 2002): 80–107.

11. William Copley, quoted in Jud Yalkut, "Toward an Intermedia Magazine," *Arts Magazine*, Summer 1968, 14.

12. Yalkut, "Toward an Intermedia Magazine," 14.

13. See, for example, the editorial "Magazines after McLuhan," *Print*, July-August 1970, 19.

14. Marshall McLuhan, *The Medium Is the Massage* (New York: Bantam Books, 1967), 41.

15. Nam June Paik, "Utopian Laser TV Station," *Radical Software*, no. 1 (1970): 14.

16. Advertisement for *Aspen*, *Evergreen Review*, no. 76 (March 1970).

17. Marshall McLuhan, "Understanding Magazines," *Print*, July-August 1970, 20.

18. Unsigned review of *Aspen*, *Time*, June 7, 1968, 66.

19. The advertisement section in issues 1 to 4 reflects the publication's initial demographic in the upscale vacation community of Aspen, Colorado, consisting largely of brochures for luxury consumer goods such as liquor, clothing, and cosmetics, as well as communication technologies.

By contrast, *Aspen* 5+6 contained just a few advertisements—for *Artforum*, Wesleyan University Press, Something Else Books, and Great Bear Press, plus a brochure for Bolex Super-8 projectors.

20. "*Aspen*—Denial of Second Class Mail Privileges," dockets of U.S. Postal Service, April 9, 1971, and August 20, 1971. United States Postal Service, http://www.usps.com/judicial/1971deci/pod3-59.htm and http://www.usps.com/judicial/1971deci/3-59.htm (accessed June 16, 2010).

21. Brian O'Doherty, interview with the author, New York, December 4, 2001. O'Doherty was introduced to Phyllis Johnson by David Dalton.

22. Brian O'Doherty, notes for *Aspen* 5+6, 1967, in the artist's possession.

23. Marcel Duchamp, "Regions Which Are Note Ruled by Time and Space ... ," edited version of "A Conversation with Marcel Duchamp," television interview conducted by James Johnson Sweeney, NBC, January 1956, in *The Essential Writings of Marcel Duchamp*, ed. Michel Sanouillet and Elmer Peterson (London: Thames and Hudson, 1975), 136.

24. Because it was a double issue, *Aspen* 5+6 cost eight dollars (at a time when an issue of *Life* magazine cost thirty-five cents, a movie ticket one dollar, a paperback book two dollars, and a vinyl LP around three dollars). *Aspen*'s actual circulation is unknown. A 1968 review of the magazine claimed that it had 20,000 subscribers (unsigned review of *Aspen*, *Time*, June 7, 1968, 66). Brian O'Doherty's notes for *Aspen* 5+6 also indicate that he was at one point planning to produce the issue in an edition of 15,000 to 20,000. While it is possible that the first issue of *Aspen* was produced in numbers close to this size, given the relatively large number of copies of this issue that are still extant, later issues, which are exceedingly rare, were almost certainly produced in much, much smaller editions. Also, many issues of *Aspen* 5+6 were missing the films because money ran out to produce enough copies of it, according to O'Doherty.

25. Brian O'Doherty, *Inside the White Cube: The Ideology of the Gallery Space* (Berkeley: University of California Press, 1976), 15. The original articles were "Inside the White Cube: Notes on the Gallery Space, Part I," *Artforum*, March 1976, 24–30; "Inside the White Cube: Notes on the Gallery Space, Part II: The Eye and the Spectator," *Artforum*, April 1976, 26–34; "Inside the White Cube, Part III: Context as Content," *Artforum*, November 1976, 38–44.

26. George Kubler, "Style and the Representation of Historical Time," *Aspen*, no. 5+6 (Fall 1967): n.p.

27. See Hans Rudolf Zeller, "Mallarmé and Serialist Thought," *Die Reihe*, no. 6 (1964). According to Graham, both he and Sol LeWitt were reading *Die Reihe* in the 1960s: Dan Graham and Benjamin Buchloh, "Four Conversations: December 1999–May 2000," in Marianne Brouwer, ed., *Dan Graham: Works 1965–2000* (Düsseldorf: Richter Verlag, 2001), 71.

28. Dan Graham, "The Artist as Bookmaker II: The Book as Object," *Arts Magazine* 41, no. 8 (Summer 1967): 23.

29. Robert Morris, "Notes on Sculpture, Part 2," *Artforum*, October 1966, 21.

30. Brian O'Doherty, interview with the author, New York, December 4, 2001.

31. Donald Judd, "Specific Objects," *Arts Yearbook* 8 (1965): 78.

32. Ibid.

33. For an account of the role of time in minimalism and its relationship to Fried's criticism that is central to my argument here, see Pamela Lee, *Chronophobia: On Time in the Art of the 1960s* (Cambridge: MIT Press, 2004).

34. Michael Fried, "Art and Objecthood," in Gregory Battcock, ed., *Minimal Art: A Critical Anthology* (New York: E. P. Dutton, 1968), 144.

35. Dore Ashton, "New York Commentary," *Studio International*, May 1968, 272.

36. Fried, "Art and Objecthood," 140.

37. Roland Barthes to Brian O'Doherty, August 10, 1967, letter in the possession of Brian O'Doherty. (My translation.)

38. Roland Barthes to Brian O'Doherty, October 29, 1967, letter in the possession of Brian O'Doherty.

39. Roland Barthes, "The Death of the Author," reprinted in *Image-Music-Text* (New York: Hill and Wang, 1978), 146.

40. Brian O'Doherty, notes for *Aspen* 5+6, 1967, in the artist's possession.

41. Barthes, "The Death of the Author," 142.

42. Sol LeWitt, "Serial Structure #1," *Aspen*, no. 5+6 (Fall 1967): n.p.

43. Barthes, "The Death of the Author," 147.

44. Fried, "Art and Objecthood," 146.

45. Roland Barthes to Brian O'Doherty, June 27, 1968, letter in the possession of Brian O'Doherty.

46. Brian O'Doherty, interview with the author, New York, December 4, 2001.

47. Benjamin Buchloh, "Conceptual Art 1962–1969: From the Aesthetic of Administration to the Critique of Institutions," *October* 55 (Winter 1990): 107. For a detailed discussion of *Schema's* particular importance in this regard, see Alexander Alberro, "Structure as Content: Dan Graham's *Schema* (March 1966) and the Emergence of Conceptual Art," in Gloria Moure, ed., *Dan Graham* (Barcelona: Ediciones Poligrafa, 1998), 12. Alberro claims that *Schema* instantiates "not only the most radical critique of the conception of the work of art as an original, uniquely produced object that will appear in the 1960s, but also the emergence of Conceptual art."

48. Unsigned review of *Aspen*, *Time*, June 7, 1968, 66; Barthes, "The Death of the Author," 143.

49. Dan Graham, "Other Observations," in Brouwer, *Dan Graham: Works 1965–2000*, 97.

50. Ibid.

51. Ibid.

52. According to Graham, *Aspen* 8 was a folder instead of a box because of the magazine's financial difficulties at that point. Graham, conversation with the author, New York, June 3, 2007.

53. Jack Burnham, "Real Time Systems," *Artforum*, September 1969, 50.

54. Dan Graham, "Editorial Statement," *Aspen*, no. 8 (Fall-Winter 1970–1971): n.p.

55. Ibid.

56. Ibid.

57. Barthes, "The Death of the Author," 143.

58. Marshall McLuhan, *The Gutenberg Galaxy* (Toronto: University of Toronto Press, 1962), 125.

59. Graham, "Editorial Statement."

60. Ibid.

61. For an account of the importance of Norbert Wiener's theory of feedback to 1960s art, see Lee, *Chronophobia*, 218–256.

62. For a discussion of models of feedback in the context of 1960s art, see David Joselit, *Feedback: Television against Democracy* (Cambridge: MIT Press, 2007).

63. Graham, "Editorial Statement."

64. Ibid.

65. Unsigned review of *Aspen*, *Time*, June 7, 1968, 66.

66. "*Aspen*—Denial of Second Class Mail Privileges," docket of April 9, 1971. United States Postal Service, http://www.usps.com/judicial/1971deci/pod3-59.htm.

67. Here I am drawing on Rosalind Krauss's understanding of medium as self-differing or differential. See Krauss, *"A Voyage on the North Sea": Art in the Age of the Post-Medium Condition* (London: Thames and Hudson, 1999).

68. My own search for Phyllis Johnson (which I recount here partly to save others the time and trouble) began in 2001, when I was writing my dissertation. I spoke with many of the artists, designers, writers, and guest editors who contributed to *Aspen*, all of whom remembered her vividly, but none of whom knew what had happened to her. I had virtually given up hope of finding her when I met Roger Conover, executive editor at the MIT Press, who, it turned out, had also been searching for *Aspen*'s elusive publisher (and who encouraged me to write this book). Without Roger's help and contagious determination, I doubt I would have pursued what at times seemed like a wild goose chase. Along the way, I contacted historical societies, museums, and libraries; examined legal documents pertaining to the incorporation of Roaring Fork Press; spoke with numerous individuals in Aspen; and encountered false leads, uncanny coincidences, mistaken identities, and many, many wrong numbers. Finally, thanks to Roger's suggestion, I consulted the archives of the Aspen International Design Conference at the Getty Research Library Special Collections, where I discovered Johnson's married name, Phyllis Glick, listed among the attendees of the 1964 conference. Knowing her married name allowed us to track down other documents: Roger found 1987 correspondence relating to her work at the Sunnyside Senior Residence in Glenwood Springs, Colorado; a phone call to the residence turned up individuals who knew her in the 1980s in Glenwood Springs; and we found a later address in Honolulu, Hawaii, where she and her husband moved in 1988. Eventually I located her obituary ("Phyllis Glick, 75, writer, world traveler," *Honolulu Advertiser*, July 13, 2001, B2) and spoke with several of her friends in Honolulu, who provided further details about Glick's later years. While the mystery is solved, questions remain: Why did she so completely cut off ties with the New York art world? What happened to any correspondence or documents related to *Aspen*?

After searching for her for so many years and thinking about her and her magazine, I feel as if I came to know Phyllis Johnson, despite never having met her. David Dalton recalled, "my impression of her at the time was of a straight, middle-class kind of a lady. But very smart, and very hip—in a sense, a visionary" (Dalton, telephone conversation with the author, December 2002). She was passionate about her magazine and its potential as an alternative space for art. In the transcript from the legal hearing in which *Aspen* was denied second-class postage (cited earlier), she explained: "we got the young artists who have pretty much dropped out, they don't have any contact with the 'Establishment' galleries, but they do have a very rich art life going. We got together a group of people that we felt were representative of this group, and thought it was important to show what is going on there."

I wonder if Phyllis Johnson's absence from history reflects, in part, a certain modesty about her own contributions—an interpretation corroborated by those who knew her personally and described her unpretentious nature. However, beyond the personal level, her story seems emblematic of how the activities of editing and publishing are so often invisible or unacknowledged, despite being so crucial to the historical record of others. One of the goals of this book is to recognize the importance of those activities.

Chapter 3

1. For a critical account of the crossover between conceptual art and experimental poetry in the 1960s, see Liz Kotz, *Words to Be Looked At: Language in 1960s Art* (Cambridge: MIT Press, 2007). For a historical account of concrete poetry, see Mary Ellen Solt, *Concrete Poetry: A World View* (Bloomington: Indiana University Press, 1968).

2. Leo Steinberg, "Jasper Johns: The First Seven Years of His Art," in *Other Criteria: Confrontations with Twentieth-Century Art* (New York: Oxford University Press, 1972), 32.

3. Vito Acconci, "10 (A Late Introduction to *0 to 9*)," in Vito Acconci and Bernadette Mayer, eds., *0 to 9: The Complete Magazine: 1967–1969* (Brooklyn: Ugly Duckling Presse, 2006), 7.

4. Ibid.

5. Bernadette Mayer, email to the author, July 28, 2008.

6. Robert Smithson, "Language to Be Looked At and/or Things to Be Read" (Dwan Gallery press release, June 1967), in *Robert Smithson: The Collected Writings*, ed. Jack Flam (Berkeley: University of California Press, 1996), 61.

7. Program of Poetry Events at Robert Rauschenberg's Loft, May 25, 1968, Vito Acconci Archive, Brooklyn, New York.

8. Program, for Friday, June 13, 1969, Paula Cooper Gallery, Vito Acconci Archive, Brooklyn, New York.

9. Vito Acconci, interview with the author, May 24, 2008.

10. Bernadette Mayer, "Rock, Paper, Scissors," in Acconci and Mayer, *0 to 9: The Complete Magazine*, 13.

11. Bernadette Mayer, "Cave of Metonymy," *Oculist Witnesses*, no. 3 (1976): n.p.

12. Acconci, "10 (A Late Introduction to *0 to 9*)," 8.

13. Daniel Kane, *All Poets Welcome: The Lower East Side Poetry Scene in the 1960s* (Berkeley: University of California Press, 2003), 58.

14. Ibid., 36–45.

15. Mayer, "Rock, Paper, Scissors," 13.

16. Acconci, interview with the author, May 24, 2008.

17. Acconci, "10 (A Late Introduction to *0 to 9*)," 9.

18. Acconci, interview with the author, May 24, 2008.

19. Acconci, "10 (A Late Introduction to *0 to 9*)," 9.

20. Acconci, interview with the author, May 24, 2008.

21. Vito Acconci, untitled poem ("reading") and untitled poem ("writing"), *0 to 9*, no. 4 (June 1968): 54–55.

22. Acconci, "10 (A Late Introduction to *0 to 9*)," 8.

23. Vito Acconci, interview with the author, June 7, 2007.

24. Sol LeWitt, "Sentences on Conceptual Art," *0 to 9*, no. 5 (January 1969): 4.

25. I discuss Siegelaub's "July/August 1970" in the epilogue. For more on Siegelaub, see Alexander Alberro, *Conceptual Art and the Politics of Publicity* (Cambridge: MIT Press, 2003).

26. Douglas Huebler, statement in Seth Siegelaub, *January 5–31, 1969*, exh. cat. (New York: Seth Siegelaub, 1969), n.p.; quoted in Alberro, *Conceptual Art and the Politics of Publicity*, 130.

27. Seth Siegelaub, "On Exhibitions and the World at Large," interview by Charles Harrison, in Gregory Battcock, ed., *Idea Art: A Critical Anthology* (New York: E. P. Dutton, 1973), 168.

28. Douglas Huebler, in Konrad Fischer and Hans Strelow, *Prospect 69* (Düsseldorf: Kunsthalle Düsseldorf, 1969), 26; quoted in Alberro, *Conceptual Art and the Politics of Publicity*, 77.

29. Robert Barry to Vito Acconci, April 2, 1969, o to 9 Archives, Fales Library and Special Collections, New York University, New York City.

30. Lee Lozano, "General Strike Piece," *o to 9*, no. 6 (July 1969), 57.

31. Lee Lozano, "Dialogue Piece," *o to 9*, no. 6 (July 1969), 10.

32. Acconci, interview with the author, June 7, 2007.

33. Acconci, interview with the author, May 24, 2008.

34. Acconci to Opal Nations, February 1968, *Strange Faeces*, no. 2 (1968): n.p.

35. Kate Linker, for example, writes of Acconci's transition from poetry to performance: "Gradually he began to work himself out of the poetry context and to shift his attention to activity off the page, performed in 'real space.'" Kate Linker, *Vito Acconci* (New York: Rizzoli, 1994), 14. Frazer Ward likewise writes that Acconci "stepped off the page—the space of writing—and began to operate as a visual artist in the space of the world." Frazer Ward, "In Private and Public," in *Vito Acconci* (London: Phaidon, 2002), 18.

36. Craig Douglas Dworkin, "Fugitive Signs," *October*, no. 95 (Winter 2001): 100.

37. Vito Acconci, "Introduction: Notes on Performing a Space," *Avalanche*, no. 6 (Fall 1972): 4–5.

38. See Richard Kostelanetz, "Why Assembling," in Bill Henderson, ed., *The Publish-It-Yourself Handbook: Literary Tradition & How-To* (Yonkers: Pushcart Book Press, 1973), 83–94.

39. *Street Works I* (March 15, 1969), in which twenty artists participated, took place for twenty-four hours over a twenty-block area in midtown Manhattan. *Street Works II* (April 18) involved forty artists during one hour on one square block. Seven hundred artists were invited to participate in *Street Works III* on May 25, 1969. The citywide *Street Works IV* was sponsored by the Architectural League of New York for three weeks in October, and *World Works (Street Works V)* took place in December 1969. See John Perreault, "Taking to the Street," *Village Voice*, October 16, 1969, 15–16.

40. John Perreault, "Street Works," *Arts Magazine*, December 1969–January 1970, 18.

41. Ibid.

42. Acconci, interview with the author, May 24, 2008.

43. Vito Acconci, *o to 9 and Back Again: An Interview with Vito Acconci by Thurston Moore* (Florence, MA: Ecstatic Peace, 2006).

44. Vito Acconci, interview by Richard Prince, *BOMB*, no. 36 (Summer 1991), reprinted in Betsy Sussler, ed., *BOMB: Speak Art!* (New York: New Art Publications, 1997), 189. For an excellent discussion of this aspect of Acconci's work, see Frazer Ward, "Some Relations between Conceptual and Performance Art," *Art Journal* 56, no. 4 (Winter 1997).

Chapter 4

1. *Avalanche* moved to 93 Grand Street in early 1971. It started in Sharp's Gramercy Street apartment.

2. Willoughby Sharp, interview with the author, June 25, 2001.

3. See Pamela Lee's discussion of the bureaucratization of artistic identity in SoHo in the late 1960s and early 1970s in Lee, *Object to Be Destroyed: The Work of Gordon Matta-Clark* (Cambridge: MIT Press, 1998). Here Lee points to the 1964 loft law, which legalized the inhabitation of loft spaces by artists as part of an urban renewal scheme, as creating an official legal definition for the artist. This identity has special significance in light of the "official" attempt to use art as a tool in the gentrification SoHo. The state-sanctioned definition of the artist and the legalization of lofts in this sense, as Lee points out, "did not just bureaucratize the artist's identity as organized around the terms of institutions and property. It effectively barred a large section of lower-income residents (largely non-white) from inhabiting the area." Lee, *Object to Be Destroyed*, 97. In light of such observations, the *Avalanche* portraits function to blur precisely those social categories that the loft law enforces.

4. The print run of the first issue was 5,000, and it ranged from 4,000 to 6,250 thereafter.

5. Sharp, interview with the author, June 25, 2001. Prior to founding *Avalanche*, Sharp was tangentially involved with the Yippies.

6. Liza Béar, "Artist in Residence: Liza Béar and Hans Haacke on Willoughby Sharp (1936–2008)," *Artforum*, March 2009, 60.

7. Thomas Leavitt, "Earth Art: Symposium at White Museum, Cornell University," in *Robert Smithson: The Collected Writings*, ed. Jack Flam (Berkeley: University of California Press, 1996), 187.

8. Robert Smithson, interview by *Avalanche*, "Discussions with Heizer, Oppenheim, Smithson," *Avalanche*, no. 1 (Fall 1970): 67.

9. Jackie Winsor, quoted in Liza Béar and Willoughby Sharp, *The Early History of Avalanche: 1968–1972* (London: Chelsea College of Art and Design, 2005), 10.

10. Béar and Sharp, *The Early History of Avalanche*, 10.

11. Sharp, interview with the author, June 25, 2001.

12. Béar and Sharp, *The Early History of Avalanche*, 11.

13. Robert Smithson, "Hidden Trails in Art," in *Robert Smithson: The Collected Writings*, 366.

14. Liza Béar, "Experimental Magazines and International Avant-Gardes 1945–1975," panel discussion chaired by David Little, Museum of Modern Art, New York, December 11, 2006.

15. Sharp, interview with the author, June 25, 2001.

16. Carl Andre, interview by *Avalanche*, *Avalanche*, no. 1 (Fall 1970): 24.

17. Liza Béar in Béar and Sharp, *The Early History of Avalanche*, 2.

18. Willoughby Sharp and Paul Maenz, "Statement," in brochure for Kineticism Press (New York: Kineticism Press, 1966), quoted in Suzaan Boettger, "The Lost Contingent: Paul Maenz's Prophetic 1967 Event and the Ambiguities of Historical Priority," *Art Journal* 62, no. 1 (Spring 2003): 35–36. Kineticism Press published Sharp's 1968 Air Art exhibition catalog and a small monograph on Zero artist Günther Uecker.

19. Liza Béar, email to the author, February 14, 2010.

20. Robert Pincus-Witten, interview in Amy Newman, *Challenging Art: Artforum 1962–1974* (New York: SoHo Press, 2000), 396.

21. Liza Béar, telephone conversation with the author, April 19, 2010.

22. Throughout the late 1960s and early 1970s, Sharp made frequent trips to Europe, where he met Beuys, Yves Klein, and Piero Manzoni. When he attended the Cologne Art Fair in 1970, he brought the galley proofs from *Avalanche* with him and showed it to dealers such as Paul Maenz and Konrad Fischer, several of whom took out advertisements. And when European dealers came to New York, they would visit the *Avalanche* headquarters and pour over the transparencies on the light tables, thus gaining exposure to American artists who were not yet showing any place, and would ask to be introduced to them. Willoughby Sharp, interview with the author, June 25, 2001.

23. Though they were instrumental in its formation, Sharp and Bear never officially became part of the Art Workers' Coalition. Liza Béar, telephone conversation with the author, April 19, 2010.

24. Art Workers' Coalition, "13 Demands," in *Documents 1* (New York: Art Workers' Coalition, 1969), 13.

25. Carl Andre, "A Reasonable and Practical Proposal for Artists Who Wish to Remain Free Men in These Terrible Times," in *An Open Public Hearing on the Subject: What Should Be the Program of the Art Workers Regarding Museum Reform and to Establish the Program of an Open Art Workers' Coalition* (New York: Art Workers' Coalition, 1969), 30.

26. Jeffrey Lew and Alan Saret, interview by *Avalanche*, "112 Greene Street," *Avalanche*, no. 2 (Spring 1971): 13. For a history of 112 Greene Street, see also Robyn Brentano and Mark Savitt, eds., *112 Workshop, 112 Greene Street* (New York: New York University Press, 1981).

27. Lew and Saret, interview by *Avalanche*, 13.

28. Ibid.

29. Liza Béar in Béar and Sharp, *The Early History of Avalanche*, 6.

30. In the beginning Liza Béar transcribed all of the interviews and then edited them in close collaboration with the artists; later they hired Linda Lawton to transcribe interviews.

31. "'… a Kind of a Huh?' An Interview with Edward Ruscha by Willoughby Sharp," *Avalanche*, no. 7 (Winter/Spring 1973): 30–31.

32. H. P. Grice, "Logic and Conversation" (1975), in A. P. Martinich, ed., *The Philosophy of Language* (Oxford: Oxford University Press, 2001), 175.

33. Lawrence Weiner, interview by Willoughby Sharp, *Avalanche*, no. 4 (Spring 1972): 67, 72.

34. Vito Acconci, interview by Liza Béar, *Avalanche*, no. 6 (Fall 1972): 72–73.

35. Yvonne Rainer, interview by Liza Béar and Willoughby Sharp, *Avalanche*, no. 5 (Summer 1972): 56–58.

36. Liza Béar, email to the author, January 27, 2010. Béar would in fact go on to become a filmmaker and a film critic. Her interviews with filmmakers are collected in Liza Béar, *Beyond the Frame: Dialogues with World Filmmakers*, vol. 2 of *The Making of Alternative Cinema* (Westport, CT: Praeger, 2007).

37. Liza Béar, "Joel Shapiro Torquing: A Dialogue with Liza Béar," *Avalanche*, no. 12 (Summer 1975): 15.

38. Ibid., 18.

39. Ibid.

40. Laurie Anderson, interview with Joan Simon, in Mary Jane Jacobs, ed., *Gordon Matta Clark: A Retrospective* (Chicago: Museum of Contemporary Art, 1985), 18.

41. Sharp, interview with the author, June 25, 2001.

42. Lawrence Alloway, "Artists as Writers, Part II: The Realm of Language," *Artforum*, April 1974, 32.

43. Liza Béar, telephone conversation with the author, April 19, 2010.

44. Not every gallery had four-week rotations; Leo Castelli, for example, rotated its exhibitions on a three-week schedule. However, according to Marcus Ratliff, who designed the advertisements for Castelli and numerous other galleries in the late 1960s and 1970s, the printing schedule of art magazines was a matter to which dealers paid a great deal of attention, attempting to ensure that the circulation of publicity would be linked to the timing of shows. Marcus Ratliff, telephone conversation with the author, April 2004.

45. For an account of the Food restaurant and the significance of the role of social interaction and sociability in the SoHo alternative art scene, see Lee, *Object to Be Destroyed*. Also see Catherine Morris, *Food: An Exhibition by White Columns, New York* (Münster: Westfälisches Landesmuseum für Kunst und Kulturgeschichte, 1999).

46. Béar and Sharp, *The Early History of Avalanche*, 10.

47. Sharp, interview with the author, June 25, 2001.

48. Here I am referring to the ephemeral nature of so much of the performance art and conceptual art from the late 1960s and 1970s. Certainly I do not mean to imply that this work has vanished from history for good—a fact for which we have *Avalanche* in part to thank.

Chapter 5

1. Walter Robinson, interview with the author, May 22, 2008.

2. Edit deAk and Walter Robinson [Edward Pursor, pseud.], "Polemic," *Art-Rite,* no. 8 (Winter 1975): 2. "Edward Pursor" was a pseudonym the editors sometimes used for their collectively written articles.

3. Stephanie Edens, "112 Greene," *Art-Rite,* no. 3 (1973): 3.

4. Stephanie Edens, "Artists Space," *Art-Rite,* no. 5 (Spring 1974): 4.

5. Lucy Lippard, *Six Years: The Dematerialization of the Art Object from 1966 to 1972* (1973; repr., Berkeley: University of California Press, 1997), 263.

6. For a history of the alternative space, see Julie Ault, ed., *Alternative Art New York, 1965–1985* (Minneapolis: University of Minnesota Press, 2002); Phil Patton, "Other Voices, Other Rooms: The Rise of the Alternative Space," *Art in America*, July-August 1977, 80–89; Kay Larson, "Rooms with a Point of View," *ARTnews*, October 1977, 32–38.

7. Brian O'Doherty, quoted in Larson, "Rooms with a Point of View," 34–35.

8. In 1972, under Chairman Nancy Hanks and Visual Arts Program Director Brian O'Doherty, the National Endowment for the Arts amended its granting categories, adding among other things a "workshop program" specifically designed to subsidize alternative spaces, and a "services to the field" category, under which artists' publications were generally funded. For a history of the role of the NEA in the rise of the alternative space, see Brian Wallis, "Public Funding and Alternative Spaces," in Ault, *Alternative Art New York*.

9. Brian O'Doherty, "National Endowment for the Arts: The Visual Arts Program," *American Art Review* 3, no. 4 (July-August 1976): 68.

10. Edit deAk and Walter Robinson, "Alternative Periodicals," in Bridget Reak-Johnson, ed., *The New Artspace* (Los Angeles: Los Angeles Institute of Contemporary Art, 1978), 39.

11. Howardena Pindell, telephone interview with the author, September 27, 2009.

12. Howardena Pindell, "Alternative Space: Artists' Periodicals," *Print Collectors Newsletter* 4 (September- October 1977): 99.

13. Edit deAk, quoted in Alan Moore, "The Art-Writing of *Art-Rite*," galleys for unpublished article for *Artforum*, September 1974, Getty Research Institute, Special Collections, n.p.

14. Edit deAk and Walter Robinson, quoted in Moore, "The Art-Writing of *Art-Rite*."

15. *Art-Rite* editors, quoted in Moore, "The Art-Writing of *Art-Rite*."

16. Many thanks to Roger Conover for drawing my attention to the possibility of this intriguing connection between *Art-Rite* magazine, Art-Rite angel hair, and *Angel Hair* magazine.

17. For an excellent account of the ironies of conceptual art's reliance on various forms of publicity, see Alexander Alberro, *Conceptual Art and the Politics of Publicity* (Cambridge: MIT Press, 2003).

18. Linda Nochlin, letter to the editor, *Art-Rite*, no. 3 (1973): 14.

19. DeAk and Robinson, "Polemic," 2.

20. Lucy Lippard, letter of recommendation, in Reak-Johnson, *The New Artspace*, 55.

21. Walter Robinson, interview with the author, May 22, 2008.

22. Ibid.

23. Edit deAk, quoted in Richard Alpert, "Art Periodical Conference: 80 Langton Street, San Francisco, California," *La Mamelle* 2, no. 4 (February 1977): 14.

24. Edit deAk, quoted in Moore, "The Art-Writing of *Art-Rite*," n.p.

25. Edit deAk, quoted in Alpert, "Art Periodical Conference," 14.

26. Walter Robinson, interview with the author, May 22, 2008.

27. Edit deAk and Walter Robinson, memo sent out with *Art-Rite* 17, Getty Research Institute, Special Collections.

28. Edit deAk and Walter Robinson, project description from a grant application, excerpted in Reak-Johnson, *The New Artspace*, 55. While the first issue of *Art-Rite* was given away, the second and third issues carried a price of thirty-five cents. Also, while the magazine was always made available for free in galleries, the editors later gingerly solicited subscriptions, announcing, "*Art-Rite* is free in artists' neighborhoods in New York and we intend to keep it that way. But we do need more income to continue publishing, and we would suggest that those who can afford it subscribe, or perhaps give a subscription to out of town friends." Memo, Getty Research Institute, Special Collections.

29. Walter Robinson and Edit deAk, letter sent out with *Art-Rite* 17, Getty Research Institute, Special Collections.

30. Edit deAk, "Copy," *Artforum*, February 1980, 92.

31. Edit deAk, telephone conversation with the author, November 28, 2008.

32. Ibid.

33. DeAk and Robinson, project description from a grant application, excerpted in Reak-Johnson, *The New Artspace*, 55; Walter Robinson, quoted in Moore, "The Art-Writing of *Art-Rite*," n.p.

34. DeAk and Robinson, "Alternative Periodicals," 38.

35. Art-Rite Publishing Company, grant application, published in Reak-Johnson, *The New Artspace*, 54

36. Lucy Lippard, letter of recommendation, in Reak-Johnson, *The New Artspace*, 55.

37. "The First and Last, One and Only Conceptual Artist," *Art-Rite*, no. 2 (Summer 1973): 3.

38. Edit deAk, Joshua Cohn, and Walter Robinson [Edward Pursor, pseud.], "Big Boys Downtown," *Art-Rite*, no. 1 (April 1973): 2.

39. Edit deAk and Walter Robinson, untitled statement in "A Survey of Contemporary Art Magazines," *Studio International*, September/October 1976, 150; Edit deAk, quoted in Moore, "The Art-Writing of *Art-Rite*," n.p.

40. Unsigned review, *Art-Rite*, no. 5 (Spring 1974): 6.

41. Christo also literally wrapped magazines, as in his *Der Spiegel Magazine Wrapped* (1963), in which he wrapped the magazine in transparent polyethylene with twine and scotch tape.

42. Dorothea Rockburne, telephone conversation with the author, June 9, 2009.

43. Rosalind Krauss, "Sense and Sensibility: Reflection on Post '60s Sculpture," *Artforum*, November 1973, 43–52.

44. Irving Sandler, in Claudia Gould and Valerie Smith, eds., *5000 Artists Return to Artists Space: 25 Years* (New York: Artists Space, 1998), 23.

45. Flyer for "PersonA," Edit deAk Archives, Getty Research Institute, Special Collections.

46. Edit deAk, in Gould and Smith, *5000 Artists Return to Artists Space*, 37.

47. Ibid.

48. Ibid.

49. Martin Beck, "Alternative: Space," in Ault, *Alternative Art New York*. Beck discusses alternative spaces of the 1970s in relationship to sociologist Henri Lefebvre's theory of space as a form of social production. See Henri Lefebvre, *The Production of Space*, trans. Donald Nicholson-Smith (Cambridge, Mass.: Blackwell Publishers, 1991).

50. Larson, "Rooms with a Point of View," 33.

51. Brian O'Doherty, *Inside the White Cube: The Ideology of the Gallery Space* (Berkeley: University of California Press, 1976), 96.

52. DeAk and Robinson, project description from a grant application, excerpted in Reak-Johnson, *The New Artspace*, 55.

53. DeAk and Robinson, "Alternative Periodicals," 39.

54. Edit deAk, Joshua Cohn, and Walter Robinson, "Reorganizations," *Art-Rite*, no. 3 (1973): 4.

55. Edit deAk, quoted in Moore, "The Art-Writing of *Art-Rite*," n.p.

56. Ibid.

57. DeAk, Cohn, and Robinson, "Reorganizations," 4.

58. Jürgen Habermas, *The Structural Transformation of the Public Sphere*, trans. Thomas Burger (Cambridge: MIT Press, 1989), 41.

59. Unsigned, "Alan Suicide: Downhome Organic Technology," *Art-Rite*, no. 1 (April 1973): 3.

60. A.R., "Anarchitecture in Englewood: Clean Cut," *Art-Rite*, no. 6 (Summer 1974): 4.

61. Masthead, *Art-Rite*, no. 10 (Fall 1975).

62. Edit deAk, email to the author, October 21, 2009.

63. Edit deAk and Joshua Cohn, quoted in Moore, "The Art-Writing of *Art-Rite*," n.p.

64. Ibid.

65. Ibid.

66. Edit deAk, "Why and When Did *Art-Rite* Stop?," interview by Monica Sprüth, *Eau de Cologne*, no. 1 (1985): 14.

67. "The Critics: L.A. in N.Y.C.," *Art-Rite*, no. 1 (April 1973): 7–8; "The Critics: Pincus-Witten," *Art-Rite*, no. 3 (1973): 7.

68. "Lucy Lippard: Freelancing the Dragon," *Art-Rite*, no. 5 (Spring 1974): 16.

69. Ibid., 19.

70. Ibid., 18.

71. Ibid.

72. Lucy Lippard, "Interview with Lucy R. Lippard on Printed Matter," by Julie Ault, December 2006, Printed Matter, http://printedmatter.org/researchroom/essays/ault.cfm (accessed March 27, 2007). During the 1970s the term "artist's book" was frequently used to encompass other kinds of artists' publications as well, including artists' magazines. See for example Martha Wilson, "Artists' Books as Alternative Space," in Reak-Johnson, *The New Artspace*.

73. Lucy Lippard, "The Artists' Book Goes Public," *Art in America*, January-February 1977, 41.

74. Ibid., 40.

75. Edit deAk, quoted in David Frankel, "The Rite Stuff (on *Art-Rite*)," *Artforum*, January 2003, 117.

76. Editorial statement, *Art-Rite*, no. 14 (Winter 1976–1977): 5.

77. Carl Andre and Hollis Frampton, "On Certain Poems and Consecutive Matters" (March 3, 1963), in *12 Dialogues: 1962–63*, ed. Benjamin H. D. Buchloh (Halifax: Nova Scotia College of Art and Design, 1980), 79; quoted in Liz Kotz, *Words to Be Looked At: Language in 1960s Art* (Cambridge: MIT Press, 2007), 151. See Kotz's discussion for an incisive analysis of Andre's poetry.

78. Lucy Lippard, untitled statement, *Art-Rite*, no. 14 (Winter 1976–1977): 10.

79. Linda Nochlin famously raised this issue in her essay "Why Have There Been No Great Women Artists?" (1971), reprinted in Linda Nochlin, *Women, Art and Power and Other Essays* (New York: Westview Press, 1988), 147–158.

80. Peter Uwe Hohendahl, "Recasting the Public Sphere," *October*, no. 73 (Summer 1995): 44.

81. For further reading on the role of magazines in the feminist art movement, see Corinne Robbins, "The Women's Art Magazines" (1979), in Hilary Robinson, ed., *Feminism-Art-Theory 1968–2000* (Hoboken, N.J.: Wiley-Blackwell, 2001); and Carrie Rickey, "Writing (and Righting) Wrongs: Feminist Art Publications," in Norma Broude and Mary Garrard, eds., *The Power of Feminist Art* (New York: Harry N. Abrams, 1996).

82. Editorial statement, *Heresies*, no. 1 (January 1977).

83. The founding members of Printed Matter were Edit deAk, Sol LeWitt, Lucy Lippard, Walter Robinson, Pat Steir, Irena von Zahn, Mimi Wheeler, and Robin White. Carl Andre joined the group slightly later.

84. See Edit deAk and Walter Robinson, "Printed Matter and Artists Books," *LAICA Journal*, no. 13 (January-February 1977): 28–30.

85. Lippard, "Interview with Lucy R. Lippard on Printed Matter."

86. Harley Lond, editorial statement, *Intermedia*, no. 1 (1974).

87. Lucy Lippard, "Biting the Hand: Artists and Museums in New York since 1969," in Ault, *Alternative Art New York*, 101–102.

88. Andrew Menard and Ron White, "Media Madness," *The Fox*, no. 2 (1975): 114.

89. Alan Moore, "New Voices," *Artforum*, December 1974, 63.

90. According to the National Endowment for the Arts' annual reports from the 1970s, the number of artists' magazines that were funded greatly increased during the decade. While there was no specific category for artists' publications, there were a number of ways in which publications could apply for funding. Individual artists and critics could apply for funding, but, more commonly, publications applied under the aegis of an umbrella organization, either an alternative gallery space or a nonprofit such as the Committee for the Visual Arts, Inc., or the Center for New Art Activities. Most publications were funded through the "Services to the Field" category, added in 1972, the same year as the "workshop" category. By 1979, twenty-four artists' magazines received grants. See "National Endowment for the Arts' Annual Reports," National Endowment for the Arts, http://www.arts.gov/about/06Annual/index.php (accessed September 15, 2009).

91. DeAk and Robinson, "Alternative Periodicals," 38–39.

92. Ibid., 38.

93. DeAk and Robinson, "Polemic," 2.

94. Edit deAk, quoted in Moore, "The Art-Writing of *Art-Rite*," n.p.

95. Walter Robinson and Joshua Cohn, quoted in Moore, "The Art-Writing of *Art-Rite*," n.p.

96. Alpert, "Art Periodical Conference," 16.

97. Tom Mandel, quoted in Alpert, "Art Periodical Conference," 16.

98. Edit deAk, quoted in Alpert, "Art Periodical Conference," 14, 16.

99. Walter Robinson, interview with the author, May 22, 2008.

100. DeAk, "Why and When Did *Art-Rite* Stop?," 15.

101. According to Rifka, she and Walter Robinson went to the Gem paper warehouse to choose the paper, and had the logo printed. Then she drew on the sheets, made collages, and cut some of them up. She made some copies of issue 21 into "Art Dogs," by cutting them into buns along the fold and cutting out hot dogs and sauerkraut. These were sold at Printed Matter in a white enamel pot so that people could assemble their own paper "Art Dog" for a dollar. Judy Rifka, email to the author, August 23, 2008.

102. Ingrid Sischy, "Letter from the Editor," *Artforum*, February 1980, 26.

103. DeAk, "Copy," 92.

104. Ibid.

105. As of 2009, a full run of *Art-Rite* was appraised at $25,000.

Chapter 6

1. Willoughby Sharp, "The Gold-Diggers of '84: An Interview with General Idea Toronto," *Avalanche*, no. 7 (Winter/Spring 1973): 15.

2. Ibid.

3. David Brittain, "F for Filing System: An Interview with AA Bronson," *Afterimage* 35, no. 3 (November/December 2007): 10.

4. Ibid.

5. General Idea, editorial, *FILE* 3, no. 4 (Fall 1977): 11.

6. AA Bronson, telephone interview with the author, May 24, 2009.

7. Sharp, "The Gold-Diggers of '84," 18–19.

8. Guy Debord, *The Society of the Spectacle* (Detroit: Black & Red, 1977), n.p.

9. Guy Debord to Constant, June 2, 1960, in Guy Debord, *Correspondence: The Foundation of the Situationist International (June 1957–August 1960),* trans. Stuart Kendall (New York: Semiotext(e), 2009), 355.

10. General Idea, "Homely Details of Everyday '*LIFE*,'" *FILE* 1, nos. 2 and 3 (December 1972): 5.

11. In the General Idea Archives at the National Gallery of Canada, Ottawa, a file labeled "Inspirational Materials for *FILE*" contains several clippings from *Fortune, Life,* and other magazines from the 1940s and 1950s, including an article entitled "*Life* Goes to a Fumble Party" about a guessing game for adults played in the dark in Denver, Colorado.

12. AA Bronson/General Idea, interview by Peter Hill at the Basel Art Fair, 1992, Peter Hill's Museum of Contemporary Ideas, http://www.superfictions.com/elgrecol/Bronson-GeneralIdea.htm (accessed November 2, 2009).

13. AA Bronson, "The Rise and Fall of the Peanut Party," *Art-Rite,* no. 14 (Winter 1976–1977): 44.

14. See Joselit's discussion of the Yippies' "pseudo-events" in the context of 1960s art in David Joselit, *Feedback: Television against Democracy* (Cambridge: MIT Press, 2007).

15. Rosalind Krauss discusses the fascination with mirrors and mirroring by video artists in the 1970s in relationship to media culture and makes this distinction between narcissistic practices and those that are more critical and self-reflexive; see Krauss, "Video: The Aesthetics of Narcissism," *October,* no. 1 (Spring 1976).

16. For a history of Rochdale College, see Henry Mietkiewicz, *Dream Tower: The Life and Legacy of Rochdale College* (Scarborough, Ont.: McGraw-Hill Ryerson, 1988).

17. For a general history of General Idea in the late 1960s and 1970s, see Fern Bayer, "Uncovering the Roots of General Idea: A Documentation and Description of Early Projects 1968–1975," in *The Search for the Spirit: General Idea 1968–1975,* exh. cat. (Toronto: Art Gallery of Ontario, 1997).

18. See Chuck Welch, ed., *Eternal Network: A Mail Art Anthology* (Calgary: University of Calgary Press, 1995).

19. Quoted in Brittain, "F for Filing System," 9.

20. The name *FILE* may have also alluded to General Idea's use of index cards to document their work during this period. See Bayer, "Uncovering the Roots of General Idea," 36.

21. Typescript by AA Bronson, "Granada Gazelle occupies her room …," in the Miscellaneous Manuscripts file, General Idea Archives, quoted in Bayer, "Uncovering the Roots of General Idea," 52.

22. AA Bronson, telephone interview with the author, May 24, 2009.

23. General Idea, "Three Heads Are Better," *FILE* 4, no. 1 (Summer 1978): 14.

24. Masthead, *FILE* 1, no. 1 (April 1972): 4.

25. General Idea, "Some Juicy and Malicious Gossip," *FILE* 1, no. 1 (April 1972): 3.

26. AA Bronson, Notebook, 1972–73, General Idea Archives, National Gallery of Canada, Ottawa.

27. Ken Friedman, "The Early Days of Mail Art," in Welch, *Eternal Network*, 10.

28. General Idea, *FILE* "Top Ten Chart" mailer, 1972, General Idea Archives, National Gallery of Canada, Ottawa.

29. General Idea, "New York Sugardada Tops Ten," *FILE* 1, no. 1 (April 1972): 8.

30. General Idea, "Top Ten," *FILE* 1, nos. 2 and 3 (May-June 1972): 21. "Fe-Mail-Art" was the title of issue 6 of *VILE*, which featured mail art exclusively by women.

31. General Idea, "Behind a Big Story There May Be Another One," *FILE* 1, nos. 2 and 3 (May-June 1972): n.p.

32. General Idea, "Borderline Cases," *FILE* 2, no. 3 (September 1973): 12.

33. Felix Partz, quoted in David Vereschagin, "What's the Big Idea? Interview with General Idea," *Body Politic*, no. 115 (June 1985): 29.

34. General Idea's approach to mail art was developed in close association with Image Bank. In fact, the name "Image Bank" was a double reference to both Lévi-Strauss's *The Savage Mind* and William Burroughs's *Nova Express*.

35. Claude Lévi-Strauss, *The Savage Mind* (Chicago: University of Chicago Press, 1966), 22.

36. General Idea, "Pablum for the Pablum Eaters," *FILE* 2, nos. 1 and 2 (May 1973): 24.

37. Burroughs's idea that language is a virus is pervasive in his writings. For a discussion see Douglas Kahn, "Two Sounds of the Virus: William Burroughs's Pure Meat Method," in Kahn, *Noise, Water, Meat* (Cambridge: MIT Press, 1999), 293–321.

38. General Idea, "Pablum for the Pablum Eaters," 26.

39. Image Bank, "Business as Usual at the Western Front," interview by Willoughby Sharp and Liza Béar, *Avalanche*, no. 8 (Summer-Fall 1973): 34–39.

40. Quoted in Sharp, "The Gold-Diggers of '84," 21.

41. Benjamin Buchloh makes this distinction, claiming that the ubiquitous commercial techniques of collage and montage represent a "reification" and "estheticization" of these techniques. See Benjamin H. D. Buchloh, "Allegorical Procedures: Appropriation and Montage in Contemporary Art," *Artforum*, September 1982, 43–56.

42. Though Johnson closed the New York Correspondence School in April 1973, mail art was by no means dead. Johnson continued his mail art activities through the newly formed "Buddha University," and an enthusiastic mail art network continues unabated to this day.

43. Robert Cummings, "The Letters of Robert Cummings," *FILE* 2, no. 3 (September 1973): 41.

44. Anna Banana, "*VILE* History," in *About VILE* (Vancouver: Banana Productions, 1983), 2.

45. General Idea, editorial, *FILE* 2, no. 4 (December 1973): 11.

46. For an account of the relationship between General Idea and the punk rock/new wave music scene in Toronto, see Earl Miller, "*FILE* under Anarchy: A Brief History of Punk Rock's 30-Year Relationship with Toronto's Art Press," *C: International Contemporary Art*, Winter 2005, 30–35.

47. General Idea, editorial, *FILE* 3, no. 4 (Fall 1977): 11.

48. General Idea, "Bzzz Bzzz Bzzz," *FILE* 5, no. 1 (March 1981): n.p.

49. AA Bronson/General Idea, interview by Peter Hill at the Basel Art Fair, 1992, Peter Hill's Museum of Contemporary Ideas, http://www.superfictions.com/elgrecol/Bronson-GeneralIdea.htm (accessed November 2, 2009).

50. Quoted in Sharp, "The Gold-Diggers of '84," 19.

51. General Idea, "Glamour," *FILE* 3, no. 1 (Autumn 1975): 21–22.

52. Quoted in Vereschagin, "What's the Big Idea?," 29.

53. "A Foot in the Doors of the Future," 1984 Pavillion Proposals, General Idea Archives, National Gallery of Canada, Ottawa.

54. AA Bronson, telephone interview with the author, May 24, 2009.

55. Robert Smithson, "A Tour of the Monuments of Passaic, New Jersey," in *Robert Smithson: The Collected Writings*, ed. Jack Flam (Berkeley: University of California Press, 1996), 72.

56. General Idea, "Pablum for the Pablum Eaters," 28.

57. General Idea, editorial, *FILE* 3, no. 3 (Spring 1977): 17.

58. Ibid.

59. Ibid.

60. Guy Hocquenghem, "We Can't All Die in Bed," *FILE* 4, no. 2 (Fall 1979): 34–37.

61. Robert Mapplethorpe, untitled statement, *FILE* 4, no. 2 (Fall 1979): 38–39.

62. While the Criminal Law Amendment Act of 1968–1969 had removed the most general proscription against homosexuality in Canada—a definite step forward, especially compared to the situation in the United States—the Canadian law was conditional, and continued to make sexual acts between two people of the same sex a crime under certain conditions: for example, there could be no more than two persons present, and the persons had to be over twenty-one.

63. Prior to 1958, simply publishing homosexual content in a magazine could land one in jail, at least in the United States. In 1958, the U.S. Supreme Court ruled in *ONE Inc. v. Olesen* that publications with homosexual content could be sent through the mail. See Bob Ostertag, *People's Movements, People's Press: The Journalism of Social Justice Movements* (Boston: Beacon Press, 2006), for an account of the gay and lesbian press in the United States. Also see Rodger Streitmatter, *Unspeakable: The Rise of the Gay and Lesbian Press in America* (New York: Faber & Faber, 1995).

64. AA Bronson, email to the author, July 13, 2009.

65. Obviously the gay liberation movement was much more complicated and diverse than I can do justice to here. In differentiating between the more identity-based approaches and those found in *FILE*, I do not mean to imply that the two can be neatly divided into mutually exclusive camps. If anything, the magazine attests to the wide spectrum of representational approaches that were mobilized in the struggle for lesbian, gay, bisexual, and transgender rights at this time.

66. Quoted in Vereschagin, "What's the Big Idea?," 31.

67. See AA Bronson and Philip Aarons, *Queer Zines* (New York: Printed Matter, 2008).

68. "*FILE*: The Great Canadian Art Tragedy," *The Grape*, May 24–30, 1972, quoted in Bayer, "Uncovering the Roots of General Idea," 80.

69. Judith Butler, *Bodies That Matter: On the Discursive Limits of Sex* (London: Routledge, 1993), 125.

70. Quoted in Brittain, "F for Filing System," 9.

71. General Idea, editorial, *FILE* 4, no. 2 (Summer 1978): 7.

72. General Idea, editorial, *FILE*, no. 26 (Xmas 1986): 8.

73. AA Bronson, telephone interview with the author, May 24, 2009.

74. For a discussion of General Idea's *AIDS Project* see Joshua Decter, "Infect the Public Domain with an Imagevirus: General Idea's *AIDS Project*," *Afterall*, no. 15 (Spring-Summer 2007): 97–105.

75. Quoted in Brittain, "F for Filing System," 12.

76. AA Bronson, Felix Partz, and Jorge Zontal, "Editorial: Stretch That Social Fabric," *FILE*, no. 29 (1989): 3.

Chapter 7

1. Carl Andre and Hollis Frampton, *12 Dialogues, 1962–1963*, ed. Benjamin Buchloh (Halifax: Press of the Nova Scotia College of Art and Design and New York University Press, 1980), 21.

2. Sherrie Levine, interview by Howard Singerman, *Artforum*, April 2003, 190–191.

3. Douglas Crimp, *Pictures: An Exhibition of the Work of Troy Brauntuch, Jack Goldstein, Sherrie Levine, Robert Longo, Philip Smith* (New York: Artists Space, 1977), 3.

4. Thomas Lawson and Susan Morgan, "Introduction: Various Histories of *Real Life* Magazine," in Thomas Lawson, Susan Morgan, and Miriam Katzeff, eds., *Real Life: Selected Writings and Projects 1979–1994* (New York: Primary Information, 2006), x.

5. Ibid., xii.

6. Levine, interview by Singerman, 190.

7. Thomas Lawson, "We Must Embrace Our Joys and Sorrows," *ZG*, no. 5 (1981): n.p.

8. In 1986, Janet Waegel took over and redesigned the logo, and Gail Swanlund designed the last issue.

9. Debbie DeStaffan, telephone conversation with the author, August 27, 2009.

10. Lawson, "We Must Embrace Our Joys and Sorrows," 4.

11. Thomas Lawson, interview with the author, November 1, 2008.

12. Valentin Tatransky, "Collage and the Problem of Representation: Sherrie Levine's New Work," *Real Life*, no. 1 (Spring 1979): 9.

13. Benjamin H. D. Buchloh, "Allegorical Procedures: Appropriation and Montage in Contemporary Art," *Artforum*, September 1982, 43–56.

14. Sherrie Levine, unpublished, undated statement, ca. 1980, quoted in Buchloh, "Allegorical Procedures," 52–53.

15. An excerpt from Guy Debord's *Society of the Spectacle* was published in *Wedge*, no. 2 (Fall 1982), and Baudrillard's book *Simulations* was published in English as part of Semiotext(e)'s Foreign Agent series in 1983.

16. Thomas Lawson, interview by Kate Fowle, in *Real Life Magazine, 1979–1990*, exhibition brochure (New York: Artists Space, 2007), 4.

17. Susan Morgan, interview with the author, November 1, 2008.

18. Douglas Crimp, "Pictures," *October*, no. 8 (Spring 1979): 87.

19. Thomas Lawson, "Too Good to Be True," *Real Life*, no. 7 (August 1981): 4.

20. Thomas Lawson, "Attempting Community," in *Mining for Gold: Selected Writings (1979–1996)* (Zurich: JRP Ringier, 2005), 216–217.

21. Lawson, interview with the author, November 1, 2008.

22. Susan Morgan, email to the author, January 12, 2010.

23. Lawson, interview with the author, November 1, 2008.

24. Thomas Lawson, interview by Kate Horsfield, *Profile* 4, no. 2 (March 1984): 25.

25. Lawson, interview with the author, November 1, 2008.

26. Ibid.

27. Ibid.

28. Ibid.

29. Richard Prince, interview by Steve Lafreniere, *Artforum*, March 2003, 70.

30. Thomas Lawson, "Last Exit: Painting," *Artforum*, October 1981, 40.

31. Sherrie Levine, interview by Howard Singerman, *Artforum,* April 2003, 190.

32. Thomas Lawson, "The Dark Side of the Bright Light," in *Mining for Gold: Selected Writings*, 121.

33. David Robbins, "Notes towards Film," *Real Life*, no. 7 (Autumn 1981); Richard Prince, "Primary Transfers," *Real Life*, no. 3 (March 1980): 3.

34. Lawson, interview with the author, November 1, 2008.

35. DeStaffan, telephone conversation with the author, August 27, 2009.

36. Susan Morgan, interview by Kate Fowle, in *Real Life Magazine, 1979–1990*, 9.

37. Lawson, "Too Good to Be True," 3.

38. Morgan, interview with the author, November 1, 2008.

39. Adrian Piper, "An Open Letter to Donald Kuspit," *Real Life*, no. 17/18 (Winter 1987–1988): 3, 9, 11.

40. For a discussion of Squiers's curatorial practice, see Silvia Kolbowski, "Discordant Views," in Brian Wallis, ed., *Blasted Allegories: An Anthology of Artists' Writings* (Cambridge: MIT Press, 1987).

41. Carol Squiers [Elsa Bulgari, pseud.], "Your Everyday Critic," *Real Life*, no. 6 (Summer 1981): 31.

42. Carol Squiers, telephone conversation with the author, October 29, 2009.

43. David Robbins, email to the author, October 18, 2008.

44. Laurie Simmons, *Color Coordinated Interiors: A Conversation with James Welling* (New York: Skarstedt Fine Art, 2007), 5.

45. Crimp, "Pictures," 88.

46. Helene Winer, statement, in Claudia Gould and Valerie Smith, eds., *5000 Artists Return to Artists Space: 25 Years* (New York: Artists Space, 1998), 59.

47. Lawson, "Attempting Community," 221.

48. "New York," *Real Life*, no. 1 (March 1979): 2.

49. Morgan, interview with the author, November 1, 2008.

50. See Brian Wallis, "Public Funding and Alternative Spaces," in Julie Ault, ed., *Alternative Art New York, 1965–1985* (Minneapolis: University of Minnesota Press, 2002).

51. See Sandy Nairne, "The Institutionalization of Dissent," in Reesa Greenberg, Bruce W. Ferguson, and Sandy Nairne, eds., *Thinking about Exhibitions* (New York: Routledge, 1996).

52. Irving Sandler, interview with Sandy Nairne, June 1993, in Ferguson and Nairne, *Thinking about Exhibitions*.

53. Helene Winer, quoted in Deborah C. Phillips, "New Faces in Alternative Spaces," *Artnews* 80, no. 9 (November 1981): 96.

54. One of the main reasons Winer left Artists Space was because of the rule that any individual artist could have only one show there, and she wanted to show the same artists more than once. Helene Winer, telephone conversation with the author, November 7, 2008.

55. Thomas Lawson, email to the author, January 12, 2009.

56. For an excellent discussion of this changing notion of the alternative space, see David Little, "Colab Takes a Piece, History Takes It Back: Collectivity and New York Alternative Spaces," *Art Journal* 66, no. 1 (Spring 2007): 60–74.

57. Group Material, "Caution! Alternative Space!" (1982), in Kristine Stiles, ed., *Theories and Documents of Contemporary Art* (Berkeley: University of California Press, 1996), 894.

58. Walter Robinson and Carlo McCormick, "Slouching toward Avenue D," *Art in America,* Summer 1984, 159.

59. Lucy Lippard, "Archival Activism," *Museum of Modern Art Library Bulletin,* no. 86 (Winter 1993–1994): 5.

60. Craig Owens, "The Problem with Puerilism," *Art in America,* Summer 1984, 162–163.

61. Walter Robinson, "The Quest for Failure," *Real Life,* no. 15 (Winter 1985–1986): 9.

62. David Salle, statement, in Gould and Smith, *5000 Artists Return to Artists Space,* 92.

63. Among the grants that were vetoed by the NEA during the 1980s, for example, was a joint proposal by the Heresies Collective and Political Art Documentation and Distribution to support forums with politically engaged artists and critics. See Carol Vance, "Reagan's Revenge: Restructuring the NEA," *Art in America,* November 1990, 49–55.

64. Lippard, "Archival Activism."

65. Lawson, interview with the author, November 1, 2008.

66. Peter Nagy, "Brie Popcorn," interview with David Robbins [pseudonym Rex Reason], *Real Life,* no. 11/12 (Winter 1983–1984): 30.

67. Karen Benson, "Art Stars: Out of the Studios, into the Glossies," *ZG,* no. 8 (1985): 4.

68. Robinson, "The Quest for Failure," 6.

69. Ibid., 9.

70. Lawson, interview with the author, November 1, 2008.

71. Ibid.

72. Thomas Lawson, "No Bull," *Real Life,* no. 20 (1990): 2.

73. Ibid.

74. Lawson, interview by Kate Fowle, in *Real Life Magazine, 1979–1990,* 14.

Chapter 8

1. Lucy Lippard, interview by Ursula Meyer, December 1969, in Lippard, *Six Years: The Dematerialization of the Art Object from 1966 to 1972* (1973; repr., Berkeley: University of California Press, 1997), 6.

2. Georg Schöllhammer, editorial, *Documenta Magazine No 1–3, 2007 Reader* (Cologne: Taschen, 2007), n.p.

3. Claire Bishop, "Writer's Bloc," *Artforum,* September 2007, 415.

4. For a critique of the Western bias through which conceptual art has been historicized, see Luis Camnitzer, Jane Farver, and Rachel Weiss, eds., *Global Conceptualism: Points of Origin, 1950s–1980s*, exh. cat. (New York: Queens Museum of Art, 1999).

5. Seth Siegelaub, "On Exhibitions and the World at Large: A Conversation with Seth Siegelaub," interview by Charles Harrison, in Gregory Battcock, ed., *Idea Art: A Critical Anthology* (New York: E. P. Dutton, 1973), 171.

6. Ibid.

7. The exhibition reflected *Studio International*'s larger commitment to covering both conceptual art and international developments under editor Peter Townsend from 1965 to 1975. See Jo Melvin, "Peter Townsend and *Studio International*: Notes from Inside the Archive," *Art Monthly Australia*, September 2006, 26–28.

8. See Darko Šimičić, "From *Zenit* to *Mental Space*: Avant-garde, Neo-avant-garde, and Post-avant-garde Magazines and Books in Yugoslavia, 1921–1987," in Dubravka Djurić and Miško Šuvaković, eds., *Impossible Histories: Historical Avant-gardes, Neo-avant-gardes, and Post-avant-gardes in Yugoslavia, 1918–1991* (Cambridge: MIT Press, 2003), 294–331.

9. See Valery Gerlovin and Rimma Gerlovina, "Samizdat Art," in Charles Doria, ed., *Russian Samizdat Art* (New York: Willis Locker & Owens, 1986), 67–192; and Géza Perneczky, *The Magazine Network: The Trends of Alternative Art in the Light of Their Periodicals, 1968–1988* (Cologne: Edition Soft Geometry, 1993).

10. See Martha Hellion, *Artist's Books; Ulises Carrión: Personal Worlds or Cultural Strategies* (Madrid: Turner; New York: D.A.P., 2003); Felipe Ehrenberg, Magali Lara, and Javier Cadena, "Independent Publishing in Mexico," in Joan Lyons, ed., *Artists' Books: A Critical Anthology and Sourcebook* (New York: Gibbs M. Smith, in association with Visual Studies Workshop Press, 1985); Cuahtémoc Medina, "Publishing Circuits," in Olivier Debroise, *The Age of Discrepancies: Art and Visual Culture in Mexico, 1968–1997* (University City, Mexico: Universidad Nacional Autónoma de México and Nashville Turner Publishing, 2007).

11. The repressive political conditions in Latin America likely influenced the pervasiveness of mail art and assembling practices there from the 1960s to the 1980s, since these practices did not depend on official venues and more easily evaded censorship. These practices still led to the imprisonment of several artists, including the Uruguyan artist Clemente Padín, who published the important mail art publication *Ovum*. See Luis Camnitzer, *Conceptualism in Latin American Art: Didactics of Liberation* (Austin: University of Texas Press, 2007).

12. Friedrich Heubach, quoted in Christine Mehring, "Continental Schrift: The Story of *Interfunktionen*," *Artforum*, May 2004, 180.

13. See Serge Guilbaut, *How New York Stole the Idea of Modern Art* (Chicago: University of Chicago Press, 1985).

14. As Christine Mehring points out in her excellent discussion of American art in Germany in the 1960s, fifty-seven of the artists at Documenta 4 were from the United States, while only eighteen were from Germany. See Christine Mehring, *Blinky Palermo: Abstraction of an Era* (New Haven: Yale University Press, 2008), esp. ch. 4, "Metal Pictures, 1973–1977: Playing with American Art."

15. Friedrich Heubach, editorial statement, *Interfunktionen*, no. 1 (1968), title page. (My translation.)

16. Friedrich Heubach, editorial statement, *Interfunktionen*, no. 1 (1968), 4. (My translation.)

17. Ibid., 3. (My translation.)

18. Benjamin Buchloh, "Magazine Mentality and the Market," *Art Monthly*, October 1976, 4–5.

Among the European magazines Buchloh discusses are *Art Press* and *Peinture/Cahiers Théoriques* in France, *Magazin Kunst* and *Das Kunstwerk* in Germany, and *Flash Art* in Italy.

19. Friedrich Heubach, "*Interfunktionen*, 1968–1975," in Gloria Moure, ed., *Behind the Facts: Interfunktionen, 1968–1975* (Barcelona: Ediciones Polígrafa, 2004), 47.

20. Ibid., 57.

21. Friedrich Heubach, email to the author, December 2, 2008.

22. Heubach, "*Interfunktionen*, 1968–1975," 49.

23. Ibid.

24. Benjamin Buchloh, "A Survey of Contemporary Art Magazines," *Studio International,* September/October 1976, 168.

25. Heubach, "*Interfunktionen*, 1968–1975," 49.

26. Ibid., 51.

27. Heubach, email to the author, December 2, 2008.

28. Benjamin Buchloh, interview with the author, May 29, 2008.

29. See Phyllis Tuchman, "American Art in Germany: The History of a Phenomenon," *Artforum,* November 1970, 58–69. Also see Mehring, *Blinky Palermo,* esp. ch. 4.

30. Buchloh, interview with the author, May 29, 2008.

31. According to Graham, his dealer, John Gibson, sent Heubach the article, and Heubach presumably did the layout for *Interfunktionen.* Graham, interview with the author, June 4, 2009.

32. Dan Graham, "Schema (March, 1966) Notes," *Interfunktionen,* no. 8 (1972), 29.

33. Friedrich Heubach, statement, *Interfunktionen,* no. 9 (1972): n.p.

34. Heubach, email to the author, December 2, 2008.

35. Ibid.

36. Buchloh, interview with the author, May 29, 2008.

37. Daniel Buren, "Critical Limits" (1970), in Buren, *Five Texts* (New York: John Weber Gallery, 1974), 38.

38. Daniel Buren, "caption," in Kynaston McShine, ed., *Information,* exh. cat. (New York: Museum of Modern Art, 1970), 30.

39. The first time Buren used a printed publication as the medium of his work was for the catalog of "Prospect 68," organized by Konrad Fischer and Hans Strelow in Düsseldorf in 1968. In addition to *Interfunktionen,* he has created works for *Studio International, Extra, Artforum,* and *Tri-Quarterly.*

40. Daniel Buren, email to the author, June 11, 2009.

41. Buchloh, interview with the author, May 29, 2008.

42. See Rosalind Krauss, *A Voyage on the North Sea: Art in the Age of the Post-Medium Condition* (London: Thames & Hudson, 2000).

43. For an excellent discussion of these issues as they play out in *Eau de Cologne,* see Johanna Burton, "A Will to Representation: *Eau de Cologne,* 1985–1993," in Rhea Anastas and Michael Brenson, eds., *Witness to Her Art* (New York: Bard College Center for Curatorial Studies, 2006).

44. Buchloh, interview with the author, May 29, 2008.

45. Ibid.

46. For a discussion of this aspect of Kiefer's *Occupations* series, see Lisa Saltzman, *Anselm Kiefer and Art after Auschwitz* (Cambridge: Cambridge University Press, 1999).

47. Buchloh, interview with the author, May 29, 2008.

48. Benjamin Buchloh, quoted in Mehring, "Continental Schrift," 179; restated by Buchloh in interview with the author, May 29, 2008.

49. Ibid.

50. Benjamin Buchloh, "Beuys: The Twilight of the Idol, Preliminary Notes for a Critique," *Artforum*, January 1980, 35–43; reprinted in Buchloh, *Neo-Avantgarde and Culture Industry: Essays on European and American Art from 1955 to 1975* (Cambridge: MIT Press, 2000), 48.

51. Amy Baker Sandback, "Salad Days: Editing the '80s," interview by David Frankel, *Artforum*, April 2003, 227.

Appendix

1. George Kubler, "Style and Representation of Historical Time," *Aspen* 5+6 (Fall 1967): n.p.

2. Stéphane Rona, editorial, *+–o*, no. 42 (October 1986): 5.

3. Anne-Marie Rona, email to the author, November 2, 2009.

4. Michel Aphesbero and Danielle Colomine, artists' statement and press release for Printed Matter, April 29, 2000.

5. Jochen Gerz, email to the author, March 12, 2009.

6. Gina Covina and Laurel Galana, "Frontiers," *Amazon Quarterly* 1, no. 1 (Fall 1972): 5.

7. Bob Witz, letter to the author, December 12, 2008.

8. Cliff Baldwin, "The *¡Aqui!* Story," http://www.cliffbaldwin.com/aqui/bg.html (accessed September 5, 2009).

9. Peter Cook, "Some Notes on the Archigram Syndrome," in Pasqual Shoenig and Dennis Crompton, *A Guide to Archigram 1961–74* (London and Vienna: Academy Editions and Vienna Kunsthalle Wien, 1994), 25.

10. Willi Bongard, statement in "A Survey of Contemporary Art Magazines," *Studio International*, September-October 1976, 146.

11. Brian O'Doherty, *Inside the White Cube: The Ideology of the Gallery Space* (Berkeley: University of California Press, 1976), 96.

12. Editorial, *Art Communication Edition*, no. 6 (1978).

13. Frank Gaard, quoted in Michael Fallon, *Five Geniuses: Scott Stack, Richard Brewer, Frank Gaard, Herb Grika, Leon Hushcha*, exh. cat. (Minneapolis: Minneapolis Institute of Arts, 1977).

14. Editorial statement, *Artpolice* 3, no. 1 (1979), n.p.

15. Edit deAk and Walter Robinson, "Alternative Periodicals," in Bridget Reak-Johnson, ed., *The New Artspace* (Los Angeles: LAICA, 1978), 63.

16. Igor Makarevich, "A/Ya Magazine," in *East Art Map: Contemporary Art and Eastern Europe*, ed. IRWIN (London: Afterall, 2006), 282–283.

17. Naoyoshi Hikosaka, email to the author, October 12, 2009.

18. Rasheed Araeen, email to the author, May 16, 2010.

19. Rasheed Araeen's "Preliminary Notes for a Black Manifesto" appeared in the first issue of *Black*

Phoenix (January 1978). Despite his doubts, it was later published in *Studio International* 194, no. 1 (1978): 58–67.

20. Rasheed Araeen and Mahmood Jamal, "Editorial," *Black Phoenix* 1 (January 1978), n.p.

21. Flyer for *Bomb*, collection of Liza Béar.

22. Betsy Sussler, telephone conversation with the author, October 13, 2009.

23. Quoted in *Chrysalis*, no. 1 (1977).

24. Rimma Gerlovina and Valeriy Gerlovin, email to the author, April 3, 2009.

25. Ibid.

26. Stephen Willats, statement in "A Survey of Contemporary Art Magazines," 161–162.

27. Editorial, *Control*, no. 5 (1969).

28. Barry Hale, review of Les Levine's *Culture Hero Masterprint*, in *Artscanada*, February-March 1971, 57.

29. Edgardo Antonio Vigo, quoted in Magdalena Pérez Balbi, "Movimiento Diagonal Cero: Poesía experimental desde La Plata (1966–1969)," *Escaner Cultural: Revista virtual de arte contemporáneo y nuevas tendencias*, September 2006, http://revista.escaner.cl/node/277 (accessed November 2009).

30. James Hugunin, email to the author, June 2, 2009.

31. David Greenberger, "Foreword," The Duplex Planet, http://www.duplexplanet.com/visitorcenter.html (accessed May 16, 2010).

32. Leonard Abrams, phone conversation with the author, May 14, 2010.

33. See Jonas Mekas, "Notes on George Maciunas' Work in Cinema," *Visible Language* 26, no. 1–2 (Winter-Spring 1992): 125–132.

34. See Simon Anderson, "Fluxus Publicus," in Joan Rothfuss, Elizabeth Armstrong, and Janet Jenkins, eds., *In the Spirit of Fluxus*, exh. cat. (Minneapolis: Walker Art Center, 1993).

35. Josip Vaništa, quoted in Darko Šimičić, "From *Zenit* to *Mental Space*: Avant-garde, Neo-avant-garde, and Post-avant-garde Magazines and Books in Yugoslavia, 1921–1987," in Dubravka Djurić and Miško Šuvaković, eds., *Impossible Histories: Historical Avant-gardes, Neo-avant-gardes, and Post-avant-gardes in Yugoslavia, 1918–1991* (Cambridge: MIT Press, 2003), 316.

36. Josip Vaništa, "The Gorgona," in Božo Bek, ed., *Gorgona*, exh. cat., Gallery of Contemporary Art, Zagreb (Zagreb: Galerije grada Zagreba, 1977), 159.

37. Josip Vaništa, quoted in Šimičić, "From *Zenit* to *Mental Space*," 318.

38. *Integration* 1, 12–13.

39. Guy Debord to Constant, June 2, 1960, in Guy Debord, *Correspondence: The Foundation of the Situationist International (June 1957–August 1960)*, trans. Stuart Kendall (New York: Semiotext(e), 2008), 63.

40. Andy Warhol, in Amy Sullivan, interview with Mark Frechette and Daria Halprin, *Interview* 1, no. 1 (1969): 34.

41. Andy Warhol, statement, Howardena Pindell Papers, The Museum of Modern Art Archives, New York.

42. Barbara Ess, interview by Nancy Princethal, quoted in Nancy Princethal, "Barbara Ess: Machine Dreams," *Print Collector's Newsletter* 21, no. 5 (November-December 1990): 169.

43. Naoyoshi Hikosaka, email to the author, October 12, 2009.

44. William Leavitt, email to the author, September 19, 2009.

45. Sarenco, editorial, *Lotta Poetica*, no. 1 (1975); quoted in Melania Gazzotti and Nicole Zanoletti, "*Lotta Poetica*: The Magazine, the Artists, and Their Aims," in *Lotta Poetica: Artisti e una revista*, exh. cat. (Milan: Fondazione Berardelli, 2009), 6.

46. Paul de Vree, editorial, *Lotta Poetica*, no. 1 (1975); quoted in Gazzotti and Zanoletti, "*Lotta Poetica*," 6.

47. Ibid.

48. Gerhard Johann Lischka, email to the author, November 12, 2009.

49. This English translation of *Macula*'s editorial statement appeared in "A Survey of Contemporary Art Magazines," 171.

50. Yve-Alain Bois, "Le Toucher Juste," *Grey Room* no. 20, 93n2. Also for an account of the role of Hubert Damisch in the founding of *Macula*, see Yve-Alain Bois, "Tough Love," *Oxford Art Journal* 28, no. 2 (2005): 245–255.

51. Group of Six, statement, *Maj 75*, issue A (1975), quoted in Šimičić, "From *Zenit* to *Mental Space*," 318.

52. In 1959, the Judson literary quarterly *Exodus* was published under the aegis of the Judson Studio. This anthology of poetry, edited by Howard Hart and sold in local bookstores, included poems by William Godden, Robert Hanlon, and John Williams. Volumes I, II, and III of *Exodus* were published in the spring of 1959, the fall of 1959, and the summer of 1960, respectively. *Exodus* later became *The Judson Review*, edited by Rev. Al Carmines and Don Katzman. Volume I of *The Judson Review* was published in 1963 and included the poetry of Jackson Mac Low, Diane Wakoski, and Joel Oppenheimer.

53. Charles Bernstein, "For *M/E/A/N/I/N/G*," *M/E/A/N/I/N/G*, no. 1 (1986): 3.

54. Lucio Pozzi, email to the author, August 25, 2009.

55. Ibid.

56. Herman de Vries, letter to the author, September 14, 2009.

57. Jennifer Oille, statement in "A Survey of Contemporary Art Magazines," 117.

58. Heinz Zolper, email to the author, July 6, 2009.

59. Editorial foreword, *Présence Africaine*, nouvelle série, no. 1–2 (April-June 1955).

60. Quoted in Christoph Schifferli, ed., *The Japanese Box: Facsimile Reprint of Six Rare Photographic Publications of the Provoke Era* (Paris: Edition 7L, 2001), 14.

61. Ibid., 16.

62. Karl Jirgens, "20th Anniversary Editorial," *Rampike* 10, no. 2 (1999): 3.

63. Françoise Mouly, "A *Raw* History, Part One," ed. Bill Kartalopolous, *Indy Magazine* (Winter 2005), http://web.archive.org/web/20080411221103/64.23.98.142/indy/winter_2005/raw_01/index.html (accessed May 15, 2010).

64. The final three issues of *Raw* (volume 2) were printed in a smaller, digest-sized format, and published by Penguin Books.

65. Art Spiegelman and Françoise Mouly, *Read Yourself Raw* (New York: Random House, 1990), n.p.

66. Julien Blaine, email to the author, December 5, 2009.

67. Editorial statement, *Rok*, no. 1 (1969), quoted in Miško Šuvaković, "Conceptual Art," in Djurić and Šuvaković, *Impossible Histories*, 101.

68. Gerhard Theewen, interview by David Brittain, *Salon*, boxed reprint (Cologne: Salon Verlag, 2007).

69. Sidney Geist, interview by Hubert Grehan, *Scrap*, no. 2 (1960), n.p.

70. Carter Ratcliff, "SMS: Art in Real Time," in *SMS: A Collection of Original Multiples*, exh. cat. (New York: Reinhold-Brown Gallery, 1988).

71. William Copley, quoted in Jud Yalkut, "Towards an Intermedia Magazine," *Arts*, Summer 1968, 14.

72. Karl Gerstner, introduction to Marcel Wyss's "Trans-variations," *Spirale*, no. 9 (1964), n.p.

73. Timothy Silverlake, email to the author, July 23, 2009.

74. Linda Hasselstrom, email to the author, May 13, 2010.

75. Editorial statement, *The Tiger's Eye*, no. 3 (March 1948): 75.

76. Ibid.

77. Editorial statement, *The Tiger's Eye*, no. 1 (October 1947): 76.

78. Ibid., 53.

79. Prospectus for *The Tiger's Eye*, no. 2, quoted in Pamela Franks, *The Tiger's Eye: The Art of a Magazine* (New Haven: Yale University Art Gallery, 2002), 63.

80. Herbert George, email to Roger Conover, January 22, 2009.

81. Ibid.

82. Herbert George, email to Roger Conover, January 29, 2009.

83. Ibid.

84. Michael Andre, statement in "A Survey of Contemporary Art Magazines," 183.

85. Anna Banana, "*VILE* History," *VILE*, no. 8 (also called *About VILE*) (1983): 2.

86. Ibid.

87. Ibid.

88. Tom Marioni, interview with the author, June 24, 2009.

89. Brian Wallis, email to the author, September 2, 2009.

90. Ibid.

91. Ibid.

92. Leonard Koren, *13 Books* (Berkeley: Stone Bridge Press, 2001), 25.

93. Ibid., 28.

94. Peter Plagens, interview with the author, New York, November 12, 2001.

95. Koren, *13 Books*, 33.

96. Cynthia Navaretta, statement, Howardena Pindell Archives.

97. Cynthia Navaretta, email to the author, August 3, 2009.

98. Michael McClard, email to the author, November 29, 2009.

99. Otto Piene and Heinz Mack, *Zero* (Cambridge: MIT Press, 1973), xx.

100. Otto Piene, email to the author, October 4, 2009.

101. Rosetta Brooks, editorial, *ZG*, no. 1 (1980).

102. Judith Wong, email to the author, November 17, 2010.

SELECTED BIBLIOGRAPHY

I list here sources that specifically address the topic of artists' magazines, conceptual art publications, and closely related phenomena.

Aarons, Philip, and A. A. Bronson, eds. *Queer Zines.* Exh. cat. New York: Printed Matter, 2008.

Aarons, Philip, and Andrew Roth, eds. *Numbers: Serial Publications by Artists.* Zurich: JRP-Ringier; New York: PPP Editions, 2009.

Alberro, Alexander. *Conceptual Art and the Politics of Publicity.* Cambridge: MIT Press, 2003.

Alberro, Alexander, and Blake Stimson, eds. *Conceptual Art: A Critical Anthology.* Cambridge: MIT Press, 1999.

Alloway, Lawrence. "Artists as Writers," Parts I and II. *Artforum,* March 1974, 30–35; April 1974, 30–35.

Anderson, Simon. "Fluxus Publicus." In Elizabeth Armstrong and Joan Rothfuss, eds., *In the Spirit of Fluxus.* Minneapolis: Walker Art Center, 1993.

Armstrong, David. *A Trumpet to Arms: Alternative Media in America.* Cambridge: South End Press, 1981.

Ault, Julie, ed. *Alternative Art New York 1965–1985.* Minneapolis: University of Minnesota Press, 2002.

Battcock, Gregory. "Documentation in Conceptual Art." *Arts Magazine,* April 1970, 42–45.

Battcock, Gregory, ed. *Idea Art: A Critical Anthology.* New York: E. P. Dutton, 1973.

Buchan, David. "The Canadian Artists' Press." In Karen McKenzie and Mary F. Williamson, eds., *The Art and Pictorial Press in Canada: Two Centuries of Art Magazines.* Toronto: Art Gallery of Ontario, 1979, 40–45.

Buchloh, Benjamin. "Conceptual Art 1962–1969: From the Aesthetic of Administration to the Critique of Institutions." *October,* no. 55 (Winter 1990): 105–143.

Buchloh, Benjamin. "Moments of History in the Work of Dan Graham" (1978). In *Neo-Avantgarde and Culture Industry: Essays on European and American Art from 1955 to 1975.* Cambridge: MIT Press, 2000.

Castleberry, May. "The Magazine Rack." *Afterimage,* March 1988, 11–13.

Celant, Germano. *Book as Artwork 1960/72.* London: Nigel Greenwood, 1972.

Clay, Steven, and Rodney Phillips. *A Secret Location on the Lower East Side: Adventures in Writing, 1960–1980.* New York: New York Public Library and Granary Books, 1999.

Cohen, Ronny. "Seeing between the Pages." *Artforum,* February 1980, 50–52.

Colomina, Beatriz, and Craig Buckley. *Clip, Stamp, Fold: The Radical Architecture of Little Magazines 196x to 197x.* Barcelona: Actar; Princeton: Media and Modernity Program, Princeton University, 2010.

deAk, Edit, and Walter Robinson. "Alternative Periodicals." In *The New Artspace.* Los Angeles: Los Angeles Institute of Contemporary Art, 1978.

Dot Dot Dot, no. 1 (2000). Special Issue on Graphic Design Magazines.

Drucker, Johanna. *The Century of Artists' Books.* New York: Granary, 1995; 2nd ed. 2004.

Duncombe, Stephen. *Notes from Underground Zines and the Politics of Alternative Culture.* London: Verso, 1997.

Fawcett, Trevor, and Clive Phillpot, eds. *The Art Press: Two Centuries of Art Magazines*. London: Art Book Company, 1976.

Friedman, Ken. "Notes on the History of the Alternative Press." *Lightworks*, Winter 1977, 41–47.

Fawcett, Trevor, and Clive Phillpot, eds. *Figuring the Word: Essays on Books, Writing, and Visual Poetics*. New York: Granary Books, 1998.

Gerlovin, Valeriy, and Rimma Gerlovina. "Samizdat Art." In Charles Doria, ed., *Russian Samizdat Art*, 67–192. New York: Willis, Locker & Owens, 1986.

Gibson, Ann Eden. *Issues in Abstract Expressionism: The Artist-Run Periodicals*. Ann Arbor: UMI Research Press, 1990.

Goldstein, Ann, and Anne Rorimer. *Reconsidering the Object of Art: 1965–1975*. Exh. cat. Los Angeles: Museum of Contemporary Art, Los Angeles, 1995.

Held, John, Jr. *Mail Art: An Annotated Bibliography*. Metuchen, N.J.: Scarecrow Press, 1991.

Heller, Steven. *Merz to Émigré and Beyond: Avant-Garde Magazine Design of the Twentieth Century*. New York: Phaidon Press, 2002.

Hoffberg, Judith. *Umbrella: The Anthology 1978–1998*. Santa Monica: Umbrella Editions, 1999.

Hoffman, Frederick J., Charles Allen, and Carolyn F. Ulrich. *The Little Magazine: A History and a Bibliography*. Princeton: Princeton University Press, 1946.

Kotz, Liz. *Words to Be Looked At: Language in 1960s Art*. Cambridge: MIT Press, 2007.

Kurowski, Travis, and Gary Percesepe, eds. *Mississippi Review* 36, no. 3. Special Issue on Literary Magazines, Fall 2008.

Lauf, Cornelia, and Clive Phillpot. *Artist/Author: Contemporary Artists' Books*. New York: Distributed Art Publishers, 1998.

Leiber, Steven. *Extra Art: A Survey of Artists' Ephemera, 1960–1999*. Santa Monica: Smart Art Press, 2001.

Linker, Kate. "The Artists' Book as an Alternative Space." *Studio International*, January 1980, 75–79.

Lippard, Lucy. *Six Years: The Dematerialization of the Art Object from 1966 to 1972*. 1973; repr., Berkeley: University of California Press, 1997.

Lyons, Joan, ed. *Artists' Books: A Critical Anthology and Sourcebook*. New York: Gibbs M. Smith, in association with Visual Studies Workshop Press, 1985.

McKenzie, Karen, and Mary F. Williamson. *The Art and Pictorial Press in Canada: Two Centuries of Art Magazines*. Toronto: Art Gallery of Ontario, 1979.

Medina, Cuahtémoc. "Publishing Circuits." In Olivier Debroise, ed., *The Age of Discrepancies: Art and Visual Culture in Mexico, 1968–1997*. University City, Mexico: Universidad Nacional Autónoma de México; Nashville: Turner Publishing , 2007.

Meyer, Ursula. *Conceptual Art*. New York: E. P. Dutton, 1972.

Moore, Alan. "New Voices." *Artforum*, December 1974.

Moseley, Catherine, ed. *Conception: Conceptual Art Documents 1968 to 1972*.Exh. cat. Norwich, England: Norwich Gallery, Norwich School of Art and Design, 2001.

Ostertag, Bob. *People's Movements, People's Press: The Journalism of Social Justice Movements*. Boston: Beacon Press, 2006.

Perneczky, Géza. *Assembling Magazines 1969–2000*. Budapest: Arnyekkotok Foundation, 2007.

Perneczky, Géza. *The Magazine Network: The Trends of Alternative Art in the Light of Their Periodicals, 1968–1988*. Trans. from Hungarian by Tibor Szendrei. Cologne: Edition Soft Geometry, 1993.

Phillpot, Clive. "Art Magazines and Magazine Art." *Artforum*, February 1980, 52–54.

Pindell, Howardena. "Alternative Space: Artists' Periodicals." *Print Collector's Newsletter* 8 (4) (September-October 1977): 96–121.

Pindell, Howardena. "Artists' Periodicals: An Event for 1984 or Page 2001." *Art Journal* (Summer 1980): 282–283.

Price, Seth. "Dispersion." 2002. www.distributedhistory.com/Dispersion2008.pdf.

Robins, Corinne. "The Women's Art Magazines" (1979). In Hilary Robinson, ed., *Feminism-Art-Theory*. London: Blackwell Publishers, 2001.

Rorimer, Anne. "Siting the Page: Exhibiting Works in Publications—Some Examples of Conceptual art in the USA." In Michael Newman and Jon Bird, eds., *Rewriting Conceptual Art*, 11–26. London: Reaktion Books, 1999.

Saper, Craig. *Networked Art*. Minneapolis: University of Minnesota Press, 2001.

Šimičić, Darko. "From *Zenit* to *Mental Space*: Avant-garde, Neo-avant-garde, and Post-avant-garde Magazines and Books in Yugoslavia, 1921–1987." In Dubravka Djurić and Miško Šuvaković, eds., *Impossible Histories: Historical Avant-gardes, Neo-avant-gardes, and Post-avant-gardes in Yugoslavia, 1918–1991*, 294–331. Cambridge: MIT Press, 2003.

Stosuy, Brandon, ed. *Up Is Up but So Is Down: New York's Downtown Literary Scene, 1974–1992*. New York: New York University Press, 2006.

Studio International 193, no. 983 (September-October 1976). Special Issue on Art Magazines.

Šuvaković, Miško. "Conceptual Art." In Dubravka Djurić and Miško Šuvaković, eds., *Impossible Histories: Historical Avant-gardes, Neo-avant-gardes, and Post-avant-gardes in Yugoslavia, 1918–1991*, 210–245. Cambridge: MIT Press, 2003.

Triggs, Teal. *Fanzines*. San Francisco: Chronicle Books, 2010.

Turner, Fred. *From Counterculture to Cyberculture: Stuart Brand, the Whole Earth Network, and the Rise of Digital Utopianism*. Chicago: University of Chicago, 2006.

Walker, John A. "Periodicals since 1945." In Trevor Fawcett and Clive Phillpot, eds., *The Art Press: Two Centuries of Art Magazines*, 4–52. London: Art Book Company, 1976.

Welch, Chuck, ed. *Eternal Network: A Mail Art Anthology*. Calgary: University of Calgary, 1995.

Wilson, Martha. "Artists' Books as Alternative Space." In *The New Artspace*. Los Angeles: Los Angeles Institute of Contemporary Art, 1978.

INDEX

Page numbers in boldface indicate illustrations.

as artistic medium, 94, 97
and art market, 111–117
and *Art-Rite*, 121, 134
and Art Workers' Coalition, 101–103
beginnings, 100–101
circulation, 91
covers, 91, **92**, **93**, 101, **102**
and earth art, 94–95
editorial impetus, 91–95, 101–103
ending, 117
and European coverage, 101
funding, 117, 118–119
and gender, 107
graphic design, 95–96, 100–101
and *Interfunktionen*, 213
interviews, 104–111
"Rumbles" and "Messages" sections, 114
and SoHo artistic community, 91, 94–97, 103–104,
114–117
title, 94
Axe, 242
A/Ya, 206, 242, **242**
Aycock, Alice, 97
Azimuth, 203, 243, **243**

Baer, Jo, **62–63**
Bainbridge, David, 237
Baldessari, John, **22**, 23, 114
This Is Not to Be Looked At, **22**, 23
Baldwin, Cliff, 234
Baldwin, Michael, 59, 237
Balloon Newspaper, 243
Balthazar, André, 253
Banana, Anna, 157, 162, 308, **308**
Bann, Stephen, 261
Baptiste, Jules, 192
Baracks, Barbara, 244
Barnabus Rex (New York bar), 183
Baroni, Vittore, 236
Barowitz, Elliott, 239
Barr, Alfred, 23, 52
Barry, Judith, 188
Barry, Robert, 71, 79–83
Barthes, Roland, 49, 53, 55–58, **56**, 64
Bartlett, Jennifer, 131
Baselitz, George, 197
Bašičević, Dimitrije (Mangelos), 245
Basquiat, Jean-Michel, 197
Battcock, Gregory, 15–16
Baudrillard, Jean, 181

Bay Area Dadaists, 151
Bealy, Allan, 243
Béar, Liza, 91–119, **96**, **118**. *See also Avalanche*
on 93 Grand Street, 95
and Art Workers' Coalition, 101–103
on *Avalanche*, 94, 100, 104, 114
interview with Acconci, 107
interview with Shapiro, 107–111
Beck, Martin, 132
Beckett, Samuel, 28, 49
Beckley, Bill, 215
Bee, Susan, 277
Beers, Sally, 313
Beijeren, Geert van, 235
Belcher, Alan, 172, 173
Benglis, Lynda, 25–26, **25**
Benjamin, Walter, 2–3, 6, 48
Benson, Karen, 197
Benzene, 194, 243
Berman, Wallace, 43, 295, **295**
Bertholo, René, 271
Bertini, Gianni, 273, 277
Beuys, Joseph, 101, **102**, 207, 212, 213, 224
Bienvenue, Marcella, 249
Big Deal, 142, 244
Bijutsu Shihyō, 205, 244, **244**
BILE, 162, 244, **244**
Birnbaum, Dara, 189
Bishop, Claire, 202
Bishop, Isabel, 290
Bit, 205, 245
Bit International, 205, 206, 245, **245**
Black Art, 142, 246
Black Mountain Review, 69
Black on White, 246
Black Phoenix, 205, 206, 246
Blaine, Julien, 205, 234, 255, 293
Blast, 194, 247
Bleckner, Ross, 173
Blok, 247
Blumenthal, Lyn, 287
BMPT Group (Buren, Mosset, Parmentier, Toroni),
205
Boa, 3, 203, 247
Bochner, Mel, 16, 79, 129
and *Aspen* 5+6, 49, 52, 54
magazine articles and interventions, 31, 34–39
Bode, Arnold, 207
Bode, Sigmund (Brian O'Doherty), 53
Body Politic, 41, 170